ISLAM IN THE SUBCONTINENT

MUSLIMS IN A PLURAL SOCIETY

Islam in the Subcontinent

Muslims in a Plural Society

MUSHIRUL HASAN

MANOHAR
2002

First published 2002

© Mushirul Hasan, 2002

ISBN 81-7304-451-1

Published by
Ajay Kumar Jain for
Manohar Publishers & Distributors
4753/23 Ansari Road, Daryaganj
New Delhi 110002

Typeset by
A J Software Publishing Co. Pvt. Ltd.
New Delhi 110005

Printed at
Lordson Publishers Pvt. Ltd.
Delhi 110007

In Memory of
SARVEPALLI GOPAL

زندگی کیا ہے عناصر میں ظہورِ ترتیب
موت کیا ہے انہیں اجزاء کا پریشاں ہونا

Contents

Tables

Acknowledgements

I have substantially revised and updated all the papers in this volume. Some have even been rewritten to make them accessible to the reader. The introduction is based on some of my earlier writings. The next essay 'Resistance and Acquiescence in North India: Muslim Responses to the West' is a substantially revised and enlarged version of my paper published in Mushirul Hasan and Narayani Gupta (eds.), *India's Colonial Encounter: Essays in Memory of Eric Stokes*, New Delhi, 1993. Since then, Gulfishan Khan has published *Indian Muslim Perception of the West During the Eighteenth Century*, Karachi, 1998, a well-researched monograph. I have also made use of the unpublished paper 'Eroticizing Europe' by Mohammad Tavakoli-Targhi, an Iranian scholar based in the US. Rosie Llewellyn-Jones, *Engaging Scoundrels: True Tales of Old Lucknow*, New Delhi, 2001, has interesting references to Abu Talib and his work.

• 'The Myth of Unity: Colonial and National Narratives' was originally published in David Ludden (ed.), *Contesting the Nation: Religion, Community and the Politics of Democracy in India*, Philadelphia, 1996.

• Versions of my paper 'Traditional Rites and Contested Meanings: Sectarian Strife in Colonial Lucknow' have appeared in *The Indian Economic and Social History Review*, Vol. 27, 2, 1990; Violette Graff (ed.), *Lucknow: Memories of a City*, New Delhi, 1996, pp. 114-35; Mushirul Hasan (ed.), *Islam, Communities and the Nation: Muslim Identities in South Asia and Beyond*, New Delhi, 1999, pp. 341-66.

• Two of my papers that were originally published in Mushirul Hasan (ed.), *Communal and Pan-Islamic Trends in Colonial India*, New Delhi, 1985, have been combined into one, and appear under the title 'Mediating the External: Pan-Islamism and Nationalist Renewal'. By far the most analytical study of the khilafat movement is by Gail Minault, *Religious*

Symbolism and Political Mobilization in India, New York, 1982; M. Naeem Qureshi, *Pan-Islam in British Indian Politics: A Study of the Khilafat Movement, 1918-1924*, Leiden, 1999, is a massive researched work. Though Francis Robinson has plotted the trajectory of the movement in the United Provinces, our knowledge of developments in other regions is still inadequate. The part played by the ulama of Firangi Mahal and the Barelwi school are discussed in Usha Sanyal, *Devotional Islam and Politics in British India: Ahmad Riza Khan Barelwi and his Movement, 1870-1920*, New Delhi, 1996, and Francis Robinson, *The Ulama of Farangi Mahall and Islamic Culture in South Asia*, New Delhi, 2001. *My Life: A Fragment: An Autobiographical Sketch of Maulana Mohamed Ali*, edited and annotated by me, is quite instructive. So are the essays in Mushirul Hasan (ed.), *Islam, Communities and the Nation: Muslim Identities in South Asia and Beyond*.

• '*My Life: A Fragment*: Mohamed Ali's Quest for Identity in Colonial India' was originally published in *Islam, Communities and the Nation: Muslim Identities in South Asia and Beyond*, New Delhi, 1999, pp. 57-96.

• 'Representations of Indian Nationalism: Ideology and Praxis of Azad and Mohamed Ali' was originally published in Mushirul Hasan (ed.), *Islam and Indian Nationalism: Reflections on Abul Kalam Azad*, New Delhi, 2001 rpt., pp. 77-99. Some sections of this chapter have been substantially modified.

• 'Congress Muslims and Indian Nationalism, Dilemma and Decline, *c*. 1928-1934' was originally published in Jim Masselos (ed.), *Struggling and Ruling: Indian National Congress 1885-1947*, New Delhi, 1986.

• 'Religion, Politics and Partition' was my Introduction to the volume *India's Partition: Process, Strategy and Mobilization*, New Delhi, 2001 rpt. I have introduced substantial stylistic changes without, of course, tampering with the overall thrust of my argument. I have also provided some additional information.

• 'The Muslim Mass Contact Campaign: a Strategy of Political Mobilization' was originally published in Richard Sisson and Stanley Wolpert (eds.) *Congress and Indian Nationalism: The Pre-Independence Phase*, Berkeley, 1988, pp. 198-222.

- 'The Local Roots of the Pakistan Movement: The Aligarh Muslim University' is a revised and enlarged version of the paper originally published in A.K. Gupta (ed.), *Myth and Reality: The Struggle for Freedom in India, 1945-47*, New Delhi, 1987. This version is close to what appeared in Mushirul Hasan (ed.), *Knowledge, Power and Politics: Educational Institutions in India*, New Delhi, 1999.

- 'Memories of a Fragmented Nation: Rewriting the Histories of India's Partition', was originally published in Mushirul Hasan (ed.), *Inventing Boundaries: Gender, Polities and the Partition of India*, New Delhi, 2000, pp. 26-46, and reprinted in Amrik Singh (ed.), *The Partition in Retrospect*, New Delhi, 2000, pp. 339-60; *The Annual of Urdu Studies*, University of Wisconsin-Madison, No. 15, Part I, 2000, pp. 263-86; S. Settar and Indira B. Gupta (eds.), *Pangs of Partition: The Human Dimension*, New Delhi, 2002, pp. 171-90. The essay does not cover the historical writings on the Bengal province, especially Bangladesh where the histories of Partition are being written differently since 1971. For a recent insight and references to other works, see Willem van Schendel and Erik Jan Znrcher (eds.), *Opting Out of the Nation: Identity Politics in Central, South and West Asia*, London, 1998.

- A slightly modified version of the paper 'Divided Nationhood: India's Partition Revisited' was published in K.N. Panikkar, Terence J. Bryce and Utsa Patnaik (eds.), *The Making of History: Essays Presented to Irfan Habib*, New Delhi, 2000, pp. 550-7. An enlarged version appeared in Mushirul Hasan (ed.), *Inventing Boundaries*, pp. 1-25.

- 'Moradabad Riots, 1980: Causes and Meanings' was jointly written with Satish Saberwal. It was originally published in A.A. Engineer (ed.), *Communal Riots in Post-Independence India*, Bombay, 1984. We visited Moradabad on 8-10 January; and then again on 29-31 January 1981.

- 'Competing Symbols and Shared Codes: Inter-Community Relations in Modern India' was originally published in Sarvepalli Gopal (ed.), *Anatomy of a Confrontation: The Babri Masjid-Ramjanmabhumi Issue*, New Delhi, 1990. A number of major works have appeared since then. For example, Gyan Pandey (ed.), *Hindus and Others: The Question of Identity in India Today*, New Delhi, 1990; Nilanjan Mukhopadhyay, *The Demolition: India at the Crossroads*, New Delhi, 1994; A. Nandy, S. Trivedi, S. Mayaram and A. Yagnik, *Creating a nationality—the*

Ramjanmabhumi movement and fear of the self, New Delhi, 1995; Rajeshwari Ghose, *In Quest of a Secular Symbol: Ayodhya and After*, Hong Kong, 1996. Both *South Asia*, Vol. 17, 1994, and *Asian Survey*, Vol. 33, No. 7, July 1993, brought out special issues on the Ayodhya tangle and its aftermath. Furthermore, the demolition of Babri Masjid generated lively debates on Hindu nationalism, and on secularism and its future in India. For example, Tapan Basu, Pradip Dutta, Sumit Sarkar, Tanika Sarkar and S. Sen, *Khaki Short and Saffron Flags: A Critique of the Hindu Right*, New Delhi, 1993; Peter van der Veer, *Religious Nationalism: Hindus and Muslims in India*, Berkeley, 1994; David Ludden (ed.), *Contesting the Nation: Religion, Community, and the Politics of Democracy in India*, Philadelphia, 1996; Christophe Jaffrelot, *The Hindu Nationalist Movement and Indian Politics 1925 to the 1990s*, London, 1996, is by far the most authoritative work on the subject; Gerald James Larson, *India's Agony over Religion*, New Delhi, 1997; Achin Vanaik, *Communalism Contested: Religion, Modernity and Secularisation*, New Delhi, 1997; Rajeev Bhargava (ed.), *Secularism and its Critics*, New Delhi, 1999, and Rajeev Bhargava, A.K. Bagchi and R. Sudarshan (eds.), *Multiculturalism, Liberalism and Democracy*, New Delhi, 1999.

• 'The Changing Position of the Muslims and the Political Future of Secularism in India, *c.* 1947-1986' was originally published in T.V. Sathyamurthy (ed.), *Region, Religion, Caste, Gender, and Culture in Contemporary India*, New Delhi, 1996, Vol. 3, pp. 200-28. Some additional information is included in this version. In January 2001, the Planning Commission constituted a Working Group on 'Empowering the Minorities' under my chairmanship. I have appended excerpts from that report as Appendix II to update some of the points discussed in this paper.

• 'India and Pakistan: Why the Difference?' was originally published in Mushirul Hasan and Nariaki Nakazato (eds.), *India's Unfinished Agenda: Nation-Building in South Asia*, New Delhi, 2001, pp. 309-44. I wrote this paper during my stay at the University of Virginia, Charlottesville, from January to May 2000. I am grateful to Walter Hauser for his intellectual support and to Douglas Verney for his comments.

For his painstaking editing and indulgence, I am beholden to B.N. Varma and to Ramesh Jain, as always, for his support and understanding.

15 August 2002   MUSHIRUL HASAN

PART I

PART I

1

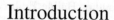

Introduction

When the American historian David Lelyveld started researching at Aligarh in 1967 I, an undergraduate at the university's History department, dutifully attended lectures on medieval India. Here a whole new world was being opened up by scholars with exceptional skills. But unfortunately, we were not acquainted with late-nineteenth-century trends in north India, some of which left an indelible stamp on Aligarh's Muhammadan Anglo-Oriental College. There was no mention of its founder, Saiyid Ahmad Khan, or the intellectual activities of his companions at Aligarh and Delhi. Shibli Numani, Altaf Husain Hali and maulvi Zakaullah were distant figures: they did not figure in an otherwise elaborate curriculum. We read the *Babur-Nama* but not the *Asar ul-Sanadid*. Hindi poets—Kabir, Rahim and Raskhan—were introduced but not Mir Taqi Mir, Sauda and Mirza Asadullah Khan Ghalib. Stocked with numerous scholarly monographs authored by members of the department, the seminar library had few books on Aligarh's more recent history. Nobody had even tried to replicate, in the context of the Aligarh movement, Susobhan Sarkar's seminal work on the Bengal renaissance. I wondered why this was so. I did not ask. I merely sensed that the history of Islam in India during the colonial period was forbidden territory. At the beginning of the present millennium it is probably much the same at the Aligarh Muslim University, though social and cultural histories are being written elsewhere in India (Sumit Sarkar, *Writing Social History*, New Delhi 1997).

Joining Delhi's Jamia Millia Islamia in 1978, I found that the private papers of its two illustrious founders—Mohamed Ali and M.A. Ansari— had been retrieved from a damp basement by my father, Professor Mohibbul Hasan, just a few years ago. I also discovered that a serious history of the institution, described by free India's first prime minister as 'a lusty child of the Non-Co-operation [Movement]', did not exist. Nor did there exist a scholarly assessment of those 'self-sacrificing workers' who were, in the words of Gandhi, 'staunch Muslims and equally staunch nationalists'. Mohamed Ali's long-winded speeches and writings were first compiled, somewhat indifferently, by a retired diplomat and published in Lahore. The Turkish author Halide Edib (who lived in the Ansari household in 1935 and delivered lectures at the Jamia Millia Islamia), wrote the only readable accounts of Dr. M.A. Ansari. So did Jawaharlal Nehru in his autobiography, published in 1936.

This scholarly inertia has also gripped traditional centres of learning. The fortunes of Lucknow's Firangi Mahal, once home to several erudite religious thinkers of Awadh, have not improved since Independence and Partition. And though the Dar al-ulum remains a major theological seminary with a powerful ideological base and an extensive network of schools and colleges in South Asia, scholars at Deoband have yet to produce a scholarly history of an institution that has, for well over a century, influenced the intellectual and religious currents in the subcontinent. The same is true of Lucknow's Nadwat al-ulama. Though the Germany-based scholar Jamal Malik has recently produced a weighty account of Nadwas' history, the late Saiyid Abul Hasan Ali Nadwi almost single-handedly interpreted the political, intellectual and religious trends among Muslims in north India.

Scholars must be alerted to the neglect of an important component of north India's past. It is equally important to remind them that scholarly interventions are essential in order to unfold the variety and diversity in Indian Islam, examine the mixed experiences of its adherents, and reveal the deep internal divides and schisms, as well as tangible areas of interaction with castes and communities. Such researches will, doubtless, remove many misleading and stereotyped ideas associated with the nature and character of Islam and the structure of Muslim communities in South Asia.

The task is an awesome one for several reasons. For one, India's Partition had a curiously mixed intellectual impact. In an attempt to highlight their contribution to the freedom struggle, scores of writers connected with formal groups and organizations, notably the Dar al-ulum at Deoband and the Jamiyat al-ulama, dwell on their nationalist past. But serious scholars are reluctant to study the lives of 'defeated' men and 'lost' causes. The ideals and activities of 'nationalist Muslims' are either not taken into account or submerged within the rationalizations of the 'victors'. Saiyid Ahmad Khan—whose contribution to education and reform matched the intellectual stride of Bengal's early reformers and their contemporaries in Egypt and Syria—is an embarrassment because of his image as the progenitor of Muslim nationalism. The movement he generated among 'Aligarh's First Generation' is virtually written off for having stimulated communitarian ('communal' in common parlance) and pan-Islamic consciousness. The khilafat upsurge is regarded as a mere pan-Islamic outburst reinforcing the image of a 'community' with extra-territorial loyalties, while Muslim 'separatism' and the clamour for a separate Muslim nation are underlined to illustrate a specifically 'Muslim tendency' to organize separately as an exclusive religious entity.

The intellectual milieu after Independence has influenced the choice of, and preference for, certain themes. A number of historians, mostly Marxists, produced seminal works on the colonial economy, on economic nationalism, and on peasant as well as working-class movements. On the other hand, the dominant historiographical trends until the 1970s allowed little space for research on religion, culture, and intellectual life. Such themes, especially those perceived as being outside the framework of 'medieval India', were not seen as a part of the historian's agenda. This may explain why Kunwar Muhammad Ashraf, though endowed with a sharp analytical mind, failed to complete his projected study on Indian Muslims, or that a generation of scholars, especially at Aligarh and Allahabad, studied the economic, agrarian and institutional histories of medieval India to the exclusion of other themes. Professors Khaliq Ahmad Nizami and Saiyid Athar Abbas Rizvi were notable exceptions, but their writings were overshadowed by the Marxist writers.

India's Partition raised the most fundamental historical and sociological issues, but these have not been adequately analysed within studies on nationalism. Aziz Ahmad, Abid Husain, A.A.A. Fyzee, K.A. Nizami, Saiyid Athar Abbas Rizvi, and Muhammad Mujeeb opened up, for the first time after Independence, new areas of research on law, religion and politics and on the histories of ideas and movements. Yet, academic circles in India were neither prepared nor intellectually equipped (most have no knowledge of Persian and Urdu) for a serious engagement on those issues they underlined in their writings.

The result is for everybody to see. The intellectual advance has taken place in the West but not in South Asia. Islam in the subcontinent and its dynamic interaction with local, indigenous traditions remains a peripheral area of research in the country, and outside the college or university curriculum. One turns to David Lelyveld and C.W. Troll to renew acquaintance with 'Aligarh's First Generation'; to Barbara Metcalf,

Francis Robinson (*The Ulama of Farangi Mahall and Islamic Culture*, New Delhi, 2001, and his *Islam and Muslim History in South Asia*, New Delhi, 2000) and Usha Sanyal to uncover the histories of Deoband, Firangi Mahal, and the Barelwi 'schools'; and to Gail Minault for highlighting reformist trends and movements among north Indian Muslims towards the end of the nineteenth century, and, recently, documenting the history of women's education. Rafiuddin Ahmed, Claudia Liebeskind (*Piety on Its Knees: Three Sufi Traditions in South Asia in Modern Times*, New Delhi, 1998), Susan Bayly, Paul Brass, Stephen Dale, Sandria B. Freitag, David Gilmartin, Ayesha Jalal, Jamal Malik, Asim Roy, Ian Talbot—all based in universities outside India—have explored a number of significant areas and added depth to our understanding of Islam in South Asia. David Lelyveld's research, for one, resulted in the finely crafted, broadly erudite and innovative work: yet, not a single scholar at the Aligarh Muslim University has pursued the themes he outlined more than two decades ago.

II

Lelyveld's principal concern—one that commands wide assent now-adays—was to understand what it meant to be a Muslim in the nineteenth-century, how that cultural/social identity changed meaning in colonial India, and how it was articulated in that context. The Aligarh College is his focal point as a formally organized, self-consciously created social establishment, founded 'with the defined goal of carrying out transitions of identity and loyalty suitable to the special circumstances of British India'. But much more than this, *Aligarh's First Generation: Muslim Solidarity in British India* (1978) analyses an important group whose role in the nationalist movement has been condemned instead of being understood.

Lelyveld's book—that can still open up new vistas of research—is firmly rooted in history and sociology. Social history is his chief interest, though political themes are also skilfully integrated in his narrative. Not all his conclusions command equal assent; nor is his delineation of situations and problems free from the obscurities of sociological jargon. Yet, readers will find major aspects of his area of study better explained than ever before. Many writers have followed his methodology and framework of analysis; many study the same issues in other contexts; some acknowledge their debt to him; some do not. But discerning readers are likely to be impressed by Lelyveld's contribution to the ongoing debates, some of which have been underlined—though from different perspectives—in recent writings.

To what extent have such writings led to a reappraisal of existing approaches and interpretations? In other words, where does one situate them within the corpus of historical and sociological literature? Or, is it still the case that India's Muslims are treated as a special category for historical exploration?

I have argued elsewhere that social science scholarship and historiography since the 1980s have generated new approaches into different aspects of Indian society: change, variety, and difference have been highlighted in researches conducted under Marxist, post-modernist and subaltern approaches. But research on Muslims is still mired within traditional frameworks, and still dominated by widely accepted stereotypes. (Such trends will be accentuated by the 11 September 2001 terrorist assault on the World Trade Center and the Pentagon.) Colonial categories of knowledge, as applied to the Muslim communities, have been questioned but not changed. Consequently, ideas and movements associated with them are categorized as revivalist rather than reformist, communal rather than secular, separatist rather than nationalist, and finally, reactionary rather than progressive. In this scheme, the ideas and actions of Saiyid Ahmad Khan and his associates are placed within the same binary opposition. The stereotypical figure of the Saiyid as the architect of Muslim separatism, mesmerized by the British, remains unaffected by the knowledge of his reformist endeavours and his role in introducing rationalist ideas and English education in the last quarter of the nineteenth-century.

Similarly, men like Altaf Husain Hali, maulvi Nazir Ahmad and Sheikh Abdullah—all engaged in the project of 'reforming' Muslim women—find little mention in either conventional or unconventional histories and critiques of nationalism and separatism. The old explanations are presumed to unravel and delineate their conduct; it is all too readily assumed that they were imbued with 'reactionary' or 'communal' ideas. There is still talk of a 'Muslim mind', a 'Muslim outlook', and an inclination to construe a 'Muslim identity' around Islam, which is invariably on the wrong side of the binary divide. A sense of Otherness is, consequently, conveyed in such images and polarities.

Notice, for example, how the expression—'nationalist Muslims'—is widely in vogue to describe the activities of those Muslims who were wedded to a broadly secular polity and to the ideal of composite nationality. Its inappropriateness lies in the majoritarian view, a view that ascribes patriotism/nationalism to the vast majority of non-Muslims and not to others. If others share the sentiment, this is grudgingly recognized as an exception rather than the rule. Thus, the 'nationalist Muslims' are treated not only as exceptional individuals, but placed within a separate domain of enquiry and often outside the so-called nationalist discourse. When the Indian state commemorates their memory to advertise its secular credentials, the intellectual resources of specifically Muslim organizations and institutions are pressed into service to organize seminars and conferences. In this way the partition of the nation's heritage proceeds uninterruptedly.

The question is this: if, for example, Ajmal Khan, Ansari and Maulana Azad were 'nationalist Muslims', surely Gandhi, Jawaharlal Nehru and Vallabhbhai Patel were 'nationalist Hindus' by much the same logic. If religion is the criterion for categorizing an individual or a group, then how does one define the identity of a kisan or a trade union leader? Was Muzaffar Ahmad, founder of the Communist Party of India, a 'nationalist Muslim', and P.C. Joshi, also a leading figure in the communist movement, a 'nationalist Hindu'?

There are other widely-held beliefs and assumptions: for instance, the oft-repeated view that orthodoxy represents 'true' Islam, whereas liberal and modernist currents are secondary or peripheral to the more dominant separatist, communal, and neo-fundamentalist paradigms. Hence the focus on traditional revival, on religious revivalism, and on fundamentalist stirrings. When it comes to studying the Muslim communities, the dominant orthodox paradigms are ones that tend to get underlined most often. Contrariwise, heterodox trends—which contest the definition of a 'Muslim identity' in purely religious terms (in the context of imperial institutions), and which refute the popular notion that Islamic values and symbols provide a key to the understanding of the 'Muslim world view'— are not.

Consider another area where, despite the wide range of a rich secondary literature, certain views continue to influence popular beliefs and perceptions. Time and again one is reminded of the pervasive impact of Islam on its adherents, their concern to defend values enshrined in the Koran and the *Hadith*, and their trans-national links with a Muslim fraternity. Time and again one is also led to believe that the major preoccupation of a Muslim is praying, going on pilgrimage, and observing other religious rituals. Time and again we are told that Muslims, more than any other religious entity, attach importance and value to their religio-cultural habits and institutions, and therefore they are more prone to paying heed to Islamist ideas and movements.

Doubtless, theologians, publicists and itinerant preachers invoked the solidarity of the *umma* and other Islamic symbols to cultivate pan-islamism, religio-revivalism, and Muslim nationalism. Notice, how small groups of Muslims in Kanpur took to the streets when a portion of a masjid in the city was demolished in 1913. Notice, too, how the ulama and sections of the professional classes stimulated Muslim sentiments over the khilafat and the holy places. Or consider their stout resistance to interference in Muslim family law, exemplified in the opposition to the Sarda Marriage Bill of 1929, and after Independence, to the Indian Supreme Court's judgement on Shah Bano, and to the demolition of the Babri Masjid on 6 December 1992.

Doubtless, these are important facets, but their significance should not be overstated to construct a unified Muslim structure of consciousness or a singular Muslim community acting in unison to achieve common goals. Why is it *exceptional* if some Muslims, falling prey to colonial enumerations and definitions and their own fanciful theories, regarded themselves as an indivisible component of a religious collectivity? Other communities have nurtured similar self-images. Else, how shall we explain the activism of the Hindu Mahasabha, the RSS, and the numerous Hindu caste associations? What does one make of the nineteenth-century movements in Bengal, Maharashtra and Punjab, and their deepening anxieties over the future of, or the evangelical threat to, their 'Hindu identity'? The historian Susobhan Sarkar commented on 'the obsession with Hindu traditions which helped to keep the men of our [Bengal] renaissance aloof from the masses': this requires elaboration.

At the heart of the Arya Samaj's brand of reconstruction and reform was the object of restoring the supposedly pristine purity of Vedic culture and civilization. The 'Tilak school' in Maharashtra and the leading architects of the Swadeshi movement in Bengal, including Aurobindo Ghose and B.C. Pal, were re-thinking their Hindu heritage and meeting the challenges of modern thought by assimilative-creative processes. The Cow question—one that occupied centrality in the Gandhian discourse as well—was nothing but an evocative symbol of Hindu resurgence in northern and western India. The crusade for Hindi *in opposition to Urdu* was as much linked with government employment as with a widely perceived symbol of Hinduized identity. The historian Romila Thapar shows how the emergent national consciousness appropriated an

Orientalist construction of Hinduism as the heritage of Hindu culture. The need for formulating a Hindu community became a requirement for political mobilization, when representation by religious community gave access to political power and economic resources.

Muslim groups, too, appropriated certain elements from Islam to legitimize their claim to a greater share in the existing power structures. In reality, though, communitarian mobilization, though ultimately successful, failed to obliterate internal differentiations among Muslims. Although religious ties endowed them with a semblance of unity, they were none the less remarkably fragile and unable to override other forms of identity. The links binding Muslim groups with other social classes, though occasionally strained, proved in the end to be demonstrably more powerful and enduring. Hindu-Muslim ill-will in the 1940s was exacerbated, yet, traditional cross-communal associations were revived in the aftermath of the Partition. This is, indeed, part of the reason why India's secular fabric has remained intact more than five decades after Independence.

Second, it must be borne in mind that a Muslim, like his counterpart in any other community, has many acts to perform, and many diverse roles to play. He is not genetically or culturally cast in the role of a religious crusader or a relentless defender of the faith. Besides following Islam by birth and training, a Muslim, or for that matter a Hindu or a Sikh, is a peasant or a landlord, an agricultural worker or a landless labourer, a worker or an industrialist, a student or a teacher, a litigant or a lawyer, a Shia or a Sunni, a Deobandi or a Barelwi. Why, then, harp on his Muslim and Islamic identity and ignore the secular terms in which he relates to more immediate socio-economic needs, and his wide-ranging interactions with his class and not just with his brethren? While the depth and nature of this interaction is debatable, they do not justify an absolute Muslim/Islamic consciousness. If, as we are told, centuries of common living and shared experiences could not create composite solidarities, how could a specifically Muslim self-consciousness emerge out of such multiple and diverse experiences?

Muhammad Ali Jinnah believed he had the answers. So did the Jamaat-i Islami. But there were other explanations as well that were boldly constructed around secular and pluralist conceptions and counterposed to an essentialist view of Indian Islam. Though the tenability of some of those theories were critically scrutinized after the Partition, the basic tenor and thrust of liberal-left arguments is validated by serious and objective scholarship. Scholars, artists and creative writers, in particular, continue to contest the two-nation theory; they unfold the past to discover elements of unity, cohesion and integration, and provide historical legitimation for multi-culturalism and religious plurality. Prominent amongst these are people with pronounced liberal, socialist, and Marxist leanings.

Quite a few intellectuals—Muhammad Mujeeb, Muhammad Habib, A.A.A. Fyzee, Saiyid Abid Husain, Humayun Kabir, K.G. Saiyidain— did much the same after the Partition. They carried forth the inconclusive debates of the post-1857 decades when the ulama and the liberal intelligentsia, being confronted with the external political and religio-cultural threat of colonialism, were constrained to sketch out a role for themselves and reflect on the internal weaknesses within a religious tradition that had strong revivalist precedences as well as liberal and reformist tendencies. They did this because certain key aspects in those debates bore contemporary relevance, and pertained to how Muslims situated themselves in a world brutally shattered by the Partition. The nature of this engagement in pre- and post-Independence India must be explored for a rounded view of the political and intellectual currents embracing the Muslim communities. This is attempted in the following chapters.

Any discussion based on scriptures or on the corpus of knowledge inherited from the theologians cannot explain how Islam, or for that matter any other religion, has been historically *experienced* and *observed* by its adherents. The critical issue is not the apologetic defence of Islam and its tenets—a project that is at any rate pursued relentlessly by theologians of all hues—but to challenge scholarly attempts to 'essentialize' civilizations. The real task at hand is to draw attention to the enormous diversities and the variety of beliefs and practices, the multiple levels at which a Muslim relates to the temporal and spiritual world in day-to-day living, and the currents of change, reform and innovation influencing the course and direction of quite a few Muslim societies the world over. In a nutshell, the collective experience of Muslim polities and societies, rather than segments of it, needs to be considered in plotting their socio-historical evolution. Isolated and sporadic campaigns of Islamic purification, howsoever significant they may have appeared at a given moment, must be seen in perspective and not invoked to lend credence to misleading theories on Islam and Muslim identity.

It needs to be recognized that Islam is not a static point of reference, its interpretations have changed over time, and powerful pluralist visions have shaped Muslim communities in India and elsewhere. Such an approach enables us to challenge, among other things, the distorted vision of the future offered by scholars like Samuel P. Huntington, the author of *The Clash of Civilizations and the Remaking of World Order*. His central argument, developed around the eternal and essential faultlines between Christian and Islamic civilizations, though influential, stands repudiated in several academic circles. So also his view that the survival of the West depends on Americans 'reaffirming their Western identity and Westerners accepting their civilization as unique not universal, and uniting to renew and preserve it against challenges from non-western societies'. Such views reinforce stereotypes of Islamic revivalism and of Muslims, and predispose the reader to view the relationship of Islam to the West in terms of rage, violence, hatred, and irrationality.

Most of us need to take Muslims into account: an end to the neglect that Barbara Metcalf calls 'too little', and all of us need to build a history that does not make 'Islam' prior to the stereotypical thinking she calls 'too much'. Also, rather than creating difference, we need to draw boundaries around common social and political structures, situating Muslims squarely within the complex world of the opportunities and constraints, motivations and tastes they share with everyone else. (Presidential Address: 'Too Little Too Much. Reflections on Muslims in the History of India', *Journal of Asian Studies*, 54, 1995, pp. 951-67).

Contemporary politics in India is characterized by a preoccupation with communitarian identities, chauvinistic ideologies, and movements that exacerbate religious differences. More attention needs to be given to ideologies and movements that have, in the past or in the present, tried uniting Hindus and Muslims thereby furthering the post-colonial agenda of social transformation. Furthermore, we need to locate the social norms, cultural patterns and political responses of Muslim groups in relation to what Aziz Ahmad described as an 'Indian environment'. Prominent political and religious figures need to be situated within a perspective that would enlarge our appreciation of their role as well as prevent their appropriation by denominational groups. This is surely how the contribution of people like Hakim Ajmal Khan, Ansari, Azad, Rafi Ahmed Kidwai and Khan Abdul Ghaffar Khan can be evaluated. This is surely how a nation, desperately in search of symbols of unity, can pay tribute to those men and women who nursed the vision of a secular and democratic Hindustan.

Our own effort to reflect on the changing and varied portraits of Muslim communities in the subcontinent has been vindicated by the rich harvest of literary material gathered in, *Image and Representation: Stories of Muslim Lives in India*, edited by Mushirul Hasan and M. Asaduddin (New Delhi: Oxford University Press, 2000). We have selected most of the stories on the basis of how best they invoke and construct images of Muslims, chronicle our times, articulate many intimate yet historically unfamiliar points of reference, and represent the lived experiences of Muslims in various regions and socio-economic locations. What these literary representations and the nature of their life reveal is the variety of forms, style, language and symbols adopted by different writers. Neither the forms nor the lives they portray derive from a supposedly homogeneous and unbroken tradition.

2

Resistance and Acquiescence in North India: Muslim Responses to the West

When I reflect on the want of energy and the indolent dispositions of my countrymen, and the many erroneous customs which exist in all Mohammedan countries and among all ranks of Mussulmans, I am fearful that my exertions will be thrown away. . . . It may consequently be concluded, that as they will find no pleasure in reading a book which contains a number of foreign names, treats [*sic*] on uncommon subjects, and alludes to other matters which cannot be understood at the first glance, but require little time for consideration, they will, under pretence of zeal for their religion, entirely abstain and refrain from perusing it.

MIRZA ABU TALIB KHAN, *Travels of Mirza Abu Taleb Khan in Asia, Africa, and Europe during the years 1797 to 1803*

Decadence has brought us to a sorry pass; adversity far and wide lays us low. Our honour has long since vanished from the world, and no hope of revival is in sight. One hope alone sustains us now we are laid low; we live on in the expectation of paradise after death.

Too inept to travel, too spineless to journey, we know nothing of what God's creation holds. The four walls of our home which we see before our eyes are for us the limits of human habitation—like fish in a tank, for whom its limits bound their whole world.

ALTAF HUSAIN HALI, *Mussadas-i maddo-jazr-i Islam (Mussadas-i Hali)*

Any number of scholarly works delineate the responses of the Muslim aristocracy, the ulama and the literati to the first major incursion of a European power into India.[1] The late Aziz Ahmad was the first to dwell on this theme in his seminal study of *Islamic Modernism in India and*

Pakistan. Muhammad Mujeeb, former vice-chancellor of Delhi's Jamia Millia Islamia, added fresh insights through his lucid analysis of, among others, Mirza Abu Talib 'Londony's' *Masir-i Talibi fi Bilad-i Afrangi*, Lutfullah's (b. 1802) *Autobiography*, and Mirza Ihtisamuddin's *Shigurf Nama-i Velayet*.[2] In this paper, my concerns are twofold. First, to shift the focus from 'revivalist' and 'fundamentalist' trends in the first-half of the nineteenth-century—extensively covered in secondary literature—to the presence of alternative currents of thought. This may provide a corrective to the essentialist view, which was part of the colonial stereotype, that Muslims were so steeped in their religion and so firmly anchored in Islamic traditions that anything Western or modern was inimical to their world view. Secondly, I wish to underline both the elements of continuity as well as the variety of responses to the West. This places in perspective the ongoing debates on identity politics in the nineteenth century.

I

Most thinking Muslims of the late nineteenth and early twentieth-centuries looked at the events of the past hundred years as a historical catastrophe for their religion. The notion of *umma*, resting on the utopian concept of a unified belief system and ritualistic structure, lost its validity as the house of Islam stood hopelessly fragmented and doctrinally polarized. As the colonial powers established their political hegemony, the beleagured Ottoman sultan remained the sole surviving symbol of resistance to Western imperialism. Many educated Indian Muslims, swayed by the pan-Islamic ferment, rose to defend the sultan and his empire. By the time their passions cooled, the khilafat bubble had burst, the empire had withered away, and the khalifa/sultan was far removed from Constantinople. '*Chhak kar di Turk-i Nadaan ne khilafat ki Qaba*' (Alas, the naive Turk has cut to pieces the khilafat robe), wrote a distraught Muhammad Iqbal.[3]

The trauma of decline, a recurrent theme in world-wide Islamic litera-ture, was expressed in a variety of ways. In some places it was mani-fested in militant assertions of Islamic identity, a stricter conformity to the Koran and the *Sunna*, and a call for a return to the pristine Islam of the early days of the orthodox khalifas. In other places, most notably in West and North Africa, there was greater consciousness of the internal degeneration of Muslim society and an awareness of the positive lines of reconstruction through an integration of modern ideas and institutions with the bases of Islam.[4] In advocating such a course, early Islamic modernism encouraged the import of Western thought and educational initiatives, and offered partial justification for the Western intellectual influences that were already there and were bound to come anyway.

In the Indian subcontinent, early reformist trends were either dormant or suffered from ambiguity until Saiyid Ahmad Khan advocated, in the tradition of his Egyptian counterpart Muhammad Abduh, integrating the modern scientific world view with the injunctions of the Koran. The theme of decline mattered to him a great deal, though his own discourse was remarkably free of ceaseless lamentations over the eclipse of Muslim power and the declining Muslim civilization. Others did so with unfailing regularity and with great effect. Altaf Husain Hali, acutely sensitive to the departed glory of Islam and its followers, wrote: 'We have eclipsed,' he bemoaned, 'the fame of our ancestors' name. Wherever we set one foot our countrymen are ashamed of us. We have squandered the high honour that our ancestors won, and have lost the nobility of our Arab forbears.'[5] 'With my unskilful mirrors', he stated in his preface to a book, 'I have built a house of mirrors, in which our people can see their face and form reflected.'

There was, in addition, a good deal of soul-searching, and many earnest attempts to ask what had gone wrong, a question Shah Waliullah had raised amid the ruins of the Mughal empire. Few could claim to have the right answers. And fewer still, when faced with the reality of foreign rule, could decide on how best to cope with the colonial encounter, withstand the ideological assault of the Christian West, and acquire the strength to confront Europe and become part of the modern world. There were varied responses, each one being seriously debated. When the poet Mirza Ghalib reached Delhi in 1810 he found the conflict between the 'traditionalists' in religion and the 'radical' reformers 'raging vigorously'.[6] When maulvi Karimuddin (b. 1821) of Panipat visited Delhi he found 'the fountain of knowledge' flowing in every direction.[7] He referred to the setting up of new printing presses in Delhi. These gave spurt to publications and stimulated interest in contemporary social and political issues.

Early responses to colonial rule were, predictably, mixed. Nineteenth-century historical literature is replete with instances of resistance to and rebellion against the 'infidels'. Some tangible expressions of opposition to the new symbols of authority was the *fatwa* of Shah Abdul Aziz, eldest of Waliullah's son, the adventurist campaigns of the *mujahidins* in the Frontier region, the Faraizi movement of Haji Shariat-Allah in Bengal, and the involvement of some prominent ulama in the 1857 revolt. Islam provided a ready-made conceptual framework for such wide-ranging reactions.

Equally intense was the stubborn resistance to the proselytizing activities of Christian missionaries and their denigration of Islam and its Prophet, to the influx of unorthodox ideas which threatened to undermine religious beliefs, and to what Abu Talib described as 'that overbearing insolence which characterizes the vulgar part of the English in their conduct of Orientals'. There was, moreover, strong and pungent criticism of unabashed British expansionist designs. Like so many others his generation, Ghalib's sense of pride was wounded by the annexation of Awadh. 'Although I am a stranger to Awadh and its affair,' he wrote on 23 February 1857, 'the destruction of the state depressed me all the more, and I maintain that no Indian who was not devoid of all sense of justice could have felt otherwise.'[8] 'No doubt,' observed Saiyid Ahmad a year later, 'men of all classes were irritated at its (Awadh) annexation, all agreed in thinking that the Honourable East India Company had acted in defiance of its treaties, and in contempt of the word which it had pledged.'[9]

Nineteenth-century movements of revivalism and reform symbolized anger and indignation against political subordination and the cultural hegemony of the 'outsiders'. They were grounded in the belief that the Islamic community enjoyed an autonomy of its own requiring no mediation. Thus, Islam in India had to be purged of Hindu accretions, and its followers to be equipped to combat the pernicious influence of the West through the unchanging social and religious codes enunciated in the Koran and the *Hadith*. The conception of community, still in its embryonic form, had to be revitalized and its lost pride restored through a carefully devised educational scheme. Such was the rationale behind the founding of the Dar al-ulum at Deoband. The institution, inspired by the ideas of Waliullahi school and conforming to Hanafi codes, delivered hundreds of rulings (*fatawa*) a year to guide the faithful and maintain a close vigil on their social and religious conduct.[10] On a lesser scale, Lucknow's Firangi Mahal, the seminary founded in Aurangzeb's reign (1658-1707), performed the same role. These interventions were designed to bring about an uniformity of belief and practice, rejuvenate and revitalize the slackening faith of the believers, define the place and status of the Muslims in a Western-dominated cultural and intellectual milieu, and cement the bonds of unity in an otherwise stratified community.

Saiyid Ahmad spurned the 'traditionalist' world view. In his generation, he was among the few to recognize the presence of a powerful colonial force in the subcontinent, and, for that reason, laid stress on *ijtehad* (interpretation) and not *taqlid* (conformity), on innovation, reforms and change rather than on unquestioning adherence to the *Shariat*. Drawing upon the Islamic intellectual heritage and his own reading of the contemporary political scene, he endeavoured to convince the British that the Muslims were loyal subjects. Importantly, he told his co-religionists that they would gain much more by cooperating with the government and learning from them than they would by carrying on with futile resistance or withdrawing into a sulk. They were not to live as the British themselves lived, but to carve out a place for themselves within the establishment. To do this, they were not required to adopt nineteenth-century British liberalism, but only to accept some of its values as at least a second-best substitute for the vanished Muslim glories.[11]

Muslim theologians found this a bitter pill to swallow. Denouncing the Aligarh reformer, they called him a *nechari* and an apostate. But Saiyid Ahmad ignored such blunt criticism and the rude *fatawa*. At the end of the day, the grand old man of Aligarh emerged a clean winner and his message embodied, in large part, the *ijma* (consensus) of succeeding Muslim generations in the subcontinent. His interpretation of Islam became part of the mental frame of educated Muslims, including those trained and tutored in the traditional centres of learning. Those who condemned him had to eat their words. Those who chided him sent their own children to the college he founded at Aligarh, a town (also known as Koil) in western Uttar Pradesh (hereafter UP), situated 79 miles south of Delhi. 'The world has seen,' stated Hali in a moving tribute to his intellectual mentor, 'how one man has aroused a whole land, one man saved a caravan from destruction, and small boats sinking ships to the shore . . . Hidden among the gravel there are pearls to be found; and mingled in the sand are particles of gold.'[12]

As the nineteenth-century wore on, it became increasingly clear that there was little prospect of successful military resistance, and little hope of fulfilling the dream of establishing a *Dar al-Islam*. Just as the collapse of the Mughal empire had upset the uncertainties of the previous era, the coming of the British created eddies of uncertainty in certain circles. Yet, a broad consensus existed in favour of an Anglo-Muslim rapprochement as opposed to the repudiation of everything Western. Much before Saiyid Ahmad, the *sajjada nashin* of certain Sufi shrines in Punjab had assisted the British during the siege of Multan in 1848-9.[13] Nor did the Muslims of Bengal stir, a fact noted by Canning (1812-62), the governor-general at the time of the 1857 upheaval. In Punjab, they joined with Sikhs and the tribesmen of Kohat to form part of the reinforcements for the British troops on the Ridge outside Delhi. In the North-Western Provinces, 'the Mahomedans have, I think, behaved better than might have been ex- pected . . . and that the result, far from bringing to light a chronic Mahomedan conspiracy, has been to show that we have not in that class of our subjects that formidable danger that has been sometimes apprehended'.[14] The historian Eric Stokes explained how the economic and political ties of members of Muslim learned families helped moderate their response to cries for *jihad*. Only in the vicinity of Thana Bhawan, north of Delhi, did the poverty of the petty gentry and a strong ideological impulse from local religious leaders, who later helped set up the Dar al-ulum in Deoband, forge a 'truly' Islamic response.[15] The heroics supposedly performed by the ulama, catalogued in *Ulama-i Hind Ka Shandar Maazi*, was no more than a latter-day idealized construction.[16]

New generations grew up for whom foreign rule was an unchanging fact of life, whether they liked it or not. For some time, since the British perpetuated the administrative patterns of the Mughals, including the use of Persian as official tongue, the presence of a handful of Britishers at the top made relatively little difference in day-to-day routine. In judicial and revenue employ, except in the highest posts, Muslims held their own in Bengal until the middle of nineteenth-century, in the region of modern UP for a generation thereafter. Likewise, while the landed classes proved vulnerable to British-induced changes in some areas, it was not so in others. In Bengal, Muslims did not become as insignificant a proportion of the new landed class as their numbers among the population might suggest. In UP, the 'Islamic gentry' in the *qasbahs* remained well-entrenched in the lower levels of the British service during the early nineteenth-century; the Muslim landlord class exercised an influence and power that persisted well into the next century.[17]

Some Muslims quickly sensed that their community could no longer live in a stable and self-sufficient system of inherited culture: their need was now to generate the strength to survive in a world dominated by 'Others'. A large number of them explained the reasons for the strength of Europe to demonstrate that Muslims could adopt European concepts and methods without being untrue to their belief. Although this realization eventually diluted opposition to and softened hostility towards the British, the earliest signs of change is broadly reflected in the careers of Mirza Abu Talib and Lutfullah (1802-74), the two outstanding representatives of early nineteenth-century north India.

II

Abu Talib spent his early years in Murshidabad at the court of Muzaffar Jung. With the accession of Asaf al-Daula (r. 1775-97) he returned to Awadh as *amildar* of Etawah and other districts. He also served as a revenue official under Colonel Alexander Hanny in Gorakhpur, and spiritedly defended his revenue administration in *Tafzih al-Ghafilin*, a history of Awadh under Asaf al-Daula. Later employed by Nathaniel Middleton, the English Resident (1773-82), and connected with Richard Johnson in managing the confiscated jagirs of the Begums of Awadh, his superiors were impressed with his robust attitude to life, his scholarly disposition, and his sensitivity to the winds of change blowing in the areas under Company rule. A Scotsman, Captain David Richardson, recognized these traits in his personality and arranged for his travel to Europe.[18]

On 7 February 1799, Abu Talib sailed from Calcutta to Europe where he visited England, France, Turkey, and other countries, returning to India in August 1803. He reached London on 21 January 1800, the starting point of his trip to other parts of England. He set out on his return journey on 7 June 1802, travelling through France, Constantinople, Baghdad, Karbala, Najaf and the Persian Gulf to 'describe the curiosities and wonders . . . (and) give some account of the manners and customs of the various nations (he) visited, all of which was little known to the Asiatics'.[19]

The Mirza was received with warmth and courtesy. He had an audience with George III and Queen Charlotte, met the old colonial hands—Warren Hastings (1754-1826), Cornwallis (1738-1805) and Charles Metcalf (1785-1846)—and interacted with literary figures and artists. Known as 'The Persian Prince', the press followed him everywhere. 'I declare', he wrote, 'I never assumed the title; but I was so much better known by it than by my own name, that I found it in vain to contend with my godfather.'[20] He was courted, entertained lavishly, and his wit and repartees were apparently the subject of conversation in the politest circles.[21] He was perfectly at ease in such circles, enjoying 'every luxury my heart could desire', drinking 'exquisite' wines, and visiting operas in the company of 'ladies of quality'. He viewed the visit to playhouses as an 'employment of sensuality', and detailed the arrangement of the stage, seats, spectacles, and spectators. He even drew a blueprint of the playhouse in Dublin. He was taken in by the beauty of the women, and their grace in dancing; his senses 'charmed' by the variety and melody of their music. Exhilarated by the coolness of the climate and devoid of all care, the Mirza wrote about how he 'gave' himself 'up to love and gaiety'.[22] On his return journey home he visited the shrines of the Shia *imams*, Hazrat Ali, Imam Husain, and his son Imam Zainul-Abidin, and sought their forgiveness for his sins in Europe. He also composed two elegies in praise of Ali and his son Imam Hasan.

Returning to Calcutta on 4 August 1803, Abu Talib put together his notes and diaries to write a truly 'monumental assessment' of Anglo-Saxon civilization.[23] Written nearly a quarter of a century before the impressions of the Egyptian scholar-educationist Rifa al-Tahtawi, *The Travels of Mirza Abu Taleb Khan* was one of the first introductions to modern Western civilization. 'I believe this is the first time,' wrote Abu Talib's translator, 'the genuine opinions of an Asiatic, respecting the institutions of Europe, have appeared in the English languages.'[24] Translated by Charles Stewart, Professor of Oriental Languages in the East India Company's college at Hertford, the *Masir-i Talibi fi Bilad-i Afrangi* was published in 1810, in two volumes, by Boxbourne, London. A French translation (*Voyages du Prince Persan Mirza Abul Taleb Khan*) appeared in Paris in 1812, the year when the Persian text was published by his son Mirza Husain Ali; its second version a year later. The same year a German translation was out in Vienna.[25]

Lutfullah, who visited England nearly half a century later,[26] agreed with some of Abu Talib's impressions of the West. Both were struck by the progress in mechanical inventions, the tangible benefits of the industrial revolution, and by the organization and functioning of mills, iron foundries and hydraulic machines. 'On entering one of the extensive manufactories in England,' recorded Abu Talib, 'the mind is at first bewildered by the number and variety of articles displayed therein; but, after recovering from this first impression, and having coolly surveyed all the objects around, every thing appears conducted with so much regularity and precision, that a person is induced to suppose one of the meanest capacity might superintend and direct the whole process.'[27] In fact, the 'sixth excellence' of the English people, according to him, 'is a passion for mechanism, and their numerous contrivances for facilitating labour and industry'.[28] He was fascinated by the fire extinguishing 'machines',[29] and by the art of printing, 'the utility of which may not appear at first sight to be Asiatic'.[30] Likewise, Lutfullah admired the bridges in London:

The first objects that engaged our attention were the enormous bridges in the city, especially the iron bridge, and the swinging bridge. It astonished us greatly to see large masses of cast iron regularly fixed and nicely cemented together in these useful fabrics. The country, we felt convinced, must have some inexhaustible mines of this metal, which is so necessary for man; for, besides these bridges, iron appears to be used profusely. No house seemed to be without iron railings, iron bars, and some houses are even roofed with iron, and some gardens hedged with iron bars.[31]

Consider, too, Abu Talib's description of Woolwich:

I there saw several large ships on the stocks; and such stores of timber, iron canvas etc. that had the war (Anglo-French) continued for ten years longer, they would not have required a fresh supply. I was particularly attracted by the mode of casting the cannon-balls and shells; also by the manner of boring and shaping the exterior surface of the guns at the same time, all done by the motion of a wheel turned by a steam-engine, which so facilitated the work, that an old woman or a child might have performed the rest of the operation.[32]

Clearly, the impact and potentialities of the industrial revolution sensitized Abu Talib to its implications. Attributing Britain's economic superiority over the Napoleanic empire to industrial technology and its military success to the navy, he stated: 'The great perfection to which the English have brought their navy is, doubtless, the chief cause of their prosperity, and the principal source of all their wealth.'[33] Likewise, he attributed Britain's conquest of Egypt and other colonies to 'the prowess of their own arms', and to their being formidable on shore as at sea. In this way he thus recognized the importance of sea-power more than eighty years before the publication of Mahan's classical work on the subject.[34]

Abu Talib attributed Britain's industrial revolution to the system of government, to the country's vibrant social and cultural ethos, and to the 'national character' of its people. He commended the unwritten British constitution underlining its monarchical, aristocratic and democratic character, and the respect for individual freedom protected by the British Law; 'liberty may be considered as the idol or tutelary deity of the English; and I think the common people here enjoy more *freedom* and equality than in any other well-regulated government of the world'.[35]

During his stay he went several times to the Houses of Parliament, and was astonished to discover that this was a legislative assembly, with the duty of enacting laws to regulate both civil and criminal matters. The English, he explained to his readers, unlike the Muslims, did not accept any divinely revealed holy law to guide them and regulate their lives in those matters and were therefore reduced to the pitiable expedient of making their own laws 'in accordance with the exigencies of the time, their own dispositions, and the experience of their judges'.

Abu Talib took great interest in the education of English women and their freedom. He mentioned six spheres where the liberty of the Asian women appeared 'less than that of Europeans', though he also pointed to those spheres where they had more rights. Likewise, Mirza Ihtisamuddin (Mirza Itesa Modeen, *Shigurf namah-i-Valaet, or, Excellent intelligence concerning Europe: being the travels of Mirza Itesa Modeen in Great Britain and France-e Velaet*, translated by James Edward Alexander, London, 1872), who visited England in 1765, praised the status of women, their devotion to education, and their quest for knowledge. 'They are not like the people of this country,' he wrote, 'who repeat Hindi and Persian poems in praise of a mistress's face, or descriptive of the qualities of the wine, of the goblet, and of the cup-bearer, and who pretend to be in love.' He was, moreover, impressed with women unveiled in the public sphere, and attracted to the spectacle of male-female intimacy in public parks. This is how he describes the scenes near the Queen's palace in London:

On Sunday, men, women, and youths, poor and rich, travelers and natives resort here. This park enlivens the heart, and people overcome with sorrow, repairing thither, are entertained in a heavenly manner, and grieved hearts, from seeing that place of amusement, are gladdened against their will. On every side females with silver forms, resembling peacocks, walk about, and at every corner fairy-faced ravishers of hearts move with a thousand blandishments and coquetries; the plain of the earth becomes a paradise from the resplendent foreheads, and heaven (itself) hangs down its head for shame at seeing the beauty of the loves. There lovers meet without fear of the police or of rivals, and gallants obtain a sight of rosy cheeks without restraints. When I viewed this heavenly place I involuntarily exclaimed:

> If there is a paradise on earth,
> It is this, oh! It is this.
>
> (*Gar firdows bur ru-ye zamin ast*
> *hamin ast va hamin ast va hamin ast*)

At the same time, Abu Talib noticed widespread poverty, social inequalities, the disparities between the rich and poor, and the effects of a high cost of living,[36] rates of taxation on the common people, and the enormous national debt.[37] He criticized the unsavoury role of commercial magnates and proprietors of joint stock firms enjoying large extra-constitutional powers. He found, much to his dismay, that the privileged sections of society were 'puffed up with their power and good fortune for the last fifty years',[38] and had no idea of how the 'flame, though . . . smothered by a heap of fuel thrown on it, breaks out in the sequel with the greatest violence'.[39] Concerned that no attempt was being made to alleviate the sufferings of those people in London who had 'assembled in mobs on account of the great increase of taxes and high price of provision, and were nearly in a state of insurrection', he opined that this attitude 'betrays a blind confidence'.[40] Instead of meeting the 'danger' and preventing disaffection, the English people waited for the misfortune to arrive: 'such was the case with the late King of France, who took no step to oppose the Revolution, till it was too late.'[41]

In delineating the features of the British 'national character', both Abu Talib and Lutfullah highlighted their sense of honour and prestige, their concern for and recognition of merit, and their cautious, law-abiding, disciplined, and courteous nature.[42] He mentioned, with implied approval, that instead of rushing ahead with changes the British proceeded slowly and cautiously. Yet, he castigated them for their 'want of chastity',[43] criticized the want of faith in religion,[44] and upbraided the upper classes for being complacent and haughty. Contemptuous of their passion for wealth and their preoccupation with worldly affairs,[45] he disapproved of their insularity, their contempt for the customs of other nations, and the preference they gave to their own.[46] He reminiscenced how

in London, I was frequently attacked on the apparent unreasonableness and childishness of some of the Mohammedan customs; but as, from my knowledge of the English character, I was convinced it would be a folly to argue the point philosophically with them, I contended myself with parrying the subject. Thus, when they attempted to turn into ridicule the ceremonies used by the pilgrims on their arrival in Mecca, I asked them, why they supposed the ceremony of baptism, by a clergyman, requisite for the salvation of a child, who could not possibly be sensible [sic] what he was about. When they reproached us for eating with our hands; I replied, 'There is by this mode no danger of cutting yourself or your neighbours; and it is an old and a true proverb, 'The nearer the bone, the sweeter the meat': but, exclusive of these advantages, a man's own hands are surely cleaner than the feet of a baker's boy: for it is well-known, that half the bread in London is kneaded by the feet. By this mode of argument I, completely silenced all my adversaries, and frequently turned the laugh against them, when they expected to have refuted me and made me appear ridiculous.[47]

Although receptive to some of the new ideas, Abu Talib distanced himself philosophically from the West and found much that was of enduring quality in his own intellectual traditions. Rooted in his own soil, he derived inspiration and strength from the values he had inherited and imbibed in late eighteenth-century Awadh society without, of course, sharing the scepticism of some of his own contemporaries towards Western ideas and institutions. He noticed the social transformation taking place in the industrialized nations of Europe, and commented on its world-wide impact.

Abu Talib's religious identity was unassailable; it was a major component of his ideological orientation. But he did not find religious categories of much help when it came to understanding either Awadh society or delineating the contours of Western polities, economy and society. If anything, he attached importance to the diverse economic forces moulding attitudes and shaping the destiny of humankind. Thus, in analysing the ancien régime in France and his contemporary Awadh society, he referred to the growing disparities between various classes and to the widening economic disparaties. Implicit in his narrative is the view that the key factor leading to the collapse of the ancien régime was the exacerbation of class differentiation. He wondered why such an upheaval had not occurred in Awadh in spite of excessive taxation, the tyranny of the land-lords, the impoverishment of the peasantry, a fall in production, and in land revenue realization. It is not without significance that he attributed the passivity of the oppressed to the role of religion, and to British pol-icies which buttressed the wazir and averted the immediate collapse of his kingdom.

Abu Talib belonged to a declining aristocracy. But, like so many people of his social background, he tried to make the best of the opportunities available under the Company's dispensation. This was a pointer to his generation of Muslims, as indeed to the generations thereafter, who were faced with an inescapable dilemma *vis-a-vis* British rule. Eschewing a defiant posture towards the colonizers, he acknowledged the inevitability of change and the necessity of softening belligerent attitudes towards foreign rule. For this reason he adhered to his resolve, despite fears of being villified and ridiculed, to inform his countrymen about the political and economic conditions, the industry, and the social and cultural life of the British who had come to preside over India's destiny. He hoped that many of 'the customs, inventions, sciences, and ordinances of Europe, the good effects of which are apparent in their countries, might with great advantage be initiated by Mohammedans'.[48] In this respect, at least, he was a fore-runner of the ideas of Saiyid Ahmad Khan, the major catalyst of social and educational reforms among India's Muslims in the last-quarter of the nineteenth-century.

III

Representing the scribal class—those serving the regional and local bureaucracies under the Mughals and their British successors—Abu Talib and Lutfullah were not the only ones favouring rapprochement with the British in India or seeking government patronage. Muhammad Khan of Bilgram joined the foreign department of the governor-general in the early days of Company rule.[49] Ghalib's uncle, Nasrullah Beg Khan, served the Company in the Anglo-Maratha war of 1802-3 as commander of a contingent and received a life jagir from the British commander-in-chief, Lord Lake.[50] The father of nawab Mustafa Khan Shefta (b. 1806), Ghalib's fellow-poet, received estates for resolving the disputes between Lord Lake and the Maratha commanders.[51] In this way, the British continued with the Mughal traditions of granting jagirs and *inam* lands for political loyalty and military services. For thirty years after the Maratha war of 1802-3, the holders of such grants were left relatively undisturbed. For a generation after 1803, a gentlemanly existence in something like the old style was thus possible in upper India for those Muslims who were ready to serve the British as auxiliary cavalry and as subordinate revenue and judicial officers.[52] Bishop Heber's *Narrative* for 15 September 1824 contains a British collector's impression of 'a new order rising from the middling classes' to replace that of 'very many ancient families . . . gone to decay'.[53]

The 'middling classes' were drawn from those enterprising groups who were prepared to make the most of what little there was. They were, to begin with, small in numbers. Yet, they formed a major component of what was, until the last-quarter of the nineteenth-century, the Muslim intelligentsia in north India, the harbinger of reforms and social change. They contributed, as in the case of their counterparts in Bengal and Maharashtra, to the efflorescence of modern learning, which C.F. Andrews described as the 'Delhi Renaissance'.[54] They pioneered the Aligarh movement, where the first generation of students and teachers set the tone and tenor of powerful intellectual ideas in the twentieth century.[55] They were also the first to promote Western education and the learning of sciences among Muslims through organizations—the Anjuman-i Himayat-i Islam in Punjab, the Muhammadan Literary and Scientific Society, and the Central National Mohammedan Association in Bengal. Hali would have had them in mind when he spoke of 'men of feeling', 'men of sympathy', 'men of worth'. 'Amongst these heedless sleepers,' he wrote, 'some are awake'. 'In the taverns are some who are still sober. These are men who are not like the rest of their group. Among the worthless are still some men of worth.'[56]

Education was the key to success, a passport to government service. Though most Muslims defiantly stayed away from British schools and colleges, there were others who acquainted themselves with Western languages and literature, philosophy and science. As early as 1775-6, Mirza Ihtisamuddin, who travelled to Europe in the year of the Treaty of Allahabad between Clive (1724-74) and Shah Alam (1759-1806),[57] visited the laboratories and observatories in London. 'In England,' he wrote, 'it would be extraordinary if the arts and sciences did not flourish (from their being encouraged). Now in India, if a person by a long course of study were to acquire knowledge, so as to excel the world, yet he would remain despised and contemned [*sic*]: he would neither acquire honour nor respect, and in the end misfortune and misery would overtake him.'[58] In 1788, Tipu Sultan (r. 1783-99), the ruler of Mysore, wanted one of his sons to be educated in France. The French authorities approved of the idea, but suggested that the prince should learn to read and write French, learn a little calculus and some arithmetic before leaving for Paris.[59] In 1794, Mirza Ahmad Khan of Broach, a town in Gujarat, reached Paris, learnt French in three months, and translated *The Declaration of the Rights of Man* into Persian. He then presented his work to the Committee of Public Safety, which had it deposited in the *Bibliotheque Nationale*. This translation was the first in any oriental language.[60] Such works were channels through which knowledge of the new world of Europe travelled to India.

Tafazzul Husain Khan (d. 1800), long associated with the Company as well as the Awadh nawabs, compiled important mathematical works, and translated into Persian Newton's *Principia*. Officials in Calcutta commended his command over the English language, and his knowledge of European literature and philosophy.[61] His successor, Saadat Ali Khan (r. 1798-1814), founded an observatory in Lucknow. Both Ghaziuddin Haider (r. 1814-27) and Nasiruddin Haider (r. 1827-37) patronized Western and Oriental philological studies. According to Bishop Heber, the former had 'a strong taste for mechanics and chemistry' and constructed a laboratory in Lucknow.[62] Speaking of a breakfast at the Residency at which Ghaziuddin Haider was present, Heber (who visited Lucknow in 1824) noted that the King talked about steam engines and a new device, invented by an English engineer in his pay, of propelling ships by a spiral wheel at the bottom of the vessel. He also explained his acquaintance with English books read to him in Hindustani by his aides-de-camp.[63] Nasiruddin, inheriting such scientific and artistic tastes, hired an English tutor to make himself at home in English culture. He built an observatory in the charge of an English Astronomer-Royal, a colonel Wilcox.

Finally, the Fort William College in Calcutta encouraged literary and scientific learning all over India. A resident of the city, Mansher Khesumul Riya, wrote to the *Calcutta Journal* on 13 April 1820:

I am a Mooslem of this city, who by early instruction in the English language, have acquired access to the general literature with which that tongue is adorned, and am enabled to enjoy the numerous publications which advocate the cause of liberty.

Lutfullah wrote his *Autobiography* in English, 'the first (and) almost the best autobiography by an Indian in English'. He had read Gibbon, a Latin book on the customs and institutions of the Turks, and a *Universal History* by some Dr Philip Prince.[64] A lesser known person, Abdur Rahim Dahri (1785-1850), travelled from Gorakhpur in eastern UP to acquire proficiency in English at the Fort William College. He wrote widely, including a pamphlet on the virtue of studying the English language and disseminating Western thought. He insisted, in a memorandum submitted to Warren Hastings, that modern education be introduced through the medium of English. Abdur Rahim spent the last years of an extraordinary career as an English teacher at Fort William College.[65] For him the civilization of the West did not appear wholly alien; Muslims could move towards it without any sense of being untrue to themselves or their faith.

The Madrasa Aliyah flourished in Calcutta. Among its beneficiaries were Saiyid Ameer Ali, author-historian, and Abdur Rahim, a judge turned politician. The Delhi College, an early and significant enterprise in secular education, was established in 1825 with two branches: an English branch where English language and literature and modern European sciences were taught and an Oriental branch in which not only Arabic, Persian and Sanskrit were taught but geography, mathematics and sciences as well.[66] By far the most popular side of the education offered in Old Delhi College was that which dealt with science. Maulvi Zakaullah, in his old age, used to tell C.F. Andrews 'with kindling eyes how eagerly these scientific lectures were followed'.[67] The doctrines of ancient philosophy taught through the medium of Arabic were 'thus cast in the shade before the more reasonable and experimental theories of modern science. The old dogma . . . that the earth is the fixed centre of the universe was generally laughed at by the higher students of the Oriental as well as by those of the English Department of the college.'[68]

The Delhi College was the nucleus of a group which tried re-evaluating inherited doctrines and beliefs. Take maulvi Karimuddin, whose book provided the basis of Farhatullah Beg's modern Urdu classic, *Delhi ki Akhri Shama* (The Last Mushairah of Delhi). He belonged to a family of maulvis, left his home town Panipat to join Delhi College in 1839, and set up a printing press to meet the growing demand of writers trying to express, in Urdu and English, their consciousness of themselves and their place in the modern world.[69] Consider, too, the career of Munshi Shafaqatullah, an English teacher in Bareilly. He translated Chamber's introduction to the sciences, as also a well-known work on astronomy, natural philosophy, geology, and other sciences. It was entitled *Khulsatul-Ulum*.

There was another noticeable trend: influential groups in various regions, especially those needing a fresh imprimatur from each ruling power, made the colonial government work. Thus, many *sajjada nashins* in rural Punjab agreed to be incorporated into the framework of the British administration, often playing leading roles as *ziladars*, honorary magistrates, and district board members. By early twentieth-century, they had become an integral part of the class of rural intermediaries on whom British rule rested in the area.[70] In Sind, the British constructed a political system hinging on the cooperation of landed elites, of whom the pirs made up a sizeable proportion. Sarah Ansari has established how both sides took advantage of the system and how the pirs, in particular, discovered new ways of increasing their power and prestige. The very section of the élite which, in theory, had most to lose from being too closely associated with the administration, found that there was much to gain from maintaining a good working relationship with their new 'infidel' rulers. They managed to retain an aura of spiritual aloofness at the same time as making the most of the benefits of cooperation. In the long run, their willingness to participate in the colonial system helped endow pir families with the resilience needed to cope with British rule.[71]

The British realized, particularly after 1857, that the crucial task in maintaining their rule was to be able to react quickly and sensitively as power flowed from one group to another in response to processes of economic, social, or even ideological change. The imposing edifice of colonial government rested on delicate political relationships with powerful and influential groups in a myriad localities.[72] Though wary and distrustful of the Muslims, the British co-opted some of them into administrative and bureaucratic structures. They were to form the pillar of the raj during the inter-War years during the twentieth century.

Some ulama, following an old established tradition of pliancy and conformism, accepted British rule. Some others were, however, made of sterner stuff, falling into the colonial stereotype of being bigoted, fanatical and intransigent. Shah Abdul Aziz had declared India as *Dar al-harb*; so the Friday and Id prayers could not be performed as congregational prayers. 'From here (Delhi) to Calcutta,' he announced, 'the Christians are in complete control.' This pronouncement sustained Saiyid Ahmad Shaheed's exertions against the British, and legitimized other nineteenth-century movements against their rule, even though the *fatwa*, read in its totality, conveyed different meanings to different people and was, therefore, subject to diverse interpretations. Muhammad Ismail, the nephew of Abdul Aziz, recommended a *modus vivendi* with the British as long as they did not interfere with the religious freedom of the Muslims.

In the early days of Company rule, such positions may well have prompted Fazl-i Rasul Budauni, Mufti Sadruddin, Fazl-i Haq Khayrabadi and a section of the Firangi Mahal family to serve the Company, take up jobs in institutions, and accept government titles. There were many more Muslim divines in the nineteenth-century who held the view that India was *Dar al-aman* (land of peace) as the British allowed the Islamic Personal Law to be applied to the Muslims in cases of inheritance, succession, gifts, *auqaf*, marriage, divorce, parentage, guardianship, and maintenance. They invoked the Koranic verse—'Obey God, obey His Prophet, and obey those in authority over you'—to argue that the duty of obedience to a legitimate authority was not merely one of political expediency but a religious obligation. The ulama availed of the opportunities either left by the British policy of non-interference with religion, or created by the development of communications, printing and the press. This enabled them to propagate their teachings more widely and, with their considerable resources and knowledge of Islamic traditions, confront Christian missionaries and the forces inimical to Islam. Saiyid Ahmad Shaheed's *Siral al-Mustaqim* (The Sacred Path) and Muhammad Ismail's *Taqwiyat al-Iman* (Strengthening the Faith) were printed in lithographic editions thus receiving wider circulation than had hitherto been possible.

Nineteenth-century Indian Islam did not produce scholars like Rifa Badawi, Rafi al-Tahtawi, Khayar al-Din, or Abduh, who reinterpreted the Islamic Law in the direction of conformity with modern needs and endeavoured to adapt the *Shariat* to new circumstances. Yet, India's ulama, while jealously guarding their exclusive right as guardians of a fixed and established tradition, grudgingly came to terms with British rule. In the aftermath of the 1857 revolt, in particular, they acquiesced in rather than repudiated Pax Britannica. Deoband's Dar al-ulum, founded in a spirit of compromise rather than opposition to colonial rule, rested on an unstated principle: if living in the nineteenth-century world demanded changes in the Islamic ways of life, the ulama must try to make them while remaining true to themselves and their faith.

IV

Hali's repeated pleas and exhortations, couched in his *Mussadas*, summed up a major strand in the thinking patterns of the north Indian literate Muslims in the nineteenth century. He wrote:

No man wishes evil to your faith and religion. No man attacks the Traditions and the Koran. No man seeks to harm the pillars of your community. No man seeks to prohibit you from the commands of the Holy Law. Say your prayers without fear in your places of worship, and let the call to prayer ring out in your mosques.

The roads to travel and trade lie open. None blocks the roads to crafts and industry. The roads to the acquisition of learning are lighted. The roads to the gaining of wealth are made level. . . .

Know the words of this peace and freedom. For the paths to advancement have been cleared in every direction, and the age is the friend of all who would travel upon them. The cry comes persistently from every side, 'There is no enemy to dread, no highway robber to fear: come out and take the road, for the roads are safe!' ↙

Many caravans have long been on the move. Many more are loading up their burdens. Many are in agitation at the movement all round them. . . . You alone amongst them are still sunk in heedless sleep. Take care, lest in your heedlessness you fail to reach your goal![73]

Ghalib announced the tidings of the dawn and pointed the way to the light of the sun.

> The harp player, when he strikes the chord
> One can see what he is after,
> Happiness lies concealed behind the veil of sorrow,
> Not for wrath does the washerman beat the cloth.[74]

NOTES

1. A. Yusuf Ali, 'Muslim Culture and Religious Thought', in L.S.S. O'Malley (ed.), *Modern India and the West: A Study of the Interaction of their Civilization*, Oxford, 1941; Muhammad Mujeeb, 'First Impressions of Western Culture on Indian Muslims', in H. Rao (ed.), *South Asian Studies I*, New Delhi, 1965; Aziz Ahmad, *Islamic Modernism in India and Pakistan, 1857-1964*, Cambridge, 1967; Muhammad Mujeeb, *The Indian Muslims*, London, 1967; S.A.A. Rizvi, 'The Breakdown of Traditional Society', *The Cambridge History of Islam*, Vol. 2, Cambridge, 1970; Peter Hardy, *The Muslims of British India*, Cambridge, 1972; Mujeeb Ashraf, *Muslim Attitudes towards British Rule and Western Culture*, New Delhi, 1982; Peter Hardy, 'Islam in South Asia', in Raphael Israel (ed.), *The Crescent in the East: Islam in Asia Major*, New Delhi, 1985, rpt.

2. Mujeeb, *Indian Muslims*, pp. 491-501.

3. Mushirul Hasan, *Nationalism and Communal Politics in India, 1885-1930*, Delhi, 1991; Mushirul Hasan, *A Nationalist Conscience: M.A. Ansari, the Congress and the Raj*, New Delhi, 1987.

4. On these themes, Albert Hourani, *A History of the Arab Peoples*, London, 1991; and his *Arabic Thought in the Liberal Age, 1798-1939*, London, 1962; Fazlur Rahman, *Islam*, London, 1966; Deliar Noer, *The Modernist Muslim Movement in Indonesia, 1900-1942*, London, 1973; Wilhelm Halbfass, *India and Europe: An Essay in Understanding*, State University of New York Press, 1990; Edward Mortimore, *Faith and Power: The Politics of Islam*, London, 1982.

5. *Musaddas-i Hali*, pp. 43-4, in Aziz Ahmad and Grunebaum (eds.), *Muslim Self-Statement*, p. 95.

6. Ralph Russell and Khurshidul Islam, *Ghalib 1797-1869*, Vol. I: *Life and Letters*, London, 1969, p. 31.

7. Akhtar Qamber, *The Last Mushairah of Delhi*, New Delhi, 1979, p. 39.

8. Russell and Khurshidul Islam, *Ghalib*, p. 134.

9. Saiyid Ahmad Khan, *History of Bijnor Rebellion*, translated with notes and introduction by Hafeez Malik and Morris Dembo, New Delhi, 1982, p. 15.

10. For Muslim revivalist movements in the nineteenth and early twentieth centuries, see Mohiuddin Ahmad, *Saiyid Ahmad Shahid*, Lucknow, 1975; S.A.A. Rizvi, *Shah Abdul Aziz and his Times*, Australia, 1983; Qeyamuddin Ahmad, *The Wahhabi Movement in India*, revd. edn., New Delhi, 1992; Rafiuddin Ahmed, *Bengal Muslims 1871-1906: A Quest for Identity*, New Delhi, 1981; Asim Roy, *The Islamic Syncretistic Tradition in Bengal*, Princeton, N.J., 1983. For Deoband, see Barbara Daly Metcalf, *Islamic Revival in British India: Deoband, 1860-1900*, Princeton, N.J., 1982.

11. Marshall G.S. Hodgson, *The Venture of Islam: The Gunpowder Empires and Modern Times*, Vol. 3, Chicago, 1974, p. 335, and C.W. Troll, *Sayyid Ahmad Khan: A Reinterpretation of Muslim Theology*, New Delhi, 1978.

12. *Musaddas-i Hali*, pp. 83-5, quoted in Ahmad and Grunebaum (eds.), p. 98.

13. David Gilmartin, *Empire and Islam: Punjab and the Making of Pakistan*, Berkeley, 1988.

14. Hardy, *Muslims of British India*, pp. 67-9.

15. Eric Stokes, *The Peasant Armed: The Indian Rebellion of 1857*, edited by C.A. Bayly, Oxford, 1986, p. 240.

16. Mushir U. Haq, *Muslim Politics in Modern India, 1857-1947*, Meerut, 1970, and Metcalf, *Islamic Revival in British India*, pp. 81-5.

17. Anil Seal, *The Emergence of Indian Nationalism: Competition and Collaboration in the Later Nineteenth Century*, Cambridge, 1968, Chap. 7; Francis Robinson, *Separatism among Indian Muslims: The Politics of United Provinces' Muslims, 1860-1923*, Cambridge, 1975; Hardy, *Muslims of British India*, pp. 36-50; Mushirul Hasan, *Nationalism and Communal Politics*, pp. 12-20; C.A. Bayly, *Rulers, Townsmen and Bazaars: North Indian Society in the Age of British Expansion, 1770-1870*, Cambridge, 1983, pp. 190-1.

18. Abu Talib was the son of Haji Muhammad Beg, who fled from Tabriz in his youth, lived in Isfahan in order to escape the tyrannies of Nadir Shah, and settled in Lucknow. The Haji led a troubled life until his death at Murshidabad in 1768. Misfortune also struck his son who, after some years of service in Etawah and Gorakhpur, became a victim of the machinations of his detractors in the Awadh court. He lost his job and his yearly allowance. From 1787 to 1797 he journeyed to Calcutta thrice and sought the help and intervention of senior Company officials into his affair. He met the governor-general, Cornwallis, and his successor, John Shore. 'During the three years of expectation which I passed in Calcutta', wrote Abu Talib, 'all my dependents and adherents, seeing my distress, left me; and even some of my children, and the

domestics brought up in my father's family, abandoned me'. For biographical information, T.W. Beale, *An Oriental Biographical Dictionary*, London, 1894, p. 32; Colin C. Davies, *Encyclopaedia of Islam*, new edn., p. 152; Mujeeb, *Indian Muslims*, pp. 491-2; Humayun Kabir, *Mirza Abu Talib Khan*, Patna: The Russell Lecture, Patna College, 1961.

19. *Travels*, p. xiv.
20. Ibid., p. 111. Wherever he went, Abu Talib aroused interest and curiosity. Nearly half a century before him, Mirza Ihtisamuddin had similar experiences during his stay in England. People were attracted by his robe and turban, the sash tied around his waist and the dagger in his belt. 'Whenever I attempted to go abroad, crowds accompanied me, and the people in the houses of the bazars thrust their heads out of the windows and gazed at me with wonder.' Mirza Ihtisamuddin, *Shigurf Nama-i Velayet*, translated from the original Persian by James Edward Alexander, London, 1827, p. 40.
21. *Travels*, p. 75.
22. Ibid. Notice his description of a party hosted by the Mayor of London, where he spent 'one of the most delightful nights I ever passed'. He was 'gazing all the time on the angelic charms of Miss Combe, who sat in that assemblage of beauties like the bright moon surrounded with brilliant stars'. Ibid., p. 155.
23. Ahmad, *Islamic Modernism*, pp. 6-7.
24. Charles Stewart, in *Travels*, p. xiii.
25. In 1791, Abu Talib produced an edition of *Diwan-i Hafiz*, and shortly after, a compendium account of ancient and contemporary poets (*Khulasat al-Afkaar*). He was himself a poet and there is a manuscript of his *Diwan* in the Bodleian. His collection of poems were edited and translated into English by George Swinton. It was published in 1807 under the title *Poems of Mirza Abu Talib Khan*. He also composed a *mathnawi*, available in the Edinburgh University Library, a medical treatise (*Miraj al-Tauhid*) on astronomy with a prose commentary, a book entitled *Lubb al-Siyar*, and *Tafzih al-Ghafilin* (English translation by W. Hoey, 1888), a history of Awadh under Asaf al-Daula, an important source for the careers of Hyder Beg and the various English residents.
26. Lutfullah belonged to a distinguished Sufi family of Malwa. But the fortunes of the family dwindled to such an extent that 'we sold all we had, and sometimes starved for a day or so, after which we obtained but some food through our own hard labour'. The family travelled to Baroda, Ujjain, Gwalior, and Agra until it reached Delhi in early 1817. Soon thereafter, Lutfullah found odd jobs in the course of his extensive travels. He developed his reputation as a teacher of Arabic, Persian and some Indian languages, notably Marathi, and was *en rapport* with young Britishers of the ICS. In March 1844, he accompanied Mir Jafar Ali Khan, son-in-law of the nawab of Surat, to England. His *Autobiography*, acclaimed in England, was written in 1854 and dedicated to colonel W.H. Sykes. It was later edited by Edward B. Eastwick and published in London, in 1857.

His first reaction on reaching London was:

> Here (7, Sloane Street) we settled after our long voyage from the middle of the globe to the end of the world, where the sun appears, far to the south, as weak as the moon, and the polar star nearly vertical; where the country all over is fertile, and the people ingenious, civil and active; where the language, customs, and manners are entirely different from our own; where, in fine, the destiny of our sweet native land lies in the hand of some twenty-five great men (Directors of the East India Company). It cannot be, I am sure, without the will of that one Supreme Being that this island, which seems on the globe like a mole on the body of a man, should command the greater part of the world, and keep the rest in awe.

Autobiography, p. 406. Reprinted in India under the title *Autobiography of Lutfullah: An Indian's Perception of the West*, with an introduction by S.A.I. Tirmizi (Delhi, 1985).

Equally interesting is his comment on a dissection taking place at the St. George's Hospital. He wrote:

> Here I became convinced that a great part of what I had studied in 'Galen's Anatomy' in Persian and Arabic was founded upon fancy and conjecture, and that it was impossible for anybody to acquire a thorough knowledge of this most useful study for mankind, without the practical course of dissection.

Autobiography, p. 415.

27. *Travels*, p. 121.
28. Ibid., p. 182.
29. Ibid., p. 184.
30. Ibid., p. 110.
31. *Autobiography*, p. 407.
32. *Travels*, pp. 114-15.
33. Ibid., p. 112.
34. Mujeeb, *Indian Muslims*, p. 498; Kabir, *Mirza Abu Talib*, pp. 10, 24.
35. *Travels*, p. 129.
36. Abu Talib found that 'living is very expensive in England; and a good appetite is a serious evil to a poor man'. He listed the prices of meat and bread to illustrate his point. Ibid., p. 112.
37. It is remarkable that a man of his background and his limited experience of Awadh recognized the 'evil' of National Debt. 'Let the creditors of Government be assembled', he proposed, 'in the presence of the Parliament; and let the Minister, clearly and dispassionately, explain to them, that the state of affairs is arrived at such a crisis, that is impossible the nation can continue longer to pay the amount of the enormous taxes which oppress them; that a revolution is to be apprehended; that the first act of the leaders of the revolution certainly will be *to cancel the national debt*, and that the rich may consider themselves fortunate if left in possession of their real wealth; that the national

debt, being thus cancelled, they, the creditors, will lose *the whole* of their property invested in the funds; and therefore it will be much wiser to enter into an immediate compromise, and relinquish a part'. Ibid., pp. 165-6.

38. Ibid., p. 168.
39. Ibid., p. 179.
40. Ibid., p. 168.
41. Ibid., p. 169.
42. Ibid., p. 181. Also, Lutfullah's comment, *Autobiography*, p. 433.
43. *Travels*, p. 175.
44. Ibid., p. 178.
45. Ibid., p. 169.
46. Ibid., p. 177.
47. Ibid., p. 178.
48. Ibid., p. xv.
49. Bayly, *Rulers, Townsmen and Bazaars*, p. 356.
50. Peter Hardy, 'Ghalib and the British', in Ralph Russell (ed.), *Ghalib: the poet and his age*, London, 1972, p. 56.
51. Russell and Khurshidul Islam, *Ghalib*, p. 67.
52. In an interesting observation, Andrews recorded that the intrusion of the West did not make much difference to maulvi Zakaullah's lifestyle. 'None of his outward manners and customs had been changed, and he remained outwardly the most conservative man in Delhi. His dress, his habits, his domestic life, his religious life—all that he valued most dearly—remained unalterably eastern.' C.F. Andrews, *Maulvi Zakaullah of Delhi*, New Delhi, 1928 edn., p. 118.
53. Hardy, 'Ghalib and the British', p. 55.
54. Andrews, *Zakaullah of Delhi*.
55. David Lelyveld, *Aligarh's First Generation: Muslim Solidarity in British India*, Princeton, N.J., 1978.
56. *Musaddas*, pp. 83-5, in Ahmad and Grunebaum (eds.), p. 100.
57. He travelled to Europe as a representative of Shah Alam, who wanted a British protective force at Allahabad. The identity of his companion, Captain 'S', is not known. Nor is there much information on Mirza Ihtisamuddin. What we know is that the sea voyage took them to Mauritius, and around the Cape of Good Hope to Europe where the Mirza stopped briefly in France. The book—*Shigurf Nama-i Velayet*—is a commentary on his travels and impression of England and Scotland written after his return to India. It was translated from Persian into English by James Edward Alexander and published in London in 1827.
58. *Shigurf Nama-i Velayet*, p. 70.
59. Mohibbul Hasan, *History of Tipu Sultan*, Calcutta, 1971, 2nd revd. and enlarged edn.
60. Mohibbul Hasan, 'An Indian Prince and the French Revolution', *Iran Society Silver Jubilee Souvenir*, 1968.

61. Michael H. Fisher, *A Clash of Cultures: Awadh, The British and the Mughals*, New Delhi, 1987, p. 70.
62. Yusuf Ali, 'Muslim Culture and Religious Thought', p. 391. See also Fisher, *A Clash of Cultures*, pp. 172-3.
63. Ibid., p. 397.
64. Mujeeb, *Indian Muslims*, p. 497.
65. For details of Abdur Rahim Dahri's life and career, see Ashraf, *Muslim Attitudes Towards British Rule*, pp. 190, 261.
66. Barbara Metcalf, *The Islamic Revival*, pp. 72-3.
67. Andrews, *Zakaullah of Delhi*, p. 42.
68. Ibid., pp. 38-40.
69. *The Last Mushairah*, pp. 39-40.
70. Francis Robinson, 'Ulama, Sufis and Colonial Rule in North India and Indonesia', in C.A. Bayly and D.H.A. Kolff (eds.), *Two Colonial Empires: Comparative Essays on the History of Indonesia in the Nineteenth-Century*, Dordrecht, 1986, p. 19.
71. Sarah F.D. Ansari, *Sufi Saints and State Power: The Pirs of Sindh, 1843-1947*, Cambridge, 1992, pp. 53-6.
72. Robinson, *Separatism Among Muslims*.
73. *Musaddas*, pp. 43-4, in Ahmad and Grunebaum (eds.), p. 96.
74. K.M. Ashraf, 'Ghalib and the Revolt of 1857', *Rebellion 1857: A Symposium*, New Delhi, 1957, p. 256.

3

The Myth of Unity:
Colonial and National Narratives

> Of all the great religions . . . Islam alone was borne forth into the world on a great wave of forceful conquest. . . . There was seldom a pause in the consolidation of Mahomedan power, seldom a break in the long-drawn tale of plunder and carnage, cruelty and lust, unfolded in the history of the earlier dynasties that ruled India.
>
> VALENTINE CHIROL, *India Old and New*

> You never ceased proclaiming that Islam spread by the sword.
> You have not deigned to tell us what it is the gun has spread.
>
> AKBAR ALLAHABADI in Ralph Russell,
> *The Pursuit of Urdu Literature: A Select History*

> Hinduism, with its love of images and symbols, and its polytheism, and Islam, with its strict Unitarian faith and its strong iconoclastic principles, are at opposite poles.
>
> REGINALD CRADDOCK, *The Dilemma in India*

A disquieting feature of the *Hindutva* wave was not just the demolition of the Babri Masjid but the way Hindu propagandists conjured up the image of a community outside the 'national mainstream'. Muslims were depicted as aggressive fundamentalists and demonized as descendants of depraved and tyrannical medieval rulers who demolished temples and forcibly converted Hindus to Islam. They were portrayed as 'fifth columnists' tied to the world of Islam, held responsible for the country's vivisection in August 1947, and depicted as proceeding hand in glove with the Congress and left-wing formations in a concerted endeavour to undermine Indian/Hindu culture and civilization.

The reading of what Muslims are and the vain hope of how they ought to have been is echoed with unfailing regularity. Equally familiar are images of the Muslims and the reconstruction of their history. What is less clear is how certain images and constructions, having gained currency during the second half of the nineteenth-century, continue to enjoy widespread appeal and acceptance. How is it that the image of the Other has not altered or modified over time? Why did alternative ideologies fail to construct a different paradigm? Does the explanation lie in the Muslim intelligentsia's own assertion of a unity of interest and ideals, and in its conviction that all Muslims were part of an indivisible community with a monolithic mind? Or is it simply that they were logical victims of their own myth-making, claiming for themselves an alien culture, if not origin, and being so regarded by others? I am inclined to agree with the last point, though the critical issue is how the colonial government fostered the growth of such ideas and helped sections of the Muslim intelligentsia to etch a certain image of themselves. I also believe that the etching of 'nationalistic' images of India's Muslims was just as important as the colonial framework that defined and categorized 'Indian Muslim society'.

Any number of scholarly studies, Edward Said's *Orientalism* included, are replete with instances of Islam's representation as a hostile and aggressive force, of Muslim societies being caricatured as rigid, authoritarian, and uncreative.[1] Quite a few British writers in India, some occupying government positions, perpetuated a repertoire of such images, construing Indian Islam as an emblem of repellent Otherness, 'the faith of a body of savage marauders and conquerors, who swept over the land . . . in a series of cruel raids, bringing rapine and destruction in their train'.[2] The sultans of Delhi and their Ottoman counterparts in Constantinople suffered much the same fate at the hands of several writers. Projected as the great iconoclasts, they were considered tokens of evil and scapegoats for issues with which they had no connection. Bishop Heber, who stayed in India from 1823 to 1826, wanted Hindus to be constantly reminded 'that we did not conquer them, but found them conquered, that their previous rulers were as much strangers to their blood and to their religion as we are, and that they were notoriously far more oppressive masters than we have ever shown ourselves'. Valentine Chirol, in charge of the foreign department of the *Times* (London) from 1908 to 1912, observed that 'with the monumental wreckage of those early Mohamedan dynasties, steeped in treachery and bloodshed, the plain of Delhi is still strewn'.[3]

Travellers, missionaries, administrators, and ethnographers[4] transposed the same imagery to Victorian India. According to their images, Islam was static and dogmatic, its adherents conservative, haughtily contemptuous of things 'modern', and under the influence of an obsolete system of education.[5] The Earl of Ronaldshay opined that, 'a candid Muhammadan would probably admit that the most powerful factors in keeping the majority of Moslems aloof from the educational movement of the day were pride of race, a memory of bygone superiority, religious fears, and a not unnatural attachment to the learning of Islam'. Major-general Stockley Warren, who retired in 1885, reminisced in these terms on his reaction to a Muslim 'coolie' who would not have brandy for medicinal purposes: 'These men I presume we shall ultimately civilize, make them Christians and drunkards, and lead them to liberty' (British Library).[6] The civil servant E.C. Bayley told the viceroy Northbrook in 1864 that the standard of 'Muslim morality' was not pitched very high, and that the 'corruptions' in their manners and social habits preceded their contact with the Europeans.[7]

A 'community' steeped in religious obscurantism was prone to treat the government with contempt and hostility. Recollecting the 1857 days in north India, Arthur Owen added a stereotype to those of the 'wily Mahratta' and the 'crafty Brahman', reporting that the 'sensual Mohammadan' fanatically believed that 'if one of their creed falls in battle against the infidels, Christians in particular, he is immediately translated to the garden of paradise'.[8] Nearly half a century after 1857, Bampfylde Fuller, the first lieutenant-governor of the new province of East Bengal and Assam, discovered an undertone of Muslim hostility to their Christian rulers: 'Of such men it may be truly said that at heart they are disloyal, and probably await their opportunity for manifesting their feelings in hostile acts.'[9]

Owen, Fuller, and other British functionaries believed that Islam in the subcontinent was indelibly stamped by its early history, particularly by its original social carriers, and that Islamic values, inherently hostile to the West, caused Muslim estrangement from the government. The call to wreak a special vengeance upon Muslims in the wake of the so-called Wahhabi movement and the 1857 revolt manifested how things 'Islamic' were constructed, located, categorized, and connected in British India.

Another common belief was that the British presence irked Muslims on account of the latter's close identification with the erstwhile ruling classes. They preserved in their blood the pride of a conquering race and cherished hopes of re-establishing their rule. 'Most Indian Mussulmans', commented one writer, 'cherished in their hearts some memory of the days when their fathers were the masters of India, and they believe, rightly or wrongly, that if ever the English power were shaken they would regain their old dominance'. A closer look reveals that the evidence in support of such contentions was thin. Most Muslims had no cause to be enthused by the glory of the Mughal era or to mourn its end. The fact that a Shah Waliullah or a Mirza Ghalib bemoaned its decline should not be treated lightly, but it should also not be construed as a generalized or undifferentiated 'Muslim response'. Similarly, it was patently hollow for Harcourt Butler, governor of UP (1918-20) during the high noon of British imperialism, to raise the spectre of a Muslim 'conspiracy' to overthrow the British with the aid of their 'virile' co-religionists in India and overseas.[10]

Doubtless, some Muslims at the turn of the century nursed such illusions. There were, likewise, isolated instances of elites or their interlocutors seeking an external Muslim imperium for help in reconsolidating their local or regional authority. In 1759, Shah Waliullah turned to Ahmad Shah Durrani (Abdali) to rescue India for Islam; later, Saiyid Ahmad of Rae Bareli corresponded with Central Asian rulers to recognize his khilafat. In general, however, British officials knew from their long administrative experience that most Muslims were prepared to make the colonial government work and gain benefits from its structures. Yet, colonial mentalities stuck to inherited frameworks, conjuring the image of a belligerent community with extra-territorial loyalties. 'The world is full of groups relying on their connection with some dominant "race" elsewhere', commented G.T. Garrat. 'The claim is natural enough, but the English, in accepting this picture of the Moslems as a race apart, seem to have been misled by a writer of genius (Rudyard Kipling), who had, however, a journalist's flair for the picturesque, and who always saw the Peninsula in terms of the Punjab.'[11]

The generalities extended to an appraisal of Indian Islam, the structure of the Muslim 'community', and the nature of its interaction with the Hindus. Some Britishers found it easy to get on with the Muslims at a social level as opposed to 'the Hindu, with his glib tongue, his pliant brain and back, his fantastic social rites, and his incomprehensible religion'.[12] They also found it easy to comprehend the essentials of their faith, 'built on Jewish foundations and devoid of the crudities and subtleties of Brahminism'.[13] But most were ill-informed and crude in their exposition. They believed, for example, that Islam south of the Himalayas remained, to all intents and purposes, the same as in other parts of the world, and that its adherents were a well-knit religious entity, acting as a monolith and keeping the desert faith pure in the land of 'idolaters'.[14] Muslims were, for this reason, endowed with 'cultural coherence', a real sense of unity transcending considerations of race, class, language, and region, and 'an essential community of thought and point of view that on occasion is able to speak with authority through its representative bodies'.[15] 'The solidarity of Islam was a hard fact against which it was futile to run one's head.'[16] The governor of Bengal, the province where most Muslims lived in British India, illustrated the strength of the call of Islam—'a call which rings insistently in the ears of the devout Muslims, whether of India or elsewhere, drowning the call of country and all else'. He put forward the official view, unchanged for nearly a century, that

the ethnic pageant which passes across one's vision as one travels over India is made up of many tableaux. There is one such tableau which at once arrests attention because of the many points of contrast which it provides with the rest of the procession. . . . It is a tableau in which we see represented a religion, a civilization and culture, and an outlook differing profoundly in all material respects from those of Hinduism.[17]

Such a view hardly conformed to the reality. Islam in its Persian-Arabic attire had never made much sense to the masses. That is why its 'cultural mediators' were constrained to make the Islamic traditions more meaningful to the converts in syncretic and symbolic forms.[18] In the process, the pristine purity of dogmas and tenets, which the Faraizis in Bengal and the *mujahidins* in the north-west tried in vain to restore, was tailored to suit the people's spiritual and material urges. Local customs and heterodox traditions found a place in the corpus of beliefs and religious practices. This was reflected in the diversity of religio-cultural observances, as also in the variety of political and economic experiences. The medieval sultans may have wanted to erect a uniform religio-cultural system and impose religious authority from 'great' or 'middle' traditions, but geographic distances and particularistic localism inhibited them. In the end, the 'Islamic little tradition' developed, with its roots firmly anchored in Indian soil and autonomous from all centralized political control.[19] The itinerant preachers imposed their will sporadically in certain pockets, as in rural Bengal, but their impact was transient.

Charles Alfred Elliot reported from Unnao, close to Lucknow in UP, that there was a strong tendency among Muslims to assimilate in all externals with their Hindu neighbours. He found them wearing dhotis and using '*Ram Ram*' as the mode of salutation.[20] Fuller, likewise, wrote on Hindu influences among Muslims: in purely agricultural districts, he commented, the people not 'only understood each other's systems, but the systems often seem to overlap'. Hindus and Muslims cheerfully attended each other's festivals and sang each other's songs.[21] Lytton, Bengal's governor in the 1920s, commented on the rank and file of the communities in the province getting on well with each other in all daily business of life.[22] O.M. Martin, having served in Bengal from 1915 to 1926, emphatically stated that Hindu-Muslim mutual dependence and friendship were an old and cherished tradition.[23]

Such knowledge and understanding were neither reflected in concrete political decisions nor translated into constitutional decrees. In the constitutional plans, which broadly reflected the colonial assumptions about Indian society, the Mapilla Muslim appeared indistinguishable from Kipling's sturdy Pathan; the landed élite of Awadh was no different from the Tamil-speaking Muslim merchant; E.M. Forster's Cambridge buddy Saiyid Ross Masood was cast in the same mould as a *karkhandar* (artisan) in Delhi's old city; Shias and Sunnis, Bohras and Khojas, the Barelwis and the Deobandis were all part of pan-Indian Islam; even though politically, as Bishop Heber noted from long experience in central India, the Bohras were 'agreeing far better with Jains and Rajpoots than their Sunnite rivals'.[24]

It is true that conventional wisdom about Muslims and established theories about their role in the 1857 revolt were questioned by George Campbell, second-in-command to James Outram after the capture of Lucknow, W.W. Hunter, the Bengal civilian, and W.S. Blunt, an old-fashioned patriot shocked by the vulgarity of new imperialism.[25] But according to the viceroy, Dufferin, the followers of Islam were still 'a nation of 50 million, with their monotheism, their iconoclastic fanaticism, their animal sacrifices, their social equality and their remembrance of the days when, enthroned at Delhi, they reigned supreme from the Himalayas to Cape Cormorin'.[26] A decade after Dufferin wrote this, Anthony Macdonnell, lieutenant-governor of UP, treated Muslims with the same degree of suspicion and hostility. He found theological seminaries, such as Lucknow's Nadwat al-ulama, promoting disaffection and sedition. His pronounced belief that all Muslims were loyal to the Ottoman khalifa added fuel to the wild notions already present about pan-Islamism and its pervasive appeal the world over. What Macdonnell failed to grasp was that pan-Islamic sensibilities were heightened by the colonial government to bolster its imperial interests in the Balkans, and that there were any number of influential Muslims who denied the Turkish sultan's claim to be a khalifa. Political rights, Saiyid Ahmad Khan had said, 'were more important than religious traditions, and so long as the Muslims lived freely under British rule they would remain good subjects'. He agreed with maulvi Zakaullah that the Muslims should not look to foreign countries for guidance, since 'for a thousand years, our own religion of Islam had been intimately bound up with India; and in India, Islam has won some of its greatest triumphs, for its own popular form of civilization'.[27] Saiyid Mehdi Ali (nawab Mohsinul Mulk), Saiyid Ahmad's close friend and principal of the Aligarh College, made clear that Turkey's sultan could not exercise any of the powers and prerogatives of the khalifa over India's Muslims, who were in no way bound by their religion to obey him.[28]

Though British functionaries perpetuated the myth of the pervasive influence of pan-Islamism, overseas writers visiting India, including the Turkish author Halide Edib, thought differently. She insisted that Muslim allegiance to England during World War I

demolished a strong historical myth—it showed that political pan-Islamism was a mere bogey. The attachment of the Indian Muslim to the interests of his country was a greater reality than his solidarity with Muslims outside India. *It may be useful for Western powers with Muslim colonies to realize that there is a distinct sense of nationhood separate from their religious life.* The Indian Muslim would resent an Afghan-Muslim domination and fight it; the Arab-Muslim would resent a Muslim-Turkish domination and fight it as much as he would any non-Muslim domination, if he ever got his independence.[29] (italics mine)

The direction and flow of 'Muslim politics', guided first by Saiyid Ahmad and later by the Muslim League, went towards compromise and accommodation with the government. Most modern and traditionally educated Muslims, for whom the Faraizi or the Barelwi adventures were faint memories, recognized the need to change attitudes and generate the strength to survive in a world dominated by colonialism. The ulama, many of whom were harshly treated as arch enemies of the British, made it clear after 1857 that adjustment with rather than repudiation of the raj was their main plank.

In his views on pan-Islamism, Macdonnell was out of sympathy with the official line, which had grudgingly veered around two sets of convictions. One was based on the bizarre belief that the Muslims had to be won over because they were so terrible and fear-inspiring.[30] The other rested on pragmatic imperial considerations. How could so many Muslims, some wielding power and influence in certain areas, be alienated for so long? They had to be enlisted 'as allies and auxiliaries',[31] courted to thwart nationalist aspirations, and encouraged to counter rabble-rousers in the

Indian National Congress. Viceroy Lord Northbrook was told by the colonial office to remove any 'just cause of [Muslim] complaint, because, in the event of any action against Russia, our allies must be the Mohametans of Central Asia, Afghanistan, and of Russia'. Viceroy Lord Mayo's note of 26 June 1871 on Muslim education indicated a change in imperial policy in this direction;[32] and Mayo's successor, Northbrook, received kudos for 'doing great good in directing attention to the long and grievously neglected subject of Mussalman education'.[33] After the 1857 difficulties with Muslim policy in India, Mayo began to fill the cup of reconciliation, Northbrook held it out.

The Simla deputation of October 1906—masterminded by the Aligarh College principal W.A.J. Archbold—paved the way for establishing the Muslim League. It was seen, for this reason, as a decisive break with the silent policy of the earlier decades. The reforms of 1909 established separate electorates for Muslims, along with reservations and weightages, and thus gave birth to a religio-political community, sections of which began to see themselves in the colonial image of being unified, cohesive, and segregated from the Hindus. Separate electorates put a formal seal of approval on the institutionalized conception of Muslim political identity and contributed to the forging of communitarian identities that were, both in conception and articulation, profoundly divisive and inherently conflict-oriented. An otherwise diverse community was thus homogenized, like a 'caste' or a 'tribe', so that it could be suitably accommodated within political schemes and bureaucratic designs. The self-styled Muslim leaders could thus stake their claims to be represent an 'objectively' defined community and contend with others for government patronage, employment, and political assignments. In this way, the ideological contours of the future Pakistan were delineated by British opinion and policymakers long before Jinnah expounded his two-nation theory.

The same process extended to the formation of caste-cluster consciousness and caste politics. By viewing caste categories as units of patronage and proscription, the government forced a predictable response: those seeking patronage or protesting proscription had to speak in the name of the bureaucratically recognized category. In such circumstances, the emergence of 'caste' publicists, spokesmen, and associations say more about the manner in which the foreign rulers viewed Indian society and sought to come to terms with it and the agility of the Indian response than it does about the ubiquity of 'caste' sentiment.[34]

The Montagu-Chelmsford Reforms (1919) projected the same colonial assumptions. The Act of 1935 held out the prospect of a divided nation and implicitly endorsed the hitherto hazy notion of an incipient Muslim nation. Indeed, if the British were to incline overmuch towards the Muslim League in the early 1940s, it was in part because their own political framework left them with little choice except to depend on League leaders. They had, after all, laid the foundations of a state-support realm enabling influential Muslims to define their 'community' on their own terms and to extract statutory concessions and guarantees almost at will. The structures of governance offered them much greater space for articulating sectional interests.

The Muslims in the Congress were put in an awkward position. The official, colonial definition of a community ran contrary to secular, territorial nationalism and undermined their moral authority. They were greatly constrained and unable to operate from a position of strength, because their conception of nationhood had no place in the constitutional blueprint. The overall thrust of British policies, especially after 1909, led to their political isolation. A man of Ansari's stature was virtually prevented from attending the Round Table Conferences in London. Rank communalists, on the other hand, were feted, and welcomed with open arms.[35] Congress Muslims like Azad were 'the wrecking horse', just because Jinnah, whose own status was far from assured, insisted on their exclusion from the Simla conference and from the interim government.[36] Jinnah's plea, which did not go unheeded in official quarters, was that no one but a Muslim Leaguer could represent the 'Muslim interests'. This moment in history must have been relished by the surviving architects of the 1909, 1919, and 1935 constitutions.

In the final analysis, the British bequeathed the Indian republic a truncated nation, a distorted perspective, a series of blurred images, and a number of vague and undifferentiated categories. These need to be challenged, contested, and refuted vigorously and consistently. If the history of intercommunity relations is to be rewritten, it has to steer clear of colonial paradigms, and freed from the stranglehold of an intellectual tradition, orientalist or otherwise.

II

A good number of educated Muslims in the last quarter of the nineteenth-century longed for an 'objective' assessment of their history and sociology and a rigorously argued repudiation of certain popular notions about their community and their creed. Who could they turn to? Not the theologians or the formal body of ulama, many of whom explicitly challenged the ideological tenets of the modern age. They were no doubt trained to debate and defend matters of faith but were ill-equipped, on account of their limited concerns, training, and religious orientation, to match orientalist scholarship. The intervention of scholars based in Aligarh, Delhi, Patna, and Calcutta was far more impressive and in tune with Western intellectual pursuits. The Aligarh College, for one, was a visible embodiment of the victory of forward-looking forces. It was here that movements of reform were consummated. A typically Aligarh version of reformed Islam, based on nineteenth-century liberalism and humanism, grew up in opposition both to the orthodox stream and to the popular syncretism of the masses.

Yet, the intellectual energy released by Saiyid Ahmad, Shibli Nomani, Hali, Zakaullah lost momentum once the reformist trends became increasingly intertwined with political controversies. The ambition of an average student, drawn from the landed class and the upper crust of the bourgeoisie, was government service. His pride was soothed, thanks to early pan-Islamic stirrings, on his being reminded that he was a unit in the great democracy of Islam, and in testament to this brotherhood, he jauntily wore the Turkish fez on his head.[37] Aligarh produced, for the most part, cautious pedagogues instead of a few thinkers of surpassing boldness. There appeared a cloud, to borrow Clifford Geertz's expression, of not terribly distinguished and usually rather unoriginal academicians.[38] This was also true of other centres of learning. Once the newly emergent Muslim bourgeoisie developed a vested interest in the power structures, the initial thrust given to reformist ideas was considerably diluted.

The few who stayed out of the charmed circle of government servants and addressed themselves to issues of reform and innovation were unable to correct colonial stereotypes or stir a debate comparable, in depth and vigour, to what occurred in Turkey under the aegis of the Young Turks. Part of the reason was their self-image of being part of a community—a monolith *umma*—that remained, or was normatively expected to remain, the same across spatial divisions and temporal boundaries. Time and again, this theme was powerfully expressed across a number of élite scholastic factions, especially of Sunni Islam, for which Sufi and syncretic practices and Shi'ism in general were just so many deviations from the norm. Time and again, the theme of eternal and unmitigated Hindu-Muslim hostility was echoed. So also the view that 'internal' differences among groups of Hindus and/or Muslims were secondary and irrelevant to the more fundamental religious cleavage. If Muslim intellectuals had examined such convictions in the light of their normal way of living, they would have discovered ample evidence of great 'internal' political, moral, and social tensions and their disruptive effects. In this way, they would have understood themselves better and made their cultural anxieties and political concerns intelligible to others.

What about nationalist writers, historians, social reformers, and political activists? Did they conceptualize the Indian social reality differently? Or question the Muslim élite's highly exaggerated and romanticized assessment of its historic role and destiny? Did they refute colonial stereo-types and set right the image of a static community, sunk in torpid medievalism, insulated from the winds of change, influenced by the diktat of the mullahs, tied to the Islamic community, susceptible to pan-Islamic influences, and organized, despite internal differentiations, on a pan-Indian basis?

Sections of the intelligentsia were expected to redefine the terms of the debate, not so much on Muslims or on Indian Islam, but on inter-community relations. They were required to harness their intellectual resources to demonstrate that the Muslims, both in their historical and contemporary settings, were part of and not separate from the Indian reality, and that the colonial stereotypes were constructed on false premises. This was a necessary pre-condition for establishing their all-India credentials, as also to hasten the process of nation-building with Muslims as co-partners. They had to contend, moreover, with a problem summed up by Gulshan and Chandra, the two fictional characters in Firoz Khan Noon's novel *Scented Dust* (1942), and to bridge the gulf separating the followers of Islam and Hinduism. 'Do not carry away the idea', Gulshan told Chandra,

that I think ill of you for your ignorance, because there are thousands of us Hindus, men and women, who are as ignorant of the great Muslim religion and its philosophy as you are of ours. You will meet millions amongst us, who know no more about Islam than that it introduced into India loose trousers and a spouted pot for ablutions. There are also millions amongst us who know no more about the Hindu culture than what is represented by *langoti* (jockstrap dress) and *dal-roti* (lentil and bread/vegetarian diet). It is only the irascible, fiery and short-tempered who speak evil of other people's religions.[39]

III

There are numerous tracts and treatises on Hindu-Muslim intermingling, on social and cultural fusion, and on the commonality of intercommunity interests. There was, likewise, an enlightened conception of state and society grounded in the values of tolerance, syncretism, and fraternal living. One can also discern a wide range of liberal, eclectic, and radical ideas and movements from Raja Rammohun Roy to Jawaharlal Nehru that transcended communitarian barriers and fostered intercommunity linkages. Some were creatively expressed in the poetry of Rabindranath Tagore and the young Muhammad Iqbal. There were serious initiatives, such as the one taken by C.R. Das in Bengal, to resolve the communal deadlock.

Broadly speaking, however, a tentative survey of the vast and amorphous 'nationalist' literature reveals the uncritical acceptance of colonial constructions, their political legitimation through pacts, accords, 'unity' conferences, and the inner religio-cultural tensions within the nationalist paradigm. As a result, subcontinental themes on communal peace and understanding, shorn of their rhetorical value, ceased to be a major reference point in creating or articulating a truly national consciousness. This requires elaboration.

First and foremost, the intellectual understanding of the evolution of Islam in India and its followers was sketchy, superficial, and marred by a majoritarian perspective. The upper castes, who were convinced of their own superiority in the realm of ideas and thought, considered Islam a rather crude approach to the problems of philosophy and metaphysics.[40] There were, consequently, no serious interpreters of Islam, no counterparts of Al-Beruni, Amir Khusro, Malik Muhammad Jaisi, Abul Fazl, Raskhan, Rahim, or Dara Shikoh. M.N. Roy, the Marxist activist, expressed surprise that Hindus and Muslims, having lived together for so many centuries did not appreciate each other's culture and religion; that the Muslims, even after living in the country for many centuries, were 'generally considered to be an extraneous element'; and that educated Hindus were blissfully ignorant of 'the immense revolutionary significance of Islam'. He concluded that a radical change in mutual attitudes 'would shock the Hindus out of their arrogant self-satisfaction, and cure the narrow-mindedness of the Muslims of our day by bringing them face to face with the true spirit of the faith they profess'.[41]

Nineteenth-century writers and reformers, many of whom grudgingly came to terms with the Muslim presence, accepted the 'knowledge' derived from the medieval chroniclers and translated by British historians. Thus, they treated the Muslim intrusion as an aberration or a break in the continuity of Brahmanic traditions; equated Indian culture with Vedic culture; Indian philosophy with Vedic, Puranic, and the Upanishadic; and Indian religion with Hinduism.[42] Most accounts focused on the Muslim ruling élites, their military exploits and glittering durbars, and ignored the subtle fusion of 'little traditions' at the Sufi shrines in particular and in the rural hinterland generally. Islam had no Max Mueller to detail how its dogmas and tenets were gradually incorporated into regional and local belief structures and rituals; how Muslims—most converted to Muhammad's religion at different points of time—and for different reasons, were integrated with the rest of the population through a tangible and clearly identifiable historical process. Islam was mistakenly viewed as part of the 'great tradition'—codified, rigid, unchanging, insular, and close to external influences. Its followers, whether converted or not, were cast in a specifically Muslim/Islamic mould. Regardless of economic status, caste, language, or regional affinity, their identity was understood, defined, and described in strictly textual terms.

K.M. Panikkar, otherwise identified with the liberal stream, commented that 'the organization of Islam in India was . . . frankly communal, and its outlook was governed by the single fact of ensuring to the Islamic nation in India its independence and authority'. Muslims constituted a society everywhere and were much more than a religious minority. Their culture and way of life was different from the Hindus and other communities around them. 'Unlike the Christians who, though they profess a different religion, are not in their way of life different from the Hindus, the Muslims, whether in the south of Kerala or in Kashmir, represent a culture of their own.'[43]

Islam's militancy and inflexible doctrinal structure was a theme in and a major component of the Arya Samaj movement. Its founder, Swami Dayanand Saraswati, was a relentless critic of Islam and his celebrated text, *Satyarth Prakash*, inspired anti-Islamic polemics in much of Punjab. 'The Quoran, the Quoranic God and the Muslims', according to him, 'are full of bigotry and ignorance.'[44] Pandit Lekh Ram, Swami Shraddhanand, and Lala Lajpat Rai carried forward the Swami's polemics, subjected the Koran to severe criticism, depicted Muhammad as a man of dubious sexual ethics, and interpreted Islam as a religion sanctifying war and the slaughter of non-believers.[45] 'When I considered how devoted a Muslim is to his religion', wrote Lajpat Rai, whose father turned Muslim for a while, 'how he regards the propagation of Islam as a bounden duty and how he believes that the highest reward is attached to converting a man to Islam, I can well imagine what great pressure must my father's Muslim friends have brought to bear upon him . . . and how often they must have tried to induce him to become a Mussalman openly.'[46]

Such views correspond to the oft-repeated colonial axiom that orthodoxy rather than heterodoxy had a more direct and profound impact on the Muslims, and that they were deeply committed to fulfilling their

Islamic obligations. What distinguished them from others was their crusading zeal, their inclination to wage *jihad* against non-believers, and their abiding commitment to spreading their faith.

Invoking the past lent credence to such a reconstruction by major literary writers, though by no means all, who contrasted the glory of pre-medieval India with the oppressive character of 'Muslim dynasties'. Quite a few Marathi writers were, thus, concerned with the overall degradation of Hindus during Muslim rule, and with Islam's pernicious influence on their social customs. Gopal Ganesh Agarkar (1856-95), Gopal Hari Deshmukh (1823-92) and Vishnushastri Chiplunkar (1850-82) thought that Muslims were bullies and fanatics, because violence and aggression was the essence of their civilization.[47] Bal Gangadhar Tilak, the fiery politician-writer, sought to build a Maratha identity through a conscious choice of historical figures and symbols that evoked memories of Muslim oppression and exploitation. His essentialist endeavour to define Muslims through constant references to Mahmud of Ghazni, Alauddin Khilji, Timur, Aurangzeb, and Ahmad Shah Abdali created a major religious divide in Maharashtra society and provided ideological coherence to the Hindu Mahasabha and the RSS, two of the most militant Hindu organizations in the 1930s and 1940s.

Noted Hindi writers like Bharatendu Harishchandra (1850-85), Pratap Narain Misra (1856-94), Radha Charan Goswami (1859-1923), and Kisorilal Goswami (1866-1932) portrayed medieval rule as a chronicle of rape and abduction of Hindu women, the slaughter of sacred cows, and the defilement of temples. Bharatendu referred to the 'wounds in the heart' kept fresh by the sight of Aurangzeb's mosque that stood beside the sacred Vishwanath temple in Varanasi.[48] Two closely related themes figure in his and some of his contemporaries' works: the downtrodden, long-suffering Hindu, and the dominant, oppressive Muslim. In his play *Nildevi*, Muslim characters display cruelty, cowardice, treachery, bigotry, and debauchery, while Hindus, though sometimes portrayed as meek and submissive, demonstrate courage, honour, and fidelity.[49]

Kisorilal, following some notable British historians, described in his novel *Tara* (1902) the depraved conditions at the court of Shahjahan in Agra: intrigues, scenes of illicit love, murder among Muslims.[50] Misra and Radha Charan chastised Muslims as the 'abominably impure mlecchas' and damned them as rank outsiders. Both denounced the medieval rulers—'those mad elephants'—who 'trampled to destruction the flourishing lotus-garden of India', slaughtered cows with impunity, and prevented Hindu religious processions.[51]

Bankim Chandra Chattopadhyay looked upon medieval India as a period of bondage, and interpreted the Hindu chieftain's resistance to the Mughals as a form of national resistance. Muslim rule brought neither material nor spiritual improvement to India. Instead, he saw in Islam a quest for power and glory, devoid of spiritual and ethical qualities, irrational, bigoted, devious, sensual, and immoral, and a complete anti-thesis of his 'ideal' religion.[52] Bhudev Mukhopadhyaya (1827-94), on the other hand, questioned this version and described it as a mischievous fabrication of British historians. In his view, the Delhi sultans contributed significantly to the emergence of an inchoate consciousness of community among Indians. Emphasizing the ties that bound Muslims with the rest of the population, he underlined that Islam in the subcontinent was quite different from Islam elsewhere both in doctrine and in internal social practices.[53] Romesh Chandra Dutt, who wrote a major denunciation of British economic policies, avoided the familiar portrayal of Muslims as innately wicked and bloodthirsty. In *The Lake of Palms*, an English translation of the Bengali text, he avoided, generally, the more or less brazen confrontation of Hindus and Muslims and the attendant display of an anti-Muslim bias that provided the staple for his historical novels;[54] nevertheless, the picture of Muslims as alien emerges strongly in his novels and fiction. Muslims were not quite 'one of us', but enemies of 'our' country and religion.[55]

The Bengali intelligentsia of Nirad C. Chaudhuri's generation absorbed the spirit of such writings. 'Nothing was more natural for us', commented Chaudhuri, 'than to feel about the Muslims in the way we did'. They were told, even before they could read, that the Muslims had ruled and oppressed the Hindus, spread their religion with the Koran in one hand and a sword in the other, abducted Hindu women, destroyed temples, and polluted sacred places. 'As we grew older we read about the wars of the Rajputs, the Marathas, and the Sikhs against Muslims, and of the intolerance and oppression of Aurangzeb.'[56] On the other hand, the pukka sahib nurtured in the Victorian traditions believed in the benevolence of the British intentions and lamented, in no uncertain terms, the eclipse of the empire. The British empire in India was and 'remains one of the central facts of universal history and the concrete evidence that the British people have discharged one of their primary roles in history. They could not disinterest themselves in it without abrogating their historical mission and eliminating themselves from one of the primary strands of human evolution.'

Bengali thinkers, according to Chaudhuri, based their lifework on the formula of a synthesis of Hindu and European currents. Islamic trends and 'Muslim sensitivities' did not touch the arc of their consciousness. They stood outside as an 'external proletariat'.[57] If they wanted to enter the Bengali cultural world, they could do so 'only after giving up all their Islamic values and traditions'. In this way, the new Indian/Bengali culture of the nineteenth-century built a perimeter of its own and put specifically Muslim influences and aspirations beyond the pale.[58]

Nirad Chaudhuri was no different. Intellectually, the European mind was outraged by the Hindus precisely in those three principles which were fundamental to its approach to life, and which it has been applying with ever greater strictness since the Renaissance: that of reason, that of order, and that of measure. Discussing E.M. Forster's *A Passage to India*, his main criticism was that the major Indian character, Aziz, and most of the supporting Indians were Muslims. Nirad Babu believed that Forster did this because he shared the liking the British in India had for the Muslims, and the corresponding dislike for the Hindus. So that Dr Godbole, the chief Hindu character in the novel, was not an exponent of Hinduism but a clown.

Though a self-proclaimed liberal humanist, Chaudhuri nursed an arrogant contempt for and deep-seated hostility towards the Muslims in Calcutta, where he spent most of his life.[59] It was just the same in Kishoreganj, now in Bangladesh. He became conscious of a new kind of hatred for the Muslims during the Swadeshi movement. A cold dislike for them 'settled down in our heart, putting an end to all real intimacy of relationship'.[60] He rejoiced at Italy's attack on Tripoli in 1911. He was pleased—'so that the Muslims would be taught a lesson'—when Turkey joined the German side at the end of 1914.[61] 'Strongly anti-Muslim in 1920' owing to the khalifat upsurge, Chaudhuri was uneasy with the 'menacing assertiveness' of the Bengali Muslims and 'repelled' by the thought of living in a province where Muslims would be a dominant social and cultural entity.[62] His verdict: Muslims constituted a society of their own with a distinctive culture and could not be absorbed into a unified nation. For this reason, 'no historical argument was too false or too foolish to be trotted out by the Hindus to contest the demand of the Indian Muslims to have their own way of life'.[63] Chaudhuri declared, 'When I see the gigantic catastrophe of Hindu-Muslim discord of these days I am not surprised, because we as children held the tiny mustard in our hands and sowed it very diligently. In fact, this conflict was implicit in the very unfolding of our history, and could hardly be avoided'.[64] Whenever he saw a burqa-clad person, he apostrophized her mentally: 'Sister! You are the symbol of your community in India.' The entire body of the Muslims, according to him, was under a black veil. And his advice to them was to immigrate to Pakistan. 'There is something unnatural in the continued presence of the Muslims in India and of the Hindus in Pakistan, as if both went against a natural cultural ecology.'

The following description, which must not be conveniently dismissed as an illustration of Nirad Chaudhuri's 'eccentricity', sharply reflects the images of Muslims:

One day I saw a procession of Muslim divines trooping into Sarat Babu's house. I was quite familiar with the modern Muslim dress, but had no idea that these learned Muslims wore different clothes. They did, for they had green gowns on and big turbans on their heads. . . . We, the educated and urban Bengalis . . . did not even imagine that such persons existed in Bengal. I with my knowledge of Islamic painting could only assume when I saw them that they were crude incarnations of the Muslim divines I had seen portrayed in Persian or Mughal miniatures. . . . Their faces were grave, and even stern. One face struck me very forcibly. It was pinched and peevish, but of an incredible ferocity. The eyes were large, black, and burning, and in that emaciated face they looked even blacker and larger. . . . He looked like an ill-dressed Robespierre, the sea-green Incorruptible. Sarat Babu's house was not only crowded for the occasion with these survivals of Islam, but even reeked of them.[65]

Such representations of Muslims did not augur well for the nationalist agenda of welding various communities, along with castes, regions, and linguistic units, into a unified nation. The rise of the Congress movement, in particular, imposed serious demands on its leaders to define the contours of multiculturalism and religious pluralism so as to keep intact the fragile social fabric that was being steadily undermined by British policies, as well as by the Hindu-Muslim revitalization campaigns. Otherwise, the Congress project of creating a composite nationality on liberal and secular values was bound to run into serious difficulties. Nehru rightly emphasized that 'only by thinking in terms of a different political framework—and even more so a different social framework—can we build up a stable foundation for joint action'.[66]

IV

Nehru's perspective was influenced by his cosmopolitan family back-ground, his education in England, his social and cultural ambience in Allahabad, his long-standing friendship and political camaraderie with Ansari, Azad, Saiyid Mahmud, Khaliquzzaman, Tassaduq Ahmad Khan

Sherwani, and Abdul Majid Khwaja. He was a product of, and his sensibilities were influenced by, the cultural norms and intellectual ambience of the Urdu-speaking élites of the Indo-Gangetic belt. As a student at Trinity College, Cambridge, he was in close touch with Fabian socialists in London. Such interactions widened his intellectual horizon and enriched his appreciation of political and social transformative processes around the globe. He could thus place in perspective the rapid changes taking place in Muslim countries like Egypt, Turkey, and Iran. Discussions with Azad and other Muslim scholars helped him understand Indian Islam and medieval Indian history better. In *The Discovery of India* (1946), he analysed late-nineteenth-century reformist currents among Muslims in a manner no other nationalist leader did during his lifetime, appreciated Saiyid Ahmad Khan's initiatives, commented on the nationalist stir among the young Muslim intelligentsia of north India, noted the 'sensation' created by Azad—'this very youthful writer and journalist'— and assessed Iqbal's impact on the younger generation of Muslims.[67]

More than anything else, Nehru was aware that the social, educational, and economic backwardness of most Muslims was not because of any innate failing, but because of historical and sociological factors.[68] He knew, so he said, more about their hunger and poverty than those who talked in terms of percentages and seats in councils. That is because he claimed to be in greater touch with them than most Muslim leaders. How could he then accept the League's pretentious claims? How could he recognize Jinnah as the 'sole spokesman'? The League leadership at the top deliberately sought refuge in the name of religion to avoid discussing problems of the common man.

A simple fact that eluded most of Nehru's comrades was that Indian society was at no stage structured around religious solidarities or polarized along 'communal' lines. Nehru's exceptionally eclectic mind grasped this reality. He believed that intercommunity conflicts, as and when they occurred, were counterpoised to the quiet, commonplace routines in which communities intermingled. Cross-community linkages rather than religious ties influenced the direction in which patronage, authority, and economic relations flowed into everyday life. Consequently, he recognized the need to reinforce traditional linkages through 'mass contact' and a radical socio-economic blueprint. He recognized, moreover, the importance of reducing class disparities, creating opportunities for upward mobility, and making the masses aware of their mutual interdependence, their shared historical experiences, and their common concerns, interests, and destiny.

The impulse behind Nehru's brainchild, the Muslim Mass Contact Campaign, launched in March 1937, was to approach the Muslims not as a collective fraternity but as a segment of an otherwise impoverished population. The principal motivation was to convince them that they did not constitute a 'nation', and that their fortunes were not tied to their Muslim brethren per se, but with fellow artisans, peasants, and workers in other communities. Nehru dialogued with Jinnah on these lines, questioned the rationale of 'Muslim nationalism' in a society traditionally anchored in cultural and religious pluralism, and criticized the construct of a 'Muslim identity' in religious terms. He tried in vain to delink issues of proportion and percentages of seats with the more basic and fundamental contradictions between nationalism and colonialism. He expected Jinnah to draw his constituency into this just and legitimate struggle as co-citizens and not as a preferential religio-political 'community'. The two-nation idea made no sense; it was not more than a reversion to some medieval theory.

Why only two I do not know, for if nationality was based on religion, then there were many nations in India. Of two brothers one may be a Hindu, another a Moslem; they would belong to two different nations. These two nations existed in varying proportions in most of the villages in India. They were nations which had no boundaries; they overlapped. A Bengali Moslem and a Bengali Hindu, living together, speaking the same language and having much the same traditions and customs belonged to a different nation.[69]

There was much ambiguity and fuzziness in nationalist thinking about the corporate identity of the Muslims. Nehru removed some of it. He made clear: 'when we enter the political plane, the solidarity is national, not communal; when we enter the economic plane, the solidarity is economic'.[70] In what way, he asked, were the interests of the Muslim peasant different from those of the Hindu peasant? Or those of a Muslim labourer from those of his Hindu prototypes? The ties that bound people were common economic interest and, in the case of a subject country especially, a common national interest.[71] If the country began to think and act on these lines, the 'myth' of communalism would disappear along with the pseudo-religious mentality.[72] Communalism was not the power it was made out to be: it was a mere creation of educated classes in search of office and employment. The 'communal question' was essentially one of protecting their interests. Religion was just a useful stalking-horse for this purpose.[73] 'The real conflict,' according to Nehru, 'had nothing to do with religion, though religion often masked the issue, but was essentially between those who stood for a nationalist—democratic—socially revolutionary policy and those who were concerned with preserving the relics of a feudal regime. In a crisis, the latter inevitably depend upon foreign support which is interested in preserving the status quo.'[74]

The basic premise of Nehru's argument was valid. He was right in arguing that religious solidarity should not be the basis for political activism or that religious symbols of disunity should be shunned in Congress mobilization campaigns. The alternative strategy, worked out by Tilak in Maharashtra or the Swadeshi leaders in Bengal, had created fissures in the liberation struggle, alienated Muslims in these regions, and weakened the appeal of secular nationalism. Though not the only fervent champion of secular nationalism, Nehru raised the standard of debate on the subject not on the strength of abstract principles of Western democracy, which is a commonly leveled charge against him, but in relation to his perception of and insights into wider social and political processes. There is no reason to believe that his perceptions were flawed or to find fault in his vision. There is no reason to doubt his motives or intentions.

Nehru's ideas ran contrary to Jinnah's two-nation theory, just as they conflicted with the protagonists of a Hindu nation. Some of his own Congress colleagues were, consequently, uncomfortable with his 'pro-Muslim' proclivities. Haunted by the bogey of pan-Islamism, they insisted that the fortunes of the Islamic world counted far more with Muslims than did their country's political regeneration. They harped on Muslims' aggressive instincts and the militancy of their faith. When they agreed to the Lucknow pact (December 1916) and similar accords, they did so on the assumption that Muslims were, after all, a separate religious and political entity.[75] In this way, they quietly legitimized what were later derided as 'separatist' and 'communal' demands. In so doing, they jettisoned their own moral authority to challenge the colonial assumptions outlined in the Acts of 1919 and 1935, and created the space, sometimes unwittingly but mostly consciously, for certain strident sectional claims to be accommodated in the Congress political agenda. The political language in which such accommodation was expressed and the energy derived from recognizing the Muslims as a distinct political unit implied that the basic terms of reference precluded any lasting solution of the communal tangle.

The Congress was sensitized to this reality after the Muslim outcry over certain policies adopted by its ministries in UP, Bihar, and Bombay. But it was too late to retrace its steps. With the political currents flowing in different directions, the Congress agenda could not be written afresh in the post-War years without the Muslim League, the votaries of a Hindu nation, and the British who still held the scales. There were not just 'two parties', as Nehru had mistakenly announced in 1937, but as many as four parties who had jumped into the fray. Nehru and his socialist comrades swallowed this bitter pill when they helplessly witnessed the collapse of the Muslim Mass Contact Campaign.

I do not intend to portray the image of an always liberal, enlightened, largely innocent Muslim community—'sinned against' but hardly ever 'sinning'. Nor is it intended to suggest that their fortunes or misfortunes could be explained solely in terms of the unremitting, overwhelming power and prejudice of the British and 'Hindu' intelligentsia. Sections of the Muslim intelligentsia have made their own history at least as much as others have made it for them—that they have not made it very well should engage social scientists.

It is therefore important to examine the depth, vigour, and variety of Muslim revivalism, to consider why the idea of a singular community appears in Muslim writings, to explore how Islamic ideas moulded élite perceptions, and to analyse why Islamic symbols of disunity were sometimes preferred to Indian historical symbols of unity. We need to acquaint ourselves more fully with the Muslim educational system, 'the master institution', in the words of Clifford Geertz, in the perpetuation of an Islamic tradition, and in the creation of an Islamic vision.[76] In this context, the part played by the itinerant preachers and the ulama requires detailed investigation, not just as models of 'Islamic conduct' or as interpreters of the *Shariat* but also as leaders of a political 'community' in the making. We need to delineate, just as Saiyid Ahmad, Hali, Iqbal, and Azad did, the implications of their social conservatism in a society that was rapidly changing under colonial rule, and also the consequences of their resistance to innovation and change and their suppression of dissent and interpretation (*ijtehad*). The issue, which sometimes escapes notice in some writings on Muslims in Western scholarship, is of considerable significance to the citizens of South Asia generally and to the Muslim communities in particular.

Finally, it is necessary to deconstruct the language of minorityism and uncover the motives of those who practiced modern-day politics in the name of the *millat* they purported to represent, but whose main aim was to wield political power and to use Islam and communitarian solidarity as a shield to cover their designs. The general implication of this idea was summed up by Chandra in her conversation with her lifelong friend Gulshan. 'You see, my dear,' she said, 'a man will use any old argument to achieve his object in all walks of life, and this communal discord is a very useful and good stick with which our men-folk can beat the old India goat—her political progress'. Troubled by the communal cleavage, she remarked angrily: 'This Hindu-Muslim discord only exists because it pays our men-folk to keep it going.'[77]

What we ideally need is a triangular narrative in which the Muslim is not a privileged victim but as much an actor as the others. The main thrust of this discussion is to identify points of convergence between the colonial and nationalist discourses and to argue that, despite various constraints, it was still possible to challenge Hindu majoritarianism and Muslim nationalism. Surely, there was a wide range of options available. If one were to evolve, in the spirit of Ghalib's quintessential message,[78] as an independent/autonomous discourse, this would have entailed discarding the communal categories created by the raj and also ignoring the Muslim élite's own image and representation of itself. There were, objectively speaking, profound historical and sociological reasons for doing so. The fact that this was not done in a concerted and systematic manner weakened the cause of eclectic and secular ideologies.

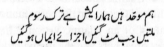

My creed is oneness, my belief is abandonment of rituals.
Let all communities dissolve and constitute a faith.

MIRZA GHALIB

NOTES

1. Edward W. Said, *Orientalism*, London, 1978; Normal Daniel, *Islam and the West: The Making of an Image*, Edinburgh, 1960; Aziz Al-Azmeh, *Islams and Modernities*, London, 1993.

2. W. Crooke, *The North-Western Provinces of India: Their History, Ethnology, and Administration*, New Delhi, 1897, 1975 rpt., pp. 258-9.

3. M.A. Laird (ed.), *Bishop Heber in Northern India: Selection from Heber's Journal*, Cambridge, 1971, p. 64. 'With the monumental wreckage of those early Mahomedan dynasties, steeped in treachery and bloodshed', commented Valentine Chirol (1852-1929), journalist in charge of the foreign department of *The Times* (1908-12), 'the plain of Delhi is still strewn'. *India Old and New*, p. 3.

4. The literature on the subject is vast, though its fuller analysis is awaited. For clues and insights see Daniel, *Islam and the West*, pp. 266-85; A.J. Greenberger, *The British Image of India: A Study on the Literature of Imperialism 1880-1960*, London, 1969; Hardy, *Muslims of British India*, pp. 1-2, 62-91; Robinson, *Separatism Among Muslims*, pp. 164-73; Lelyveld, *Aligarh's First Generation*; Gyanendra Pandey, *The Construction of Communalism in Colonial India*, New Delhi, 1990; Clinton Bennet, *Victorian Images of Islam*, London, 1992; Carol A. Breckenridge and Peter van der Veer (eds.), *Orientalism and the Postcolonial Predicament*, New Delhi, 1994; David Ludden (ed.), *Contesting the Nation: Religion, Community and the Politics of Democracy in India*, Philadelphia, 1996; P.K. Datta, *Carving Blocs: Communal Ideology in Early Twentieth Century Bengal*, New Delhi, 1999; Michael R. Anderson, 'Islamic Law and the Colonial Encounter in British India', in Chibli Mallat and Jane Connors (eds.), *Islamic Family Law*, London, 1990; Avril Powell, *Muslims and Missionaries in Pre-Mutiny India*, London, 1993); Lucy Carrol, 'Colonial Perceptions of Indian Society and the Emergence of Caste(s) Associations', *Journal of Asian Studies*, Vol. 27, 2, February 1978; and Kenneth Jones, 'Religious Identity and the Census', in N.G. Barrier (ed.), *The Census in British India*, Delhi, 1981, pp. 83-5.

5. Sidney Low, *A Vision of India*, London, 1911, p. 281. Low was an eminent journalist and writer. His book was well received by *The Times* in London, and by Curzon and Morley. And the comment of the Earl of Ronaldshay, Bengal governor (1917-22): 'A candid Muhammadan would probably admit that the most powerful factors in keeping the majority of Moslems aloof from the educational movement of the day were pride of race, a memory of bygone superiority, religious fears, and a not unnatural attachment to the learning of Islam.' *India: A Bird's-Eye View*, London, 1924, p. 235.

6. Reminiscences (typescript), Mss. Eur. C-607, India Office Library and Oriental Collection, London (hereafter BL). The Major retired from service in 1885.

7. E.C. Bayley to Northbrook, 10 July 1874, Northbrook papers, Mss. Eur. C-144/17, BL.

8. Arthur Owen, 'Recollections of a Veteran of the Days of the Great Indian Mutiny of 1857', Lahore, 1915, 2nd edn., Mss. Eur. 239/120, BL.

9. Bampfylde Fuller, *India The Land and Its People*, pp. 41 and 124, and his *The Empire of India*, London, 1913. And the view that 'the Mahomedan star is not in the ascendant, and his position wars with his religion. That enjoins conversion by the sword if need be, and an almost fierce intolerance of the idolater. His whole entourage therefore is galling.' Low, *Vision of India*, p. 281; also, Flora Annie Steel, *India*, London, 1905, p. 180.

10. Harcourt Butler, 'The Country, Peoples, Language and Creeds' in John Cumming (ed.), *Modern India: A Co-operative Survey*, Delhi, 1932, p. 15; G.T. Garrat, *An Indian Commentary*, London, 1929, p. 172, basing his assessment on the dubious testimony of the Khoja spiritual leader, the Aga

Khan; Low, *Vision of India*, p. 281; *Speeches, by Harcourt Butler delivered at the M.A.O. College, Aligarh, on 25 November 1919*, Allahabad, 1921, pp. 140-1; and his *India Insistent*, London, 1931, p. 38; and Lelyveld, *Aligarh's First Generation*, pp. 9-10.

11. Garrat, *Indian Commentary*, p. 173.

12. As opposed to 'the Hindu, with his glib tongue, his pliant brain and back, his fantastic social rites, and his incomprehensible religion. . . .' Low, *Vision of India*, p. 281.

13. George Lumley to Linlithgow, 14 December 1939, L/P&J/8/645, BL.

14. Bampfylde Fuller, *Studies of Indian Life and Sentiments*, London, 1910, p. 125. The unifying force of Islam, commented Fuller, 'has checked schism, and religious divisions are few in number'. See also W.W. Titus, 'The Reaction of Muslim India to Western Islam' in John R. Mott (ed.), *The Muslim World Today*, London, 1925, p. 93; Claude H. Hill, 'Religion and Caste in India', in *India and the Durbar*, London, 1911, p. 210. He was editor of *The Times*.

15. Henry Whitehead, *Indian Problems in Religion, Education, Politics*, London, 1924. He was Bishop of Madras before becoming a Fellow of Trinity College, Cambridge; Garrat, *Indian Commentary*, p. 172.

16. Lawrence, second Marquess of Zetland, *Essays*, London, 1956, p. 119. See also T.W. Holderness, *Peoples and Problems of India*, London, 1911, p. 127.

17. Ronaldshay, *India: A Bird's-Eye View*, p. 214.

18. Asim Roy, *The Islamic Syncretistic Tradition in Bengal*, p. 249.

19. The argument is based on Frank C. Darling, *The Westernization of Asia: A Comparative Political Analysis*, Boston, 1939, pp. 21-9.

20. C.A. Elliot, *Laborious Days*, Calcutta, 1892, p. 28.

21. Fuller, *Studies*, pp. 130-1; Edward Thompson, *The Reconstruction of India*, London, 1930, p. 234.

22. Earl of Lytton, *Pundits and Elephants: Being the Experiences of Five Years as Governor of an Indian Province*, London, 1942, p. 172; Garrat, *Indian Commentary*, pp. 175-6, 181.

23. Memoirs of O.M. Martin (typescript), Centre for South Asian Studies, Cambridge (hereafter CSAS).

24. Bishop Heber first came in contact with the Bohras—'by far the wealthier and more industrious party'—in Rajasthan. He found them to be 'peaeable and orderly merchants and tradesmen' with considerable 'influence and privileges' in Central India. His other interesting observation was that the Bohras were 'agreeing far better with both Jains and Rajpoots than their Sunnite rivals'. *Bishop Heber in Northern India*, p. 282.

25. James Outram, *Memoirs of my Indian Career*, London, 1893, p. 397. He emphatically denied that there was a Muslim insurrection or that Muslims were a formidable danger to the government. He was unhappy at their 'exclusion' and 'degradation'. He insisted that 'each section of people in each district must be judged by their acts, and not otherwise; and that they

should be fairly judged—not by a foregone prejudice, but with an equal mind'. W.W. Hunter, *Indian Mussalman: Are they Bound in Conscience to Rebel against the Queen?*, Calcutta, 1945 edn., p. 123. Unlike the great majority of his compatriots, Blunt studied Islam and followed the fortunes of Muslim societies with an open mind. Of his book *The Future of Islam*, he wrote: 'In it I committed myself without reserve to the Cause of Islam as essentially the "Cause of God" over an immense portion of the world, and to be encouraged, not repressed, by all who cared for the welfare of mankind.' His sympathy for Islam eventually led him to champion the Arab cause against European intervention and Ottoman injustices. Rana Kabbani, *Europe's Myths of Oriental Devise and Rule*, London, 1986, pp. 96-7.

26. Dufferin's Minute of Nov. 1988, quoted in Hardy, *Muslims of British India.*

27. Annemarie Schimmel, *Islam in the Indian Subcontinent*, Leiden, 1980, p. 197.

28. *Eminent Mussalmans*, Madras, n.d., p. 91.

29. Halide Edib, *Inside India*, London, 1937, pp. 317-18.

30. Edward Thompson to Wedgewood Benn, 31 Dec. 1930, L/PO/6/74 (ii), BL.

31. Alfred Lyall to Morley, 4 Feb. 1909, quoted in Robinson, *Separatism Among Muslims*, p. 170. This view could sometimes get mixed up with the articulation of worldwide imperial interests. For example, in the 1870s, the viceroy was told by the colonial office to remove any 'just cause of [Muslim] complaint, because, in the event of any action against Russia, our allies must be the Mahometans of Central Asia, Afghanistan, and of Russia'. To Northbrook, 21 Feb. 1873, Northbrook papers, Mss. Eur. C-144/21 (1) BL. Similar views were expressed during the First World War.

32. Hardy, *Muslims of British India*, p. 90; and Lelyveld, *Aligarh's First Generation*, p. 12.

33. Rev. J. Long to Northbrook, 19 July 1873, Northbrook papers, Mss. Eur. C-144/21 (1). The secretary of state told the viceroy on 23 October 1882: 'If there be any real special grievances which affect the Muslim population which we can fairly remove, by all means let it be done.'

34. Lucy Carroll, 'Colonial Perceptions of Indian Society', p. 249. For the implications of separate electorates and the claims of Muslims as 'an objectively-defined Muslim community', Farzana Shaikh, *Community and Consensus in Islam*, pp. 90, 157-9; and David Gilmartin, 'Democracy, Nationalism and the Public: A Speculation on Colonial Muslim Politics', *South Asia*, 14, 1, 1991, p. 125.

35. Hasan, *A Nationalist Conscience.*

36. Pethick-Lawrence to Cripps, 30 Sept. 1939, in Nicholas Mansergh (ed.), *The Transfer of Power, 1942-7*, London, 1969, Vol. 1, p. 629. See also my edited volume, *Islam and Indian Nationalism: Reflections on Abul Kalam Azad*, Delhi, 1992, pp. 93-4. The Simla conference was convened by the viceroy, Wavell, to resolve the political issues at the end of war in Europe, but it broke down. 'So my efforts to bring better understanding between the parties have

failed and have shown how wide is the gulf', noted the viceroy.

37. Jawaharlal Nehru, *An Autobiography*, London, 1936, p. 464; Hardy, *Muslims of British-India*, pp. 103-4. Rafiq Zakaria, *Rise of the Muslims in Indian Politics: An Analysis of Developments from 1885 to 1906*, Bombay, 1970, p. 351, quoted in Asma Barlas, *Democracy, Nationalism and Communalism: The Colonial Legacy in South Asia*, Boulder, CO, 1995, p. 148.

38. Nehru and M.N. Roy were in substantial agreement over Aligarh's role after the death of Saiyid Ahmad Khan. I am fascinated by M.N. Roy's reflections, the more so because he arrived at certain important conclusions without any close contact with the university or its scholars. The communist leader pointed out that Aligarh failed to produce youthful elements holding social and political ideas similar to the Hindu intellectuals who conceived of a political nationalism as expressed in the Congress. While the early generation of the Hindu intelligentsia imbibed progressive social and political views, the Aligarh alumni belonged to the landed aristocracy with social and political tendencies that were predominantly feudal. Roy concluded that 'the absence of a class cohesion was responsible for the political divergence between the Hindus and Muslims. . . . Elements so diverse socially could not unite in a national movement.' M.N. Roy, *India in Transition*, Bombay, 1971 rpt., p. 222.

39. Firoz Khan Noon, *Scented Dust*, Lahore, 1941, p. 293. This novel was written at the request of an English friend to acquaint him with some of the con-temporary themes in Indian politics and society. A leading landlord of Punjab, the author played a key part in the Muslim League.

40. Jawaharlal Nehru, *The Discovery of India*, Calcutta, 1946 rpt., p. 225.

41. M.N. Roy, *The Historical Role of Islam*, Delhi, 1981 rpt. This book was first published in 1939 but written in jail in the early 1930s. It was translated into Hindi as *Islam ki etihasik bhoomika* by Chandrodaya Dixit, Bikaner, 1988. A devout follower of Jainism wrote: 'To ascertain the truth about the teaching of Islam, and to separate its valuable gems from valueless stones as also from glittering pebbles, so that its beauty may be brought in the limelight of public notice.' Champat Rai Jain, *The Lifting of the Veil or the Gems of Islam*, Bijnor, 1931.

42. K.M. Panikkar, *The Foundations of New India*, London, 1963, p. 56. Such views were endorsed by quite a number of liberal and secular scholars as well as politicians before and after independence—for example, the contention that 'the great principles of Islam did not afect Hinduism as a whole' or that the 'social structure of Hinduism remained almost unaffected by 700 years of association with Islam'. K.M. Pannikar, *Asia and Western Dominance*, London, 1953, p. 240. In fact, '700 years of Islamic authority over the Indo-Gangetic plain . . . had left Hinduism in a state of depression. It was the religion of a subject race, looked down upon with contempt by the Muslims as idolatry.' *The India We Served*, p. 127, and the Early of Ronaldshay, *The Heart of Aryavarta: A Study of the Psychology of Indian*

Unrest, London, 1925, p. 2. Likewise, it was common to identify India with Hinduism and with 'Hindu culture' and 'Hindu civilization'. This was a classic British theory reinforced by Indologists of different intellectual pedigrees. 'To me', wrote Walter Roper Lawrence, 'India is Hindu, and whatever the picture of "India Reformed" may have been in the minds of the imaginative men who made the rough sketch, in the finished work the Brahman will be the central and the striking figure.'

43. Panikkar, *Foundations*, pp. 55, 60; see S. Radhakrishnan, *Eastern Religions and Western Thought*, London, 1940 edn., p. 339; and the comment of a senior Congress leader: 'The Muslims are an all-India community. Whether organised in one overall organisations or not, it often feels the identity of the interests of its members and acts unitedly where its minority rights are concerned.' J.B. Kripalani, *Minorities in India*, Calcutta, n.d., p. 40.

44. J.T.F. Jordens, *Dayananda Saraswati: His Life and Ideas*, Delhi, 1978, p. 268.

45. K.W. Jones, *Arya Dharma: Hindu Consciousness in 19th-Century Punjab*, Berkeley, 1976, pp. 145, 150; J.E. Llwellyn, *The Arya Samaj as a Fundamentalist Movement: A Study in Comparative Fundamentalism*, New Delhi, 1993, pp. 104-8.

46. V.C. Joshi (ed.), *Lajpat Rai: Autobiographical Writings*, New Delhi, 1965, p. 14.

47. B.G. Gokhale, 'Hindu Responses to the Muslim Presence in Maharashtra', in Yohanan Friedmann (ed.), *Islam in Asia*, Vol. 1: *South Asia*, Jerusalem, 1984, pp. 162-7.

48. Sudhir Chandra, 'Communal Consciousness in Late 19th Century Hindi Literature', in Mushirul Hasan (ed.), *Communal and Pan-Islamic Trends in Colonial India*, New Delhi, 1987, pp. 180-95.

49. Christopher R. King, 'Hindu Nationalism in the Nineteenth Century U.P.', in Dhirendra K. Vajpeyi (ed.), *Boeings and Bullock-Carts: Essays in Honour of K. Ishwaran*, New Delhi, 1990, pp. 187, 191; see also Yogendra Malik, 'Reflections of Inter-Communal Relations through Hindi Fiction', in Vajpeyi (ed.), *Boeings and Bullock-Carts*, Chap. 9; R.S. McGregor, 'A Hindu Writer's Views of Social, Political and Language Issues of his Time: Attitude of Harischandra of Banaras (1850-1885)', *Modern Asian Studies*, Vol. 25, 1, 1991, pp. 91-100.

50. P. Gaeffke, *Hindi Literatue in the Twentieth Century*, Wiesbaden, 1978, p. 27.

51. Sudhir Chandra, *The Oppressive Present: Literature and Social Consciousness in Colonial India*, New Delhi, 1992, p. 120.

52. Partha Chatterjee, *Nationalist Thought and the Colonial World: A Derivative Discourse*, New Delhi, 1980, p. 77; Tapan Raychaudhuri, *Europe Reconsidered: Perceptions of the West in the Nineteenth Century World*, New Delhi, 1988, pp. 188-9; Tanika Sarkar, 'Imagining Hindurashtra: The Hindu and the Muslim in Bankim Chandra's Writings', in Ludden (ed.), *Contesting*

the Nation, pp. 162-84. For a different interpretation. see Sisir Kumar Das, *The Artist in Chains: The Life of Bankim Chandra Chatterjee*, New Delhi, 1984, Appendix C: 'A Muslim Baiter?'

53. Sudipta Kaviraj, 'The Reversal of Orientalism: Bhudev Mukhopadhyay and the Project of Indigenist Social Theory'. Vasudha Dalmia and H. von Stietencron (eds.), *Representing Hinduism: The Construction of Religious Traditions and National Identity*, New Delhi, 1995, pp. 253-82; Ray-chaudhuri, *Europe Reconsidered*, pp. 41-3.

54. Sudhir Chandra, 'Towards an Integrated Understanding of early Indian Nationalism', in Alok Bhalla and Sudhir Chandra (eds.), *Indian Responses to Colonialism in the 19th Century*, New Delhi, 1993, p. 18.

55. Sudhir Chandra, 'The Lengthening Shadow: Secular and Communal Consciousness', in Bidyut Chakrabarty (ed.), *Secularism and Indian Polity*, New Delhi, 1990.

56. Nirad C. Chaudhuri, *The Autobiography of an Unknown Indian*, New York, 1951, p. 227.

57. It has been noted that the peasants, most of whom were Muslims, never entered Bankim's fictional mind. While commenting on the present in polemical prose, Bankim could see the Hindus and the Muslims both as sections of the oppressed masses but in his historical novels the Muslim was always perceived as the alien. Meenakshi Mukherji, 'Rhetoric Identity: History and Fiction in Nineteenth Century India', in Bhalla and Chandra (eds.), op. cit., p. 35. See also Pradip Kumar Datta, 'Dying Hindus: Production of Hindu communal common sense in early 20th century Bengal', *EPW*, 19 June 1993, pp. 1305-25; and Tanika Sarkar, 'Imagining Hindu Rashtra', op. cit.

58. Chaudhuri, *Autobiography*, pp. 226-7.

59. Ibid., p. 228.

60. Ibid., p. 232.

61. Nirad C. Chaudhuri, *Thy Hand, Great Anarch! India, 1921-1952*, Delhi, 1987, p. 37.

62. Ibid., p. 466.

63. Ibid., p. 39.

64. Chaudhuri, *Autobiography*, p. 225.

65. Chaudhuri, *Thy Hand, Great Anarch!*, p. 469.

66. Nehru, *Autobiography*, p. 137.

67. Nehru, *Discovery of India*, pp. 297-305.

68. Ibid., p. 340.

69. Nehru, *Discovery of India*, pp. 341-2.

70. To Mohammad Ismail Khan, 26 Dec. 1927, S. Gopal (ed.), *Selected Works of Jawaharlal Nehru* (hereafter *SWJN*), Delhi, 1976, Vol. 8, p. 203.

71. Statement to the press, 10 Jan. 1937, ibid., Vol. 8, p. 12.

72. Presidential Address at Punjab National Conference, Amritsar, 11 Apr. 1928, ibid., Vol. 3, pp. 225-6.

73. Ibid., Vol. 8, p. 120.
74. Nehru, *Discovery of India*, p. 343.
75. Hasan, *Nationalism and Communal Politics*, pp. 102-3.
76. Clifford Geertz, 'Modernization in a Muslim Society: The Indonesian Case', in Robert N. Bellah (ed.), *Religion and Progress in Modern Asia*, New York, 1965, p. 95.
77. Noon, *Scented Dust*, p. 282.
78. Russell, *Pursuit of Urdu Literature*, p. 71.

4

Traditional Rites and Contested Meanings: Sectarian Strife in Colonial Lucknow

The truth is that in those days the whole year was spent waiting for
Muharram. . . . After the goat sacrifices of Baqr Id the preparations for
Muharram began. Dadda, my father's mother, started to softly chant elegies
about the martyrs. Mother set about sewing black clothes for all of us; and
my sister took out the notebooks of laments . . . and began to practice them
to new airs. In those days film music had not taken grip of *nauha* melodies.
They were simple and at the same time deep, like the folk-music of villages
and small towns, and when my sister, mother, or an aunt wore black clothes
and stood up to recite,

> Sleeping spoke out the dreaming Sakina,
> The lord's breast's no more, so no more Sakina . . .

the wrists supporting the book of *nauhas* were immediately transformed.
It seemed to the listeners as if the lament was issuing straight from the jail
in Damascus where Imam Husain's sister Zainab was trying to comfort his
beloved daughter Sakina in a subterranean dungeon. . . . I don't know about
Lucknow—I don't even know about Ghazipur—but I certainly do know
that among the Saiyid families of Gangauli, Muharram was nothing less
than a spiritual celebration.

RAHI MASOOM REZA, *The Feuding Families of Village Gangauli*

As darkness descended on Lucknow, once a prized city of Awadh, some
people huddled together in a cafe or on the terraces with their eyes fixed
on the distant horizon. After a long and anxious wait, the city comes alive:
the moon is sighted in the middle of dark clouds hovering over the Gomti
river. The deafening sound of crackers from Nakhaas and the loud and
clear call for prayers from Shah Najaf mark the beginning of the holy

month of Muharram. Lakhnavis would observe the next ten days with solemnity. They would, moreover, reaffirm their unflinching devotion to those Islamic principles for which Imam Husain, grandson of the Prophet of Islam, and his companions laid down their lives on the banks of the river Euphrates in AD 680. Once more, they would, in their imagination, rally round those gallant men and women at Karbala who kept the Islamic flag flying without capitulating before the evil and tyrannical forces. They would once again desire to share in their *karb* (pain) and *bala* (trial). The ritual recreation of Karbala creates an environment that, in Clifford Geertz's terms, can 'establish powerful, pervasive, and long-lasting moods and motivations in men by formulating conceptions of a general order of existence and clothing those conceptions with such an aura of factuality that the moods and motivations seem uniquely realistic'.

Come day one of Muharram and life in Lucknow comes to a standstill. Perfume and tobacco shops wear a deserted look. Trade is no longer brisk. Business has slackened. The busy and noisy bazaars of Aminabad and Nakhaas are subdued. The city is robbed of its buoyancy and festive look. Meer Hasan Ali, an English lady married to a Shia and living in Lucknow in the 1820s, contrasted the profound stillness of an extensively populated city with the incessant bustle usual at all other times.[1]

The change is also manifested in other ways. Women, including the newly-wed, remove their jewellery, their bangles and flashy clothes; 'the hair is unloosed . . . and allowed to flow in disorder about the person; the coloured pyjamahs (loose trousers) and duppattas (long scarf) are removed, with every other articles of their usual costume, for a suit that, with them, constitutes mourning—some choose black, others grey, slate, or green'.[2] Comfort, luxury and convenience are set aside. The *pallung*, the *charpoy* (the two descriptions of beds) and the *musnad* are removed. Instead, women of all classes use a date mat or simply sleep on a matted floor.[3] Men are equally abstemious, sporting white *angarkhas* (a combination of the *jama*, a collarless shirt and *balabar*) or *achkans* (knee-length tunics) in dark shades. Poets, accustomed to regaling large audiences with *ghazals*, switch to writing *marsiyas* (elegies) and *soz* (dirges). Their chief patrons, the rajas and nawabs, abandon their favourite pastimes to lead a life of piety. Their palaces, *havelis* and forts bear a sombre look during Muharram.

Courtesans and their retinue in the Chowk area put away their musical instruments, their *ghungrus*, *payals* and the *tabla*. Umrao Jan Ada's 'Khanum' commemorated Husain's martyrdom on a more elaborate scale than any other courtesan in Lucknow, decorating the place of mourning

with banners, buntings, chandeliers and globes. She was herself an accomplished *soz-khwan* (reciter of dirges). The most celebrated profes-
sionals dared not perform in her presence.[4] Her account finds resonances
in Attia Hosain's description of her visit down 'the forbidden street whose
balconies during the first days of Muharram were empty of painted,
bejewelled women when visitors climbed the narrow stairs only to hear
religious songs of mourning'.[5] There was the glass *tazia,* the miniature
domed tomb, shining, gleaming, reflecting the light of many crystal lamps.

The city's black clad men and women set aside their daily chores to
sorrow for the martyred Imam and his loyal and courageous companions.
They marched through the lanes and bylanes in fervent lamentation
chanting 'Ya-Husain, Ya-Husain', rhythmically beating their chests, self-
flagellating, carrying replicas (*tazia*) of Husain's tomb, his coffin (*taboot*),
his standards and insignia (*alam* and *panja*) and his horse (*dul-dul*). One
of the most impressive religious spectacles, commented William Crooke,
was the long procession of *tazias* and flags streaming along the streets
with a vast crowd of mourners, who 'scream out their lamentations and
beat their breasts till the blood flows or they sink fainting in an ecstasy of
sorrow'.[6] Notice, the following description:

The sun was high above the church steeple when we heard the distant chanting,
'Hasan! Husain! Hasan! Husain! Haider!' It came nearer and the measured sound
of bare hands striking bare breasts, the monotonous beat of drums and cymbals
made my heart beat with a strange excitement. Then the barefooted, bareheaded
men came in view following the *tazias* carried shoulder-high. There were *tazias* of
peacock's feathers, of glass, of sugar, of bright-coloured paper, intricate, beautiful
arched domed, some as high as telegraph poles, others from poor homes so small
that they could be held on one man's head, all hurrying to join the main procession
at the allotted time, for burial or, consecration.[7]

Such devotional activities in public were just a small part of Muharram
ceremonies. The imambaras (literally, the house of Imam), symbolizing
Lucknow's Shia past and present, served as central organizing spaces,
physical statements uniting the populace of the city,[8] symbols of communitarian solidarity, and as platforms for articulating individual and
collective experiences. Here the gatherings (*majlis*) were structured, ad-
hering to a pattern laid down by the Shia nawabs of Awadh. Beginning
with *soz-khwani* (recitation without the aid of musical instruments), a
majlis would be followed by a sermon or *marsiya-khwani* (reading of
elegy), a style of rendering inspired by the legendary Lucknow poet, Mir
Anis (1802-75) and conclude with short dirges. 'As soon as the impressive and heart-rendering notes of dirges were chanted by Mir Ali Hasan

and Mir Bandey Hasan', wrote the essayist-novelist Abdul Halim Sharar (1860-1926),

hundreds of men from élite families began to sing them, and then the women of noble Shia families also intoned them with their matchless voices. Matters have now reached the stage that during Muharram and on most days of mourning, heart-rending sounds of lamentation and the melodious chanting of dirges can be heard from every house in every lane in old Lucknow. In every alley one will hear beautiful voices and melodies which one will never forget.[9]

The sermon is an elegiac account of the episodes in the Karbala story, a moving narrative of the pain, anguish, and agony of Husain and his companions. Year after year speakers detail the sequence of events, retaining the order in which individual members of Husain's family were killed. Thus the sixth of Muharram is connected with Husain's young nephew, the seventh with his 18-year old son, the eighth with the brave and devoted brother Abbas, the ninth with the 6-month old son Ali Asghar, and the tenth with Imam Husain's own martyrdom. Qasim, Ali Akbar, Abbas, Ali Asghar and Husain himself exemplified the enormity of the tragedy; so that days linked with their martyrdom convey deep meanings, special attachments, and associations. Their experiences, narrated by an *alim* or a *mujtahid*, move audiences (*azadars*) to mourn, wail and lament, beat their chests (*matam*), and, in this way, share in the sufferings of the martyrs by self-deprivation and mortification. Again, the novelist Attia Hosain captures the mood in Lucknow:

It was the ninth night of Muharram. On the horizon there was a glow as of a forgetful sun rising before moonset. The glow of a million lamps from the illumi-nated Imambaras where *tazias* and banners were laid to rest, lit the sky, and the city was alive, crowds forgetful in that bright beauty of the month of mourn-ing . . . . When he (Asad) read of the agonies of thirst of the children of the Prophet, cut off from the river by their enemies, the women sobbed softy. Ustaniji began beating her breast, saying 'Hassan-Husain' softly, with a slow rhythm. Ramzano stared at her strangely and joined in. The others still sobbed softly.[10]

Ten days of mourning ceremonies culminate on *Yaum-i Ashura* with the *Majlis-i Sham-i Ghariban* at the famous Ghuframab Imambara, the final mournful tribute to the *Saiyid-ash-Shuhada* (Lord of the Martyrs). The final curtain is drawn on Chehlum, the fortieth day. Sharar described a procession of women carrying *tazias* at the Talkatora Karbala. All were bareheaded and their hair hung loose. In the centre a woman carried a candle. By its light a beautiful, delicately formed girl read from some sheets of paper. She chanted a dirge along with other women. Moved by the 'stillness, the moonlight, those bareheaded beauties and the soul-rending notes of their sad melody', he heard the following lament as the group passed through the gates of the shrine:

> When the caravan of Medina, having lost all
> Arrived in captivity in the vicinity of Sham
> Foremost came the head of Husain, borne aloft on a spear
> And in its wake, a band of women, with heads bared.[11]

II

Muharram, Husain and Karbala signified different things to different sections of Lucknow society. Some saw in the observances the potential for political mobilization. The khilafat leadership and the votaries of Pakistan could therefore employ the paradigm of Karbala and harness the most evocative themes of Shi'ism to provide depth to their movements.[12] Husain's martyrdom also served, to the Shias of all times and in all places, as an everlasting exhortation to guard their separate identity, and to brave their numerical inferiority in the face of firmly established and sometimes oppressive majorities. It made sense, according to Hamid Enayat, on two other levels: first, in terms of a soteriology not dissimilar to the one invoked in the case of Christ's crucifixion—just as Christ sacrificed himself at the altar of the cross to redeem humanity, so did Husain allow himself to be killed on the plains of Karbala to purify the Muslim community of sins; and second, as an active factor vindicating the Shia cause, contributing to its ultimate triumph. When one adds to all this the cathartic effect of weeping as a means of releasing pent-up grief over not only personal misfortune but also the agonies of a long-suffering minority, then the reasons for the popular appeal of Muharram ceremonies become apparent.[13]

Husain stirred the passions and sensitivities of several groups. On the night of ninth Muharram, groups of women, largely Hindus, moved about the villages wailing and reciting, mostly improvised lyrics, on the epic tragedy. Urban and rural Hindus venerated Husain, incorporated his cult into their rituals,[14] offered flowers and sweets at local Karbalas, participated in processions, decorated and kept *tazias*, and sought Husain's intercession to cure the diseased, avert calamities, procure children for the childless or improve the circumstances of the dead. The Imam's trial and tribulations inspired faith in a universal nemesis ensuring justice for the oppressed souls. In popular belief and mythology he was the Ram of

Ayodhya carrying his crusade into the wilderness; his brother Abbas personified Lakshman—devoted, energetic and brave; his sister Zainab and wife Um-i Kulsoom, the surviving witnesses to the slaughter at Karbala, were cast in the image of Sita, caring, dutiful and spirited. Yazid, the Umayyad ruler and Husain's persecutor, was Ravana, greedy, corrupt, ambitious, cruel, and ruthless.

W.H. Sleeman found Hindu princes in central and southern India, 'even of the brahmin caste', commemorating Muharram with 'illuminations and processions . . . brilliant and costly'. In Gwalior, a Hindu state, Muharram was observed with splendid pomp. So also in Baroda, where the ruler sent an exquisite prayer carpet of pearls to Mecca.[15] Travellers discovered Hindus clothed in green garments and assuming the guise of faqirs.[16] So did Jafar Sharif.[17] A Hindi newspaper reported in July 1895 that Muharram had passed off peacefully in Banaras. 'When it is Hindus who mostly celebrate [sic] this festival, what fear can there be?'[18] In Lucknow, 'thousands of Hindus chanted dohas along with the Shias and Sunnis'.[19] Shiva Prasad kept a tazia in a specially prepared shed. On the tenth of the month, the elaborate man-high tomb made of bright-coloured paper and tinsel was carried to its burial in procession. The Muslim servants recited dirges, while Shiva Prasad and his sons followed in barefooted, bareheaded respect.[20]

This was not all. Munshi Faizuddin's reminiscences, published in 1885, described Muharram rites in the court of the last two Mughal emperors.[21] So does Saiyid Ahmad Dehlawi's (b. 1946) Rusum-i Dehli (Rituals and Traditions of Delhi), written some decades later.[22] The Sunni raja of Nanpara had Shia ulama read to him elegies for Husain.[23] In Allahabad, Sunnis took out 122 of the 220 tazias.[24] Rural Muslims, Crooke declared in 1897, joined the Muharram observance 'almost without distinction of sect'.[25] A Western scholar of Indian Islam was struck by the Shia influences on 'the length and breadth of the Sunni community'.[26] In a small north Indian princely state, a British civil servant found every Muslim guild—the painters, the masons, the carpenters, the weavers—having their own tazias and their own troupes of actors and mourners who reproduced scenes of the struggle at Karbala.[27] Here and elsewhere, Shia-Sunni relations were not structured around sectarian lines. Regardless of the polemics of the ulama and the itinerant preachers, bonds of friendship and understanding remained intact among Shias and Sunnis of all classes. Most shared a language and literature and a cultural heritage. This is probably why Sharar declared that no one in Lucknow ever noticed who was a Sunni and who a Shia.[28]

Lucknow was, both before and during the nawabi rule, relatively free of religious insularity or sectarian bigotry. The Shia nawabs took their cue from their Sunni overlords in Delhi to create a broad-based polity and a cosmopolitan cultural and intellectual ethos. They adhered to the policy of *sulh-i kul* (peace with all), pioneered by the Mughal emperor Akbar. Wajid Ali Shah is reported to have said that 'of my two eyes, one is a Shia and the other is a Sunni'. Sunni officials occupied important positions in the middle and lower echelons of government department. The highest officials in Wajid Ali Shah's court, including the vazir and paymaster, were Sunnis. Sunni officers also managed the Sibtainabad Imambara and the *baitul buka* (house of lamentation).[29] Generally speaking, the Awadh rulers provided both a liminal cultural glue and a set of structural lines of schism along which conflict could be routed.[30]

Shia-Sunni controversies did not plague most princely states. Several Shia families from Awadh, such as the Saiyids of Bilgram, sought and secured lucrative positions in Hyderabad. Shia-Sunni marriages were commonly contracted in princely states like Rampur, as also in *taluqdari* families. Shias and Sunnis forged a common front in literary and political associations, acted in unison during the Urdu agitation against the April 1900 Nagri resolution of the government in UP, and shared the Muslim League platform. They were one in agitating over the Kanpur mosque, the Aligarh Muslim University issue, and, much to everybody's surprise, on the khilafat question. The raja of Mahmudabad, a devout Shia, kept these causes alive. He patronized the 'young party', funded their newspapers and their agitations. James Meston, lieutenant-governor of UP, reported that a 'clique of noisy and aggressive Muslims of the young party made the raja's house their headquarters and lived and agitated at his expense'.[31]

Urdu prose and poetry, too, offers no clue to polarized Shia-Sunni sentiments. The writings of Saiyid Ahmad Khan, Hali, Shibli, maulvi Zakaullah, maulvi Nazir Ahmad and Abdul Halim Sharar were free of sectarian claptrap. In 1889, Sharar wrote *Hasan aur Anjalina*; Shia-Sunni relations was its theme. The great Urdu poet Asadullah Khan Ghalib wore no sectarian badge, no sectarian colour. He was 'a pure unitarian and true believer'. Suspected by some to be a Shia and by others as a *tafzili* (one who, though a Shia, acknowledges the pre-eminence of Ali), Ghalib revelled in the ambivalence. In fact, there was some confusion at his death as to whether his funeral rites should follow Shia or Sunni rituals.

Dakhni and modern Urdu poetry were both rich in *manqabat*, poems in praise of Ali, and in *marsiyas*, authored by both Shias and Sunnis. Husain is everybody's hero, the embodiment of Islamic virtues of piety, courage and commitment. He laid down his life but did not compromise with a bloody-minded tyrant presiding over a degenerate political and social order. His exemplary courage inspired Mohamed Ali, the volatile khilafat leader, to observe that while Yazid won on the bank of Euphrates it was Husain who 'reigned and still reigns over the hearts of a faith of God's human creation, while the soul of humankind in its entirety applauds the victory and final triumph of the victims of Karbala and shall continue to do so. . . .'[32]

Qatl-i Husain asl me marg-i Yazid hai
Islam zinda hota hai har Karbala be baad.

Husain's assassination, in reality, symbolizes the death of Yazid.
Islam is revived in the wake of every Karbala.

Iqbal echoed similar sentiments: 'Strange and simple and colourful is the story of Kaaba; its end is Husain, its beginning Ismail.' Husain was a model of the Perfect Man who becomes a martyr in his strife for God's unity against the rulers of the world. Every age brings forth a new Yazid, but resistance to tyranny, as evident in Husain's legendary example, is incumbent upon every believer.[33] Employing the paradigms of Husain and Karbala, Iqbal sent forth the message:

Nikal kar khanqahon se ada kar rasm-i Shabbiri.

Emerge from the confines of the Khanqahs and,
re-enact the example set by Husain.

All of this underlined the importance of Husain, Muharram and Karbala as living and vibrant symbols of India's composite cultural interaction, the intermixing of religio-cultural strands, and the fusion of religious beliefs and practices. Yet, by the end of the nineteenth century, such representations of unity gradually gave way to symbols of discord. They served, in the hands of the politician-priest combine, to heighten sectarian consciousness, assert judicial and political rights, and widen areas of competition and disharmony. Each side came to nurse profound grievances about the other based on mutually exclusive interpretations of history.

The first ominous sign surfaced around 1906, when some Sunni zealots constructed their own local Karbala at Phoolkatora on the north-eastern edge of Lucknow, opposite the existing one in Talkatora. The fires of sectarian unrest were then stoked by the public praise (*madhe sahaba*) of the three khalifas—Abu Bakr, Umar and Usman—whom the Shias regarded as 'usurpers' of Ali's claim to be the successor of the Prophet.

The Shias retaliated with a vilification (*tabarra*) campaign. Sunni preachers, on the other hand, declared Muharram observances as acts of *biddat* (heresy). They exhorted their followers to avoid them scrupulously.[34] Zafarul Mulk, secretary of the Lucknow Madhe Sahaba Committee, declared *taziadari* 'deleterious to the spiritual and temporal well-being of the Muslims'.[35] The nature of the Shia-Sunni engagement inevitably led to the appropriation of certain symbols and the rejection of others.

The writing on the wall was clear; Muharram was no longer a common symbol of veneration but an exclusively Shia concern both in its format as well as in the composition of the participants.[36] By the 1930s, its popular appeal had considerably diminished, though less so in the rural hinterland.[37] A powerful symbol of unity was transformed into a potent vehicle for sectarian mobilization; in consequence, Shia-Sunni strife became much more common in certain north Indian towns than Hindu-Muslim riots. Shia-Sunni frictions were sparked off in Lucknow in the 1880s and 1890s and 1907-8. 'The feeling of tension between the Sunnis and Shias of Lucknow had reached its climax', reported the *Gauhar-i Shahwar* in April 1907.[38] Allahabad, Banaras and Jaunpur witnessed widespread violence. What began as small-scale skirmishes during the last quarter of the nineteenth century (many went unnoticed in official despatches because they were listed in the category of 'Native Societies and Religious and Social Matters' in the 'Selections from the Native Newspapers') escalated into bloody feuds involving scores of people and turning several areas, including Lucknow and its adjoining districts, into a cauldron of sectarian animus.

The lines of cleavage were sharply demarcated by the mushroom growth of sectarian organizations, such as the Anjuman-i Sadr-us Sudoor, floated by maulana Saiyid Agha Husain in 1901, and the Anjuman-i Jafariya, established by the Saiyids of Barha four years later. A Shia conference was set up in October-December 1907, some months after the Muslim League came into being. There was much talk of 'Shias of light' leading the way and mitigating the economic and educational backwardness of their community. Some conveyed their grievances to the British government, including the viceroy.[39]

The depth of sectarian feelings surfaced at the first Shia Conference in 1907. Delegates delivered fiery and intemperate speeches against the Sunnis. The atmosphere was so vitiated that Gulam-us Saqlain, editor of *Asr-i Jadid*, left the meeting in disgust. The hardliners seized the initiative in renaming the organization as the Shia Political Conference, petitioned the government in December 1909 to enumerate the Shia population separately in the census, and insisted on their separate and distinct identity.[40] The conference, initially formed to foster cultural and educational goals, turned into a powerful vehicle for articulating sectional political goals.

In the mid-1930s, the Shia Political Conference, now firmly controlled by Saiyid Wazir Hasan, the architect of the Congress-League scheme of December 1916, rallied round the Congress and supported the Muslim Mass Contact Campaign, Jawaharlal Nehru's brainchild. At the same time, it continued to clamour for separate representation in the legislative councils, a demand spurred by the defeat of two Shia candidates in the 1937 elections. The *Sarfaraz*, a Shia weekly from Lucknow, attributed their defeat to the 'venomous' Sunni propaganda and called for safeguarding Shia 'national and political rights'.[41] The Anjuman-i Tanzimul Muminin expressed lack of faith in the Muslim League, a body controlled by the 'Sunni Junta'. So did Saiyid Ali of the Shia Students' Conference. The Majlis-i Ulama, held at Lucknow on 5 July 1945, endorsed the memorandum sent by Hosseinbhoy A. Laljee to Wavell as well as the Congress High Command. The Shia Federation threatened to organize strikes, boycotts and demonstrations if its demands were not fulfilled.[42]

These were empty threats. Although sections in the Congress sympathized with Shia aspirations, they were not willing to raise the 'Shia case' in negotiating with the British and the League. Likewise, the government had no reason or compulsion to recognize the Shias as a major political force. 'We cannot give them special help' was how an official reacted. 'We cannot contemplate', commented a senior member in the Home department, 'treating religious sub-division of Muslims as a new minority'. Inevitably, the future editors of the transfer of power documents ignored Shia petitions in their compilation. 'Not wanted: I don't think we need bother at all with those cables from the Shias.'[43]

III

Lucknow was the scene of violent Shia-Sunni riots in 1938-9. These were a sequel to a protest movement, launched in May 1935, against an official suggestion to forbid *madhe sahaba* on certain days.[44] The agitation gained intensity a year later. It turned violent in May-June 1937, with frenzied mobs in Lucknow and Ghazipur going on a rampage. Trouble in Ghazipur was instigated by some Sunnis from Jaunpur. Enraged mobs burnt and looted property, and killed at will. The summer of discontent rumbled on. Sectarian strife, hitherto dormant, became a common occurrence in the daily lives of Lakhnavis.[45]

More trouble was fuelled during the next two years against a committee's ruling against *madhe sahaba* in Lucknow.[46] Husain Ahmad Madani, principal of the Deoband seminary, along with some other Jamiyat al-ulama leaders, advocated civil disobedience. Thousands courted arrest. Although a fervent advocate of secular nationalism and a principled critic of the 'two-nation theory', the Maulana stirred sectarian passions. He spoke at a public meeting in Lucknow on 17 March 1938, sharing the platform with the firebrand Maulvi Abdul Shakoor, head of the Dar al-Muballighin, and Maulana Zafarul Mulk, the chief exponent of *madhe sahaba* in Lucknow.[47] Elsewhere, the Ahrars and the Khaksars developed common cause with the Jamiyat al-ulama. The mercurial Khaksar leader, Allama Mashriqi, mobilized his followers from different places, although police vigilance made sure that not many sneaked into the city's municipal limits.[48] The Ahrars, fresh from their successful agitation against the maharaja of Kashmir, organized bands of volunteers (*jatha*) in Lucknow. They came from neighbouring Malihabad, Kanpur, Delhi, Meerut, and from as far as Peshawar. By the end of March 1939, hundreds were arrested. 'Tension in the city', wrote Lucknow's deputy-commissioner, 'has increased and is now nearing breaking point.'[49]

On 30 March, the Congress ministry bowed to such pressures and allowed *madhe sahaba* on *Barawafat*, the Prophet's birthday. While Sunni leaders promptly called off civil disobedience and organized a 30,000 strong *Barawafat* procession to register their victory, the Shia confidence in the Congress ministry was jolted. The *Sarfaraz* chided G.B. Pant and his ministerial colleagues for their capitulation.[50] An impression gained credence that the Congress had played a 'double game' by contravening established conventions in Lucknow, sowed the seeds of Shia-Sunni dissension, and stoked the fires of sectarian unrest to weaken the Muslim League's claim to represent the Muslim community. This was not an uncommon occurence. C.A. Bayly's study has shown how the Muslim leadership in Allahabad, poorly integrated into both the formal and informal system of power, had become an object of attention for political orators to exploit sectarian fissures.[51]

The Shias responded angrily to the ministerial decree. A large crowd assembled a day after at the imposing Asaf ud-Daula Imambara, indulged in *tabarra*, and excitedly climbed the upper stories of the gateway. Some rushed towards the nearby Tila Mosque, though the police blocked their onward march. Pandemonium prevailed; others set fire to nearby shops. A free exchange of brickbats ensued, and people waved weapons they had acquired from the *shamianas* and palisades. The police opened fire, dispersed the mob, and imposed curfew.[52] The scholar S. Khuda Bukhsh (b. 1842) was anguished to see a posse of police with glistening bayonets in Lucknow. 'Well might we heave a deep sigh at sight such as this? Has time turned its (Islamic) precepts of brotherly love and fraternal unity into sad, mocking derision? These were the mournful thoughts as my carriage glided down the road.' He was sorry that . . . the fabric of Islam is torn by dissensions, fierce and bitter; and that nobody was trying to restore peace, concord and harmony among Muslim. What a noble sight it is to see the police officers interfere at Muharram between the followers of the Prophet to prevent a breach of peace.[53]

Harry Haig, lieutenant-governor of UP, felt that sanctioning *madhe sahaba* set up among Shias conditions of intense emotional hysteria and stiffened their resolve to indulge in *tabarra*.[54] As he had foreseen, Shias assembled each day at the Asafi Imambara, recited *tabarra* on the Husainabad Road, and then courted arrest chanting '*Ya Ali*', '*Ya Ali*'. Tension mounted each day. 'No one knows', wrote an exasperated official in March 1939, 'from hour to hour—let alone from day to day—what will happen next.'[55]

There were other outward signs of protest. The Shia *mujtahid*, Maulana Nasir Husain, threatened to court arrest. So did the wife of Wazir Hasan, member of an influential family, and their son Saiyid Ali Zaheer.[56] Trouble spread to other areas as well. Volunteers from Agra, Kanpur, Fyzabad, Bara Banki and Rampur sneaked into Lucknow in early April to assist their beleaguered brethren. Plans were set afoot in Rae Bareli to congregate in Lucknow on *Barawafat* and participate in the planned *tabarra* agitation.[57] A batch of burqa-clad women from Rae Bareli turned up at Kazimain, a predominantly Shia locality, to court arrest, though the Shia *mujtahid* ultimately dissuaded them from doing so.[58] In August, Shias of Kanpur observed hartal against the police firing in Lucknow, wore badges on their arms, and fluttered black flags on their houses. Riots also broke out in Banaras.[59] A report published in August 1941 suggested that the 'attempt to find a solution to the Shia-Sunni dispute in Lucknow appears to have been abandoned'.[60]

Nehru, having spent some time in Lucknow trying to resolve the Shia-Sunni deadlock, commenting on the tactlessness of his colleagues in dealing with the disputes. 'I fear there has been much bungling about this issue', he wrote to Maulana Azad, who was not consulted before the UP ministry executed a volte-face. The matter was decided, he told the Maulana, 'without full consideration of the consequences'.[61] Rajendra Prasad, having been closely associated with some leading Shias of Bihar, such as Ali Imam, Husain Imam and Sultan Ahmad, was equally wary of the consequences. He observed:

I presume the Shias will continue civil disobedience and will be courting jail.... It must be very distressing to put nine thousand people in jail who are apparently not opposed to the government and many amongst whom are widely respected for one reason or the other. What troubles me even more is the propaganda which is gaining ground that the Congress stands to create division amongst Musalmans and what I apprehend is that after a time both will be more united against the Congress than they have ever been before.

Rajendra Prasad added that the Shias were ardent nationalists and the Shia Political Conference had consistently acted in unison with the Congress. For these reasons, the ministry should not have allowed anti-Congress sentiments 'to grow in any community and more so in a community sympathetically inclined'.[62]

IV

The Shias were few in number, not exceeding 4 per cent in any of the provinces in British India (Tables 4.1-2). They were most numerous in Lucknow and the satellite townships. Here, the imambaras and mosques stood as reminders of Shia domination under the nawabs. Elsewhere in UP, they were unevenly distributed in Jaunpur where the Sharqis once held sway, in Machhlishahar,[63] Bilgram, Sandila, Allahabad, Jalali in Aligarh district,[64] Jansath in Muzaffarnagar, Moradabad, Amroha, Sambhal, Budaun, and Rampur.[65] The nawab of Rampur and the raja of Mahmudabad and his kinsmen in Bilehra and Bhatwamau were Shias. Successful professional men were few, although some like Hamid Ali Khan, a Lucknow lawyer, Saiyid Raza Ali, Saiyid Ghulam-us-Saqlain, Saiyid Wazir Hasan and his son, Ali Zaheer, Saiyid Hyder Mehdi, Congressman and chairman of the Allahabad Improvement Trust, occupied prominent positions in public life. Some achieved fame as writers and poets in the early 1940s or thereafter, notably Saiyid Ehtesham Husain of Lucknow; Khwaja Ahmad Abbas, a descendant of Hali; Saiyid Sajjad Zaheer, son of Wazir Hasan and co-founder of the Progressive Writers' Movement; Ali Sardar Jafri of Balrampur state, an Aligarh student expelled from the university in the mid-1930s for his radical activities; and the poet Kaifi Azmi, who spent years in Bombay in the company of socialists and communists.

Yet, the success of such men does not reflect the condition of their Shia brethren, many of whom lagged far behind their Sunni counterparts. They were few in the professions, and fewer still in trade and commerce. The

Table 4.1: Shia and Sunni Population in India, 1921

Provinces and princely states	Muslim population	Shias	Sunnis
		(percentage)	
Assam	2,219,947	Nil	100
Baluchistan	773,477	1	96
Bengal	25,486,144	1	99
Bihar and Orissa	3,706,277	1	99
Bombay	4,660,828	3	88
CP and Berar	528,032	2	98
Madras	2,865,285	2	94
NWFP	2,084,123	4	95
Punjab and Delhi	12,955,141	2	97
Baroda	162,328	10	88
Kashmir	2,548,514	5	95
Rajputana and Ajmer	1,002,117	2	98

Source: Census of India, 1921, Vol. 1, p. 120.

Note: Figures for Bombay, Baroda and Rajputana and Ajmer include Khojas, Bohras, and in some cases, even Memons.

Table 4.2: Distribution of Shia and Sunni Population in UP, 1882

Division	Percentage of total Muslim population	
	Shias	Sunnis
Agra	1.5	98.5
Allahabad	5.3	94.7
Banaras	2.0	98.0
Faizabad	3.6	96.4
Jhansi	0.8	99.2
Lucknow	10.7	89.3
Meerut	2.3	97.7
Rae Bareli	1.8	98.2
Rohilkhand	1.6	98.4
Sitapur	1.7	98.3

Source: Census of India, NWFP and Oudh, 1882, Vol. 1, p. 74.

substantial group of poverty-stricken *wasiqadars* clung to the crumbling remains of their ancestral environs. In ghettos, or in the narrow lanes and alleys of Lucknow and Allahabad. In 1913, there were 1,661 *wasiqadars* in Lucknow, many living very much in the past. Some held durbars till as late as the early 1920s.[66] Their condition symbolized the decline of a class which owed its survival to nawabi patronage. Other Shia groups were not able to move up the ladder because they were poorly equipped to seize the opportunities in trade, business, professions and government service. Meston commented that the Shias were 'a community backward beyond all normal degrees of backwardness'.[67]

There can be no doubt that Shia-Sunni estrangement was related to the decline of the Shia aristocracy in the second half of the nineteenth century, the impoverishment of their less privileged brethren, and the relative prosperity of some Sunni groups which deepened Shia anxieties about their future.[68] They were estranged from a world dominated by the 'Other'. The British contributed to this process insofar as they gave legal definition to the Shia-Sunni divide. The approval or ban of religious commemorations, arbitration of disputes, and regulating religious procession routes transformed latent doctrinal differences into public, political and legal issues.[69] An even more powerful current at work towards the end of the nineteenth century appeared in the form of religio-revivalism, affecting the structure of both inter-as well as intra-community relations. Therefore, it is necessary to locate the Shia-Sunni schism in Lucknow, notwithstanding its local specificity, in the context of the countrywide religio-revivalist trends and tendencies.

It is widely known that the cow-protection societies, the Hindi Pracharni Sabhas and the Arya Samaj movement were designed to homogenize Hindu society with the aid of common cultural and religious and symbols. Similar currents, some in response to the intellectual and cultural hegemony of the West but most in reaction to Hindu revitalization campaigns, began to influence the Muslim educated classes as well. Towards the end of the nineteenth century, in particular, the notion of a sharply defined communitarian identity, distinct and separate from others, had acquired some degree of legitimacy among the *ashraf* Muslims. In the political and educational domain, Saiyid Ahmad Khan, despite his eclectic world view, plotted his trajectory within a communitarian framework. The Aligarh College, the All-India Muhammadan Educational Conference, the Urdu Defence Associations, and the Muslim League were concerned to create a Muslim identity in the public and private spaces.

Such concerns were matched by a concerted drive to create an ordered, unified, and cohesive religious community within the Islamic paradigm. Such was the goal of the founders of the Dar al-ulum at Deoband and the Nadwat al-ulama in Lucknow. Asserting their role as interpreters and guardians, they insisted, through sheafs of *fatawa*, on imposing a moral and religious code consistent with Koranic injunctions and free of accretions and interpolations. Not surprisingly, over 200 books listed in London's British Library catalogue, compiled by J.M. Blumhardt in 1900, dealt with ceremonial religious observances and includes compendia of religious duties, treatises on lawful and unlawful actions and collections of religious precepts. In a nutshell, the growth of the printing press, the proliferation of vernacular newspapers, and the expanding educational networks served as powerful instruments for restructuring an ideal community that would conform to and reflect the Islamic ethos that prevailed during the days of the Prophet and his immediate successors, the first four Khalifas.

Initially confined to north India, the Islamic resurgence spread to other areas rapidly. Religious revivalism, conducted under the aegis of the *faraizis*, had already swept the rural Muslims in the Bengal countryside. The dominant strain of the Islamization drive there and elsewhere was to reject composite and syncretic tendencies and to create, instead, a pan-Islamic or a specifically pan-Indian Muslim identity. Rafiuddin Ahmed has shown how religious preachers prompted the masses to look beyond the borders of Bengal in quest of their supposed Islamic past and attach greater importance to their 'Muslim' as opposed to their local or regional identity. This new emphasis proved crucial to the subsequent emergence of a measure of social cohesion in a diversified and even culturally polarized community.[70]

In relation to the Hindu 'Other', the meaning of being a Muslim was translated through late nineteenth-century religious and political idioms. Shias and Sunnis, on the other hand, discovered new symbols of identity in the form of separate graveyards, separate mosques, separate schools, and separate religious and charitable endowments.[71] These institutions defined the boundaries within which Shias and Sunnis were required to stay apart. They were to live as separate entities in a world fashioned primarily by the religio-political leadership. Attempts to disturb the status quo encountered strong resistance.

Sunni Islam was just as much 'corrupted' by the incorporation of Hindu beliefs and customs, as by the adoption of Shia practices. So a campaign was mounted, at the turn of the nineteenth century, to question shared cultural, religious and intellectual paradigms and revive those controversies that had been dormant for long. The *madhe sahaba* processions were, for example, organized with much greater fanfare in Fatehpur, where Maulana Saiyid Abid Husain first started the practice in 1901, and in Lucknow around 1908-9 with the backing of Maulana Saiyid Ainul Qazat, tutor of both the Firangi *alim* Maulana Abdul Bari and Maulvi Abdul Shakoor, one of the chief architects of the Sunni agitation in Lucknow.[72]

There was, in addition, a concerted move to discourage Shia-Sunni marriage, to portray Shias as promiscuous heretics, and as traitors to the country and to Islam. Frequently singled out as traitors were Mir Sadiq, diwan of Tipu Sultan, Mir Alam, diwan of Hyderabad, Mir Jafar, diwan of Siraj ud-Daula, and the Bilgrami family.[73] 'Among the people classed as Muslim', observed Zafarul Mulk,

the Shias and the Ahmadis are the two sects which have basic differences with Muslims and are a constant source of internecine trouble and discord. . . . *It would be a real gain to the health of the body politic of Islam if these two sects were lopped off and treated as separate minorities.*[74] (italics mine)

The central theme, underlined years later by an *alim* of Nadwat al-ulama, was the impropriety of giving 'vent to one's feeling of sorrow through wailings and lamentation' and crying over a past event.[75] Around 1933-9, considerable polemical literature surfaced against *azadari*.[76] *Taziadari* was denounced as *bida* and *haram*.[77] In February 1939, the Tahaffuz-i Millat sought permission to take out small processions to dissuade Sunnis, by word of mouth, from *taziadari*.[78] Sharar, who bemoaned Shia-Sunni differences, observed how Abdul Shakoor perfected the art of public debates (*munazirah*) with his Shia counterparts.[79]

The indictment of Muharram rites was by no means a new development; on the other hand, the severity with which it was done in Lucknow during the 1930s had few historical precedents. It is true that orthodox Sunni treatises were critical of the Shias and averse to their practices. In the sixteenth century, Shaikh Ahmad Sirhindi, the chief exponent of the Naqshbandi *silsilah* in India, began his career by writing a pamphlet against them. Shah Waliullah, one of the foremost original thinkers in the history of Indian Islam, discussed the question of whether Shias were *Kuffar*, apostates, or just immoral. Shah Abdul Aziz wrote a highly polemical book in 1889 to prevent 'Sunnis from straying away from their faith in polemics with the Shias'. Deoband's Dar al-ulum, inspired by Waliullah and his disciples, was antithetical to Shia beliefs and practices. Saiyid Ahmad's invitation to Deoband's founders met with an emphatic refusal: they would not associate with a college that had room for Shias.[80] One of its foremost ulama, Husain Ahmad Madani, shared this antipathy, though he was, at the same time, a major proponent of secular nationalism. Yet, the diktat of an *alim* here or a theologian there did not undermine those values and customs that people had shared for generations. There were other schools of thought in Sunni Islam advocating reconciliation and rapprochement. In fact, many of the Shia *mujtahids*, including the renowned Maulvi Dildar Ali, were products of the Firangi Mahal in Lucknow, and there were, moreover, forces within Sufi Islam that cemented unity and integration.

Sectarianism in the 1930s, however, was of a distinct nature. The debates were no longer restricted to the khilafat. Nor were the age-old controversies confined to the learned and holy men. The energy released during the decade, spurred by newly-started organizations wedded to separate Sunni and Shia world views, substantially altered the structure of social relations. They imposed severe strains on the overall consensus that had been achieved through long-standing social cultural and economic networks. People were encouraged to transgress traditional codes of conduct and behaviour and organize themselves as a separate entity in opposition to the 'Other'. The emotional charge deepened the intensity and depth of sectarian conflicts, competition, and rivalries.

The Shias were not far behind in fortifying their claims. They tried, first of all, to rejuvenate their educational institutions which had virtually collapsed in the absence of nawabi patronage. They regarded the college at Aligarh as a 'Sunni' institution, though Saiyid Ahmad had, in recognition of Shia-Sunni differences, made a provision for teaching Shia theology. They had no theological seminary of their own. And because entry to Deoband or Nadwa was restricted to Sunni students, those Shias aspiring to become religious leaders received education not in India but in Iran and Iraq. Thus Saiyid Abdul Qasim Rizvi (d. 1906) studied in Lucknow and Najaf in Iraq. Back in Lahore, he promoted Usuli Shi'ism in the second half of the nineteenth century, founded congregational prayer mosques in the city and further north in Peshawar, built edifices for commemorating Husain's martyrdom, and establishing an *imami* seminary in Lahore with the backing of nawab Ali Raza Khan Qizilbash, a wealthy Shia landowner of Iranian origin.[81] Maulana Saiyid Ali Naqi (1903-88), a descendant of the learned Ghuframab family, also studied in Iraq. He returned to Lucknow in 1932, founded the Imamia Mission, and launched a weekly magazine *Payam-i Islam*. Many of his writings in the mid-1930s were in defence of *azadari*.[82]

The establishment of the Nadwat al-ulama led to the founding of a Shia school in Lucknow. The scheme of a Shia college, floated in March 1914, was the brainchild of Fateh Ali Khan Qizilbash, a landowner of Lahore with large estates in eastern UP, but was backed by nawab Hamid Ali Khan of Rampur and the UP government. The idea caught on fast. By mid-June 1916, Rs. 3,17,410 was raised. Because contributions came mainly from UP, there were demands to locate the college in the same province. The Syeds of Jansath in Muzaffarnagar district preferred Meerut. So did Rampur's nawab, though his preference for a city so far removed from his own area of influence is incomprehensible. Some suggested Agra, so that students 'do not imbibe political ideas in tender age and may cause inconvenience and trouble to the government'. But most settled for Lucknow, where the college gates were opened in 1917.[83]

Shia societies mushroomed in every quarter of Lucknow, the hub of Shia intellectual and cultural life. Prominent amongst them were the Madrasatul-Waizeen, organized on the lines of the Shibli Academy at Azamgarh and funded by the raja of Mahmudabad; the Imamia Mission, set up by Maulana Ali Naqi; and the Tanzimul-Muminin, the Shia answer to the Tahafuzz-i Millat, which was patronized by affluent manufacturers of tobacco and perfumes like Muhammad Umar and Asghar Ali, Muhammad Ali. These bodies were backed by an aggressive Shia-owned press—the *Sarfaraz*, an organ of the Shia Political Conference, *Shia*, printed in Lahore, and *Asad*, *Nazzara*, and the *Akhbar-i Imamia*, published fortnightly.[84]

With the country heading towards greater Hindu-Muslim friction, sectarian competition began to resemble inter-community conflicts. Not surprisingly, the process structuring sectarian conflict paralleled that of Hindu-Muslim friction in other urban centres of UP. This was, in part, because Sunnis and Shias of Lucknow could draw on the reservoir of experiences and models developed in the subcontinent during that period. That is, the nationwide impetus to defining one's community in relation to the other provided material that could be used by both groups of Muslims.[85] In general, such tendencies were not countered by a parallel ideological crusade, though individuals like Azad tried in vain to cement the divide, heal the wounds, and keep the recalcitrant parties in check.[86]

The Congress in UP also tried to defuse the mounting sectarian tensions in Lucknow, though most settled for a 'divide and rule' policy doling out concessions first to Shias and then to Sunnis. This strategy worked for a while. Shia leaders, having rallied round the Congress in the past, expected to be rewarded for their loyalty. The bulk of Sunni leaders were, on the other hand, enthused by Pant's gesture on 30 March 1939. They stayed put in the Congress. But their support, having been tied to short-term communitarian interests, was rapidly eroded when the Muslim League raised new hopes and expectations in the early 1940s.

Both the context and the reference point of the Shia and Sunni leaders were rapidly eroded by the powerful drive for a separate 'Muslim nation'. The forces of an overriding and hegemonic 'Muslim nationalism' subsumed sectarian allegiances. A British official had urged the Shias in 1946 'to sink their fortunes with the Sunnis and be treated as Muslims'.[87] So they did. Once the creation of Pakistan became imminent, the Shias and Sunnis hitched their fortunes to the Muslim League bandwagon, and undertook their long trek towards the promised *Dar al-Islam* (Land of Islam). They emerged from the ruptures of history to find that their strength lay in forging ahead, and exploring new options in the future homeland. They were tantalized by this new ideal, exemplified by a new leader. The ideological conflicts were, however, carried over to the new nation, where the inconclusive debates resumed with the same intensity and fervour.

NOTES

1. Meer Hasan Ali, *Observations on the Mussalmans of India*, New Delhi, 1982 rpt., p. 30.
2. Ibid., p. 46.
3. Ibid., p. 43.
4. Mirza Muhammad Hadi Ruswa, *Umrao Jan Ada*, translated by Khushwant Singh and M.A. Husain, Hyderabad, 1982, p. 48.
5. Attia Hosain, *Sunlight on a Broken Column*, New Delhi, 1992, p. 64.
6. W. Crooke, *The North-Western Provinces of India: Their History, Ethnology, and Administration*, New Delhi, 1975 rpt., p. 263.
7. Attia Hosain, *Sunlight on a Broken Column*, p. 72.
8. J.R.I. Cole, *Roots of North Indian Shi'ism in Iran and Iraq: Religion and State in Awadh 1772-1859*, Berkeley and Los Angeles, 1988, p. 98; and Freitag, *Collective Action and Community*, p. 237.
9. A.H. Sharar, *Lucknow: The Last Phase of an Oriental Culture,* translated and edited by E.S. Harcourt and Fakhir Hussain, London, 1975, p. 149.
10. Attia Hosain, *Sunlight on a Broken Column*, p. 68.
11. Sharar, *Lucknow: The Last Phase*, pp. 149-50.
12. See Hasan, *Nationalism and Communal Politics*, and my *Legacy of a Divided Nation*.
13. Hamid Enayat, *Modern Islamic Political Thought*, London, 1982, p. 20; and V.J. Schubel, 'Karbala as Sacred Space among North American Shia', in Barbara Daly Metcalf (ed.), *Making Muslim Space in North America and Europe*, Berkeley, 1996, pp. 186-204; Farnk Korom, 'Identity on the Move: A Trinidadian Shia Ritual in Transnational Perspective', unpublished

paper presented at North Carolina State University, Raleigh, 22-5 May 1997.

14. Cole, *Roots of North Indian Shi'ism*, pp. 116-17.

15. P.D. Reeves (ed.), *Sleeman in Oudh: An Abridgement of W.H. Sleeman's Journey Through the Kingdom of Oude in 1949-50*, Cambridge, 1971, pp. 158-9; Walter Roper Lawrence, *The India We Served*, London, 1928, pp. 292-3; Fuller, *Studies on Indian Life and Sentiment*, pp. 125-6; W.S. Blunt, *India Under Ripon: A Private Diary*, London, 1909, p. 72.

16. Freitag, *Collective Action and Community*, p. 259.

17. Jaffur Shureef, *Qanoon-e-Islam*, translated by G.A. Herklots, Madras, 1863, p. 123; see also Omar Khalidi, 'The Shias of the Deccan: An Introduction', in *Hamdard Islamicus*, Vol. 15, No. 4, 1992.

18. Nita Kumar, *The Artisans of Banaras: Popular Culture and Identity 1880-1986*, Princeton, N.J., 1988, p. 216.

19. Sharar, *Lucknow: The Last Phase*, p. 149.

20. Attia Hosain, *Phoenix Fled*, New Delhi, 1993, p. 176.

21. Munshi Faizuddin, *Bazm-i Akhir*, New Delhi, 1986, pp. 63-6.

22. Saiyid Ahmad Dehlawi, *Rusoom-i Delhi*, New Delhi, 1986, pp. 178-80.

23. Cole, *Roots of North Indian Shi'ism*, p. 105.

24. C.A. Bayly, *The Local Roots of Indian Politics—Allahabad 1880-1920*, Oxford, 1975, p. 81; for Bilgram, Saiyid Athar Raza Bilgrami, 'Bilgram Ki Azadari', in *Islam aur Asr-i Jadid*, Delhi, Vol. 25, No. 2, April 1993. For a brilliant description, Rahi Masoom Reza, *The Feuding Families of Ganguli*, trs. from Hindi by Gillian Wright, New Delhi, 1994.

25. Crooke, *The North-West Provinces of India*, p. 263.

26. Murray T. Titus, *Indian Islam*, Oxford, 1930.

27. Penderel Moon, *Strangers in India*, London, 1943, pp. 86-7.

28. Sharar, *Lucknow: The Last Phase*, pp. 74-5.

29. Ibid. This is not to suggest that the Awadh rulers did not express their solidarity with the Shias or that the Shias were not given preference in appointments. Fisher, *A Clash of Cultures*, pp. 65-6.

30. Ibid., p. 250.

31. Meston to Chelmsford 20 Aug. 1917, Meston papers (1), BL.

32. Mohamed Ali to A.A. Bukhari, 19 Nov. 1916, in Mushirul Hasan (ed.), *Mohamed Ali in Indian Politics: Select Writings 1906-1916*, Vol. 1, New Delhi, 1985, p. 301.

33. Quoted in A. Schimmel, *Gabriel's Wing: A Study into the Religious Ideas of Sir Muhammad Iqbal*, Leiden, 1963, p. 167.

34. Selection from Native Newspaper Reports UP (hereafter SNNR), for the week ending 19 Dec. 1936, and 20 Mar. 1937.

35. Zafarul Mulk, *Shia Sunni Dispute: Its Causes and Cure*, Servants of Islam Society Publication No. 3, n.d., p. 1.

36. The process was not confined to Lucknow; for Bombay, see Jim Masselos,

'Change and Custom in the Format of the Bombay Muharram during the 19th and 20th Centuries', *South Asia*, Australia, Dec. 1982, p. 61; and for Banaras, see Nita Kumar, *The Artisans of Banaras*, p. 216.

37. C. Khaliquzzaman, *Pathway to Pakistan*, p. 149. Referring to Bakhshu's *tazia* procession in Lucknow, Sharar commented: 'Nowadays, because of the quarrels between Shias and Sunnis, this procession lost its original form', Sharar, *Lucknow: The Last Phase*, p. 151.

38. April 1907, SNNR, UP, 1907.

39. *Surma-i Rozgar*, 1 Feb. 1907.

40. *Asr-i Jadid*, Meerut, Oct.-Dec. 1907.

41. *Sarfaraz*, 6, 7 and 13 May 1939.

42. Saiyid Ali to Jawaharlal Nehru, 6 Dec. 1945, Jawaharlal Nehru papers, Vol. 4, NMML; Hosseinbhoy A. Laljee's Cablegram to Wavell, 6 Apr. 1945, in *Shia Muslim's Case*, Bombay, n.d., pp. 1-2, 6-96; L/P and J/8, 693; Transfer of Power papers, L/P and J, 10/64, BL.

43. 18 Feb. and 16 Dec. 1946, 16 Dec. 1974, ibid., L/P7/J, 10, 64.

44. Note by the Intelligence Department on the Shia-Sunni controversy in Lucknow, Home Poll. D., File No. 75/6, NAI.

45. Shia-Sunni riots broke out in May-June 1937. The provincial government believed that the Shias provoked them to indicate that any change introduced in their past practices would be resisted. Harry Haig to Linlithgow, 7 Jun. and 4 Jul. 1937, 2-4 Jun. 1938, 10 and 23 Oct. 1939, L/PJ/5/264-6.

46. The government appointed the Piggot Committee (1907) to regulate Muharram observances. This was followed by the Justice Allsop Committee recommendations of 15 Jun. 1937. The high court judge endorsed the Piggot Committee's report on *madhe sahaba*. Government Gazette of the UP, Extraordinary, 28 Mar. 1939, L/P and J/ File No. 265, pp. 139-50, BL.

47. G.M. Harper to Jasbir Singh, 18 Mar. 1939, General Administration Department (GAD), File No. 65, Box 607, UP State Archives, Lucknow. Harry Haig reported that Madani insisted that the Sunnis should be allowed to assert their right to recite *madhe sahaba*. To Linlithgow, 23 Oct. 1939, L/P/266.

48. Haig to Linlithgow, 6 Sept. 1939, L/P and J/5/26.

49. Jasbir Singh to Harper, 24 Mar. 1939, UPSA.

50. *Sarfaraz*, 30 Mar. 1939.

51. Bayly, *Local Roots*, p. 130.

52. Harper to chief secretary, 16 Mar. 1939, GAD, File No. 65, Box No. 607, UPSA.

53. *Essays: Indian and Islamic*, London, 1912, pp. 215 and 273-4.

54. Haig to Linlithgow, 18 Apr. 1939, Linlithgow papers (microfilm), New Delhi.

55. Jasbir Singh to Harper, 13 Mar. 1939, UPSA.

56. Wazir Hasan's wife was chairman of the All-India Shia Women's Association.

57. Harper to chief secretary, 16 Mar. 1939, UPSA.

58. Ibid.
59. *Pioneer*, 24 Aug. 1939, Kanpur's superintendent of police reported a Shia-Sunni riot and the impending threat of the Ahrars to take out a *madhe sahaba* procession defying government orders, 10 Jun. 1939, Diaries, Harold Charles Mitchell papers, BL. For Banaras, Charles Allen (ed.), *Plain Tales from the raj*, London, 1981, pp. 246-7.
60. L/P and J/5/272. See also fortnightly report, second half of Mar. 1940, L/P and J/5/270. In 1943, Sunnis in Lucknow tried to revive the *madhe sahaba* agitation and defy the ban on the *Barawafat* procession which fell about the middle of March. This led to the externment of some Sunni leaders from Lucknow. Fortnightly report, second half of Jan. 1943, L/PJ/5/272.
61. Nehru to Azad, 17 Apr. 1939, *SWJN*, Vol. 9, pp. 334-5.
62. To Nehru, 16 May 1939, Valmiki Choudhary (ed.), *Dr Rajendra Prasad: Correspondence and Select Documents*, Vol. 3, New Delhi, 1984, p. 77.
63. 'Many of the respectable Mussalmans of Jaunpur and the town Machhlishahar belong to this (Shia) denominaton.' *District Gazetteer (DG)*, UP of Agra and Oudh, Vol. 28, Allahabad, 1908, p. 85.
64. For Syeds of Jalali, see Saiyid Muhammad Kamaluddin Husian Hamadani, *Siraj-i Manir*, Aligarh, 1978.
65. *DG*, Muzaffarnagar, Vol. 3, pp. 114-15; *DG*, Sitapur, Vol. 11, pp. 105-6.
66. Sarojini Ganju, 'The Muslims of Lucknow, 1919-39', in K. Ballhatchet and J. Harrison (eds.), *The City in South Asia: Pre-Modern and Modern*, London, 1980, p. 286.
67. UP Govt. (Education Department), File No. 398, 1926, UPSA.
68. Imtiaz Ahmad, 'The Shia-Sunni Dispute in Lucknow', in Milton Israel and N.K. Wagle (eds.), *Islamic Society and Culture: Essays in Honour of Professor Aziz Ahmad*, New Delhi, 1983; Ganju, 'The Muslims of Lucknow', pp. 290, 292.
69. Keith Hjortshoj, 'Shi'i Identity and the Significance of Muharram in Lucknow India', in Martin Kramer (ed.), *Shi'ism: Resistance and Revolution*, London, 1987, p. 291.
70. Ahmed, *The Bengali Muslims*, p. 184.
71. As early as 1871, Shias and Sunnis, in separate formal representations, demanded 'distinct and separate burial grounds'. V.T. Oldenburg, *The Making of Colonial Lucknow 1856-1877*, Princeton, N.J., 1984.
72. Zafarul Mulk, *Shia-Sunni Dispute*, op. cit., p. 11.
73. Omar Khalidi, op. cit., pp. 39-40.
74. Zafarul Mulk, op. cit.
75. S. Abul Hasan Ali Nadwi, *The Mussalman*, Lucknow, 1974 edn., p. 65.
76. See, for example, Proscribed Publications (Urdu), 52, 93, 139, BL.
77. SNNR, UP for the week ending, 19 Dec. 1936, and 20 Mar. 1937.
78. Jasbir Singh to Harper, 10 Feb. 1939, UPSA.
79. Sharar, *Lucknow: The Last Phase*, p. 95.
80. Lelyveld, *Aligarh's First Generation*, p. 134; see also, S.A.A. Rizvi, *Shah Abd*

Al-Aziz, p. 256. For Deoband, Metcalf, *Islamic Revival in British India*, and Sharar, *Lucknow: The Last Phase*, p. 95, for a brief history of public debates in Lucknow.

81. See 'Introduction', in J.R.I. Cole and Nikkie R. Keddie (eds.), *Shi'ism and Social Protest*, New Haven, 1986, pp. 66-7; Cole, op. cit., pp. 288-9, and Freitag, op. cit., p. 263, for the contribution of Maqbul Ahmad to reformist tendencies among Shias.

82. This information is based on Salamat Rizvi, *Saiyid al-ulama; Hayat aur Karnamen*, Lucknow, 1988.

83. 'Establishment of a Shia college at Lucknow', 25 Oct. 1917, UP Govt. (Education), File No. 398, 1926, UPSA; Fateh Ali Khan to Meston, 21 Oct. 1915, File No. 136/15, Meston papers. The raja of Mahmudabad and Saiyid Wazir Hasan were the only two prominent Shias who initially opposed the Shia college. They believed it would weaken the Aligarh Muslim University movement, and accentuate Shia-Sunni differences.

84. For a summary of 'Shia Awakening', Rizvi, *A Socio-Intellectual History*, Chap. 5.

85. Freitag, *Collective Action and Community*, p. 249.

86. Azad was deputed by the Congress High Command to resolve the impasse. His personal stature aided the process of reconciliation. The Shia ulama, in particular, agreed to suspend the *tabarra* agitation at his instance.

87. 16 Dec. L/P and J/8/693, 1946.

PART II

PART II

5

Mediating the External:
Pan-Islamism and Nationalist Renewal

خاک وطن کا مجھ کو ہر ذرّہ دیوتا ہے

Every grain of the dust of my country is a god to me.

MUHAMMAD IQBAL

It is widely known, though scarcely recognized that sections of the Indian Muslim intelligentsia have been sensitive to their fraternal links with their co-religionists in other countries, following their history, detailing their accomplishments, and, at the same time, lamenting their decline. And when Islam fell on evil days owing to the convergence of European powers on the heartland of the Muslim world in the nineteenth-century, the heritage of the past—expressed in Hali lamenting the 'ebb' of Islam, in Shibli's pan-Islamic anguish, and in Iqbal's nostalgic ode to once-Arab Sicily—stood forth as a symbol of community pride.

Interest in Turkey's welfare continued: each time it was involved in a war—the Russo-Turkish war of 1877-8 or the Graeco-Turkish war of 1897—Indian Muslim groups launched fund drives, reaffirmed their loyalty to the sultan of Turkey, and offered prayers for his well-being. 'If the Muhammadans of the world were compared to the human body', wrote the *Akhbar-i Am*, 'the Sultan would be the heart and brain.'[1] Anthony Macdonnell, lieutenant-governor of UP, noted the 'great sympathy with Turkey partly due to incitement from outside India and partly spontaneous, and I think it has been growing for some time and is fostered in Mohammedan schools'. Agra's commissioner told him that many more people than formerly had taken to wearing the Turkish fez, indicating how the wind was beginning to blow.[2]

The 'incitement from outside' came from two distinct sources. In the first place, the British government exploited pro-Turkish feelings to secure Indian Muslim loyalty, as in 1857, and to bolster 'the sick man of Europe', as they did from the Crimean war of 1853-6 onwards, in order to thwart Russian encroachments. Then, Turkey's sultan, Abdul Hamid II (1842-1918), sent his agents to India, as to other lands, to rally Muslim support and enthusiasm for his feeble regime which was threatened by external aggression and internal strife.

Saiyid Ahmad Khan disputed Hamid's claim to the khilafat. The pan-Islamic surge threatened to destroy his effort to strengthen the Anglo-Muslim alliance; so he spoke against the Turcophilia among his Muslim brethren, arguing that they were legally bound to obey the writ not of an external Muslim khalifa but of the British government. Such exhortations fell on inattentive ears, for the sympathy in favour of Turkey was fairly widespread in parts of northern India. When nawab Mohsinul Mulk, one of Saiyid Ahmad's successors at the Aligarh College, opposed the holding of pan-Islamic meetings on the campus a section of the press castigated him as a 'downright sycophant'.[3]

The most bitter criticism came from an unexpected quarter—from that celebrated roving reformer, teacher and political agitator, Jamaluddin al-Asadabadi 'al-Afghani'.[4] He regarded the Aligarh reformer's religious views and his educational programme as ancillaries to his political servitude to British interests, and chided him for relying on the British instead of joining hands with the nationalists. Afghani considered Saiyid Ahmad as his main adversary in India, opposed to pan-Islamism, isolating India's Muslims from the rest of *Dar al-Islam*, especially from the Turks, and hostile to the conception of a universal Muslim khilafat.

Afghani spent the greater part of his life travelling from one country to the other propagating the doctrine of political unification of the Muslim world, known as pan-Islamism. His life, one of endless wanderings, touched and deeply affected Muslims in the last quarter of the nineteenth century. His pan-Islamic views inspired various activist groups in different lands and lives on patiently, if amorphously, in the aspirations of many Muslims.[5] It is also curious that the only instance where his political programme of combined radicalism, modernism, nationalism and pan-Islamism ever became a serious political programme of an active opposition was in the khilafat agitation in India, years after his death.[6]

The power of Afghani's appeal was felt in the first decade of the twentieth-century. Among those who came under his spell was Shibli who visited Istanbul in 1893, received a medal from the khalifa, and established contacts with Afghani's co-worker and disciple, Muhammad Abduh.[7]

His pan-Islamic ideas were echoed in Hali's *Musaddas*, and his strong advocacy of the co-existence of diverse religious faiths was in accord with Mohamed Ali's idea, expressed in 1923, of the 'Federation of Faiths'. Ansari developed his view of a natural solidarity beyond the nation: that which binds together all the peoples of the east threatened by the west.[8] At the khilafat conference held on 27 December 1922, he referred to the need for an Asiatic Federation to promote solidarity among the peoples and countries of Asia with a view to rescuing them from the political and economic bondage of Europe.[9] Afghani had advocated this idea more than two decades earlier.

Afghani also influenced Iqbal and Azad. The former was attracted most of all by his endeavour to find in Islam a means of unity for resisting the domination of the West, and shared his desire to express unity on the religious basis of Muslims as a supra class and a supranational unity. On the eve of and during World War I, he tied his hopes for liberation from colonial dependency to pan-Islamic solidarity. This was reflected in his poem *Shama awr Shair* (The Candle and the Poet), written in 1912.[10] In his reply to the *Shikwa* (Complaint of God) he strikes the same note:

> The trouble that is raging in the Balkans
> Is a message of awakening to the forgetful
> Thou may'st think it the means of vexing thy heart
> But in reality it is a test of thy self-sacrifice and self-reliance.

Afghani's influence on Azad can be seen from the time of his stay in Constantinople and Cairo, and his close relations with the Al-Manar group of Syrian and Egyptian scholars. Azad developed the anti-imperialist thrust in his writings in the *Al-Hilal*, a paper inspired by the *Urwat al-wuthqa* (The Indissoluble Link), an anti-imperialist journal Afghani published in collaboration with Abduh. He, too, bitterly attacked Saiyid Ahmad Khan's attitude to the khilafat, and argued on the authority of the Koran that *jihad* was obligatory against those who had occupied even a part of the *Dar al-Islam*. Political loyalty was due to the Ottoman khalifa and obedience to the *khilafat-i mulki* (monarchial khilafat) was therefore binding on the Muslims.[11]

Azad provided greater ideological coherence to those Muslim activists who were beginning to come to terms with Indian nationalism and its anti-colonial strain. He stood strongly for inter-communal harmony citing the Prophet Muhammad's covenant with some Jews as a valid historical precedent for an integrated alliance with the Hindus. He argued that joining in common action with one category of non-Muslims, the Hindus, against another category of non-Muslims, the British, was obligatory. In a similar vein, Ansari quoted the *Sura-i Mumtahanah* (60: 8-9) from the Koran to argue that Indian Muslims should behave 'righteously, affectionately and in a friendly manner towards all those non-Muslims who are neither at war with Muslims nor are they assailants intending to invade or occupy their territories'.[12]

Views on a peaceful *modus vivendi* with the Hindus were representative of Afghani's position that a religious link did not exclude national links with men of different faiths. In fact, he had urged his Muslim audience to cooperate with the Hindus and cultivate 'good relations and harmony in what pertains to national interest'.[13] In his article published in the Hyderabad journal, *Muallim-i Shafiq*, he invoked not only the universal Islamic but also national sentiments with special emphasis on Hindu-Muslim unity. And just as he helped awaken Egyptian nationalism by appeals to the ancient glories of the past, so in India, even when talking to a primarily Muslim audience, he invoked the glory of the Indian Hindu past.[14] This appeal to take pride in a Hindu past was no different from Afghani's earlier appeal to Egyptian Muslims to derive inspiration from pre-Islamic Egyptian greatness. In both cases he wanted to create an effective basis for solidarity against the colonizers.[15]

The message was taken serious note of and found echoes in the political activism of the khilafatists. Various theories were worked out to remove the widespread notion that the pan-Islamic idea implied a break with nationalism. Admittedly, the term nationalism had different, though allied, shades of meaning. But the ideologues of the khilafat movement did not find an inherent inconsistency between their pan-Islamic creed and territorial nationalism. They argued, instead, that their objective of independence from foreign rule—central to the pan-Islamic ideology—had an obvious nationalist dimension. In fact the idea itself was bound to the concept of an emerging Indian nation. They pointed out that, in spite of their pan-Islamic ambition, they always had their own Indian community most clearly in mind and were not oblivious to its trials and tribulations. The emblem used on the khilafat delegation stationery—made up of overlapping twin circles of equal size, with the word 'khilafat' on one and the word 'India' on the other—symbolized their loyalty to the nationalist cause, their vision of a free India, and the Muslim countries liberation from foreign domination. Ansari was able to establish a link between British colonial policies in India and the larger interests of the Western nations in exploiting the weaker nations of the East and in perpetuating 'the bondage and slavery of Asiatic people'. 'It is, therefore, not only a question of India's honour and freedom', he said in December 1920, 'but of a great struggle for the emancipation of all the enslaved Asiatic people from the thraldom of the West.'[16]

The relationship between the Indians and the Turks was in the nature of a compact, because both were subjected to colonial rule. For this reason, Azad observed that the problem of the khalifa was part of the larger issue of British imperialism. Khilafat workers must win India's liberty by means of non-cooperation; only then would they be able to save the khalifa.[17] Mohamed Ali offered the same advice: Muslims must fight for swaraj by plunging into the non-cooperation campaign with their non-Muslim brethren, for only in this way would it be possible to achieve the khilafat aim.[18]

Mohamed Ali made the most passionate attempt to demonstrate that pan-Islamism and nationalism were compatible.[19] His intention was to prove that, objectively speaking, Muslim reactions to events in Turkey deepened their involvement in the anti-colonial struggle in India and brought them closer to the Congress movement under Gandhi's leadership. He argued, furthermore, that they had a pre-eminent sense of community in their *Weltanschaung*, and especially so in India, where their adherence to Islam made them unique and gave them their 'communal consciousness'. He did not, however, believe that being a Muslim he was any less Indian. His religious beliefs, as indeed his commitment to nationalism, never appeared to him to be incompatibles.[20] He could—and must—be true to both Islam and India. To further prove that his loyalty to Islam and to his country was compatible, he explained that 'where India is concerned, where India's freedom is concerned, where the welfare of India is concerned, I am an Indian first, an Indian second, and nothing but an Indian'.[21] Doubtless, individuals, if not groups, were able to easily swing back and forth between pan-Islamic and local nationalist appeals, depending upon which was a more appropriate anti-imperialist weapon in a specific Indian situation.

The khilafat movement has often been denounced on the grounds that its emphasis on Muslim values and extra-Indian loyalties stood in the way of genuine Hindu-Muslim unity. It is also pointed out that those Muslims who accepted Gandhi's leadership were motivated by religious consideration, and their alliance with nationalist forces was of an ephemeral and opportunistic nature. The roots of this assumption lay in the unexpressed postulate that Muslims were unpatriotic because they were moved only by loyalty to the invisible theocracy of which God was the ruler, and that they had developed a nationalism of their own which was Islamic in tone and content. 'Under the circumstances', observed the Congress and Hindu Mahasabha leader, B.S. Moonje, 'how can peace and amity now grow between the Hindus and the Muslims unless either the Hindus surrender and become a consenting party to the Islamic Mission or if they are equally determined to preserve their essentially scientific identity separate from the one-sided Nationalism of the Muslims.'[22]

Setting aside the theological debate centred round the supposed contradiction between Indian nationalism and 'Islamic nationalism', what deserves consideration is the process that enabled the khilafat movement to merge itself into a general political struggle that far outstripped its pan-Islamic limitations.

This is exemplified in the composition and the shared concerns of the khilafat committees, local Congress bodies, kisan sabhas, and Home Rule leagues. 'There is nothing to choose locally,' commented an official, 'between a gathering under the auspices of the kisan sabha or of the khilafat committee. Both movements appear to have been completely captured by the non-cooperation party.'[23] This was not just a joyful demonstration of the newly-found sense of solidarity, but an awareness of the 'extraordinary stiffening-up' of a demoralized, backward, and broken-up people taking part in disciplined, joint action on a countrywide scale.[24]

In several areas, peasant unrest was not just tagged on to the khilafat and non-cooperation programme, but the khilafat committees and the kisan sabhas provided a tangible sign of acting in unison in attacking their common identifiable enemy—the landlord—who was perceived as an ally of the government. Here lay the danger in government's assessment, a fact referred to when the secretary of the Rae Bareli khilafat committee spoke at a kisan sabha meeting on 6 February. 'What might have been in its way a harmful and beneficent movement', observed an official, 'is in danger of being rapidly perverted into a vehicle for virulent abuse of and violent agitation against the government.'[25] Evidence of the potentially dangerous alliance came from other areas as well. A kisan sabha rally at Faizabad, held on 20-1 December 1920, was probably organized by khilafat workers.[26] Local khilafat activists—Lal Muhammad and Maulvi Riasat Husain—addressed a similar gathering at village Salethu in Maharajganj on 2 February 1921. Amid Saiyid, a local khilafat agitator, organized a meeting at village Balla in the same police station a week earlier.

A notable feature of such meetings were the common demands of the kisans and the khilafatists, on the one hand, and the attainment of the swaraj ideal, on the other. Words like 'khilafat', 'kisan ekta', 'swaraj', 'Gandhi' conjured up in the minds of the people a picture of bringing about a better world under the direction of better leaders.[27] Thus maulvi

Salamatullah of Firangi Mahal stated at a kisan sabha meeting that peasant interests would be protected only after the khalifa's dignity and prestige was restored. Kamaluddin Jafri, the Allahabad-based lawyer, linked the redressal of peasant grievances with the attainment of swaraj under the Congress directive. He moved a resolution at a kisan sabha conference at Akbarpur in Faizabad district; it had the support of Hafiz Alam and Muhammad Nabi of Tanda, important activists of eastern UP.[28]

In assessing the historical significance of the khilafat movement, it is equally important to reckon with the Congress-khilafat-League alliance at the national level as well as the bonds of friendship forged at other levels of society. All three organizations met in the same city and around the same time; both the khilafat and the League bodies took their political cue from the Congress, and mostly endorsed its decisions. The 1918 League session echoed the Congress demands, and, as in the Congress so in the League, wrote an intelligence officer, 'the moderates have lost all control'.[29] The same spirit prevailed a year later. Anti-British spirit, emphasized a government report, reigned supreme.[30] In July 1920, the League insisted on the Congress holding its session first so that it could decide 'the course of action which it should recommend to the Muslims of this country'.[31]

Such demonstrations of political unity were matched by spontaneous expressions of communal harmony. In Delhi and Punjab, Prem Sabhas and the Anjuman-i Islam worked strenuously to ensure the peaceful observance of religious festivals.[32] Zafar Ali Khan captured the spirit of the time in the verse:

> *Aai hain Aasman se chal kar woh quwaten*
> *Jo Muslim-o-Hunood ko sheer-o-shakar karen*

Heavenly forces have helped to forge the bonds of friendship between the Hindus and the Muslims.

Or by Agha Hashr:

> *Ho gaeen bikhri hui einten baham tamir ki*
> *Mil gaee har ek kari tooti hui zanjir ki*
> *But-shikan wahdat-parast ek jism ek jaan ho gaye*
> *Ghul hua duniya me phir kafir Musalman ho gaye*

The disjointed pieces have been put in order again
The links of the broken chain have been discerned
The idol-worshippers and the iconoclast have joined hands
There is a dinning clamour that the kafirs have again embraced Islam.

Finally, Akbar Allahabadi wrote:

Na Maulana me laghzish hai na sazish ki hai Gandhi ne
Hilaya ek rukh unko faqat maghrib ki andhi ne

Maulana has not blundered, nor has Gandhi hatched conspiracies;
What blows them on the same course is the gale of Western policies.

Short-lived as this unity was, the fact that it was accomplished indicated the strength and fervour of the nationalistic spirit of which it was the outward expression. 'The scenes that were enacted before my eyes', wrote the secretary of the Bengal khilafat committee, 'made me feel that the artificial barriers that had long been preventing the two major communities of the country to come together, had been miraculously swept away by the onrush of the all-embracing non-cooperation movement.'[33]

II

Ae barq aaj shola-fishan kyon nahin hai tu
Ae raad aaj garm fughan kyon nahin hai tu
Ae abr aaj girya kunan kyon nahin hai tu
Darya-I qahr aaj rawan kyon nahin hai tu
Islam aaj kufr ke narghe men aa gaya
Badal siyah rang ka Kaaba pe chha gaya.

O the thunderbolt why don't you scatter flames?
O the lightning why thou wailest not?
O the clouds why weepest not thou?
Why is it that the river of curse is a frozen puddle and flows not?
Islam has been swamped and overwhelmed by the unbelief
And the Kaaba has been engulfed by darkness.

Proscribed Publications (8), British Library, London.
Also, see 142, 152, 153

It will not do to treat the outburst of religious and nationalistic fervour as an artifact.[34] Its explanation must take into account the importance of the unifying powers of religious symbols in Indian Islam,[35] and the ability of the ulama of Firangi Mahal, Deoband and the Nadwat al-ulama to press them into service.[36] They were, indeed, at the heart of Muslim concern over Turkey and the holy places. From their *madaris* and mosques, they emerged on the national scene to dominate the khilafat agitation, and provided the much needed legitimacy to a cause which had little chance of being sustained by the Western-educated Muslims.

Who were the ulama? Where did they come from? What made them an important group in Muslim society? We must examine these questions in order to understand the significance of their participation in the khilafat movement.

Islam did not provide for a priesthood or a comparable religious institution. Gradually, however, a body of men developed with specialized religious functions—chiefly readers and reciters of the Koran, and also experts in recording the sayings and doings (*Hadith*) of the Prophet. These were the ulama—literally those who possess knowledge (*ilm*). They were not a separate class, but a body of people belonging to every social level. They formed 'an unnumbered aggregate of academicians of all degrees of learning and intelligence', with special interest in and knowledge of the Koranic exegesis (*tafsir*), the science of Prophetic tradition (*ilm-i Hadith*), jurisprudence (*fiqh*) and theology (*ilm-i kalam*). Indeed the hallmark of an alim was his learning in these subjects. According to Fakhr-i Mudabbir, a fourteenth century chronicler at the Delhi court, the ulama owed their special status to their knowledge. He observed:

All people know that after the apostles and prophets rank the truthful persons (*siddiqin*), martyrs (*shahidin*) and scholars (*aliman*). The scholars are included in the category of siddiqis and have preference over the martyrs. The Prophet has said: 'The *ulama* are the heirs of the prophets'. The world exists on account of the piety of the learned. The laws of *sharia'a* . . . are enforced by them . . . and things illegal and not sanctioned by the *sharia'a* are suppressed by them.[37]

Such a glorified image was not entirely a product of Fakhr-i-Mudabbir's fantasy but was, indeed, grounded in Muslim ethics; it helps to explain the special position occupied by the ulama in Muslim society.

The ulama dominated the upper echelons of religious hierarchy, manned the judicial and ecclesiastical services, and wherever there was a mosque—and every Muslim locality had one—the *imam*, the *khatib*, the *muhtasib* and the *muftis* represented an interest which received state recognition. Some were actually an integral part of the medieval Indian state and shared in the control of the vast revenues of the land; they were consulted and used for foreign negotiations, and took part in the politics and revolutions of the palace. The ulama established matrimonial alliances with the ruling houses, purchased property, and emulated the nobles (*amirs*) in lavish expenditure. Tradition classified them as *ulama-i duniya* as opposed to the *ulama-i akhrat* who led an abstemious life of pious devotion to religious learning and eschewed entanglement in materialistic pursuits and political affairs. The *ulama-i duniya*, on the other hand, were totally mundane in their outlook, aspired for wealth and worldly prestige, and mixed freely with the ruling élite.[38] Their relationship with the sultans was generally harmonious, not least because ties of mutual self-interest bound them together.

The ulama were indispensable allies of the Delhi sultans, for they secured for them the one important element of authority which force alone could not achieve—legitimacy. The sultans needed sanction for their monarchical and despotic rule and expected the ulama to give a favourable ruling in the light of the *Shariat*. The ulama, in turn, seemed to agree that it was far more important to preserve Muslim society and its distinctive way of life than to endanger the unity of that community and the ordered practice of religious duties by encouraging resistance against an impious ruler. For this reason, some taught the faithful a dull stagnation in matters of belief and the acceptance of political autocracy, knowing all the time that almost everything the sultans did as persons and as rulers violated the *Shariat*.[39] To protect their interests and to retain their social status, they chose to become the creatures of the state.[40]

The establishment of British supremacy, however, turned the ulama world topsy-turvy. Educational reforms, the reorganization of law courts, the growth of local governments, the spread of secular ideas, and, above all, the separation of religion and government, steadily reduced their influence in Muslim society. In his address to the first Congress of Nadwat al-ulama in April 1895, Shibli lamented:

Gentlemen! In the days of the Muslim rule the worldly as well as the religious affairs of the Muslims were in the hands of the *ulama* . . . the reins of the affairs of the community relating to both this and the next world were in the hands of the *ulama*. Now that things have changed , and worldly affairs have come under the authority of (the British) government, we have to see what relationship the *ulama* have with community. . . .[41]

Strongly opposed to the government's encroachment upon Muslim educational institutions and its interference with the Islamic personal law, the ulama asserted the pre-eminent position of the *Shariat* and claimed for themselves the sole right to interpret its meaning for all groups and classes. They submitted memoranda, sent deputations to the government on this point,[42] set up centres of learning to prevent the influx of subversive ideas from the religiously alien and 'morally inferior' British, and took tangible steps to put a premium on unorthodox thought and learning, which was calculated to undermine the position of the ulama. Thus the Nadwat al-ulama aimed to defend Islam against 'contemporary times'.[43] To maintain uniformity in belief and practice, it sought to determine what was true or desirable in the light of the Koran and *Hadith*.

Traditionally, the *madaris* were the basis of Muslim education. Their curriculum, which remained largely unchanged over the centuries, included Arabic and Persian languages and literature, logic, philosophy, Islamic Law, *Hadith*, and commentaries on the Koran. Aurangzeb reprimanded his former teacher for having taught him Arabic, grammar and philosophy rather than subjects more practical for a future ruler, but his criticism had little effect. In the eighteenth century, Mulla Nizamuddin Sihalawi introduced the *Dars-i Nizamia*,[44] the standard syllabus and the basis for instruction in many institutions. Regarded as the most comprehensive form of orthodox education, the *Dars-i Nizamia* was adopted by some of the famous *madaris* in the eighteenth century. These functioned essentially as schools of theology and as strongholds of orthodoxy. With their traditionalist course of studies, the curriculum was confined to purely religious sciences (*maqulat*) with a bit of grammar and literature. Along with *Hadith*, *fiqh*, *kalam* and *tafsir*, the Koran has remained at the heart of the curriculum and its memorization the highest scholastic attainment.

The *makatib*—smaller institutions than the *madaris*—were usually of two kinds: the first of a purely religious character in which the rituals and the tenets of Islam were taught, and the second of a more secular type in which some Persian literature was also introduced. The most important of the first type was established at Deoband soon after 1857. Conforming to the doctrines of the Hanafi school, its goal was to train well-educated ulama who, as prayer-leaders, writers, preachers and teachers, would maintain religious identity and cultural homogeneity. The Nadwat al-ulama, founded as a middle of the road institution between the extremes of Aligarh's 'secularism' and Deoband's rigid conservatism, adhered to the *Dars-i Nizamia*; it failed to combine both religious and secular types of education.[45] The institution developed conservative contours, and its students became generally indistinguishable from those of Deoband in their theological and intellectual outlook.

The Dar al-ulum and the Nadwa endeavoured to make Muslims aware of their Islamic identity, maintain the charismatic or divinely-instituted structure of the community, and preserve the special field of religious interpretation and instruction.[46] Over the years, the ulama resisted the secularizing tendencies. They continued wearing the medieval attire, and their turbans and flowing gowns made them stand out as symbols of conservatism in a society that was becoming less Islamic and more secular. Most still clung desperately to the vestiges of their religious identity, jealously guarding their theological strongholds. Obsessed with significant minutiae of ritual and engaged in fruitless disputations, they excelled in denouncing each other, and dubbing the adherents of other schools of thought as ignorant, irreligious and atheistic.[47]

Yet, they continued to make their presence felt through mosques and shrines, *makatib* and *madaris*. Above all, as guardians, transmitters and authorized interpreteres of the *Shariat*—which comprehends Muslim beliefs, rituals, public and personal law—they played a variety of roles. When, in doubt, the believers turned to them for the definition of controversial points of the doctrine, and their opinion was sought on a wide variety of subjects, ranging from divorce and inheritance to disputes over property. Rashid Ahmad Gangohi, for example, gave rulings on request that it was lawful to learn English if there was no danger to religion, that it was unlawful to take interest from a Christian, and to use money-orders and bills of exchange which contain the element of interest. He also declared the wearing of a cross or a *topi* to be sinful.[48] Such rulings were rarely flouted—at least not openly.

Given their role in regulating religious and social life, it is not surprising that, in small towns and villages where the Muslim population was more susceptible to religious exhortations through local mosques and *madaris*, the ulama provided the inspiration behind a burst of khilafat activity. They succeeded in doing so because of their dominant religious hegemony which transcended class and caste divisions and enabled them to develop an extensive network of social connections ranging from the Awadh *taluqdar* to the impoverished Muslim peasant in East Bengal. It is true that they were frequently attacked for their conservatism, and just as often blamed for the backwardness of the Muslim peoples, but their support was regularly sought by politicians who realized their value, even if it was in the negative sense, of preventing them from showing active opposition or from making adverse religious pronouncements.[49] The promoters of the Aligarh Muslim University, for instance, adopted a conciliatory attitude towards the Muslim divines in order to allay their fears about the future character of the institution; their support was necessary to convince the government that the university movement was backed by influential Muslim groups. Likewise, professional men who dominated the Muslim League after 1911, needed the ulama to rally public opinion around their brand of agitational politics;[50] so they wooed the ulama and allayed their fears about the League's *la-dini* (religion-less) character. This enabled the dividing line between the Western-educated and the orthodox to be blurred, and with it were buried their doctrinal feuds and personal animus. The younger Muslims, observed UP's lieutenant-governor, 'try to work with the priests, hoping through them to influence the mob. For the time being, however, it would be idle to deny that they have attained success'.[51] Other developments, some to be covered in the following two chapters, added thrust to the converging courses in politics of the modern and the traditionally-educated.[52]

The ulama responded favourably to these overtures mainly because they were politically unorganized and unaccustomed to political life. Moreover, their bitter doctrinal disputes created fissures in the apparent solid phalanx of orthodoxy, and prevented them from moving in unison to defend their interests.[53] By 1911, however, they were rudely awakened by the growing threat to Islam, an awakening which coincided with, and was also to a certain extent caused by, the political upheaval in Turkey. They were conscious that they must now be active in addressing themselves to the current anxieties, political, social and religious, of Indian Muslims, or else watch true Islam as they understood it, and their own claims to guide the community, get diluted by default. Such a realization led some to assiduously cultivate the Western-educated Muslim intelligentsia—college students, lawyers, journalists and teachers—who had some experience of conducting constitutional politics, and, in the words of Mohamed Ali, 'to pocket their pride and in a way even accept the lead of men whom they had but a generation ago finally consigned to perdition'.[54]

An early move was initiated by Maulana Mahmud Hasan, an alim convinced of the need to further greater fraternity between the alumni of Deoband and Aligarh.[55] The Jalsa-i Dastarbandi, convened in 1910 and attended by a delegation from Aligarh led by Aftab Ahmad Khan, and the Jamiat al-Ansar, founded by Ubaid-Allah Sindhi, a Sikh convert to Islam, was the fruition of such early efforts. These initiatives were followed by the establishment of the Anjuman-i Khuddam-i Kaaba in May 1912. This was the beginning of the generality of the ulama's formal participation in Indian politics in their capacity as religious leaders. The Anjuman provided, after all, the basis for an alliance between leading ulama of all shades of opinion and the modern educated, and illustrated that, on purely religious issues, the alim and the modernized Muslim could strive together for common ends. The orthodox and the anglicized 'were drawn together and as in a flash of lightning, saw that after all they were not so unlike each other as they had imagined'.[56] 'Once more', observed Mohamed Ali:

Muslim society in India presented a level of uniformity and the bitterest opponents of a generation ago stood shoulder to shoulder. . . . If even a decade previously anyone had ventured to foretell such a result, he would have been laughed at for such a fantastic prophesy. . . .[57]

The men of 'New Light' or *Nai Raushani* began using the existing networks of religious organizations and institutions for propagating pan-Islamism. In March 1914, Mohamed Ali, Ajmal Khan and Ghulam us-Saqlain (d. 1915), editor of *Asr-i Jadid,* served on the committee to enquire into the affairs of Nadwat al-ulama. M.A. Ansari was elected president of the Anjuman-i Islamia, Ghazipur, a position mostly occupied by the local maulvis. In December 1918, Ansari and Shuaib Qureshi, son-in-law of Mohamed Ali, addressed a meeting at Delhi's Jama Masjid in support of the Muslim League. In return for such concessions, the League began airing the specific religious demands of the ulama.[58] At the same time, Firangi Mahal's leading alim, Abdul Bari, rallied around Gandhi during the Rowlatt satyagraha, lent support to the passive resistance movement, and submitted to his leadership during the khilafat agitation. Writing to Gandhi in 1919, he observed: 'Thanks are due to your kind special attention for the success of the Day of Prayer and Hindu-Muslim unity. Your personality and behaviour are deeply affecting Muslims in general and religious sections in particular. A group of ulama have written to me specially to pay their homage to you.'[59] In November 1920, he again declared: 'I have accepted his (Gandhi) support in getting our aims fulfilled and for that purpose I think it is necessary to follow his advice. . . . *I know that the strength of Islam lies in association with him*' (italics mine).[60]

Although such a subservient posture irked some ulama, particularly Saiyid Ahmad Raza Khan of Bareilly and the Bahr al-ulum ulama of Firangi Mahal, such men were few and wielded limited influence at least during the popular pan-Islamic upsurge. Most favoured accommodation with the Congress, and welcomed Gandhi as their political guide and benefactor.

III

During the first decade of the twentieth-century, Shibli and Azad strongly challenged the notion of separating religion from politics, arguing that 'a very large part of the national life is in the ulama right of ownership and they alone have or can have absolute sway over it'.[61] Addressing the first Congress of Nadwat al-ulama, Shibli berated the ulama for being lackadaisical, and urged them to combine and organize themselves to offer an enlightened interpretation of religion, reorganize Arabic and Persian studies, exert pressure on the government to revise its legal policy, and control and efficiently administer *wakfs*.[62] All this entailed an active and vigorous involvement in politics. In 1912, his disciple, Azad, guided the ulama with the following advice:

The question whether political discussion should be separated from religious education is very important. But you must know that this is the foundation on which we intend to build the whole edifice of *Al-Hilal*. If you say that the arch is not beautiful we may try to alter its shape, but if you wish that the key-stone should be removed, then we cannot accede to your wishes. *There will be nothing left with us if we separate politics from religion.*[63] (italics mine)

This was common talk in the early 1920s. Maulana Sajjad suggested to Abdul Bari that the ulama should 'take the reins of politics in their own hands and cross their voices with those in authority' in order to establish their religious supremacy, and fulfil their higher aim of protecting Islam from Western imperialism.[64] Maulvi Kifayatullah of Delhi echoed similar sentiments at the Muslim League meeting in December 1918. He declared, '. . . in Islam religion and politics are not two separate things. For a long time they were together, but probably those who have received modern education think that they are separate from one another. This, however, is a wrong concept: they think that they should monopolize politics and leave religion for the ulama.'[65]

Words were soon translated into deeds. The ulama thronged to the League session to assert the voice of orthodoxy, assumed leadership of the khilafat agitation, and contributed to its ever more radical development. Soon after, they called upon the believers to wage *jihad* against the government, boycott foreign goods, and migrate (*hijrat*) to the *dar al-Islam*. They exercised their right to issue *fatwa* freely using the Koran and *Hadith* as powerful weapons to gain the adherence of the masses who accepted them as infallible. Abdul Bari endorsed the *fatwa* on non-cooperation. So did Azad: he also authored the *fatwa* on *hijrat*. The maulvis of Sukkur in Sind, inspired by Abdul Bari's *istifta* (questionnaire) of January 1919, declared the Jazirat al-Arab as a sacred place 'wherein non-Muslims cannot rule or remain in possession'.[66] In Bengal, a *fatwa* forbade Muslim participation in peace celebrations.[67] Doubtless, the *Muttaffiqa fatwa*, which made non-cooperation mandatory on all Muslims, was opposed by Maulana Ashraf Ali Thanwi, Ahmad Raza Khan and the Bahr al-ulum party of Firangi Mahal. But their opposition, often inspired by cynical government officials, failed to stem the pan-Islamic tide.[68]

The ulama were not content with sheafs of *fatawa,* but travelled extensively enjoining the faithful to wage *jihad.*[69] The Majlis-i Ulama of Madras toured the presidency to incite Muslim emotions on the khilafat issue and, in May 1920, the United Provinces' Ulama Association despatched students to preach *jihad* in the *mofussil.* A few months earlier, Abdul Bari and Shaukat Ali toured Gujarat together preaching the sanctity of the khilafat; later Azad joined them on a tour of Sind.[70] In the N.W.F.P., they established *Shariat* tribunals in a few places and a national school at Utmanzai.[71] In Bengal, the ulama, having held aloof from politics, were eventually drawn into the boycott movement'.[72] In UP, educational centres became the main foci of agitations. Nadwat al-ulama and the Dar al-Musaniffin at Azamgarh were amongst them.

The Nadwa came under suspicion during the Graeco-Turkish war.[73] Pan-Islamic activity was intensified during the Balkan wars and the khilafat and non-cooperation movements.[74] In November 1920, students urged the trustees to refuse the government grant sanctioned by J.P. Hewett, lieutenant-governor of UP from 1907 to 1912. From December 1920 to March 1921, they raised money for the khilafat fund and formed volunteer corps in the towns of Bihar and the UP.

The Dar al-Musaniffin, founded by Shibli in 1913 to promote the publication and translation of historical, religious, and scientific works, also turned into a pan-Islamic stronghold. This was mainly due to Saiyid Sulaiman Nadwi, one of Shibli's pupils at Nadwa. In April 1920 he spoke at Kanpur urging Muslims to give up their lives for protecting the holy places. In 1920, he joined the khilafat delegation to London. He wrote to Abdul Bari that, if Muslims wanted to liberate Kaaba, they would have to liberate India first: 'The political emancipation of India', he noted, 'was a religious duty.'[75]

Masud Ali Nadwi, too, turned the Dar al-Musaniffin into 'an extremist political institution', and a centre for political activism in Azamgarh district.[76] His influence extended to many small towns in the region, such as Mau, Sarai Mir, and Pharuja. Mau was predominantly inhabited by Muslim weavers who, under the leadership of Abdul Aziz, a barber, Maulvi Muhammad Sabir, the *imam* of the local mosque, Maulvi Abdullah, and Maulvi Zamir, were in the forefront of the non-cooperation drive. They pressed honorary magistrates in the area to resign and the local Islamia College to renounce its government aid. In Sarai Mir, on the other hand, khilafat activities were centred around the Arabic school. Here the managers, the staff and the students campaigned enthusiastically in the neighbouring villages to explain the significance of the *fatwa* issued by Abdul Bari and Azad.[77]

IV

قیامت تک وہ سرداری کے قابل ہو نہیں سکتے

Doomsday will come before they are fit to lead.

AKBAR ALLAHABADI

'Take great care', the *Independent* of Allahabad warned its readers on 3 June 1920, 'that the control of the khilafat movement does not fall entirely within the hands of theologians and divines.'[78] Others apprehended that the presence of Muslim divines was fraught with danger.[79]

By early 1921, the warning signals were proving to be prophetic. At the Meerut All-India Khilafat Conference in April 1921 some ulama objected to Hindus being involved in the khilafat movement, and demanded, moreover, the widening of its scope in accordance with the *Shariat*.[80] This was followed by Abdul Bari's warning that Muslims were ready to desert Gandhi and adopt violent methods for redressing their grievances.[81] In May 1921, Darul Qaza courts (House of Justice) mushroomed in parts of Bihar and the N.W.F.P., and the call for *jihad* against the British was heard loud and clear in the countryside.[82] In March, the Jamiyat-i-ulama-i-Hind, founded in November 1919, declared that it was *haram* (sinful) for a Muslim soldier to serve in the army.[83] The Karachi Khilafat Conference on 8-10 July simply endorsed this resolution, introduced by Maulana Husain Ahmad Madani and supported by the Ali brothers, Pir Ghulam Mujaddid, a Sindhi follower of Abdul Bari, and Maulana Nisar Ahmad of Deoband.[84]

Gandhi did not sympathize with this radical strain, fearing that militancy would lead to violence and consequently destroy the credibility of his technique of non-violent non-cooperation. Aware of the signs of discontent amongst Hindu Congressmen following the Moplah riots in August 1921, he was anxious that the khilafat leaders should not alienate them. But men like Abdul Majid Budauni (d. 1931), Ghafoor Ahmad and Nisar Ahmad did not buy his argument. On 21-2 December, their followers demanded an immediate adoption of civil disobedience. Considerable friction occurred before Ansari, Azad, and Ajmal Khan persuaded them to grudgingly accept that Gandhi, 'the recognized leader of all Indians considered that the time was not yet ripe for civil disobedience'.[85]

The showdown came in December 1921 when Hasrat Mohani proposed that the Congress and the Muslim League should strive to attain 'complete independence', and that, if martial law was imposed, Muslims would either have to abandon non-cooperation or face the bullets and bayonets. In the latter event, violence was the natural course to adopt in self-defence. This epitomized the tension between Gandhi's ideal of satyagraha and the khilafatists adoption of it as a political technique. Gandhi himself created this tension, despite his laments about Muslim motives, by making non-violence the pre-condition of his support for the movement.

Gandhi argued that complete independence could not be incorporated in the Congress creed without Hindu-Muslim unity being accomplished. The Congress backed Gandhi rather than Hasrat, as did the League's Subjects Committee on 30 December. 'If Gandhi does not favour complete independence', stated Maulana Abdul Majid, 'we would advise him to join the illustrious group *of jee-huzoors* who would welcome him with open arms.'[86] These were harsh words reflecting the growing rift between

Gandhi and the Muslim priests. With the Ali brothers still in prison, there seemed little hope of a reconciliation. The Moplah riots along the Malabar coast of south India was the last straw.

In the midst of the heated controversy generated by the Moplah riot, Gandhi suspended civil disobedience on 5 February 1922. 'The whole conception of civil disobedience', he informed the Congress Working Committee (CWC), 'is based upon the assumption that it works in and through its non-violent character. . . . I personally can never be a party to a movement half violent and half non-violent.' Three other reasons influenced him to call off civil disobedience; firstly, the patchy success of the movement, second, the resolutions passed at the Karachi Khilafat Conference in July 1921 and the violent and xenophobic speeches made by the ulama; finally, the growing feeling in Congress circles that the party should extricate itself from the travail of non-cooperation. In such a climate, the suspension of civil disobedience suddenly became a political necessity.

Gandhi's decision took the sting out of the khilafat agitation. Hasrat Mohani rejected the Bardoli programme on the ground that, if religion enjoined violence, a policy of non-violence could not be adopted.[87] At the Jamiyat al-ulama conference held in Ajmer, Abdul Bari assailed the Mahatma and the Bardoli resolution.[88] Such attacks continued even after Gandhi's arrest on 10 March 1922. When he returned from prison in February 1924, his interest—whatever little was left—in the khilafat movement had evaporated. When asked to nominate a Hindu to join a khilafat deputation to Angora, the Mahatma pointed out that it would be 'out of place' for any Hindu to do so.[89] How ironical that less than five years earlier he had urged his co-religionists to support the 'just cause of the Muslims', and said: 'for the Hindu not to support them (Muslims) to the utmost would be a cowardly breach of brotherhood'.[90]

The khilafatists had yet another surprise in store. On 21 November 1922, the Turkish National Assembly at Ankara separated the khilafat from the sultanate. And since the maintenance of the khalifa's temporal power was one of the main objects of their movement, this action by a purely Muslim body completely took the wind out of its sails. In March 1924, Mustafa Kamal Pasha burst the khilafat bubble. Its immediate result was the disruption of the khilafat party. From 1918 to 1922, religious zeal and the overwhelming anti-British bias had united various groups, but once the initial euphoria had worn thin the inherent contradictions in the alliance revealed the division among the ranks of the ulama, as also among the other Muslim groups. The Jamiyat al-ulama split, with Nisar Ahmad of Kanpur and Abdul Majid Budauni joining the *tanzim* movement; they also founded a parallel organization of Jamiyat-i-ulama-i-Hind in Kanpur.[91]

The rapprochement between the political and religious wings of the khilafat movement also collapsed in part because international developments had undermined its *raison d'être*, and, in part, because there was no sound basis for a permanent adjustment of diverse and, in some cases, conflicting interests.[92]

Soon enough, the Muslim divines disappeared from the national arena. Having once mobilized new groups, roused their religious fervour, and articulated their grievances, they were now like a contrary jack-in-the-box refusing to retire, to seek new outlets for their energy, and to build something positive out of their experience. Some doggedly kept the khilafat movement gasping, but most, including the ulama of Deoband, entered the arena of religious controversies and organized the *tabligh* and *tanzim* societies as a counterpart to *shuddhi* and *sangathan*.

The khilafat agitation had provided the ulama with a distinct enemy and goals; when the enemy and goals proved elusive other whipping boys and solutions were found. Much of their interests, geared to religious goals, remained, because they seemed to be the hope for their vision of the Muslim community. In consequence, they reverted to their former religious preoccupations. The Jamiyat al-ulama, despite its nationalist sympathies, concerned itself with securing safeguards against interference with the *Shariat* and guarantees for its propagation and implementation.[93] The ulama of Firangi Mahal, too, failed to adapt themselves to the changing realities of Indian politics, leading to Abdul Bari's estrangement from the Congress. In August 1923, he complained: 'The position of the Muslims has been rendered very awkward. Those who pretended to be our friends at one time and made a catspaw of the ulama now seem anxious to get rid of them.'[94] Abdul Bari was right. In the aftermath of civil disobedience, the issues concerning the leaders were of a political nature; so the services of the ulama were no longer required. They were bluntly told not to dabble in politics. The poet Akbar Allahabadi would have said:

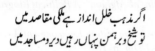

If religion hinders in pursuing the country's goals
Then the Shaikhs and Brahmans should remain confined
in temples and mosques.

Khaliquzzaman summed up the widespread confusion in the ranks of various influential Muslim groups in the following words:

The history of the next sixteen years of Muslim India is a mass of confusion and a chapter of political benightedness. The disruption of the khilafat organisation was like a breach in the embankment of the flowing stream of Muslim mass emotion, which diverted it into several petty streams, some leading to desert lands there to dry up, some flowing by zig-zag routes to meet the original bed in their headlong march and some others rushing towards the mighty ocean to drown themselves. To try to find any consistency, sound reasoning or logical method in Muslim politics during that period would be utterly fertile. We were divided between ourselves. . . .[95]

NOTES

1. *Akhbar-i Am*, 14 Mar. 1895, Punjab Native Newspaper Reports.
2. Quoted in Hardy, *Muslims of British India*, p. 177. W.S. Blunt (1840-1922) was told on the eve of his visit to India that he should not say anything against the sultan of Turkey because his name 'was now venerated in India as it has not formerly been'. Blunt, *India Under Ripon*, p. 13.
3. *Jasus* (Agra), 14 July 1906; *Al-Aziz* (Agra), 28 July 1906, UPNNR.
4. Afghani was in India from 1857 to 1865. He came again in 1879 to spend three years in Bombay, Hyderabad, Bhopal and Calcutta. The purpose of his visit was to 'meet with all the *navvabs* and princes and ulama and grandees of that land and to explain to them one by one the results that are manifested from unity and solidarity in the whole world and the injuries that have appeared from division and disunity; and to caress their ears with the mystery of the *hadith*, the faithful are brothers; and to express inspiring and prudent words and to attract the friendship and cooperation of the learned and the eloquent; and to breathe into them the new spirit of love of nationality and to rend the curtain of their neglect to explain to them the place of the luminous Sultanate in the world of Islam; and to reveal and make manifest to this group the fact that the perpetuation of religion depends on the perpetuation of this government. And in all the mosques of the famous cities I shall light a flame in their inner hearth by means of appealing sermons and *hadiths* of the Best of the Prophets, and I shall together burn out their patience and long-suffering.'
   Nikkie R. Keddie, *Sayyid Jamal al-Din 'al-Afghani': A Political Biography*, Los Angeles, 1972, pp. 134-5.
5. Aziz Ahmad, *Studies in Islamic Culture in the Indian Environment*, London, 1964, pp. 55-6; Keddie, *Sayyid Jamal al-Din*, p. 167.
6. Fazlur Rahman, *Islam*, London, 1966, p. 227.
7. Keddie, *Sayyid Jamal al-Din*, p. 26. It is not right to argue, as Elie Kedourie has, that Afghani's reputation and influence was to a large extent posthumous and was the work of disciples, or else of academic writers and publicists 'eager to discover trends and precursors' to magnify the importance of their subjects. Elie Kedourie, *Afghani and Abduh: An Essay on Religious Unbelief and Political*

Activism in Modern Islam, London, 1966, p. 3. There is adequate evidence to indicate his influence on his contemporaries, and greater evidence of his impact on subsequent political and intellectual movements in Muslim countries. Aziz Ahmad and Keddie, too, write of Afghani's limited influence. According to them, the people he met exercised no political or religious influence among Muslims, and his articles, published in an obscure journal of Hyderabad, did not cause any stir at the time. But their own evidence does not warrant this conclusion; in fact, the works of W.C. Blunt point to Afghani's influence. Kedourie's cynical view of Afghani becoming a 'British agent' is typical of his attempt to denigrate him and to underplay the role of ideology in politics.

8. Ahmad, *Islamic Modernism in India and Pakistan*, p. 129.

9. Hourani, *Arabic Thought*, pp. 118-19.

10. H.N. Mitra (ed.), *The Indian Annual Register (IAR)*, 1923, Vol. I, p. 921.

11. L.R. Gordon-Polonskya, 'Ideology of Muslim Nationalism', Hafeez Malik (ed.), *Iqbal: Poet Philosopher of Pakistan*, New York, 1971, pp. 115-16.

12. Ahmad, *Studies in Islamic Culture*, p. 67. For Afghani's influence on one of Azad's devoted followers, see Abdul Ghaffar, *Jamaluddin Afghani*, in Urdu, New Delhi, 1941. Afghani's stay in India is referred to on pp. 12-13, 16-17, 35-7. Also, Schimmel, *Gabriel's Wing*, p. 21.

13. S.S. Pirzada (ed.), *Foundations of Pakistan*, Vol. I, p. 547.

14. Hourani, *Arabic Thought*, p. 118.

15. Keddie, *Sayyid Jamal al-Din*, pp. 155, 159-60.

16. Ibid., p. 160.

17. Pirzada (ed.), *Foundations of Pakistan*, Vol. 1, pp. 545-6.

18. W.J. Watson, 'Muhammad Ali and the Khilafat Movement' (unpublished MA thesis, 1955, McGill University), p. 64.

19. Muhammad Ali, *His Life, Service and Trial*, Madras, n.d., p. 151.

20. *IAR*, 1923, Vol. 2. p. 30.

21. Hasan, *Mohamed Ali: Ideology and Politics*, p. 115.

22. Ibid., p. 115.

23. 7 Aug. 1926, Moonje Dossier, Pad No. 35, National Library, Calcutta.

24. GAD, File No. 50, 1921, Box No. 135, UPSA. All subsequent references, unless otherwise stated, are drawn from the same file.

25. Nehru, *An Autobiography*, p. 76.

26. Note on Rae Bareli disturbances, op. cit.

27. M.H. Siddiqi, *Agrarian Unrest in North India: The United Provinces 1918-22*, New Delhi, 1978, p. 149; Kapil Kumar, *Peasants in Revolt: Tenants, Landlords, Congress and the raj in Oudh*, New Delhi, 1984, pp. 146-65.

28. This idea was beautifully summed up in the verse of Mohmamad Haider, a school teacher in Pilibhit. He wrote:

Jama do qaum ka sikka baja do deen ka danka
Mohamed, Shaukat-o-Gandhi ke Pairokaar ho jao

Swadeshi se karo raghbat bidesi se karo nafrat
Ki jis se muflisi ho door aur zardaar ho jao

Let the respect for the nation be restored
  and the trumpet of the faith heralded
Follow Mohamed (Ali), Shaukat and Gandhi
Adopt all that is swadeshi and shun that which is from outside
So that you may remove poverty and achieve self-reliance.

PROSCRIBED PUBLICATIONS (43)

Also, see the collection of poems in *Bulbulan-i Hurriyat* in Proscribed Publications (47). The collection was published by the khilafat committee in Jaunpur.

29. Police Dept., File No. 51-N, 1921, UPSA. Note by Lakhte Husain and Jagannath, 28 Jan. 1921, op. cit.
30. Home Poll. B, Jan. 1919, 160-3, NAI.
31. WRDI (Jan. 1920), Home Poll. Deposit, Feb. 1920, 52, NAI.
32. *Tribune*, 13 Oct. 1919; *Fateh* (Delhi), 1 July 1920; Swami Shraddhanand, *Inside Congress*, Bombay, 1946, pp. 68-70.
33. Abul Hayat, *Mussalmans of Bengal*, Calcutta, 1966, p. 37.
34. Robinson has argued that the professional Muslim groups exploited the khilafat issue to promote their personal and political interests. '. . . the professional politicians', he insists, 'had continually to manufacture issues and to whip up agitations to keep their newspapers going, their organisations active and their coffers full. . . . The issues were religious, usually pan-Islamic: these were the only sure sources of the money they needed.' Robinson, *Separatism Among Muslims*, p. 354.
35. For an elaboration of this argument, Hasan, *Nationalism and Communal Politics*.
36. The standard works on the role of the ulama are by I.H. Qureshi, Peter Hardy, W.C. Smith, Leonard Binder, Z.H. Faruqi and Mushir U. Haq. The most detailed account, however, is that of Qureshi, *Ulema in Politics*, Karachi, 1974 edn.
37. Quoted in K.A. Nizami, *Some Aspects of Religion and Politics in India during the Thirteenth Century*, Bombay, 1961, p. 150.
38. Ibid., p. 152.
39. For a useful critique of the role of the ulama in early medieval India, see Mujeeb, *The Indian Muslims*. For a useful assessment of their activities in Pakistan, see L. Binder, *Religion and Politics in Pakistan*, California, Berkeley, 1963.
40. In the nineteenth century, the traditional idea of a partnership between ruler and ulama was brought up to date by, among others, Rafi al-Tahtawi (1801-73) of Egypt. Hourani, *Arabic Thought*, p. 76.
41. Robinson, *Separatism Among Muslims*, p. 275.
42. The ulama of Firangi Mahal asked for special treatment in judicial matters by the establishment of special courts presided over by Muslim officials. Note

by W.S. Marris, 17.11.1918, Montagu papers, Mss. Eur. 523 (34), BL.

43. *Makatib-i Shibli*, Azamgarh, 1928, Vol. 1, p. 329.

44. Mujeeb, *Indian Muslims*, pp. 407-8.

45. This was the time when scholars like Rafi al-Tahtawi in Egypt and Khayr al-Din (1810-89) in Tunis urged the ulama to come to terms with the new learning and be in touch with the spirit of the times. Hourani, *Arabic Thought*, pp. 92-3.

46. Shibli argued that the Muslim community could only develop if the ulama exercised control over its secular and spiritual existence. S.M. Ikram, *Mauj-i-Kawsar*, Lahore, 1970 edn., p. 233.

47. M. Manzar and R.A. Khan, *Deoband awr Bareilly ke ikhtilaf wa Naza par faisla kun munazara*, Sambhal, 1966.

48. Hardy, *Muslims of British India*, p. 171; Ahmad, *Islamic Modernism*, p. 105.

49. For example, there were vigorous attempts by the Congress leaders to enlist the support of the ulama during the civil disobedience movement in 1930-1. Note by D. Gladding, Officiating Deputy-Secretary to Government of India, 3 July 1931, Home Poll. A, Aug. 1931, 189, NAI. The Government of India, on the other hand, was anxious to counter the efforts of the Congress leaders. The services of the Muslim landowners were utilized to keep the ulama 'straight'. In Apr. 1930, the nawab of Chhatari went on a mission to Deoband 'in order to use his own influence to keep them (*ulama*) going astray'. This loyal servant of the raj was obviously acting on the advice of his master. Hailey to Cunningham, 26 Apr. 1930, Mss. Eur. C. 152, Irwin papers (24), BL.

50. In March 1915, Meston analysed how the professional men and the ulama came to terms with each other. According to him, 'the young educated Muslim is restless and dissatisfied with everybody. His quest is for a cause, a call, something that he can be proud of, something which at small cost will retrieve his self-esteem and restore the glories of his race. This he finds in his religion. It gives him a link with great traditions. It may not be an ethical bond, but it is a militant bond; *in hoc signo vinces*. . . . At this point he comes in contact with the priest. Hence arises pan-Islamism.' Meston to Hardinge, 25 Mar. 1915, Hardinge papers (89). The *Nai Roshni* of Allahabad, edited by Wahid Yar Khan, emphasized the importance of cooperating with the ulama in the struggle against the government's repressive policies. Similarly, the *Mohammadi* of Calcutta suggested that the task of rousing the Muslim masses to the impending danger to the Islamic world should be undertaken by the ulama. It observed: 'Let the *alim*, betake themselves to work. Let the first steps in this great national work be begun in the mofussil, and let it be explained from each village mosque. *Nai Roshni*, 23 Dec. 1917 UPNNR 1917; *Mohammadi*, 23 Apr. 1920, BENNR 1917; *Intikhab* (Gujranwala), 10 Jan. 1920, PUNNR 1920.

51. Meston to Hardinge, 25 Mar. 1915, Hardinge papers (89).

52. See *Nationalism and Communal Politics* (1979), Chap. 2.

53. For an insight into the nature of differences, see Robinson, *Separatism Among Muslims*, pp. 268-71. For personal and rivalries amongst the ulama in Deoband, see Gail Minault, *The Khilafat Movement*. A number of leading ulama kept aloof from the khilafat and non-cooperation movements and criticized their fellow divines for associating with the Hindus. Maulana Ahmad Raza Khan of Bareilly was one of them. In 1921, he formed the Jama'at-i-Ansar-ul-Islam to counter pan-Islamism and convened a conference for that purpose. The first conference of the Jama'at was addressed by Maulana Mohammed Miyan (1892-1956) of *Khanqah-i Barkatia* in Marehra, a small town in Etah district of UP. The Maulana vigorously opposed the khilafat agitation, advocated cooperation with the British and denounced the khilafatists, including Abdul Bari, for associating with Gandhi and other Hindu Congressmen. In Sind, the pirs were equally divided. The pir of Kingri, for instance, not only opposed non-cooperation, but also advised his *murids* to remain loyal to the government. Pir Rashidullah, another influential Muslim divine, held aloof from the movement because it was 'initiated and controlled by Hindus'. WR (Sind), 9 Apr. 1921, J.C. Curry papers, CSAS, Cambridge.
54. Mushirul Hasan (ed.), *Mohamed Ali—My Life: A Fragment*, p. 84.
55. Faruqi, *The Deoband School and the Demand for Pakistan*, London, 1963, pp. 56-7.
56. *My Life: A Fragment*, p. 85.
57. Ibid., p. 84.
58. See, for instance, Maulvi Muhammad Ahmad to Sheweth, 30 Oct. 1917, Meston papers Mss. Eur. F. 136 (19).
59. Abdul Bari to Gandhi, n.d., Firangi Mahal papers (FM), Lucknow.
60. Statement of Abdul Bari, n.d., ibid. (From internal evidence it must refer to the Jamiyat i-ulama session in Oct. 1920.)
61. *Khutbat-i Shibli*, pp. 29-33, quoted in S.M. Ikram, *Modern Muslim India and the Birth of Pakistan, 1858-1951*, Lahore, 1965 edn.
62. Ahmad, *Islamic Modernism*, pp. 109-10; Smith, *Modern Islam in India*, p. 39.
63. *Al-Hilal*, 8 Sept. 1912, quoted in Mushir U. Haq, *Muslim Politics in Modern India, 1857-1947*, Meerut, 1970, p. 72.
64. A.M.M. Sajjad to Abdul Bari, 4 Dec. 1918, *Naqqush*, Lahore, p. 91.
65. Cited in Qazi Abdul Ghaffar, *Hayat-i-Ajmal*, Aligarh, 1950, p. 185.
66. *Tribune*, Lahore, 21 Mar. 1919.
67. *Mohammadi*, Calcutta, 12 Dec. 1919, Bengal Native Newspaper Reports, 1919.
68. Qureshi, *Ulema in Politics*, p. 271.
69. Diary of the Earl of Ronaldshay, 16 May 1919, Ronaldshay papers, Mss. Eur. D. 609(1), BL.
70. For details, P.C. Bamford, *Histories of the Khilafat and Non-cooperation Movements*, Delhi, 1974, rpt.; Brown, *Gandhi's Rise to Power*.
71. Bamford, *Histories*, p. 151.

72. FR (Bengal), Nov. 1921, Home Poll. Deposit, Dec. 1921, 18, NAI.
73. Fears that the *Nadwa* had a pan-Islamic influence helped to deny Shibli a C.I.E. in 1911.
74. J.P. Hewett to Dunlop Smith, 27 Jan. 1908, and C.P. Della Fosse to O'Donnell, 8 Feb. 1914, GAD, 1908, File No. 79, UPSA.
75. Gracey to Lambert, 8 Jan. 1926, GAD, 1921, File No. 1074, ibid.
76. Ibid.
77. Note by R.W. Bigg, 7 Dec. 1920, ibid.
78. Robinson, *Separatism Among Muslims*, p. 316.
79. Some writers, particularly in Pakistan, have argued that it was a mistake to involve the ulama in the khilafat movement. For example, Abdul Hamid, *Muslim Separatism in India: A Brief Survey, 1858-1947*, Lahore, 1971, rpt., pp. 151-2, and M. Noman, *Rise and Growth of the All-India Muslim League*, Allahabad, 1942, pp. 213-14.
80. WRDCI, 11 Apr. 1921, Home Poll. Deposit, June 1921, 54, NAI.
81. Abdul Bari said in June 1921 that his community held non-violent non-cooperation as 'a useful weapon to get our grievances redressed, but we never committed ourselves to always adhere to this principle'. Home Poll. 1921, 45, NAI.
82. Bamford, *Histories,* pp. 168-9.
83. Ibid., p. 165.
84. Weekly Report (Sind), 8 Oct. 1921, J.C. Curry papers.
85. Bamford, *Histories*, p. 177.
86. *Zul Qarnain,* 20 Jan. 1922, UPNNR, 1922.
87. Home Poll. Feb. 1922, 18, NAI.
88. Home Poll. 1922, 501, NAI.
89. Mahadev Desai, *Day-to-Day, with Gandhi*, Varanasi, 1968, Vol. 4, p. 22.
90. *CWMG*, Vol. 17, p. 350.
91. Qureshi, *Ulema in Politics*, p. 302.
92. Faruqi, *Deoband School*, p. 36.
93. See Peter Hardy, *Partners in Freedom—and True Muslims: The Political Thought of some Muslim Scholars in British India, 1912-1947*, Lund, 1971.
94. Statement to the Press, 20 Aug. 1923, Abdul Bari papers.
95. Khaliquzzaman, *Pathway to Pakistan*, p. 76.

6

My Life: A Fragment
Mohamed Ali's Quest for Identity
in Colonial India

Mohamed Ali was a controversial figure for his contemporaries and for posterity. Government officials associated him with the 'extreme faction of the Muslim community', the 'Advanced Party' and the 'hot headed Nationalist Party'.[1] He led a clique of noisy and aggressive Muslims of the 'young party', who made the raja's house (raja of Mahmudabad) their headquarters and lived and agitated at his expense.[2] He fomented trouble wherever he went, reported the viceroy. He persuaded some students at the Lahore Medical College to raise the tribes against the government in Afghanistan, and caused 'discontent' at Aligarh's M.A.O. College. That is why he and brother Shaukat Ali were prevented from entering Punjab and UP.[3]

In recent years some historians have seen in Mohamed Ali a charmer and nothing more; a politician greedy for power, an irresponsible declaimer who drove himself and his followers from one disaster to another. He is charged with inspiring the 'Young Party' Muslims to manufacture issues and whip up agitations to keep their newspapers going, their organizations active, and their coffers full.[4]

There are other images as well: the image of an energetic, talented and charismatic figure devoted to Islamic resurgence the world over. Writers in India stress Mohamed Ali's commitment to Hindu-Muslim unity, his adherence to the Congress movement, his passion for the country's freedom.[5] Scholars in Pakistan, on the other hand, eulogize him as one who contributed 'to the march of the Muslim nation on the way to its final destination'.[6] They romanticize the story of his life and extol his achievements, some real but mostly imaginary. Schools, colleges and streets in Karachi and Lahore are named, as in Delhi, Aligarh and Bombay, after him. Indeed, Maulana Mohamed Ali 'Jauhar', the *Rais al-Ahrar* (Leader of the Free Peoples), is one of the most popular and venerated figures in Pakistan.

What lends credence to such images is the construction of a community's identity around leaders who had the energy, drive and the skills to articulate the Muslim/Islamic world-view from public platforms.[7] Therefore, Mohamed Ali, more than Saiyid Ahmad Khan or Maulana Azad, is commonly perceived to be more sensitive than others to the predicaments of the Islamic world and more stridently committed to its well-being.[8] He attracts greater notice also because he possessed to the full the resources of traditional oratory—its repertoire of tricks. Few orators or political journalists had his combination of qualities: his range of articulate emotions, his capacity for analytical argument, his pathos, fantasy and wit, and his power to marshall all these towards ends clearly discerned and passionately desired. His considerable poetic talent, which combined with his fervour and the desperate situation in which Turkey found herself after the First World War, created in him a feeling of impending martyrdom.[9] 'Such sufferings and privations as ours', he wrote, 'have only too often been the lot of mankind, in all ages and climes.'[10]

1. سکھایا تھا تمہیں نے قوم کو یہ شور و شر سارا
جو اسکی انتہا ہم ہیں تو اسکی ابتدا تم ہو

> It is you (Saiyid Ahmad Khan) that had
>   taught the community its mischiefs;
> If we are its culmination;
>   you are its commencement.

MOHAMED ALI, in 1923

Mohamed Ali was born on 10 December 1878 in Rampur where his grandfather Sheikh Ali Baksh served as a petty official in the court of nawab Muhammad Yusuf Khan. He aided the British in quelling the disturbances at Bareilly and Moradabad in 1857, and received a *khilat* two years later and a *muafi* or a rent-free land with an annual income of Rs. 13,000. The family reaped the rewards of loyalty even after Ali Baksh's death in 1867. Abdul Ali (1848-80), his son, enjoyed the patronage of Rampur's nawab. But he died of cholera in 1880 leaving Abadi Bano

Begum, then only 28 years of age, the responsibility of bringing up her five sons and a daughter. The begum's family—in direct succession to a number of nobles connected with the Mughals—had suffered in 1857. Her father changed his name and lived for several years as a refugee in the Rampur state territory. The British confiscated much of the family's property.[11]

Abadi Bano was undeterred by the family's limited resources and the heavy debt incurred by a spend-thrift husband. When approached by Azimuddin Khan, general of Rampur forces, she agreed to send her eldest son to Bareilly.[12] Mohamed Ali recalled:

How she managed to bring up her six little children and how she, an uneducated *purdah* lady, as education is understood in these days, managed to educate us better than our educated and richer uncles educated their own children, is a remarkable story which it is not through egotism that I would like to relate. . . . This miracle was not accomplished without personal privations that would do credit to a hermit living in a cave. It is not, therefore, egotism that has suggested this tribute to a mother's memory, but the sense of a heavy debt that can never be paid off. . . .[13]

In the graph of Mohamed Ali's life, the steep arc of youth is missing; we see only the flattened curve of maturity. We see him studying a few Persian classics, reading the Koran in Arabic, and observing the religious rituals in a Sunni home. While in Aligarh (1890-8), he is found writing for the college magazine, sharing Shaukat Ali's love for 'the noble and manly game of cricket', and nursing the ambition of securing 'a nomination for the post of Subordinate Magistrate or Land Revenue Collector'.[14] The 'Big Brother' was impressed with his 'unexpected success' at the BA examinations and arranged for his education in England. In Mohamed Ali's own words, 'So before the proverbial nine days of wonder were over, I was on the high seas in the Indian Ocean in the teeth of a raging monsoon, bound for England. . . .'[15]

Within weeks of his arrival in September 1898, Mohamed Ali made his way into English middle class society with the help of the family of T.W. Arnold, who had taught philosophy at the Aligarh College, and its controversial principal, Theodore Beck. Fazl-i Husain, also in England, found him to be 'a jolly good fellow, very quick in making friends'. They spent 'exceedingly pleasant evenings' discussing literary, philosophical and political issues.[16]

Mohamed Ali reached Oxford on 11 October to study modern history at Lincoln College. He matriculated a year later and secured a second in 1902, missing a first in history by a narrow margin.[17] He impressed his

tutors with his vigour, common sense and resourcefulness.[18] James
Williams, his guru in Roman and English law, noticed his 'great capacity
for acquiring and remembering information'.[19] His paper on *Macbeth* was
written by 'a man of ability, capable of thinking for himself'. Yet these
skills did not equip him to qualify the civil service examination, 'thanks to
an English spring, and a youngman's more or less foolish fancy'.[20] Success
eluded him even after returning to India in 1902. Having failed to secure
a teaching position at Aligarh owing to sordid manipulations, he opted for
the Education department in Rampur, a position for which his tutors in
Oxford had found him suitable. But his brief and inglorious innings ended
in November 1902, when he sought refuge in Baroda.

Gaekwad Sayaji Rao, the ruler, regarded the new recruit as one on
whose shoulders he could place the burden of administrative work, the
man who got papers drawn up, orders sent out, correspondence carried on
and records kept. But colleagues in Baroda, as in Rampur, resented his
initiative, drive, and his proximity to the Gaekwad. Though Mohamed Ali
kept himself in the public eye by writing and speaking at conferences, he
was set to leave for Bhopal by the end of 1906.[21] Dunlop Smith, private
secretary to the viceroy, urged him to stay: 'I quite understand that your
surroundings are not always congenial, but after all whose are in every
respect.'[22] Around this time Mohamed Ali printed the *Thoughts on the
Present Discontent*: it was based on articles published in the *Times of
India* and the *Indian Spectator*. He despatched a copy to the viceroy, hoping
that it 'would meet with the sympathy and encouragement which India
has learnt to associate now with the name of Edward the Peace-Maker'.
The viceroy endorsed its contents and wished the book the wide circulation
it deserved.[23]

Mohamed Ali stayed in Baroda until 1910, though his heart was not at
rest.[24] Activity and companionship were the drugs he craved for. The drab
and routine work in the Opium department offered no solace to his buoyant
and exuberant spirit. He yearned for the *mehfils* where he could transmit
the flame of his intellectual excitement to others. 'I am fed up with this
state . . . (and) tired of this job', he told his Aligarh friend Saiyid Mahfuz
Ali.[25] He was conceited about his Oxford degree, and contemptuous of
those who sported degrees from Indian universities. He submitted, as he
did with monotonous regularity during his internment a few years later,
long representations to his superiors commending his own abilities,
demanding higher pay, and criticizing those placed above him. 'In spite
of being an Indian and having received a very similar education to the
rest of the Baroda officials,' he complained to the Gaekwad, 'I found that

I differ from them in almost everything, and that it was difficult if not impossible for me to be received by them as one of their own number.'[26] Shaukat Ali, himself a civil servant in the Opium department, felt that his younger brother had crossed the limits of discretion; he admonished him 'to curb yourself a little—you have to work with certain people and you cannot always have your way. If I was your boss, I would strongly object to your correspondence. It borders on insubordination.'[27]

For the time being Dunlop Smith and Harold A. Stuart, the home member, held out the prospect of a government job. But hopes were soon turned into despair when told that 'the expenses of an Indian private secretary would (not) be justified at present', and that Mohamed Ali's lack of experience of detective work was a bar for a posting in the Home department.[28] Though Michael O'Dwyer, later governor of Punjab, recommended him to the nawab of Jaora, this small princely state could hardly assuage Mohamed Ali's thirst for participation in great events, even in a subordinate capacity.[29]

A career in journalism was the only option, the only avenue through which Mohamed Ali could prove to be of 'any appreciable use to it (Muslim community), while still earning a livelihood'.[30] His journalistic ventures, beginning with the *Comrade* on 14 January 1911, were successful. His articles were laced with long and tedious quotations, and tended to be verbose and repetitive. Yet he created for himself a broad-based readership because he wrote, just as he spoke, passionately. The *Comrade*, manned by some of his friends and protégés from Aligarh, grew in size; its circulation shot up to 8,500 copies. Its office in Kucha-i Chelan in the old city became a political salon after the paper moved from Calcutta to Delhi, the new capital of British India. 'No paper has so much influence with the students as the *Comrade*, and no individual has the authority over them which is exercised by Mohamed Ali', reported the UP government in 1914.[31] When he wanted to stop publishing the *Hamdard* at the beginning of his internment, Wilayat Ali, the well-known columnist, begged him not to do so: 'I do not approve of your decision and I do not think many will. . . . You cannot imagine what the loss of *Hamdard* will mean to us— the Musalmans.'[32] Wilayat Ali recognized, as did others, that the *Comrade* and *Hamdard* contributed to a general awakening of educated Muslims who read and financially supported them.[33]

The *Comrade*, more than the *Hamdard*, voiced some of Mohamed Ali's main concerns; for example, the promotion of the Aligarh College, his alma mater. He wanted the college to serve as a common centre where Muslims from all over the world would congregate and energize a common

Islamic consciousness to uphold Muslim interests in India and overseas.[34] Thus, his maiden speech in 1908 on the subject, modelled on the style of Edmund Burke and with quotations from Latin, Arabic, Persian, Urdu and English literature, proved to be the swan song of the first phase of the Muslim University movement.[35]

Mohamed Ali supported—some said fomented—a students' strike in 1907. His involvement in college affairs, a story detailed by David Lelyveld, Gail Minault and Francis Robinson, made him the *bete noire* of the board of trustees. The British staff complained to the English novelist E.M. Forster, then visiting India, that they were neither 'trusted to give the help they had hoped nor could they make some way with the students— not much, owing to the influence of the *Comrade*, a forward Islamic newspaper'. The Muslims 'had an air of desperation, which may be habitual, but was impressive'.[36] The college was transformed into a hot-bed of 'sedition'; officials wondered if anything could be done to prevent its students from 'being tampered with' by Mohamed Ali who, for all his professions of loyalty, was 'a dangerous malcontent', 'an element of strife'.[37]

2.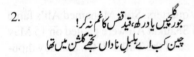

Grieve not over imprisonment in the cage, but
do not forget the actions of the plucker of the rose.
Oh foolish nightingale! When free in the garden,
When did you ever find repose?

MOHAMED ALI

I have elsewhere traced the breakup of the Anglo-Muslim *entente cordiale*, the growth of political radicalism among some Muslims, and their stridency in areas where colonial policies disturbed the *status quo* most. So have other historians. Some have examined how the anti-Muslim bias of Anthony Macdonnell, the reunification of Bengal (1911), the rejection of the Muslim University scheme (1912), and the fracas over the Kanpur mosque (1913) convinced Muslim political activists that radical self-help was a better solution than mendicancy. Much secondary literature also delineates the role of the men of *Nai Raushni* and the representatives of 'new ideals' and 'new force', many of whom endorsed the Congress policies and programme. Mohamed Ali emerged as the rallying point for such 'younger men', for he himself held the opinion that the Congress, then dominated by the 'moderates', embodied the 'genuine and vigorous aspirations which move educated India for a well-organized and common national life'.[38] He emphasized, as did Azad with greater rigour and consistency, the need for Hindu-Muslim amity and understanding. Without mutual cooperation Hindus and Muslims would 'not only fail but fail ignominiously'. He talked of a 'concordat like that of Canada' and '*a marriage de convenance* [*sic*], honourably contracted and honourably maintained'.[39] In another article—'The Communal Patriot'—he maintained that the two communities, despite their differences, should be mutually tolerant and respectful, and that eventually education and the 'levelling, liberalizing tendencies of the times' would create political individuality out of diverse creeds and races. He compared the Congress and the Muslim League to two trees growing on either side of a road:

Their trunks stood apart, but their roots were fixed in the same soil, drawing nourishment from the same source. The branches were bound to meet when the stems had reached full stature. . . . The soil was British, the nutriment was common patriotism, the trunks were the two political bodies, and the road was the highway of peaceful progress.[40]

Such views were being aired in many quarters. Still, Mohamed Ali's fame spread far and wide only after he and Shaukat Ali were gaoled on 15 May 1915 for an article entitled 'The Choice of the Turks'.[41] On that day thousands congregated to offer their Friday prayers at Delhi's Juma Masjid and 'to bid adieu to the two patriots who had done all they could to promote their cause'.[42] They were first interned at Mehrauli, then transferred to Lansdowne and, finally, to Chhindwara where they arrived on 23 November 1915 wearing 'grey astrakhan cap with large Turkish half moons in the front, also Khuddam-i Kaaba badges'. Located 'a considerable distance from their friends' and 'far removed from centres of Muhammadan feeling', Chhindwara was chosen because 'pan-Islamism is faintest' and 'the journey there from the United Provinces as regards visitors is exceedingly tedious'.[43]

The Ali brothers were well on their way towards martyrdom, with various organizations vying with each other to record their 'noble services rendered at the most psychological moment in the history of the community'. Their fame was kept fresh through many protest meetings, and also through the incident of the government's conditional offer of their release in 1917. They refused to sign the undertaking suggested by the government; instead, they signed another, adding the qualification: 'Without prejudice to our allegiance to Islam'. Leading Congressmen, especially Gandhi, also courted them and pressed for their release. The

Mahatma, having met the Ali brothers in Aligarh and Delhi in 1915 and early in 1916, assured Bi Amman—'Mataji'—that he was 'leaving no stone unturned' to secure their immediate and honourable release.[44]

Having made Hindu-Muslim unity an essential part of his mission in India since his return from Africa in 1915, Gandhi assumed that Mohamed Ali was an ideal instrument in his hand for creating a Hindu-Muslim alliance with the aim of obtaining swaraj. He was valuable to Gandhi both as an issue on which to cement a communal concordat, and also because he considered him to be a splendid example of that mingling of Hindu and Muslim cultures in the Indo-Gangetic belt.[45] His interest in Mohamed Ali's release was 'quite selfish':[46] 'we have a common goal, and I want to utilize your services to the uttermost in order to reach that goal. In the proper solution of the Mohammedan question lies the realization of Swaraj.'[47]

Gandhi's initiatives made him popular among north India's Muslims, many of whom participated in the *hartal* organized on 6 April 1919 against the Rowlatt Bills. Ansari extolled him as the 'intrepid leader of India . . . who has . . . endeared him as much to the Musalman as to the Hindu'. Mohamed Ali's younger colleagues regarded the Mahatma as a 'Tolstoy and Buddha combined', and they endorsed his non-violent programme. Satyagraha, according to Maulana Abdul Bari, was consistent with the Islamic principles.[48]

Around this time the portrayal of Mohamed Ali as a fiery and relentless anti-colonial crusader was based on the strength of his involvement in nationalist as well as pan-Islamic causes. This image is sustained in much of the secondary literature produced in India and Pakistan. In reality, however, Mohamed Ali's utterances and his frequent references to the good that was to accrue from the 'beneficent contact' with Western culture and civilization explode the myth of his being consistently hostile to the colonial government.[49] Notice, for example, how he assured Meston, whose advice he followed in shifting the *Comrade* from Calcutta to Delhi, of his 'anxious desire' to cooperate with him and other well-wishers of his country and community,[50] and pleaded, on another occasion, for 'some pegs' on which to hang his moderate stance on the annulment of Bengal's partition. He insisted that 'well-merited concessions wisely made at a suitable moment' would curb an agitation far more effectively than the strenuous efforts of Muslim leaders.[51] He even suggested that the presence of the British monarch in India should be utilized to bind still more firmly the seventy million Muslims of India to the Empire.[52] No wonder, high-ranking British officers subscribed to the *Comrade* when it began publication in Calcutta. No wonder, the viceroy Hardinge allowed Mohamed Ali to collect and advance a loan to Turkey, patronized the Delhi Crescent Society, and supported Ansari's medical mission to Constantinople.[53]

Even when officials rebuffed Mohamed Ali in London during his stay from September to 1 December 1913, he declared his loyalty and appreciated the manifold blessings of British rule in India.[54] When the war with Germany broke out, he was on the side of the British, urging India's Muslims to place their services at the disposal of the government. The article 'The Choice of the Turks' proclaimed the hope that the khalifa would stay out of the war and save his Muslim countrymen from a conflict of loyalties. Talking to Abdul Majid, the CID officer, Mohamed Ali defined his position thus:

His quarrel (Abdul Majid recorded) was not at all with the British Government. He was certainly not so advanced as Messrs. Mazharul Haq, M.A. Jinnah and Lajpat Rai. He believed that is was necessary for Muhammedans that the British Government should and would remain in India much longer than the nationalists desired. . . . The Government did not know its real enemies. They will receive in audience Lajpat Rai and other nationalists, . . . but they would consider Mohamed Ali as their enemy.[55]

Mohamed Ali's antipathy towards Pax Britannica may well have developed during his trip to Europe in 1913, though it was still not explicitly articulated. Meeting writers, journalists and civil servants enabled him to see Turkey from the outside, to observe the strife of the peninsula magnified into the terms of international politics, to watch and appraise the forces remoulding, sometimes deliberately, sometimes almost casually, the destiny of the Ottoman empire. His exchanges convinced him, perhaps for the first time in his public career, that the British were insensitive to Muslim feelings over the khilafat, and their ignorance of conditions back home was 'driving them fast to the brink of the precipice'. Hence his indignation at being denied access to senior officials of the Indian House. 'If we are unable to see even His Lordship', Mohamed Ali told John Morley, 'what could we say to our people on our return except that because some local officials were desirous that we and our co-religionists and many others in our country should be misjudged by our superiors.'[56] Furious at the lack of sensitivity, he was drawn into a kind of *egoisme a deux* in defying their stuffiness. He commented that the government, having taken Muslim loyalty and support for granted, undermined the temporal power of Islam with scant regard for Muslim religious susceptibilities.[57]

Mohamed Ali's internment was the last proverbial straw. Ziauddin Ahmad Barni, a sub-editor of *Hamdard*, traced his mentor's antigovernment stance to his confinement in Chhindwara.[58] From here, as also from Lansdowne and Betul, Mohamed Ali expounded on the government's repressive measures, targeting the ICS in particular, 'a political party perpetually in office (with) the power to crush its political opponents with all the resources of the State'.[59] He told Delhi's chief commissioner, Malcolm Hailey, that he understood 'how hateful must be a man of my character to officials of a certain type'. He recognized the implications of the Defence of India Act, 'which makes even the Archangel Gabriel liable to internment by local governments on the secret testimony of Beelzebub'.[60] In June 1915, he announced that the law under which he was interned was 'tyrannous and unjust'.[61] No government was expected in the twentieth century to claim, even by implication, the right to force a man's conscience. He dwelt on 'the spirit of tyranny', the 'gag of prodigious proportions' prepared 'for silencing more than three hundred million of God's articulate creatures'. The Rowlatt Act 'has ended the reign of law, and substituted a reign of terror in its place'.[62] As a symbol of his protest, Mohamed Ali wore half-moons in his grey cap and Khuddam-i Kaaba badge, compared with his European style of dress in previous years.

The enforced leisure made Mohamed Ali more profoundly religious, enabling him to steep himself afresh in his Islamic heritage and turn to the study of Islam—charting out an unfamiliar subject, getting at its rudiments, and exploring its nuances. In *My Life*, a document of deep religious feelings, he laments not having had access to the traditional Muslim learning. 'It is not without a feeling of deep shame that I have to confess, we boys and girls born and bred in Muslim households were taught far less of our religion than most English boys and girls of our age and position.' He bemoaned that Aligarh 'furnished' students with 'little equipment in the matter of knowledge of faith'. Though he attended Shibli Numani's lectures and referred to the elation of sitting in the principal's hall attending these lectures with all the dignity of a quasi-'Undergrad', the Koran practically remained a closed book, and the traditions of the Prophet were no more than a name. In the seclusion of his internment at Mehrauli, however, he found in Maulvi Nazir Ahmad's translation of the Koran 'the consolation and contentment that was denied to us outside its pages'.[63] He discovered, after years of ignorance of his Islamic heritage, that the Koran was a 'perennial of truth' and offered a 'complete scheme of life, a perfect code of conduct and a comprehensive social policy . . .'. As a result, the main tenets of Islam, which were earlier 'little more than a bundle of doctrines and commandments', acquired 'a new coherence and, as it were, fell suddenly into place, creating an effect of units such as

I had never realized before'. *Tauhid* grew upon him as a personal reality, man in the dignity of his 'service' as viceregent of God, and himself as part of this great strength. This was Mohamed Ali's 'unique discovery in that small volume revealed some thirteen centuries ago to an Arab of the desert whose name I bore'.[64]

Mohamed Ali read the *Sihah-i Sittah*, a compilation of the Prophet's traditions (*Hadith*), the works of Imam Ghazali, Arnold, Shibli, the person who made the symbols of Islam a living reality for the Aligarh students, and the poems of Jalaluddin Rumi and Iqbal. He experienced 'an exquisite thrill of delight' reading *Asrar-i Khudi* (Secrets of Self), especially because its author Iqbal expressed 'the same basic truth of Islam, which I had in a blundering sort of way discovered for myself'.[65] Studying Islamic history enabled him to see its great men as figures to whom he could talk, and its crises as guides to action in current affairs.[66] Studying Islam was conventional enough for men like Saiyid Ahmad Khan, Shibli and Azad who did so with greater scholarship, but none with a greater personal need. Mohamed Ali recollected: 'Since I first commenced the study of the Koran I have read a fair amount about Islam from the point of view of Muslims and also of their critics; *but nothing that I have read has altered the significance of Islam for me to which I had stumbled in the first few months of our internment eight years ago'*[67] (italics mine). To Gandhi, he wrote:

Whatever else my internment may or may not have done, it has I believe set the soul free, and that compensates me for so many items on the wrong side of the account. What I could dimly perceive before I now realize with distinctness, and it is this, that the whole aim and end of life is to serve God and obey His commandments. . . . I confess I had never before grasped this truth in all its fullness. . . . *Internment made us seek refuge in the Holy Koran, and for the first time, I have to confess it, I read it through and with new eyes.*[68] (italics mine)

In Mohamed Ali's view there was just one world of Islam regardless of caste, class, linguistic and regional variations, one vast brotherhood stretching across the continents. This was summed up by the *Comrade* on 18 January 1916.

It is not only one God, one Prophet and one Kaaba that the Muslims of the world have in common, but in every degree of longitude and latitude they hold the same views of the relations of husband and wife, of parent and child, of master and slave and of neighbour and neighbour. . . . They follow among all races the same laws of marriage, divorce and succession. And they do this in the twentieth century of the Christian era exactly as they did in the sixth and hope to do so to the last syllable of recorded time. . . . There is still the one God to worship and the one

Prophet to follow . . . , always one unaltered and unalterable Book to soothe and to stimulate, and the one Kaaba to act as the magnetic pole for all true believers from all points of the compass.

Underlining the primacy of religious loyalty, Mohamed Ali argued that Muslims have had a pre-eminent sense of community in their *Weltanschauung*, and especially so in India, where their adherence to Islam made them unique and gave them their 'communal consciousness'. 'I have a culture, a polity, an outlook on life—a complete synthesis which is Islam', he stated in his magisterial style at the London Round Table Conference in 1930. 'Where God commands', he added, 'I am a Muslim first, a Muslim second, a Muslim last, and nothing but a Muslim. If you ask me to enter into your Empire or into your nation by leaving that synthesis, that polity, that culture, that ethics, I will not do it.'[69] He did not believe that by being a Muslim he was any less an Indian. His religious beliefs and nationality never appeared to him to be incompatible. He could—and must—be true to both Islam and India. He explained thus: 'Where India is concerned, where India's freedom is concerned, where the welfare of India is concerned, I am an Indian first, and Indian second, an Indian last, and nothing but an Indian.' On another occasion he spelt out his position in the following words:

I am a Muslim first and everything else afterwards. As a Muslim, I must be free and subject to no autocrat who demands from me obedience to his orders in defence of those of God. . . . Faith is my motive of conduct in every act . . . and my faith demands freedom. That Swaraj will give me, but it does not demand the subjugation of the Hindu or any one else differing from me in faith. . . . My own freedom and not the enslavement of any other is my creed.[70]

In sum, whereas Mohamed Ali's earlier activities had been directed by 'communal loyalty', his motivation after his religious experiences was Islamic duty. This is not to suggest that he held his community in any lesser esteem or that its mundane welfare was less important to him. On the contrary, his awakening confirmed the rightness of what he had done in the past and made it necessary for him to intensify his endeavours along similar lines.[71]

3. ‏مت بهل هے جانو پھرتا هے فلک برسوں‏
‏تب خاک کے پردے سے انسان نکلتا هے‏

Don't think us cheap: the heavens revolve for years
To bring forth man out of the veil of dust.

Mohamed Ali's emotional disposition in religious matters had much to do with the nature and with the promptness of his response to events in Turkey. In this context his concerns cannot be doubted: the opinion that it was all feigned or that he was simply playing the pan-Islamic role cannot be defended. He passionately believed that the basis of Islamic sympathy was not a common domicile or common parentage but a shared outlook on life and culture, and that the khilafat stood as 'the embodiment of that culture'. He endorsed Azad's description of a 'political centre' (*siyasi markaz*), and designated the khalifa as the 'personal centre' of Islam and the *Jazirat al-Arab* as its 'local centre'. For these reasons he warned the government that,

there should be no attempt to remove, whether directly or indirectly, from the independent, indivisible and inalienable sovereignty of the khalifa, who is the recognized servant of the holy places and warden of the Holy Shrines, any portion of the territories in which such holy places and shrines are situated. . . . Nor should there be any such attempt to dismember and parcel out even among Muslim Governments, or in any other manner weaken the Khalifa's Empire with the object of weakening the temporal power of Islam, and thereby make it liable to suffer, without adequate power to prevent, the curtailment of its spiritual influence through the temporal power of other creeds.[72]

Again, he stated in London:

Well, so long as there are your Bryces and your 'Big Sticks', we, too must have some sort of stick for the defence of our faith. . . . If you think you can please the Muslims of India by allowing the Turks to retain Constantinople in such a way that the khalifa is worst than the Pope . . . for he would in fact be the prisoner of people of an alien race and faith, then, ladies and gentlemen, you know very little of Islam and the Muslims, or of India and the Indians. [*Cheers*] That affront shall never be tolerated, and if you think you can make out that all this 'agitation' is 'fictitious' and 'factitious', then you will be compelling the Indian Muslim soldiery to disprove this lie in a manner that will be far too unambiguous for your tastes or for ours. Beware, beware.[73]

Mohamed Ali envisioned a renascent Islamic world in which all Muslim peoples were united in a strong Islamic world—'the super-natural Sangathan of Muslims in Five Continents'—built around the khalifa and supporting each other through that institution whenever Muslim security was threatened.[74] The new khalifa, judged from his views at the Mecca Conference in 1928, was to be based on a democratic, elective rather than a dynastic institution like the *khilafat-i rashida*. And the person chosen would be virtuous and faithful to Islam. The Muslims of the world would direct the government and be responsible for its welfare, while his brethren in India—the largest single community—would lead the fight to emancipate Islam.[75]

Mohamed Ali infused vigour into the central khilafat committee and its provincial and local units to realize the ideal of a renascent Islam. The *Hamdard* was started on 13 June 1913 to reach out to the Urdu readers. The Ali brothers travelled widely, delivered lectures, organized mass meetings, and galvanized the ulama at the Dar al-ulum in Deoband, the Firangi Mahal and the Nadwat al-ulama in Lucknow. Henceforth, they decided to play to Mohamed Ali's tune and 'to pocket their pride and in a way even accept the lead of men whom they had but a generation ago finally consigned to perdition'. The orthodox and the anglicized were drawn together. The 'temporal misfortunes' of Islam had such a profound impact that 'the wedge that Western education had seemed to insert between the ranks of the religious, and of the men of the "New Light" vanished as if by magic'. A general levelling took place 'without any dependence on the use of force or external authority'.

Mohamed Ali strengthened these ties following his release on 28 December 1919. He reached Amritsar where, in keeping with the practice that had developed during the War years, the Congress and the League held simultaneous meetings. He had been imprisoned, Mohamed Ali told the Congress, for denouncing the injustices perpetrated on India and on Islam by the British, and now he must denounce them still, even if it meant returning to prison. He expressed his readiness to sacrifice everything he had, including his life, for the sake of Allah and Islam. He made clear that Muslims were subjects of Allah and not of Great Britain. He echoed similar views in London as a member of the khilafat delegation.

The delegation, having arrived in England at the end of February 1920. For six months, it maintained an exhausting pace, spurred on by Mohamed Ali. He was the debonair gentleman, perfectly dressed, dispensing political wisdom, epigrams, jokes and anecdotes to representative audiences, impressing everyone except the British newspapers and Lloyd George— the man who mattered most.[76] He lived well 'in a nice flat with heaps of good food, taxis to go about',[77] set up meetings with British leaders, spoke at length to various bodies, and organized the publication of the *Moslem Outlook* in England and the *Echo de l'Islam* in Paris. Reaching Bombay on 4 October 1920, nearly a month after the Calcutta Congress had adopted the non-cooperation resolution, he advised Muslims to plunge into the campaign with their non-Muslim brethren to achieve the khilafat aims.

Words were soon translated into deeds. Mohamed Ali redoubled his efforts, along with Gandhi, Azad and Ansari, to induce the trustees of the

Aligarh College to give up the government grant-in-aid. When the demand was rejected, quite a few students set up a break-away national university. This is how the Jamia Millia Islamia was founded. To begin with, Mohamed Ali devoted some time to giving the Jamia a solid Islamic footing, reviving Shibli's discourses on the Koran and ensuring that 'our day began with a full hour devoted to the rapid exegesis of the Koran'. But his project in life extended far beyond the confines of a campus. Jamia was too small and too quiet a place for someone accustomed to the humdrum of national politics.[78] Predictably, he virtually abandoned the institution he had himself founded, and headed for Nagpur to address the Congress, Muslim League and the khilafat committee meetings.

Mohamed Ali was among the busiest men in India, speaking before crowds and local committees. He travelled to eastern and western India from January to February 1921. His presence at the Erode session of the Majlis-al Ulama in March heightened the khilafat euphoria, as did his presence in April at Madras where he attracted huge crowds of Hindus and Muslims. His fiery speech at Erode nearly got him into trouble again; only an apology and an assurance that violence in every form would be eschewed led the government to withdraw the prosecution. From April to August, he spoke in Meerut (9 April), Bulandshahar (12 April), Lucknow (1 May and 7 August), Moradabad (26 July and 6 August), Pilibhit and Sitapur (7 August), and Allahabad (10 August). He was joined by his mother who threw off the veil, appeared before the public and began addressing vast audiences. Her journeys brought hundreds of thousands of rupees to the khilafat fund. The whole of India was astir. A popular song of the era reflected the spirit:

بولی اماں محمد علی کی
جان بیٹا خلافت پہ دے دو

So spoke the mother of Mohamed Ali
Give your life, my son, for the khilafat.

During this tumultuous period, Mohamed Ali had an ambivalent relationship with Gandhi. Though moved by the Mahatma's interest in his release, he could neither grasp the significance of his political message nor his vision of a new social and moral order. And yet Gandhi hoped that 'on seeing the success of my experiment in non-violence, (they) will come to realize its excellence and beauty later on'. In May 1920, he referred to a distinct understanding with the Ali brothers that violence would not be allowed to go on side-by-side with non-violence.[79] Mohamed Ali confirmed in December 1923 that he would not use force even for self-defence.[80] In fact, he and other khilafat leaders chose the path of non-violent non-cooperation to 'secure the interests of their country and their faith'. From Paris, he wrote: 'I only wish that I had a Musheer (adviser) here, and if possible Fazlul Haq, though of course the best man to have is Gandhiji himself.'[81] When accused of being a Gandhiphile, he replied: 'I cannot find in any community—Jewish, Christian or any other a man who has as noble a character as Mahatma Gandhi. My *pir* and *murshid* is Abdul Bari whom I greatly respect. Yet I can say that I have not found anyone superior to Mahatma Gandhi.'[82] 'After the Prophet, on whom be peace,' he said, 'I consider it my duty to carry out the commands of Gandhiji.'[83]

While Mohamed Ali was reaffirming his loyalty to Gandhi, the khilafat conference at Karachi had earlier declared that serving in the army or police was *haram* for the Muslims. The expected happened. Mohamed Ali, the chairman, was arrested two months later. On 26 October 1922 began the trial where he made the famous statement: 'The trial is not "Mohamed Ali and six others *versus* the Crown", but "God *versus* man". The case was therefore between God and man. The whole question was "Shall God dominate over man or shall man dominate over God?".' The jury listened to his rousing speech but were impressed. He and five other Muslim leaders were sentenced to two years' rigorous imprisonment on 1 November.

4.
خاک کا پتلا ہے آدم جو کوئی اچھا کہے
عالم خاک میں برسوں تئیں وہ بات رہے

> Man was first made of clay, and if the song you sing is good
> This world of clay for years to come will listen to your voice.

Mohamed Ali was released on 29 August 1923, and in his first public address spoke of his gloom at finding on his shoulders the burden of freeing Islam and India. He said that he came out 'from a smaller prison to a large one', and that every executive member of the Congress must sign a pledge of readiness to sacrifice life itself for independence. Non-cooperation was still the main plank of his politics: 'if cooperation was "haram" according to the Islamic law two years ago, it cannot become "halal" today'. He criticized the Swaraj party and its leader, Motilal Nehru, for starting chamber practice in defiance of the Congress decision to boycott British law courts.[84] But three weeks later he himself proposed the compromise resolution at the Delhi Congress, permitting 'such Congress-

men as have no religious or other conscientious objections against entering the legislatures . . . to stand as candidates', and calling for 'united
endeavours to achieve Swaraj at the earliest moment'. He was concerned,
as he wrote to Jawaharlal Nehru who was induced to accept against his
will the Congress secretaryship in Mohamed Ali's year of presidentship,[85]
to resolve the differences among Congressmen and to unite the factions.
Appealing for unity, he stated:

Let the Provincial Congress [UP] assembly send for the sacred soil of Kashi itself
the message of the greater and more solid *sangathan*, the *sangathan* of the
National Congress. And let us go forth from this Conference truly *shuddh*,
purged of all narrowness, bigotry and intolerance in order to free our country
from the most cramping slavery—the slavery not only of the body but also of
the soul. . . . If there is anything of the old world spirituality in Kashi, let us
recommence the work of our great chief, Gandhiji, in the spirit of religious
devotion and utter unworldiness.[86]

Whatever the reasons, Mohamed Ali's teaming up with the swarajists
enraged the ulama, whose *fatwa* against council entry was being repudiated
by one of their own spokesman. The 'no-changers', too, accused their
idol of having betrayed the Mahatma's heritage. The front-rank Communist
leader, M.N. Roy, summed up his resentment:

Much was expected of Mohamed Ali. . . . The hope had been dashed to the ground.
The idol showed its clay feet in such a hurry that the admirers were staggered.
Mohamed Ali has failed to give the leadership which was expected of him. His
pronouncements since he came out of jail are full of mere platitudes and hopeless
contradictions. No constructive programme, no positive suggestion as to the
future of the movement is to be found in them. He authorises the removal of the
ban on the councils, but holds up the edict of the ulemas [*sic*] on the question.
He professes to be the standard-bearer of pure Gandhism, but sets his face positively against civil disobedience, without which the political programme of non-
cooperation becomes meaningless. He indulges in fearful threats against the
government, but finds the demand for the separation from the British empire
'childish and petulant'. He deplores the Hindu-Moslem feuds, but still insists
on khilafat propaganda, which contributed not a little to the success of the
enemies of national freedom in creating communal dissensions. . . . In political questions, he has absolutely no programme to suggest. He harps on the
threadbare 'constructive programme' which constructs naught but inaction.
Such is the record with which Mohamed Ali goes to Kakinada to furnish the
nationalist forces with a new direction.[87]

The main tenor of Mohamed Ali's address at Kakinada was that Hindu-
Muslim unity was still necessary if Indians hoped to realize their aims.

Similarly, non-cooperation was not outmoded even if one were to grant (only for the sake of argument) that it had failed. He also spoke of his long-standing dream of a 'Federation of Faiths', a 'United Faiths of India'. India's millions were so hopelessly divided into communities and sects that providence had created for the country the mission to solve a unique problem and work out a new synthesis, which was nothing less than a 'Federation of Faiths'. The synthesis was to be of a federal type, for the lines of cleavage were too deep to allow for any other sort of union. He added:

For more than twenty years I have dreamed the dream of a federation, grander, nobler and infinitely more spiritual than the United States of America, and today when many a political Cassandra prophesies a return to the bad old days of Hindu-Muslim dissensions, I still dream of 'United Faiths of India'. It was in order to translate this dream into reality that I had launched my weekly newspaper, and had significantly called it the *Comrade*—'Comrade of all and partisan of none'.[88]

The motives for India's Muslim efforts towards achieving swaraj were dual. They aimed at freeing India and freeing Islam. The relationship between Indians and the Turks was in the nature of a compact between countries oppressed by the same imperialism. Once India was free and her forces could not be driven to fight against the Turks, the two countries would be safe. Mohamed Ali contended that the Turks would have fought for the freedom of their co-religionists, including India's Muslims, and hence India, if they had not been so weakened. His lack of realism in assessing Turkish aims did not stop here. He pictured them fighting for an ideal khalifa, even though the Kemalist bandwagon rolled on in Turkey. He believed that once the Turks were free from their 'distractions' they would revive the glories of Umayyad or Abbasid dynasties and the pristine purity of the *khilafat-i rashida*.

Mohamed Ali's elevation to the Congress presidentship legitimized his position in nationalist circles. But within months of his exhortations at Kakinada, he began drifting away from the Congress, or, perhaps, as he would have put it, the Congress drifted away from him. This had a great deal to do with worsening Hindu-Muslim relations and the feeling in some Muslim circles that the Congress nurtured the vision of a 'Hindu Raj'. Mohamed Ali developed a point of view from which everything said or done by any Hindu was linked to the Hindu Mahasabha's influence. He saw its evil hand everywhere and its tainted mark on every forehead. Indeed, his new mentality recognized only two divisions in India, Hindu and Muslim, and not nationalist and reactionary or non-cooperating.[89] Nehru could not understand, how a Hindu or a Moslem can have any political or economic rights as Hindu or Moslem. And I cannot conceive why Moslems or Sikhs or Hindus should lay stress on any such rights. No minority should be unjustly treated. But Maulana Mohamed Ali is well aware that minorities get on well enough as a rule. It is the great majority which requires protection. A handful of foreigners rule India and exploit her millions. A handful of India's rich men exploit her vast peasantry and her workers. It is this great majority of the exploited that demands justice and is likely to have it sooner than many people imagine. I wish Maulana Mohamed Ali would become a champion of this majority and demand political and economic rights for them. But this majority does not consist of Hindus only or Moslems only or Sikhs only. It consists of Hindus and Moslems and Sikhs and others. And if he works for this majority, I am sure he will come to the conclusion that he need attach little importance to the imaginary rights of individuals or groups based on adherence to a religious creed.

Mohamed Ali's main grievance was that Gandhi, whom he had only just described as 'the most Christ-like man of our times', gave a free hand to the 'Lala-Malaviya gang'. The Congress, according to him, was no longer a national party but a Hindu one, unprepared to condemn Hindu fanatics, and unprepared to work towards the creation of a secular society. His anxieties were heightened by growing fissures in the Hindu-Muslim alliance in Bengal and Punjab, and the rapid progress of the Arya Samaj, the Hindu Mahasabha, and the *shuddhi* and *sangathan* movements. Commenting on the Delhi riot of July 1924 specifically, and on the deteriorating communal situation generally, he wrote: 'And pray Mahatmaji forgive a pang of sorrow, the cry of a well-nigh broken heart, the credit of it all goes, in the first instance, to the misguided spirit of the *sangathan* movement, and the superfluous boastings of the *shuddhi* leaders. . . . I feel sick, positively sick of it all.'[90] At the same time, the 'pseudo-nationalists', he wrote in the *Comrade* on 17 July 1924,

talk and write as nationalists and run down communals; but only in the use of counters and catchwords of nationalism are they nationalists for their hearts are narrow and they can conceive of no future for India except it be one of Hindu dominance and the existence of the Musalmans as a minority living on the sufferance of the Hindu majority, forgetting that such ill-concealed dreams can have but one interpretation, the existence of the Hindu majority itself on the sufferance of the British masters of India. It is my sad conviction that not one of these pseudo-nationalists would have talked so glibly of nationalism, majority rule and mixed electorates, if his own community had not been in the safe position of an overwhelming majority. It is they who are real culprits as narrow communalists, but since the position of their community is safe enough they mouth all the fine phrases of nationalism and parade themselves as nationalists. The Cow question provides the best topic for the exposure of their pseudo-nationalism, for in the name of nationalism they make demands on their fellow-countrymen so absurd that none has ever heard of them in any other country or nation in the world, and it is time that their nationalism was fully exposed.

The Nehru report (Appendix I) set in motion the avalanche of Mohamed Ali's eloquence against Gandhi and the Congress. Soon after returning to India from Europe in October, he described the provision of dominion status in the report as being 'inconsistent with the independent spirit of Islam'. Its implication was that the creation was God's, the country was the viceroy's or of the parliament's, and the rule was Hindu Mahasabha's.[91] 'Today', he said on 25 December 1928, 'Mahatma Gandhi and Sir Ali Imam would be sitting under our flag and over them would fly the flag of the Union Jack. The Nehru report in its preamble has admitted the bondage of servitude.' He was equally outraged that Muslim representation in the central legislature was fixed at 25 and not 33 per cent, while separate electorates and weightages were done away with.[92] In his view, separate electorates guaranteed that a small minority was not swamped by an overwhelming majority, while weightages ensured that this majority would not establish 'a legalized tyranny of numbers'.[93]

Such views mostly mirrored the fears of government servants and landowners who, having gained political leverage through separate electorates and government nomination, faced the cheerless prospect of being eased out of legislative bodies. Equally, they were alarmed by the proposal for adult suffrage. The enfranchisement of over fifteen million voters, mainly tenants, was certain to oust the landlords from the general constituencies as well. Not surprisingly, they resisted all forms of provincial advance, and insisted on having separate electorates, weightages, and 'effective' Muslim representation on autonomous institutions created by the legislatures.

Mohamed Ali, now identified with such elements, did his best to turn the tables against his detractors. The first opportunity arose on 21 December 1928. The Ali brothers, in league with some others, disrupted a meeting which was tilted in favour of the Nehru report. When similar tactics were employed elsewhere, several delegates resigned and decided to boycott the forthcoming All India Khilafat Conference that was to be chaired by Mohamed Ali. A few days later Mohamed Ali did not need to stifle opposition at the All-Parties Muslim Conference in Delhi, for this assembly of loyalists had been converted to the idea that the Nehru report had jettisoned their interests.

Mohamed Ali's presence at the Delhi conference was described as 'a tragedy of Indian public life'. *The Servants of India* commented: 'One's heart sinks at the thought that the Ali brothers should have been among the staunchest supporters of the conference.'[94] Ansari, once his comrade-in-arms, was anguished by his parleys with the 'Aga Khan and Co.' He wrote:

Ever since the Lucknow Convention many of us have been making ceaseless efforts to come to an understanding with the Ali brothers and their friends. . . . They gradually but surely went on receding from us until at last they found themselves in the company of the Aga Khan and Sir Muhammad Shafi in January last. The willingness with which they associated themselves with people whose only distinction is that they have always been reactionary in regard both to Indian and Muslim affairs was surprising. . . . Indeed the differences that in their origin concerned a few provisions of the Nehru Report have now grown into a conflict of the very outlook. This to my mind explained why the Ali brothers are adopting an irreconcilable attitude although they know very well that they are thereby strengthening the government as well as the communalists, both Hindu and Muslim. . . .[95]

A striking feature of the conference was that Mohamed Ali sat beside Muhammad Shafi who he had so often derided as a government stooge, and that the Aga Khan was cheered by Azad Sobhani whose vitriolic speeches at Kanpur in 1913 had forced the Khoja leader to quit the Muslim League. Mohamed Ali actually seconded the resolution proposed by Shafi. Likewise, leaders like Jinnah, Shafi and the Ali brothers, who had not shared a platform before, signed the 'Delhi Manifesto' on 9 March 1929 in order to persuade Muslims to stay away from the Congress meetings and processions. Nehru reacted angrily to Mohamed Ali's signing the 'Delhi Manifesto', declaring it a 'treason' against the Congress by one who had served as its president:

The ex-Presidents of the National Congress are certainly a mixed lot and not always amenable to discipline. Like the king they appear to be above the law. I had ventured to criticize a statement made by one of them forgetful of this truism in Indian politics because of my high regard for this gallant leader in the cause of Indian freedom. He has made history and, if he but will, can do so again. But just when India is stretching her limbs for another and a stiffer struggle, when drooping spirits are reviving, he cries 'halt' and calls back his regiments and battalions. And have not many of those with whom he consorts in this endeavour been the strongest bulwarks of British rule in India and the antagonists of those who strive for freedom?

In his sharp rebuttal, Mohamed Ali condemned the Congress leaders who had defied the party's decisions on non-cooperation, non-violence,

Hindu-Muslim unity, and untouchability. As a price of his cooperation, Malaviya 'wanted to place a revolver in the hands of every Hindu lady, no doubt as a token of non-violence, and of course all the Hindu-Muslim riots in which he has never said a word against Hindus are in full conformity with the Congress precepts of Hindu-Muslim unity'. He accused Motilal Nehru of 'killing non-cooperation just as he is killing the Congress today and merging it into the Hindu Mahasabha in spite of his well-known lack of Hindu orthodoxy',[96] and deplored Gandhi's endorsement of the Nehru report. Quoting from his writings of 1924 and 1925 to show that the Mahatma was converted to a different creed and striving for different goals, he pointed out:

Gandhi has defeated all Muslim attempts for a compromise. He is giving free rein to the communalism of the majority. The Nehru constitution is the legalized tyranny of numbers and is the way to rift and not peace. It recognizes the rank communalism of the majority as nationalism. The safeguards proposed to limit the high-handedness of the majority are branded as communal.[97]

Gandhi conceded that the Ali brothers 'had a fairly heavy list of complaints', and that he could not make an impression on them.[98] 'Whatever Maulana Mohamed Ali may think of me, I have nothing but kindly feelings about him. And I feel sure that time will remove misunderstandings. Having no feeling either against Islam or Mussalmans, I feel absolutely at ease', he wrote from the Yeravda Central Prison. He hoped in vain that 'if truth is in me, the brothers must capitulate'.[99] Some months earlier, Mohamed Ali had already lambasted Gandhi for 'fighting for the supremacy of Hinduism [and] the submergence of Muslims'. He refused to join 'Mr. Gandhi' not only because his civil disobedience movement was 'for making the seventy millions of Indian Muslims dependent on the Hindu Mahasabha',[100] but also doubted whether he would stick to his own programme:

Doubtless man who could suddenly call of the non-cooperation campaign at Bardoli in 1922 with the same astonishing about-face can inaugurate a civil disobedience movement in 1930. But what surety is there that he would not again order suspension, just as he did eight years ago, only a few days after serving an ultimatum to the viceroy?[101]

Moreover the country was unprepared for civil disobedience: it lacked unity, discipline, and self-control. He warned Nehru: 'Your present colleagues will desert you. They will leave you in the lurch in a crisis. Your own Congressman will send you to the gallows.'[102]

Mohamed Ali's appeal to Muslims to send delegations to London symbolized the collapse of the old alliance on which Gandhi had built the non-cooperation movement. He himself joined a delegation, led by the Aga Khan, with the conviction that critical collaboration with the British at the Round Table Conference would bring greater political benefits than 'sedition' in Congress company. But his departure was marked by gloom, for he knew that his mission was condemned as smacking of treachery by those very people with whom he had worked in the past. In fact, the Maulana felt in London that, 'his real place was in the fight in India, not in the futile conference chamber in London'.[103] In Oxford, his alma mater, he addressed students in their tail coats, talked cricket, and made them laugh. But he 'made little or no impression and quite failed to put across the case for the Muslims to a youthful but intelligent audience who were to provide a fair number of the nation's political leaders in later years'.[104] His speech at the Round Table Conference, which turned out to be his last sermon, appeared to be the raving of a man isolated, inconsolably bereaved, dying. 'I want to go back to my country', Mohamed Ali declared, 'with the substance of freedom in my hand. Otherwise I will not go back to a slave country. I would even prefer to die in a foreign country so long as it is a free country, and if you do not give me freedom in India you will have to give me a grave here.' In Mujeeb's view, Mohamed Ali's appeal to the British to give India her freedom or else he would not return alive was no more than a pathetic admission of his failure.[105]

A chronic patient of diabetes, Mohamed Ali died in London on 3 January 1931 and was buried in Jerusalem. Gandhi, whom he derided with such vehemence during the years 1928-30, had this to say at his death: 'In him I have lost one whom I rejoiced to call brother and friend and the nation has lost a fearless patriot. We had differences of opinion between us, but love that cannot stand the strain of differences is like "a sounding brass and thinking cymbal".' Nehru was equally charitable. Reflecting on his role, he observed: 'It was a misfortune for India that he (Mohamed Ali) left the country for Europe in the summer of 1928. A great effort was then made to solve the communal problem. If Mohamed Ali had been here then, it is just conceivable that matters would have shaped differently.' Nehru added:

For whatever the differences on the communal question might have been, there were very few differences on the political issue. He was devoted to the idea of Indian independence. And because of the common political outlook, it was always possible to come to some mutually satisfactory arrangement with him on the communal issue. There was nothing in common between him and the reactionaries who pose as the champions of communal interests.[106]

5. ‏مجھ کو شاعر نہ کہو میر کے صاحب میں نے
درد و غم کتنے کئے جمع تو دیوان کیا

Don't think me a poet—no, my verse
Is made of pain and grief for than you know.

Mohamed Ali was blessed with the supreme gift of expression, but he was not one to be identified with any great principle or order, or even a big idea. He relished the trappings of power, the drama of great debates, the high-sounding titles, his name echoing through history. He was too outspoken to be a good manager of people. He excelled at exposing the follies of others but had little to advocate himself; his own thinking was ruthless—he spared nothing and nobody. He had a nimble wit, but sometimes his devastating sarcasm hurt, and he lost many friends.[107] He and his brother Shaukat were 'splendid agitators and very little more'. 'They certainly are not the type of men in whom we would have much faith, were they placed to rule over us', commented Abbas Tyabji, one of Gandhi's lieutenants in Bombay.[108] Edwin Montagu, the secretary of state who had not approved of Mohamed Ali's internment, found him to be 'a quite typical specimen, full of incurable vanity'.[109]

Mohamed Ali was a passionate man, strong in his resentments as in his affections. He left a strong although not wholly pleasant impression on people who knew him, of a man devoted to his convictions. At the same time, he was obstinate, impatient in temper, and choleric in disposition; quick to anger when honour or religion was touched; wild and untameable. He was the man for the people: impetuous, dashing, irrepressible, demanding sympathy by laying his heart open, crying and raising laughter, and believing in God and God's mercy with an intensity that made him at times completely irresponsible.[110] Though he advocated a strikingly wide range of ideas, some grossly contradicted each another, some complemented one another, and some appear to have been floated simply to guage public reaction before being discarded. The Urdu scholar Maulvi Abdul Haq found Mohamed Ali ruthless and dictatorial in his public and private conduct. He had an hysterical streak in his personality, lacked consideration for friends, and was, for these reasons, incapable of carrying through his numerous enterprises. Abdul Haq's final judgement was that Mohamed Ali, although a brilliant writer and orator, 'failed' to enhance his stature and reputation in public life.[111]

In his enthusiastic, unrealistic moods, which were frequent enough, he regarded himself as a link not only between Indian Muslims and the Turks, but also between the Turks and the rest of the world.[112] He was insensitive to the implications of the Turkish revolution, which was directed against the tyrannical rule of the sultan as well as against Western imperialism. Similarly, he was unfamiliar with scholars like Ziya Gökalp, the intellectual leader of that period, who had dismissed the idea of uniting Muslim nations under one ruler as a messianic hope. That is why when Muslims elsewhere were establishing national states independent of external ties of domination, Mohamed Ali was striving to recreate the khilafat of the classical theorists.

Inviting the amir of Afghanistan to liberate India from British imperialism was an indiscrete act. On such matters Mohamed Ali seemed to be wanting to forget, as often as he could, the need to be tactful, in order that he might assert with ever greater vehemence the fact that he was a sincere believer in Islam.[113] His endorsement of the idea of Muslim migration (*hijrat*) to Afghanistan was unrealistic and politically inexpedient. His credibility suffered, moreover, on account of the scandal over the 'misuse' of the khilafat funds and his frequent outbursts that caused a breach between the khilafatists and their liberal and socialist allies in the Congress.[114] The *Comrade* was revived in November 1924, but ceased publication in January 1926. 'Poverty is pestering me', Mohamed wrote. He considered restarting the paper 'and see if I can wipe off the deficit due to those two journals [*Comrade* and *Hamdard*] or I shall retire from public life, and earn 50 rupees from tuitions'.[115] The Ali brothers, having spent more than their means, were in dire financial straits. Delhi's chief commissioner informed the viceroy that Mohamed Ali was 'thoroughly discredited and almost penniless'. He went cap in hand to his former associates and colleagues (the Karachi merchant Haji Abdullah Haroon had already donated Rs. 10,000 to revive the *Comrade*), and having failed in almost all quarters he finally secured a grant of Rs. 6,000 from the deposed maharaja of Nabha.[116] Some years later, the raja of Alwar bore his travel and treatment expenses in London. Even if these are not illustrations of Mohamed Ali's loss of credibility with his own community, they clearly reveal the gradual reversal of his fortunes.

The Congress gradually deserted Mohamed Ali;[117] yet, he clung to the much-maligned khilafat committees. His defence of Ibn Saud, who had demolished numerous sepulchers held sacred by Muslims, alienated him from his spiritual mentor, Abdul Bari, and other friends. But he was not impressed. During his visit to the Arab lands in June 1926 he discovered the squalor of Mecca and Medina, the barrenness of the surrounding land, the degeneracy of the social conditions, and the mismanagement of the *haj* traffic. Yet, he continued to insist that the khilafat committees were destined to bring about a truly Islamic rule in the Holy Land. He wanted India's Muslims to form a party around the nucleus of the khilafat group, persuade other Islamic people to their way of thinking, and ultimately achieve a united Muslim voice. He wanted them to contribute money, time, technical assistance and moral support to the Hijaz, devote themselves wholeheartedly to the reformation of the Centre of Islam, and thus earn the good requital in both worlds. He was confident of resisting Ibn Saud's arrogation of control of the Holy Land and re-establishing a genuine Islamic rule.[118]

Mohamed Ali paid scant regard to his own comrades who had followed his lead in the past but were no longer prepared to pursue his mission. His protégés in UP—Khaliquzzaman and Shuaib Qureshi—opposed his plan of sending three deputations to the Middle East.[119] In neighbouring Delhi, Ansari resigned from the khilafat committees in July 1926, stating that as an Indian owing allegiance first to the motherland he had decided to sever his ties with communal and sectional organizations.[120] In Punjab, after their success in the 1924 elections, the Muslim swarajists took less interest in the khilafat committee; the main opposition to the Ali brothers came from the khilafatists under the leadership of Saifuddin Kitchlew. Iqbal believed that the khilafat movement, in its dying moments, unfolded aspects in which 'no sincere Muslim could join for a single minute'. Turkey, he pointed out, was the first Muslim country to shake off the fetters of medieval mentality and found a way of life of her own.[121]

'Muslim identity' in a plural society had to be defined not in relation to the Islamic world but in response to the specific historical and contemporary experiences of the Muslim communities in the subcontinent. This fact, underlined in Saiyid Ahmad Khan's rejection of pan-Islamism towards the end of the nineteenth century, was creatively expressed by Azad, Ajmal Khan and Ansari. But Mohamed Ali was swayed by his own religious/Islamic rhetoric without reflecting on the wider implications of the khilafat movement on inter-community relations. He even refused to accept that his co-religionists in Turkey themselves had played the final part in destroying what he was almost single-handedly fighting to maintain. As he once put it, he had 'an inherent and almost ineradicable tendency towards diffusion and a fatal attraction for tangents'.[122] He could not build the bridges for retreat, because he did not possess the skill to do so. Instead, he aimed 'to destroy all that did not conform to his ideal, even though he could not reconstruct what he had destroyed'.[123] Although popular with those who thought it a point of honour to wear Islam on their sleeves, he ultimately undermined his own position and damaged the very causes he aspired to serve.[124]

Note on Mohamed Ali's My Life: A Fragment

Since its publication in January 1942, Mohamed Ali's *My Life: A Fragment* has been widely read in academic circles in India and Pakistan. Afzal Iqbal, the editor, secured the 'manuscript' from Mohamed Mujeeb, the vice-chancellor of Delhi's Jamia Millia Islamia, and published this 'autobiographical sketch'.

Mohamed Ali was a prolific writer; yet, he did not consider writing a book until his internment in 1923, following the famous Karachi trial. This is what he told Abdul Majid Daryabadi in 1916 while in Chhindwara, then a small town in the Central Provinces (now Madhya Pradesh):

> You suggest to me that I should write some book during my enforced leisure, and that our people expect one from me. If that is so, I am afraid they don't know me. Firstly, I have not the patient perseverance nor the temper of the researcher. Secondly, my emotions are much too strong to permit what intellect I may possess to be exerted in the writing of a book. . . . No, my friend, my brain is far too busy (and so is my heart) to allow of any leisure for such 'pastimes' as authorship.[125]

He did, however, write a great deal more than many of his contemporaries. He contributed to his own newspapers, and wrote hundreds of routine letters as an editor. Besides writing *My Life*, he wrote poems to fill a not-so-slim volume, and miscellaneous historical, literary and political pieces to fill another.[126] During his internment and his trips to Europe, he corresponded with his friends and family members.[127] These letters constitute a major corpus of pan-Islamic literature in India. They uncover major themes that concerned his generation of educated Muslims who turned to him for political inspiration and leadership.

The tone in his correspondence constantly varies from boredom and depression, on the one hand, to exhilaration and conviction on the other, now relaxed and desultory, now indulging in flights of fantasy or burlesque. A flair for the dramatic, coupled with a wry self-awareness, helped foster a temperament that allowed the fullest reins to intellectual enthusiasm while never really realizing personal ones. This complexity, not rare but fascinating in Mohamed Ali's case, is also noticeable in his speeches.

My Life is much more reflective and analytical than any of Mohamed Ali's other published writings. It is an important personal statement on how some educated Muslims lived through the turbulent decades of the

early twentieth century. It is an individual's intellectual and spiritual journey, and his engagement with a society and polity that was undergoing
rapid changes. 'Experts often write for experts,' commented Mohamed Ali,
'but I am, so to speak, "the man-in-the-street", and I write for "the man in
the street". The individual experience which I relate will make this clear,
and being typical of the history of so many Muslim lives of my generation,
it will not, I trust, be altogether lacking in interest.'

At the same time, *My Life* reflects the collective experiences of large
numbers of people who shared the author's commitment to and his passion
for 'rejuvenating' the Muslim communities in the subcontinent. It is no
doubt inadequate in many ways—verbose, incoherent, repetitive and full
of digressions. Besides, as Afzal Iqbal pointed out, of the four parts
Mohamed Ali planned to write, only the first is complete. The second
part—included by Iqbal as an appendix—is incomplete. Yet, *My Life* is a
document of considerable significance for students of modern Islam in
South Asia, its historical value enhanced by the absence of a similar text
written by any of the leading Muslim actors of the period. Maulana Abul
Kalam Azad, for one, did not write much besides his commentary on the
Koran; he expressed himself instead in the literary form of his letters,
published as *Ghubar-i Khatir.* In fact, Jawaharlal Nehru commented in
his prison diary: 'Free thinker and magnificent writer as he is, he should
have turned out a host of splendid books. Yet his record is a very limited
one.'[128]

At a time when scholars are attempting to delineate the contours of
'Muslim identity' in South Asia, Mohamed Ali's *My Life* enables us to
understand how some Muslims constructed their identity in British India.
For this reason this book invites comparison with other texts written around
the same time in other countries by Muslim scholars and publicists. At a
time when 'communalism' and 'separatism' are rearing their heads again,
My Life reveals, more than any other contemporary account, the anxieties
and aspirations of several Muslim groups in a colonial society that was
being gradually transformed as a result of far-reaching political, administrative and bureaucratic changes.

NOTES

1. Sydenham to Hardinge, 18 Mar. 1913, Hardinge papers.
2. Meston to Chelmsford, 20 Aug. 1917, File No. 136 (1).
3. Quoted in Afzal Iqbal, *Life and Times of Mohamed Ali*, p. 113. In May 1915,
   the Ali brothers were asked to remain in Mehrauli and abstain from political

meetings. They were described by Richard Burn (writing for Meston) as 'disseminators of mischief and would-be-traitors', who 'have done any amount of evil at Aligarh. They have tried to stir up trouble in Lucknow and their message is mischievous wherever they go.' Home Poll. D, Proceedings, May 1915, 36, NAI.

4. Robinson, *Separatism Among Muslims*, pp. 178-9; and Brown, *Gandhi's Rise to Power*, pp. 139-40.

5. Moin Shakir, *Khilafat to Partition*, New Delhi, 1972, pp. 70, 74, 86; S.M. Hadi, *Ali Biradaran aur Unka Zamana*, New Delhi, 1978; Shan Muhammad, *Freedom Movement in India—The Role of Ali Brothers*, New Delhi, 1978; *Aaj Kal*, New Delhi, 1978; *Jamia*, New Delhi, 'Mohamed Ali Number', Apr. 1979, Jan.-Feb. 1980.

6. Moinul Haq (ed.), *Mohamed Ali: Life and Work*, Karachi, 1978, p. 41; *Nigar*, Nov.-Dec. 1976; *Maulana Mohamed Ali Jauhar Sadi Conference*, Karachi, 1978, and for the view that the 'two-nation theory' had been forecasted by Mohamed Ali, see Ahmad, *Islamic Modernism*, p. 162.

7. Thus, an address presented to Mohamed Ali following his release from internment, stated: 'It would require a volume to enumerate in detail your services in regard to the M.A.O. College, the Muslim University, the galvanizing of the Muslim community through your brilliant newspapers, the *Comrade* and the *Hamdard* . . . the raising of funds for Muslim victims in the Balkan War, the organizing of a competent and well-equipped medical mission for the Turkish wounded. Your restoration to liberty is a mark of profound rejoicing to us. . . . Your presence in our midst will stimulate our community into the solidarity seriously imperilled during the last five years of agonizing ordeal.' *Leader* (Allahabad), 12 and 15 Jan. 1917.

8. Mazharul Haq and Ansari to Hony. Secy., Muslim League, 3 Sept. 1917; and Ansari to A.M. Khwaja, 3 Sept. 1917, in Hasan (ed.), *Muslims and the Congress*, pp. 9-10.

9. Mohamed Ali, *Kalam-i Jauhar*, New Delhi, 1938; A. Rauf (ed.), *Mohamed Ali aur Unki Shairi*, Karachi, 1963; Nur-ur Rahman (ed.), *Divan-i Jauhar*, Karachi, 1962.

10. Mohamed Ali to James DuBoulay, 18 Feb. 1919, in Hasan (ed.), *Mohamed Ali in Indian Politics*, Vol. 2, pp. 192-3.

11. The best source for Mohamed Ali's life and career is his own 'autobiography' and his articles published in the *Comrade* on 21 and 28 Nov. 1924. Much additional information is available in the works of Afzal Iqbal, Rais Ahmad Jafri, Shan Muhammad and Abu Salman Shahjahanpuri.

12. 'People wondered why any mother should be so lacking in love for her children as to send them away from home while they are still so young.' *Comrade*, 5 Dec. 1924.

13. Ibid., 21 Nov. 1924.

14. Hasan (ed.), *My Life*, p. 69.

15. Ibid., p. 70.
16. Azim Husain, *Fazl-i-Husain: A Political Biography*, Bombay, 1936, p. 20; Iqbal, *Life and Times*, pp. 31-2.
17. Mohamed Ali to Dewan Tek Chand, n.d., Mohamed Ali papers [hereafter MAP], Jamia Millia Islamia, New Delhi.
18. Testimonial of Rector, Lincoln College, 19 Oct. 1901, ibid.
19. Testimonial of James Williams, 14 Oct. 1901, ibid.
20. Hasan (ed.), *My Life*, p. 73.
21. This is revealed in his exchanges with Saiyid Mahfuz Ali. It is, however, clear that he took a keen interest in political developments. Although exaggerated claims are made about his influence on the Muslim League deliberations in Dec. 1906, he was regarded as a potentially bright recruit. In Feb. 1907, he lectured in Allahabad. A month later he prepared a text of the Muslim League proceedings which was published as 'Green Book No. 1'. This prompted an explanation from an official. 'I sent in a reply,' wrote Mohamed Ali, 'before the Council. In response, a general confidential circular was issued to government servants. They were told not to contribute articles which were likely to create communal animosity.' Mohamed Ali to Mahfuz Ali, 14 Jan. 1910, M. Sarwar (ed.), *Khutut-i Mohamed Ali*, New Delhi, 1940, pp. 252-4. For Mohamed Ali's speeches, see Home Poll. B, 149, 1913, NAI.
22. Dunlop Smith to Mohamed Ali, 31 Jan. 1907, MAP.
23. To Dunlop Smith, 5 Dec. 1907, ibid.; and G.K. Gokhale, 8 Feb. 1908, Gokhale papers (341), NAI.
24. To Mahfuz Ali, 14 Jan. 1910, *Khutut*, pp. 252-4.
25. Ibid.
26. To the Gaekwad of Baroda, n.d., MAP.
27. Shaukat Ali to Mohamed Ali, 4 Jul. 1909, ibid.
28. G.S. Clark to Mohamed Ali, 2 Nov. 1909; Dunlop Smith to Mohamed Ali, 30 Oct. 1909; H.A. Stuart to Mohamed Ali, 10 Dec. 1909, ibid.
29. *My Life*, pp. 33-4, and Mohamed Ali to the nawab of Jaora, 23 Nov. 1910, ibid.
30. Ibid., p. 34.
31. Home Poll. D., Dec. 1914, 31, NAI.
32. To Mohamed Ali, 20 Aug. 1915, MAP. See, Abu Salman Shahjahanpuri, *Maulana Mohamed Ali aur Unki Sahafat* (Maulana Mohamed Ali and his Journalism), Karachi, 1983.
33. For the influence of *Comrade*, see K.M. Ashraf, 'Aligarh ki Siyasi Zindagi', in *Aligarh Magazine*, 1953-5, p. 164. 'Throughout the country, only one voice was heard by the people of the north and the south, the east and the west, by the educated and the illiterate, the ulama and the ignorant. . . .' Abdul Majid Daryabadi, *Maqalat-i Majid*, Bombay, n.d., pp. 233-4.
34. *Comrade*, 28 Jan. 1991.
35. Gail Minault and David Lelyveld, 'The Campaign for a Muslim University',

MAS, Vol. 8, 1974, p. 145; David Lelyveld, 'Three Aligarh Students: Aftab Ahmad Khan, Ziauddin Ahmad and Mohamed Ali', *MAS*, Vol. 9, 1975, pp. 103-16, and his *Aligarh's First Generation*, pp. 330-6.

36. Quoted in P.N. Furbank, *E.M. Forster: A Life: The Growth of the Novelist, 1879-1914*, London, 1978, p. 227.

37. Hardinge to Meston, 14 Nov. 1912; Hardinge to Butler, 29 Oct. 1912; Butler to Hardinge, 3 Nov. 1912, Hardinge papers. Malcolm Hailey, chief commissioner of Delhi, described Mohamed Ali as 'the centre and inspiration of the Pan-Islamic movement'. To H.H. Wheeler, 1 May 1915, Home Poll. D, May 1915, 36, NAI.

38. *Comrade*, 30 Dec. 1911.

39. Ibid.

40. Minault, *The Khilafat Movement*, p. 19.

41. The article gave the government 'ample justification for suppressing such writings'. An official note stated on 6 Oct. 1914: 'I do not see how anyone can read the article except as a direct incitement to Turkey to go to war, and practically what it says is that if this does bring them up against Russia and France, they have no cause to love these Powers and it does not matter much. England is practically threatened if she does not evacuate Egypt, and Germany is extolled. If this is not attacking our allies and siding with our enemies it is difficult to know what it is?' Home Poll. A., Oct. 1913, pp. 142-9, NAI. The Ali brothers maintained that they were interned because they freely expressed their allegiance demanded by their Islamic faith. To viceroy, 24 Apr. 1919, MAP.

42. *Leader*, 12 and 15 Jan. 1920.

43. Home Poll. D, Proceedings, Oct. and Dec. 1915, NAI.

44. Mahadev Desai (ed.), *Day-to-Day with Gandhi* (Varanasi, 1968), Vol. 1, pp. 93, 211.

45. Brown, *Gandhi's Rise to Power*, p. 152.

46. After arriving in India, Gandhi told a khilafat meeting that he began to find out 'good Mohammedan leaders'. He was satisfied when he reached Delhi and met the Ali brothers. 'It was a question of love at first sight between us.' Speech at Bombay, 9 May 1919, *The Collected Works of Mahatma Gandhi* (*CWMG*), Vol. 15, p. 295.

47. Gandhi to Mohamed Ali, 18 Nov. 1918, ibid., p. 64.

48. Hasan (ed.), *Muslims and the Congress*, Appendix 1; Abdur Rahman Siddiqi to Mohamed Ali, 24 Mar. 1919, MAP; WRDCI, Mar. 1919, Home Poll. B, Apr. 1919, pp. 148-52, NAI; A.M. Daryabadi, *Mohamed Ali: Zaati Diary ke Chand Auraq*, Hyderabad, 1943, p. 20.

49. W.J. Watson, 'Mohamed Ali and the Khilafat Movement' (unpublished MA thesis, McGill University, 1955), p. 14.

50. To Meston, 19 Feb. 1913, MAP.

51. To James DuBoulay, 3 Jan. 1912, ibid.

52. To F.H. Lucas, 3 Jan. 1912, ibid.
53. For correspondence with the viceroy on these issues, see Hardinge papers (84); Iqbal, *Life and Times,* pp. 77-8.
54. *Comrade,* 13 Sept. 1913; and Mohamed Ali to James Le Touche, 4 Nov. 1913, MAP.
55. Quoted in B.R. Nanda, *Gandhi, Pan-Islamism, Imperialism and Nationalism,* Bombay, 1989, p. 138.
56. To John Morley, 2 Nov. 1913, MAP.
57. To Chelmsford, 24 Apr. 1919, ibid.
58. 'Maulana Mohamed Ali Jauhar', *Naqqush (Shakhsiat Number),* Oct. 1956, p. 1161.
59. To Chelmsford, 24 Apr. 1919, MAP.
60. To Malcolm Hailey, 24 May 1915, ibid.
61. Ibid., 2 June 1915.
62. To Chelmsford, 24 May 1919, ibid.
63. Hasan (ed.), *My Life,* pp. 63-4.
64. Ibid., p. 122; and Iqbal (ed.), *Selected Writings,* p. 170.
65. Ibid., p. 127.
66. A.M. Daryabadi, *Zaati Diary,* p. 14; to A.M. Daryabadi, 22 May and 25 July 1916, in Hasan (ed.), *Mohamed Ali in Indian Politics,* Vol. 1, pp. 269-76.
67. Daryabadi, ibid., p. 14; Mohamed Ali to Daryabadi, 22 May and 25 July 1916 (Urdu), Daryabadi papers, NMML.
68. To Gandhi, 20 Feb. 1918, MAP.
69. Afzal Iqbal, *Select Writings,* p. 405.
70. *Mussalman* (Calcutta), 13 May 1921.
71. Mohamed Ali's loyalty to Islam was expressed in the days before the Turko-Italian war as loyalty to the Indian Muslim community rather than to an abstract way to Allah. His communal consciousness, as he said, was far more secular than religious: his decision to take to journalism was dictated by the 'secular affairs of my country' rather than by a 'religious call'. Then, in the seclusion of his internment, he read through the Koran. Islam possessed him and he discovered the dogmas and ethical codes of his religion. After this experience, argues Watson, his motivation was 'Islamic duty' rather than 'communal loyalty'.
72. To Chelmsford, 24 Apr. 1919; Hasan (ed.), *Mohamed Ali in Indian Politics,* Vol. 2, p. 236 ; also, speech in London on 22 Apr. 1920; Iqbal (ed.), *Selected Writings,* pp. 183-93.
73. Speech delivered in London on 23 Mar. 1920, in *Selected Writings,* Vol. 2, pp. 20-1.
74. 'Islam united Muslims by offering a set of common ideals and offered the only rational basis for unity and cooperation among its followers. The sympathies of a Muslim are co-extensive with his religion because they have been bred into him by the inspiring spirit of his creed.' *Comrade,* 12 Apr. 1913.

75. Watson, op. cit., p. 55.

76. Mujeeb, *The Indian Muslims*, p. 537.

77. Mohamed Ali to Shaukat Ali, 15 May 1920, MAP.

78. Hasan, *A Nationalist Conscience*, p. 104. Mohamed Ali is reported to have said in Sept. 1923: 'I never conceived of the Jamia's growth and permanence at all. The Jamia's existence today is rather like that of the refugees and the Prophet's helpers at Medina who were lying in wait for the conquest of Mecca. Our real objective is Aligarh which some day we shall conquer.' Quoted in A.G. Noorani, *President, Zakir Husain: A Quest for Excellence*, Bombay, 1967, p. 25. On this point, see Mujeeb, 'Oral History transcript' (407), p. 35, NMML.

79. Brown, *Gandhi's Rise to Power*, p. 331, fn. 2; *Day-to-Day*, Vol. 2, p. 238.

80. Brown, *Gandhi's Rise to Power*, pp. 330-1.

81. To Shaukat Ali, 15 May 1920, MAP.

82. To Swami Shraddhanand, 26 Mar. 1924, ibid.

83. Quoted in Rajmohan Gandhi, *The Good Boatman: A Portrait of Gandhi*, New Delhi, 1995, p. 104; and speech at Lahore, in *Bombay Chronicle*, 26 May 1924.

84. In September 1923 he complained that the swarajists have 'completely gone back on the entire creed and policy of Gandhi'. 'I have been realizing every day that the leaders of the Swaraj Party want to throw Gandhism overboard without some of them having the courage to confess,' he wrote to his khilafat comrade, Saifuddin Kitchlew. He wanted him to be a peacemaker between him and the 'Gujarati friends', although he advised 'caution and restraint'. Mohamed Ali to Kitchlew, 30 Sept. 1923, Hailey papers, Mss. Eur. 220 (7-A), BL.

85. Nehru, *An Autobiography*, p. 99. 'I have just received your letter, and must "protest most indignantly" once more against your misplaced modesty. My dear Jawahar! it is just because some members of the Working Committee distrust and dislike your presence as Secretary that I like it.' Mohamed Ali to Nehru, 15 Jan. 1924, MAP.

86. Mohamed Ali to Nehru, n.d., 1923, in *A Bunch of Old Letters*, pp. 30-1.

87. G. Adhikari (ed.), *Documents of the History of the Communist Party of India*, Vol. 2, p. 181.

88. Iqbal (ed.), *Selected Writings*, p. 256.

89. Ansari to Mazharul Haq, 7 Sept. 1929; Hasan (ed.), *Muslims and the Congress*, pp. 86-7.

90. Mohamed Ali to Gandhi, 21 July 1924, MAP.

91. 'You make compromises in your constitution everyday with false doctrines, immoral conceptions and wrong ideas, but you make no compromise with our communalists—with separate electorates and reserve seats. Twenty-five per cent is our proportion of the population and yet you will not give us 33 per cent in the Assembly. You are a Jew, a Bania.' See Hasan, *Nationalism and Communal Politics* (1979 edn.), pp. 287-8.

92. Ibid.

93. In the very first issue of the *Comrade*, he had declared separate electorates to be necessary because of 'the distinct and well-defined Hindu and Muslim standpoints in regard to the common, immediate and everyday affairs of Indian life'. *Comrade*, 11 and 28 Jan. 1911, 29 Mar. 1913, 19 Jan. and 6 Feb. 1925.

94. *Servants of India*, 10 Jan. 1929.

95. Ansari to Mazharul Haq, 7 Sept. 1929, Hasan (ed.), *Muslims and the Congress*, pp. 86-7.

96. *Nigarishat-i Mohamed Ali*, quoted in Abdul Hamid, *Muslim Separatism in India*, p. 201.

97. *Times of India*, 5 Mar. 1929.

98. Gandhi to Motilal Nehru, 12 Aug. 1929, Motilal Nehru papers (G-1), NMML; see also Gandhi to Shaukat Ali, 17 Apr. 1930, *CWMG*, Vol. 43, p. 280.

99. Gandhi to Horace G. Alexander, 23 Dec. 1930, *CWMG*, Vol. 45, p. 26; *Young India*, 3 Apr. 1930, *CWMG*, Vol. 43, p. 126.

100. Quoted in Reginald Coupland, *The Constitutional Problem in India*, Oxford, 1944, pt. 3, p. 111. The position of the 'Nationalist Muslims', on the other hand, was different. This was explained by Ansari to the raja of Mahmudabad: 'Whilst, on the one hand, we consider the policy and programme of the Congress entirely ill-conceived and detrimental to the larger interests of the country today, we do not consider the campaign of civil disobedience conceived in the spirit of antagonism to the Muslims.' To the raja of Mahmudabad, 11 May 1930, Hasan (ed.), *Muslims and the Congress*, p. 121.

101. Jafri (ed.), *Nigarishat-i Mohamed Ali*, pp. 237-72.

102. Nehru, *An Autobiography*, p. 120.

103. Ibid.,

104. Benthall papers (2), CSAS, Cambridge.

105. Mujeeb, *Indian Muslims*, p. 539.

106. *CWMG*, Vol. 45, p. 203; Nehru, *An Autobiography*, p. 120.

107. Nehru, *An Autobiography*, p. 117.

108. Brown, *Gandhi's Rise to Power*, p. 276. This opinion was shared by others. One of them wrote to Tej Bahadur Sapru: 'Frankly, I am not very much interested in the Ali brothers. I do not believe in them, and to the extent that they are doing right, it is because they are either attracted by Gandhi's glamour, or they feel that they can work more effectively under the kudos of his name.' S.L. Polak to Sapru, 8 July 1981, Sapru papers, Vol. 17, p. 241. Percival Spear, who met Mohamed Ali at Delhi's St. Stephen's College in 1924, wrote: 'He was a handsome bearded man with striking eyes and clothed in flowing robes. His speech was easy, his manner ingratiating, that of a willing sufferer for a noble cause. To me he seemed to be too suave to be sincere and too insincere to be noble. In fact I took an instant dislike to

him.' Percival and Margaret Spear, *India Remembered*, New Delhi, 1981, p. 15.

109. To Chelmsford, 23 June 1920, File No. 6, Chelmsford papers. 'Why we should intern Mohamed Ali for pan-Mohammedanism', Montagu recorded in his diary on 11 Nov. 1917, 'when we encourage pan-Judaism, I cannot for the life of me understand.' S.D. Waley, *Edwin Montagu: A Memoir and an Account of his Visits to India*, Bombay, 1964, p. 141.

110. Mujeeb, *Indian Muslims*, p. 536.

111. Abdul Haq, *Chand Humasr*, Karachi, 1952 edn., p. 164. Muhammad Sadiq had described this sketch of Mohamed Ali as 'vitriolic'. *Twentieth Century Urdu Literature*, Karachi, 1983, p. 368.

112. Mujeeb, *Indian Muslims*, p. 538.

113. Azad stated that 'whatever Mohamed Ali said was quite compatible with the teaching of Islam'. Home Poll., 1921, 45, NAI. Later, of course, Mohamed Ali clarified his position in order to remove the misunderstandings in many quarters. See his presidential address, Allahabad district conference, May 1921, Home Poll., 1921, 10, NAI.

114. The Urdu poet, Brij Narain 'Chakbast' was convinced that the political turmoil in India was fomented to strengthen Islam and create conditions which would give Afghanistan the excuse to invade the country. He did not think that Muslims could be converted to Indian nationalism because of their extra-territorial loyalties. According to him, Mohamed Ali, a pan-Islamist, was not a friend of the Hindus, and that the Ali brothers used Gandhi to save their own ends. Chakbast to Sapru, 28 Apr. 1921 (in Urdu), Sapru papers. In an 'Open letter to the Maulana Sahebs', the editor of *Bharatwasi* took exception to the khilafatists designating themselves as 'Khadim-i Kaaba' (Servants of Kaaba) and not as 'Khadim-i Hind' (Servants of India). He told the Ali brothers: 'For you swarajya for India is not the first duty. You build the whole edifice on religion, while we build the entire edifice on patriotic considerations.' P. Parasram to Ali brothers, 8 July 1921, MAP.

115. *Searchlight*, 17 Apr. 1927.

116. Page, *Prelude to Partition*, pp. 104-5.

117. One of his former colleagues, Arif Husain Hasvi, resigned from the *Hamdard* because of his communal posture. *Searchlight*, 14 May 1926. Page, *Prelude to Partition*, pp. 100-1.

118. Watson, 'Mohamed Ali and the Khilafat Movement', p. 87; Ahmad, *Islamic Modernism*, p. 139; Rais Ahmad Jafri, *Karawan-i Gumgushta*, Karachi, 1971, pp. 16-18.

119. Page, *Prelude to Partition*, p. 502.

120. Ansari to Shaukat Ali, 16 July 1926, Hasan (ed.), *Muslims and the Congress*, p. 19.

121. Page, *Prelude to Partition*, pp. 503-4. For Iqbal, Schimmel, *Gabriel's Wings*, p. 47.

122. Quoted in Nanda, *Gandhi, Pan-Islamism*, p. 201.
123. Khaliquzzaman, *Pathway to Pakistan*, p. 69.
124. Mujeeb, *Indian Muslims*, p. 538.
125. 25 July 1916, Abdul Majid Daryabadi papers, NMML.
126. Rais Ahmed Jafri (ed.), *Selections from Mohamed Ali's Comrade*, Lahore, 1965, and his *Ifadat-i Mohamed Ali*, Hyderabad, n.d.; Mohammed Sarwar (ed.), *Mazameen-i Mohamed Ali*, New Delhi, 1938, 2 vols.
127. Hasan (ed.), *Mohamed Ali in Indian Politics*, 3 vols.; Shan Muhammed (ed.), *Unpublished Letters of the Ali Brothers*, New Delhi, 1979; Abu Salman Shahjahanpuri (ed.), *Siyasi Maktubat Rais al-Ahrar*, Karachi, 1978; Muhammad Sarwar, *Maulana Mohamed Ali ka Europe ka Safar*, Lahore, 1941.
128. Christmas Day—1942, S. Gopal (ed.), *SWJN*, Vol. 13, p. 39.

7

Representations of Indian Nationalism: Ideology and Praxis of Azad and Mohamed Ali

Maulana Abul Kalam Azad's ideological discourse was influenced by his knowledge of and interaction with Islamic societies, while his political praxis was determined by the specificity of India's colonial experience. At the same time, he was not swayed by a unified stream of thought or monolithic ideology. Though Islam was central to his world view, he took great pains to scrutinize and evaluate existing theories and established notions. 'There is no conviction in my heart', he wrote, 'which the thorns of doubt have failed to pierce: there is no faith in my soul which has not been subjected to all the conspiracy, of disbelief.'[1] Allegiance to his intellectual mentors was not constant as the Maulana traversed the rough terrain of religion, politics and philosophy. 'I am under no obligation', he claimed, 'for guidance to any man's hand or tongue, nor to any syllabus of education. All the guidance I have received has been from the Divine Throne.'[2] In the end, he emerged from the darkness of his inner strivings as an independent man.

The same spirit of independence was the hallmark of his public life. He was nobody's follower, not even Gandhi's. Even though religion and moral fervour bound the Mahatma and the Maulana in a common quest for swaraj, they did not share a common perspective on socio-political issues. Azad's relationship with other front-rank Congress leaders was ambivalent. This was because his political survival was not dependent on his loyalty to a Gandhi or a Jawaharlal Nehru or his alignment with or opposition to any of the Congress factions. His stature and charismatic appeal rested on his quality of mind, his unassailable loyalty to the Congress, his deep commitment to India's independence and his firm opposition to communal forces. In the words of Muhammad Mujeeb: 'He was too aloof to concern himself with persons, too intellectual to relish political small talk, too proud to think in terms of alliance, affiliation or opposition. . . . He had to be taken for what he was, with no credentials than his personality.'[3]

This chapter reflects on Azad's relationship with Mohamed Ali, a leading and popular figure who rose like a firmament on the Indian political scene. Both burst on the national stage around the same time, achieving success and prominence through their powerful writings. They voiced their community's anguish over the Balkan issue, the Kanpur mosque, the future of the university at Aligarh, and spearheaded the massive pan-Islamic upsurge. While Azad worked laboriously over sheafs of *fatawa*,[4] Mohamed Ali reached out to the common people to disseminate his ideas on a wide range of contemporary issues relating to Indian nationalism, the future of Islam, and of Indian Muslims. And when the British government put them in gaol time and time again, both reflected on their role with a sense of pride and satisfaction and derived comfort from the fact of occupying centre-stage and influencing the course of history. Azad saw himself in the same role as Jesus, a victim of unjust courts: 'At all events, how strange and glorious a place is this prisoners deck where both the greatest and the best of men are made to stand. For even so great a being as He, this was no inappropriate place.'[5]

I

The first decade of the twentieth-century witnessed the rise of a new generation of young Muslims—the men of *Nai Raushni*—with an ideology and outlook on contemporary social and political issues which was different from Aligarh's first generation. Men like Hasrat Mohani, Zafar Ali Khan, Raja Ghulam Husain, the Ali brothers and Wilayat Ali 'Bambooque' repudiated Aligarh's political legacy by acting in unison with the nationalist forces. All were graduates of the Aligarh College, where they had once learnt the lessons of loyalty at the feet of their mentor, Saiyid Ahmad Khan.

The person who did not belong to UP and was not educated in Western schools and colleges was Mohuiddin Ahmad, better known as Abul Kalam Azad. He studied at Mecca and, in 1898, when the family returned to India, he was tutored by his father Maulana Khairuddin Ahmad in the Islamic sciences. Later, he came into contact with Shibli Numani, and was exposed to the liberal, reformist writings of Egyptian scholars, Muhammad

Abduh and Rashid Rida. With his enriched intellectual experiences, he commented on contemporary issues with sensitivity in his first major journalistic venture, the *Al-Hilal*, launched in 1912, which took educated Muslims by storm with its eloquence and fervour. 'The Muslims were set on fire by his passionate words', recalled Saiyid Sulaiman Nadwi, who worked with him on the staff of *Al-Hilal* for a time in 1913.[6]

Azad strayed into the political arena in Calcutta, then in the throes of the Swadeshi agitation. Impressed by the revolutionaries,[7] he regarded their anti-imperialism parallel to similar movements in other Muslim lands: he claimed that the *Al-Hilal* was founded to propagate his nationalistic, anti-imperialistic stand. From 1912-13 until his imprisonment in 1921, he was connected with several agitations for which he was often sent to gaol. He toiled in and out of prison over a monumental *Tarjuman al-Koran* (the first volume was published in 1931), putting forward the view of the transcendental oneness of all faiths and the theology of multi-religious cooperation. He was looked upon, in spite of his youthful years, as one of the elders in the Congress, whose advice both in national and political matters as well as in regard to the communal and minority questions was highly valued. In the final phase of his life, he returned to the front rank of politics as the Congress president from 1939 to 1946, and as the symbol of those Muslims who worked for a united India. He opposed the Partition heart and soul—almost alone among the Congress stalwarts to do so. His speeches echoed the themes of his earlier life and writings: communal harmony, religious broad-mindedness, and cultural cosmopolitanism.

Mohamed Ali's career followed a familiar graph—degrees obtained at Aligarh and Oxford, followed by jobs in the princely states of Rampur and Baroda. While in service, he wrote and lectured on the contemporary political scene and took part in the foundation of the Muslim League. By the time the *Comrade* was launched, Mohamed Ali (yet to acquire the prefix 'Maulana' before his name) had gained a substantial following in his alumni, the college at Aligarh. Around this time, Azad was busy planning his journalistic assault in Calcutta, a city where the echoes of the Swadeshi movement continued to reverberate in many circles.

When the *Comrade* and *Al-Hilal* appeared, they bore the unmistakable style of their editors. Azad was not much of a stylist, but wrote authoritatively. His discourse was subtle, complex, and incisive; his style fierce, combative, and akin to the Egyptian journal *Urwat al wuthqa*. He invoked scriptural and rational arguments assaulting the position of his opponents effectively, pausing only to regret occasionally the necessity of dealing with noisome adversaries. He spoke in the language of a 'high-souled prophet', appealed to religious passions, awakened dormant spirits by invoking Islamic symbols, and urged the ulama to alter the language and tenor of their discourses. At first, he envisaged leading the Muslims at the head of a 'Party of God' (*Hizbullah*) to Indians in ousting the British. He, then, founded the Dar al-Irshad to reform the teaching methods used in religious institutions, encourage independent thinking, and to make plain to students the social applicability of their curriculum. Such activities were a necessary preliminary to Azad's emergence as a powerful political force. They were, moreover, designed to change the intellectual and political climate created by the Aligarh school.

Mohamed Ali had an equally meteoric rise, though without being an ideologue or a theorist like Azad. He was a crusader—one who sought to undo the 'wrongs' done to his community by the forces inimical to Islam. That is why he took to journalism, 'the only avenue through which I could reach a place in which I could prove of any appreciable use to it . . .'. His style was verbose, pedestrian, rambling and repetitive; yet, he had a profound influence in moulding public opinion. The Muslim intelligentsia throughout the country responded with warmth and enthusiasm to his writings.

Islam, as expressed in his life, was different from Islam as expressed in Azad's life. Yet, it was the chief source of intellectual inspiration. Mohamed Ali's early religious training involved a superficial acquaintance with the rudiments of Islam and the concomitant ritual. The family influences, too, do not appear to have been such as to have either inclined him in favour of dogmatic theology, or fostered in him independence of thought and a spirit of rebellion against the prevailing religious beliefs. His mother's gentle influence, to which Mohamed Ali owed so much in life, was exerted more in the direction of promoting his educational career than in creating around him a religious atmosphere.

The enforced leisure at Chhindwara, Lansdowne and Betul jails enabled him to steep himself afresh in his Islamic heritage and turn to the study of his religion—charting out an unfamiliar subject, getting at its rudiments, and exploring its nuances. The experience was, in some ways, similar to that of Azad. His three-and-a-half year internment in Ranchi kindled his Islam into warmth and fervour. He began writing the *Tarjuman al-Koran*, with his commentary on the opening *Surah Fatihah*, and its themes— Divine Providence, benevolence, justice, unity and guidance, *rabubiyah*, *rahma*, *adala*, *tawhid*, and *hidaya*.

Azad and Mohamed Ali asserted the transcendental truth of Islam, 'a way of life, a moral code and social polity', a complete set of rules (*qanun-i falah*), as Azad put it. They were convinced of the rightness of the Islamic ideals that offered a complete way of life for an organized community living out Allah's plan under the kind of government which had prevailed in the days of the Prophet. They were equally convinced of the compatibility of the Islamic principles with reason or science. This was Mohamed Ali's central argument in 'The Future of Islam', and of Azad's essays published in the first three issues of *Al-Hilal*. Alone among his contemporaries, Azad conceived for Islam a vital socio-political role that went against the apparently triumphant secularizing tendencies of the age, and conveyed, first to his associates and pupils and then to Indian society, the large the vibrant and comprehensive Islamic vision that had first animated his being in youth. In April 1913, he wrote in *Al-Hilal*:

Islam does not commend narrow-mindedness and racial and religious prejudice. It does not make the recognition of merit and virtue, of human benevolence, mercy and love dependent upon and subject to distinctions of religion and race. It teaches us to respect every man who is good, whatever be his religion, to let ourselves be drawn towards merits and virtues, whatever the religion or the race of the person who possesses them. . . . But above and beyond this law of universal goodwill, and I do not hesitate to own it even in this age of hypothetical impartiality, is the *jehad* of helping the cause of justice, worshiping Allah and establishing right-mindedness and justice. Islam teaches us that the purpose of the creation of man is that he should represent God on earth, keep burning the torch of truth and light.[8]

Azad's rationalism was not merely an element in his modernist, intellectual explorations, but an integral part of his traditional scholastic training. Mohamed Ali was a vigorous proponent of neo-intellectual modernism, deriving his ideas from Saiyid Ahmad in his appeal for cultivating scientific disciplines and rejecting *taqlid*. 'I have as much right to interpret God's message as any other man', he declared. Formal renunciation of a 'mildewed scholasticism' will set Islam 'right with itself'.[9] Azad echoed similar views. 'The shopkeepers of religion have given the name of religion to ignorance and *taqlid*, to prejudice and indulgence', he wrote in *Al-Hilal*. Years later, he commented:

The greatest hindrance to human intellectual progress is unquestioning acceptance of traditional beliefs . . . the first thorn of doubt which pricked my heart was against his very *taqlid*. . . . If the foundation of belief should be knowledge, why on *taqlid* and inheritance.[10]

The rationalist strain enabled Azad and Mohamed Ali to reconcile their passionate attachment to pan-Islamism with the ideological underpinnings of Indian nationalism. They viewed pan-Islamism and nationalism as compatible ideologies; so they sought to establish that their community's anguish over Turkey's future deepened their involvement in the anti-colonial struggle and brought them closer to the Congress. Azad, more than Mohamed Ali, invoked the Koran and *Hadith* to strengthen the case for non-cooperation against the British. Following closely the views of Abduh who, in his answer to inquiries from India, had endorsed inter-religious cooperation, Azad reiterated, with all the religious fervour at his command, that Muslims should be up in front, fighting for freedom. Mohamed Ali offered the same advice: Muslims must fight for swaraj with their non-Muslims brethren, for only in this way would it be possible to achieve the khilafat aim. 'If you want to release the khilafat from slavery', he stated, 'there is only one course for you and that is that you should side with the Hindus and first secure the freedom of your own country. You cannot save Islam from danger so long as you do not rule your own country.' This conviction, shared by many Muslims, enabled them to easily swing back and forth between pan-Islamic and local nationalist appeals, depending upon which was a more appropriate anti-imperialist weapon.

Mohamed Ali's first editorial pleaded for Hindu-Muslim friendship. He believed that, 'if the Muslims or the Hindus attempt to achieve success in opposition to or even without the co-operation of one another, they will not only fail, but fail ignominiously'.[11] And the *Comrade* intended to prepare Muslims to 'contribute' to territorial patriotism without compromising on their extra-territorial sympathies which is the quintessence of Islam'.[12] His misgivings about the Congress were removed in Chhindwara when he reflected on the role of Tilak,[13] and came into contact with Gandhi at Aligarh in 1915.[14] He told Saifuddin Kitchlew: 'It is Gandhi, Gandhi, Gandhi, that has got to be dinned into the people's ear, because he means Hindu-Muslim unity, non-co-operation, *swadharma* and *swaraja*, while the rest are after petty communal or local bodies, most of them tinged with personal ambitions.'[15]

Mohamed Ali's emotional disposition in religious matters had surely much to do with the nature and with the promptness of his response to events in Turkey. In this context there is no reason at all to doubt the sincerity of his indignation, aroused by the machinations of some European Powers, and his genuinely-felt emotional concern for the safety of the holy places. The opinion, presented by Francis Robinson and others, that it was all feigned, that he was simply playing the pan-Islamist, cannot be seriously defended. Calculation comes in, not in pretending an emotion which is not there, but in deciding how much of genuinely-felt emotion to release publicly; how far to let oneself go. Similarly, it is difficult to sustain the charge, rendered plausible by Mohamed Ali's complicated financial situation, that he lived off the khilafat funds.

Mohamed Ali's pan-Islamism was both instinctive and the outcome of much thought and deliberation. Central to his belief was the view, based on the concept of *umma*, that 'the basis of Islamic sympathy is not a common domicile or common parentage, but a common outlook on life and common culture', and that 'the embodiment of that culture is the khilafat'. Inspired by Azad's description of a 'political centre' (*siyasi markaz*), Mohamed Ali argued that the 'personal centre' of Islam was the khalifa and the 'local centre' was the 'Island of Arabia', the *Jazirat al-Arab*.

It was not ceremonial piety that motivated Mohamed Ali and other khilafatists to rally under the khilafat banner. The khalifa, according to the classical theorists, defended the faith, and wielded the authority to ensure that Muslims follow the *Shariat*. For this reason, the khilafat was 'the most essential institution of the Muslim community'; hence its defence a sacred duty.[16] Mohamed Ali gave the need for preserving in the institution a utilitarian quality when he told a London audience:

Well, so long as there are your Bryces and your 'Big sticks', we, too, must have some sort of stick for the defence of our faith, and to jeopardize at least the dominance of those that jeopardize the freedom of our conscience. That, and that alone is the *rationale* of our main claim that the khilafat should be preserved with adequate temporal power.[17]

He explained that Muslims were not concerned with political dominance, because the 'spiritual force of Islam' did not depend on political supremacy. What concerned them most was the erosion of Islam's temporal power to the extent that it might become 'liable to suffer, without adequate power to prevent, the curtailment of its spiritual influence through the pressures of the temporal power of rival creeds'.[18]

The defence of the khalifa and holy places was seen as the method of assuring that the *Ummat-i-Islamia* had the freedom to conform to its religious precepts. The khilafatists envisioned a renascent Islamic world, in which all Muslim peoples were united—'the supernatural sangathan of Muslims in five continents'[19]—built around the khalifa and supporting each other through that institution. The new khalifa, judged from the views expressed by Mohamed Ali at the Mecca Conference in 1928, would be based on the pattern of *khilafat-i rashida*. It would be an elective institution rather than a dynastic one, and the holder of the office would be chosen by virtue of his godliness, and his devotion to Islam. All the Muslims of the world would have a part in the direction of the government, all responsible for its welfare. Mohamed Ali was not one to recognize the dramatic changes in the 'Islamic world', the emergence of nationalism as a force, and the rejection of pan-Islamism in most countries, including Turkey. He continued to picture a new Muslim world—unified by common religious symbols and experiences—which would present a single force to whatever power attempted to jeopardize the rights of any Muslim nation.

II

So long as Islam occupied centrality in the concerns of Azad and Mohamed Ali and religious symbols retained their primacy in mass mobilization campaigns, Azad and Mohamed Ali spoke from a common platform, acted in unison, and voiced shared concerns. But once Gandhi called off civil disobedience and the Turks burst the khilafat bubble, they began to see the world around them differently.

It is, at first, hard to understand why this was so, for their differences were not so fundamental as they are sometimes portrayed in historical accounts. Admittedly, their experiences in public life were not always the same, especially in the aftermath of the non-cooperation movement. Yet, they were both engaged in a common endeavour: to define the position and status of their community in a free, composite, and plural society. In addition, they continued to play a part in Congress affairs and were engaged in resolving the communal impasse, though sometimes from a different standpoint. Mohamed Ali's views were, for example, often at odds with the Congress, but his enthusiasm for that organization was not dampened until the publication of the Nehru report in August 1928. Likewise, though engaged in verbal feuds with Gandhi and Jawaharlal Nehru, his loyalty to them never slackened. He and the younger Nehru were tied to each other by 'a bond of affection and mutual appreciation . . .'.[20] About the Mahatma, he announced in 1925 that he had identical views 'with regard to the way in which India can win her freedom'. 'I am proud to regard (him) as my chief', he had declared.[21]

Azad shared the same sense of loyalty, though it was much less pronounced in his public utterances. In the post-khilafat era, he was inspired by Gandhi, Nehru and Das, rather than by Afghani and Abduh. His writings and speeches echoed his life-long passion and yearning for India's political liberation, unity, and inter-religious understanding. At Ramgarh, the Maulana said he was prepared to accept Independence whenever available whether during war or peace; his sole object was the attainment of real Independence of Hindustan.

Why, then, the drift, or the 'parting of ways'? Was it because Azad and Mohamed Ali competed with each other to wrest the community's leadership? Were they different in temperament and style? Or, was their divide symptomatic of the ideological polarization during the post-khilafat days? There are no simple answers, though the genesis of their rift can be traced to the collapse of the khilafat and non-cooperation campaigns.

For the men of religion, the demise of the khilafat could only be explained within the legal categories of orthodox Islam. Azad set out to do so: in Islam, he pointed out, spiritual leadership was the due of God and his Prophet alone. So obedience to the khilafat was binding on all Muslims, though not in the same degree as submission to God and his Prophet. In his articles to the *Zamindar*, published in the spring of 1924, Azad opined that by abolishing the khilafat of the Ottoman dynasty, the Turkish government had merely rectified the unsatisfactory division of spiritual and temporal powers which had existed since 1922. By down-playing the importance of Turkey's action, he tried to redirect the energies of the khilafat committees into work for education, social reform and the economic progress of India's Muslims.[22]

Though traumatized by the collapse of the khilafat, there was no break in the essential continuity of Azad's political ideology: he merely adapted himself well to the changed political climate. The shift, if any, was in his framework of analysis. The Koran, the *Hadith* and the traditions of Islam had moulded his political views during the *Al-Hilal* years. Not so afterwards. He now learned to 'eliminate irrelevant religious considerations when thinking of or discussing purely political issues', and his arguments were no longer couched in theological terms but based on his understanding of social realities, and the dynamics of and his commitment to a secular polity. 'It is one of the greatest frauds on the people to suggest', he reaffirmed after Independence, 'that religious affinity can unite areas which are geographically, economically, linguistically and culturally different.' With an insight rare for those from his background, Azad argued: 'The problems of the country were economic, not communal. The differences related to classes, not to communities.'[23]

III

Azad plotted a course strewn with obstacles and difficulties. Seeking refuge in platitudinous statements was one thing, but coping with the ideological assault of the communalists was an hazardous exercise. And yet his Ramgarh speech—perhaps the most eloquent exposition of Indian nationalism ever made from a Congress platform—reaffirmed his secular vision and rebutted the two-nation theory. It could well have served as a political manifesto for those Congress Muslims who were, after Ansari's death in May 1936, in search of a leader and a programme to steer their ship through the rough currents of communalism.

In April 1940, Azad placed proposals for overcoming the constitutional deadlock and, at the same time, challenged the League's claim to be the sole representative of the Muslims. The conference resolution included a declaration beginning: 'India, with its geographical and political boundaries, is an indivisible whole and as such it is the common homeland of all citizens, irrespective of race or religion, who are joint owners of its resources'.[24]

As the Congress president, a position he had already occupied in 1923, Azad sought to narrow down the ever-increasing gulf separating the Congress and the League. He also conducted negotiations with Stafford Cripps and the viceroy, Wavell, and again, after the War, with the cabinet mission. It was a role he enjoyed most. Cripps and Wavell thought well of him and counted on his support for their plans and proposals. The former thanked Azad for his help and friendship and the 'really marvellous way in which you stuck to your guns'. He was 'absolutely convinced' that, but for the Maulana, 'no arrangement would have been come to'.[25] Wavell found Azad 'very moderate and friendly'. He added: 'I have a great respect for him, and if all these politicians were of the same quality matters would be comparatively easy'.[26] Azad reciprocated these sentiments. Complimenting Cripps for his 'courtesy, tact and resourcefulness', he referred to his own part in the negotiations. 'I may tell you', he wrote on 22 July 1946:

that my attitude was throughout governed by two considerations. I regard the advent of the Labour Party to power an event of historic importance. For the first time in history, there is the prospect of a peaceful transition to a Socialist order. I also feel that the Labour Government have on the whole been following a policy of democracy and freedom, and working for peace and stability in the modern world. I therefore felt it my duty to do everything possible to help it towards a peaceful settlement of the Indian problem.[27]

On the other hand, sections of the Congress leadership doubted Azad's negotiating skills; in fact, Nehru's election as Congress president in 1946 is said to have been an expression of lack of confidence in Azad's ability to follow the dictates of the Congress Working Committee.[28] The judgement is unfair. Azad was, as Alan Campbell-Johnson recorded on

21 December 1947, just a 'titular head of the movement during the vital negotiations with both the Cripps and the Cabinet Missions'.[29] Others like Gandhi and Nehru, backed by Patel, Rajagopalachari and Rajendra Prasad, called the shots, though Azad could bring round the AICC and the CWC to his point of view on a few issues, including the formation of a coalition government composed of both Congress and the League.[30] But, in general, Azad was expected to perform a subservient role. His own initiatives were not welcomed. On occasions, they were thwarted.[31]

In a sense, Azad's position was similar to that of his Congress Muslim comrades who held positions of authority but were rarely allowed to influence major policy decisions. This was so in 1930 when Gandhi ignored the wishes of Ansari and his Nationalist Muslim Party in launching the civil disobedience movement. Again, the Congress in general, and Nehru in particular, ignored the views of Azad on the formation of a Congress-League coalition ministry in UP. On reflection, Azad concluded that 'if the League's offer of co-operation had been accepted the Muslim League party would for all practical purposes merge with the Congress, Jawaharlal's action gave the League in UP a new lease of life'.[32] Azad may not have been right in his assessment, but he, at least implicity, gave vent to the feeling that the upper echelon of the Congress leadership paid no heed to the 'Nationalist Muslim' perspective.

Dealing with the Muslim League posed an added problem: the stout refusal of its diehards to recognize the position and status of the Congress Muslims. The Aligarh students and teachers, who had once idolized the Maulana when their pan-Islamic passions were heightened, turned against Azad. The Barelwi ulama, averse to the Jamiyat al-ulama-Congress alliance, were his sworn critics. And Jinnah, of course, refused to meet him and showed no sympathy for his viewpoint. 'Cannot you realize', he told Azad in July 1940, 'you are making a Muslim show-boy Congress president to give it colour that is national.'[33] In this way, recorded Campbell-Johnson:

Maulana Azad, a great scholar and a man of retiring disposition, has during the past ten years been a central figure of controversy. He embodied in his position and person perhaps the most important symbol of the Congress aspiration to be a nationalist as against a communal party. His status was thus the focal point of Gandhi's clash with Jinnah, who always maintained that politically no one but a member of the Muslim League could represent Muslim interests.[34]

Jinnah displayed lack of realism in insisting that the League solely represented the Muslim community. How could it be in the light of the poor performance of his party in the 1937 elections? Besides, as Wavell pointed out candidly, 'after all, there is a Congress Ministry in the Province (Bombay) with the greatest proportion of Muslims, and 1 million votes were cast *against the Muslim League at the recent election as compared with about 6 million for the League*'[35] (italics mine). Jinnah was on an equally weak turf in demanding the exclusion of the Congress Muslims from the interim government. They may not have been, in Nehru's description, the 'soul of the Congress', but they had occupied an important enough position in the country's liberation struggle. They may not have always played a pivotal role, but they remained a priceless asset to the Congress movement. Their presence vindicated the Congress stand of representing the Indian nation rather than a segment of it. How could the Congress, then, forsake its close allies for the illusory prospect of an accord with the League? How could Gandhi and Nehru, in particular, sacrifice personal friends and political expediency? 'It has now become clear', wrote the viceroy on 1 October 1946, 'that Congress are unwilling to give way on the Nationalist Muslim issue.'[36] The problem, he told Pethick-Lawrence, 'is an extraordinary intractable one'.[37] This was so because of Jinnah's obstinacy, and his refusal to give way.

Sensing the mood in the Congress circles, Cripps and Wavell urged Jinnah to give way on the question, and, in exchange, secure his other points.[38] Wavell went to the extent of explaining that the Congress would not, in fact, appoint a 'Nationalist' Muslim in the end, if Jinnah conceded their right to do so. The Congress had not given any such assurance.[39]

Azad and his Muslim comrades may have been comforted by the Congress stand, but not by the vicious communal atmosphere that gripped the country. The League campaign gathered momentum day after day, and the country was, consequently, caught up in a bitter and violent confrontation. With their limited constituency, which had steadily shrunk over the years, Azad and his followers could do little to influence the course of events. The inexorable march towards the vivisection of the Indian nation could neither be halted by an individual or a group. Nor could the communal tide be stemmed by the Mahatma or the Maulana. Besides, once the Congress agreed to the Partition Plan, the tide turned against the Congress Muslims. Ghaffar Khan protested loudly and passionately; others did so quietly. Azad maintained his studious silence and aristocratic poise at the Congress Working Committee meeting on 2 June 1947, when the Mountbatten plan for the Partition was ratified. He could do little at the time to prevent this 'abject surrender', particularly after Gandhi and Nehru dithered in the face of the communal onslaught.[40] Dispirited, defeated and detached from the humdrum of political happenings, Campbell-Johnson recorded the details of a meeting on 16 September 1947. 'Throughout this long meeting, Maulana Azad, the Moslem elder statesman in the Congress, sat silent and impassive, as he always does, looking, with his pointed beard, just like Cardinal Richelieu.'[41]

The dawn of freedom had arrived. But 'the sad face of Maulana Azad, to whom the occasion was something of a tragedy, sticking out from the sea of happy faces like a gaunt and ravaged rock'.[42] Azad could well have recalled his own passage from *Ghubar-i Khatir* which summed up the story of his life.

In religion, in literature, in politics, in everyday thought, wherever I have to go, I have to go alone. On no path can I go with the caravans of the day. . . . Whichever way I walk, I get so far ahead of the (caravan) that when I turn to look back, I see nothing, but the dust of the way, and even that is the dust raised by the speed of my own passage.

NOTES

1. Kenneth Cragg, *Counsels in Contemporary Islam*, Edinburgh, 1965, pp. 132-3, and Ian Henderson Douglas, *Abul Kalam Azad: An Intellectual and Religious Biography*, eds. Gail Minault and Christian W. Troll, New Delhi, 1998, p. 29; Abdur Razzaq Malihabadi, *Zikr-i Azad*, Calcutta, 1965, pp. 132-3. See the collection of articles in Rasheeduddin Khan (ed.), *Abul Kalam Azad: Ek Hamageer Shaksiat*, New Delhi, 1989.
2. Cragg, *Counsels*, p. 134.
3. Mujeeb, *The Indian Muslims*, p. 302.
4. For example, the *fatwa* on the boycott of government-aided educational institutions. *Khilafat*, 1 Nov. 1920.
5. Douglas, *Abul Kalam Azad*, p. 180.
6. Ibid.
7. For Azad's early political life, Rajat K. Ray, 'Revolutionaries, Pan-Islamists and Bolsheviks: Maulana Abul Kalam Azad and Political Underworld in Calcutta, 1905-1925', Hasan (ed.), *Communal and Pan-Islamic Trends in Colonial India*, pp. 101-24.
8. *Al-Hilal*, 23 Oct. 1912.
9. Mohamed Ali, *My Life*, pp. 163-4.
10. Douglas, *Abul Kalam Azad*, p. 76.
11. *Comrade* (Calcutta), 14 Jan. 1911.
12. Mohamed Ali, *My Life*, p. 46.
13. To Tilak, 12 Nov. 1916, *Mohamed Ali in Indian Politics*, Vol.1, p. 292.
14. Hasan, *Mohamed Ali: Ideology and Politics*, pp. 28-9.

15. Iqbal, *Life and Times of Mohamed Ali*, p. 308.
16. 'India's Message to France', Iqbal (ed.), *Writings and Speeches*, p. 158; *Comrade*, 13 May 1913.
17. 'A People's Right to Live', ibid., p. 171.
18. Mohamed Ali to Chelmsford, 24 Apr. 1919, MAP.
19. Mohamed Ali observed: 'Islam united Muslims by offering a set of common ideals and offered the only rational basis for unity and co-operation among its followers. The sympathies of a Muslim are co-extensive with his religion because they have been bred into him by the inspiring spirit of his creed.' *Comrade*, 12 Apr. 1913.
20. Nehru, *An Autobiography*, p. 117.
21. *Comrade*, 16 Oct. 1925; Afzal Iqbal (ed.), *Select Speeches*, pp. 331-2, 337.
22. Douglas, *Abul Kalam Azad*, p. 223.
23. Abul Kalam Azad, *India Wins Freedom: the complete version*, New Delhi, 1988, p. 248.
24. Nicholas Mansergh (ed.), *The Transfer of Power* (hereafter *TP*), 1942-7 (London: His Majesty's Stationery Office), Vol. 1, p. 293. For an account of the Conference, Humayun Kabir, *Muslim Politics, 1906-42*, Calcutta, 1944.
25. *TP*, Vol. 8, p. 103.
26. Wavell to J. Colville, 8/9 July 1946, and Note by Wavell, 19 Aug. 1946, ibid., p. 23; Datta, *Maulana Azad*, p. 171.
27. To S. Cripps, 22 July 1946, ibid., Vol. 8, pp. 102-3.
28. Sarvepalli Gopal, *Jawaharlal Nehru: A Biography 1889-1947*, Vol. 1, New Delhi, 1975, p. 326.
29. Alan Campbell-Johnson, *Mission with Mountbatten*, London, 1951, p. 254.
30. To Wavell, 9 July 1946, *TP*, Vol. 8, p. 24.
31. On differences between the Mahatma and the Maulana, first over the Quit India movement, and later over the conduct of the negotiations with the cabinet missions, see Datta, *Maulana Azad*, pp. 168, 174, 175, 176. For Gandhi's unfavourable response to Azad's proposal for alleviating Muslim fears, see Jenkins to Abell, 28 Aug. 1945, reporting on an intercepted letter from Gandhi to Azad, *TP*, Vol. 6, p. 76. Azad's own version of his differences with Nehru is quite revealing. For a refutation of the Maulana's thesis, see Gopal, *Jawaharlal Nehru*, Vol. 1, pp. 227-9, and S.R. Mehrotra, 'Nehru and the Partition of India, 1935-47', in Philips and Wainwright (eds.), *The Partition of India*, pp. 178-9.
32. *India Wins Freedom*, p. 170.
33. Datta, *Maulana Azad*, pp. 164,171; Douglas, *Abul Kalam Azad*, p. 295.
34. Campbell Johnson, *Mission with Mountbatten*, p. 254.
35. Wavell to A. Clow (Bombay), 7 Oct. 1946, TP, Vol. 8, p. 675.
36. To Pethick-Lawrence, 1 Oct. 1946, ibid., p. 634.
37. To Pethick-Lawrence, 1 Oct. 1946, ibid., p. 636.

38. Wavell to Abell, 1 Oct. 1946, ibid., p. 631.
39. Wavell to Pethick-Lawrence, 29 Sept. 1946, ibid., p. 625.
40. Pethick-Lawrence to Cripps, 30 Sept. 1939, ibid., p. 629.
41. Campbell-Johnson, *Mission with Mountbatten*, p. 194.
42. Douglas, *Abul Kalam Azad*, pp. 232-3 and 238.

8

'Congress Muslims' and Indian Nationalism, Dilemma and Decline
c. 1928-1934

In the aftermath of the Nehru report controversy, the Congress had to reckon with Jinnah's 'Fourteen Points'. Gandhi tried to soothe suspicions with the assurance that swaraj did not mean Hindu raj, and engaged with him in February and August 1929 to explore possible avenues to peace. But Lajpat Rai, Malaviya, Jayakar, B.S. Moonje, working president of the Hindu Mahasabha (1927-35), and N.C. Kelkar, urged him not to reach a solution outside the terms of the Nehru report.[1] Lajpat Rai refused to accept any modification,[2] while Jayakar pressured Gandhi not to yield on the ground that the government, as in 1919, would deliberately make any concessions part of a constitution.[3] Gandhi wrote to Motilal Nehru in anguish: 'How that can be done [resolving the communal deadlock] or whether it should be done, you know best. My mind is in a whirl in this matter. The atmosphere is too foggy for me to see clearly.'[4]

With the failure of the Gandhi-Jinnah talks and the crusade against the Nehru report gathering momentum, the Lahore Congress let the report lapse, and decided not to accept any solution of the communal problem without the concurrence of the minorities.[5] Gandhi hoped the declaration of complete independence and the launching of civil disobedience would enable leaders of various shades of opinion to draw their followers into the anti-colonial struggle. He wrote in *Navajivan*: 'If we have true freedom we will shed communal fear. Hindus and Muslims will cease to fear one another.'[6]

But soothing Muslim feelings was not enough. The issue at stake was to arrest their growing alienation from the Congress. The process, having begun soon after the khilafat movement came to a halt, was attributed to a

wide range of factors, including the failure of the Congress to curb assertive and militant expressions of Hindu nationalism. Such had been the
burden of Abdur Rahim's speech at the 1925 Muslim League session. He
argued that the Congress would jettison Muslim interests in any future
scheme of swaraj, and that their 'salvation' lay in either forging an alliance
with the government or in pursuing independent political action.[7] Such
views, echoed both in Bengal and Punjab, struck a favourable chord in
certain Muslim circles and led to, here and in other provinces of British
India, a steady decline in Muslim participation at annual Congress sessions and in national, provincial, and district committees.

Table 8.1 indicates the attendance of Muslim delegates at Congress
sessions from 1918 to 1923. Clearly, the number of Muslims gradually
dwindled from a few hundred to less than a score. Muslim representation
in the AICC was impressive, showing an increase from 11.1 per cent in
1919 to 24.5 per cent in 1923 (Table 8.2). In 1922-3, 84 of the 338 AICC
members were Muslims. By 1928, however, their number was reduced to 54
out of 332.[8] Provincial and district committees also had very few Muslim
members. In UP, only 7 Muslims served on various district committees:
1 each in Gonda, Allahabad, Jhansi, Moradabad, Faizabad, Azamgarh, and
2 in Bara Banki.[9]

In 1922-3, Motilal Nehru built his support among an influential group of
Lucknow and Allahabad based professional men: T.A.K. Sherwani, Rafi
Ahmed Kidwai, Khaliquzzaman and M.H. Kidwai.[10] In Bengal, C.R. Das
lured the khilafatists into supporting the Swaraj party by offering a set of
extravagant concessions. In consequence, his party swept the November
1923 polls, capturing an overall majority of seats, including half the
Muslim seats. Muslim backing was strongest in the eastern division
of Chittagong and the northern division of Rajshahi, the storm centres of
the khilafat movement in Bengal. Likewise, the swarajists won 10 of the

Table 8.1: Attendance of Muslim delegates at the Congress sessions, 1918-23

Year	Total no. of delegates	No. of Muslim delegates
1918	3,975	205
1919	6,717	314
1920	13,532	1,050
1921	4,201	521
1922	NA	NA
1923	1,550	111

Table 8.2: Composition of AICC, 1919-23

Religion	1919 (161 Members)	1920 (163 Members)	1921	1922 (338 Members)	1923
Hindus	139	133	124	242	248
Muslims	18	21	33	84	83
Sikhs	-	2	2	9	8
Parsees	3	4	2	-	-
Christians	1	2	2	3	3

Source: Gopal Krishna, 'The Indian National Congress, 1918-1923', D. Phil. thesis, Oxford, 1960, p. 747.

15 Muslim seats in the Calcutta Corporation elections. The Muslim vote was strongest in the city's central mercantile wards with its up-country Urdu-speaking merchants, property owners and artisans who had formed the backbone of the khilafat movement.[11]

This support was eroded once the Bengal Congress repudiated the Das pact. There were 15 Muslim swarajists in 1923; there were none in 1926. The *Mussalman* rejected the Swaraj party 'as the party which turned out to be inimically disposed towards the Mussalmans,'[12] while Husayn Suhrawardy and Abdul Karim, leading negotiators of the Das pact, led their followers in Calcutta deeper into the labyrinth of distinctly communal politics.[13] The picture was not very different in UP.[14] As against 11 Muslims nominated and 4 elected in 1923, 6 were renominated in 1926 and only 1 returned. Of the 8 swarajist Muslims returned in 1923 to the Central Assembly, only 3 were elected in 1926. Irked by Motilal Nehru's attitude towards reforms in the N.W.F.P., Saiyid Murtaza, a swarajist from Madras, accused him of sacrificing the Frontier Muslims in order to woo Lajpat Rai on the eve of the 1926 elections.[16] Muhammad Shafee Daoodi's indictment was equally harsh: 'Temporary success in your political endeavours has got greater value for you than the more enduring rapprochement of the two great communities of India.' He charged that the Congress, having gradually drifted towards the Mahasabha since 1923, had reduced itself to being its tool.[17] Both Murtaza and Daoodi quit the Swaraj party in 1926. The feeling of insecurity was so widespread that some Muslims, who had in the recent past contributed to Congress's popularity, were now arrayed among its enemies.[18]

Yet, political activity among Muslims was sporadic and fragmented. Conflicting regional, local and class interests—a consequence of the uneven development of the Muslim communities—deepened conflicts and divisions only to expose the hollowness of the leader's claim to represent all Muslims. This was reflected in the formal split between the Jinnah and the Shafi factions in the Muslim League. Any new party, whether cobbled together by the khilafatists or the Leaguers, promised to be a rickety, splintered structure that could collapse at any moment. Such was the fate of the All-Parties Muslim Conference after 1932. The organizers, like the Dutch army, were all generals but no soldiers. Members of the land-owning class, none of them was prepared to spreadhead the movement or to follow the other.[18]

Similarly, Jinnah's brave attempts to infuse some life into the Muslim League were poorly rewarded; its total membership rose from a mere 1,093 in 1922 to 1,330 in 1927.[19] 'We are disgusted', wrote the *Mussalman*, 'with the Muslim League on account of its culpable inactivity. . . . The provincial Leagues have imbibed the inactivity and the character of the parent body.'[20]

Within the Congress ranks were, however, a number of groups, who were described as 'Nationalist Muslims'. Most had been associated with the party from the days of the Rowlatt satyagraha, though the distinction between them and their detractors—the Ali brothers, Muhammad Shafi and the other organizers of the All-Parties Muslim Conference—gained currency in the mid-1920s. 'They are men', said Ansari, the principal spokesman of the Congress Muslim, 'to whom the freedom of the country from alien rule comes merely as a bad second to communal privileges.'[21]

Though the label 'Nationalist Muslim' communicates the ideology and politics of those wedded to Indian nationalist aspirations, its exclusive application to Muslims, as discussed in the introduction to this book, conjures up the false image of a community largely communally-oriented with only a handful integrated with the dominant nationalist trend. Such a label also does not account for the subtle but extremely important differences between a professed nationalist and a so-called communalist. It is thus not easy to place Mohamed Ali in this supposed dichotomous framework. Though a critic of the Congress and the Nehru report, he remained committed to swaraj. Ansari conceded that, in spite of being led into the 'camp of national reaction', the Ali brothers had not 'surrendered their loyalty to the fundamental principle of Indian politics, freedom from foreign domination'.[22]

How, then, does one describe the many Muslim groups connected with the Congress movement at various levels? It is convenient, for descriptive purposes, to identify them as Congress Muslims, though the term does not quite embrace the range of their activities in the social and education spheres. And, yet, it indicates the overall thrust of their political concerns in relation to the community, the region and the nation at large. Some like Azad and Husain Ahmad Madani, head of the Dar al-ulum at Deoband, interpreted Islam as a religion of freedom and equality, of justice, and of cooperation with and respect for all mankind.[23] Thus Madani defended full and individual Muslim participation in a struggle for India's freedom by advancing a theory of territorial nationhood for India rather than by appealing to concepts of safeguards and community confederation. He expressed his ideas in a public controversy with Iqbal shortly before the latter's death in 1938.[24]

For those trained and tutored at the Aligarh College or the institutions in Allahabad, Patna and Calcutta, the Congress expressed the popular yearning for political freedom and independence. 'If I were asked why I have such an abiding faith in Indian nationalism,' stated the Bihar lawyer-politician Ali Imam, 'my answer is that without that India's freedom is an impossibility.'[25] Such men accepted the Congress as a viable vehicle for social change rather than the communal organizations. By joining it in large numbers, observed Maulvi Mujibur Rahman at the Bakarganj District Muslim Conference in May 1931, the Bengali Muslims would take a greater part in the freedom struggle.[26] Khan Abdul Ghaffar Khan announced at a public meeting in December 1931 that the Congress party alone would free the country, feed the hungry, and clothe the naked.[27] The *Jirgah* of India, he reaffirmed, was called Congress—a common *Jirgah* of all the communities of India. Justifying his alliance with Congress he said: 'In order to save himself from the enemies did not the Holy Prophet make alliance with the Jews and the Politheists [*sic*]?'[28] His audience beamed approvingly.

Such individuals and groups spanned several provinces of British India. The Khudai Khidmatgars headed a nationalist and socially progressive movement in the frontier province. Within two years of its creation they were 2,00,000 strong.[29] Quotations from the Koran against slavery served as rallying points for nationalist enthusiasm, and the struggle to liberate the country from foreign rule became the rallying cry. 'No section of India', observed W.C. Smith, the historian of Indian Islam, 'has been more thoroughly nationalist.'[30] During civil disobedience in 1930-1 Khudai Khidmatgar activism was linked with the Congress—the connection was strengthened in August 1931 when the Afghan *Jirgah* merged with the provincial Congress committee. The local *Jirgahs* became the local Congress committees, while 'Red Shirt' volunteers merged with the Congress bodies at various levels. The whole movement was conducted in accordance with the Congress constitution, and the flag used was the Congress flag. The 'Frontier Gandhi' explained:

People complain against me for having joined the Congress by selling my nation. The Congress is a national and not a Hindu body. It is a jirga composed of Hindus, Jews, Sikhs, Parsis, and Muslims. The Congress as a body is working against the British. The British nation is the enemy of the Congress and of the Pathans. I have therefore joined it and made common cause with the Congress to get rid of the British.[31]

The intensity of civil disobedience was reflected in the number of prosecutions and convictions. Until September 1932, the figure was 5,557 in a total population of 25 lakhs. In neighbouring Punjab, the number was 1,620, though the population was more than eight times that of the N.W.F.P.[32] Convictions were also higher than the Bombay presidency (see Table 8.3). Ghaffar Khan's motto: 'We are Pakhtuns but until we attain freedom we do not deserve to be called Pakhtuns'[33] remained the rallying slogan of his followers.

The Majlis-i Ahrar-i Islam, organized in 1929 by a group of Muslims in Punjab, had its base amongst the well-to-do peasantry and the lower-middle classes. The Ahrars combined economic grievances and religious passions to formulate their militant policies,[34] thus expressing something of the old khilafat movement tradition: an ardent and explicit enthusiasm for freedom. And like the Khudai Khidmatgars, the Ahraris steadily and fervently went to jail in large numbers.[35] In Delhi, they combined with the Jamiyat al-ulama activists to organize processions, public meetings, and picket liquor shops. Clashes with the police on 11-13 March 1932 led to the arrest of Azad and Maulvi Kifayatullah and twenty-five other Muslims. Reminiscent of scenes during the Rowlatt satyagraha was a mammoth meeting at the Fatehpuri Masjid, where 4,500-5,000 Muslims endorsed Gandhi's civil disobedience movement.[36]

Table 8.3: Convictions in Bombay and the N.W.F.P.

	Conviction in January-February 1932	Convictions in March-September 1932	Total
Bombay	5,165	6,311	11,476
N.W.F.P.	4,318	1,239	5,557

Source: Home Poll. File No. 5/72, 1932, NAI.

The Ahrar party, also active in Kashmir, agitated against the Dogra ruler, maharaja Hari Singh, seeking redressal of the grievances of the Muslim subjects.[37] These were set out in the memorial submitted to the maharaja on 19 October 1931,[38] and taken note of by B.J. Glancy, chairman of a commission to enquire into the demands of the memorialists.[39] Led by Mazhar Ali, Habibur Rahman of Ludhiana, Abdur Rahman Ghazi, and Ataullah Shah Bukhari, the Ahrars sent *jathas* of red-uniformed *razakaars* (volunteers) from parts of Punjab, especially Sialkot, to Kashmir to bear pressure on the maharaja to meet their demands.[40] Large-scale rioting in Jammu on 2 November 1931, and violent clashes at Mirpur between the *jathas* and state forces, followed. British troops were deployed to quell the disturbances.

The spurt in political activity profoundly influenced Kashmir's future history. With the Ahrar agitation petering out, the Jammu and Kashmir Muslim Conference, founded in 1932, wrested the political initiative. The conference, stated its founder Shaikh Muhammad Abdullah, though Muslim in name, was 'in spirit national and concerned with the welfare of all communities.'[41] He declared in 1931 and, again, in 1935, that the country's progress depended on harmonious communal relations,[42] and that he fought for the country's emancipation. 'Let us all rise above petty communal bickerings and work jointly for the welfare of the masses,' he said.[43] In the years to come, the Muslim Conference formulated a radical 'New Kashmir' plan, and spurned the rising tide of Muslim nationalism.

In Bombay, Saiyid Abdullah Brelvi, editor of the *Bombay Chronicle*, launched the Congress Muslim Party on 8 July 1929 to induce Muslims to join the Congress.[44] His chief support lay among the urban-based politicians, such as Yusuf Meharally, editor of the English weekly *Vanguard*, Abbas Tyabji, a lawyer with a long-standing association with the Congress movement, and M.C. Chagla, also a lawyer who came to the forefront as a vociferous champion of the Nehru report. Gandhi blessed the party with the message: 'If it is fully supported and does not go to sleep, it may prove a tower of strength to the Congress and an instrument of real service to India generally and to Mussalmans in particular.'[45]

The Congress Muslim Party, though assailed by Shaukat Ali and his followers among the Urdu-speaking Muslims, garnered a fair measure of support for civil disobedience: thus, Brelvi, backed by several Muslim mercantile associations, led a mile-long procession on 2 June 1930 and chaired a meeting of about 10,000, including Hindus.[46] 'Conspicuous amongst organizers of procession and speakers at meeting', noted a government report, 'were certain Maulanas and Muslim propagandists from other provinces. To this extent, [the] procession must be regarded as success of Congress propaganda and it must be admitted that during the last *fortnight many Muhammadans have been gathered into the Congress fold*'[47] (italics mine). This is not to deny that, compared to 1920-1, Muslim enthusiasm in Bombay and elsewhere was much less. But, then, the religious passion stirred by the khilafat question was out of the extraordinary: no such issue in the early 1930s evinced the same degree of fervour.

II

The All-India Nationalist Muslim Party was formed on 27-8 July 1929. This was a sequel to the AICC meeting at Allahabad where delegates, reflecting on the political struggle being weakened by inter-communal conflicts and the attempts being made in to wean Muslims away from political activities, resolved to form themselves into a group.[48] They attributed the 'disruption' among politically-minded Muslims and their consequent apathy to a 'confused appreciation of the political obligations implicit in the fact of the community being a part of the Indian nation. Muslim political activity is now confined under the auspices of the existing Muslim institutions, to winning political responsibility as the main objective, and with freedom for the country as merely incidental thereto. Hence the need for the new party.' The NMP set out to develop a mentality above communalism, inspire into the Muslim communities greater confidence in nationalistic ideas, and create harmonious Hindu-Muslim relations.[49]

Khaliquzzaman claimed to be the founder of the NMP,[50] though existing historical evidence points to Ansari as its architect. Others closely associated with him were Rafi Ahmed Kidwai, Sherwani, Azad, Ghaffar Khan, Brelvi, Abdul Majid Khwaja, Mujibur Rahman, Saifuddin Kitchlew, and Abdul Bari of Bihar. Maulvis Kifayatullah, Muhammad Sajjad and Ahmad Said represented the Jamiyat al-ulama, while Maulana Qutubddin Wali belonged to Firangi Mahal.[51]

At its first meeting held at Sherwani's home in Allahabad on 27 July 1929, a central body was constituted: 28 members were elected from Bengal, 27 from Punjab, 3 from the N.W.F.P., 24 from UP. Committees were set up in Lucknow, Rae Bareli, Allahabad, Banaras, Faizabad, Hardoi, Bijnor, Saharanpur, Bareilly, Mahoba, Meerut, Aligarh, and Shahajahanpur.[52] In Punjab, NMP committees functioned in eight districts. There were ten in Bihar, and at least four in Bengal—Calcutta, Dacca, Bogra and Faridpur. Shamsul Huda and Ghulam Qadri headed the Dacca committee;

Mujibur Rahman, Akram Khan, K. Nooruddin and Abdur Razzack (the latter two were Calcutta Corporation Councillors) the Calcutta branch. Local branches in Bogra and Faridpur were controlled by a scattering of others who had been active in the khilafat and non-cooperation movements.[53]

On the strength of this network, the NMP claimed to represent the 'entire Muslim intelligentsia'.[54] Ansari scoffed at the League, pointing out that it had long ceased to be a reality, while the khilafat committee, once so powerful, 'was now but a shadow of its former self'. He concluded his party as the 'real representative group of the Musalmans of India today'.[55]

Such claims were exaggerated, and yet the NMP had the potential of emerging as a powerful force.[56] Hence, Ansari and his comrades staked their claim to represent the Muslims at the Round Table Conference in London. Gandhi insisted on demonstrating Congress's representative position,[57] and told the viceroy that without Ansari he would be 'perfectly helpless' in conducting Hindu-Muslim negotiations.[58] But the viceroy did not acquiesce. The Mahatma said in London that, whoever prevented Ansari from being selected as a delegate, committed a 'fatal blunder'.[59]

Actually, it was Fazl-i Husain, member of the viceroy's council, who vetoed Ansari's participation. Backed by the Muslim Conference and a section of the Urdu press, the Punjabi leader questioned the NMP's claim to represent the Muslims. 'The Muslim press has already stated', he wrote in July 1931, 'that Ali Imam and Ansari should not go as representatives of Muslims. This is the right line to take, and if it is right, there is no reason why it should not succeed.' He admired Ansari, adding, however, how 'during the last few weeks he [Ansari] seems to have done his best to convince all his friends and admirers that [his] partisanship of the Congress has deprived him of any sense of fair-play and propriety'.[60] Fazl-i Husain reserved his harsh comments for Gandhi. 'To confuse the issues, to indulge in irrelevance and to begin to talk of Muslim demands, and then talk of Congress Muslims of Dr. Ansari and so on', he wrote to friends in October 1931,

all are devices with which Hindus as well as Muslims are quite familiar . . . Gandhi's insistence upon Dr. Ansari's inclusion and his parading readiness for complete surrender in case complete unity is forthcoming have nothing new about them. They are the very old devices which the Congress, Gandhi and the Indian Hindus have been condemning in the British Government and the British statesmen. They are doing now exactly what they alleged Lord Birkenhead was doing— asking for complete unanimity and resorting to the well known principle of Divide and Rule; but Gandhi should know that the people are not so unsophisticated today as they used to be and that the game he is now indulging in is one which has been played out for some time.[61]

Ansari hated being drawn into the controversy. Gandhi, he wrote on 28 September, 'is harking back on me and wanting me even at this eleventh hour to be invited. . . . It is like a baby crying for his wetnurse'. Convinced that the government would keep the NMP unrepresented,[62] he stated:

I am positive that the government has deliberately left the Nationalist Muslim Party unrepresented . . . because they do not want the Hindu-Muslim question to be settled without their intervention.' And they know that if there is any party in India which can bring about Hindu-Muslim unity it is the Nationalist Muslim Party. It is, therefore, against their interest to have the representatives of that party at the Round Table Conference, for they would be able to cement the unity of the various parties in India and thus deprive the government from playing their trump card against the representatives of India who are pressing hard for complete freedom from the British tutelage.[63]

He felt that Gandhi should not insist on his inclusion, but Jawaharlal Nehru dissuaded him not to be 'so rash as to cable him to do what he chooses'.[64] In early October, Gandhi changed gear, arguing that Ansari will be of no use unless the Muslim delegation endorsed his selection as a delegate.[65]

Meanwhile, the NMP secured the adherence of influential Muslims who had built their reputation through years of selfless political work. Its meetings at Lucknow (18-19 April 1931), Faridpur (27-8 June 1931) and Lahore (24 October 1931) were well-attended, and its policies conveyed some sense in the N.W.F.P., Punjab, UP and Bombay.[66] 'One of the most gratifying signs of the times', commented the *Leader*, 'is the rapid growth of nationalism among Indian Muslims. . . . The impressive gathering of the nationalist Muslims at Lucknow from all parts of the country tells its own tale.'[67] The editor of the *Indian Annual Register* expressed similar views.[68]

Ansari worked feverishly to weld together the various Muslim factions and persuade them to accept the NMP's proposals. They were mainly two: joint electorates and adult suffrage;[69] on other issues there was no fundamental difference between Jinnah's 'Fourteen Points' and the NMP resolution adopted in Lucknow on 18-19 April 1931.[70] Political problems, argued the Bihar lawyer Ali Imam, were a reflex of social forces. 'If you erect an iron wall between community and community in their politics, you destroy the social fabric. . . . Nationalism can never evolve from division and dissension.'[71] Ansari, too, refused to countenance separate electorates. He wanted the measure and method of representation in the federal and provincial legislatures to be settled on the basis of joint electorates and adult suffrage,[72] and suggested a round table conference of Muslim organizations to iron out differences.[73]

Ansari's statement set the stage for the real business at hand: ongoing talks between representatives of the NMP and the Muslim Conference. On 10-12 May they met at Bhopal, discussing the vexed issue of joint *versus* separate electorates. Ansari proposed joint electorates for the first ten years with a provision for a referendum thereafter. Alternatively, 50 per cent of the seats were to be contested on the basis of joint, and the other half on the basis of separate electorates in the first general election. The arrangement was to change in the second election with two-thirds of the seats to be contested by joint electorates. Thereafter, joint electorates with adult suffrage, as proposed in the Nehru report, were to be introduced. On the other hand, Iqbal, Shafi, and Shaukat Ali insisted on joint electorates and adult suffrage after ten years, though they could be introduced earlier if a majority of legislators so desired. Their other proposal provided for five years of separate electorates with a referendum on joint electorates at the beginning of the fifth year.[74]

These discussions, announced Ansari with characteristic over-optimism, raised the prospect of a working agreement.[75] But his hopes were soon belied by the intransigence of delegates from both sides,[76] and by Fazl-i-Husain's stout refusal to endorse a compromise.[77] When talks resumed at Simla on 21 June 1931, the Punjab leader demanded separate electorates and reservation of seats for the Muslim majorities in Bengal and Punjab.[78] Ansari found the atmosphere 'very inauspicious'.[79] Hence the Simla conference accomplished little more than restating a daunting agenda of continuing problems and differences.

The blame for the failure of such meetings was placed on Ansari and his colleagues.[80] Their policies, stated the Allahabad historian and publicist Shafaat Ahmad Khan, were 'like the bloom on the peach; you touch it, and it is gone. Where is the party now? Nowhere! The exact minute and detailed account of its branches and activities may be found in the secretariat of the Indian National Congress, but so far as Muslims of India are concerned they exist only on paper.'[81] Shafee Daoodi repeated the charge: Rafi Ahmed Kidwai replied that the number of Muslims in Congress exceeded the combined strength of the provincial Leagues and khilafat committees.[82] Others excoriated the NMP for selling out the community's interest as well as the interest of Islam.[83] Ansari stoutly refuted the allegation: 'We are surely not worse Musalmans because we refuse to turn our faith into a greedy superstition or an ignoble exercise in political hide and seek. . . . Our nationalism is part of our loyalty to our faith and not a betrayal or an infidelity.'[84] Shaukat Ali, who had no pretensions to detachment and only the flimsiest to moderation, told Saiyid Mahmud: 'I consider you all to be weak men and renegades, and, yielding to the open threats of the Hindus, (to) have chosen to live at their mercy',[85] an ill-chosen way to dramatize his contention that the Congress Muslims had 'sold out' to the 'Hindus'. Ansari was unswerving in his resolve to respond to Shaukat Ali. His underlying theme was simple: religion and faith were private matters, not symbols to be exploited by partisan politicians.

The Hindu Mahasabha, too, charged that some Muslims, masquerading as nationalists, had infiltrated the Congress in large numbers in order to exert pressure from within.[86] In substance, B.S. Moonje said, there was no difference between the demands of the communalist and the nationalist Muslim.[87] C. Vijaraghavachariar, the Mahasabha president in 1931, believed that the NMP resolutions adopted at Faridpur, were 'subject to all the infirmities of the proposals of the other section of Moslems to which Mr. Jinnah's fourteen points give expression'.[88] In short, the Mahasabha's strategy was to prevent the NMP activists from extracting concessions from the Congress. This was evident during the Gandhi-Jinnah talks in 1929, and later when Tej Bahadur Sapru tried negotiating with various non-Congress groups. Moonje was morbidly apprehensive of any move to conciliate the Muslims; Jayakar insisted that the Liberals must declare themselves on the communal question, stating the limits beyond which they would not go in their engagement with the Muslims.[89]

In July 1931, Ansari, Malaviya and Sardar Sardul Singh recommended, and the Congress Working Committee adopted, a scheme purportedly based on 'undiluted communalism and undiluted nationalism'.[90] Its main features were: joint electorates and adult suffrage, with reservation for minorities of less than 25 per cent. The N.W.F.P. and Baluchistan would have the same form of government and administration as the other provinces, Sind would form a separate province provided its people bore the financial burden, and residuary powers would rest with the provinces. While Gandhi agreed, the Muslim Conference stuck to its guns.[91] The Mahasabha's rejection was equally unequivocal.[92] The Bengal Provincial Hindu Conference acted likewise.[93]

Ansari reacted angrily. The Mahasabha's nationalism, he argued, cloaked its aggressive communalism. Even with the issue squarely placed in the context of the country's interest—which is where Ansari thought it ought to be—the Mahasabha was anything but enthusiastic. He also criticized some fellow-Congressmen. Malaviya, having formed a break-away group on the issue of the Communal Award, was one of them. Ansari poured out his anger and frustration in a stream of letters to friends.

As if this was not enough. When Ansari returned to India in January 1933 after a four-month stay in Europe, he found the NMP in disarray. Khaliquzzaman had signed its death warrant in UP by founding the Muslim Unity Board.[94] In Punjab, Fazl-i Husain and the Unionists, and in Bengal Fazlul Haq and the United Muslim Party guided the course of Muslim politics leaving the NMP member crying in the wilderness. Abdur Rahman Siddiqi, one of the founders of the New Muslim Majlis, joined hands with Husayn Suhrawardy, while Mujibur Rahman, a fervent nationalist, failed to cope with the confusing plethora of Muslim factions.[95]

By 1934, the Congress Muslims stood 'divested of every shred of principle or practice on the basis of which they formed their group, and which they had proudly nailed to their masthead—of everything, all, except their name!'[96] Their party lived in the newspapers all right but beyond that it had no positive existence. Khaliquzzaman's idea that the NMP would discipline 'Nationalist Muslims' did not materialize because the remedy, he wrote, was not potent enough to eradicate the 'evil'.[97]

III

Explanations for the NMP's decline already exist.[98] Jawaharlal Nehru attributed it to the upper middle class background of its members, the absence of 'dynamic personalities' amongst them, and their method of drawing-room meetings, mutual arrangements, and pacts. At this game, the communal leaders

drove the Nationalist Muslims from one position to another, made them give up one by one, the principles for which they stood. Always the Nationalist Muslims tried to ward off further retreat and to consolidate their position by adopting the policy of the 'lesser evil', but always this led to another retreat and another choice of the 'lesser evil'. There came a time when they had nothing left to call their own, no fundamental principle on which they stood except one, and that had been the very sheet-anchor of their group: joint electorates. But again the policy of the lesser evil presented the fatal choice to them, and they emerged from the ordeal minus that sheet-anchor.[99]

To Jawaharlal's explanation, one must add the combined and sustained opposition of the Mahasabha, the Muslim Conference, and certain powerful local and regional formations in Punjab and Bengal. Sure enough, the NMP served as a platform to the Jamiyat al-ulama, the Khudai Khidmatgars, the All-India Momin Conference, and the Ahrars, but it could not present itself as a viable alternative to either the Muslim Conference or the League. It was, consequently, reduced to arbitrating between the Congress and the communally-inclined Muslim parties—a role Ansari played in the early 1930s.

The image of men like Ansari got indissolubly linked with the Hindus, and they were, therefore, pictured as 'renegades' and accused of a 'sell out'. Attempts to remove this impression were, at best, feeble. Ansari persevered doggedly, for he had a greater awareness of the need to respond to the pressures for change than a great many of his Muslim contemporaries. He also had the courage and the conviction to assert his political will, and face the daunting challenge posed by his critics. He met criticism, and at times bitter attacks, but he did not hesitate to fight it out with them. Yet, his lieutenants lacked motivation, and the determination to solve their problems of tactics, coordination or leadership; in fact, Ansari soon became aware of how wayward the elements he was seeking to fuse into one were. Used to playing second-fiddle—first to Mohamed Ali and later to Ansari—several NMP members succumbed to communal pressures; other sturned defensive, sulking when faced with the combined opposition of their detractors. This was true of Saiyid Mahmud, Khaliquzzaman, Shuaib Qureshi, and A.R. Siddiqi, all bound to Ansari by personal rather than political loyalty. Jawaharlal's experience with such leaders led him to observe in April 1937:

Our experience of the Nationalist Muslim Party in the past was not a happy one. Such half-way groupings confuse the issue and the masses are perplexed. . . . Those who agree (with the Congress) should not stand on the doorstep; they should enter the nation's chamber and take full share in shaping the nation's policy.[100]

The NMP was composed of a small number of professional men—lawyers, doctors, and journalists—who did not operate in politics from a position they could claim their own. They mainly depended on the goodwill of leading Congressmen, who encouraged them to counter the League and patronized them to lend credence to their claims of representing all Indians. This was not good enough. What was also not good enough was the preoccupation of the NMP leaders with constitutional issues. Thus, Ansari was closely associated with the All-Parties Conference; Shuaib Qureshi served as a member of the Nehru Committee; and Khaliquzzaman, Saiyid Mahmud, Sherwani and Khwaja were enmeshed in constitutional controversies which raged from the time of the first Round Table Conference and culminated in the squabbles over the Communal Award. Ultimately, however, such preoccupations led to no tangible results: such men mostly operated on the fringes of politics and were made, in the words of Shaukat Ali, a cat's paw by their Congress co-workers. Their fate was similar to that of the Liberals.

Admittedly, they formed a constituency the Congress assiduously courted in the 1920s to deepen its support. Gandhi did so during the khilafat campaign: Ansari and Ajmal Khan were adroitly used to follow a middle-of-the road policy to restrain the militant khilafatists. Later, Ansari and his associates formed valuable allies in dealing with estranged communal relations, projecting Congress policies among Muslims, and securing their electoral support.[101] Motilal Nehru tried to woo Ansari, Shuaib Qureshi, and Khaliquzzaman in the making of the Nehru report. Gandhi did the same, referring to their commitment to inter-communal harmony and insisting on Ansari's presence in London at the Round Table Conference.

Such symbolic gestures did not, however, empower the Congress Muslims to counter their detractors. Faced with the verbal assault of the Mahasabha and the Muslim Conference, they required strong ideological sustenance and political backing. This was not forthcoming. Though used on occasions, given decorative positions in the Congress hierarchy, and loudly proclaimed as devoted leaders, they were wilfully ignored during the critical negotiations in the 1930s and 1940s. Often, their viewpoint was treated with undeserved contempt.[102] This was so at the Lahore Congress in 1929. 'We found the atmosphere', wrote Khaliquzzaman,

very secretive, and when in private talks the leading Congressmen decided to throw the Nehru report into the Ravi, even Dr. Ansari was not consulted . . . Dr. Ansari, Tasadduq and myself were leaving Lahore in the evening for our destinations, humbled, disappointed and angry. . . . At the station we had enough time to decide between ourselves that the Nehru report having been drowned in the Ravi, we could not take the responsibility of shouldering the burden of fighting for the independence of India, for the Muslims were bound to consider it to be a purely Hindu fight.[103]

The self perception of the Congress Muslims was that they were, at best, bargaining counters; when not so, they were stored in the deep freeze.[104] Thus when Gandhi agreed to compromise with the Muslim leaders on separate electorates, Abdul Majid Khwaja reacted angrily. 'It means', he wrote indignantly, 'that you are prepared to surrender the Congress Muslims who have fought the battles of the country side by side with you to those Mussalmans who have done nothing except for themselves, their seats, their posts, their salaries and their lunches and dinners at the Government Houses.' Khwaja opposed both separate electorate and communal representation. The 'salvation of the Muslims', he felt, 'lies in the salvation of the motherland and the salvation of the motherland in its turn lies in the mutual trust and goodwill of the two great communities'.[105]

Ansari's exchanges with Gandhi and Motilal Nehru in 1930 illustrates his ambivalences as well as his disenchantment with the Congress. Soon after Gandhi and Motilal turned a blind eye to his criticism of the Lahore resolutions, Ansari summed up the guidelines of his political conduct:

We must not leave the Congress, nor must we do anything to weaken the Congress. After all the will of the majority must prevail, that is the only guide for any democratic institution. . . . To leave the Congress would be a crime. Therefore we must remain in the Congress and let those who believe in the present policy and programme carry on.

Again,

As . . . for joining the Liberals or the communalists it is unthinkable for you and me. The Liberals will never do anything, even though they are kicked out of the Round Table Conference . . . As regards the Muslim communalists, we have . . . extricated ourselves from them. We have formed the 'Nationalist Muslim Party' and it would be the height of unwisdom to leave that party or to cease working for its object. *To my mind, that is the only avenue left for our political activities.* We must put all our mind to it and carry on a vigorous campaign to wean the Muslims away from the influence of communalists and reactionary leaders and think and act in terms of 'nationalism'. *That is the only channel left for out political activities.*[106] (italics mine)

It is perhaps surprising to find such a straightforward, commonsense approach in a man who combined strict standards of political honesty and obligation with a passionate emotional involvement in what he was doing. This is not to argue that Ansari was right—that is an opinion which every historian of Indian nationalism will answer for himself. Still, it would not be an exaggeration to say that in opposing the Mahatma, Ansari and others who shared his views acted from conviction and, in their own opinion, would have been false to the principles which brought them into the Congress movement if they had acted otherwise.

NOTES

1. Jayakar to Gandhi, 23 Aug. 1929, Jayakar papers (437), NAI. In his reply, Gandhi assured Jayakar that he had not 'bound anybody' because he had no representative capacity. 'I simply listened to Mr. Jinnah's exposition of his position. Similarly with the Ali brothers too, I heard what they had to say. With the latter the talk turned upon their grievance against me for my reticence.' Gandhi to Jayakar, 24 Aug. 1929, *CWMG*, Vol. XLI, pp. 319 and 289.

2. Lajpat Rai to Motilal Nehru, n.d., File No. 108 (Suppl.), AICC papers. Moonje to Malaviya, 31 July 1928, Moonje to Gandhi, 5 Aug. 1929, Jayakar papers (437).

3. Quoted in Uma Kaura, *Muslims and Indian Nationalism: The Emergence of the Demand for India's Partition*, New Delhi, 1977, p. 50.

4. Ibid., p. 51.

5. CWC resolution on the communal problem, July 1931, File No. G-37/1931, AICC papers; *IQR*, July-Dec. 1929, pp. 310-11; *India in 1929-30*, p. 95.

6. 9 Jan. 1930, *CWMG*, Vol. XLVII, p. 381.

7. S. Pirzada (ed.), *Foundations of Pakistan*, Vol. 2, pp. 42-4.

8. File No. G-59, 1928, AICC papers.

9. File No. 11, 1926, ibid.

10. Motilal was a patron of such men, as indeed of other Muslims, whom he helped to find jobs. See, for instance, the case of Hakim Wali who was recommended for the post of executive officer in Banaras municipality. Motilal Nehru to T.A.K. Sherwani, 29 July 1928, File No. 60 (Suppl.), 1925-6, ibid. Motilal also ensured that the PCC's find Muslims of Congress and swarajist views to elect candidates for elections. In a directive to the Sind PCC he insisted that 'the PCC even though constituted wholly by Hindus must rise above communalism and show that it makes no distinction between National- ists whether they are Hindus or Muslims'. File No. 76 (Suppl.), 1928, ibid.

11. Kenneth McPherson, *The Muslim Microcosm: Calcutta, 1918 to 1935*, Wiesbaden, 1974, p. 80.

12. *Mussalman*, 27 Apr. 1926. Report on Native Newspapers, Bengal, Jan.-Dec. 1927, pp. 127, 204, 271.

13. McPherson, *The Muslim Microcosm*, sections 5 and 6 in Chap. 5.

14. B.N. Pandey, *Nehru*, London, 1976.

15. Idem, p. 145.

16. Page, *Prelude to Partition*, pp. 132-3.

17. Shafee Daoodi to Motilal Nehru, 26 Mar. 1929, File No. 96, Motilal Nehru papers. *The Frontier Question in the Assembly, being the statements of Pandit Motilal Nehru, MLA, Maulvi Shafi Daudi, MLA, and Saiyid Murtaza, MLA*, New Delhi, 1926.

18. Khaliquzzaman, *Pathway to Pakistan*, p. 117.

19. The membership of the All-India Muslim League was 1,093 in 1922, 1,097 in 1923, and 1,184 in 1924. *Annual Report of the All-India Muslim League*, Lucknow, n.d., Chagla papers, NMML.

20. *Mussalman*, 3 July 1930. The League, according to the 1931 annual report, was unable to perform its functions effectively because of the Muslim Conference 'which has divided our energies and caused a great deal of harm to the All-India Muslim League'. The situation remained unchanged in 1932-3 when the joint secretary warned that 'a little oversight or a little expression of inactivity on the part of Muslims today means lifelong suffering and bondage'. In order to gain members, the annual subscription was reduced from Rs. 6 to Re. 1 and the admission fee was abolished. *Annual Report of the All-India*

Muslim League for the year 1931, New Delhi, n.d., pp. 1, 4; *Annual Report of the All-India Muslim League for the years 1932 and 1933 (upto November)*, New Delhi, n.d., pp. 2, 3.

21. *Modern Review*, July 1929, p. 103.
22. Idem.
23. Smith, *Modern Islam in India*, p. 251; Faruqi, *Deoband School*, pp. 70-1.
24. Hardy, *Partners in Freedom*, p. 37.
25. *Mussalman*, 16 Apr. 1931.
26. *Liberty*, 1 June 1931, quoted in Bhola Chatterji, *Aspects of Bengal Politics in the early Nineteen Thirties*, Calcutta, 1969, pp. 14-15.
27. Home Poll. File No. 5/72, 1932, NAI.
28. Home Poll. File No. 5/54, 1932, NAI.
29. D.G. Tendulkar, *Abdul Ghaffar Khan*, Bombay, 1967, p. 116.
30. Smith, *Modern Islam in India*, pp. 266-7.
31. Home Poll. File No. 5/54, 1932, NAI.
32. Home Poll. File No. 5/62, 1932, NAI.
33. Home Poll, File No. 5/54, 1932, NAI.
34. Humayun Kabir, *Muslim Politics 1905-47 and other Essays*, Calcutta, 1969, p. 22.
35. Smith, *Modern Islam in India*, pp. 270-1.
36. Home Poll. File No. 5/46, 1932, NAI.
37. Malik Afzal Husain, *Kashmir awr Dogra raj, 1848-1931*, New Delhi, 1970 edn.
38. Among the demands listed were representation in ministries and in all grades of services in proportion to the Muslim population, religious freedom, the right to hold public meetings, and the freedom of speech and press. In other areas such as Mirpur *tahsil*, Major General R.G. Finlayson took note of the common grievance relating to high grazing tax and high rent assessments which were double of what they were in neighbouring Punjab, inadequate representation in civil administration, insufficient resources being spent on the development of the *tahsil*, and rampant corruption, inefficiency, and maladministration. Home Poll. File No. 10/28, 1932; Home Poll. File No. 5/2, 1933, NAI.
39. P.N.K. Bamzai, *A History of Kashmir*, New Delhi, 1962, pp. 660-1.
40. Home Poll. File No. 13/23, 1931, NAI.
41. Foreword by S.M. Abdullah in *New Kashmir*, New Delhi, n.d., p. 6.
42. Cited in Bamzai, p. 661: M. Ishaq Khan, *Perspectives on Kashmir: Historical Dimensions*, Srinagar, 1983, pp. 146-7.
43. *New Kashmir*, p. 6.
44. *IQR*, Jul.-Dec. 1929, pp. 350-1.
45. Ibid., p. 351.
46. Brown, op. cit., p. 137.
47. Viceroy to secretary of state, 18 Jan. 1930, Home Poll. File No. 257/V, 1930, NAI.

48. Khaliquzzaman, *Pathway to Pakistan*, p. 102.
49. *IQR*, Jul.-Dec. 1928, Vol. 2, p. 350.
50. Khaliquzzaman, *Pathway to Pakistan*, p. 102.
51. For list of those present at the Allahabad Conference, see *IQR*, Jul.-Dec. 1929; for Jamiyat al-ulama, see *Leader*, 19 Apr. 1931.
52. Funds for their support came from several sources, including the raja of Mahmudabad. He was much active in nationalist campaigns, leading the boycott of the Simon commission in Lucknow, presiding over the all-parties conference in Lucknow in September 1928, and lending his name to the list of those who endorsed the Nehru report. He also proposed launching a newspaper and invited Saiyid Abdullah Brelvi to join as editor. 'In view of the importance of the political situation and also in view of the Nehru Committee Report it is most necessary to start propaganada in right earnest to educate the people and get the report ratified by all recognized institutions.' To Brelvi, 8 Sept. 1928, Saiyid Abdullah Brelvi papers, NMML. Earlier, the raja had supported similar journalistic ventures in support of nationalist causes. The *Comrade*, the *New Era* (Lucknow), and the *Hamdam* (Lucknow) were among them. Both James Meston and Harcourt Butler tried unsuccessfully to persuade the raja to withdraw his patronage from such 'extremists' papers. Butler to the raja of Mahmudabad, 4 Sept. 1920, Mahmudabad papers, NMML.
53. *Mussalman*, 21 Mar. 1931; For Punjab, *Bombay Chronicle*, 4 July 1931.
54. Ibid., 27 June 1931; For Saiyid Mahmud's claims, *Bombay Chronicle*, 20 Apr. 1931.
55. *Modern Review*, May 1931, p. 611; A.Z. Zaidi (ed.), *The Evolution of Muslim Political Thought in India*, New Delhi, 1980, Vol. 4, p. 476. Gandhi's interview to *New Leader*, 25 Nov. 1931, *CWMG*, Vol. XLVIII, p. 333.
56. Letter to the Editor, 15 Apr. 1931, *Leader*, 19 Apr. 1931.
57. Gandhi to Irwin (tel.), 20 July 1931, *CWMG*, Vol. XLVIII, p. 158.
58. Gandhi to viceroy, 29 Aug. 1931, ibid., p. 382.
59. Interview to *Bombay Chronicle*, 14 Sept. 1931, p. 12; Gandhi to Ansari (cable), 14 Oct. 1931, *CWMG*, Vol. XLVIII, p. 148.
60. To Shafaat Ahmad Khan, 28 July 1931, 'Indian Muslims do not believe that Gandhi is serious in the matter of Muslim rights. His desire to have Ansari in London is only a continuation of his tactics at Delhi to demonstrate the existence of cleavage in Muslim opinion, while, as a matter of fact, it does not exist.' Waheed Ahmad (ed.), *Diary and Notes of Mian Fazl-i-Husain*, Lahore, 1977, pp. 213-14.
61. Ibid., p. 228.
62. To Shaukatullah Ansari, 28 Sept. 1931 (ed.), *Muslims and the Congress*, p. 129.
64. Statement to Press, 14 Sept. 1931, *CWMG*, Vol. XLVIII, p. 150; Devdas Gandhi to Jawaharlal, 2 Sept. 1931, *SWJN*, Vol. 5, p. 48, f.n. 3.
65. To Ansari, 4 Oct. 1931, *SWJN*, Vol. 5, p. 98.

66. Draft note on the success of Punjab Nationalist Muslim, n.d., Brelvi papers; 'Lucknow seldom had a bigger gathering of Mussalmans than one seen yesterday in connection with Muslim Nationalists' Conference', reported the *Tribune* of 23 July 1930, and *Indian Daily Mail*, 24 July 1930, Ansari papers.
67. Note on the Press, UP, for the week ending 23 Apr. 1931.
68. *IAR*, Jan.-June 1931, Vol. 2, p. 80.
69. For resolutions adopted at the meetings on 15-17 Apr., *Leader*, 19 Apr. 1931; *Mussalman*, 16 Apr. 1931.
70. *Mussalman*, 23 Apr. 1931.
71. Ibid., 16 Apr. 1931.
72. *Bombay Chronicle*, 27 Apr. 1931.
73. *Leader*, 19, 20, 22, and 23 Apr. 1931, Page, *Prelude to Partition*, p. 238.
74. Brelvi papers; Iqbal to Fazl-i Husain, 14 May 1931, *Letters of Mian Fazl-i-Husain*, p. 143.
75. *IQR*, Jan.-June 1931, Vol. I, p. 304.
76. Saiyid Mahmud to Nehru, 27 June 1931, Datta and Cleghorn (eds.), *A Nationalist Muslim*, pp. 115-16.
77. *IQR*, op. cit., pp. 303-6; K.K. Aziz (ed.), *The All-India Muslim Conference 1928-1935*, Karachi, 1972, pp. 75-6.
78. *Mussalman*, 25 June 1931; Page, *Prelude to Partition*, pp. 238-40; R.J. Moore, *The Crisis of Indian Unity 1917-1940*, New Delhi, 1974, p. 190; Fazl-i-Husain to Shafee Daoodi, 16 May 1931, *Letters of Mian Fazl-i-Husain*, pp. 144-8; *Bombay Chronicle*, 23 June 1931.
79. *Mussalman*, 25 June 1931; *Bombay Chronicle*, 24 June 1931.
80. The nawab of Chhatari to Fazl-i Husain, 3 July 1931, *Letters of Mian Fazl-i-Husain*, p. 158. Fazl-i Husain, who did much to undermine the possibility of a settlement, wrote that there were no Muslims in the Congress strong enough to persuade that body to act in a 'just' and 'righteous' manner. To Umar Hayat Khan Tiwana, 20 June, ibid., p. 152.
81. *IQR*, July-Dec. 1931, Vol. 2, p. 225.
82. *Leader*, 19 Apr. 1931. For Ansari's response, *Bombay Chronicle*, 6 July 1931.
83. Speech of Shaukat Ali at the UP Muslim Conference, 8 Aug. 1931, *IQR*, July-Dec. 1931, Vol. 2, p. 228.
84. *Bombay Chronicle*, 21 Apr. 1931.
85. 26 Apr. 1929, Datta and Cleghorn (eds.), *A Nationalist Muslim*, p. 94.
86. 22 Aug. 1929, Moonje Diaries, National Library, Calcutta: Moonje to Jayakar, 31 July 1926, Jayakar papers (437).
87. Speech at the Bengal Provincial Hindu Conference, *IQR*, Jul.-Dec. 1931, Vol. 2, pp. 260-1.
88. Speech at Akola, 8 Aug. 1931, *IQR*, ibid., pp. 252-3.
89. Moore, *The Crisis of Indian Unity*, p. 105.
90. *Young India*, 16 July 1931, *CWMG*, Vol. XLVII, p. 141; *Bombay Chronicle*, 13 July 1931.
91. For details, Page, *Prelude to Partition*, pp. 241-2.

92. *IQR*, Jul.-Dec. 1931, Vol. 2, p. 254.
93. Ibid., p. 261.
94. Khaliquzzaman, *Pathway to Pakistan*, pp. 119-20.
95. McPherson, *The Muslim Microcosm*, pp. 111, 121-2.
96. Nehru, *An Autobiography*, p. 139.
97. Khaliquzzaman, *Pathway to Pakistan*, p. 102.
98. K.M. Munshi, *Pilgrimage to Freedom*, Bombay, 1967, Vol. 1, p. 29.
99. Nehru, *An Autobiography*, p. 139.
100. *SWJN*, vol. 8, p. 128.
101. Thus in 1926 Ansari, Ajmal Khan, Azad, Mazharul Haq, and Shafee Daoodi appealed to the Muslim electorate of the Madras Presidency 'to stand by the Congress and to vote solidly for the Muslim candidates who stand under the banner of the Congress which is the sole common national organisation of India'. File No. G-66, 1926, AICC papers.
102. Notice Shaukat Ali's comment at the UP Muslim Conference, Allahabad. *IQR*, Jul.-Dec. 1931, Vol. 2, p. 228.
103. Khaliquzzaman, *Pathway to Pakistan*, p. 104.
104. Chatterji, *Aspects of Bengal Politics*, p. 73.
105. Khwaja to Gandhi, 12 Mar. 1931, A.M. Khwaja papers, NMML.
106. Ansari to Sherwani, 6 Jan. 1930, Hasan (ed.), *Muslims and the Congress*, pp. 90-1, and Ansari to Brelvi, 2 Apr. 1930, Brelvi papers.

PART III

PART III

9

Religion, Politics and Partition[1]

صبح آزادی

اگست ۱۹۴۷

یہ داغ داغ اُجالا، یہ شب گزیدہ سحر
وہ انتظار تھا جس کا، یہ وہ سحر تو نہیں
یہ وہ سحر تو نہیں جس کی آرزو لے کر
چلے تھے یار کہ مل جائے گی کہیں نہ کہیں

Dawn of Freedom (August 1947)

This stain-covered daybreak, this night-bitten dawn,
This is not that dawn of which there was expectation;
This is not that dawn with longing for which
The friends set out, (convinced) that somewhere
  there would be met with.

فلک کے دشت میں تاروں کی آخری منزل
کہیں تو ہوگا شبِ سُست موج کا ساحل
کہیں تو جا کے رُکے گا سفینۂ غمِ دل

In the desert of the sky, the final destination of the stars,
Somewhere there would be the shore of the sluggish wave of night,
Somewhere would go and halt the boat of the grief of pain.

جواں لہُو کی پُراسرار شاہ راہوں سے
چلے جو یار تو دامن پہ کتنے ہاتھ پڑے
دیارِ حسن کی بے صبر خواب گاہوں سے
پکارتی رہیں باہیں، بدن بلاتے رہے
بہت عزیز تھی لیکن رخِ سحر کی لگن
بہت قریں تھا حسینانِ نور کا دامن
شبک شبک تھی تمنا، دبی دبی تھی تھکن
سنا ہے ہو بھی چکا ہے فراقِ ظلمت و نور
سنا ہے ہو بھی چکا ہے وصالِ منزل و گام

By the mysterious highroads of youthful blood
When (we) friends set out, how many hands were laid on our skirts;
From impatient sleeping-chambers of the dwellings of beauty
Arms kept crying out, bodies kept calling;
But very dear was the passion for the face of dawn,
Very close the robe of the sylphs of light:
The longing was very buoyant, the weariness was very slight.
—It is heard that the separation of darkness and light
   has been fully completed,
It is heard that the union of goal and step has been fully completed;

بدل چکا ہے بہت اہلِ درد کا دستور
نشاطِ وصل حلال و عذابِ ہجر حرام

The manners of the people of suffering (leaders)
   have changed very much,
Joy of union is lawful, anguish for separation forbidden.

جگر کی آگ نظر کی اُمنگ، دل کی جلن
کسی پہ چارۂ ہجراں کا کچھ اثر ہی نہیں
کہاں سے آئی نگار صبا کدھر کو گئی
ابھی چراغِ سر رہ کو کچھ خبر ہی نہیں
ابھی گرانئ شب میں کمی نہیں آئی
نجاتِ دیدہ و دل کی گھڑی نہیں آئی
چلے چلو کہ وہ منزل ابھی نہیں آئی

The fire of the liver, the tumult of the eye, burning of the heart—
There is no effect on any of them of (this) cure for separation.

Whence came that darling of a morning breeze, whither has it gone?
The lamp beside the road has still no knowledge of it;
In the heaviness of night there has still come no lessening.
The hour of the deliverance of eye and heart has not arrived.
Come, come on, for that goal has still not arrived.

In 1970, a volume edited by C.H. Philips and M.D. Wainwright elaborated certain major themes relating to the genesis and growth of the Pakistan movement.[2] Today, 'specialists' and 'non-specialists' alike continue to grapple with much the same issues that were once a historian's delight but are now a nightmare. A case in point was the lively debate sparked off by the release of Maulana Azad's 'thirty pages' in 1989. Newspapers splashed stories on the inept handling of the 'communal' tangle by the Congress, on Jinnah's 'motives' and his use of Pakistan as a bargaining counter to extract concessions from an obdurate Congress leadership. Cryptic comments appeared on the machinations of the colonial government, specially its last representative, Mountbatten, who hastened India's Partition. The baldly stated conclusions in much of the literature that has appeared since the publication of the 'Complete Version' of *India Wins Freedom* are that Partition could have been averted if the Gandhi-Nehru leadership had been magnanimous towards the Muslim League demands, if Mountbatten's predecessors—Linlithgow and Wavell—had shown greater enterprise in devising political initiatives, and if Jinnah had been less intransigent during his dialogues with the Congress high command.

This debate—often conducted polemically and acrimoniously—goes on ceaselessly as more and more information comes to light and as individual and collective memories are revived time and time again through the medium of the vast Indian television network and its screening of popular 'serials' like *Buniyad* and *Tamas*. These are memories of broken homes and families, the wounds inflicted by Partition generally, the 'unequalled mistrust, acerbity and frenzied warfare',[3] and the 'general sense of gloom and despondency that pervaded the subcontinent'.[4]

It is tempting, even more than five decades after Independence and Partition, to reflect on the agony so many experienced, review part of the literature afresh, and explore themes for future research. The story told in the following pages leaves out many vital areas, not because I do not recognize their importance, but because they are explored elsewhere. The colonial government's policies, so central to the evolution of 'separatist' politics, is more than adequately analysed and documented.[5] Similarly, a number of studies have delineated those ideological and social forces that aided 'separatist' politics around shared values and symbols.[6] Discussed in section IV, they illustrate the different frameworks for studying communalism.

I neither detail the history of Hindu-Muslim strife,[7] though some aspects of inter-community relations are analysed,[8] nor the tortuous course of Congress-League-British negotiations leading to Independence and Partition. The Simla conference, the Cripps mission, the cabinet mission, and the Mountbatten plan do not figure in the discussion. I focus instead on the years 1937-40. I see these years as crucial to the legitimization of the League as a powerful political force and as the spokesman of an aggrieved and beleaguered 'community' which gradually distanced itself from secular nationalism, the rallying cry of the Congress, to create a separate Muslim/Islamic nation state. Fears and apprehensions generated during these critical years offered Jinnah and the League a constituency which they had not managed to secure for so long. In the months following the resignation of the Congress ministries they pressed home the political advantage thus secured.

<h1 style="text-align:center">I</h1>

The decade preceding Partition frequently escapes historical scrutiny. Part of the reason is that the genesis of Pakistan is traced, quite mistakenly, to the activities of Saiyid Ahmad Khan and his comrades at the M.A.O. College in Aligarh. They are identified as the only vocal group to raise the spectre of Hindu domination, and the first to introduce the language of minorityism. Backed by the Muslim élites of upper India, they turned to 'separatist' politics to safeguard their interests which had come under threat from British educational policies, bureaucratic reforms, and powerful Hindu revivalist campaigns. Muslim government servants and landowners, in particular, whose power was most obviously reduced by the pressure of change in the late nineteenth century, organized the Simla deputation (1 October 1906) and founded the Muslim League (December 1906).[9] Their insistence on separate electorates and reservations, coupled with their concern to defend deeply-cherished religio-cultural symbols, which were being gradually drawn into the public arena and contested by Arya Samajists and Hindu Mahasabhites, was designed to create the space for a distinct Muslim identity in politics. Colonial policies, which began tilting in·favour of the Muslims from the days of Mayo (1822-72) and Dufferin (1826-1902), legitimized such initiatives through an accommodation of sectional interests in the Act of 1909 and thereafter.[10]

This is a familiar story told in several different ways—the story of the pressure placed on the Islamic gentry by the rise of monied men and the resurgence of Hindu landholding communities;[11] the dreaded fear of majority rule, vividly described by Saiyid Ahmad in his 1883 speech on a local self-government bill for the Central Provinces;[12] and the apprehensions caused by Hindu resurgence.[13] These factors, together with the theories and institutions for separatism developed by the religious and political leadership in the last decade of the nineteenth-century, point to the heightening of communitarian consciousness. But this process in itself was a slow and tardy one, and impeded by the differentiated structure of the 'community', its regional and local diversities, and by deep-rooted sectarian and doctrinal disputes. No amount of pious exhortation could bridge the wide gulf separating, say, a Muslim peasant in Mymensingh from a Muslim *taluqdar* in Awadh. Nor could religious leaders, who began playing an important role in public affairs from early twentieth century, settle their theological differences. The Barelwis and the Deobandis had little in common. The Ahmadiyas and the Ahl-i Hadith were engaged in a running battle over doctrinal matters. And the Shias and the Sunnis were estranged, especially in Lucknow, both jealously guarding their separate mosques, religious endowments and educational establishments. The lines of cleavage in north India were more sharply drawn between the Sunnis and the Shias than between Hindus and Muslims.

Thus the initiative towards the creation of a separate Muslim homeland, though spurred by the anxieties expressed by Saiyid Ahmad, had its own contextual and ideological specificity. It was the outcome of a particular scenario on the eve of and during the Second World War which altered the tenor of political discourse in India and created the space for Jinnah's manoeuvrings. A beleaguered war-time government, having refused to deal with him in the past, now turned to Jinnah for political and moral support and, in the process, legitimized his critique of the Congress claim to represent all the communities of India. The inglorious breakdown of cross-community alliances and the accompanying collapse of the coalition governments in Punjab and Bengal—the last bastions of resistance to the League—helped turn Jinnah's dream into a reality.[14] That this would happen on the midnight of 14 August 1947 was unthinkable a decade before that date.

In the 1930s, there was no blueprint of a future Pakistan, no Islamic flag, no common platform, no shared goals and objectives. Rehmat Ali's scheme, nurtured in Cambridge, was an illustration of obscurantist political eccentricity. Having caused much political embarrassment back home, it was dismissed as 'chimerical' and 'impracticable'. Iqbal's blueprint, outlined three years earlier, did not envisage a *separate* Muslim state. He did, however, make out a case for provincial autonomy in Punjab, the North-West Frontier Province, Sind and Baluchistan *within the body-politic of India* for much the same reason that had prompted the Nehru report to recommend the separation of Sind from the Bombay Presidency and to constitute the N.W.F.P. into an 'independent' administrative unit. In the same speech, Iqbal, whose patriotic poems continued to be recited and sung in schools and colleges all over India, referred to autonomous states being formed, obviously not all-Muslim, based on the unity of languages, race, history, religion and identity of common interests. He did so in the context of *'India where we are destined to live'* (italics mine). This was surely not the swan-song of the Pakistan movement.

If Pakistan was still a pipe-dream, the League was little more than a paper organization. Having been in the wilderness during the khilafat agitation, its membership had plummeted to 1,330 in 1927. The branch in Bombay, Jinnah's homeground, could only boast of 71 members.[15] The 1929 session was adjourned for lack of quorum. When Iqbal spoke at Allahabad in 1930, the meeting failed to muster the required quorum of 75 members.[16] The organizers of the 1933 session in Delhi had a busy time filling up the hall with students of the Anglo-Arabic College. The League's income that year was Rs. 1,318, with 92 out of the 300 council members under notice to pay their arrears of membership.[17] Halide Edib commented, in 1935, that no one talked of the League as an arbiter of Muslim destiny.[18]

The leadership was fragmented, battered and bruised by frequent splits caused by factional feuds. Nawabzada Liaquat Ali Khan, credited with having persuaded Jinnah to return to India in 1934, set his eyes on securing the High Commissionership in London.[19] Khaliquzzaman was placed uneasily because of his loyalty to the Nehru household in Allahabad and his ambition to carve out his own sphere of influence in UP politics.[20] Nawab Muhammad Yusuf Khan solicited Malcolm Hailey's help in securing a knighthood or a place in the viceroy's executive council. His credentials were: 'I have neither spared money nor energy in creating a mentality among the landholders, the Muslims and other stable elements that their only salvation did lay in throwing their lot with the Government.'[21] The Aga Khan, mellowed after his hectic lobbying at the Round Table Conferences in London, was busy promoting the idea of a Vatican City in the territory of a protected ruler either in India or in the Persian Gulf.[22] And Jinnah, crestfallen after the rebuff he received at the national convention in December 1928, nursed his political wounds at his Hampstead home.[23] In 1934, the year he returned to Bombay, Hailey commented that Muslims had 'too many third-class leaders. There was no solidarity in the community, more so after the Communal Award which removed the sense of danger and prevents reunion under a strong leadership.'[24]

Some signs of revival followed Jinnah's return, and some endeavours to refurbish the League's image and rescue it from the political wilderness came to light. Yet, there was no evidence to indicate that the League had emerged as a political adversary or a force powerful enough to challenge the hegemony of the Congress. When the raja of Mahmudabad, a close friend of Sarojini Naidu, Tej Bahadur Sapru and the Nehrus, joined the League in 1936, he believed that the Congress and the League 'were like two parts of the same army fighting a common enemy on two fronts'.[25]

The raja's belief was grounded in hard facts. The Congress and the League had berated the Act of 1935. They shared, despite the perceived clash of ideologies, a perspective on political and agrarian issues. The League manifesto, minus its rhetoric, endorsed major Congress policies: the manifesto showed as much awareness of the people's needs as that of the Congress. In UP, the League and the Congress even put up Muslim candidates for the elections. Jinnah hoped that the Congress and the League, together in partnership, could inspire their followers by demonstrating that even the most intractable problem could be solved through dialogue and understanding. So, Jinnah talked of a 'united front' when the Congress accepted office in March 1937. There was no difference, he proclaimed on 18 September 1937, between the ideals of the Muslim League and of the Congress.[26]

Jinnah's own political conduct was above reproach. Liberal, eclectic and secular to the core in private and public life, he generally acted in unison with the Congress and initiated and backed proposals to break the communal impasse. 'If out of 80 million Muslims', he observed on 20 October 1936, 'I can produce a patriotic and liberal-minded nationalist block, who will be able to march hand in hand with the progressive elements in other communities, I will have rendered great service to my community.'[27] What India required, he stated a year later, was a united front. 'And then by whatever name you call your government is a matter of no consequence so long as it is a government of the people, by the people, for the people.'[28] That should explain why the viceroy thought of Jinnah as 'more Congress than the Congress', and why others regarded him as an 'arch enemy' of colonialism and a rallying symbol of secular forces.[29] Nobody expected him to foist the flag of Islam on an area supposedly defined by Iqbal and Rehmat Ali. India's unity was an ideal Jinnah still cherished.

In the face of such evidence, it is hard to make sense of Jinnah's subsequent crusade against the Congress and his repudiation of the principles he himself espoused for nearly three decades. It is much less easy to explain why, in the mid-1930s, the League was seen in some quarters as Congress' *bete noire* out on a mission to destroy India's liberation struggle. It was right to expose the League's semi-feudal orientation, but it was equally important to marry this perspective with the fact that not everybody in the League was feudal, obscurantist or religious-minded. People like Liaquat Ali Khan, the raja of Mahmudabad and Khaliquzzaman, for whom Nehru had a 'warm corner' in his heart,[30] were constantly 'torn between two loyalties'[31] but not necessarily imbued with an anti-Congress spirit or swayed by the League's religious claptrap.[32]

In 1936, Haig felt that the 'great majority of UP Muslims' had serious reservations about the Muslim League and opposed the policy of 'running a communal party'. That is why they were keen to wrest control of the provincial League, 'so as to render the All India Muslim League nugatory'. Three years later, Haig commented, despite the crucial changes in the political scenario during the intervening years, that, except for the Muslim landlords in UP, all others in the Muslim League were 'in general outlook much nearer the Congress'. 'For these reasons', he pointed out, 'if the right wing in the Congress found it necessary to strengthen themselves in this Province, they might do so by a coalition with the Muslim League rather than with landlords as such.' Read in the proper sequence of events, these observations reflect a powerful strand in UP 'Muslim politics'—a strand overlooked by other political commentators. It has also not figured in the discourses on Partition and 'communalism'.

Was it not possible to draw estranged comrades back into the Congress fold and assuage their feelings? Nehru would have said 'no' at the time. Rajendra Prasad, on the other hand, felt otherwise. Referring to the large number of 'Congress sympathizers' among the successful Muslim candidates in the 1937 elections who were willing to arrive at some settlement with Azad, he argued that 'if the proposed agreement between the Independent Muslims and the Congress had materialized, the communal animosity which the Muslim League whipped up later might never have been brought about'.[33]

Rajendra Prasad reflected on such events a decade after Independence and Partition. Jinnah did not. He had pleaded with Nehru and with Rajendra Prasad, even at the risk of being rebuffed yet again, that there was no

serious difference between him and the Congress, except that he stood for
safeguarding 'Muslim rights' against Hindu majoritarianism. Nehru
concurred. He told Meerut's nawab Muhammad Ismail Khan in November 1937: 'I do not quite know what our differences are in politics. I had
imagined that they were not great.'[34] If this was so it was an error of judgement to treat the League as a counter-force and an adversary. Instead of
making clear its own terms of secular and composite nationhood, the
Congress leaders, including the secular-minded amongst them, settled for
a soft option—one that Jinnah mentioned in his March 1940 speech at
Lahore. The 'terms' were, of course, not made explicitly clear, for they
ranged from Gandhi's 'Ram-Rahim' approach to the Malaviya-Lajpat Rai
vision of 'Hindu India'. 'Indian' nationalism was so often seen as a manifestation of a more 'genuine' expression—'Hindu nationalism'. In 1939,
Ashraf, who headed the Muslim Mass Contact Campaign, lamented that
'the Congress position regarding communal organizations and the communal activities of the Congress members has been dangerously vague
until now'.[35]

The Congress truculence over a coalition ministry was, in its historical
sequence, a political miscalculation. This is an oft-repeated argument,
perhaps a bit worn out. Yet, its validity is yet to be questioned with any
degree of conviction. Hence its mention is not out of place in tracing the
broad sequence of events.

To carry the story forward, it needs to be stressed that, as champion
of national unity and as a mediator between rival groups and warring
factions, a role performed by the Congress with such adroitness since
its inception in 1885, its leaders had two clear-cut options. These were to
reach out to the Muslim masses who, in Nehru's reckoning, had rallied
round the Congress flag in large numbers, and weaning away those Leaguers who felt dispirited after the party's poor showing in the elections. But
nothing of this kind happened. The Muslim Mass Contact Campaign,
launched amid much fanfare, petered out owing to the opposition of the
Congress right-wing, which feared an influx of Muslim activists and their
critical and unacceptable influence on party policy. The prospect of a
Congress-League coalition was, on the other hand, dimmed for reasons
that had very little to do with principles, more so because the Congress
had not just concluded pacts and agreements with the Muslim League, as
in December 1916, but also with the Akalis in Punjab.

Both Nehru and Prasad explained the 'breach of faith' in terms of
the unexpectedly large Congress majority secured in the elections. This,
according to their political calculation, made all talk of a coalition in-

defensible. In addition, Nehru referred to the feeling in Congress circles that without the League they would be freer to quarrel with Harry Haig, UP's governor, and break with him on their own terms.[36]

Nehru should have added that the Congress strategy was moulded by two conflicting forces, though each aimed to achieve a common goal— jettisoning all hopes of a Congress-League *entente*. There was, first of all, the stranglehold of the Hindu Mahasabha and other Hindu militant bodies opposed to a Congress-League rapprochement. Though acting purposefully and effectively on the strength of their following, their effectiveness derived, in large measure, from their patrons in the Congress. B.S. Moonje, the architect of the Hindu Mahasabha, stated that Vallabhbhai Patel and other right-wing Congressmen constantly urged him to 'stand firm on a variety of points in the interest of Hinduism'.[37]

The Congress strategy was, moreover, influenced by the perceptions of Congress Muslims. Wary of losing their secure and privileged position in the Congress hierarchy, they opposed, despite Azad's assertion to the contrary,[38] the idea of a coalition government in UP. Their instinct of political survival may have prompted them to do so. The socialist K.M. Ashraf, a relatively new arrival on the political stage, disapproved of 'the old methods of coalition, of pacts with Jinnah and others'.[39] The more experienced politician-journalist, Saiyid Abdullah Brelvi, berated élite forms of compromise-hatching.[40] Noble thought, yes, but quite out of tune with the realities of power politics and not quite consistent with Congress' own track record. Besides, how could Congress Muslims advocate a 'principled' posture only in relation to the League when so many of their party stalwarts paid allegiance to the Mahasabha and the RSS creed? This thought weighed heavily on their secular-nationalist conscience. Yet, they were unable to articulate it in the way Ansari had done in his indignant note of protest against Gandhi's decision to launch civil disobedience in 1930.[41] Without bothering to assess the situation independently, they accepted Nehru's harsh and ill-considered verdict on the League.

The Congress decision in the summer of 1937 created the space for the League's revival and offered Jinnah the chance to establish his hold in UP, a province that had spurned his initial overtures. With Khaliquzzaman and nawab Ismail Khan losing face and the National Agriculturist Party in disarray, Jinnah tasted victory in the erstwhile capital of the nawabs of Awadh. It was his finest hour. Appearing belligerent and impatient with his numerous detractors in the N.W.F.P., Punjab, Sind and Bengal, he lost no time humbling the recalcitrant elements. A mass contact campaign, launched under the aegis of the League, was his antidote to the Congress-sponsored programme. The person who consistently opposed the mixing of religion with politics and, for that reason, remained on the fringes during the khilafat upsurge, pressed the ulama into service, cultivated two of Deoband's renowned theologians—Shabbir Ahmad Usmani and Ashraf Ali Thanwi—and created fissures in the ranks of the ulama. The university at Aligarh turned out to be his prized trophy. What had once been a politically benign campus came to be described as the 'arsenal of Muslim India' by Jinnah.

Unwittingly, the Congress bolstered Jinnah's claim to be 'Muslim India's' sole spokesman, and aided the League to cultivate its image as a beleaguered organization, a victim of Congress machinations. Writing to the viceroy on 3 June 1939, UP's governor commented that 'Muslim solidarity would soon have been undermined' had the Congress agreed to a coalition. He added:

There are bound to be differences between Muslims on the main agrarian and economic issues. The Muslims in office would have to make themselves responsible for definite policies in regard to these matters; they would have received the support of some Muslims and aroused the opposition of others. Nothing seems to be so effective in disintegrating a party as the taking of office.[42]

Harry Haig stated an old axiom of British policy in India, which lay at the heart of the principle of dyarchy detailed in the Montagu-Chelmsford Reforms of 1919. The reckless course adopted by the Congress would have been averted had the party learnt from its own experiences with dyarchy. Bringing the League into government may well have given rise to inter-party feuds. At the same time, rejecting its representatives had the effect of creating a far broader unity among the League factions and greatly hardening their stance thereafter.

II

The coalition issue cast an ugly shadow over the Congress ministry in UP and elsewhere. There was talk of overt manifestations of aggressive Hindu nationalism, of the tyranny of a Hindu brute 'majority' over the Muslim 'minority', and a reiteration of the fear—expressed by Saiyid Ahmad Khan in the 1880s, by the Simla deputationists of 1906, and by Mohamed Ali at the Round Table Conference in 1930—that a non-Muslim majority would use its powers under democratic institutions to undermine 'Muslim interests' and offend cultural sensitivities and religious susceptibilities.

Complaints ranged from the general to the specific. There were pointed references to Hindu Mahasabhites 'in the garb of Congressites', and to 'Hindu Congress Cabinets' paying only lip service to nationalism and religious impartiality: 'The elephant tusks are only for display but it uses its real teeth for chewing its food.'[43] Reports from certain districts spoke of the 'arrogance and oppression of Hindu officials', and the coming of 'Hindu raj'.[44] In UP, Haig noticed cases against Muslim police officers being sent to the anti-corruption department. He intervened to protect Muslim officials from unjust treatment.[45] In Bombay, Roger Lumley was impatient with the arrogance of the Congress leaders in general, and with the rank and file in the districts, in particular. What, in his view, angered the Muslim leadership were the tales of woe that came up to them from Muslims in villages and towns 'where the local Congress boss has made it apparent that in his eyes Congress rule meant that he now wielded local power and that he had every intention of making things uncomfortable for the Muslim minority'.[46] Finally, the scale of Hindu-Muslim rioting led Muslim publicists to conclude: 'Never before in India's history did riots take a heavier toll of life and property within such a short space of time than during the two and a half years of Congress administration in some of the Provinces of India.'[47]

There were added grievances, mostly either localized or specific to a region—for example, the anti-Muslim bias of a welfare officer in the Delhi Cloth Mills, or the declining strength of Muslim wholesale foodgrain dealers in Delhi.[48] On the other hand, contentious issues of a general nature, such as the form of electorates, representation in services and professions, and the future of Urdu, did not bother Muslims everywhere. What irked them in Meerut was the ill-advised policy of the food control authorities causing hardship to Muslim traders in rice,[49] the punitive police tax in Budaun,[50] and the Congress alliance with textile-owners and the Mazdoor Sabha in Kanpur, an alliance forged to weaken the large Muslim working force.[51] Again, in Kanpur, they were concerned with the municipal board fanning the fires of Hindu-Muslim violence and, to add insult to injury, doling out services, contracts and scholarships to its Hindu benefactors.[52] Here and elsewhere, Muslims were aggrieved at being outside the patronage network. Finally, ill-will was sometimes engendered by incidents that could have taken place anywhere and in any other period of history—from offering prayers within the school compound, or Muslim boarders at the Etah Government High School being prevented from cooking beef and being told to participate in games during Ramzan.[53]

In Bihar and the Central Provinces, the Wardha and Vidya Mandir schemes of education, the singing of *Vande Mataram*, and the hoisting of the Congress flag were major contentious issues. Added to these were local grievances: inadequate Muslim representation in certain branches of administration,[54] dissatisfaction with the housing schemes of the Improvement Trust,[55] discrimination in disbursing loans and educational grants, and minor but incredibly trivial issues such as withdrawal of the Jabalpur riot cases of 1938, the arrest of 15 Muslims in the Chandur-Biswa murder case, and the release of a convicted Hindu in the Hoshangabad *paan* (betel) poisoning case.[56] Such incidents, even when unrelated to the policies or actions of the Congress governments, highlighted their 'tyranny'.

The Bombay ministry was held responsible for the discharge of Muslim employees in some Ahmedabad mills. But the fact of the case was that the millowners, some of whom were decidedly not free of communal prejudices and hostility towards the Muslim working force, dismissed 7,000 to 10,000 Muslim workers so as to avoid the risk of having communal trouble inside the mills.[57] They did so despite loud protests from the ministry. Likewise, the UP administration was placed in the dock for fomenting Hindu-Muslim riots in, say, Kanpur and Marehra, a small town in Etah district. As for Kanpur, aggressive action by a rowdy Muslim crowd started the chain of events leading to a bloody feud. In Marehra, ill-feeling was caused through a Congress flagpole having been bent by a *tazia*, perhaps accidentally. This led to brick throwing on the procession. All hell broke loose. Several Hindus were killed, their shops looted, and a temple desecrated. Whatever the provocation, the Muslims were undoubtedly the aggressors.[58]

So many of the grievances catalogued in the Pirpur and Shareef reports and in Dr. Ziauddin's tale of woes were by no means specific to the years of Congress rule. Riots occurred from 1893 onwards, though their frequency and intensity increased only in the aftermath of the khilafat movement. Nor was there any novelty in issues connected with the representation and form of electorates. These were advanced time and time again in Punjab, UP and Bengal, and were contested with equal vehemence. Notice the hue and cry following the Lucknow pact, or the indictment of the Swarajist party in Bengal, the relentless crusade against Fazl-i Husain's ministry in Punjab, and the denunciation of the Nehru report by the Ali brothers and the so-called 'All-India' Muslim Conference.[59]

In the mid-1930s, however, many of the old fears gained an altogether new kind of intensity because of a significant, though less visible, shift in the structural situation. What lent a sharp edge to the debate then was how power and authority, which flowed directly out of the Act of 1935,

was going to heighten competition and enlarge arenas of conflict, and
how social classes and communities, whose interests were delicately
safeguarded by the colonial authority in the constitutional arrangement,
were pitted against each other in an uneasy and sometimes antagonistic
relationship. Increasingly, local bodies were embroiled in this unlovely
struggle. In UP, where the number of municipalities had increased steadily
along with the representation of non-official Indians, there were unmistakable signs of a bitter contest to command resources in order to
reinforce patronage networks. Thus a report on municipal administration
for the year 1937-8 noted: 'The year's working was disfigured by the same
unhealthy party action and intrigue, the same interminable wrangles about
motions of no confidence, the same jobbery and injustice in connexion
with appointments, the same reckless irresponsibility in the financial
sphere.'[60] The same report pointed to 'communal dissensions exerting a
sinister influence on account of appointments, transfers and postings. A
year later the administration of over 30 municipalities was tarnished by
communal dissensions, party strife, and intrigue. Boards of Farrukhabad,
Fatehpur, Soron, Mainpuri, Mussoorie, Barant, Chandausi and Moradabad
were the worst offenders.[61]

At the same time, such dissensions were not always between Hindus
and Muslims *per se*. Haig commented on how the 'general political criti-
cisms are the stock in trade of opposition, voiced by non-Congress
Hindus just as much as by Muslims'. Thus vocal Muslim groups of his
province indicted the G.B. Pant cabinet only for the reason that they did
not have the same degree of pull and influence enjoyed by the supporters of the ministry. In essence, therefore, their grievance was not a
religious one, though it assumed an intensely communal form.[62]

The conduct of some Muslim *zamindars* illustrates how class issues
could so easily degenerate into religious squabbles, and how particularistic
concerns were so drawn into the public arena and identified with the
fortunes of an entire 'community'. Both the *taluqdars* of Awadh and the
zamindars of eastern and western UP raised the bogey of Islam to denounce
the Congress agrarian programme, including the UP Tenancy Bill, even
though they knew full well that the party in power was committed to land
reforms well before the ministry was formed, and that the Bill, piloted by
Rafi Ahmad Kidwai, was directed against an exploiting class and not
specially against the Muslim *zamindars*. Muslim landlords were a target
of attack not *qua* Muslims but *qua* opponents of the Congress and its
land reforms.[63]

Similarly, when the Bombay ministry levied property tax to pay for prohibition on *all* the urban property owners in the city, it was construed as an anti-Islamic measure on the grounds that Muslims invested savings in property rather than in stocks and shares and that they possessed a large number of religious endowments. In reality, their main grouse was against Brabourne, governor of Bombay, who had not insisted on a Muslim League minister being included in the cabinet. From that moment, the League publicists put the worst possible construction on everything the ministry did.[64]

What about the perception of those Muslims who regarded the ministry as a 'Hindu' administration, the ministers as 'renegades', and the Congress as a 'Hindu' party? It is true that the Congress record was not without blemish. The Wardha and Vidya Mandir schemes of education were ill-conceived.[65] The neglect of Urdu in UP and Bihar, notwithstanding the pro-Urdu sentiments of Gandhi and Nehru, was deliberate.[66] So was the systematic exclusion of Muslims from district and provincial Congress committees. The presence of Hindu militants in the ranks of the Congress was not unusual, but their overbearing attitude was a major irritant and a source of considerable discord. Ramgopal Gupta, secretary of the district Congress committee in Mahoba, Hamirpur, reported:

The other day the Education Committee of the District Board elected a Hindu Chairman as a result of coalition among the Hindu members on the cry of danger to Hinduism. The defeat of the Muslim candidate through Hindu communalism has angered the Muslim public who cannot distinguish between a Mahasabhite Hindu and a Congressite Hindu.[67]

Ashraf highlighted some other irritants as well. He pointed out how the Congress ignored 'the Muslim sentiment in matters of detail and permitted a number of things to happen which gave the [Congress] annual session a distinctly Hindu appearance'. The League papers emphasized that there were no Urdu posters or Urdu signposts to guide the delegates, no gates and arches named after Muslim leaders, and finally, that propaganda for cow-protection and Hindi was conducted in Congress Nagar. Ashraf regarded these as 'trifles' but conceded the need to make the right gestures. 'Considering its psychological effect on the Muslim visitors,' he observed, 'and particularly in view of the fact that a number of Muslim papers have made it a point to exaggerate to a willing audience, we must take every precaution that the Congress session in Mahakoshal meets all possible susceptibilities.'[68]

In the light of the League's charges, it is an awesome task to prepare a balance sheet of the ministry's performance. Yet, it is worth the effort so as to place the League's Congress-baiting in perspective and uncover the motives behind its well-orchestrated campaign.

It is an undeniable fact, often ignored in secondary literature, that the Congress and its allied partners embarked upon an ambitious programme of legislation, especially to protect the interests of the cultivating class.[69] In the N.W.F.P., *naubat chaukidari* was done away with. The Agricultural Debtors' Relief Act limited the rate of interest realized by moneylenders and cancelled interest due to creditors on 1 October 1937.[70] In UP, the Tenancy Bill was a significant piece of legislation and a forerunner of the abolition of *zamindari* in 1952. In CP and Berar, the Relief of Indebtedness Act, the CP Revision of Land Revenue of Estates Act, and the CP Tenancy (Amendment) Act were examples of radical legislation. The governor of the province admitted that 'there was much of value in the Congress programme and undoubtedly the Congress as a body was striving towards the objective of a better India'.[71] In Orissa, efforts were made to place the tenant in a position of independence, free him from his contract with the landlord, and provide credit and relief from debt.[72] And finally, in Bombay the Agricultural Debtor's Relief Act turned out to be the 'most important legacy left by the legislatures'. The governor's impression was that the ministry was 'inspired by a real ideal of service to the public', and that its performance 'was certainly not bad. And when one takes into account the strange circumstance of . . . the fact that the Ministers, and most legislators, had practically no previous experience of their tasks . . . it was remarkably good and held out promise for the future.'[73]

UP's governor believed—and there is little reason to doubt his opinion—that the provincial ministry had performed admirably in communal matters, and that some of its policies, such as the Rural Development Scheme, benefited the Muslims.[74] They fared well in public services, occupying 39.6 per cent of the posts in the Provincial Executive Service, 25 per cent in the Judicial Service, and 24.4 per cent of Class I positions in the UP Agricultural Service (Table 9.1). Not surprisingly, the governor did not have to use his special powers to protect the 'beleaguered' Muslims. The story was no different in CP, Bihar, and Bombay. The CP Muslims 'have hitherto suffered little, if any, serious injustice at the hands of the Congress Ministry'. The governors of Bihar and Bombay sent out similar reports,[75] observing that the ministers were usually anxious to err on the side of generosity wherever 'Muslim interests' were affected. The Bombay ministry withdrew the textbooks prescribed by the Jamia Millia Islamia and its vice-chancellor Zakir Husain. It also refused to ban cow-slaughter. The CP government allowed Muslim donors to finance Urdu schools for Muslim boys on lines similar to those of Vidya Mandirs and

Table 9.1: Hindu and Muslim Representation in UP Public Services

Services	Hindus		Muslims	
	Number	Percentage	Number	Percentage
Civil				
Executive Service	175	52.5	132	39.6
Tahsildars	106	54.99	84	43.6
Naib Tahsildars	117	55.9	87	44.1
Agricultural Service				
Class I	9	64.2	3	24.4
Class II	32	76.0	5	12.0
Subordinate	401	73.3	137	25.0
Police				
DSP	28	56.0	14	28.0
Inspectors	105	46.4	68	30.0
Sub-Inspectors	1,029	54.2	832	43.8
Head Constables	898	35.2	1,638	64.4
Naiks	884	51.5	883	47.9
Constables	14,063	53.00	12,289	46.4
Educational Service				
Class I	11	73.3	4	26.7
Class II	78	73.6	14	13.2
Subordinate Service:				
Teaching branch	1,062	69.0	372	24.2
Inspecting branch	169	64.0	85	32.2
Judicial Service	159	72.0	55	25.0
Medical Service				
Civil Surgeons	25	83.3	4	13.3
Medical Officers	78	75.0	21	20.1
Assistants	271	80.4	61	18.1
Service of Engineers				
Class I	3	60.00	1	20.0
Class II	21	72.4	3	10.4
Subordinate	104	91.0	8	7.0
Income Tax Department				
Class I and II	24	61.5	12	30.7
Forest Service	12	57.0	4	19.0
Rangers	87	80.5	20	18.5
Deputy-Rangers	175	74.4	59	25.1
Co-operative Societies				
Gazetted Officers	5	62.5	3	37.5
Subordinate	120	77.0	36	22.9

Source: Address by G.B. Pant to members of the UP Press Consultative Committee, 11 January 1939, L/P&J/8/686, BL.

Note: Grants made to Muslim institutions by the Education Department (excluding grants made by local boards) for 1938-9 amounted Rs. 3,83,201. This included a special grant Rs. 48,396 made out to Arabic *madrasas*.

extended official support to such schools (*Bait al-Islam*).[76]

All said and done, however, there is no denying the fact that Muslim grievances existed, and that it was exceedingly difficult to dissipate these by any process of reasoning. After two and a half years of Congress rule, they were embittered by instances (very difficult for the most part to prove, but nevertheless symptomatic of the atmosphere that prevailed) of their oppression. Side by side was the growing realization of the importance, from their point of view, of the Congress claim to be the sole mouthpiece of Indian opinion and the sole party to negotiate with the raj, and an anxiety to secure their own position before their bargaining capacity with Pax Britannica deteriorated further. The result was, of course, seen in the League's consolidation, and the pitching of its demands on a very much higher level.

The demands were that future constitutional arrangements should be made not on the basis of population but on the basis of communities, that the Muslims be treated on complete equality with the Hindus, and that no constitutional change be made without the approval of the two communities. In basing demands on communities rather than parties, the League drew mileage from the Hindu Mahasabha contesting the Congress claims, and the scheduled castes demanding to be treated separately. This was the first tangible step towards delineating the contours of the Pakistan demand. It was very much the outcome of the Congress ministries. The League's only success was in making this perception look *real*.

III

Jinnah raised the war cry at Lahore, the city with a glorious history of cultural synthesis and integration. The mild, moderate statesman, tutored in the liberal traditions of Dadabhai Naoroji, spoke angrily and defiantly, sending out alarm signals all around. Much to the consternation of the Congress Muslims, including Azad who had only just set out his political agenda for his co-religionists at Ramgarh, Jinnah talked of 'two nations', and of Muslims having 'their homelands, their territory and their state'. Refuting the theory of a plural, composite nationhood, he argued that it was a 'dream' for Hindus and Muslims to evolve a common nationality. They belonged to two different civilizations which were based on conflicting ideas and conceptions. Yoking together two such 'nations' under a single State 'would lead to growing discontent, and the final destruction of any fabric that may be so built up for the government of such a State'.

These were ominous remarks; yet, they did not lower the final curtain on the prospect for a united India. Although the crusade against 'Hindu India' had been launched amid cries of '*Allah-o-Akbar*', the syntax and import of the phrases used in the 'Pakistan Resolution' were obscure. The silver lining was that Jinnah had, albeit consciously, refused to define his nation and had thereby left his scheme open to diverse interpretations. The viceroy regarded it as 'very largely in the nature of a bargaining. . . . Half the strength of his [Jinnah's] position is that he has refused to define it and I am quite certain that he would refuse to define it now if asked to. . . .'[77] E.J. Benthall, president of the Bengal Chamber of Commerce and an astute political observer, commented in March 1940 that Jinnah did not want to be dragged into the details of the Pakistan scheme in order to avoid being tangled up in interminable discussions, possibly to the disadvantage of his own case. After an hour-long conversation with him, Jinnah refused to be pinned down to future constitutional proposals: 'his main interest was to keep Congress out while he builds up power and influence.'[78] Resignation of the Congress ministries, combined with the domestic and global compulsions of the British government during the World War, enabled the future Quaid to play his 'Pakistan' card to out-manoeuvre his opponents and detractors. Having been rebuffed and rejected by the Congress leadership for well over a decade, he had at long last earned his moral right and established his political claim to be heard as the chief, if not the sole, spokesman of 'Muslim India'.

Yet, initial reactions to the 'Pakistan Resolution' did not bring much comfort to the League diehards. Sikander Hyat Khan, averse to Jinnah's intrusion into his political territory, was disturbed, as the resolution drafted by him at Lahore provided for definite links with the Centre so as to preserve India's national unity.[79] In Bombay, Muslim leaders saw little in Jinnah's scheme to bolster their self-confidence: 'the best that any Muslim has said . . . is that Jinnah is using it [Pakistan] as a bargaining weapon',[80] an impression not easy to dispel in other quarters as well. As late as the spring of 1946 when Mirza Ismail, the knighted dewan of Mysore, was asked if Jinnah was serious about Pakistan, he said: 'no, it was a move in the political game'.[81] In UP, too, the Pakistan idea was long held to be a bargaining move, 'a counter demand to that of the Congress'.[82] The nawab of Chhatari, architect of the UP National Agriculturist Party, was unsure how the Lahore resolution would protect Muslims in 'Hindu-majority provinces'.[83] Many Muslims in such areas were decidedly unhappy at the prospect of Partition.[84] Their fears were confirmed when they discovered that Jinnah's Pakistan simply provided a homeland for those living in majority areas but not elsewhere.[85]

There were still others—the socialists, the Congress Muslims of Azad's generation, the ulama in the Jamiyat al-ulama, the Ahrars, the Shias, the Khudai Khidmatgars and the Momins—who doggedly adhered to their vision of a united India.[86] The All-India Ahrar Conferences, held in 1943 and 1945 and attended by maulana Ataullah Shah Bukhari and Mazhar Ali Azhar, denounced Jinnah's plan to divide the country. The Momin Conference, convened in September 1945 by its charismatic leader, Abdul Qayyum Ansari, took a similar stand. The slogan of Pakistan, stated Ansari, was 'invented' by well-to-do Muslims to grind down their impoverished co-religionists. The nationalist concerns of the Jamiyat al-ulama, which had already declared complete independence as its goal in 1939,[87] was reflected in the activities of learned and distinguished men like maulanas Husain Ahmad Madani, Ahmad Said, and Kifayatullah. They were insulted, rebuffed and violently attacked,[88] but refused to capitulate to the forces of political reaction and religious fanaticism. Their role must not be written off or relegated to a historian's footnote. In the evolution of a composite, nationalist ideology, the turbaned men with flowing gowns had as much role to play as their counterparts among the Western-educated intelligentsia.

Finally, some of Jinnah's own close associates quibbled and hesitated. Ismail Khan and the nawab of Chhatari, friends of the Nehrus, decided to stay put in India. Khaliquzzaman and the raja of Mahmudabad, brought up in the liberal and composite ethos of Lucknow and Allahabad, dithered for long. But when the reality, so to speak, dawned on them, they journeyed to Pakistan with a sense of unease and remorse. Like so many of their generation, they were pained to bid adieu to the symbols of their faith—the great Imambaras of Lucknow and Matiya Burj, the sacred shrines at Ajmer and Delhi, and the *dargahs* at Bansa-*Sharif*, Rudauli, Kakori and Dewa-*Sharif* in Awadh. They were agonized, as reflected in their diaries and memories, to snap their ties with Lucknow and Delhi, the cities of Mir Anis and Ghalib, or the *qasbahs* in Awadh which served as centres of cultural and intellectual life.

There were, indeed, memories on both sides of the fence, memories of living side by side for generations with a shared heritage, memories of friends and of long-standing associations. The birth of Pakistan severed cultural ties and fragmented an intellectual tradition which was neither 'Hindu' nor 'Muslim' but, in its essence, Hindustani. Quratulain Hyder's Urdu novel *Mere Bhi Sanamkhane* ('My Temples Too'), published in 1947, captured the anguish of a group in Lucknow whose dream of a united India was shattered by the grim and tragic happenings in 1946-7. What was there for them to celebrate at the fateful midnight hour or at the dawn of Independence? Which country did an author like Saadat Hasan Manto belong to? India or Pakistan? When he sat down to write he tried in vain to 'separate India from Pakistan and Pakistan from India'. He would repeatedly ask himself: 'to whom will now belong what had been written in undivided India? Will that be partitioned too?' Other Urdu writers and poets, too, conveyed their agony and experiences in their own inimitable styles. Khwaja Ahmad Abbas, a key figure in the Progressive Writers' Movement, bemoaned the 'death' of one's country. 'Who killed India?' he asked indignantly: '. . . that an imperialist power planned the dismemberment of our country is not surprising. The wonder and the tragedy is that India should have been killed by the children of India.'[89]

IV

So, why did a Pakistan come about which served the interests of most Muslims so poorly? Why did an ill-defined and vague concept sway the masses in such large numbers? What enabled Jinnah to create and popularize the symbol of a separate Muslim nation? Why did the Congress, having championed national unity with such gusto, capitulate without offering much resistance to the two-nation theory? Was it a case of 'betrayal', as Azad pointed out retrospectively, or an implied recognition of the failure of secular nationalism? Or should we search for clues in two of Nehru's statements?—one made in April 1940 when he told Malcolm Darling, a civil servant, that he would accept Pakistan rather than not have freedom,[90] and the other in 1960 when he confessed to the author, Leonard Mosley: 'The truth is that we were tired men and we were getting on in years . . . the plan for partition offered a way out and we took it. . . .'[91] Or, perhaps, in a highly suggestive post-facto justification of Congress acquiescence to the country's vivisection: in an appeal to the Indian electorate on the eve of the first general election in 1952 it was stated:

The price of freedom was Partition. The Congress and its leaders resisted the idea of Partition till the last moment and they yielded only when they realized that the alternative was indefinite perpetuation of foreign rule or civil war or both. The short experiment of coalition government with the Muslim League in 1946-7 demonstrated that no real co-operation was possible between the secular nationalism of the Congress and the narrow communalism and the two-nation theory of the Muslim League. *A strong and stable Central Government could be established by peaceful means only through Partition. . . . It should not be forgotten that without Partition there might have been no transfer of power at all, or the whole of India might have been involved in a civil war the consequences of which would have* been *infinitely more tragic than the sad events of the latter half of 1947.*[92] (italics mine)

Some of these questions, as indeed the clues offered by the election appeal of 1952, have been tackled from a wide range of perspectives. There are, first, those who see Muslim nationalism linked with the demand of a nationality apprehensive of its future in a Hindu-dominated federal structure, and who regard secular nationalism out of place in a society where the 'divisive forces have proved much more dynamic than the cohesive ones'.[93] They find Hindu-Muslim antagonism 'embedded in the historical logic of India'. Farzana Shaikh argues that the call to Partition was driven by a long history of ideas that saw the Muslims as an exclusive political entity separate from others, an 'awareness of the ideal of Muslim brotherhood, a belief in the superiority of Muslim culture, and a recognition of the belief that Muslims ought to live under Muslim governments'.[94]

Such an interpretation, coupled with crude expositions of the two-nation idea, are grounded in the mistaken belief that the ideologues of Muslim nationalism had shared paradigms or a common Islamic framework for determining the place and status of Islam and of Muslims in the subcontinent. Did Mohamed Ali and Ansari share the same world view? Did Muzaffar Ahmad, one of the founders of the communist movement in India, and Fazlul Haq have a common discourse? Was Azad's secular vision and Jinnah's two-nation idea compatible? Was there no difference in the perspectives of the ulama of Deoband, Nadwat al-ulama, and Firangi Mahal? Moreover, even if one were to recognize, for the sake of argument, a common theme across the political spectrum, what place does one assign to the Ahrars, the Khaksars, the Khudai Khidmatgars, of the Momin Conference, the Shia Political Conference and the Jamiyat al-ulama?[95] Their presence communicates forcefully the message that Indian Muslims had a strong secular and nationalist tradition as well which ought not to be forgotten, and that their perspective should not be submerged beneath the rationalizations of the 'victors', the founders of Pakistan.[96]

Furthermore, the two-nation theory is grounded in the mistaken belief that Hindus and Muslims constitute exclusive, autonomous entities, with no common points of contact and association, and that religious loyalty gains precedence over bonds of relationship based on inter-social connections, cross-cultural exchanges, and shared material interests. A corrective to an approach that underlines the primacy of religion is required in order to understand the movement towards Partition in its specific context and not as a 'logical' sequel to developments dating back to the pre-colonial era.

'Communalism' or 'separatism', both in their latent and overt forms, only touched limited groups in certain areas. Their impact was, moreover, transient, for groups embroiled in inter-religious feuds at a given moment could be seen living harmoniously at other times. The governor of Bengal, where Hindu-Muslim conflicts were almost endemic, commented on the rank and file of the two communities co-existing peacefully. 'Only at rare intervals', he added, 'when religious feelings became inflamed, that they treat each other as enemies and clashes occur.'[97] Recent studies reveal the fusion of Hindu and Muslim 'folk' worship, with the practices and teachings of the high or 'orthodox' Islamic tradition and the participation, as in the case of the Muslim weavers of Banaras, in public ceremonials relating to particular Hindu figures.[98] There are also instances, such as the one from Bahraich in eastern UP where the outbreak of cholera in 1930 prompted Muslims to join in great force to worship the goddess Bhawani to induce her to remove the pestilence, which illustrate that religious barriers could be transcended and strict codes of behaviour transgressed.[99] Or the way Islamic ceremonies relating to birth, marriage and death were observed in many areas, though the 'outer labels' were sometimes discarded to make the rituals and practices look 'Islamic'.[100] 'The rigidity of intolerance on view', stated the 1921 Census report, 'which is a marked feature of the religion of Islam in its purer form, does not extend to the masses, who are quite willing to recognize and assist the efforts of their neighbours to keep on peaceful terms with unknown powers'.[101]

Much work needs to be done on the historical development of Islam and of the various Muslim communities scattered across the subcontinent. On the basis of existing studies, we can safely trace the strength of composite and syncretistic tendencies, though their growth and progress were neither unilinear nor unimpeded. Islam in Kashmir developed a resilient tradition of its own, incorporating many social and cultural practices of pre-Islamic origin.[102] Islam in Punjab provided a repertoire of concepts and styles of authority which served to encompass potentially competing values, including the values of tribal kinship, within a common Islamic idiom.[103] Islam took many forms in Bengal and assimilated values and symbols not always in conformity with Koranic ideals and precepts. The cultural idioms, rooted in the Koran and the *Hadith* (traditions), underwent a rapid transformation, giving birth to a set of popular beliefs and practices which, in essence, represented the popular culture of rural Bengal rooted in the pre-Islamic past.[104] Finally, Islam in south India evolved a tradition of worship marked by a striking capacity to accommodate itself to indigenous patterns of faith and worship. Islam gained a foothold because of its capacity to forge links with the religions and peoples of the wider society, and to offer a form of access to the divine which could be grasped and built upon through means already present within these societies. This interpenetration was neither 'degenerate' nor a product of superficial accretions from Hinduism. The sharing of belief and practice was, in fact, built up into a dynamic and expensive religious system.[105]

Nationalist writers in the 1940s and thereafter were wedded to the concept of composite nationality, a quintessential feature of India's liberation struggle, and laid stress on cultural assimilation and social intermingling between Hindus and Muslims. Perhaps they painted an idyllic picture, and disregarded elements of discord and disharmony. Still, the essential thrust of their argument—that the followers of different religious creeds had co-existed peacefully even in turbulent times—was profoundly true. Nehru's reflections in Ahmednagar jail and Azad's introspection at Ramgarh are as relevant today as they were in the 1940s. India's Partition did not make their perspective any less relevant.

In his book published in 1971, Anil Seal, the doyen of the 'Cambridge School', questioned the common assumption which marred historical narratives of previous decades, that the Indian Muslim 'community' formed a bloc of peoples whose conditions were generally equal, whose interests were generally the same, and whose solidarity was generally firm. Unevenness of socio-economic development, he argued, produced disparities between Muslims in different provinces and between Muslims in the same province, just as it was doing between Hindus. In 'so shapeless, so jumbled a bundle of societies, there were not two nations, there was not one nation, there was no nation at all, what was India?—a graveyard of nationalities and the mother of new nationalisms struggling to be born'.[106]

Following the same framework, Paul Brass argued that the ideology of Muslim separateness did not flow out of the objective differences between Hindus and Muslims but out of the use made of those differences through a conscious process of symbol selection. Nor was it the consequence of the objective circumstances of Muslims in UP, who were better placed than Hindus in urbanization, literacy, English education, social communications and government employment.[107] Francis Robinson arrived at similar conclusions; the threat of becoming backward, rather than backwardness itself, encouraged UP Muslims to organize themselves separately. Their influence in the province helped them to do so with much effect.[108] More recently though, Robinson has sought to establish a 'fundamental' connection between Islamic traditions and 'political separatism'.[109]

Until the 1980s, UP was seen as the heartland of Hindu and Muslim revitalization movements, and the chief arena where competing elites devised and followed their political trajectory within communitarian frameworks. Historians have since turned to regions outside the Indo-Gangetic belt to explore the terrain of elite politics within formal imperial structures. David Page detailed the profoundly divisive effects of the Montagu-Chelmsford Reforms in Bengal and Punjab. His story is about how Hindu-Muslim antagonism became a permanent feature of provincial politics, how 'communal' interests were consolidated around 'communal' issues, and how 'Muslim attitudes' were formed towards the emergence of provincial autonomy and the eventual withdrawal of imperial control.[110] Ian Talbot and David Gilmartin carry the story further to trace the roots of Partition in Punjab. In Talbot's analysis, the 'decisive shift' takes place as late in the day as the 1946 provincial elections, when landholders tilted the balance in favour of the League.[111] Gilmartin, on the other hand, examines the evolution of support for the Pakistan movement in terms of a search for ideological identity amid the severe contradictions established by colonial rule. The Pakistan movement remains essentially a paradox to Gilmartin: millennarian tendencies and Islamic revivalism on the one hand; political objectives shaped by the structures of the colonial state on the other. Yet, many of the political pressures that produced Pakistan—and led to Punjab's partition—originated outside the province. The events of 1947 in Punjab owed much to the broader currents that brought the decline of the British empire, the rise of the Congress, and the rapid progress of the League in other parts of India. Indeed, Jinnah's political ascendancy, which in its beginnings owed little to Punjab, ultimately shaped events there deeply. But in the end the Punjabi Muslims decided their own future, for the creation of Pakistan could not be denied.[112]

Studies of this nature lay bare the main contours of political 'separatism' in the critical regions of British India, establish the linkages between provincial and national leaders, and trace the strength of social/cultural inter-connections as instruments of mobilization. The appeal of ideology—nationalist or otherwise—is best mirrored in the specific context of a region. So also its use by the political and religious leadership.

Regional studies do not, in any way, diminish the value of other works that concentrate on all-India leaders and organizations, and unfold the happenings at the apex. For example, Anita Inder Singh manages to fill in some of the gaps in our knowledge of the interplay of British, Congress and Muslim League strategies. She assesses, with much sensitivity, the attitudes and tactics of the three parties in the negotiations for the transfer.

of power and the factors that induced the Congress and the British to accept the idea of Pakistan.[113] It is not very often that the story of such negotiations is told with such clarity and objectivity.

R.J. Moore provides useful insights into the official mind in Delhi and Whitehall. *The Crisis of Indian Unity* deals with the problems of wresting freedom from the British and keeping the country united in the wake of the Pakistan demand. *Churchill, Cripps and India* and *Escape from Empire* trace the evolution of the Labour party's policies to solve the many-sided Indian problem.[114] Read together with the earlier versions and interpretations of Leonard Mosley, Penderel Moon, V.P. Menon, H.V. Hodson and P.S. Gupta,[115] Moore's researches cover important aspects of British policy and strategy towards Independence and Partition.

Many of the themes delineated in their writings figure in a work of outstanding merit—Ayesha Jalal's *The Sole Spokesman: Jinnah, the Muslim League and the Demand for Pakistan.* It is by far the most refined statement on this cataclysmic and violent event. Raising the standard of debate, she underlines the importance of Jinnah's cleverly disguised manoeuvres and the significance of keeping the terms of the Lahore Resolution vague and amorphous. The critical importance of her work lies in presenting the resolution as a tactical manoeuvre and in her success in elevating this interpretation basically from the realm of doubts and speculations and giving it academic authenticity and credibility.[116] Equally important is the way in which she uncovers the provincial world of Bengal and Punjab to argue that behind the simple cry of Pakistan lay a host of complex and conflicting interests, some of which had very little to do with the shape Pakistan was going to assume in Jinnah's guarded exposition in March 1940 or thereafter. Finally, her summation of Mountbatten's role is a powerful indictment of a man who made such tall claims for so modest a 'feat'—conducting an administrative operation that left hundreds of thousands dead and rendered millions homeless. His 'great operation' was an ignominious scuttle enabling the British to extricate themselves from the awkward responsibility of presiding over India's 'communal madness'.

There are, however, notable gaps in an otherwise fascinating exposition. Part of the reason why this is so is because Jalal's perspective is based on high politics and diplomacy. Jinnah occupies centrestage in her narrative, with provincial leaders rather than interest groups extracting their price for supporting the Quaid. That is why the sense of a growing movement, drawing its constituents from different regions and social classes at various stages of its progress and development, is missing. Also missing is a perspective on the ideological content of the movement, on the social base of the League, its mobilization techniques, and its ability to use Islam as a rallying symbol with such great effect. Both Talbot and Gilmartin have argued how the linking of Islamic appeals to social and economic grievances and their transmission through the all-important rural idiom of *biradari* and Sufi networks succeeded in transmitting the League's message from its strongholds in the towns to the countryside, which had the bulk of the voters.

Jalal's version of the Congress' part in the making of Pakistan is one-sided, because her book is almost solely based on official sources, on League records, and on Jinnah's private collection. While it is possible to argue, as Asim Roy does, that the Congress steadily and deliberately worked itself up to a position where Jinnah was forced to take his 'Pakistan' and leave the scene for good,[117] the nature of its political intervention still awaits careful historical scrutiny.

While Jalal marshals an array of facts to establish Jinnah's popularity and the League's acceptability, she does not mention that Pakistan was not everybody's dream and Jinnah not everybody's Quaid. It is a lesser known fact that, in terms of the actual number of votes secured and against the background of the tremendous build up to Pakistan, 'nationalist Muslim' groups did not fare too poorly in the 1946 elections (Table 9.2). Their performance in some UP constituencies, such as Bahraich (south), Meerut (east), Gorakhpur (east) and Pilibhit was, in fact, comforting.

Table 9.2: Votes Polled in the Muslim Constituencies

Parties	Seats contested	Votes polled	Percentage
Muslim League	64	5,15,229	64.70
Congress	29	1,07,877	13.54
Nationalist Muslims	32	1,14,686	14.39
Ahrars	2	10,154	1.27
Sunni Board	1	11,188	1.40
Shia Conference	2	5,847	0.73
Khaksars	3	176	0.02
Independents	30	31,491	3.95

Sources: L/PJ/8/478 and L/PJ/8/483, British Library, London.

Though Congress stalwarts like Rafi Ahmad Kidwai lost in Rae Bareli, success came to Nisar Ahmad Khan Sherwani in Mainpuri and Etah, Bashir Ahmad in Bijnor south-east, and Hafiz Muhammad Ibrahim in Garhwal and Bijnor north-west. Some additional gains were possible had the Congress put up Muslim candidates in the general urban and rural constituencies, and if its nominees were chosen with care. It was a mistake, for example, to pit Abdul Aleem of the Aligarh Muslim University against Haji Muhammad Shakoor in the Jaunpur-Gorakhpur constituency. Similarly, Aftab Ali was too weak a candidate to be pitted against Jamshed Ali Khan, the nawab of Baghpat and a recent convert to the League creed. A more formidable rival could have performed better at the hustings.

In any case, asking people to sit on judgement on the partition plan, which had already been thrashed out during the prolonged confabulations at the viceregal lodge, was an act of deception, a monumental fraud. The die was cast, more so after the 1946 elections which were held under a restricted franchise but were treated as the people's final verdict. The predictable collapse of the interim government and the fire of violence in Bihar and Bengal, which nobody tried to extinguish,[118] offered to every party an opportunity and an excuse to hammer out the modalities of transferring power to two separate nations. Never before in South Asian history did so few decide the fate of so many. And rarely did so few ignore the sentiments of so many in the subcontinent. A distraught eye witness to the trauma of 1946-7 recalled on the eve of her departure from Rajshahi: 'Tears began to flow, I realized for the first time that the part of Bengal which had been my home was no longer my home. It was a foreign land. . . . The underlying feeling was that we were being driven from our own country. . . . We were angry with both Nehru and Jinnah for not handling the situation properly.'[119] Such impressions need to be reflected in our historical discourse. Only then will it become clear that, in the ultimate analysis, it does not matter whether, in the penultimate phase of the League crusade, Jinnah bargained for a separate nation or not. What mattered was his articulation of the two-nation idea and his successful mobilization strategies. The whims and personal idiosyncrasies of individuals do not give birth to new nations. The conjunction of forces and circumstances do. For many of us in the subcontinent, still confronted with and troubled by the bitter legacy of Pakistan, the critical and unresolved issue is how Jinnah and the League secured the support of so many Muslims in so short a time.

Does the explanation lie in UP society and polity? In the evolution of ideas, reinforced by colonial policies, from the days of Saiyid Ahmad Khan? In the unequal contest between Hindu and Muslim revitalization movements? In the conflict between the symbols of Kaaba and Kashi? In the self-perception of a minority community placed in a disadvantageous position in relation to the power structures? In the manipulation of religious and cultural symbols by competing elites? Jalal does not address herself to these possibilities. In any event, she does not think, though it is nowhere explicitly stated in her book, that in making Jinnah the 'sole spokesman' of 'Muslim India' the part played by the UP Muslims was of any consequence. She does not attach much importance to the role of Muslim landlords, the students and teachers of the university at Aligarh, described by Jinnah as the 'arsenal of Muslim India', a section of the Deobandi ulama, and the leading priests of the Barelwi school who had much following amongst the weavers, artisans, and other entrepreneurial groups in the *qasbahs*. Did Jinnah not have such groups in mind when he spoke of those 'who spread the light when there was darkness in the majority provinces. It is they who . . . suffered for you in the majority provinces, for your sake, for your benefit and for your advantage.'[120] These were comforting remarks, though one cannot help concluding with a not-so-comforting thought—never before in South Asian history did so few divide so many, so needlessly.

NOTES

1. The use of the expression 'secular nationalism' in this chapter in the context of India's nationalist struggle may be contested on the grounds that nationalism and its secular dimension was associated with an amalgam which ranged all the way from Gandhi to V.D. Savarkar. I have consciously used the expression because, in theory at least, the Congress and its allies in the left parties and groups subscribed to secular values and were committed to the building of a secular society, a legacy bequeathed to the makers of India's constitution. It is of course arguable that Jinnah tried to fashion a particular variant of secular nationalism for the Indian Muslims, in the perspective of 'modern' ideas of ethno-territorial nationhood and self-determination. I am inclined not to agree with this view for reasons made clear in this introduction.
2. *The Partition of India: Policies and Perspectives, 1935-1937*, London, 1970.
3. G.D. Khosla, *Stern Reckoning: A survey of the events leading up to and following the partition of India*, New Delhi, 1989, p. vii.
4. K.A. Abbas, *I Am Not an Island: An Experiment in Autobiography*, New Delhi, 1987; A.K. Gupta (ed.), *Myth and Reality: The Struggle for Freedom in India, 1945-7*, New Delhi, 1987.

5. Robinson, *Separatism Among Muslims*; Bipan Chandra, *Communalism in Modern India*, New Delhi, 1984; Gyanendra Pandey, *The Construction of Communalism in Colonial North India*, New Delhi, 1990; Freitag, *Collective Action and Community*.

6. Hardy, *Muslims of British India*; Robinson, *Separatism Among Muslims*; S. Gopal (ed.), *Anatomy of a Confrontation: The Babri Masjid-Ramjanam-bhumi Issue*, New Delhi, 1991; K.N. Panikkar (ed.), *Communalism in India: History, Politics and Culture*, New Delhi, 1991.

7. Suranjan Das, *Communal Riots in Bengal, 1905-1947*, New Delhi, 1991, and Gyanendra Pandey, 'In Defence of the Fragment: Writing about Hindu-Muslim Riots in India Today', *EPW*, Annual Number, 1991.

8. I have discussed this aspect in detail in 'Competing Symbols and Shared Codes: Inter-Community Relations in Modern India', below.

9. Robinson, *Separatism Among Muslims*.

10. Hasan, *Nationalism and Communal Politics*.

11. Bayly, *Rulers, Townsmen and Bazaars*, pp. 456-7.

12. For an extract of the speech, Philips (ed.), *The Evolution of India and Pakistan*, p. 185.

13. A substantial monograph on Hindu revivalist movements is still awaited, though some of the aspects are adequately covered in J.R. McLane, *Indian Nationalism and the Early Congress*, Princeton, N.J., 1987 (for an excellent account of the cow-protection movement); Kenneth W. Jones, *Arya Dharm: Hindu Consciousness in 19th-Century Punjab*, California, 1976 and J.T.F. Jordens, *Dayananda Sarasvati: His Life and Ideas*, New Delhi, 1978, for the Arya Samaj movement; Robinson, *Separatism Among Muslims*, pp. 66-82, for Hindu nationalism; D.A. Low (ed.), *The Indian National Congress: Centenary Hindsights*, New Delhi, 1985. And Gyanendra Pandey, 'Hindus and Others: the Militant Hindu Construction', *EPW*, 28 Dec. 1991.

14. It is a comment on fluctuating loyalties that Fazlul Haq, who was so virulent in denouncing the Congress ministries, had this to say after his fallout with Jinnah. He wrote that the Muslim League had roused Muslim passions against the Congress and the Hindus through ceaseless propaganda and 'clever distortion of facts'. Muslims were 'naturally drawn towards the Muslim League as the only organized political body among the Muslims and their only heaven [*sic*] of refuge against Hindu oppression'. British imperialist policy favoured such a development as it 'expected to be able to set off the Muslim League against the political ascendancy of the Congress'. The result 'is that the Muslim League has now got a foothold in the land which is not justified by the extent to which it can truly claim to be representative of Muslim interests'. A.K. Fazlul Haq, *Bengal Today*, Calcutta, Dec. 1944, p. 46.
    It is equally significant that Fazlul Haq, the champion of 'Muslim interests', was prepared to forego this role and fill the vacancy in the viceroy's council created by the death of Sir Akbar Hydari. He wanted the viceroy to give him a chance 'to serve my king and my country in a position of much greater

responsibility than that I have yet occupied in my activities in the provincial sphere'. To Linlithgow, 12 Jan. 1942, Linlithgow papers (125/124), BL.

15. The membership was 1,093 in 1922, 1,097 in 1923, and 1,184 in 1924. *Annual Report of the All India Muslim League*, Lucknow, n.d. Khaliquzzaman recalled how the League merely lived on paper during the khilafat days and how afterwards a 'new set of Nawabs' wrested control of the body. 'They merely attended the annual sessions and received praise from their equally honourable hosts for having undertaken the journey in a first-class compartment at great inconvenience to themselves, and their staying as guests in good, well-decorated buildings with the most delicious dishes to devour and plenty of pans (betels) and cigarettes to chew and smoke.' The proceedings were duly sent to the Press, though long before the British officials received from their own inner sources news of every word spoken at the meeting. 'The end of the session was the end of the organization for the year and no one took notice of what had been said except in the critical record of the Government of India.' *Pathway to Partition*, pp. 137-8.

16. I have cited an eyewitness account of the session in 'Congress Muslims and Indian Nationalism, Dilemma and Decline 1928-34', below.

17. Sayeed, *Pakistan: The Formation Phase*, p. 176.

18. Halide Edib, *Inside India*, p. 348.

19. Liaquat Ali Khan to Willingdon, 14 Sep. 1934, Samuel Hoare papers (4), BL.

20. Harry Haig took special note of the factional struggles in the UP Muslim League and keenly followed the moves of Khaliquzzaman, 'an extremely astute and ambitious man'. Haig to Linlithgow, 2 Dec. 1936, Harry Haig papers (microfilm), NMML.

21. Malcolm Hailey to Melville, 14 Mar. 1934, Hailey papers (E 220/27B), BL.

22. Hoare to Willingdon, 8 Mar. 1935, Samuel Hoare papers (4).

23. Jinnah's stay in London from 1930 to 1934 is covered in Wolpert, *Jinnah of Pakistan*, pp. 119-33.

24. To the nawab of Chhatari, 15 Feb. 1934, Hailey papers (27-A), and Haig to Linlithgow, 29 Oct. and 2 Dec. 1936, Jan. 1937, Haig papers.

25. Raja of Mahmudabad, 'Some Memories', in Philips and Wainwright (eds.), *The Partition of India*, p. 387.

26. Quoted in Mujahid, pp. 230-1, and Zaidi, 'Aspects of Muslim League Policy', pp. 290-1. Some writers do not share such a view. Notice the observation that in 1936-7 a clash between Congress and the League, spearheaded by Nehru and Jinnah, lay in the logic of history'. Bimal Prasad, 'Congress versus the Muslim League 1935-1937', in Sisson and Wolpert (eds.), *Congress and Indian Nationalism*, p. 309.

27. *Civil and Military Gazette*, March 1936, quoted in Zaidi, 'Aspects', p. 230.

28. Pirzada (ed.), *Foundations of Pakistan*, Vol. 2, p. 267.

29. See raja of Mahmudabad, 'Some Memories', in Philips and Wainwright (eds.), *The Partition of India*, p. 384, and the impressions of some prominent

individuals associated with Jinnah. For example, M.R.A. Baig, *In Different Saddles*, Bombay, 1967 and M.C. Chagla, *Roses in December: An Autobiography*, Bombay, 1977; Kanji Dwarkadas, *India's Fight for Freedom, 1913-1937*, Bombay, 1966, and his *Ten Years to Freedom*, Bombay, 1968.

30. Nehru hoped that Khaliq would some day break from 'the reactionaries who surround him'. To Abdul Wali, 30 Mar. 1937, AICC papers (G-5, K.W. i, 1937).

31. Khaliquzzaman to Nehru, 29 June 1937, AICC papers (G-61, 1937).

32. To Linlithgow, 21 May 1936, Linlithgow papers (11-B), Haig to Linlithgow, 10 June 1939, Haig papers.

33. Rajendra Prasad, *Autobiography*, New Delhi, 1957, p. 446.

34. Cited in Zaidi, 'Aspects', p. 256.

35. To Mohanlal Saxena, 5 Sept. 1939, AICC papers (Misc. 30, 1937).

36. Linlithgow to Zetland, 29 Mar. 1940, L/PJ/8/50-B, BL; Rajendra Prasad put forth the same reasons in his *Autobiography*, pp. 446-7.

37. B.S. Moonje, quoted in Linlithgow to Zetland, 17 Sept. 1940, L/PJ/8/507.

38. A.K. Azad, *India Wins Freedom: The Complete Version*, New Delhi, 1988, p. 170. For a different version, S. Gopal, *Jawaharlal Nehru: A Biography 1889-1947*, Vol. 1, New Delhi, 1975, p. 22.

39. To Brelvi, 5 May 1937, AICC papers (G-67/1937).

40. To Ashraf, 5 May 1937, ibid. Also, Abdul Wali (of Bara Banki in UP) to Nehru, 28 March 1937, AICC papers (G-5, K.W. i, 1937).

41. See Hasan, *A Nationalist Conscience*.

42. Draft letter in enclosure: Haig to Linlithgow, 3 June 1939, Haig papers.

43. *Haqiqat* (Lucknow), *Hamdam* (Lucknow), UPNNR, week ending 4 Sept. 1939.

44. *Hamdam*, UPNNR, week ending 18 Dec. 1937.

45. Haig to Linlithgow, 6 Dec. 1939, L/PJ/8/645.

46. F.V. Wylie to Linlithgow, 14 Dec. 1939, L/PJ/8/645.

47. There was a marked deterioration in communal relations, affecting large parts of the north and centre of India. There was rioting in CP on the occasion of Dussehra (Oct. 1937) and at Jabalpur on Holi (Mar. 1938). This was followed by a whole series of riots spreading from the south-west corner of Berar, right across the Jabalpur district in the extreme north-east of CP. In UP there were riots at the Dadri fair in Ballia (20 November 1937), Banaras (15 Mar. 1938), Tanda (25 Aug. 1939), Allahabad (17 Mar. 1938) and at Kanpur (7-15 Feb. 1939). The casualties in the Banaras and Kanpur riots were high. See *It Shall Never Happen Again* (Department of Publicity & Information, All-India Muslim League, New Delhi, 1946). This is a collection of articles published in *Dawn*, with a foreword by Qazi Muhammad Isa, president of the Baluchistan Muslim League. Riots in UP and Bihar are described in Ashiq Husain Butalwi, *Hamari Qaumi Jaddo-Jehad (Our National Struggle): January 1939 se December 1939 tak*, Lahore, 1968; Maulana Basituqqal Ghori, *Meri Sarguzasht ya Congress ka Raaz*, Unnao, 1938. Publications like

Uriyaan-e Muraqqa, Budaun, 1939 described the riots in Bareilly and Budaun districts.

48. All-India Muslim League papers (hereafter AIML papers) (12), History of the Freedom Movement Archives, University of Karachi.

49. The lead was taken by the district Muslim League in Saharanpur, one of the largest centres of rice industry in UP.

50. L/P&J/8/86.

51. *Al-Bashir* (Etawah), UPNNR, week ending 4 Dec. 1939.

52. *Hamari Awaaz,* UPNNR, week ending 20 Nov. 1937; *Sarguzasht* and *Asia,* UPNNR, week ending 4 Dec. 1937; *Haq,* UPNNR, week ending 11 Dec. 1937.

53. *Hamdam,* UPNNR, week ending 18 Dec. 1939.

54. F.V. Wylie to Linlithgow, 24 Dec. 1939, L/P&J/8/645; Saiyid Iftikhar Ali, *Working of the C.P. Congress Ministry* (Nagpur, n.d.).

55. Hallet to Brabourne, 6 Sept. 1938, Linlithgow papers (126/1010).

56. Wylie to Linlithgow, 2 Dec. 1939, L/P&J/8/645.

57. Roger Lumley to Linlithgow, 23 Jan. 1940, L/P&J/8/686.

58. Haig to Linlithgow, 10 May 1939, Haig papers.

59. See Hasan, *Nationalism and Communal Politics,* Chap. 5.

60. *Report on the Municipal Administration and Finances in the UP of the Year 1937-38,* Allahabad, 1940, p. 9.

61. Ibid., 1938-9, p. 9.

62. To Linlithgow, 10 May 1939, Haig papers.

63. Ibid.

64. Lumley to Linlithgow, 14 Dec. 1939, Linlithgow papers (107).

65. Ashraf to Saiyid Mahmud, 14 June 1938, and Ashraf to Azad, 3 Sept. 1938, AICC papers (Misc. 30/1937).

66. Aftab Ahmad (from Calcutta) to Azad, n.d., ibid.

67. Ramgopal Gupta to Ashraf, 3 July 1937, AICC papers (38/1938). Such unholy alliances were quite common. This made it difficult for Muslim Congressmen to secure a position in the Congress hierarchy at the provincial and district levels. Cases from Nagpur, the stronghold of the RSS and the Hindu Mahasabha, were reported by Manzar Rizvi to the secretary, Nagpur PCC, 24 June 1938, ibid. Ashraf was greatly upset with the outcome of a by-election in a Muslim constituency in Amritsar. The Congress candidate was defeated owing to an alliance between the party bosses and the Hindu Mahasabha. 'I could go on multiplying instances', wrote Ashraf, 'to prove that the Congress machinery is fast disintegrating and our provincial and district Congress committees are more or less confident that no direction will come from the Centre and in any case they will be left free to do what they please in a given situation.' To Narsinh, 4 June 1938, ibid. Fida Husain Sherwani, cousin of the Congress stalwart, T.A.K. Sherwani, commenting on the lack of pre-paredness on the eve of the election, shared his anguish with Nehru: 'I have all the time been feeling that my enthusiasm for the Congress is second to none

including yourself and Mahatma Gandhi but this heartless neglect of us by the so-called socialist party in power has made me believe for the last three days that a Mussalman has no place in the Congress and that a good and true Mussalman like myself has no alternative but to commit suicide.' To Nehru, 30 June 1937, AICC papers (G-61/1937).

68. Ashraf to the secretary, reception committee, Mahakoshal sessions, Jabalpur, 25 July 1938, AICC papers (Misc. 30/1937).

69. This is not to deny the inadequacy of some legislative enactments or implementation. Many Congress supporters were, in general, quite dissatisfied with the performance of the ministries in certain spheres. There are many reasons why this was so. But in the case of one UP minister, Sampurnanand, the predicament was succinctly expressed. 'We have to work', he wrote in *Congress Socialist*, 'within the four walls of the Government of India Act, against which we revolt with every fibre of our being. It is not easy. We feel like kicking over the traces. Believe me, not one of the ministers I know does not, immersed in his files, pine for the old days. We live in an atmosphere of unreality. There are many of us who would like to get out of it. But there we are. To my knowledge, there is no historical parallel to the circumstances in which we accepted office. A people struggling for national Independence, meaning to continue to fight for it, stop half-way to accept administrative responsibility! This is a contradiction in our position which creates difficulties.' Quoted in J.C. Donaldson to Puckle, 16 Sept. 1938, Linlithgow papers (101).

70. George Cunningham to Linlithgow, 19 Nov. 1941, ibid. (109).

71. Henry Twynam to Linlithgow, 10 Mar. 1941, ibid.

72. Hawthorne to Linlithgow, 6 Jan. 1942, ibid.

73. Roger Lumley to Linlithgow, 11 Apr. 1942, ibid. See Rani Dhavan Shankardass, *The First Congress Raj*, New Delhi, 1982, for the Bombay ministry.

74. In Sitapur, the Rural Development movement was of help to Muslim weavers as well as the Hindu cultivators. Besides, out of the 789 rural development organizers 20 per cent were Muslims recruited from rural areas. Considering that the Muslim population in UP was largely concentrated in the towns this was by no means a low percentage. Haig to Linlithgow, 10 May 1939, Haig papers; Hallet to Linlithgow, I Jan. 1940, Linlithgow papers (125/103).

75. Wylie to Linlithgow, 18 Apr. 1939, Hallet to Linlithgow, 8 May 1939, L/P&J/8/686. *The Central Provinces and Berar Government at Work*, Nagpur, 1939.

76. Wylie to Linlithgow, 24 Dec. 1939, L/P&J/8/645.

77. Linlithgow to Amery, 2 May 1943, L/P7J/8/512 (part 2).

78. E.J. Benthall papers, File Nos. 12 & 19, CSAS, Cambridge.

79. Malcolm Darling to Linlithgow, 25 Apr. 1940, L/P&J/8/506 (part B). Also, the anguish of Khizar Hyat Khan who felt that Pakistan, deeply tinged as it was with religious prejudice, was getting at a point at which it could not be resisted. He wanted the British government to define 'Pakistan' and to reject

the idea if found unreasonable. But Linlithgow did not agree. The government's response, in his view, would convey to the League and the Hindu Mahasabha the mistaken impression of its bias in favour of either position. He told the secretary of state for India: 'I fear Khizar and his friends will have trouble with the Muslim League, and Khizar may be . . . much less qualified to deal with it than Sikander.' Linlithgow to Amery, 2/4 May 1943, L/P&J/8/512 (part 2).

80. Governor of Bombay to Linlithgow, 30 Mar. 1940, ibid.

81. 'Punjab Memories 1910-1941' (typescript, 1971), James Penney papers, CSAS.

82. Enclosure 2 in: governor of UP to governor-general (telegram), 31 Mar. 1940, Linlithgow papers (125/108). The viceroy referred to the 'uncertainty of the Muslims and the leaders as to where they stand and what policy they are to pursue'. Linlithgow to Haig, 17 Apr. 1939, Linlithgow papers (125/102).

83. To Jinnah, n.d. (probably written in early Jan. 1940), L/P&J/8/507. The role of the nawab of Chhatari illustrates how personal or class interests rather than ideology dictated political preferences. In August 1934 he suggested the revival of the defunct All-India Muslim Conference. In April 1936 he broke away from the League Parliamentary Board to revive a 'mixed Party in preference to a Muslim communal Organisation'. But his subsequent experiences compelled him to re-think his position *vis-a-vis* the National Agriculturist Party and the League. Chhatari to Linlithgow, 4 Aug. 1936, Linlithgow papers (125/11B); Chhatari to Hailey, 28 Oct. 1936, Hailey papers (220/28C).

84. Linlithgow to Amery, 6 April 1940, L/P&J/B/506 (B).

85. In an anonymous letter to *Dawn* dated 19 Jan. 1948, a correspondent who styled himself 'A Musulman' enquired from the newspaper's readers whether or not refugees from India such as himself had been cleverly duped by the creation of Pakistan: the country was surely meant not for them but rather for the people of Punjab, Sind, Baluchistan and Bengal alone. Quoted in Sarah Ansari, *MAS*, Vol. 24, 4, 1990, p. 819.

86. The Haripura session of the Congress in February 1938 took special note of the growth in anti-imperialist feelings among the Muslims. In November 1939, Nehru listed a large number of Muslim organizations which had rallied round the Congress. 'So you will see', he informed Krishna Menon, 'that it is quite absurd to talk of the Congress facing the Muslims. I am quite sure that as matters develop, large numbers of Muslims will be with us.' Report of the Indian National Congress, Haripura, Feb. 1938, p. 7; Nehru to Krishna Menon, 8 Nov. 1939, *SWJN*, Vol. 10, pp. 230-2.

87. Statement of the Working Committee of the Jamiyat al-ulama. Home Dept. (Political), File No. 37/1939, NAI.

88. The League rowdies insulted and, in some cases, physically assaulted leaders of the Jamiyat al-ulama and the Central Muslim Parliamentary Board. Azad was ill-treated in Delhi and Aligarh. His friend, Abdur Razzaq Malihabadi, editor of *Hind*, was attacked in Calcutta. Maulanas Muhammad Quddus and

Muhammad Ismail escaped a murderous assault in Gaya. And in Saidpur (Bengal), the police and a handful of volunteers prevented Husain Ahmad Madani, president of the Jamiyat, from being lynched by an angry mob.

89. Abbas, *I Am Not an Island,* p. 280.

90. Darling to Linlithgow, 25 Apr. 1940, L/P&J/8506 (B).

91. Leonard Mosley, *The Last Days of the British Raj,* London, 1961, p. 77.

92. *Vote Congress—Congress and the Welfare State* (published by the Central Publicity Board, New Delhi, n.d.).

93. Ahmad, *Islamic Culture,* p. 74.

94. Farzana Shaikh, *Community and Consensus in Islam: Muslim Representation in Colonial India, 1860-1947,* Cambridge, 1989, p. 230.

95. For an elucidation of the role of some of these groups, see my *A Nationalist Conscience,* and my introduction to *Islam and Indian Nationalism: Reflections on Abul Kalam Azad,* New Delhi, 1992.

96. See the reviews of *A Nationalist Conscience* by Francis Robinson, *Modern Asian Studies,* 1989, pp. 609-19, and by P.G. Robb, *Bulletin of the School of Oriental and African Studies,* Vol. 1, 1991, pp. 104-25.

97. Earl of Lytton, *Pundit and Elephants: Being the Experiences of Five Years as Governor of an Indian Province,* London, 1942.

98. Judy F. Pugh, 'Divination and Ideology in the Banaras Muslim Community', in K.P. Ewing (ed.), *Shariat and Ambiquity in South Asian Islam,* New Delhi, 1988; Sandria Freitag (ed.), *Culture and Power in Banaras: Community, Performance and Environment 1800-1980,* New Delhi, 1989.

99. *Census of India,* 1931, p. 515.

100. Rafiuddin Ahmed, 'Conflicts, and Contradictions in Bengali Islam', in Ewing (ed.), *Shariat and Ambiguity,* p. 134, and the excellent study of Asim Roy, *The Islamic Syncretistic Tradition in Bengal,* Princeton, N.J., 1983.

101. *Census of India,* 1921, p. 115.

102. M. Ishaq Khan, 'Islam in Kashmir: Historical Analysis of its Distinctive Features', in C.W. Troll (ed.), *Islam in India: Studies and Commentaries,* New Delhi, 1985, and his 'The Significance of the Dargah of Hazratbal in the Socio-Religious and Political life of Kashmiri Muslims', in C.W. Troll (ed.), *Muslim Shrines in India: Their Character and Significance,* New Delhi, 1989.

103. David Gilmartin, 'Customary Law and Shariat in Punjab', in Ewing (ed.), *Shariat and Ambiguity,* p. 44.

104. Rafiuddin Ahmed, 'Conflicts and Contradictions in Bengal Islam', in ibid., p. 115.

105. Susan Bayly, *Saints, Goddesses and Kings: Muslims and Christians in South Indian Society 1700-1900,* Cambridge, 1990, pp. 13-14.

106. Seal, *The Emergence of Indian Nationalism,* p. 339.

107. Brass, *Language, Religion and Politics in North India,* pp. 178ff.

108. Robinson, *Separatism Among Muslims,* Chap. 1.

109. Francis Robinson, 'Nation Formation: The Brass Thesis and Muslim

Separatism', and reply by Paul Brass, *Journal of Commonwealth and Comparative Politics*, Vol. 15, 3, pp. 215-34.

110. Page, *Prelude to Partition*.

111. Ian Talbot, *Punjab and the Raj and Provincial Politics and the Pakistan Movement, 1849-1947*, New Delhi, 1988.

112. David Gilmartin, *Empire and Islam: Punjab and the Making of Pakistan*, London, 1988, and its review by Sarah Ansari, *Modern Asian Studies*, Vol. 24, 4, 1990.

113. *The Origins of the Partition of India 1936-1947*, New Delhi, 1987.

114. *The Crisis of Indian Unity 1917-1947*, Oxford, 1974; *Churchill, Cripps and India 1939-1945*, Oxford, 1979, *Escape from Empire: The Attlee Government and the Indian Problem*, Oxford, 1989.

115. For a useful bibliographical survey, see A.K. Majumdar, 'Writings on the Transfer of Power', in B.R. Nanda (ed.), *Essays in Modern Indian History*, New Delhi, 1980.

116. Asim Roy, 'The High Politics of India's Partition: The Revisionist Perspective', in Hasan (ed.), *India's Partition*.

117. Ibid., p. 123.

118. Commenting on the massacre of August 1946 in Calcutta, Leonard Mosley remarked: 'A few weeks later, however, you would have found it difficult to believe that anyone (with the possible exception of Mahatma Gandhi) had taken any notice of them at all. Not the Hindus. Not the Muslims. Not the British.' Mosley, *The Last Days of the British raj*, p. 40. I believe one should attach some weight to Azad's judgement that 'the people of India had not accepted Partition. In fact their heart and soul rebelled against the very idea. I have said that the Muslim League enjoyed the support of many Indian Muslims but there was a large section in the community which had always opposed the League. They were naturally deeply cut by the decision to divide the country. As for the Hindus and Sikhs, they were to a man opposed to Partition. . . .' *India Wins Freedom*, p. 224. At the same time, it must be said that the Maulana, like everybody else, readily agreed to the Partition plan. In the crucial meeting of the Congress Working Committee held on 2 June 1947, he, according to Ram Manohar Lohia, a special invitee to the meeting, 'sat in a chair throughout the two days of the meeting in a corner of the very small room which packed us all, puffed away at his endless cigarettes and spoke not a word'. According to Lohia, barring four persons—himself, Jayaprakash Narayan, Ghaffar Khan and Gandhi—'none spoke a word in opposition of Partition'. And though the Mahatma 'turned to Mr. Nehru and Sardar Patel in mild complaint that they had not informed him of the scheme of Partition before committing themselves to it', he stopped well short of obstructing 'a leadership united for acceptance'. Quoted in Rajmohan Gandhi, *Patel: A Life*, Ahmedabad, 1992, p. 402.

119. H. Ghoshal, 'The Memsahib I could never be', CSAS, p. 8.

120. Pirzada (ed.), *Foundations of Pakistan*, Vol. 2, p. 224.

10

The Muslim Mass Contact Campaign: A Strategy of Political Mobilization

From the days of the Lucknow Pact (1916), the Congress leadership expressed eagerness to negotiate with a handful of Muslim politicians in order to arrive at a consensus on major political and constitutional issues. The logic of such negotiations stemmed from the belief that India's Muslims were entitled to certain concessions and safeguards because of their distinct political identity and because their interests were different from those of other groups in society. As I have discussed earlier, the political language within which such accommodation was expressed and the energy that derived from a recognition of this conception of society necessarily implied that the very terms of reference precluded any lasting solution to the communal tangle. At the same time, by negotiating with Muslim politicians whose organizational base and political stature were by no means assured, Congress perpetuated its legitimacy as spokesperson of the whole community—a recognition that flowed largely from the organizational and political structures within which the Congress leadership was itself elaborated. Rather than forcing these so-called leaders into a situation where they had, as it were, to demonstrate their implied support, Congress consistently refused to draw out the conditions for such a confrontation, from an apparent desire not to weaken the integral and unified nature of the national movement. It also feared that the consequences of such a confrontation would reveal a divide too profound to remedy. Since national integrity was Congress' cardinal political assumption, such a confrontation had to be avoided.

The collapse of the Congress-khilafat alliance in 1922-3, the revival of communal bodies, and the recrudescence of widespread Hindu-Muslim riots exposed the limitations of Congress' approach. Some contemporary commentators believed that the Hindu-Muslim alliance was artificially cemented on the 'unreliable foundations of religious sentimentalism'. 'The present debacle,' noted the Communist Party of India manifesto, 'was a foregone conclusion of such ill-starred movement.' 'The Congress programme,' observed another manifesto, 'has to be denuded of all sentimental trimmings. . . . The object for which the Indian people will fight should not be looked for somewhere in the unknown region of Mesopotamia or Arabia or Constantinople, it should be found in their immediate surroundings—in their huts, on the land, in the factory. Hungry mortals cannot be expected to fight indefinitely for an abstract ideal.'[1]

Later attempts to revive the spirit of the khilafat days through widely publicized unity conferences and hastily concluded pacts failed to resolve the communal deadlock: such was the fate of the so-called Indian National Pact (1923), the Das Pact (1923), and the Nehru report (1928).[2] Likewise, Gandhi's 'Ram-Rahim' approach and his initiatives in the form of fasts, such as the one undertaken during the bloody Kohat riots of 1924, did not improve deteriorating communal relations.[3]

The problem of attracting Muslim support became an issue within Congress as well. Writing to Ansari, whose own efforts to bring about communal rapprochement were noteworthy, Gandhi conceded in early 1930 that the Hindu-Muslim problem was to be approached 'in a different manner from the one we have hitherto adopted—not, as at present, by adjustment of the political power but by one or the other acting on the square under all circumstances'.[4] In a more candid recognition of Congress' failure, Motilal Nehru observed that 'no amount of formulae based upon mutual concessions . . . will bring us any nearer Hindu-Muslim unity than we are at present'. 'It is my firm conviction,' he continued, 'that Hindu-Muslim unity cannot be achieved by preaching it. We have to bring it about in a manner which will accomplish it without either Hindus or Muslims realizing that they are working for unity. *This can only be done on an economic basis and in the course of the fight for freedom from the* usurper'.[5] (italics mine)

Motilal's formulation was close to that of his son, Jawaharlal, but did not reflect the thinking of most Congress leaders, who persisted with the belief that the surest and perhaps the easiest way of coming to terms with the Muslim communities was to settle the controversy over the issue of joint versus separate electorates, reservation of seats in legislatures, especially in the Muslim-majority provinces of Bengal and Punjab, weightage to Muslims in provinces where they were in a minority, separation of Sind from the Bombay Presidency, and the introduction of reforms in the N.W.F.P. Resolution of the controversies centred around these demands was not easy, as became evident from the deliberations of the All-Parties National Convention and the Round Table Conferences in London. A new approach was thus called for to resolve the communal impasse, to draw Muslims into the Congress fold, and to reach over the heads of Muslim politicians to the rank-and-file Muslim voter. The lead was given by the CWC meeting, held at Wardha on 27-8 February 1937, to discuss the plan of Muslim mass contacts. Nehru took the initiative and, on 31 March 1937, urged provincial Congress committees:

> to make a special effort to enrol Muslim Congress members, so that our struggle for freedom may become even more broad-based than it is, and the Muslim masses should take the prominent part in it which is their due. Indeed when we look at the vital problem of independence and of the removal of poverty and unemployment, there is no difference between the Muslim masses and the Hindu or Sikh or Christian masses in the country. Differences only come to the surface when we think in terms of the handful of upper class people.[6]

The October 1937 session of Congress approved Nehru's plan, pointing out that its aim was to protect the religious, linguistic, and cultural rights of the minorities in order to ensure their participation in the political, economic, and cultural life of the nation.[7]

Organization of the Mass Contacts Campaign

The plan of Muslim mass contacts was in some ways different from previous mobilization campaigns. To begin with, it was based on a series of fresh assumptions that questioned the efficacy of negotiating with a handful of Muslim politicians for short-term political gains. 'We have too long thought in terms of pacts and compromises with communal leaders, and neglected the people behind them', observed Nehru. He called it a 'discredited policy' and hoped that Congress would not revert to it.[8] He also rejected the earlier religio-political initiatives, such as Congress' support to the khilafat cause, in favour of establishing direct contact with the Muslim masses. On the basis of an optimistic—some may say misleading—assessment of the outcome of the 1937 elections, the high command felt that if the party could obtain support from a great majority of Hindus, it could also win over Muslims. Experience during the election campaign reinforced this optimism. Both Rajendra Prasad and Nehru were convinced that in many provinces Muslims appreciated Congress policies.[9] Constrained by various factors, however, Congress could not realize their latent sympathy and take advantage of the 'new interest and awakening'.[10] The remedy, then, was to explain and project its programme, to impress on poor Muslim villagers that they would not lose under the Congress dispensation as their interests were identical with those of the Hindu poorer classes, and to convey the message that their real champions were not the landlords and lawyers of the Muslim League. With a degree of persistence it could thus wean the masses away from the League and draw them into the Congress fold.

On 31 March 1937, Nehru set out his ideas on 'The need for greater contacts with Muslims', directed Congress committees to concentrate on enrolling Muslims, and suggested taking in hand the work of increasing contacts with Muslim masses living in rural and urban areas.[11] The AICC set up a cell to control and direct activities relating to propagate Congress' programme through newspaper articles and pamphlets, and to counteract anti-Congress propaganda. Kunwar Muhammad Ashraf, one of Nehru's most trusted lieutenants, headed the cell. Impressed with Nehru's 'language of Marxism', Ashraf felt that 'we were on the threshold of a fresh mass struggle'. He seemed convinced that 'any honest and consistent anti-imperialist struggle led by the Congress would wean away the Muslim masses from the growing influence of Jinnah and the revived Muslim League'.[12]

The campaign was launched amid much fanfare. Ashraf went on a countrywide tour, addressing innumerable meetings at which he referred to the mass contact programme as a 'decisive state' in Congress' history—'the state of revolutionary mass action'.[13] He exhorted Congressmen to form ward and *mohalla* committees to take up the day-to-day struggle of the masses and advised them to organize peasants, industrial workers, and the unemployed on the basis of Congress' programme.[14] He challenged the notion of a Muslim community with an exclusive and distinct political and social personality; the fundamental contradiction, according to him, was between the class interests of Muslim leaders and the political and economic demands of the Muslim masses; the 'religious outlook' obscured this fundamental division in Indian Muslim society.[15] Using Marxist phraseology, Ashraf tried to dispel the notion that Indian Muslims could achieve freedom on their own. Political experience, in his opinion, demonstrated that the Muslims could build their own strength through the national struggle and not by organizing themselves on a communal basis. Politics was dictated essentially by class interests, and efforts to obscure class differentiation led to the suppression of the exploited elements.[16] The anti-imperialist struggle of the exploited and poor masses in India was 'essentially one and indivisible' and could not be carried out 'on the basis of separate political organizations working within a particular community'. Indian Muslims should join this struggle by participating in the Congress— 'the only joint organization of the Indian exploited masses which interprets and organizes this struggle'.[17]

Ashraf's strenuous efforts were backed by Nehru, who, with his usual flair and aplomb, set out to combat League propaganda, and extended support to the launching of an Urdu periodical 'to give the Urdu-knowing public the ideological message of the Congress to fight all sectarian tendencies'.[18] He rebutted Jinnah's charge that the policy of mass contact was fraught with grave consequences.[19] To boost the campaign, he turned to the Jhansi-Jalaun-Hamirpur by-election where Nisar Ahmad Khan Sherwani was pitted against his League rival, Rafiuddin Ahmad. He attached significance to this election because Sherwani's victory would give a 'tremendous fillip' to its crusade against communalism. 'I want to tell you,' he wrote to Sherwani on 30 June 1937, 'that we regard your election campaign as a most important one and I hope that you and all Congressmen in Bundelkhand will realize this fact and do their utmost in it.'[20] Words were matched with action. Nehru placed Rafi Ahmed Kidwai in charge of the election campaign and mobilized friends and political comrades to take part in electioneering, urging them to 'work in earnest' and give 'all your great energy to this election'.[21] Nehru's own energy, drive, and resourcefulness was truly remarkable.

Although Sherwani lost and the League rejoiced at its unexpected victory, Nehru referred to some positive gains that enhanced Congress' prestige and strength: the party contested a Muslim seat after many years; its candidate secured the majority of votes in Orai and Jhansi, which formed two of the three districts in the constituency; and the rural votes of peasants were almost entirely cast for Congress. For these reasons the Bundelkhand election was 'one of the most encouraging sign of times. It points to the inevitable growth of the Congress among the masses, both Hindu and Muslim.'[22] Gandhi shared Nehru's optimism, pointing out that the election gave rise to the hope that 'if we plod away we can effectively take the Congress message to the Mussalmans'.[23]

The outcome of the election, some prophesied, would place the mass contact programme in jeopardy. Such fears were unwarranted. Reports from some parts of the country indicated an unexpectedly favourable response, leading Nehru to announce that the Congress efforts to increase our contact with the Muslim masses proved rewarding.[24] What pleased him and surprised many was the enthusiasm of newly mobilized groups such as the Ahrars,[25] the Khudai Khidmatgars, and the socialists. They spearheaded the mass contact campaign in N.W.F.P. and Punjab with the active backing of leaders who wielded considerable influence in certain areas and were known for their involvement in nationalist politics. They included Ghaffar Khan and his brother Khan Saheb, Saifuddin Kitchlew of Rowlatt satyagraha fame, the socialist Mian Iftikharuddin, Muhammad Alam, Fazal Din, and Babu Muhammad Din. They attended a meeting in early May 1937 when mass contact committees were first formed in Punjab.[26] A series of conferences held in the following month and addressed by Ashraf and Sajjad Zaheer also had a 'favourable impact on many Muslims'. Impressed by the success of one such gathering in Lahore, the Punjab PCC decided to hold a number of such meetings in the province to attract Muslims to the Congress.[27] Such organized activity spelt danger to the Punjab Unionist Party and the Muslim League. They combined to launch a counter-offensive in order to keep their political base intact.[28] Their fierce reaction reflected a recognition of the growing strength and popularity of the mass contact programme in the N.W.F.P. and Punjab.

In UP, the mass contact programme appealed to Muslims in places such as Aligarh, Lucknow, Allahabad, Budaun, Pratapgarh, Ghazipur, and Shamli in Muzaffarnagar district, while in Jaunpur, for instance, 'the fresh wave is not being passed unobserved and we are sure that the Congress would open a way to us in approaching the masses'.[29] Equally noticeable was the favourable impression on the students of Aligarh Muslim University; the ulama of Deoband; the Shias of Lucknow, Jaunpur, and Amroha; and the Ansaris of Ghazipur and Mirzapur connected with the All-India Momin Conference.[30] Here, too, the Muslim League sensed danger, and Harry Haig, who succeeded Malcolm Hailey as UP's governor, noted that its leaders were 'alarmed at the Congress attempts on the Muslim masses' because they 'feel very strongly that if the community is to retain its individuality, no efforts must be spared in resisting the attempts of the Congress to absorb them'.[31] The raja of Mahmudabad informed his political mentor, Jinnah, that Congress was exploring all avenues of approaching the Muslim masses, and would intensify its efforts in that direction; so 'it was essential that we have funds so that we may try to put up an organization analogous to the very efficient and aggressive organization of the Congress'.[32]

In other parts of the country the drive to enroll Muslims met with success. In neighbouring Delhi the groundwork for the prosecution of the mass contact campaign was prepared by Congress socialists such as Faridul Haq Ansari and Asaf Ali, and Muslim divines such as maulvis Abdul Majid and Ahmad Said, both associated with Congress from the time of the Rowlatt satyagraha. 'There has been a marked change in the attitude of Muslim masses,' stated a Congress report, 'and primary membership among them has also increased.'[33] An 'Enrolment Week' observed in Bombay resulted in 500 Muslims joining Congress.[34] In Bihar the efforts were equally rewarding, especially in Patna, Champaran, and Purnea. Here Kisan Sabhas, the Students' Federation, the Muslim Independent Party, and the Jamiyat al-Momineen were in the forefront of the mass contact campaign.[35] Finally, the *mohalla* and city mass contact committees in Calcutta, Burdwan, and Comilla—all in Bengal—fared well. By May 1937 over 1,000 Muslims joined the Congress in the suburbs of Calcutta.[36]

Several organizations, representing a wide range of provincial, local, sectional, and religious interests, supported the mass contact programme to express their solidarity with Congress. This was true of the Jamiyat al-ulama, dominated by the pro-Congress faction of Husain Ahmad Madani and Kifayatullah; the Shia Political Conference, founded in 1929 with a strong base among the small but influential Shias of Lucknow, Amroha, Bilgram, and Jaunpur; the All-India Ahl-i Hadis League;[37] and regional parties and groups, such as the Khudai Khidmatgars, the Ahrars in UP and Punjab, and the Momin Conference in parts of UP and Bihar. Rallying the Shias, made possible by two important *fatawa* issued by their *mujtahids* in Lucknow and Jaunpur, was the handiwork of a Shia, Wazir Hasan, who took advantage of estranged Shia-Sunni relations in UP to draw the Shias into the Congress movement.[38] Estranged from the Sunni-dominated Muslim League and irked by the violent outbursts over the *madhe sahaba* controversy in 1935-6, the Shias hoped to receive a better deal from UP's Congress ministry.[39]

The Allahabad conference, held on 15-16 May 1937, brought some of these groups on a common platform. Thus Abdul Majid Khwaja, Nehru's contemporary at Cambridge, as well as Wazir Hasan, who had chaired the Muslim League session in May 1936 and had since returned to the Congress fold, appeared alongside Muslim divines such as maulanas Hifzur Rahman and Ahmad Said, and avowed socialists and communists such as Sajjad Zaheer, Mian Muhammad Iftikharuddin, Z.A. Ahmad, and Ashraf. There was much patriotic fervour, reminiscent of the early 1930s when conferences of the Nationalist Muslim Party were held in different parts of the country. There was talk of extending 'unconditional support' to Congress, and speeches made on the theme of inter-communal unity elicited much interest. Reference was made to the League's unrepresentative character, and its leadership—'these upper class gentlemen'—were castigated for their reactionary policies and their 'theories of inactivity and cowardice'.[40] This conference, masterminded by Ashraf and Azad, was a notable feat, the like of which was accomplished only once during the khilafat movement; it was also a significant one in terms of being the first organized expression of Muslim support for Congress in the 1930s.

Leadership and Representation

Lack of adequate evidence makes it difficult to relate the protagonists of the mass contact campaign to their social, occupational, and political backgrounds. A rough survey, however, indicates that they were mostly urban based and drawn largely from the professional classes: lawyers, students, and teachers sharing socialist and Marxist ideas; journalists such as Saiyid Ali Ahmad, editor of a leading Patna-based weekly *Itehad*; Saiyid Abdullah Brelvi and Muhammad Nazir, editors of the *Bombay Chronicle* and *Mussawir*, respectively; Mujibur Rahman, founder and editor of the leading Calcutta newspaper *Mussalman*; Hayatullah Ansari, editor of the *Hindustan Weekly*, published first from Lucknow and later from Delhi; and Muhammad Ismail and Muhammad Jafri, editors of the Delhi papers *Daily Qaumi Akhbar* and *Millat*. Some sections of the mass contact leadership had been associated with Congress from the khilafat days and were connected with the Nationalist Muslim Party and the Congress Muslim Party, organizations founded in early 1929 to canvas support for the Nehru report; others were drawn during the 1930-2 civil disobedience movement.

Among the most vociferous mass contact campaigners in UP were young and brilliant lawyers, journalists, teachers, poets, and writers. Most of them were educated either in Aligarh or in British universities. Having been tutored in Marxism-Leninism, they shared a common commitment to the revolutionary transformation of society through an alliance with radical elements in Congress. They brought a Marxist perspective to communalism that was markedly different from both the religious-oriented approach of the khilafatists and that of the Congress Muslims of Ansari's generation, whose efforts to achieve Hindu-Muslim reconciliation found fruition merely in unity conferences, pacts, and short-term agreements. They rejected communal categories that they believed had been superimposed by the British to create fissures in the mass struggle, and regarded any rapprochement with the self-styled Muslim leaders as counter-productive. The Congress, they argued, deserved support because it favoured abolition of the *taluqdari* system and liquidation of rural indebtedness and insisted on relief for the landless and the unemployed. The League, in contrast, was allied with the British government and engaged in promoting the interests of the privileged classes; thus, its real contradiction, according to Ashraf, 'lies in the fact that a few landlords and reactionaries want to exploit the backward Muslim masses for the redemption of their privileges and a fundamentally reactionary political outlook'.[41] In sum, then, their emphasis was not so much on 'mere honeyed phrases and appeals couched in eloquent and winsome phraseology to the communities to live in amity and grace', but rather on the unity and solidarity of the peasants and workers in their struggle against the British government and its collaborators.

Those Muslims who advocated this position represented a powerful ideological strand among the Muslim intelligentsia. Prominent amongst them were Ashraf, who rose to political prominence in the 1930s as a member of the Congress Socialist Party (CSP) in charge of the minorities cell in the Congress; Z.A. Ahmad, an Aligarh graduate who joined the Economic Information Department of the AICC as secretary (1936-7) and was a member of the National Executive of the CSP from 1937 to 1940; Faridul Haq Ansari, cousin of M.A. Ansari, one of the founder members of the CSP and convener of the Mass Contact Committee in Delhi; Hayatullah Ansari of Firangi Mahal in Lucknow, a graduate of the Aligarh Muslim University and editor of the pro-Congress *Hindustan Weekly* from 1937 to 1942; Ansar Harvani, also an Aligarh graduate with the distinction of being both the founder and general secretary of the All-Indian Students' Federation (1936-9); Husain Zaheer, son of Wazir Hasan, educated in Lucknow, Oxford, and Heidelberg; and Husain's brother, Sajjad Zaheer, and young poets and writers such as Kaifi Azmi, Khwaja Ahmad Abbas, and Ali Sardar Jafri, who was expelled from Aligarh University for organizing a political strike in 1936. The support of such men gave the mass contact campaign in UP an ideological thrust that was lacking in earlier Congress efforts at popular mobilization.[42]

Equally vital was the part played by the Jamiyat al-ulama. Founded in the wake of the khilafat agitation in December 1919, its alliance with Congress, although strained in the aftermath of non-cooperation, remained largely intact. This was evident in 1930-2, when the Jamiyat favoured 'Muslims working shoulder to shoulder with their brethren in the fight for freedom' and its leaders such as Husain Ahmad Madani, Ahmad Said, Ataullah Shah Bukhari, Hifzur Rahman, and Moinuddin joined the ranks of satyagrahis. In June 1937 some of them worked for the Congress candidate in the crucial Bundelkhand election and toured various parts of UP to promote the Mass Contacts campaign.

In August 1937 Husain Ahmad Madani, president of the Jamiyat al-ulama, appealed to his community to join Congress in the fight for freedom'[43] and a year later propounded his theory of composite nationalism in *Mutahhidah qaumiyat awr Islam* (composite nationalism and Islam). In his letters to Iqbal he argued that the word *quam* could be applied to any collective group regardless of whether its common characteristics were religion, common habitat, race, colour, or craft. It should be distinguished from *millat*, which refers to a collectivity with a *Shariat* or *din*. Indian Muslims were fellow nationals with other communities and groups in India, although separate from them in religion. At present, he said, nations are made by homelands, as England, for instance, where members of different faiths constitute one nation. Madani argued that freedom from British rule was necessary for the welfare of Islam, so that Muslim religious duties could be properly performed. The Muslims were not strong enough to win this freedom for themselves, but needed the help of non-Muslim communities. He wanted independence for India so that Muslims could freely express their religious personality, enjoy a truly Islamic system of education, and remove corruption from their social life by abolishing British-made laws.[44] On 3-6 March 1939, the Jamiyat called for cooperation with Congress 'according to Islamic principles and dictates of wisdom and foresight', and urged Indian Muslims to enlist as primary members of Congress and participate in its activities—'as it is the only constitutional way to reach the goal of independence and achievement and protection of religious and national rights of Mussalmans'.[45]

Madani's sympathy for the Congress and his advocacy of Indian nationalism represented a trend set by maulana Mahmud Hasan, principal of the Dar al-ulum at Deoband. In the mid-1930s, however, these views were vigorously challenged by Madani's two distinguished colleagues, Ashraf Ali Thanvi and Shabbir Ahmad Usmani, and by the theologian-politician, maulana Abul Ala Mawdudi. In a series of articles in the monthly journal, *Tarjuman al-Koran*, Mawdudi first related the history of the Muslims in India, debunking Congress secularism, and showing the unsuitability of India for democratic rule. In the *Tahrik-i Azadi-i Hind awr Mussalman* (1939), he concluded that the Muslims and the Congress movement had absolutely nothing in common, and indicted the Jamiyat for its acquiescence in the mass contact campaign—a campaign directed toward the 'total disintegration' of the Muslim community and intended to convert the Muslim masses to Marxism.[46]

While Mawdudi and his ilk viewed the idea as a challenge to the traditional Muslim belief that Islam pervaded every sphere of human

activity, and Congress advocated secular politics, Jinnah, who was averse
to mass politics, viewed mass contact as a deliberate attempt to divide the
Muslims and break the League by 'falsely representing that the Congress
alone has the monopoly to champion and fight for the freedom of India'.[47]
The Leaguers saw in the Congress campaign a threat to their very existence and felt that, unless they organized themselves like the Congress
and won over the Muslim masses, they might find that, Congress had
walked away with their flock. For this reason the UP Muslim Parliamentary
Board chalked out its own plan to enroll 25 per cent of the adult population
of the province in just three months.[48] In September 1937, the raja of
Mahmudabad suggested a plan of action to be worked out by men 'with
determination and consciousness'.[49] Although Congress and the League
had existed as separate organizations for a long time, never before was
there such a rivalry between them for association with the Muslim masses.[50]

The importance of the ulama-League protest and the significance of
their counter-offensive cannot be ignored or dismissed; nevertheless, it is
crucial to take note of the ascendancy of the pro-Congress elements in the
Jamiyat, forcing men such as Ashraf Ali Thanvi and Shabbir Usmani to
resign from that body to fall in line with the Muslim League. Madani and
Kifayatullah guided the affairs of the Jamiyat; others merely followed their
lead. Also, the progress of the mass contact campaign was not greatly
hampered by the virulent propaganda of Jinnah and his newly found allies
among the ulama. By mid-1938, as Table 10.1 indicates, a hundred
thousand Muslims were enrolled as primary members of the Congress
outside UP, Bengal, and the N.W.F.P.[51] Of these, 25,000 were from Bihar,
15,000 from Madras, and 13,995 from Punjab.

Table 10.1: Enrolment of Muslim Primary Members by 1938

Ajmer	477
Andhra	2,832
Assam	425
Bihar	25,000
Bombay	1,346
Delhi	1,114
Gujarat	1,600
Kerala	2,574
Maharashtra	3,894
Punjab	13,995
Sind	1,000
Madras	15,000

The Failure of Peasant Mobilization

It is a mistake to argue, a view held by writers in Pakistan and uncritically accepted by historians of Indian nationalism, that the Muslim community rejected the mass contact campaign unequivocally. The evidence marshalled herein demonstrates that, despite vigorous opposition from certain quarters, the campaign enjoyed success in some parts of UP, Bihar, Bengal, and Punjab. It failed, however, to have much of an impact in rural areas. This was due not to a resolute or determined Muslim opposition; it reflected the limited nature of Congress mobilization. Significantly, Muslim peasants and other underprivileged groups in the countryside, the very sections supposedly mobilized on a massive scale, were largely ignored, with efforts concentrated instead on enlisting urban-based ulama and the professional classes.[52]

What Nisar Ahmad, an advocate from Bahawalpur, observed on 31 March 1937, remained largely true of Congress' strategy in the years to come. Congress, he complained, had not reached the masses—'the backbone of the community' who, besides being familiar with the names of Gandhi and Mohamed Ali, were ignorant of 'everything else'.[53] Ashraf, too, conceded in mid-1938 that the mass contacts work in various provinces was 'totally unorganized' and that no *substantial effort was made to come in direct contact with the Muslim masses in large numbers*'[54] (italics mine). The pattern was thus similar to that from 1930 to 1932, when the Congress leaders minimized civil disobedience propaganda in areas with a high proportion of Muslims in the population in order to avoid igniting communal passions.[55] They did the same in the mid-1930s, although for different reasons and with far more serious implications.

Another important conclusion that emerges from our analysis is not only strikingly different from standard accounts of the mid-1930s but is also inconsistent with the popular belief that, by 1937-8, most Muslims were arrayed against the Congress and had rallied around the League banner. This is not to say that Hindu-Muslim antagonism was not fairly widespread nor to deny Jinnah's success in capitalizing on the 'wrongs' done by the Congress ministries, but to underline that in 1937-8 neither did there exist a sharp communal political solidarity among Muslims. In Bengal, Punjab, and UP, a common Muslim political identity had yet to crystallize, and the League struggled to acquire legitimacy. The Krishak Praja Party in Bengal and the Punjab Unionist Party, organized essentially on cross-communal lines, maintained their ascendancy well until the mid-1940s, thwarting Jinnah's attempts to undermine their linkages. Likewise, there was no clear sign of a complete polarization in UP, and little evidence of the so-called Muslim drift into the League. Hindu and Muslim land-lords, although torn by personal feuds and jealousies, continued to act in unison to protect their landed interests against the UP Tenancy Bill; in fact, the Hindu-Muslim landlord combination works reasonably well in the National Agriculturist Party. Powerful landlords—the nawab of Chhatari, nawab Jamshed Ali Khan of Bagpat, and nawab Muhammad Yusuf of Jaunpur were more concerned to protect their class interests, represented by landlords' organizations, than their communal interests, represented by the League.

Doubtless, the ulama of the Barelvi and Firangi Mahal schools hitched their fortunes to the League bandwagon, and yet most Deobandi ulama joined forces with the Congress. The Jamiyat sponsored, in April 1940, an Azad Muslim Conference which, in opposition to the demand for a separate Muslim state, declared India as 'the common homeland of all its citizens irrespective of race and religion'. Representing at that time a substantial number of Muslims, the conference protested against the Paki-stan idea and against the use made of the Muslims by the British govern-ment and others as an excuse for political inaction. Allah Bux Soomro, premier of Sind and president of the conference, stated that to regard 'Muslims as a separate nation in India on the basis of their religion was un-Islamic'.[56]

The Muslim University at Aligarh mirrored some trends. K.G. Saiyadain, who joined the institution in 1919 and was on the staff of the Teachers' Training College from 1926 to 1938, recalled his participation in the 'great Jubilee debate in 1926 when the students of the university endorsed with great acclaim a policy of united nationalism'. Campus politics in the 1930s remained unchanged, with men such as T.A.K. Sherwani, Khaliquzzaman, Shuaib Qureshi, and A.M. Khwaja—all graduates of Aligarh and closely associated with Nehru and the Congress movement in UP—enjoying a greater following than leaders with communal proclivities. Most office-bearers of the influential Students' Union belonged to the radical alumni circles, anti-British and pro-Congress; the 1936 students' strike against the university's repression of nationalist activities as well as the opposit-ion to a move initiated in the Students' Union in the same year to form an All-India Muslim Students' Federation, was organized in Aligarh; the widely circulated *Aligarh Magazine* retained its pro-Congress bias; and the theme of national unity and communal harmony—central to Mirza Samiullah Beg's (nawab Mirza Yar Jung Bahadur) Convocation Address of December 1938—continued to evoke a ready response in Aligarh. The mass contact campaign also struck a favourable chord in wider Aligarh circles. Its chief protagonists in UP, Bihar, and the N.W.F.P. were Ghaffar Khan, A.M. Khwaja, Saiyid Mahmud, N.A.K. Sherwani, Zakir Husain, Ashraf, Ansar Harvani, Hayatullah Ansari, and Sardar Jafri—all either educated at or closely connected with Aligarh.[57]

The political climate in the country in general, and in UP in particular, was thus no less conducive for the success of the mass contact campaign than in 1930-1, when Congress launched civil disobedience. True, there was now much evidence of mounting communal pressures and increased communal strife. It is also true that the 'highhandedness' of the Congress ministries was bitterly attacked; so was the singing of *Vande Mataram*, the hoisting of the tricolor flag, the introduction of Wardha and the Vidya Mandir schemes of education, which implied a Hindu orientation, the exclusion of Muslims from local bodies, the imposition of Hindi at the expense of Urdu, and the recurrence of communal riots. Yet, Congress was still able to count on the support of several powerful Muslim groups in the N.W.F.P., UP, and Bihar, a fact that explains why the progress of mass contact work caused panic in League circles and led Jinnah to launch a counter-offensive.

The Collapse of the Campaign

Ashrafuddin Chowdhury, editor of the Comilla newspaper *Naya Bangla* and an associate of Subhas Chandra Bose, wanted to know whether the 'Congress Secretariat' would take up the mass contact work seriously and earnestly or whether it would remain 'a mere paper propaganda'.[58] He should have known better. Within two years of its launching, the mass contact campaign ran into serious trouble, not so much due to the League's opposition or the lack of Muslim support, but because of Congress' own reluctance to pursue it with any vigour or sense of purpose. In the early summer of 1939, mass contact committees were scrapped, signifying the unhappy ending of a campaign that was started amid much hope and enthusiasm.

Why did this happen? Some suggest that the programme, devoid of any social and economic content, offered 'too little too late';[59] others argue that it remained largely on paper, and secularist, and radical rhetoric in the end alarmed Muslim vested interests without winning over the Muslim masses.[60]

Part of the explanation must reckon with the fact that the idea was Nehru's brainchild, and he alone, along with some of his trusted comrades, pressed it relentlessly until it formed part of the Congress agenda. Few Congress members shared his enthusiasm. Gandhi disapproved and preferred to proceed cautiously through constructive work among the Muslim masses by both Hindu and Muslim workers.[61] Nehru's socialist allies, too, argued that their concern was with the masses, not as Hindus or Muslims but as peasants and workers of all communities.[62] The idea of a separate mass contact campaign for the Muslims, however, was consistent with the structure of Congress politics and its strategy of mobilization; in fact, it was a logical consequence of the approach followed from the time of the Lucknow Pact when the Congress leaders, in effect, recognized the distinct political identity of the Muslims.

The most bitter criticism came from the Congress right wing. Their opposition was symptomatic of the ideological rift with the socialist Nehru, and based on the fear that the success of mass contact would further bolster Nehru's image and provide him, as in the case of Gandhi during the khilafat days, with a solid Muslim base. They girded themselves to resist the campaign that threatened their political dominance and raised the chances of Nehru's Muslim, socialist, and communist allies dominating the Congress. G.B. Pant, chief minister of UP, thus argued that it was 'not necessary to lay emphasis on the Muslim mass contact' and advised Nehru that Congress should stick to its old policy and creed of representing the 'masses of India regardless of caste or creed'.[63] At the same time, he explained that he was busy securing the 'goodwill and cooperation' of the Muslims by appointing them to high government positions. 'Two of the six Hon'ble Ministers and three out of the twelve Parliamentary Secretaries,' announced a government report, 'have been appointed from the Muslims'.[64] Likewise, J.B. Kripalani, general secretary of Congress, brusquely chided Riyazul Mustafa of Bulandshahar for having 'subscribed yourself as the secretary of the Muslim Mass Contacts Committee . . . as there are no such things in the Congress', and directed the UP PCC to ensure that 'such committees are disbanded'.[65] More discreet critics such as Morarji Desai pointed out that it was neither 'expedient' nor 'prudent' to implement the scheme in Gujarat on the false plea that there were no Muslim workers through whom the work could be done. 'If non-Muslims take up the work,' he wrote, 'it will meet with no response and will perhaps give rise to a dangerous counter-propaganda.'[66]

These were not exceptional or isolated instances. In several parts of UP, such as Agra, Bareilly, and Meerut, there were complaints of inactivity and 'idleness' on the part of mass contact committees; in some cases their activities were hampered by shortage of funds and lack of any organized or coordinated line of action.[67] 'What is being done by the local Congress for mass contact?' asked an agitated secretary of the Young Muslim Party in Meerut. 'How many leaders have been called to Meerut for this object? How many Muslims have been enrolled here as Congress members? *So far I think the Congress diary is nearly blank.*'[68] The Bombay-based socialist Yusuf Meharally was equally disappointed with the indifference of the Congress committees, while a number of Calcutta Muslim leaders were dismayed by the Bengal PCC's reluctance to pursue the campaign and enroll Muslims.[69] They sought the intervention of Nehru, the leader whose integrated secular outlook inspired them most.

The drive to enroll Muslims did not make much headway also because several leading Congressmen had unpleasant memories of the khilafat and non-cooperation days when the Mahatma pandered to the religious sentiments of the Muslims and allowed them to dictate Congress policies. With mass contact making rapid progress, they were now faced with the cheerless prospect of yet another Muslim 'influx'.[70] Fearful that with Nehru's backing and Gandhi's grudging support Muslims would wrest major concessions, the Congress right wing, in alliance with the Hindu Mahasabha, fiercely attacked the mass contact programme in an attempt to thwart its success. Part of their strategy was to starve mass contact committees of funds, to fill them with their trusted lieutenants, and to ensure that Muslims were kept out of provincial and district Congress committees.[71] In Aligarh, for instance, Nehru got wind of the plan to exclude the only two Muslims who filed their nominations out of the fifty DCC seats. He intervened to set matters right. In Budaun, there was quite a furore when Idris Khan Lodi, associated with Congress for nearly two decades, was not allowed to contest a PCC seat. Lodi resigned in disgust, along with seventy-five other Muslims. In Mahoba and Hamirpur, the Hindu members forged a coalition on the cry of danger to Hinduism to defeat a Muslim candidate from being elected to the Education Committee of the district board. 'The defeat of the Muslim candidate through Hindu communalism,' wrote Ramgopal Gupta, secretary of the DCC, 'has angered the Muslim public who cannot distinguish between a Mahasabhite Hindu and a Congressite Hindu.' Finally, in the vital Bundelkhand and Amritsar by-election the Congress right wing worked against two Congressmen of long standing—Nisar Ahmad Khan Sherwani and Saifuddin Kitchlew—and contributed to their defeat. Such belligerence could hardly inspire confidence among the Congress Muslims, who braved the fierce and bitter attacks of the League, resisting pressures to desert the Congress camp and becoming part of the communal front.[72]

The success of the mass contact campaigns—as, indeed, of any such initiative—depended on the active backing of provincial and district Congress committees. This was not easily forthcoming. One of the reasons—one that constantly figured in the Muslim-owned Urdu press—was that these bodies were often controlled by men with close links with the Hindu Mahasabha and other overtly communal organizations.[73] In Gorakhpur a Holi procession, with spears, swords, and sticks on display, was led by senior office-bearers of the DCC 'reacting very badly on the position of the Congress Muslims and on the prospect of Congress work in general'.[74] In Budaun and Bareilly, districts with large Muslim populations, local Congressmen exacerbated communal tensions, while in Dehradun an indignant Khushi Lal, chairman of the municipal board, warned Nehru of serious consequences if Congressmen fomented communal troubles, and 'try to impose a social boycott of all the Muslims for the sins, imaginary or real, of one or two'.[75] Lal was right. The presence of such elements in Congress made the task of drawing Muslims into the nationalist fold difficult and diminished chances of accomplishing Hindu-Muslim amity.

Congress' one and only attempt to isolate the communal elements failed. On 11-16 December 1938, the CWC declared, probably at the initiative of Ashraf and his socialist comrades,[76] the Hindu Mahasabha and the Muslim League as communal organizations and debarred *elected* members of Congress committees from serving on similar committees in the Mahasabha and the League.[77] This decision, adopted somewhat belatedly, elicited much interest, and PCCs and DCCs all over the country wanted to know whether they could exclude the Hindu Mahasabhites. 'In our belief,' wrote the secretary of the Bengal PCC, 'Congress organization will suffer very much in prestige and hold over the masses if Congress members be allowed to be members of the Hindu Mahasabha organizations.'[78] J.B. Kripalani, Congress' general secretary, ignored such views, however, and gave an interpretation that defeated the purpose of the CWC's resolution. He wrote to the secretary of the Bengal PCC:

You must remember Article V(c) in the constitution refers not to primary members of any communal organization but to members of elected committees. There is therefore nothing in the Congress constitution, even if the working committee named some organizations as communal, in the sense contemplated by Article V(c) to prevent ordinary primary members of such organization from being office holders in the Congress organization.[79]

Inconsistent with the spirit of the CWC resolution, this interpretation gave a free hand to communal groups to move in and out of the Congress with ease and to meddle in its affairs brazenly. Congress' own position regarding communal organizations and the communal activities of its members remained dangerously vague.

Summary

The mass contact campaign was Congress' last serious attempt to mobilize Muslims in a joint struggle against colonial rule. Although based on a set of assumptions that did not adequately take into account the presence of the 'third party', this campaign, conceived at a crucial historical juncture, was a significant move in the right direction. Pursued purposefully, it had the potential of weaning large sections of the Muslim communities away from the Muslim League camp, a point so well made by some contemporary observers.[80] There can be no doubt about the problems that Nehru and other protagonists of mass contacts were confronted with: the stout resistance of Jinnah, the lukewarm support of their own party comrades, and communal animosities manifest in Hindu-Muslim rioting and other forms of antagonism. These problems were not insurmountable, however, as would appear from Nehru's own assessment. The League, after all, was weak, divided, and disorganized, and its leader, Jinnah, did not yet command widespread allegiance in Punjab, UP, and Bengal. Congress, however, enjoyed a fair measure of goodwill, a fact that places Jinnah's outburst against mass contact and the League's endeavors to arrest its progress, in perspective. Its inability to consolidate the gains of the year 1937 to 1938, was a sure case of letting an opportunity slip by. By letting the mass contact campaign peter out, Congress allowed Jinnah, perhaps involuntarily, to take advantage of deteriorating communal relations and rally his community around the symbol of a Muslim homeland; in fact, Ashraf suggested many years later that one reason why the League 'turned overnight into a full-fledged manager' was because Congress abandoned the struggle of mass contact for ministry-making.[81]

NOTES

1. G. Adhikari (ed.), *Documents of the History of the Communist Party of India,* Vol. 1: *1917-1922,* New Delhi, 1971, p. 345; Vol. 2: *1923-1925,* New Delhi, 1974, p. 210.
2. For details see, Hasan, A *Nationalist Conscience.*
3. Hasan, *Nationalism and Communal Politics.*
4. Statement by Gandhi on 16 February 1930, Hasan (ed.), *Muslims and the Congress,* p. 101.

5. Ibid., pp. 103-4.
6. *SWJN*, Vol. 8, p. 123. All references are drawn from this volume.
7. Deepak Pandey, 'Congress-Muslim League Relations 1937-9: "The Parting of the Ways"', *MAS*, Vol. 12 (1978), p. 643.
8. *SWJN*, Vol. 8, p. 128.
9. For Rajendra Prasad statement, *Bombay Chronicle*, 26 Apr. 1937.
10. *SWJN*, Vol. 8, p. 123.
11. Ibid.
12. Horst Kruger (ed.), *Kunwar Muhammad Ashraf: An Indian Scholar and Revolutionary 1903-1962*, Berlin: Academie-Verlag, 1966, pp. 112-13. Ashraf's excitement was shared by his associates. His comrade, Sajjad Zaheer, one of the founders of the Progressive Writers' Movement, recalled: 'As I belonged to the same Allahabad group of young Indians who had then arrived from Europe after finishing their education there, I wish to record here the feeling of hopefulness in and enthusiasm for . . . the success of our revolutionary mission with which we and a large number of young Indian intelligentsia were moved during that time.' Sajjad Zaheer, 'Recent Muslim Politics in India and the Problem of National Unity', in S.T. Lokhandwala (ed.), *India and Contemporary Islam*, Shimla: Indian Institute of Advanced Study, 1971.
13. AICC papers, File No. 30/1937, Misc., p. 15.
14. AICC papers, File No. 48/1937, p. 155; *Hindustan*, 10 Oct. 1937, p. 5.
15. AICC papers, File No. 13/1937, p. 39.
16. To Hassan Habib, editor of *Agra Citizen* (Agra), 15 Jul. 1938, AICC papers, File No. G-67/1938, pp. 17-21.
17. Resolution proposed by Ashraf and Z.A. Ahmad at the 1938 Haripura session of the Congress, AICC papers, File No. G-103/1938.
18. *Bombay Chronicle*, 10 Jul. 1937; *SWJN*, Vol. 8, p. 156.
19. *SWJN*, Vol. 8, 25 Apr. and 23 May 1937, pp. 125, 131-2.
20. Ibid., 30 Jun. 1937, p. 138. Also see letters to R.V. Dhulekar, 30 Jun. 1937, and to Rafi Ahmad Kidwai, 1 Jul. 1937, pp. 139, 146.
21. To A.G. Kher and Manilal Pande, 30 Jun. 1937, *SWJN*, Vol. 8, pp. 140-1.
22. To Rajendra Prasad, 21 Jul. 1937, *SWJN*, p. 167; statement to the press, 25 Jul. 1937, *SWJN*, Vol. 8, p. 171; *Bombay Chronicle*, 27 Jul. 1937.
23. To Nehru, 30 Jul. 1937, *CWMG*, Vol. LXV, p. 445.
24. Circular to PCC's, 10 Jul. 1937, *SWJN*, Vol. 8, p. 156. 'The Mussalmans of UP and Punjab,' reported the *Bombay Chronicle*, 3 Jun. and 1 Nov. 1937, 'are rallying round the Congress in large numbers much to the discomfiture of big landlords and the Muslim Leaguers.'
25. S. Tufail Ahmad Manglori, *Ruh-i Raushan Mustaqbil*, Budaun, 1946, p. 132; M. Rafique Afzal, *Political Parties in Pakistan: 1947-1958*, Islamabad, 1976, pp. 27-8; statement of Anwar Sabri, secretary of the UP Provincial Ahrar Committee, in *Leader*, 8 Apr. 1937; resolution of the Provincial Ahrar

Conference, Lucknow, *Bombay Chronicle*, 19 Apr. 1937. See Smith, *Modern Islam in India*, pp. 270-6.

26. *Leader*, 6 and 12 Jun. 1937.

27. AICC papers, File No. P-24(i)/1937, p. 8.

28. *Bombay Chronicle*, 8 May 1937.

29. Ahmad Khan president DDC to Ashraf, 24 Jul. 1938 (in Urdu); Muhammad Aqil to Ashraf, 30 Apr. 1937 (in Urdu); and Hargovind Singh to Ashraf, 29 Jun. 1937, respectively, in AICC papers, File No. 42(B)/1937, Misc., p. 378, File No. 42(i)/1937, p. 557.

30. Aftab Ahmad Khan to Ashraf, 26 Apr. 1937, AICC papers, File No. 11/1937, Misc., p. 279; Fazalbhoy, editor of the university magazine, in *Bombay Chronicle*, 24 May 1937. The Momin Conference was established in 1926 in order to focus on the separate and distinct interests of the weavers, variously known as Ansari and Momin. The conference, with its headquarters in Kanpur, claimed to have a membership of 2 lakhs with over 500 branches in UP alone. Abdul Qaiyum Ansari to Rajendra Prasad, 9 Oct. 1939, Jawaharlal Nehru papers (hereafter cited as Nehru papers), File No. 136, part 2, NMML. For further details, Manglori, *Ruh-i Raushan Mustaqbil*, pp. 143-4.

31. Haig to Linlithgow, 7 and 24 May 1937, Haig papers.

32. The raja of Mahmudabad to M.A. Jinnah, 8 Aug. 1937. Shamsul Hasan collection, Karachi.

33. Annual Report of the Delhi PCC for 1937, AICC papers, File No. P-25/1937, p. 60. *Leader*, 21 Apr. 1937.

34. Report for the month of Sept. 1937, AICC papers, File No. P-24(i)/1937, p. 13. By Dec. 1937, 3,894 Muslims joined Congress in Maharashtra. Report of the Maharashtra PCC, 8-31 Dec. 1937, AICC papers, File No. P-25/1937, p. 101. 'The Muslim Leaguers of our province', reported Brelvi, editor of the *Bombay Chronicle*, 'are whipping themselves into furious activity. . . . Some local friends are even holding out threats of violence if we go on spreading our contacts with the masses.' To Ashraf, 5 May 1937, AICC papers, G-67/1937, p. 101.

35. Wali Hasan to Ashraf, 20 Jun. 1937; Saiyid Mahmud and Abdul Bari organized meetings, lectures, and conferences; so did Maulvi Nizamuddin, president of the Champaran branch of the Muslim Independent Party. *Bombay Chronicle*, 19 Apr. and 18, 26 Jun. 1936. Significant also was the support extended by the provincial Jamiyat al-Momineen. Hakim Wasi Ahmad to Rajendra Prasad, 12 Mar. 1937 (telegram), Valmiki Chaudhary (ed.), *Dr. Rajendra Prasad Correspondence and Select Documents*, New Delhi, 1984, Vol. 1, p. 30.

36. *Bombay Chronicle*, 18 May 1937. For an optimistic assessment of the work Calcutta Mass Contact Committee, see Manzoor Ahmad to Ashraf, 13 July 1938 (in Urdu), AICC papers, File No. 42/1937 (1), pp. 117-18.

37. *Bombay Chronicle*, 25 Nov. 1937. The Ahl-i Hadis accepted the entire corpus of the Prophet Muhammad's *hadis* (traditions) and rejected the four juristic

schools: Hanafi, Shafai, Maliki, and Hambali. Ahmad, *Islamic Modernism*, pp. 113-22.

38. *Leader*, 25 Apr. and 9 Jun. 1937.

39. *Sarfraz* (Lucknow), 17 Aug. 1937, AICC papers, File No. 49/1937, Misc., p. 160.

40. *Leader*, 18 May 1937; AICC papers, File No. 12/1937, Misc., pp. 43-5. For Jinnah's criticism of the Allahabad conference, *Bombay Chronicle*, 20 Apr. 1937.

41. *Leader*, 15 Apr. 1937; AICC papers, File No. 31/1937, Misc., pp. 39, 207.

42. Leaders of the CSP were strong supporters of a more general mass contacts strategy.

43. *Bombay Chronicle*, 3 June and 16 Aug. 1937; AICC papers, File No. 30/1937, Misc., p. 585.

44. The summary is based on Hardy, *Muslims of British India*, pp. 227-8.

45. *Leader*, 8 Mar. 1939.

46. Qureshi, *Ulema in Politics*, pp. 335-8.

47. *Bombay Chronicle*, 20 Apr. 1937. The Pirpur Report (1938) also charged that the aim of mass contact was 'to destroy Muslim solidarity and create disruption in the community', and to 'lure' Muslims into the Congress fold by following a policy of 'divide and rule'. For Shaukat Ali's outburst, *Bombay Chronicle*, 28 Dec. 1937, and Sayeed, *Pakistan: The Formative Phase*, pp. 89-90.

48. *Bombay Chronicle*, 20 Apr. 1937.

49. The raja of Mahmudabad to Jinnah, 24 Sept. 1937, Shamsul Hasan collection.

50. Khaliquzzaman to Nehru, 29 June 1937; AICC papers, File No. G-1/1937, p. 173.

51. AICC papers, File No. G-22/1938.

52. Some Muslims, such as Fahimuddin Noori, a regular contributor to the Delhi paper, *Alaman,* opposed the ulama being pressed into service. Their intervention in politics, he observed, would eventually prove 'harmful'. To Ashraf, 20 Apr. 1937 (in Urdu); AICC papers, File No. 41/1937, p. 173. For the role of ulama, especially in the Bundelkhand elections, AICC papers, File No. 30/1937, pp. 583-5.

53. AICC papers, File No. 41/1937, p. 27. Abul Hayat, one of Bengal's most consistent nationalists, regretted that the Congress leadership 'persistently neglected to pay heed to the needs and aspirations of the Muslim masses and always tried to come to a settlement with the top leaders of the Muslim League'. Abul Hayat, *Mussalmans of Bengal*, Calcutta, 1966, pp. 65-6.

54. AICC papers, File No. G-22/1938.

55. Pandey, *Ascendancy of the Congress*, p. 149.

56. For his role, *Bombay Chronicle*, 18 and 26 June 1937.

57. The role of the Muslim intelligentsia is the subject of a separate study. See my, 'Nationalist and Separatist Trends in Aligarh, 1915-47', *Indian Economic and Social History Review*, Vol. 22 (1985), pp. 1-33.

58. To Ashraf, 16 Apr. 1937, AICC papers, File No. 26/1937, Misc., p. 9.
59. Pandey, *Ascendancy of the Congress*, p. 151; Deepak Pandey, 'Congress-Muslim League Relations', pp. 643-9; Hardy, *Muslims of British India*, p. 227; Sayeed, *Pakistan*, pp. 89-90.
60. Sumit Sarkar, *Modern India, 1885-1947*, New Delhi: Macmillan, 1983, p. 354; Bipan Chandra, *Communalism in Modern India*, New Delhi, 1984, p. 300.
61. *SWJN*, Vol. 8, p. 225.
62. B.P.L. Bedi, 'Communalism Enters Congress', *Congress Socialist*, 12 June 1937.
63. Nehru papers, Vol. 79, part I, pp. 65-6; V.N. Tiwary to Nehru, 7 Jan. 1939, Nehru papers, quoted in Deepak Pandey, 'Congress-Muslim League Relations', p. 649. For opposition of Mohanlal Gautam, see proceedings of the executive council of the UPPCC held at Allahabad on 20 June 1937, recorded in UPPCC papers (microfilm), Reel No. 2, NMML.
64. AICC papers, File No. 1/1937, p. 41.
65. 7 Jan. 1939, AICC papers, File No. P-20/1938, pp. 329, 341.
66. To Ashraf, 26 June 1937, AICC papers, File No. 49/1937, p. 129. Ashraf's view, however, was that the 'average Mussalman hesitates to join the Congress not because he has any inherent dislike but because he is ignorant of what the Congress stands for'. To Morarji Desai, 5 June 1937, p. 133.
67. Manzer Siddiqi, editor of *Asia*, to Ashraf, 10 Sept. 1938, AICC papers, File No. 30/1937, Misc., p. 179; Damodar Swarup Seth to Ashraf, 20 Aug. 1937, AICC papers, File No. 42/1937 (2), p. 381; and Shamsul Huda, secretary, Barabazar Congress Committee, to Ashraf, AICC papers, 48/1937, Misc., p. 73. A.K. Azad's pamphlet *Congress and Mussalmans* could not be distributed for lack of funds; AICC papers, File No. 11/1937, p. 65.
68. AICC papers, File No. 47/1937, p. 62 (italics mine).
69. Yusuf Meharally, 'Non-Congress Ministries in the Melting Pot', *Congress Socialist*, 26 Mar. 1938, p. 223; S.M. Ahmad to Ashraf, 19 Aug. 1937 (in Urdu), AICC papers, File No. 47/1937, p. 85.
70. In anticipation of Congress' electoral victory in Bijnor and the expected Muslim entry into the party in large numbers, B.S. Moonje proposed to Bhai Parmanand and raja Narendranath that all the Hindu Mahasabhites should join Congress to counteract the effect of such an influx. See *Bombay Chronicle*, 9 Nov. 1937. Notice the comment of the Urdu daily *Hind:*, 'Responsible Congressmen,' wrote the Calcutta paper, 'have never countenanced the entry of Muslims in the Congress and they have in fact encouraged communalism.' Nehru to president, Bengal PCC, 10 Apr. 1937, AICC papers, File No. 49/1937, Misc., p. 251.
71. Manzar Rizvi of the Political and Economic Information department brought this complaint to the notice of the secretary, Nagpur PCC. Such reports also reached the AICC office from Jabalpur, Hamirpur, and Bulandshahar. For

relevant information, see AICC papers, File No. 30/1937, Misc., pp. 63, 429; File No. 38/1938, p. 99. For Aligarh, see File Nos. P-20(2)/1938-9, p. 276; for Budaun see, Ashraf to K.D. Malaviya, 12 Jan. 1939, AICC papers, File No. 30/1937, Misc., p. 81, and Mahoba and Hamipur, 3 July 1937, AICC papers, File No. 38/1938, p. 99.

72. Fida Ahmad Khan Sherwani attributed the defeat of his brother Nisar to the 'ruthless' neglect of Congress and reached the conclusion that 'a Mussalman has no place in the Congress'. To Nehru, 30 June 1937, AICC papers, File No. G-61/1937, pp. 197-9. See K.C. Nigam to Ashraf, 26 July 1937, AICC papers, File No. 42(2)/1937, p. 391.

73. Ashraf was posted with such news. The president of the Jessore Hindu Sabha, he was informed, was also a prominent member of the provincial, district, and town Congress committee. There were reports of an alliance between V.D. Savarkar, one of the founders of the Hindu Mahasabha, and the speaker of the Central Provinces Assembly. The links of many UP Congressmen, such as Malaviya, with Hindu communal and revivalist causes is fairly well known. This was, incidentally, the strain of many editorial comments. See *Din Duniya Weekly* (New Delhi), in Urdu, 11 Feb. 1937; AICC papers, File No. 41/1937, Misc., p. 107; Saiyid Hasan Baqai, editor of *Peshwa*, an Urdu monthly, to Ashraf, 5 Aug. 1937, in Urdu, AICC papers, File No. 47/ 1937, Misc., p. 123; *Hilal* (Bombay), AICC papers, File No. 47/1937, Misc., p. 81. Abbas Husain, editor of *Akhbar Qaum wa Risala-i Tamaddun*, to Nehru, 19 Apr. 1937, AICC papers, File No. 41/1937, Misc., p. 169. Also, references in Ashraf to Azad, 3 Sept. 1938, AICC papers, File No. 30/1937, Misc., p. 213, and M. Umar Khan to Ashraf, 8 May 1937, AICC papers, File No. P-5/1948, pp. 77-81.

74. To A.K. Azad, 27 June 1938, AICC papers, File No. 30/1937, Misc., p. 399.

75. Ashraf to Lal Bahadur Shastri, 5 Apr. 1939, AICC papers, File Nos. 6(1)/ 1937, P-20(2)/1938-9, pp. 273-7 and 193.

76. Ashraf to Mohanlal Saxena, 3 Sept. 1938, AICC papers, File No. 30/1937, Misc., pp. 209-10.

77. Resolution of the CWC, Wardha, 11-16 Dec. 1938, AICC papers, File No. P-1/1938.

78. Ashrafuddin Chowdhury to Kripalani, 16 Aug. and 20 Sept. 1938, AICC papers, File No. P-5/1938.

79. To Chowdhury, 6 Oct. 1938, AICC papers, File No. P-5/1938, p. 101.

80. Dube Rai to Ashraf, 19 Dec. 1937, AICC papers, File No. 54/1937, Misc., p. 399; Faridul Haq Ansari, 'Communalism Clarified', *Congress Socialist*, 19 Feb. 1938, pp. 122-3; Hayat, *Mussalmans of Bengal*, p. 65.

81. Kruger, *Kunwar Muhammad Ashraf*, pp. 413-14.

11

The Local Roots of the Pakistan Movement: The Aligarh Muslim University

One of the author's earliest memories is of the arrival in our ancestral village in northern India of three young men carrying the Muslim League flag—the Islamic crescent and star on a deep green background. The three were students from Aligarh University. They planted the flag in the village square and a crowd of little boys gathered around them. . . . Within an hour our quiet village had been turned into a 'Pakistan Village'. . . . Every piece of green material our mother could find was made into Muslim League flags. . . . A few months later they [parents] all walked in their bare feet and some carried their aged and sick parents on the backs to the polling booth four miles away to vote for the Muslim League and Pakistan. This was repeated all over India. Seldom in History have so few inspired so many with so little effort.

KALIM SIDDIQUI, *Conflict, Crisis & War in Pakistan*

This chapter seeks to examine, with the aid of hitherto unexplored materials from the Sir Saiyid Archives at Aligarh and the Shamsul Hasan collection in Karachi, how and why the Pakistan idea caught the imagination of people who were far removed from the mutual bickering at the national scene. By focusing on the Aligarh Muslim University, I endeavour to analyse how and why an important centre of nationalist activity during the khilafat and non-cooperation days was so quickly transformed into the 'arsenal' of 'Muslim India' and the 'emotional centre' of the Pakistan demand.

The choice of the university is dictated by its critical role in creating a Muslim intelligentsia in north India and its overall impact on their intellectual and political activities. The M.A.O. College, founded by Saiyid Ahmad Khan in 1886, headquartered the Muhammadan Educational Conference and hosted five of its eleven sessions. It was the arena in which Muslim opinion was created and in which the Muslim leadership in UP assembled. The agitation against the Nagri resolution of 18 April 1900 was led, organized and dominated by the Aligarh Muslims, while the Simla deputation of October 1906, a catalyst for the formation of the Muslim League in December that year, was also an act of the Aligarh elders. Just before its elevation to the status of a university in 1920, the college was in the forefront of the great post-War agitation on behalf of the Turkish khalifa. Finally, it attained new heights of practical and symbolic prominence in the 1940s as a centre for mobilizing a powerful Muslim response to the Pakistan movement. In the words of the Aga Khan,

often in civilized history a university has supplied the springboard for a nation's intellectual and spiritual renaissance. . . . Aligarh is no exception to this rule. But we may claim with pride that Aligarh was the product of our own efforts and of no outside benevolence, and surely it may also be claimed that the independent, sovereign nation of Pakistan was born in the Muslim University of Aligarh.[1]

II

The foundation of the college marked the fulfilment of Saiyid Ahmad Khan's dream to equip his co-religionists for government employment and to make them 'worthy and useful subjects of Crown'. But soon after his death in 1898, this most 'benighted' and conservative of institutions responded to the political currents prevailing in the country. The agitation against the Nagri resolution, followed by the students' strike of February 1907, confronted the British with serious dissidence and a trend to steer the Muslim communities on a course different from the one chartered by the Saiyid. The Aligarh students, sensitized to the political upheaval in the wake of Bengal's partition, were beginning to throw to the winds all the caution that had been enjoined upon them by their mentor.

Political activity on the campus was heightened during and after World War I. Funds were raised for the beleaguered Turkey, and prayer meetings organized for the Turkish armies and the Anjuman-i Khuddam-i Kaaba.[2] Four Aligarh graduates joined Ansari's medical mission to Constantinople. At least one Aligarh Old Boy—Mahendra Pratap—was involved in the 'Silk Letter Conspiracy' and headed the provisional government in Kabul.[3] In September-October 1920, Gandhi and his khilafat partners chose Aligarh to garner support for non-cooperation.[4] The Mahatma reached the campus on 12 October and, according to an eye-witness account, spoke to the students haltingly in Hindustani. He tried to find the right words, but 'his accent seemed droll to his "pseudo-sophisticated" audience who did not agree with him, for their political and economic background and affiliations did not predispose them to accept his radical new doctrine of non-cooperation'.[5] The first shot misfired. He then appealed to the trustees:

to decline any further Government grant, disaffiliate the great institution of which you are the trustees and reject the charter of the Moslem University. The least that the Aligarh boys can do, if you fail to respond to the call of Islam and India, is to wash their hands clean of an institution acknowledging the aegis of Government that has forfeited all title to the allegiance of Islam and India and to bring into being, a larger, nobler and purer Aligarh that would carry out the most cherished wishes of its great founder.[6]

Brought up in the tradition of sturdy loyalty to Pax Britannica, the trustees paid no heed to his plea. They had already decided, much before receiving Gandhi's letter of 24 October, to run their college on 'old established lines' and make their Muslim brethren 'worthy and useful subjects of the British Crown'.[7] For once, they had their taste of revenge. Having failed to curb Mohamed Ali's influence in Aligarh during the past few years, they drew satisfaction from his isolation. Most trustees rallied round the principal, Dr Ziauddin Ahmad, and agreed with his decision to use the big stick to isolate the pan-Islamists and the Anjuman-i Khuddam-i Kaaba, co-founded by Abdul Bari and Shaukat Ali.[8]

The khilafat contingent, led by Ansari, Azad Subhani, Azad, and the Ali brothers, returned to Aligarh on 23 October and addressed numerous meetings. On this occasion, there was a change of heart. A graduate student wrote to Ziauddin that his doubts had been 'removed within the last four or five days', and that he would continue his studies only if the college was 'nationalised' [sic]. Otherwise, he was 'ready to face the doom awaiting my non-cooperating brothers'.[9] Another student from Azamgarh, impressed by the speeches of Azad and Azad Subhani, decided to join the non-cooperators.[10] Amidst fiery and passionate speeches, resolutions, promises and assurances, many more responded—estimates range from 200 to 700[11]—to the call of non-cooperation and enrolled themselves with the newly-founded Jamia Millia Islamia.

This mood remained unchanged until the mid-1930s despite the escalation of Hindu-Muslim violence and the growing rift between the Congress and the League. In general, campus politics was not marred by religious polarization. K.G. Saiyadain, who joined the university as a lecturer in

1925, participated in the Jubilee debate where his fellow-students spoke in favour of Indian nationalism.[12] He himself argued, in the presence of luminaries like the Aga Khan, Jinnah and Ali Imam, that his community should not organize themselves on communal lines but must work together with the nationalist forces for the country's freedom and progress.[13] In 1931, Tofail Ahmad Manglori, a distinguished Aligarh alumni, critiqued the Muslim demand for separate electorate, arguing that the real cause for the communal tangle was the recognition of special interests 'which appears to have dimmed the national outlook'. He proposed a constitution that would safeguard minority rights by 'correct redistribution of India with compact homogeneous zones, autonomous in character and with as few central subjects as circumstances permit'.[14] Most office-bearers of the influential students' union belonged to the radical alumni circles, anti-British and pro-Congress; the *Aligarh Magazine* retained its pro-Congress stance until its charge was handed over to Muhammad Noman Zuberi, a law student with League sympathies.[15] In 1930, the vice-president of the union exhorted his audience to

turn ourselves into the biggest, the most disciplined, the most educated and the most united army that India possesses, to fight against the evils that have made India the laughing stock of the world and let nobody say that Aligarh lagged behind anybody in India's battle of freedom. . . . To be indifferent towards anything that happens in a depressed country like India is criminal. To be ignorant of one's own political status is far worse than death. And not to think of and dream of a brilliant future for one's own country is a state which will reduce one to a lifeless mass of flesh.[16]

Support for nationalism combined comfortably with socialist commitments. The themes of capitalist exploitation, class conflict, and of revolt against imperialism, figured in the writings of former Aligarh graduates like Hasrat Mohani, Sajjad Hyder Yaldaram, Wilayat Ali 'Bambooque', Qazi Abdul Ghaffar, and Abdur Rahman Bijnori.[17] The younger generation often turned to Marxist writers and poets for political and intellectual inspiration. Saiyid Muhammad Tonki, who later turned to 'Islamic socialism' under the influence of Hasrat Mohani, received M.N. Roy's writings 'which discussed the Russian revolution, the reality of the socialist system, and the weakening of big empires as a result of capitalist and imperialist exploitation'. He and Ashraf often discussed 'what a socialist system might achieve in India'.[18] Nasim Ansari of Firangi Mahal in Lucknow and an intermediate class student in 1947 recalled how socialism 'carried the same poetic and romantic appeal as the poetic blasphemy in the work of Hafiz, Ghalib and Hasrat Mohani'.[19] Finally, the Progressive Writers' Association, formed in the mid-1930s, represented the continuation and development of the literary and political trends set by many writers connected with Aligarh. Their writings gave Urdu literature a vital stimulus, a new vigour, and a liberating consciousness.[20]

Political debates were conducted in and around the hostels. The revolutionary poems of Josh Malihabadi, Asrarul Haq 'Majaz' and other younger poets filled the Aftab Hall, the focal point of much radical activism and the venue of public lectures delivered by local Congress stalwarts like Maulvi Abu Bakr Muhammad Shish (d. 1941), chairman of the Sunni theology department from 1925 to 1940. He caused a furore by chairing a Congress meeting in Jaunpur.[21] The 1936 students' strike against the suppression of nationalist activities was triggered in Aftab Hall,[22] as also the moves to prevent the All-India Muslim Students' Federation (AIMSF) from forming its branch in Aligarh.[23] In December 1937, one of its residents declared support for the All India Students' Federation (AISF) and his stout opposition to the setting up of a Muslim organization in the university.[24]

Just a few later, however, campus politics was in the throes of a dramatic change. Emboldened by the spate of successfully organized League conferences in Delhi and the neighbouring districts,[25] the AIMSF[26] arrived on the scene with its strident demand for removing teachers holding 'socialistic' and 'atheistic' ideas. As a result, a few radical teachers were dismissed, some were told to fall in line; others were eased out of administrative positions and replaced by the Leaguers. 'Dangerous' books, like those of James Harvey Robinson on rationalism and Freud's on religion, were removed from the Lytton Library, *purdah* was reintroduced in an institution which had once led the crusade for the emancipation of women,[27] and the students' union platform was denied to the communists. K.M. Ashraf was, for instance, ridiculed when he intervened in a meeting addressed by Zafar Ali Khan, the editor of the Lahore newspaper *Zamindar*. 'The treatment meted out to Dr. Ashraf', stated the vice-president of the union, 'must serve as a warning to the Communists and the unscrupulous nationalists who may venture to speak on this platform, for the students are ever prepared to vindicate the honour of their religion, community and Alma Mater.'[28] Criticism of the League was suppressed with an iron hand. Thus an article by Khwaja Ahmad Abbas, a law student, was not published. A.B.A. Haleem, the pro-vice-chancellor, stated that 'Pakistan has been adopted as a creed by the great bulk of the Muslim community in India and the publication of the article in the *Aligarh Magazine* was sure to be exploited by the critics of the University and the opponents of the movement'.[29] Clearly, young students poured 'their idealistic zeal into the emotionalism of Pakistan and discussed rational arguments with the contentment of religious authoritarianism, and its scorn'.[30]

The Lahore resolution, followed by the lectures of Jinnah and Liaquat Ali Khan delivered at Aligarh in the summer of 1940,[31] generated fresh hopes and excitement. The students' body promptly endorsed the resolution as its official creed;[32] in this way, the Aligarh boys' adolescent pride in their institutional identity got easily and temporarily merged with the League's politically-oriented search for a collective identity.[33] They soon started claiming that the Pakistan scheme was itself shaped and crystallized by them, and that they were privileged to express 'the hidden feelings of the Muslim nation'.[34] Their new fervour led to a flurry of activity. Associations and debating societies, including a Buchha Muslim League to train children, mushroomed;[35] the University City League, established in 1937 and controlled by Saiyid Abdus Sattar Kheiri, a professor of German, gained a new lease of life; the 'Duty Society' was revived;[36] the AIMSF launched a quarterly journal—*Awakening* in English and its Urdu version *Bedaari*; the *Aligarh Magazine* carried scores of articles in support of Pakistan and Jinnah.[37] Indeed, the Quaid's visits to Aligarh were celebrated with much fanfare. Large crowds gathered at the otherwise sleepy railway station and crackers were laid on the track so that when the engine of the Kalka Mail passed over them, it seemed that a gun salute had been fired to welcome him.[38] His leadership 'created a spirit of obedience to the command of our Leader', for he was not just the voice of a 'Muslim Nation' but also personified its sense of 'persecution' by the 'Hindu-dominated' Congress.[39] 'The walls of the Strachey Hall', commented an AIMSF activist, 'had echoed with the voices of great men right from the days of Sir Saiyid. These voices were now silent. A new voice had begun to be heard there in the later nineteen-thirties, and during the last decade before independence it was the only political voice that mattered at Aligarh: it was the voice of Muhammad Ali Jinnah.'[40]

The reasons for gravitating towards the League had much to do with the League's refurbished image, its widening financial and recruitment base, the frustration and anger caused by the Congress rebuff to the League on the coalition issue,[41] and the resentment triggered by the Congress ministry in UP. There was talk of overt manifestations of aggressive Hindu nationalism, of the tyranny of Hindu brute majority, and of how the Congress policies jarred upon Muslim sensibilities. The ministry, headed by G.B. Pant, was accused of forcing cow-protection upon the Muslims, pushing the use of Hindi, interfering with Muslim worship, and fanning the fires of communal violence.[42]

Jinnah drew political mileage from these trends, as also from the pan-Islamic ferment in the early 1920s that had heightened religious consciousness, reinforced the community's perception of being unified and cohesive, and made it susceptible to religious appeals. When the going was tough, the Aligarh-based scholars, many having invoked the theme of a separate Muslim identity in their polemical defence of the khilafat cause, found it intellectually convenient to defend the two-nation theory.[43] Likewise, the 'communal consciousness' of the students which 'was far more secular than religious' when Mohamed Ali was a student,[44] expressed itself in a vigorous movement of Muslim nationalism.

In retrospect, it was an error of judgement to mobilize a highly stratified and differentiated community around pan-islamic symbols that mattered so little to the Muslim communities. No wonder, the khilafat issue faded in their memory after a few years. No wonder, they parted company with their erstwhile allies after civil disobedience was called off and the khilafat was abolished in Turkey.[45] The structure of Hindu-Muslim unity, so assiduously built by Gandhi, also crumbled. This was foreseen by, among others, the early communist movement. It was argued then and later that the basis of Hindu-Muslim unity, built on the 'unreliable foundations of religious sentiment', was artificial.[46] Attributing the root cause of Hindu-Muslim antagonism to religion, it was observed:

it may be comparatively easy to fire politically backward people with religious fanaticism; but it is impossible, even dangerous, to base a political movement on such unreliable grounds. . . . If the hostility against British imperialism is made a religious issue, the hostility thus aroused can at any moment turn into antagonism among the two great Indian communities as they do not profess the same religion. It is precisely what happened now.[47]

Finally, Jinnah's own endeavours to gain a foothold in the university yielded immediate rewards. He sedulously cultivated Ziauddin, maintained regular contacts with the AIMSF,[48] offered funds to the Muslim University City League, made frequent visits to Aligarh,[49] and won over the tall poppies in the Aligarh Old Boys' Association. Khaliquzzaman was his prized trophy in UP. Though associated with the Congress and the Nehru household for nearly a decade, in the early 1930s he began flirting with the League for advancing his political career.[50] In June 1937, Nehru chided him for working against the Congress candidate in the Bundelkhand election.[51] 'Is it not strange,' he wrote, 'that in this conflict men like Wazir

Hasan and Husain Ahmad [Madani] should be ranged on the progressive side and that you should be on the side of the reactionaries.'[52] A few months later Khaliquzzaman tried to justify his stand when he visited Aligarh. 'I was feeling a little nervous', he wrote,

because the students had known me as a khilafatist and a Congressman and they might not appreciate the circumstances in which I had undertaken the opposition to [the] Congress. I began slowly narrating to them step by step the negotiations carried on by me with the Congress, resulting ultimately in the terms and conditions imposed by the Congress for a coalition with the Muslim League and finally took out a copy of the document which had been handed over to me by Maulana Abul Kalam Azad. While reading it I could see the effect on the boys. By the time I had finished I felt that I had won the day.[53]

For Jinnah's project to succeed, it was equally vital to secure the adherence of the leading Muslim landlords of Aligarh and the neighbouring Bulandshahar district, many of whom had a voice in local and provincial affairs. Influential men like the nawab of Chhatari, Haji Muhammad Ismail Khan, nawab Muzammilullah Khan and the nawab of Pahasu used the university platform to maintain their predominance, furthered Saiyid Ahmad Khan's dream of an institution with close links with the government, and promoted their own goals as landlords. They thus voiced their anxieties over the implications of the new constitutional reforms. The reforms, they stated in their address,

will transfer a large measure of power and responsibility to the vote of the majority and it is natural for those who are in the minority to feel anxious about their future. We, as educationists, are concerned with these reforms in so far as we have to train our future generation to enable it to appraise the benefit of good and progressive government, to live as law-abiding citizens and to become, some day, leaders of public opinion.[54]

The rise of Hindu-Muslim antipathies in the mid-1930s created deep fissures in the landlord fraternity; in consequence, many of its tall poppies succumbed to communal pressures.[55] Harry Haig noted this trend in May 1937, though he hoped that the 'non-Congress Hindus' would not be tempted to join the communal organization, namely, the Hindu Mahasabha, and thereby jettison the prospect of the 'non-Congress Muslims and Hindus' acting in unison.[56] The simple fact that eluded the lieutenant-governor was that a number of Hindu *taluqdars* had already taken part in reorganizing the Oudh Liberal League in 1935, a body committed to protecting the 'legitimate Hindu interests'.[57] Likewise, quite a few Muslim *taluqdars*, especially the raja of Mahmudabad, revived and reorganized the Muslim League.[58] Some did so because of their commitment to the idea of an Islamic republic; others to protect themselves from the anti-landlord policies of the Congress ministries and the socialist rhetoric of Nehru and his comrades. The fears and grievances of such men were summed up by nawab Muhammad Yusuf of Jaunpur who wrote to Jinnah: 'I and Moslem zemindars look up to you to protect our fundamental rights and save them from economic ruination or elimination in U.P.'[59]

III

Admittedly, some demurred at the League movement and a few voices of protest mingled with the jubilant welcome accorded to Jinnah during his visits to Aligarh. Several writers and historians wanted the communal tangle to be resolved within a secular framework,[60] while the two-nation theory remained an anathema to committed Congress, socialist and communist activists.[61] 'The communists have openly come out in the field', reported a Leaguer in early 1943, 'preaching communist doctrines, distributing communist literature and their organ of the People's War, and enrolling members of the League. They have established a regular centre at the house of a professor and some other professors are secretly supporting them.'[62] This was an exaggerated assessment, for opposition to the League was considerably diluted in Aligarh and elsewhere after the Communist Party of India backed the Pakistan demand on the principle of 'national self-determination'.[63] Yet, Jinnah reacted to this 'disturbing' trend in Aligarh: 'I should have thought that Aligarh is now strong, well-knit and organized enough to resist any mischief that may be created against us.' He told friends 'to face any attempt to disrupt the Aligarh solidarity'.[64]

Soon thereafter, the League machine got rapidly into gear. Liaquat Ali Khan, Aligarh's Old Boy and president of the UP Muslim League, set up fourteen libraries in various hostels to propagate his party's message;[65] the University League published pamphlets on the Pakistan movement;[66] and an army of National Guards demonstrated Aligarh's solidarity with the 'Muslim cause'.[67] This burst of activity was not all hot air and un-coordinated action. In May 1944, a blistering attack was launched on the pro-Congress Nationalist Muslim Majlis started by Abdul Majid Khwaja and Shaukatullah Ansari, Dr Ansari's son-in-law. They were challenged to speak at the university, 'representing the cream of Muslim intelligentsia of India'.[68] A League camp, organized in October 1944, was the raja of Mahmudabad's brainchild. The *Aligarh Magazine* pub-lished a 'Pakistan Number' in 1945 to silence its detractors,[69] while the

AIMSF conference condemned the Sergeant Scheme of Education, and backed the proposal of Muslim emigration from Bengal to Assam.[70]

Such initiatives contributed to the League's ascendancy in Aligarh. The two-nation theory, with its emphasis on division and conflict in Hindu and Muslim 'cultures' and 'civilizations', began to make greater sense than the painstaking researches of historians underlining multiculturalism in medieval India.[71] An undergraduate student declared that 'Hindus and Muslims represented two different cultures and civilizations—one rooted in Islam and the other being the synthesis of the Central Asian and Indian traditions'.[72] In 1945, Abdus Sattar Kheiri argued that no other 'nation' possessed so many factors and attributes which constituted a Muslim nation in India, and that India's Muslims had no 'natural bonds of affection' with the Hindus. 'They will achieve Pakistan,' he wrote, 'and the independence of India for themselves, for the Hindus, and for all those to whom the independence of India is dear.'[73] A.B.A. Haleem and Moinul ·Haq in Aligarh and Ishtiaq Husain Qureshi in the Delhi University reinforced such ideas through their researches. Haleem launched the Historical Research Association in 1940 to collect material for bringing out a 'reliable history of India relating to the Muhammadan period'.[74]

By all accounts, the Aligarh students played a critical role in the 1945-6 elections to the central and provincial legislative assemblies. The election was, as is well-known, 'a kind of rehearsal for the bigger fight later on',[75] while Jinnah had to vindicate his claim as the 'sole spokesman' of 'Muslim India'. Haunted by the electoral debacle in 1937, he and his comrades left nothing to chance. They organized fund-raising missions, launched many newspapers, and enlisted the support of the ulama, the pirs of Sind and Punjab, and a large body of students and teachers to broaden their base.[76]

Aligarh's response to the elections—'a matter of life and death—'[77] was impressive. Elaborate plans were put in place to mobilize Muslims in the countryside and equip young students for campaigning.[78] Those touring Punjab during December 1945 attended such a camp and heard lectures on Islam, Islamic history, the League, and the religious background to the demand for a separate Muslim nation.[79] Omar Ali Siddiqi, who headed the Aligarh group in Punjab, raised the spectre of a bloody civil strife in the land of the five rivers, reminiscent of the battle of Karbala, and urged his audience to rally round the League to save the imminent destruction of the 'Muslim Nation'.[80] In other areas, the Aligarh students harped on familiar themes to make public the wrongs, real or trivial, suffered by the Muslims under the Congress governments in UP and Bihar. Exaggerated accounts of Hindu atrocities, based on the Pirpur and Shareef reports, were disseminated. Reference was made to Muslim children being made to sing the *Vande Mataram*, to the exaltation of Hindi and the accompanying attack upon Urdu, for many UP Muslims the heart and soul of their culture, the exclusion of Muslims from local bodies and government service, and the loss of Muslim lives in communal riots.[81] The whole campaign was marked by instinctive hostility towards Hindus and towards the idea that there should be any reconciliation with them except, on the terms laid down by Jinnah. Its scale and intensity, comparable only with the khilafat agitation, was aided by a large contingent from Aligarh.[82] By the end of 1945, 225 students canvassed in Punjab, 75 in UP, 25 in the N.W.F.P., and 7 in Bengal.[83] In early 1946, an additional 250 students campaigned in Assam, Sind, and Punjab.[84] An ebullient M.B. Mirza, dean of the science faculty, declared: 'So far all the students [are] united and working under one Leader, one Party and one Flag.'[85]

The intervention of the Aligarh boys tilted the balance in several constituencies.[86] In Hardoi, the League candidate secured 'a walk-over by hundreds over the Nationalist candidate due to the selfless work of the Muslim university students';[87] in Meerut, some 500 students made a difference.[88] Liaquat Ali Khan conceded that they had 'contributed largely towards the success which we have achieved in the elections'.[89] The final tribute came from Jinnah himself. 'I have been following the wonderful work that the Aligarh boys have done,' he wrote, 'you have proved what I said, that Aligarh is the arsenal of Muslim India.'[90]

IV

Students alone did not form the arsenal of the League. Jinnah was also backed by the university administration, headed by Ziauddin and his two influential colleagues: A.B.A. Haleem, chairman of the History department and pro-vice-chancellor since February 1935, and Obaidur Rahman Khan Sherwani, member of the UP legislative assembly and the university treasurer.[91] Ziauddin ruled Aligarh with an iron hand, organized factions, stifled dissent, and employed coercive methods to curb Congress activists.[92] Allied with the colonial government whose interests he served in public life, the Cambridge-educated administrator had been a relentless critic of the non-cooperation campaign in Aligarh.[93] In the 1930s, he sought the moral support of Fazl-i-Husain and the Aga Khan to isolate the AISF and the Congress activists.[94] The Aga Khan concurred. 'I have never looked upon Aligarh or UP', wrote the Khoja leader, 'as the leadership [sic] of Islam but I do understand here with its geographical position midway between Pakistan and Bengal how important it is that the Congress should not capture our Centre.'[95] In 1936, Ziauddin denied admission to the organizers of a students' strike, led by Ali Sardar Jafri, Jalil Abbasi, Khalilul Rab and Zamir Siddiqi, for his mission was to 'suppress their feelings of nationalism and patriotism'.[96] A similar fate awaited other students 'with progressive social and political views'.[97] In September 1938, one of them was found guilty of agitating against the authorities and for publishing a pamphlet against a provost and some staff members.[98] He could thus boast that the Congress was lying low in Aligarh, and that he had advised students 'to boycott every person who misleads the Mussalmans'.[99] He reaffirmed his loyalty to Jinnah in August 1947, claiming that he had been working for him for nearly a decade and that he would cheerfully follow his command. To serve the 'national cause', he offered to resign the vice-chancellorship and the legislative assembly membership.[100] But his offer came a bit late in the day. A massive student agitation, led by a group of militant Leaguers who accused the vice-chancellor for disrupting their activities and turning the university into a 'hot-bed of intrigues',[101] led to his resignation on 26 December 1946. Having used students on many previous occasions to consolidate his own personal gains, Ziauddin eventually paid a price for his own machinations. His reinstatement, the honorary secretary of the students' union told Jinnah, 'will be a great betrayal of this university and the Muslim youth'.[102]

Closely allied with Ziauddin were teachers like Jamiluddin Ahmad, lecturer in English and convenor of the committee of writers of the League; M.B. Mirza, a zoologist with a D. Phil. from Frankfurt (1927-8), provost of Aftab Hall (1942-4), and dean of the science faculty;[103] Abdus Sattar Kheiri, who headed the pro-German group in Aligarh;[104] and Muhammad Afzal Husain Qadri, a Cambridge graduate, member of the League and the Aligarh-based education sub-committees.[105] Qadri was involved in making proposals for 'a whole-hearted and more effective struggle' in realizing the ideal of Pakistan.[106] Education was his main concern. 'You have given them [Muslims] the lead to become a consolidated nation,' he wrote to Jinnah, 'and to struggle for an independent national existence. It is for you now, Sir, to give them the lead for their future being and advancement also, viz., Muslims should have throughout their own system of education, and they should have their own separate institutions, *so far as possible.*'[107]

The insistence on a new education policy was designed to counter the Wardha scheme of basic education, devised by Zakir Husain and blessed by Gandhi. Though the idea was to combine manual work with mental training and shift the emphasis from mere literary to vocational efficiency, the League propagandists dubbed the scheme as a diabolical plot designed to 'de-Islamize the Muslim nation',[108] destroy Muslim culture, and impose the domination of the Congress. So that Qadri, who published an alternative scheme for primary Muslim education in 1940,[109] claimed to have succeeded in establishing its 'evil effects' and, at the same time, persuading Muslims to plan and run their own system of education.[110]

Around the same time, some Aligarh scholars mooted several schemes of Muslim autonomy within the Indian federation and of independent Muslim states. In August 1939, Qadri and Zafarul Hasan, the philosophy professor, came up with an extraordinarily naive and unrealistic proposal for the Indian Muslims—'a nation by themselves'—who faced the cheerless prospect of being enslaved into a single all-India federation with an overwhelming Hindu majority at the Centre. They demanded a repartition of India 'on the only fundamental and valid principle of division, viz., Nationality, and to get India divided into Muslim India and Hindu India'. They proposed three sovereign states in British India: north-west or Pakistan, Bengal, and Hindustan. The principalities within these states or exclusively on the frontier of one of them would be attached automatically, while those adjoining more than one state had to choose their attachment. But Hyderabad must recover Berar and Karnatak, and with its restored territories, become a fourth sovereign state, 'the southern wing of Muslim India'. Pakistan would include the four north-western provinces, Kashmir and other adjacent states, Bengal would embrace the existing province, including the districts of Purnea and Sylhet but excluding the districts of Howrah, Midnapur, and Darjeeling. Both Pakistan and Bengal would be Muslim states. Hindustan would compromise the rest of India but within it two new autonomous provinces—Delhi and Malabar—should be formed, with strong Muslim minorities. The three states would have separate treaties of alliance with Britain and a joint court of arbitration to settle dispute between themselves or between them and the Crown.[111]

The Hasan-Qadri scheme (Appendices 11.1 and 11.2) was endorsed by ten Aligarh professors, who felt that it 'offered the right outline on which the future India must be reconstituted', and satisfied the 'just claims of the two nations inhabiting India'. 'It appears', they continued, 'as if Providence has in His mercy offered an opportunity to Muslims of India to launch a reasonable plan of political partition—*political partition* which is the only solution of their problem. *It is our bounden duty to fight for it to a man.*' A few months later, two of them—Zakiuddin and Burhan Ahmad—joined Zafarul Hasan and Ubaidullah Durrani, leaders of the Khaksar organization in Aligarh, in repudiating Gandhi's criticism of the two-nation theory. In their statement, they pointed out that neither the fear of British bayonets nor the prospect of a bloody civil war would weaken their determination to achieve 'free Muslim states' in Muslim-majority areas. It is noteworthy that Jinnah relied upon this Aligarh petition for selecting the rhetoric of his classic exposition of the two-nation theory.[112]

In the wake of India's Partition, Zafarul Hasan, Qadri, Haleem, Noman, and Jamiluddin Ahmed, who had voted for the creation of a state whose constitution and political life would be Islamic, joined hundreds of Aligarh students on the long trek to Pakistan. With their goal accomplished, they could draw comfort from their own part in its making.

V

After Independence and Partition, the university at Aligarh was left rudderless with some of its well-known teachers rushing to Karachi in search of greener pastures. The number of students dropped from 2,497 in 1946-7 to 1,753 a year later.[113] Those who stayed behind in India had a rough time, for it was not easy to disentangle the institution from its Muslim League past. They were harassed and harangued, and called upon to prove their loyalty. For years, wild rumours were afloat of Pakistani officials recruiting students to the army, of arms and ammunition being stored on the campus, and of bombs being recovered from the hostels. Demands were also made in the UP assembly and parliament to close down the university. But Nehru, India's first prime minister, and Azad, the education minister, resisted the Hindu communalist onslaught. In 1948, Nehru persuaded Zakir Husain to quit the Jamia Millia Islamia and join the Aligarh University as its vice-chancellor. This was a smart move, for Zakir Husain proved to be extremely successful in fulfilling the demands of his new assignment. He worked imaginatively and creatively, revived the dampened spirits of teachers and students alike, isolated the last remnants of the Muslim League ideology, and placed the university on a sound footing.

In 1947, Aligarh had four faculties and twenty-one departments; in 1964, there were seven faculties and 5,000 students. Today, the number of students has risen to well over 17,200 with a teaching faculty strength of 1,209, seventy-six departments and four colleges, including those for medicine and engineering. The non-plan expenditure exceeds Rs. 6,048 lakh.

There is little doubt that the university has surged ahead, despite many setbacks, in its quest to establish its distinct identity and meet the educational needs of the Muslim communities. Though its overall academic performance has been patchy in many areas and violence and discipline have marred campus life in recent decades, the institution has expanded vastly since Independence. Aligarh graduates, who were once tempted to seek employment in neighbouring Pakistan, are now comfortably placed in business, industry and the professions in India and elsewhere. Go to a district town in UP and you see the familiar sight of BA (Alig.). Travel to Birmingham in England or Cleveland in the United States and you will find the Aligarh Old Boys' Association listed in the telephone directory. Here and elsewhere, far removed from the humdrum of campus life, the 'Aligarians' regard themselves as a closely-knit community. Whether in Sydney or in Toronto, they congregate every year on 17 October to celebrate 'Sir Saiyid Day', fraternize with each other wearing the black *achkan* (*sherwani*) with the university monogram, recall the festive occasion brought by the annual exhibition held in the civil lines in close proximity to the district jail, revive memories of the years spent in Sir Saiyid, Viqarul Mulk or the Mohsinul Mulk Hall, and take much pride in being part of the Old Boy network.

Aligarh has so far negotiated with its past and succeeded in creating a niche for itself in the country's academic structures. And yet, it faces the uphill task of preparing the fraternity of teachers and students to meet the challenges of the next millennium. It needs to complete Saiyid Ahmad's unfinished agenda of fostering liberal and modernist ideas and take the lead, once and for all, in debating issues of education, social reforms and gender justice. It needs to interpret Islam afresh in the light of world-wide intellectual currents, respond to the winds of change just as the Saiyid had done, guide the 120 million Muslims, and equip them to cope with the harsh realities of life. This is what the great visionary Saiyid Ahmad would have expected it to do. With the Jamia Millia Islamia, its closest counterpart, unable to rise to the occasion during its lazy existence since Independence, the university can no longer shirk its responsibilities.

abhi manazil-i dasht-o-daman kuch aur bhi hain

NOTES

1. *The Memoirs of Aga Khan: World Enough and Time*, London, 1954, pp. 34-5; see also, *A History of the Freedom Movement*, Karachi, 1970, Vol. 4, pp. 249-99.
2. For accounts of politics in Aligarh during these years, see K.M. Ashraf, 'Aligarh ki siyasi zindagi', *Aligarh Magazine* (Special issue: Aligarh Number), 1953-4–1954-5, pp. 163-6; Khaliquzzaman, *Pathway to Pakistan*, pp. 17, 21; Hasan, *Mohamed Ali: Ideology and Politics*, pp. 17-20; R.A. Siddiqui; *Ashufta Bayani*

Meri, New Delhi, 1977 edn.; Mukhtar Zaman, *Students' Role in the Freedom Movement*, Karachi, 1978; Hasan (ed.), *Mohamed Ali in Indian Politics*, Vol. 1.

3. A sum of Rs. 6,000 was raised by January 1920 and handed over to the Central Khilafat Committee. Mushtaq Husain to principal, 17 Jan. 1920, File No. 62-B, Sir Saiyid Academy (hereafter SSA), Aligarh Muslim University, Aligarh.

4. For the impact of the non-cooperation, see S.Y. Shah, *Higher Education and Politics in Colonial India*, New Delhi, 1996, pp. 256-9.

5. K.G. Saiyadain, *Gandhian Idea on Education: Their Relevance to our Times*, New Delhi, n.d., pp. 6-7; S.M. Tonki, *Aligarh and Jamia: Fight for National Education*, New Delhi, 1983, p. 50.

6. *CWMG*, Vol. 18, p. 369.

7. Proceedings of the Syndicate meeting, 10 Oct. 1920, File No. I/1, 1920-1, SSA.

8. D. Lelyveld, 'Three Aligarh Students: Aftab Ahmad Khan, Ziauddin Ahmad and Muhammad Ali', *MAS*, Vol. 9, 2, 1975, p. 238.

9. M.A. Husain to Ziauddin, 24 Oct. 1920, SSA.

10. Nurul Hasan to Ziauddin, n.d., ibid.

11. Home Poll. A. Dec. 1920, 210-16 and K.W., NAI. According to Sheikh Muhammad Abdullah, a strong critic of the non-cooperation movement, 700 students left the college. *Mushahidaat wa Tasuraat*, Aligarh, 1969, p. 295. On 27 Oct., 14 graduates, 37 4th year, 21 3rd year, 52 2nd year and 35 1st year students wrote to the principal as 'firm adherents of the non-cooperation movement'. Tonki, *Aligarh and Jamia*, p. 72.

12. K.G. Saiyadain, 'Aligarh—A Retrospect and a Prospect', in Saiyid Muhammad (ed.), *The Aftabs' Memoirs Special*, Aligarh, 1975-6, p. 55.

13. Abbas, *I am not on Island*, pp. 50-1.

14. Tofail Ahmad, *The Solution of the Indian Communal Problem*, Aligarh, 1931, p. 2. Notice that Tofail Ahmad also wrote the *Mussalmanon ka Raushan Mustaqbil*, published in 1937, which was a sympathetic exposition of the principles of Indian nationalism.

15. He was appointed editor for the session 1937-8. A notification to this effect was issued by the pro-vice-chancellor after much deliberation. File No. 7/18, 1937-8 (Academic), SSA.

16. *Aligarh Magazine* (English), Jan.-Aug. 1930, pp. 56-7; Abbas, *I am not an Island*, pp. 59, 66.

17. K.R. Azmi, 'Urdu Shair wa Adab me Aligarh ka hissa', in Naseem Qureshi, *Aligarh Tehrik: Aghaaz ta Imroz*, Aligarh, 1960, pp. 313-53. Note that Majaz wrote poems like *Inqilab* (Revolution), *Sarmayadari* (Capitalism), *Khwab-i Sehar* (Dream of Tomorrow) which echoed the political trends in Aligarh. Ehtisham Husain, 'Majaz: Fikro-o-fan ke chand pahlu', *Aligarh Magazine 1955*, in A.K. Kasimi (ed.), *Intikhab Number 1975-76*.

18. Saiyid Muhammad Tonki, in Horst Kruger (ed.), *Kunwar Muhammad Ashraf: An Indian Scholar and Revolutionary 1903-1962*, Berlin, 1966, p. 344.

19. Nasim Ansari, 'Aligarh Muslim University, 1935-1947: Recollections of a Student', in Parshotam Mehra, Narayani Gupta and Rajiv Lochan (eds.), *Society, Religion and the State: Identity Crisis in Indian History*, New Delhi, n.d., p. 94.
20. Ibid., pp. 94, 98.
21. M.A. Zuberi, *Ziya-i Hayat*, Karachi, n.d., p. 160.
22. As 'ring-leaders' of the strike Ali Sardar Jafri and Jalil Abbasi were refused admission in 1937. The latter, according to the pro-vice-chancellor, was 'guilty of repeated acts of indiscipline, and was repeatedly reprimanded, warned and forgiven'. A.B.A. Haleem to K.M. Ashraf, 5 Oct. 1937, File No. 12, 1937, AICC papers. Jafri eventually completed his degree at the Lucknow University.
23. Its founder at Aligarh were Muhammad Noman, Abul Lais Siddiqui, and Ali Jawaad. The AIMSF was formed to counter the activities of the Congress and the AISF, and to 'create a common platform for the Muslim students of the universities and colleges in all the provinces of the country with a view to bringing about closer social contact, better cultural, political, economic and religious understanding, and a deeper sense of common relationship'.
24. *Indian Annual Register*, July-Dec. 1937, Vol. 2, p. 466. The first session of the AIMSF was held in Calcutta on 27-8 Dec. 1937. Jinnah presided.
25. The UP League conference was held in Gorakhpur on 18 Mar. 1939 with nawab Muhammad Ismail Khan as president. A month later, the Meerut division of the League held its conference chaired by Jinnah. On 8 Apr., the raja of Mahmudabad chaired the Delhi provincial Muslim League conference. See *IAR*, Jan.-Mar. 1938, Vol. 1, p. 372.
26. The number of students in Mar. 1940 was 1,717. Registrar to Director of Public Instruction, UP, 24 Sept. 1940, File No. 8/2, 1940-1, SSA.
27. Smith, *Modern Islam in India*, pp. 181-2.
28. Statement by M.M. Sayeed, 16 Nov. 1937, File No. 7/5, 1937-8 (Academic), SSA.
29. Haleem to F.J. Fielden, 29 Aug. 1941 and 29 Nov. 1941, File No. 7/18, 1941-2 (Academic), SSA.
30. Smith, *Modern Islam in India*, pp. 181-2.
31. Jinnah and Liaquat Ali Khan were invited by the Students' Union in Apr. 1940. Their visit was followed by that of Zafar Ali Khan, Rizwanullah, secretary of the UP Provincial League, and other Muslim League leaders. Report by Muhammad Mohsin Siddiqui, honorary secretary, students' union, 2 Dec. 1940, File No. 51, 1940-1 (Executive), SSA.
32. Zaman, *Students' Role in the Pakistan Movement*, p. 49.
33. Masoodul Hasan, 'Some Glimpses of the University in the Forties', Saiyid Muhammad (ed.), *The Aftabs' Memoirs Special*, p. 69. ·
34. Zaman, *Students' Role in the Freedom Movement*, p. 49.
35. Fasihuddin Ahmad to Jinnah, 5 Dec. 1942, Jinnah to Fasihuddin, 9 Dec. 1942, *The Quaid-e-Azam Papers*, Lahore, 1976, p. 247.

36. The membership of the University Muslim League rose to 1600 in 1944. Freedom Movement Archives, University of Karachi, Vol. 356, part xiii. M. Mukhtar Azad to Jinnah, 23 Sept. 1942, ibid., p. 241.

37. For instance, Saiyid Hamid, 'Iqbal and Politics', *Aligarh Magazine* (English), Special Number, 1939-40, 48, 1, p. 305; Ashkar Husain, 'Hindustan ke siyasi ikhtilaf ka haal', Mar. 1944, 22, 1, p. 60; Muhammad Afzal Mahmood, 'Pakistan ka iqtisadi wa siyasi pahlu', pp. 70-1, 79, ibid.; Jamiluddin Ahmad, *Indian Constitutional Tangle*, Lahore, 1941; *Is India one Nation?*, Aligarh, 1939; Muhammad Noman, *Muslim India: Rise and Growth of the All India Muslim League*, Allahabad, 1942.

38. Nasim Ansari, op. cit., p. 95.

39. *Aligarh Magazine* (English), 1943-4, 52, p. i.

40. Zaman, *Students' Role in the Freedom Movement*, p. 48.

41. Khaliquzzaman, *Pathway to Pakistan*, p. 195.

42. *Aligarh Magazine* (in Urdu), Mar. 1939, 17, 1, p. 6; *History of the Freedom Movement*, Vol. IV, pp. 1-50.

43. Muhammad Noman, *Whither India?* Serial No. 1, n.d.

44. Mohamed Ali, *My Life: A Fragment*, p. 22.

45. *Nationalism and Communal Politics in India*, Chap. Six.

46. Adhikari (ed.), *Documents of the History of the Communist Party of India*, Vol. 2, p. 210.

47. Ibid., p. 211.

48. In a message to the Aligarh MSF, Jinnah referred to his speech in which he appealed to the Muslim intelligentsia to 'take off your coats' and 'sacrifice all that you can and work selflessly, earnestly and sincerely' for the Muslim community. To S.A.M. Naqshbandi, 6 Dec. 1941, Sharifuddin Pirzada (ed.), *Quaid-e-Azam Correspondence*, Karachi, 1977, Vol. 2, p. 182.

49. According to Athar Parvez, then a student at Aligarh, Jinnah was worshipped (*parastish*) in Aligarh around 1941. At that time there were just a few nationalists among students, none enlisted among teachers. *Aligarh se Aligarh tak*, New Delhi, 1977, pp. 28, 31. In April 1942, the University Court decided to confer upon Jinnah the Honorary Degree of Doctor of Law. Jinnah, however, refused to accept the honour of the plea 'that I have lived as plain Mr Jinnah and I hope to die as plain Mr Jinnah. I am very much verse to and title or honours and I will be more happy if there was no prefix to my name.' Jinnah to Ziauddin Ahmad, 4 Oct. 1942, Shamsul Hasan Collection (hereafter SHC), Karachi University Archives, Karachi.

50. Harry Haig spoke of Khaliquzzaman's 'manoeuvres' in his correspondence with the viceroy, especially on the eve of Ministry-making in UP. To Linlithgow, 7 May 1937, Haig papers.

51. Nehru to Khaliquzzaman, 27 June 1937, S. Gopal (ed.), *SWJN*, Vol. 8, pp. 135, 142.

52. Ibid., 1 July 1937, p. 144.

53. Khaliquzzaman, *Pathway to Pakistan*, p. 195.

54. Address presented to Harry Haig, 27 Jan. 1937, *Addresses and Speeches relating to Aligarh Muslim University, Aligarh, from January 1920 to June 1937*, Aligarh, 1937, p. 67.
55. P.D. Reeves, 'Landlords and Party Politics in the United Provinces, 1934-7', in Low (ed.), *Soundings in Modern South Asian History*, p. 272.
56. Haig to Linlithgow, 5 May 1937, Haig papers.
57. Reeves, op. cit., p. 273.
58. Ibid.
59. To Jinnah, 14 Jan. 1946, SHC.
60. The writer Rasheed Ahmad Siddiqi, for example, was unhappy at the deterioration in Hindu-Muslim relations. In his reminiscences (*Apni Yaaden*), published in the *Aligarh Magazine* of March 1944, he regretted that the two communities asserted their communal rights as opposed to the national interests.
61. Ashraf listed a number of writers, poets, and political activists who belonged to Congress, Socialist and Communist circles. Ashraf, 'Aligarh awr Siyasat-i Hind', op. cit., p. 191. See also Ansari, op. cit., p. 102.
62. Jamiluddin Ahmad to Jinnah, 1 Jan. 1943, SHC.
63. Hasan, *Legacy of a Divided Nation*, pp. 112-3.
64. Jinnah to Jamiluddin Ahmad, 9 Jan. 1943, ibid.
65. *Aligarh Magazine*, 1943-4, p. 109.
66. The two well-known pamphleteers were Muhammad Numan and Jamiluddin Ahmad.
67. For instance, sixty 'National Guards' were raised at Aligarh to attend the Karachi session of the Muslim League in 1943. *Aligarh Magazine*, 1943-4, p. iv.
68. Statement by Jamiluddin Ahmad, n.d., SHC.
69. Zaman, *Students' Role in the Freedom Movement*, p. 45.
70. Ibid., p. 46.
71. Muhammad Habib, 'An Introduction to the Study of Medieval India, 1000-1400 A.D.', *Aligarh Magazine*, Jan.-Mar. 1931, pp. 5-20.
72. Ibid., Mar. 1944, p. 60.
73. *National States and National Minorities* (Pakistan Literature Series No. 1, Lahore, 1945).
74. *Minutes of the Annual Meeting of the University Court*, 7 Apr. 1940, p. 20.
75. Ziauddin also wrote pamphlets dealing with the administration of railways, financial and economic policies, and the development of industries in the Pakistan area. Ziauddin to Jinnah, 17 Aug. 1946, SHC. The election committee consisted of M.B. Mirza, chairman, Ubaidur Rahman Khan Sherwani, Manzar-i Alam, president of the Muslim University Muslim League, and Jamiluddin Ahmad, convenor.
76. For details of the mobilization campaign, see *Legacy of a Divided Nation: India's Muslims Since Independence*, Chap. 3.

77. Iqbal Masud to Jinnah, 24 Sept. 1945; M.A. Humayun to Jinnah, 16 Aug. 1946, SHC.

78. Ziauddin also wrote pamphlets dealing with the administration of railways, financial and economic policies, and the development of industries in the Pakistan area. Ziauddin to Jinnah, 17 Aug. 1946, SHC. The election committee consisted of M.B. Mirza, chairman, Obaidur Rahman Khan Sherwani, Manzar-i Alam, president of the Muslim University Muslim League, and Jamiluddin Ahmad, convenor.

79. I.A. Talbot, 'Deserted Collaborators: Political Background to the Rise and Fall of the Punjab Unionist Party, 1923-1947', *The Journal of Imperial and Commonwealth History*, Oct. 1982, Vol. XI, 1, f.n. 44, p. 93.

80. *Dawn*, 19 Dec. 1945.

81. Ibid.

82. Jamiluddin Ahmad to Jinnah, 1 Dec. 1945, SHC. An activist claimed: 'We have gone into the mohallas, villages, and even to the houses and have left some abiding impressions.' Qadir to Jinnah, 28 Nov. 1945, SHC.

83. Manzar-i Alam to Jinnah, 17 Dec. 1945, ibid.

84. Manzar-i Alam to Jinnah, 16 Jan. 1946, ibid.

85. Baber Mirza to Jinnah, 8 Feb. 1946, ibid.

86. For detailed reports of electioneering conducted by Aligarh students and teachers, see *Dawn*, 1, 9, 11, 12, 22, 27, 30, 31 Dec. 1945.

87. Ibid., 3 Dec. 1945.

88. Ali Ahmad Faziel to Jinnah, 2 Dec. 1945, SHC.

89. Liaquat Ali Khan to Manzar-i Alam, 2 Dec. 1945; K.R. Khan, offg. secy., UP, Muslim League Parliamentary Board, to Manzar-i Alam, 28 Nov. 1945, ibid.

90. Jinnah to Zahid Husain, 5 Dec. 1945, ibid.

91. As the acting vice-chancellor, he asked Jinnah to lay the foundation stone of the proposed medical college and hospital. To Jinnah, 23 Feb. 1947, in Zaidi (ed₁), p. 71.

92. He was in constant touch with the lieutenant-governor's and kept them posted with the developments on the campus. His role in the university affairs was far from exemplary. As the pro-vice-chancellor, he led a faction against Aftab Ahmad Khan, the vice-chancellor (1924-9). In a pamphlet circulated in December 1926, Aftab Ahmad Khan observed: 'I tried my best to work with him [Ziauddin] but bitter experience has opened my eyes as it has shown me the other side of his personality.' *Aligarh Mail*, 19 Feb. 1927; *The Aligarh of Today*, Aligarh, n.d., pp. 4, 64. The Rahimtoola Enquiry Committee (1927) also indicted Ziauddin and referred to his use of Aligarh as a 'stepping stone to political advancement'. The root cause of the 'Present Discontent', according to the committee, was the personal differences between Aftab Ahmad Khan and Ziauddin, irregularities and disregard of the Act, Statutes and Regulations prompted by the 'interests of petty faction and intrigue' and the appointment of 'a large proportion of men of insufficient academic qualifications'. *Report of the AMU Enquiry Committee*, Oct. 1927, Aligarh, n.d. This

led to Ziauddin's resignation in Apr. 1925. But he turned to Aligarh to continue his intrigues against the new vice-chancellor S.R. Masood (1929-32). A severe indictment of Ziauddin was made by Faiyaz Khan, member of the University Court and the UP legislative council. In his letter of resignation from the University Court, he stated: 'I have been watching with concern the affairs of the Aligarh Muslim University since the days of the Rahimtoola Committee, which put its finder on the right spot, when it diagnosed that the main cause of the decadence of Aligarh was the factious spirit which you, as pro-vice-chancellor, were largely responsible for creating in the life of the University.' To Ziauddin, 5 Sept. 1942, Freedom Movement Archives, University of Karachi.

93. Hasan, *Nationalism and Communal Politics in India*, pp. 182-3.

94. Zuberi, *Ziya-i Hayat*, p. 170.

95. The Aga Khan to Fazl-i-Husain, 14 Jan. 1936, Waheed Ahmad (ed.), *Letters of Mian Fazl-i-Husain*, Lahore, 1976, p. 481.

96. 'Appeal' (Printed), p. 19, File No. 13, 1937, AICC papers.

97. Ashraf to A.B.A. Haleem, 26 July 1937. Ashraf tried to raise the issue in the legislative assembly through his friend, Husain Zaheer. Ashraf to Husain Zaheer, 3 Aug. 1937, ibid. The extent to which the authorities were sensitive to the Congress movement is evident from the fact that they kept a close watch on the contents of books distributed by the students' union as prizes for debating competitions. Note by S.M. Ahsan, registrar, 25 May 1939, File No. 7/5, 1939-40 (Academic), SSA.

98. A.B.A. Haleem to M.A. Ghani, 30 Sept. 1938, File No. 1/4, 1938-9, ibid.

99. Ziauddin to Jinnah, 30 Nov. 1945, SHC.

100. Ziauddin to Jinnah, 17 Aug. 1946, ibid.

101. Ghayurul Islam to Jinnah, n.d., ibid., and Abid Ahmedali to Jinnah, 20 February 1947, in Z.H. Zaidi (ed.), *Quaid-i Azam Muhammad Ali Jinnah Papers: Prelude to Pakistan*, Vol. 1, part 1, Islamabad, 1993, pp. 4-6.

102. 22 Feb. 1947, ibid., p. 42.

103. Baber Mirza, married to a German lady, was suspected to be the chief link in the Nazi-Khaksar connection. According to the intelligence department, he gave a pro-Nazi lecture in Aligarh after returning from Germany in December 1938. This was published as 'Modern Germany—A Lesson to India' in the Muslim University League Publication Series. Towards the end of March 1939, he stated that Germany would soon be the liberator of India. Home Poll. File No. 21/65, 1939, NAI; Home Poll. File No. 111, 1940, NAI.

104. The 'red-hot' Nazi in Aligarh was Abdus Sattar Kheiri. He was involved in pro-German propaganda for which he received funds and literature through the Allianz and Stuttgarter Insurance Bank and other agencies. He launched *The Spirit of Time* in June 1938, which was 'anti-Communist, pro-Muslim and pro-Nazi in tone'. Home Poll. File No. 21/65, 1939, NAI. Sattar and his German wife, Fatima, were detained in Sept. 1940. The League pressed for their release; so did Jinnah who wrote to Maurice Mallet, lieutenant-

governor of UP, on 12 Oct. and 28 Nov. 1943. The Kheiris were released in Oct. 1944. See Saiyid Shamsul Hasan, *Plain Mr Jinnah*, Karachi, 1976, pp. 266-7.

105. Qadri, a resident of Budaun, was educated in Aligarh. He joined the University of Cambridge in 1936 and wrote a thesis on 'The Development of Locusts and Allied Insects' in May 1938 with the distinguished scientist, I.D. Imms. His research work at the Cavendish Laboratory was highly commended.

106. Qadri to Jinnah, 4 Feb. 1943, ibid.

107. Qadri to Jinnah, 5 Dec. 1943, ibid.

108. Qadri to Jinnah, 22 Nov. 1943, *Quaid-e-Azam papers*, p. 161.

109. Ibid.

110. Qadri to Jinnah, 28 Apr. 1943, SHC.

111. This summary is based on R.J. Moore, 'Jinnah and the Pakistan Demand', *MAS*, July 1982, Vol. 17, 4, Oct. 1983, pp. 541-2.

112. Ibid., p. 546.

113. *Report of the AMU Enquiry Committee*, Aligarh, 1961, p. 13.

APPENDIX 11.1

CONFIDENTIAL

DR AFZAL H. QADRI'S SCHEME

The Problem of Indian Muslims and Its Solution

The Government of India Act of 1935 and therein the proposed All India Federation as well as the partial working out of it in the form of Provincial Autonomy have brought the Muslims of India face to face with the gravest danger, viz., the annihilation of their specific national identity.

There is little need of explaining at length what this Act means. It hurls down the 90 million Muslims of India under the heels of the perpetual domination of a Hindu majority at the Centre, reduces the Muslim majority provinces to the status of mere vassals and leaves the Muslim minority provinces entirely at the mercy of the Hindu majority. Its fundamental fault is that it does not recognize the undeniable fact that the Muslims of India are a Nation distinct from Hindus, vitally opposed to the latter in their outlook and aspirations and incapable of being merged into any other so-called nation, Hindu or no Hindu.

The London Times (India No., 1 April 1937) commenting on the Government of India Act of 1935 wrote that undoubtedly the difference between Muslims and Hindus is not merely that of religion in the strict sense of the word, but also that of law and culture—that they may be said indeed to represent two entirely distinct and separate civilizations; however in the course of time the superstitions will die out and India will be moulded into a single nation. To this homily of the *London Times* one cannot but demur, for the 'superstitions' that shall have to die out are exactly the characteristic features of the Islamic culture and the contributions of Islam to India; without the shadow of a doubt the All India Federation will, within the space of a generation, bring about total annihilation of the specific Islamic outlook, culture, and language and will mould the Muslims after the will of the Hindus. Unequivocal signs of this are making themselves felt in the Muslim Mass-Contact programme of the Indian National Congress as well as the various educational schemes like the Vidya Mandir and the Wardha schemes, the drive for Hindi, and other

* A.H. Qadri collection, Vol. I, Box No. 25, Freedom Movement Archives, Karachi, University of Karachi.

urban and rural movements recently inaugurated under the auspices of that nationally-minded [*sic*] body.

Therefore, it is absolutely obligatory on us, the Muslims, that we must do our utmost to save our national identity in India and to safeguard our interests. We must win independence and equality for Muslims and should in no case acquiesce in their subjugation, whether planned by Hindus or the British, or even if agreed to by certain Hinduized anti-British Muslims.

To realize this great object I beg to offer, in the following, a scheme for your careful consideration. But before coming to it I must state the principles on which it is based. I am convinced that we Muslims of India must insist persistently and strenuously on them, namely,

1. That the Muslims of India are a nation by themselves—they have a distinct national entity wholly different from the Hindus and other non-Muslim groups; indeed, they are more different from the Hindus than the Sudetan Germans were from the Czechs;
2. That the Muslims of India have got a separate national future and their own contribution to make to the betterment of the world;
3. That the future of the Muslims of India lies in complete freedom from the domination of the Hindus, the British, or for the matter of that, any other people;
4. That the Muslim majority provinces cannot be permitted to be enslaved into a single All India Federation with an overwhelming Hindu majority in the Centre; and
5. That the Muslims in the minority provinces shall not be allowed to be deprived of their separate religious, cultural and political identity, and that they shall be given full and effective support by the Muslim majority provinces.

Now, in order to save the Muslim Nation in India we have to demand a repartition of India on the only fundamental and valid principle of division, viz., Nationality, and to get India divided into Muslim India and Hindu India further we must do all we can to safeguard the interests of our nationals living in Hindu India. On this principle British India must be divided into three wholly independent and sovereign states.

1. North-West India, including the Punjab, the N.W.F. Province, Sindh, and Baluchistan;
2. Bengal, including the adjacent district of Purnea (Bihar) and the Sylhet Division (Assam), but excluding the south-western districts of Howrah

and Midnapore (Burdwan) and the north-western district of Darjilling; and

3. Hindustan, comprehending the rest of British India. Inside Hindustan there must be formed two new autonomous provinces;

  (a) Delhi Province, including Delhi, Meerut Division, Rohilkhand Division and the district of Aligarh (Agra Division); and

  (b) Malabar Province, consisting of Malabar Coast. Further, all the *Towns* of Hindustan with a population of 50,000 or more shall have the status of a Borough or Free City.

Also, in Hindustan Muslims in *villages* shall have to live together in considerable numbers.

The Indian States: The Indian or native states included inside the boundaries of any of the above three proposed States or exclusively on the frontier of one of them, ought to be attached to that State.

Those bordering on more than one of the three States should have the option of joining any of the adjoining States.

Hyderabad with its old dominions Berar and Karnatik to be at sovereign state.

A map is herewith attached in which the proposed division of India is visualized. Some explanatory remarks may be added.

North-West India will include several native states, e.g. Qalat, Jammu and Kashmir, Bahawalpur, Khairpur, Patiala, Jhind, Nabha, Kapurthala, Malerkotla, Faridkot, and the Simla Hills States. With the inclusion of Kashmir,it may well be called 'Pakistan' as it has been for some years past.

The Pakistan Federation will be a Muslim state. It will include about 25 millions of Muslims, i.e. more than 60 per cent of the total population. It is a self-sufficient unit on the basis of geographical, economical and political considerations. The realization of this federation will open a new and living future for the Muslims of India and will have a far-reaching effect on the whole of the Islamic world. The Pakistan will form the north-western wing of Muslim India.

The Hindus and Sikhs are the two non-Muslim minorities in Pakistan. They will have the same cultural, religious and political safeguards granted to them as the Muslims will have in Hindustan. It will be of greater advantage for the Sikhs to be in this State than in an All India Federation as envisaged by the Government of India Act of 1935, for they will be relatively in much larger proportion in their province and in the Centre.

The claim of Pakistan to form a separate federation cannot be challenged by any one on any reasonable ground; and if not conceded, the Muslims of these provinces will leave no stone unturned and will carry on the struggle by all means at their disposal until their goal is achieved.

The new Bengal will again be a Muslim State. It will contain more than 30 million Muslims, i.e. 57 per cent of the whole population. New Bengal can be entirely self-sufficient on account of its natural wealth and agricultural richness. It will be equal to France in area as well as in population. Because of having no component provinces, it will be no Federation. However, it will be a Sovereign State, having a status analogous to Burma, and will be the eastern wing of Muslim India.

Hindustan will be a Hindu State. It will have a population of 245 millions. It will include about 23 million Muslims, forming a minority of 10 per cent. It is our duty to safeguard their interests politically as far as it is at present possible. We must consequently insist on the formation of two new provinces inside Hindustan, one in the north and the other in the south, viz., Delhi and Malabar respectively.

In the newly constituted province of Delhi there will be more than 3.5 millions of Muslims, forming about 38 per cent of the total population. Indeed they will still be a minority. However they will be such an important minority as cannot easily be swept aside by the Hindu majority. Being highly cultured and educated as the Muslims of these parts are, and having their boundaries close to the Muslim Federation of Pakistan, they will be in a much stronger position to guard their interests than otherwise. Aligarh, the centre of Muslim education, must be included in this province, for we cannot afford to leave it unprotected inside the remaining portion of the U.P. which will be overwhelmingly Hindu.

The southern or Malabar province will comprise the southern part of Madras presidency especially that lying adjacent to Malabar Coast. This part is well populated by Muslims. There are about 1.4 million Muslims in it, forming about 27 per cent of the total population. They have large trading interests in this province and possess an eminent cultural position. Moreover, they are a virile race and being such an important minority can look after their interests far better than they can at present.

In Hindustan the Muslims largely live in cities and in considerable numbers, we cannot afford to leave them entirely at the mercy of the Hindu government. Therefore, it is necessary to protect their interests. Left to themselves they can fight their battle with the Hindus of those towns. All that can be done for them at present is to eliminate the undue interference of the provincial and central Hindu governments. This can well be done by giving the status of Free Cities or Boroughs to large towns of a population of 50,000 and more. They shall have their own police and magistracy, and they may have powers to legislate and execute on local manners to a large extent. In this way the interests of about 1.25 millions of Muslims of Hindustan can be protected.

The Muslims in the rural area of Hindustan must be persuaded not to remain scattered in neglegible minorities, as they do at present, in different villages. They must be induced to aggregate in villages with a preponderant Muslim population. In this way alone can their cultural as well as economical interests be protected. A number of useful and constructive programmes for social, educational and economical improvement may at once be launched in rural areas of Hindustan for the sake of this object as well as for the immediate amelioration of the conditions of Muslims residing therein.

The afore-mentioned three states of Pakistan, Bengal and Hindustan should enter into a defensive and offensive alliance on the following bases:

1. Mutual recognition and reciprocity.
2. That Pakistan and Bengal be recognized as the homelands of Muslims, and Hindustan as the homeland of Hindus, to which they can migrate respectively, if and when they want to do so.
3. In Hindustan the Muslims are to be recognized as a nation in minority and part of a larger nation inhabiting Pakistan and Bengal.
4. The Muslim minority in Hindustan and non-Muslim minorities in Pakistan and Bengal will have (i) representation according to population; and (ii) separate electorates and representations at every state, together with effective religious, cultural and political safeguards guaranteed by all the three states.

Note: Separate representation according to population may be granted to all considerable minorities in the three States, e.g. Sikhs, non-caste Hindus, etc.

5. The All India Muslim League will be the sole official representative body of the Muslims in Hindustan.

Each of these three independent states, Pakistan, Hindustan and Bengal will have separate treaties of alliance with the Great Britain and separate Crown Representatives, if any. They will have a joint Court of Arbitration to settle any dispute that may arise between themselves or between them and the Crown.

Hyderabad commands a position which is exclusive amongst Indian States. It is even now recognized as an ally by the British Government, and its Ruler addressed by the distinctive title of His Exalted Highness. In truth it is a sovereign state by treaties. Berar and Karnatik were taken from it by the British for administrative reasons. Now, when the British are giving the control of India to its rightful owners, they must return to Hyderabad its territories, and recognize Hyderabad expressly as a sovereign state, at least as sovereign as Nepal. Karnatik will restore a sea coast to Hyderabad, and Hyderabad will naturally become the southern wing of Muslim India.

Muslim University,	MOHD. AFZAL HUSAIN QADRI,
Aligarh.	M.Sc., Ph.D. (Alig.), Ph.D. (Cantab).

APPENDIX 11.2

Muslim University,
Aligarh.
.... September 1939

Dear Sir,

We beg to place before you our proposals about the problem of Indian Muslims and its solution. It is needless to assure you that they are the outcome of our most earnest efforts and extremely serious deliberations lasting over a number of years. The proposals mentioned below rest on the following fundamental theses, which we strongly believe admit of no alteration, if a just and honourable solution of the Hindu-Muslim problem is at all to be sought:

1. That the 90 millions Muslim of India constitute a distinct nation by themselves and as such must possess complete independence and the right of self-determination.
2. That the Muslim majority provinces are the embodiments of the hope and future of Muslims in India, and as such cannot be permitted to be enslaved in an All-India Federation under the perpetual domination of a Hindu majority in the centre.

*A.H. Qadri collection. The typescript of this representation includes the names of Abdus Sattar Kheiri and Syed Zafarul Hasan.

For permission to include these documents, I am obliged to the Director of the Freedom Movement Archives at the University of Karachi, Karachi.

3. That the future of Muslims in the minority provinces lies in their own determination to guard their separate political and cultural entity and the support they receive from their brethren in the majority provinces.

4. That the Hyderabad State represents the symbol of a thousand years old empire of Muslims in India. It is a sovereign State on the basis of every historical, political and constitutional consideration. The Muslims of India, therefore, cannot tolerate any attempt to undermine the sovereignty of H.E.H. the Nizam of Hyderabad.

We sincerely believe that our proposals will meet your approval and will enlist your fullest support and sympathy for the cause of our national future.

Your faithfullies,
The Authors.

We have carefully considered the 'Aligarh Scheme' as drafted by Professor Dr. Syed Zafarul Hasan and Dr. Afzal Husain Qadri, and fully discussed it with them in principle and in detail. We are convinced that it offers the right outline on which the future India must be reconstituted. It goes to satisfy as much the just claims of the two nations inhabiting India, viz., Muslims and Hindus, as seems to be apparently possible.

We have also studied the Scheme of Dr. Abdul Latif with sympathy and with care. However, we are afraid that Scheme does not satisfy the essential requirements of such a Scheme. Dr. Abdul Latif conceives of the whole of India as one political entity. That will necessarily give the Hindus overwhelming majority at the Centre and, therefore, effective sovereignty of the whole country. In one India, the Muslims, who shall be in a minority of 25 per cent scattered throughout the country, must but live as a subject nation. This cuts at the very root of all hope for Indian Muslims. They must in no case agree to it.

Further, Dr. Abdul Latif would create so many cultural zones and corridors by means of large scale migrations and thereby save Muslim culture. The idea is a pleasing one, but we do not think that such large scale migrations are practical politics. Moreover, to contemplate, in course of time, total denudation of Hindustan from Islamic influences by wholesale migration of Muslims, would contravene the very mission of Islam in this world and its spirit of expansion. However, the Aligarh Scheme does not exclude migration, if necessary; nor the creation of cultural zones, if feasible. It has room for and absorbs in itself this aspect of Dr. Abdul Latif's Scheme.

The Aligarh Scheme gives complete independence to 25 million Muslims in the north west, and 30 million Muslims in the east; while it provides semi-independence to 5 million Muslims in Malabar and around Delhi. Moreover, it procures respectable existence in Hindustan for about 13 lakhs of Muslims living in smaller towns. And for the remaining 22 million Muslims living in smaller towns and villages of Hindustan, the Scheme urges reasonable rights and safeguards which are calculated to make their existence self inside the ocean of Hindu population.

Now when the question of the constitution of India is most likely to be reopened the time is propitious for a new Scheme. It appears as if Providence has in His mercy offered an opportunity to Muslims of India to launch a reasonable plan of Political Partition—Political Partition which is the only solution of their problem. It is our bounden duty to fight for it to a Man.

The Aligarh Scheme seems to us to present the best solution of the problem, and we offer ourselves as the whole-hearted supporters of it.

Amiruddin Kedwaii,
B.A., L.L.B. (Alig.),
Hony Secretary,
All India Muslim Conference.

Dr. Zaki Uddin,
M.Sc. (Cantab), Ph.D. (Alig.),
Dr. Phil. (Bon.).

Umar Uddin
M.A., B.T. (Alig.).

Dr. Burhan Ahmad Faruqi,
M.A., Ph.D. (Alig.).

Zafar Ahmad Siddiqi,
M.A. (Alig.).

Jamil-uddin Ahmad,
M.A. (Alig.).

Masud Makhdum,
M.A. (Alig.).

Muddassir Ali Shamsee,
M.A., LL.B. (Alig.).

12

Memories of a Fragmented Nation:
Rewriting the Histories of India's Partition

Today I am asking Waris Shah to speak from the grave,
To turn the page of the book of love.
   Once the daughter of the Punjab wept, and you wrote endlessly.
Today Lakhs [1,00,000] of daughters are weeping
   and they are imploring you Waris Shah
Get up, you who sympathise with our grief, get up and see your Punjab.
Today there are corpses everywhere, and the Chenab is filled with blood.
Somebody has mixed poison in all the five rivers,
The rivers we use to water our fields. . . .

When I think of Lahore, I go back to the days of my youth
   just before the Partition.
Life then was so romantic, slow, deep and beautiful.
   Really, they were good times, they were great times.[1]

I hope that one day . . . displaced families on both sides of the fence will at
least be able to freely cross the borders and show their grandchildren where
their grand parents had once lived and belonged. The day such a change
comes about, I shall be the first to cross the Wagah or Hussainiwallah
border posts to take my grand-daughter to Lahore, and show her the home
of my youthful dreams – 91, Garden Town.[2]

The countdown to 15 August 1997, India's fiftieth year of Independence,
generated an extraordinary interest in plotting the history of Partition.[3]
One wonders why painful memories and traumatic experiences were
revived on such an occasion, why the nostalgia, why the celebration of
the dead?[4] Was it because there was not much to celebrate? Or did the
occasion itself finally sensitize us to the painful legacy of a brutal past.

Amrita Pritam, the noted Punjabi writer who lived in Lahore before moving to Delhi in 1947 and whose celebrated poem quoted in the epigraph became one of the most influential and representative works of Partition, recalled: 'What I am against is religion—the Partition saw to that. Everything I had been taught—about morals, values and the importance of religion—was shattered. I saw, heard and read about so many atrocities committed in the name of religion that it turned me against any kind of religion. . . .'[5]

Sure enough, a common refrain in popular and scholarly writings was that the country's division was a colossal tragedy, and a man-made catastrophe brought about by hot-headed and cynical politicians who failed to grasp the implications of division along religious lines.[6] For a change, the focus was on the popular experiences of violence and displacement,[7] on the impact of Partition on the lives of hundreds of millions, including the trauma of women,[8] and the great variety of meanings they attached to the upheaval in and around their homes, fields and factories.[9] Indeed, the inclination to sideline the tall poppies in the debates expressed the growing disillusionment with high politics and its post-colonial practitioners.

The mood reflected in popular literature was decisively against the leaders and their inability to resolve their perennial disputes over power-sharing. Doubtless, the colonial government's role in heightening Hindu-Muslim rivalries and the implications of Bengal's partition in 1906 were recounted. So also the political blunders committed by Wavell (1883-1950) during his inglorious years in the viceregal lodge, the impetuousness of Mountbatten who revelled in his role as arbiter, the destiny of millions sitting light on him, the collapse of the law and order machinery which was kept in a state of readiness to protect the Europeans but not the hapless victims of a civil war, and, finally, the demarcation of the border by a British jurist who had neither been to India nor shown interest in Indian affairs.[10] 'Nothing could illustrate', commented the senior journalist Ajit Bhattacharjea, 'the callous haste with which Partition was pushed through more strikingly than the last-minute arrangements to demarcate the border.'[11]

According to the same writer, the onus nonetheless rested on the Indian leaders, many of whom ensured that the transfer of power was not delayed and were therefore 'unaware and uncaring of the human cost of cutting a border through the heart of populous provinces'.[12] Illustrating Nehru's 'lack of touch with grassroots reality' and his 'self-delusion' that Pakistan would be compelled by its limitations to return to the greater Indian fold,[13] Bhattacharjea recalled what Nehru told the author Leonard

Mosley. 'We were tired men', India's first prime minister said in 1960,

and we were getting on in years too. Few of us could stand the prospect of going
to prison again—and if we had stood out for a united India as we wished it, prison
obviously awaited us. We saw the fires burning in the Punjab and heard of the
killings. The plan of Partition offered a way out and we took it. . . . We expected
that Partition would be temporary, that Pakistan was bound to come back to us.[14]

With the focus on high politics, the same old story does the rounds
with unfailing regularity. The engagement continues to be with the 'major'
political actors, who conducted their deliberations lazily in cosy surroundings and presided over the destiny of millions without their mandate. One is still encumbered with the details of what went wrong and who
said what from the time the first Round Table Conference was held in
London in 1930. Thanks to the publication of the voluminous transfer of
power documents and the works of Gandhi, Nehru, Jinnah, Patel and
Rajendra Prasad, the spotlight remains on the 'mystery' behind the
protracted and tortuous negotiations triggered by the Cripps offer and
the cabinet mission.[15] The bitter and acrimonious exchanges thereafter,
which have all along dominated the historiography on nationalism, 'communalism' and 'Muslim separatism', continue to haunt present-day
writers. The search for the 'guilty men', based on personal reflections/
memories or the blunt testimony of the socialist leader Ram Manohar
Lohia and the guarded 'revelations' of Maulana Azad, goes on relentlessly.[16] As a result, the historians' history of partition 'is not a history of
the lives and experiences of the people who lived through that time, of the
way in which the events of the 1940s were constructed in their minds, of
the identities and uncertainties that partition created or reinforced'.[17]

These concerns are not so widely reflected in Pakistan, where the
'Partition issue', so to speak, was resolved well before 1947 by the weight
of the two-nation theory.[18] The result is for everybody to see. Although
Jinnah of Pakistan has been elevated to a high pedestal, he would remain,
unless rescued from his uncritical admirers, a lonely figure in the pages of
history and in the gallery of nation-builders. If the desire is to come to
terms with his political engagement and explain his extraordinary success,
it is not at all helpful to press him into service to establish Pakistan's
identity as an Islamic State. Likewise, the use of religious symbols, long
forsaken by that country's bureaucracy and military establishment, can
hardly serve as the starting point for a meaningful dialogue on Partition.

The engagement of several writers in India, though sometimes marred
by a majoritarian perspective, centres around secular nationalism, the main

inspiration behind much of liberal-left activism from the 1920s onwards. Their chief concern, though nowadays pooh-poohed in the 'post-modernist' discourse, is to examine why the secular elites and their ideologues, whose presence is grudgingly recognized across the ideological divide, failed to mediate between those warring factions/groups who used religion as a cover to pursue their worldly goals and ambitions. While detailing the cynical games played out on the Indian turf by the British, the League, and the self-proclaimed 'nationalists' of every variety, they do not spare the Congress stalwarts, Gandhi, Nehru and Patel included, for failing to guide the movements they initiated away from the forces of reactionary communalism.[19] They marshal a wide array of sources to comment on Hindu communalists preventing the national movement from becoming truly inclusive. They also point to Gandhi's role in introducing religion into politics, the anti-Muslim proclivities of the Hindu right, led by Patel in the 1940s, the *Hindutva* agenda of the Hindu Mahasabha, the Arya Samaj, and the Rashtriya Swayam Sewak Sangh (RSS), and Nehru's arrogance and haughtiness in dealing with Jinnah and the Muslim League. At a time when the League was flexing its muscles, India's first prime minister is said to have jettisoned the plan for a Congress-League coalition in 1937 and dimmed the prospect of an enduring Hindu-Muslim coalition in Indian politics. The mainstay of the argument is that the country's vivisection could have been avoided had Nehru acted judiciously at such critical junctures in the 1940s.[20]

Though such impressions rest on questionable assumptions, they cannot be brushed aside.[21] The real difficulty lies with the grand narrative itself and the tendency to generalize on the basis of the actions of a few. While the grand narrative illuminates several facets of the Pakistan story, it fails to take into account the complexities and subtleties of institutional and structural changes introduced by the colonial government, as also the impact of socio-economic processes on caste, class, and religion-based alignments. One does not, moreover, get a sense of why the two-nation theory was floated in March 1940 and not earlier, why and how different forms of identities and consciousness got translated into a powerful campaign for a separate Muslim homeland, why Partition created ten million refugees, led to the death of over a million people, and resulted in sexual savagery, including the rape and abduction of 75,000 women.

Finally, the grand narrative does not reveal how the momentous happenings in August-September 1947 affected millions, uprooted from home and field and driven by sheer fear of death to seek safety across a line they had neither drawn nor desired. Clearly, the issue is not whether a million or more died or whether only 33 per cent of the country's population was affected by the communal eruption. The essential facts, as pointed out by the chief of the governor-general's staff, were that 'there is human misery on a colossal scale all around and millions are bereaved, destitute, homeless, hungry, thirst—and worst of all desperately anxious and almost hopeless about their future'.

In order to probe those areas which directly or indirectly impinged on the sudden and total breakdown of long-standing inter-community networks and alliances, it is necessary to locate the Partition debates outside the conference chambers. Without being swayed by the paradigms set by the two-nation theory or the rhetoric of Indian nationalism, it is important to examine why most people, who had so much in common and had lived together for generations, could turn against their neighbours, friends and members of the same caste and class within hours and days.

Such tragedies have taken place in the former state of Yugoslavia, but it is unclear why they have gone unnoticed at research centres in the subcontinent, especially in areas worst affected by gruesome violence and migration. Is it because the ghosts of Partition should be put to rest and not exhumed for frequent post-morterms? Or, is scholarship on the subject itself is so woefully inadequate and contentious that it fails to excite the imagination of young graduates?

Perspectives and attitudes on such vexed matters are bound to differ, though scholars in Pakistan tenaciously adhere to the belief that the creation of a Muslim nation marked the culmination of a historical process. Perhaps, it is hazardous to contest such inherited wisdom in a society where nationality is still defined, often clumsily, in purely Islamic terms, and religious minorities, Hindus and Ahmadiyas (Qadianis) included, are left to stew in their own juice. Perhaps, Partition does not convey the same meanings in Lahore and Islamabad as it does to some people living in Delhi, Lucknow, Calcutta, and Dacca. It is not bemoaned, for understandable reasons, as an epic tragedy but celebrated as a spectacular triumph of Islamic nationalism. After all, why should people inhabiting the fertile districts of western Punjab or the rugged Frontier region mourn the break-up of India's fragile unity or lament the collapse of a common cultural and intellectual inheritance? Some beleaguered *muhajirs* may still want to recall their friendships and associations in Hindustan (*guzashta bada-paraston ki yaadgar koi*), trace their intellectual and cultural links with Lucknow or Delhi, and occasionally revive memories of a bygone era by dipping into the writings of Manto, Ahmed Ali, Josh Malihabadi, Quratulain Hyder and Intizar Husain.[22] Yet, the nostalgia for what has already become an imaginary homeland or the identification with Lucknow's grand *imambaras* or with the sufi shrines of Khwaja Muinuddin Chishti at Ajmer and Nizamuddin Auliya in Delhi is gradually fading away with the passage of time and the passing of a generation. The Badshahi mosque, standing majestically as a symbol of India's secular dream, is as distant and remote as the Masjid-i Qartaba, the theme of Iqbal's melodious poem. Aminabad in Lucknow or Ballimaran in Old Delhi are far removed from the imagination of a generation nurtured in a different social and cultural milieu.

The differences in approaches and perspectives should not, however, stand in the way of developing a common reference point for rewriting the *histories* of an event that cast its shadow over many aspects of state and society in the subcontinent. Despite decades of mutual suspicions and antipathies leading to a mindless arms build up and contributing to the backwardness and appalling poverty of the region, it is still possible for the peoples, rather than the governments, to make sense of the poignant writings of creative writers and poets and to reflect on how and why a generation was caught up in the crossfire of religious bigotry, intolerance and sectarianism. Such an exercise can be undertaken without calling into question the legitimacy of one or the other varieties of nationalism.

For the initiative to get off the ground, it may be useful to revisit the old-fashioned theories on the syncretic and composite trajectory of Indian society, and detail, as the writer Krishna Sobti did in an interview, the shared values and traditions that had enabled diverse communities to live harmoniously for centuries.[23] It is not necessary to be swayed by the 'nationalist' historians who portray an idyllic picture of Hindu-Muslim relations during the pre-colonial days in order to strengthen inter-community ties during the liberation struggle. It is nonetheless important to underline the fusion and integration of the Hindu communities at different levels and the value they attached to religious tolerance and pluralism in their day-to-day living.[24] In so doing, one can put to rest those speculative theories that lend respectability to British colonialism and offer a corrective to the distorted Islamist or the *Hindutva* world views which have, in equal measure, created widespread confusion in the minds of the common people and, in the process, caused incalculable damage to state and civil society.

The conclusions flowing from such formulations are bound to differ, yet the urgency to underline the commonality of interests amongst large segments of the population must be felt in India where *Hindutva* could well be the new *mantra* of civil society in the foreseeable future, and in neighbouring Pakistan, where ethnic and sectarian strife, combined with deep-seated regional and linguistic cleavages, reveal the limits of an agenda tied to wild and imaginary notions of Muslim/Islamic brotherhood or solidarity.

II

The following three impressions are drawn from a period when Hindu-Muslim relations had reached their lowest watermark. The first is of Malcolm Darling, a civil servant in Punjab for many years. During his travel in 1945-6, he found much similarity between the Hindu and Muslim communities in the tract between the Beas and Sutlej and the Chenab and Ravi rivers. He noticed, something he would have done on numerous occasions during his long career as a British civil servant, how often Hindus, Muslims and Sikhs had a common ancestor in a village, how a Hindu from Karnal proudly announced that the Muslim inhabitants of the fifty neighbouring villages belonged to his clan and were prepared to return to the Hindu fold on the one condition that the Hindus would give them their daughters in marriage. Although the condition was refused, Hindus and Muslims of the area continued to interchange civilities at marriage, inviting the mullah or the Brahman, to share in the feasting. Malcolm Darling wondered how Pakistan was to be fitted into these conditions. 'What a hash politics threatens to make of this tract', he observed, 'where Hindu, Muslim and Sikh are as mixed up as the ingredients of a well-made pilau (rice cooked with fowl or meat).'[25]

Muhammad Mujeeb, the vice-chancellor of Delhi's Jamia Millia Islamia, had a similar experience in Bihar soon after the orgy of violence had taken a heavy toll of human lives. While visiting the grave of a sufi saint on the bank of the river Ganga, he found that the Muslims living in the shrine had already abandoned the place. But soon a group of Hindu women appeared. They performed the same rituals that their ancestors had observed for generations. It appeared 'as if nothing had happened that affected their sentiments of veneration for the tomb of a Muslim saint'.[26]

Finally, consider the reports of Phillips Talbot, written for the Institute of Current World Affairs in New York on the eve of Independence and published recently in the daily newspaper, *The Hindu*. For one thing, Talbot was struck by the countrywide expression of Hindu-Muslim cordiality during the Independence celebrations.

For twenty long and bloody weeks after 16 August 1946, Hindus avoided entering Muslim neighbourhoods and *vice versa*. Communal clashes and deaths were daily occurrences. Yet at the climax of Independence celebrations this week, Hindus and Muslims mixed together freely. Many Hindus visited mosques on the 18th and distributed sweets to Muslims who were observing their Id festival. . . . It was a spectacular truce, if not a peace treaty, between the two communities. Similarly, in Delhi and Bombay I saw Hindus and Muslims playing hand in hand. Reports of the same nature came from most places except the still-troubled Punjab.[27]

Talbot's own explanation was that the political parties desired peace and friendship between the communities, though he laid greater stress on 'the popular revulsion against the constant dislocation and actual fear of life during the last year'. 'Terror', he added,

is an enervating emotion. I've seen neighbourhoods so distraught by the medieval lack of personal security that they could not think of nothing else. I think that people everywhere used the excitement of the celebrations to try to break the vicious cycle of communal attacks and retaliations. How permanent the change may be is yet to be seen.[28]

Such impressions need to be drawn into the discussions on Partition so that the past is not judged through our recent encounters with Hindu-Muslim violence in India. It is just as important to delineate the multiple strands in the Muslim League movement, underline its complexity, assess its ideological orientation afresh, and explore the mobilization strategies adopted by Jinnah after he returned from his home in Hampstead to plunge into the humdrum of Indian politics. In addition to having greater access to source materials, this is an opportune moment, fifty years after In-dependence, to revise and reconsider established theories on Partition, introduce a more nuanced discourse, and stay clear of the conventional wisdom that we, the generation born after Independence, have inherited on the theme of 'communal' politics generally, and the Pakistan move-ment, in particular. As 'old orthodoxies recede before the flood of fresh historical evidence and earlier certitudes are overturned by newly detected contradiction', this is the time to heal 'the multiple fractures which turned the promised dawn of freedom into a painful moment of separation'.[29]

For example, one of the points adequately documented, though not sufficiently considered in secondary literature, is that not everyone who raised or rallied around the green flag was uniformly wedded to or inspired by a shared ideal of creating an Islamic society. The reality is that many were pushed into taking religious/Islamic positions, while many others, especially the landed classes in Punjab and UP, used the Muslim League as a vehicle to articulate, defend, and promote their material interests. In fact, the intensity of emotions expressed in the 1940s, which is so often invoked in the subcontinent to create popular myths and stereotypical images, had more to do with the political and economic anxieties of various social classes than with a profound urge to create a *Shariat*-based society. Today, the issue is not the legitimacy of a movement but to place in perspective the dynamics of power-politics in a colonial context. In fact, a rounded picture of the Pakistan movement is possible only if we are able to contest the exaggerated claims made in the name of Islam, then and now, by the Islamists and the proponents of the two-nation theory.

In sum, the clamour for a separate nation, though pressed vigorously in the post-War years with much popular backing and enthusiasm, was raised not so much by the Muslim divines, many of whom were waiting on the fringes of Indian politics to intervene on behalf of Islam, but by the vociferous professional groups in UP, Bihar, the princely state of Hyderabad, and the small but upcoming trading and banking communities in Gujarat, Bombay, and Calcutta. Interestingly enough, the Muslim landlords of UP were the first to raise the banner of revolt against the League; in fact, the nawab of Chhatari and nawab Muhammad Yusuf of Jaunpur broke away from the Muslim League Parliamentary Board in April 1936 in order to revive 'a mixed party in preference to a Muslim communal organization'.[30] They changed course once the Congress ministry adopted the UP Tenancy Bill and Nehru and his comrades became more and more strident in their socialistic pronouncements. These men were not concerned to defend the Koranic injunctions which they probably flouted every day of their life. Nor were they interested in the welfare of poor Muslims, victims of their oppression and exploitation. Their chief goal was to defend their landholdings, orchards, havelis, palaces and, above all, the nawabi paraphernalia built through the courtesy of their British benefactors. Notice the following conversation between Saleem and his father Hamid in Attia Hosain's (died in January 1998) celebrated novel *Sunlight on a Broken Column*:

Saleem was saying, 'In the final analysis, what you are facing is the struggle for power by the bourgeoisie. It is not really a peasant's movement, but when it comes to a division of spoils even class interests are forgotten. For example the four hundred or so Taluqdars insisted the British should give them higher representation than the thousands of other landlords.'

'It is not a question of numbers alone', protested Uncle Hamid, sitting up and waving his pipe in negation. 'We Taluqdars have ancient rights and privileges, given by a special charter, which we have to safeguard. . . .'

'Yes, yes, of course. One respects tradition. One fights for one's self, one's interests. But you cannot expect the tenants to love you for it.'

'That is because so-called reforms are destroying the personal ties between landlord and peasant. Surely a Government and its changing officers cannot have personal relations or traditional ties with the tenants? With whom are the people in constant touch? Their landlords or local political leaders?. . .'

'How can landlords but be uneasy at the thought of such reserves of power being vested in officials at a time when it is uncertain what class of persons will obtain political power?. . .' (Uncle Hamid)

Saleem could not let an argument die an unnatural death. He began, 'What you said, father, about the landlords' fear of abolition is the crux of the matter. This fear for their existence is the basis for the formation of a new parry which is interested in keeping the status quo intact, that is favoured by the British and is fundamentally opposed to progressive, national movements. . . .'

'Words? Theories! Irresponsible talk!' Uncle Hamid burst out. 'I am a part of feudalism, and proud to be. I shall fight for it. It is my heritage—and yours. Let me remind you of that. And that you enjoy its 'reactionary' advantages. You talk very glibly of its destruction, but you live by its existence. It is, in fact, your only livelihood.'[31]

No wonder, the landed elements in UP, as also the Jamaat-i Islami and some sections of the ulama connected with the Barelwi 'school', Nadwat al-ulama, Firangi Mahal and Deoband, hitched their fortunes with the Muslim League at different points of time and for different reasons. Their overall strategy, one that suited the raj during and after World War II, was to masquerade their hidden agenda and project the Congress, their main rival in the political world, as a 'Hindu' party inimical to Islam. Once the League bandwagon rolled on, other aggrieved groups, especially those who had failed to secure employment, contracts or seats on regional and local bodies, jumped into the fray as the defenders of the faith.

Still, Pakistan was not everybody's dream. Nor was Jinnah everyone's Quaid (leader).[32] In this respect, one should not, as is generally the case with both the Hindu and Muslim majoritarian discourses, lose sight of the perspectives of those who were intellectually committed to secular nationalism or were actively engaged in repudiating the two-nation theory. Their voices, which have been stifled by 'secular' as well 'communal' histories, should not be relegated to a historian's footnote. Indeed, the part played by those Muslims, who are patronizingly described as 'Nationalist Muslims', the Khudai Khidmatgars in the N.W.F.P., who were eventually let down by the dispirited Congress leadership on the eve of Independence, the ulama of Deoband and the Momins in Bihar, should not be submerged beneath the rationalization of the 'victors'. Their main contribution, exemplified by Azad's exemplary conduct and performance,[33] lay in keeping alive the vision of a secular India. These 'marginal' voices should be recovered to rewrite the histories of Partition.[34]

For these and other reasons, it would be appropriate to ask if the Muslim League movement was as cohesive and unified as it is made out to be by some writers in India and Pakistan. If the Congress was faction-ridden and ideologically fragmented, so was the League.[35] This is illustrated by the depth and intensity of jealousies and internal discord in the organization, the regional groupings, the *Ajlaf-Ashraf* divide, the Shia-Sunni strife in many places, and the unending doctrinal disputes between the theologians, especially the followers of the Barelwi and the Deobandi 'schools'. Such differences, though conveniently overlooked in the histories of the freedom movement in Pakistan, were real and not imaginary. If so, it will not do to portray the Muslim Leaguers as earnest and self-sacrificing crusaders or equate them with the *muhajirs* or *ansars* of the Prophet Muhammad. What is perhaps challenging, as indeed intellectually rewarding, is to probe those critical areas where the 'faithful', despite having projected themselves as a community acting in unison, were themselves so hopelessly split. Such an exercise, far from reducing or tarnishing the reputation of historic figures, will enrich our knowledge and understanding of a complex phenomena. Arguably, if we know our leaders better and question their reading of the authentic and vibrant histories of shared memories and experiences, we may not repeat their mistakes and errors of judgement which cost the nation dearly at the stroke of the midnight hour on 14-15 August 1947.

III

The decision about the creation of Pakistan had just been announced and people were indulging in all kinds of surmises about the pattern of life that would emerge. But no one's imagination could go very far. The sardarji sitting in front of me repeatedly asked me whether I thought Mr. Jinnah would continue to live in Bombay after the creation of Pakistan or whether he would resettle in Pakistan. Each time my answer would be the same, 'Why should he leave Bombay? I think he'll continue to live in Bombay and continue visiting Pakistan.' Similar guesses were being made about the towns of Lahore and Gurdaspur too, and no one knew which town would fall to the share of India and which to Pakistan.[36]

In the specific context of the Pakistan movement, the professed ideology of the nation state itself, though celebrated on both sides of the border, had no significant impact on or relevance to the millions living in India or Pakistan. Contrary to the exaggerated claims made in both countries, most people were either indifferent to or unconcerned with the national borders or the newly-created geographical entities that were being laboriously created. National borders were political constructs, and imagined projections of territorial power. Although they appeared in deceptively precise forms, they reflected, at leat initially, merely the mental images of politicians, lawyers, and intellectuals. Their practical consequences for most people were quite different.[37] Rajinder Sachar, jurist and human rights activist who has spent a lifetime struggling with his memories of Lahore, recalled: 'One day I ran into a Muslim villager who had come to Lahore all the way from Sargodha looking for my grandfather, a well-known criminal lawyer. Poor chap he didn't realize that Partition had taken place and that the Hindus had left. It just shows how long it took for the implications of Partition to sink in.'[38] Indeed, though such people were repeatedly fed with ill-informed and biased views, they were neither committed to the land of *Aryavarta* nor the *Dar al-Islam*. They had no destination to reach, no mirage to follow. Even though the trains had started carrying people to their death-traps, they were unclear whether Lahore, with its splendid Mughal monuments, beautiful gardens and boulevards, would be part of India or Pakistan. They did not know whether Delhi, the city of Mir Taqi Mir and Mirza Ghalib, would remain in Gandhi's India or Jinnah's Pakistan. Manto captures the mood in his brilliant story 'Toba Tek Singh', a character from the lunatic asylum. This is what he writes:

As to where Pakistan was located, the inmates knew nothing. That was why both the mad and the partially mad were unable to decide whether they were now in India or in Pakistan. If they were in India where on earth was Pakistan? And if they were in Pakistan, then how come that until only the other day it was India?. . .

Those who had tried to solve this mystery had become utterly confused when told that Sialkot, which used to be in India, was now in Pakistan. It was anybody's guess what was going to happen to Lahore, which was currently in Pakistan, but could slide into India any moments. It was still possible that the entire sub-continent of India might become Pakistan. And who could say if both India and Pakistan might not entirely vanish from the map of the world one day? . . .

Just before sunrise, Bisham Singh, the man who had stood on his legs for fifteen years, screamed and as officials from the two sides rushed towards him, he collapsed on the ground.

There, behind barbed wire, on one side, lay India and behind more barbed wire, on the other side, lay Pakistan. In between, on a bit of earth which had no name, lay Toba Tek Singh.

The paradox of how borders simultaneously separate and unite is discussed elsewhere.[39] The significance of Manto's description lies in describing an existentialist reality—the separation of people living on both sides who had a long history of cultural and social contact—and the pradoxical character of borders being a metaphor of the ambiguities of nation building.[40] He, in essence, offered a way of correcting the distortions inherent in state-centred national histories. Finally, 'India' or 'Pakistan' were mere territorial abstractions to most people who were ignorant of how Mountbatten's plan or the Radcliffe Award would change their destinies and tear them apart from their social and cultural moorings. In their world view, there was no nationalism, religious or composite. They were blissfully unaware that their fate, which had rested in the hands of the exploiting classes for centuries, would be settled after Mountbatten's three days of 'diplomacy' leading to the 3 June Plan, and that the frontiers would be decided by Cyril Radcliffe in just seven weeks and 'a continent for better or worse divided'.[41] They had no clue whatsoever that these vain, insensitive and conceited representatives of the Crown, having received the mandate from Clement Atlee's Labour government to preside over the liquidation of the most important imperial possession of all time, would abandon them in mid-ocean 'with a fire in the deck and ammunition in the hold'. Nobody had warned them how Mountbatten's mentor Winston Churchill had, likewise, sat with T.E. Lawrence and the Emir Faisal in Cairo as colonial secretary in 1922 drawing nation states on the map of what had previously been the Ottoman empire. But, then, how were they to know that the colonial powers divide people and territories when in ascendancy, as also in retreat.

IV

For a long time I refused to accept the consequences of the revolution, which was set off by the Partition of the country. I still feel the same way; but I suppose, in the end, I came to accept this nightmarish reality without self-pity or despair. In the process I tried to retrieve from this man-made sea of blood, pearls of a rare hue, by writing about the single-minded dedication with which men had killed men, about the remorse felt by some of them, about the tears shed by murders who could not understand why they still had some human feelings left. All this and more, I put in my book *Siyah Hashye*. (Saadat Hasan Manto)[42]

Everytime I visited Amritsar, I felt captivated. But the city this time presented the look of a cremation ghat, eerie and stinking. . . . The silence was so perfect that even the faint hiss of steam from the stationary engine sounded a shriek. . . . The brief stoppage seemed to have lingered into eternity till the engine whistled and gave a gentle pull. . . . We left Chheharta behind and then Atari and when we entered Wagah and then Harbanspura everyone in the train felt uplifted. A journey through a virtual valley of destruction has ended when finally the train came to a halt at Platform No. 2—Lahore, the moment was as gratifying as the consummation of a dream.[43]

Scores of writers reveal the other face of freedom, the woes of divided families, the agony and trauma of abducted women, the plight of migrants and the harrowing experiences of countless people who boarded the train that was supposed to take them to the realization of their dream, but of whom not a man, woman or child survived the journey. A Zahid in Attia Hosain's *Sunlight on a Broken Column* or a Saddan in Masoom Reza Rahi's *Aadha Gaon* (Half-a-Village) offer a vivid and powerful portrayal of a fragmented and wounded society.[44] What political debate will never fully do—and the reason we so badly need the literature—is defeat the urge to lay blame, which keeps animosity alive. Only such a literature can truly evoke of the sufferings of the innocent, whose pain is more universal, and ultimately a vehicle of more honest reconciliation than political discourse.[45]

Board the *Peshawar Express* or the *Train to Pakistan* to discover the implications of what happened before and after the fateful, midnight hour. Consider the exchanges between Choudhry Muhammad Ali, a well-known landlord of Rudauli in Barabanki district (UP) and his daughter who left her father to settle in Karachi, or the correspondence of Brahm Nath Dutt, father of the historian V.N. Datta, to capture the poignancy of the moment. Turn to Rahi's Gangauli village—a world where people are seen to be wrestling to come to terms with competing ideologies—in order to uncover how the intricate and almost imperceptible way in which the politics of Partition worked its way into the interstices of people's consciousness.[46] Read Attia Hosain's *Sunlight on a Broken Column* or *Phoenix Fled* to discover how the Pakistan movement split families on ideological lines and created fears and uncertainties in the minds of people. To read her novel and collection of short stories is, 'as if one had parted a curtain, or opened a door, and strayed into the past'.[47]

Indeed, if the *histories* of Partition are to be rewritten, there are several reasons why we must judiciously draw upon the intellectual resources made available to us by such creative writers. They expose the inadequacy of numerous narratives on Independence and Partition, compel us to explore fresh themes and adopt new approaches that have eluded the grasp of social scientists, and provide a foundation for developing an alternative discourse to current expositions of a general theory on intercommunity relations. Their strength lies in representing a grim and sordid contemporary reality without drawing on religion or a particular community as the principal reference point. In their stories, the experiences of each community distinctly mirror one another, indeed reach out to and clutch at one another. No crime, no despair, no grief in exile belongs uniquely to anyone.[48] In the words of Krishna Sobti, whose best-known Hindi writings on Partition are *Sikka Badal Gaya* and *Zindaginama*, the fiction written about that cataclysmic event preserved 'essential human values'.[49] That is probably why we emerge from the literature with a mistrust toward group solidarity of an oppositional bent. If so we must emerge at the same time, paradoxically, with a conviction to oppose such mistrust with trust in the goodness of the human life-urge wherever we find it. Indeed,

we emerge from the literature as searchers of such trust. If we find it in the solitary dissidence of even a singly person, we feel obliged to offer him or her our companionship. And if we find it stitched into whole communities, we come away not necessarily more pious, but inspired. The literature as a whole seeds pathos for the suffering and inhumanity of the Partition, and related instances of cultural chauvinism, but not merely so. It also sprouts a countervailing protest, a voice of justice that must be the surging of our humanity itself—something greater than our bestiality—within us. In this sense the literature does what religious leaders in each community failed to do: to make communities forces for the affirmation of humanity broadly. . . . If religious politics worked nefariously in favour of Partition, it was because an ecumenical religious politics never de-veloped. We are in a different position than the men and women of August, 1947. Our choices are not limited to exile, death or resignation. . . .[50]

In other words, if creative writings on Partition can still stir the individual and collective imagination of sensitive readers in the subcontinent, there is no reason why people on both sides of the Wagah border cannot share the anguish of Faiz Ahmad Faiz[51] and, at the same time, echo the optimism and plea of Ali Sardar Jafri expressed in the following lines:

> *Tum aao Gulshan-i Lahore se chaman bardosh,*
> *hum ayen subha Banaras ki raushni lekar,*
> *Himalaya ki hawaon ki taazgi lekar,*
> *Phir uske baad ye puchen ke kaun dushman hai?*

> You come covered with flowers from the Garden of Lahore
> We bring to you the light and radiance of the morning of Banaras,
> the freshness of the winds of the Himalayas,
> And then we ask who the enemy is?

NOTES

1. Krishna Sobti, in conversation with Alok Bhalla, in Geeti Sen (ed.), *Crossing Boundaries*, New Delhi, 1997, p. 78.
2. N.N. Vohra, '91, Garden Town', ibid., p. 54.

3. Some years ago, the historian Gyanendra Pandey complained that the history of violence accompanying Partition had not been written. Ashis Nandy bemoans that the finest creative minds of India had maintained a profound, almost cultivated silence about Partition and the bloodbath. *Times of India*, 20 July 1997. See, Urvashi Butalia on the 'Official Silence', *Hindu*, 21 Sept. 1997. My principal interest in this essay centres around articles published in newspapers, magazines and journals during the fiftieth year of Independence. I have, however, used scholarly writings, mostly published in 1996-7, to comment on the theme of Partition.

   The Delhi-based weekly newsmagazine, *Outlook*, brought out a special issue on 28 May 1997. *The Asian Age*, edited by M.J. Akbar, published extracts from books on Partition, personal memories, recollections and interviews. See, for example, the reports of the Reuters correspondent Don Campbell who arrived in India in March 1947 and spent the next 15 months in Delhi. The coverage in the newspaper *The Hindu* (Delhi) was also quite extensive. The impressions of Phillips Talbot, an American, were particularly interesting.

4. For example, Urvashi Butalia, 'Blood', *Granta* (London), Mar. 1997; Sunil Mehra, 'Sufferers and Survivors', *Outlook*, 28 May 1997, pp. 32-3; 'Bridging a Great Divide', *India Today*, 18 Aug. 1997; Anita Mukhopadhya, 'The Last Journey', *The Hindu*, 31 Aug. 1997; Ajeet Cour, 'I've seen rootless trees wobbling and walking', *Hindustan Times*, 4 Jan. 1998; C.M. Naim, 'Pakistan or Hindustan', *Communalism Combat*, Sept. 1997; 'India's unforgettable divide', *Guardian* (London), 30 July 1997; Iqbal Masud, 'Dream Merchants, Politicians & Partition: Memoirs of an Indian Muslim', New Delhi, 1997.

5. *Femina* (Bombay), 1 Aug. 1997.

6. For example, Patrick French, *Liberty or Death: India's Journey to Independence and Division*, London, 1997.

7. See, for example, Gyanendra Pandey, 'Community and Violence', *EPW*, 9 Aug. 1997, and his 'Partition and Independence in Delhi: 1947-48', *EPW*, 6 Sept. 1997; also, Azhar Abbas, 'The Twice Displaced', *Outlook*, 28 May 1997, p. 66. For insights into ethnic violence in Sri Lanka in 1983 that had many features in common with the Hindu-Muslim riots before and after Independence, S.J. Tambiah, *Ethnic Fratricide and the Dismantling of Democracy*, Chicago, 1986.

8. Urvashi Butalia, *The Other Side of Silence: Voices from the Partition of India*, New Delhi, 1998; Ritu Menon and Kamla Bhasin, *Borders & Boundaries: Women in India's Partition*, New Delhi, 1998.

9. Hasan, *Legacy of a Divided Nation*, and *India Partitioned: The Other Face of Freedom*, New Delhi, 1997, 2nd rev. edn.

10. For a critique of Mountbatten, see N.N. Vohra, '91, Garden Town' and F.S. Aijazuddin 'Same to Same' from a different perspective, in Sen (ed.), *Crossing Boundaries*.

11. *Outlook*, 28 May 1997. Notice the following letter of Cyrill Radcliffe to his

son: 'I thought you would like to get a letter from India with a crown on the envelope. After tomorrow evening nobody will ever again be allowed to use such stationery and after 150 years British rule will be over in India. . . . I am going to see Mountbatten sworn as the first governor-general of the Indian Union . . . and then I station myself firmly on the Delhi airport until an aeroplane from England comes along. Nobody in India will love me for the award about the Punjab and Bengal and there will be roughly 80 million people with a grievance who will begin looking for me. I do not want them to find me. I have worked and travelled and sweated—oh I have sweated the whole time.' Quoted in Sunil Khilnani, *The Idea of India*, London, 1997, p. 201.

12. Ajit Bhattacharjea, 'Cyril's Scalpel', *Outlook*, 23 July 1997, p. 8.

13. Thus the following view: 'Looking back 50 years, the haste and self-delusion of Congress and Muslim leaders that contributed to the bloodiest religious cleansing in history emerges with disturbing clarity.' *Outlook*, 28 May 1997.

14. Mosley, *The Last Days of the Raj*, p. 77.

15. For example, the presidential address delivered by Professor V.N. Datta at the Indian History Congress held in Madras, 1996.

16. Kuldip Nayar, 'Was Pakistan Necessary?', *Indian Express*, 15 Aug. 1997, and his 'Partition: An Inevitability', *The Hindu* (Special Issue on 'India!'), Aug. 1997. For earlier accounts of 'who is to blame?', see Chimanlal Setalvad, *India Divided*, Bombay, n.d., pp. 4-7.

17. Gyanendra Pandey, 'The Prose of Otherness', David Arnold and David Hardiman (ed.), *Subaltern Studies VIII: Essays in Honour of Ranajit Guha*, New Delhi, 1994, p. 194.

18. This is the common refrain in the writings of Ayesha Jalal and Farzana Shaikh. For his critique of Jalal's work, see Pandey, 'The Prose of Otherness', pp. 209-10. And for her response, see 'Secularists, subalterns and the stigma of "Communalism": Partition historiography revisited', *The Indian Economic and Social History Review*, Vol. 33 (1), 1996, pp. 93-103. The tendency to exaggerate the difference in perspectives and to castigate each other for that reason is the hallmark of recent historiography on South Asia. Young and upcoming social scientists, many of whom have not even written their doctoral dissertations, are engaged in polemical writings. They regard this as a shortcut to establishing their scholarly reputation in the West. Ayesha Jalal's critique of my introduction to *India's Partition: Process Strategy and Mobilization*, is based on a misunderstanding of my overall argument. Yet, I respect her views and her understanding of a highly complex phenomena which should not, incidentally, be reduced to polemical exchanges among fellow-historians.

19. In a perceptive article, Aijaz Ahmad has offered a powerful critique of 'the Congress-inspired mythology'. His analysis suggests: (a) that the politics of caste and communalism was inherent in the structure of the colonial society itself; (b) that the reform movements usually contributed to solidifying such identities rather than weakening them in favour of ecumenical culture and a non-denominational politics; and (c) that the national movement itself, includ-

ing the majority of the Congress under Gandhi, was deeply 'complicit in a transactional mode of politics which involved bargaining among the elites and a conception of secularism which was little more than an accommodation of the self-enclosed orthodoxies. Given the immensity of this historical weight, the wonder is not that there was a partition but that there was one.' *The Hindu*, 'India' (Special Number), p. 28.

20. The judgement is harsh, although many contemporary observers believed that Jinnah may not have had the space to press his campaign in the United Provinces if the coalition issue was amicably resolved. The governor of UP felt that way. Harry Haig to Linlithgow, 3 June 1939, File No. 115/6, BL. See also, my introduction to *India's Partition*, pp. 12-15.

21. There is unmistakable evidence to suggest that talks for a Congress-Muslim League alliance were initiated some time in Mar.-Apr. 1937. Although Nehru had opposed 'all pacts and coalitions with small groups at the top'. (To Abul Wali, 30 Mar. 1937, AICC papers, G-5, K.W. i, 1937. Abdul Wali of Bara Banki (UP) referred to a scheme 'being hatched with the help of Pantji [G.B. Pant] and Mohanlal [Saxena] to bring about coalition between the Congress and League parties in the Assembly'. To Nehru, 28 Mar. 1937, AICC papers. The governor of UP reported on 7 Apr. that the League was looking forward to an alliance with the Congress and felt that 'at present it looks as if the new government will gradually attract to itself a fair number of the Muslim Leaguers'.

22. See Masud Hasan Shahab Dehlavi, in Mushirul Hasan (ed.), *India Partitioned*, Vol. 2, pp. 184-95.

23. Interview with Alok Bhalla, in Sen (ed.), *Crossing Boundaries*, p. 66. And the comment of J.S. Butalia, a retired journalist: 'I was born and brought up in a predominantly Muslim village, Butala. There were 300 Muslim families and only 10 or 15 Hindu homes but we lived in such close harmony that it was difficult to make out who was who. A Hindu-Muslim conflict was something we had not imagined even in our worst dreams. It is with a sense of horror and shame that I look back . . . but, finally, I am overwhelmed by nostalgia'. *The Hindu*, 'India' (Special Number), 15 Aug. 1997, p. 32. For Bengal, see Mukhopadhaya, 'The Last Journey', *The Hindu*, 31 Aug. 1997.

24. See the contributions of Rakshat Puri, Muchkund Dubey and Sumanta Banerjea, in Sen (ed.), *Crossing Boundaries*, op. cit.

25. This is quoted in full in my, *Legacy of a Divided Nation*, p. 168.

26. See Hasan, *India's Partition*, p. 405. For Punjab, see Sobti, pp. 67, 69-70. For Bengal, see Samaddar (ed.), *Reflections on Partition in the East*, and its review by Sumanta Banerjee in *Biblio*, New Delhi, Jul.-Aug. 1997, pp. 40-1; and Peter van der Veer, 'Playing or Praying: A Suf Saint's Day in Surat', *The Journal of Asian Studies*, Vol. 51, 3, Aug. 1992, pp. 545-64.

27. Phillips Talbot, 'Thus Independence came to India', *The Hindu*, 4 and 24 Aug. 1997.

28. Talbot filed this report on 10 Aug. 1947.

29. I have borrowed these lines from Ayesha Jalal, 'Secularists, Subalterns and the Stigma of "Communalism"', p. 1.
30. Nawab of Chhatari to Hailey, 28 Oct. 1936, Malcolm Hailey papers, File No. 28c.
31. Attia Hosain, *Sunlight on a Broken Column*, New Delhi, 1992 edn., pp. 231-3, 234.
32. In this respect, my reading of the Pakistan movement is different from that of Ayesha Jalal.
33. The following impression of Azad by Kanji Dwarkadas is interesting. 'Abul Kalam Azad,' he wrote, 'is dignified and level-headed, but his health is giving way. Jinnah dislikes him heartily and a few years ago he called him the "show boy" of the Congress and in private conversations Jinnah says much worse things about Abul Kalam Azad.' 'India—April 1944 to Nov. 1945: What Next', 28 Nov. 1945 (typescript), George Lumley papers, BL.
34. Pandey, 'The Prose of Otherness', p. 214.
35. In fact, Jinnah exhorted various regional groups and other factions to overcome their differences and rival claims so that the Muslim League could concentrate all its energies towards the achievement of Pakistan. 'We shall have time to quarrel ourselves,' he said, 'and we shall have time when these differences will have to be remedied. We shall have time for domestic programmes and politics, but first get the Government. This is a nation without any territory or any government.' Quoted in Sayeed, *Pakistan: The Formative Phase*, p. 297.
36. Bhisham Sahni, 'We have Arrived in Amritsar', Stephen Alter and Vimal Dissanayake (eds.), *The Penguin Book of Modern Short Stories*, pp. 180-7.
37. These lines are based on Michiel Baud and Willem van Schendel, 'Towards a Comparative History of Borderlands', in *Journal of World History*, Vol. 8, 2, 1997, pp. 211-42.
38. Quoted in *The Hindu*, 'India' (Special Number), 15 Aug. 1947, p. 28.
39. Baud and Schendel, 'Towards a Comparative History of Borderlands', p. 242.
40. Benedict Anderson, *Imagined Communities: Reflections on the Origin and Spread of Nationalism* (1983; rpt., New York, 1991); E.J. Hobsbawm and Terence Ranger (eds.), *The Invention of Tradition*, Cambridge, 1983.
41. This is a line from W.H. Auden. See Khilnani, op. cit., p. 200.
42. For my translation of *Siyah Hashye* ('Black Margins'), see my (ed.), *India Partitioned*, Vol. 1, pp. 88-101.
43. Muhammad Saeed, *Lahore: A Memoir*, Lahore, 1989, p. 94.
44. On *Aadha Gaon*, see Sudhir Chandra, 'The Harvest of Fear: A Retrospective Critique of Hindu-Muslim Relations in Two Hindi Novels', in T.V. Sathyamurthy, *Region, Religion, Caste, Gender and Culture in Contemporary India*, Vol. 3, New Delhi, 1996.
45. Jason Francisco, 'In the Heat of Fratricide: The Literature of India's Partition Burning Freshly (A Review Article)', *The Annual of Urdu Studies*, No. 2, Madison, 1996, p. 250.

46. Chandra, 'The Harvest of Fear', p. 195.
47. Anita Desai, 'Introduction', *Phoenix Fled*, New Delhi, 1988, p. viii.
48. Jason Francisco, op. cit., p. 250.
49. Geeti Sen (ed.), *Crossing Boundaries*, p. 77; and Alok Bhalla (ed.), *Stories about the Partition of India*, 3 vols., New Delhi, 1994.
50. Francisco, op. cit., p. 250.
51. This leprous daybreak, dawn night's fangs have mangled—
    This is not that long-looked-for break of that day,
    Not that clear dawn in quest of which those comrades
    Set out, believing that in heaven's wide void
    Somewhere must be the stars' last halting place,
    Somewhere the verge of night's slow-washing tide,
    Somewhere an anchorage for the ship of heartache.

13

Divided Nationhood:
India's Partition Revisited

> Ghalib died long ago, but I still remember
> his constant questioning.
> To everything he would counter
> *had it been this way*, what would have been?

Theories of nationalism have traditionally been divided into two main categories, instrumentalist and primoridialist. The former conceived nationalism as a product of élite manipulation and contend that nations can be fabricated, if not invented. The latter see nationalism as a spontaneous process stemming from a naturally given sense of nationhood. Locating India's Partition in this debate is a daunting task. In addition to the die-hards who regard the 'event' as imminent and inevitable, one has to contend with writers who have lazily settled for the two-nation theory, articulated not just by the Muslim League but also by the Hindu right.[1] Similarly, while the government's part in stoking the fires of communalism is underscored, its 'divide and rule' policy is readily invoked, rhetorically, to explain 'Muslim separatism' rather than the overt manifestations of Hindu communalism.[2]

But the more fundamental difficulty lies elsewhere—in the overall direction and orientation of research on the Muslim communities that is still mired within traditional frameworks. Though some new voices are being heard, most academic exchanges involve a range of intellectual suppositions that still rest on the belief that Muslims are an exclusive category, with a shared world view, a common outlook, and a structure of consciousness in accord with the fundamental tenets of Islam.[3] This approach underlines the primacy of culture and ideology, assigns a privileged place to Islam, and portrays the image of a community acting in unison. In other words, the emphasis is on a monolithic conception of Islamic ideology and practice or a teleology dictating the actions of the Muslims or a general acquiescence in the actions of a few. The mere fact of people being Muslim in some general sense is usually conflated with their adherence to beliefs and practices that are strictly described as 'Islamist' or 'separatist'.[4]

By now, the continued harping on such views has perpetuated the mistaken belief that the roots of the Partition lie not in the 1930s on early 1940s but in the late-nineteenth century 'Neo-Muslim modernist and separatist' tradition of Aligarh's modernism and its spokesperson Saiyid Ahmad Khan.[5]

What also plagues the Partition studies is the misplaced emphasis on, what Anthony D. Smith calls *ethno* history—the tendency to extol the heroic deeds of past national leaders and to provide a legitimizing historical perspective as the basis of the project. Hence the use, in the writings of some Pakistani scholars, of Saladin as a metaphor, a cultural construct, to compare him with Jinnah. The oddity of the comparison is apparent in the comment: 'Both Saladin and Jinnah took on the most renowned opponents of their age, almost mythical in stature. Saladin fought against Richard the Lionheart and Jinnah challenged Mounbatten, Gandhi and Nehru.'[6] Yet, this is how the writings on Partition are dignified as an academic speciality not because it contains demonstrably special features, but because they allow the historian to identify with his heroes and 'his' event.[7]

Though the adulation of Jinnah is by no means exceptional in Pakistan, historians of all hues have painstakingly profiled national parties and their leaders for decades to construct the grand narrative of India's vivisection. This exercise cannot be decried or considered unimportant: the Congress and the Muslim League were, undeniably, the key players in the decade preceding the transfer of power. Introducing a volume in 1993, I referred to the complexities of the years 1937 to 1940 embodied in the three paradoxes—the League's being catapulted to prominence after years of political wilderness; Jinnah's transformation from a secular politician to an ideologue of Muslim nationalism; and the Congress acceptance of the Partition plan with seeming alacrity, thus relinquishing its vaunted principles of national unity. Pointing to the intricacies of the conjuncture, I analysed the performance of the 1937-9 Congress ministries, including the interaction between class and communal tensions, in influencing the timing of the emergence of the Pakistan demand. I revisited the debates over the Congress truculence over a coalition ministry in UP, examined the failure of the Muslim mass contact campaign, and mapped out the political consequences of the Congress, refusal to join the war effort in 1939.[8] 'It was the war', wrote the historian Eric Hobsbawm, 'that broke India in two. In one sense it was the last great triumph of the raj—and at the same time its last exhausted gasp.'[9]

I have since argued that concentrating only on the British-Congress-League negotiations cannot unravel the complex nature of the Partition story. Similarly, individual pronouncements, party resolutions and manifestos, though a pointer to various crucial turn of events in politics and society, are not good enough. For one, they convey the impression that the subcontinental leaders occupied an unassailable place in deciding the nation's destiny on the eve of the transfer of power. The reality, obscured by dense official papers and documents, was profoundly different. 'Major' players in the high politics of the 1940s, though influential, were by no means free agents able to pursue their own or their party's agenda. Some, if not all, of their initiatives were severely curbed by those sections of their following who were embroiled in communal campaigns and affected by changing political alignments in UP, Punjab and Bengal, the eventual storm-centres of the Pakistan movement. This explains, at least in part, why Nehru's brainchild, the Muslim mass contact campaign, petered out long before the Lahore resolution was adopted amid cries of *Allah-o-Akbar*: it ran into serious trouble because district Congress committees, often dominated by Hindu Mahasabhites, girded themselves to ward off the 'Muslim influx' into the organization. Likewise, in a different context but an equally important milestone in polarizing communal sentiments, local units of the League and their ulama collaborators, imbued with a misguided zeal to expose the 'wrongs' of the Congress ministries, mounted ceaseless pressure on central leaders to celebrate 'Deliverance Day'. Amid the exuberant rejoicing and by the general expression of loathing for Congress, they demanded their pound of flesh for their 'sufferings' under a 'Hindu Raj'. 'The Deliverance Day', wrote one of Jinnah's admirers in Lucknow, 'was such a success that it was even celebrated in those quarters where the League is looked upon as a vile disease. . . . You have laid the foundation of a self-respecting nationhood for the Muslims. It (Deliverance Day) is the first concrete step that shows [*sic*] without ambiguity that there are not one but several nations in India.'[10]

Much the same energy was released, in a communally-polarized climate, whenever the prospect of a Congress-League rapprochement brightened up. Local Hindu, Muslim and later the Sikh bodies, infused with religious fanaticism and sensitive to escalating communal violence, sent out loud and clear signals to the Congress, League and Akali Dal representatives, many of whom were obliged to dispel the impression of a 'sell out'. 'So ends the second Simla Conference', the viceroy wrote in his *Journal* on 12 May 1946, 'with much the same fate as the first. I was always very doubtful about it, I have never attached the same importance as the (Cabinet) Mission to Congress and the League reaching agreement, as I was pretty sure that they never would.'[11] In the months following the Simla conference, the lonely figure of the Mahatma, forsaken by his Congress lieutenants and wilfully targeted by the Hindu right for 'appeasing' Muslims and helping to destroy Hindus and Hinduism, Gandhi wrote in October 1946: 'I know that mine is today a voice in the wilderness.' As the 'vivisection of India' became imminent, his own sense of impotence increased. 'My writ runs no more. . . . No one listens to me any more. . . . I am crying in the wilderness.'[12]

Another instance is how, to begin with, both Nehru and Liaquat Ali Khan had set their faces against any wholesale transfer of populations, but how events, rapidly becoming too large for them, dictated the course of their policy.[13]

Although the pressure on national leaders came from various quarters, the constraints on their capacity to act freely and independently need to be probed in the context of the direction, thrust, and modus operandi of the mobilization campaigns. Whether it was the Congress or the League, their initiatives often generated new fears and uncertainties in many regions though in significantly different ways. They also enlarged, thanks to the colonial structures, areas of conflict and competition. This paved the way for religious and cultural bodies, some founded in the last-quarter of the nineteenth century, to assume the mantle of community leadership and intervene stridently in national affairs. Although every single step in the process of devolution of authority, commencing with the Morley-Minto Reforms (1909) onwards, legitimized their operations, a good many 're-formist' movements, notably the Arya Samaj in Punjab or the *tabligh* and *tanzim* societies in the Indo-Gangetic belt, developed their ideas and support base outside institutional structures, colonial policies, and 'external' influences. They derived sustenance from their own complex repertoire of ideas and concepts, from their own self-image and self-representation, from their apprehension of the intrusive influences responsible for contemporary decadence, and from their overall comprehension of where they stood in a world, they believed, was dominated by the Other.

We need to know how and why this occurred; in fact, making sense of the occurrences outside the national and regional spheres requires delineating the local roots of Hindu and Muslim nationalisms. That is how we can perhaps establish how local interests, operating within sharply-demarcated religious boundaries and using their linkages with *Hindutva* or Islamist movements, mounted pressure on all-India leaders to safeguard their special claims; also, how they opposed, sometimes violently, the occasional concession being offered to their adversaries as a price for reconciliation. Their profile, location and linkages serve to explain the reasons why they occupied a vantage point in Indian politics in the mid-1940s, and why they were able to (mostly in doubt in earlier decades) prepare the groundwork for Partition well before the Union Jack was lowered in Delhi and Karachi.

Two 'conflicting forms of urban solidarity' in eighteenth and nineteenth century north India served as the foundation for nationalism and religious communalism, which so dramatically affected events in the twentieth century.[14] Sumit Sarkar noted, more explicitly, that 'the decisions and actions of [the] leaders cannot really be understood without the counterpoint provided by pressures from below'.[15] This is corroborated by the pattern of communal violence between 1905 and 1947: a transition from a phase of rioting which was relatively unorganized, less related to institutional politics and with a strong class orientation, to outbreaks connected with organized politics, exhibiting a higher degree of organization and overt communalism.[16] Sarkar has delineated, moreover, the process by which Hindu-Muslim divisions in Bengal became elaborated in the 1920s. As a result, the masses 'outstrip[ped] their leaders', while the 'specific features and collective mentalities' of the subaltern groups involved became sharply defined in relation to 'the domain of the elite politicians'. Popular notions began to define community not by a shared Bengali culture but by religious identity.[17] Much the same process is discernible among the Urdu-speaking elites of UP in the last-quarter of the nineteenth century,[18] the Sikhs in Punjab,[19] and the Jats in rural south-east Punjab in the 1920s and 1930s.[20]

It is true that localities often mirrored the regional and all-India setting, hence the argument that the political pressures leading to the partition of Punjab and Bengal originated outside the province.[21] Yet the complex and intricate processes of the formation of community-based solidarities and how, these spread their tentacles upwards, can be delineated in the 'public arena', the arena of public performance and of 'collective activities in public spaces'.[22] So it may be that the untold story lies in the dusty lanes and by-lanes of towns and cities and not only or always in the faceless metropolitan centres; in and around the bustling vernacular newspaper offices, district courts, *thanas*, municipalities; or in the seemingly benign *madaris*, *pathshalas*, mosques, temples and Sufi shrines, the focal point of mobilization in Sind and Punjab;[23] and in the highly charged and volatile precincts of *shuddhi* and Gauraksha Sabhas, the Anjuman-i Islamia's, and the *tabligh* and *tanzim* outfits. These were, undeniably, the sites where myths, memories and divisive religious symbols got invented and propagated to heighten communitarian consciousness and perpetuate the image of the Other. They were also the arenas where wide-ranging issues—some having breached the citadel of inter-community harmony towards the end of the nineteenth century—were passionately contested. Public discussions over cow-slaughter and music in front of mosques, conducted in the columns of newspapers and in printed tracts, pamphlets, journals and books, all added fuel to controversies of one kind or another.

The intricate nature of such processes can be traced to urban centres— Lucknow, Aligarh, Allahabad and Banaras—in late-nineteenth and early twentieth centuries, as also to the rough and rugged rural south-east Punjab where the Jats, having been converted to the Arya Samaj, became the votaries of *shuddhi*, Hindi and cow-slaughter.[24] The urban-rural divide, having been partially bridged by the pan-Indian ideology of re-vitalization movements, involved the separation from and rejection of earlier symbols of joint Hindu-Muslim culture, the definition and affirmation of newer communal symbols,[25] and the invention of a tradition which Christophe Jaffrelot describes, in the context of Hindu nationalism, as 'the strategy of stigmatization and emulation'.[26] This was a new and, from the liberal-left perspective, an ominous development. There had after all, been, common traditions and common reference points in the pre-colonial past, but they had not necessarily developed into the consolidated solidarities which 'Islam' or 'Hinduism' in late-nineteenth and early-twentieth century came to signify.[27] Christopher Bayly thus argued, quite rightly, that prior to 1860 there was perhaps no identifiable 'Muslim', 'Sikh' or 'Hindu' identity that could be abstracted from the particular circumstances of individual events or specific societies.[28] Accordingly, in her work on the interaction between Muslim, Hindu and Christian traditions in the south, Susan Bayly identifies a borrowing of symbols and ideas, a frequently shared vocabulary, and an interweaving of motifs within a common sacred landscape.[29]

Whatever the debate on the nature and depth of such interactions, it must be recognized that Islamization or the 'Nationalization' of Hindu traditions was triggered by factors that not only converged, but also gained salience, at a particular historical conjuncture. It is therefore imperative to properly contextualize these trends rather than read them in the light of dubious theories on the long-standing, irreconcilable Hindu-Muslim differences.

I have no common ground with those who celebrate religious nationalism or contest the pluralist/composite heritage in what has been one the most multicultural societies in the world; on the contrary, the weight of evidence, some of it assembled by British historians and ethnographers, points to a flourishing plural and synthetic civilization providing a hospitable framework within which different communities, cultures and religions have lived side by side and made their distinctive contribution.[30] Within the paradigms of secular historiography—nurtured by the liberal-left strands in Indian nationalism—my own concerns—far removed from the post-modernist discourses and the 'New' histories—are simple enough: why do a people, with a long-standing history of shared living, respond to symbols of discord and disunity at a particular historical juncture? Why was the innocence of the mind, in the words of a common man at Sakhua village in Mymensingh district, 'banished after so many days of living together? Why did the structure of the human mind change overnight?' 'How could that land become somebody else's forever', asked his/her counterpart in Bimyapher village! 'Just one line drawn on the map, and my home becomes a foreign country!'[31] Surely, 'India belongs to all of us, and we have to live and die here. But why this Partition and the exchange of population.'[32] Why did a society with its splendidly plural heritage, become the site of one of the most divisive event of the twentieth century? And last but not the least, if the nineteenth century Urdu poet Mirza Ghalib had been alive, he would have asked in his inimitable style:

When all is You, and nought exists but You
Tell me, O Lord, why all this turmoil too?

Despite the recent breakthrough in scholarship on nations and nationalism initiated by Benedict Anderson's *Imagined Communities: Reflections on the Origin and Spread of Nationalism* (1983), these questions (as pertinent today as they were at the time of Independence) need to be analysed afresh with the aid of historical and sociological insights,[33] and in the light of fresh source materials now available in the libraries and archives of India, Pakistan, and the United Kingdom.

To do so, it is important, first of all, not to read the present into the past; in other words, to shed our present-day prejudices and preconceived notions about communalism, and not be guided by the nature of inter-community relations in post-colonial India. Scholarship, although stimulated by preoccupations stemming from the present, is never sufficient in itself to modify the conceptualization of a problem or an event. For this and other reasons, it is necessary to challenge commonly-held assumptions on Islam and the Muslims, a point repeatedly underlined in my writings, delineate the multiple ideological strands amongst them, and trace the *evolution* of a Muslim political personality not in doctrinaire terms, but in the context of colonial policies and the exertions of powerful *Hindutva* and Islamist forces. Their profound impact needs to be explored, as was fruitfully done by the 'Cambridge School' in studies on Indian nationalism, in the regions and localities.

Islam, for one, can no longer be treated as a static point of reference. Contemporary scholarship has drawn attention to changing interpretations over time and the powerful pluralist visions that have shaped the Muslim (not *Islamic*) communities in India and elsewhere. Indeed, as historians and anthropologists have noted, the Islamic tradition has produced a repertoire of concepts that have been employed to validate and explain a wide variety of political, social and intellectual ideas and movements.[34] No longer can we assume, despite the rhetoric of the theologians and the publicists, the existence of a single, inalienable Muslim identity. 'I am against the identities built on religion', stated Nawal El Sadwi, the Egyptian novelist,

because the history of religion was written in the endless rivers of blood flowing in the name of God. . . . I am an Arab woman. But in my body run the rivers of Africa that flow through Africa from Jinja and Tana. I am African and Arab and Egyptian because my genes were drawn from all these, because my history goes back in Egypt for seven thousand years, to Isis and Ma'at and Noon.[35]

Much the same sentiment was expressed, though contextualized differently, by Azad. In his presidential address at the Ramgarh Congress in 1940, he declared:

I am a Muslim and profoundly conscious of the fact that I have inherited Islam's glorious traditions of the last thirteen hundred years. I am not prepared to lose even a small part of that legacy. . . . As a Muslim I have a special identity within the field of religion and culture and I cannot tolerate any undue interference with it. But, with all these feelings, I have another equally deep realisation, born out of my life's experience, which is strengthened and not hindered by the spirit of Islam. I am equally proud of the fact that I am an Indian, an essential part of the indivisible unity of Indian nationhood, a vital factor in its total make-up without which this noble edifice will remain incomplete. I can never give up this sincere claim.[36]

Generally speaking, identities in South Asian history and politics have seldom been unified; in colonial India they were increasingly fragmented and fractured. Indeed, they were not singular but multiple, and thus difficult to capture on a single axis. Constructed across different, intersecting and antagonistic sites, discourses, and practices, they are subject to a radical historicization, and are constantly in the process of making and unmaking.[37] Thus Nita Kumar focuses on the existential experiences, of the Hindu and Muslim masses based on their culture of everyday life to argue that 'identity in Banaras has not been communal in the past nor is it progressively becoming so. It is based rather on occupation, social class, and a city's tradition.'[38] An interesting insight into the community of weavers in Banaras is also provided in the following comment in Abdul Bismillah's much acclaimed Hindi novel, *Jhini Jhini Bini Chadaria*: 'There is a community of the world. There is a community of India. There is a community of Hindus. There is a community of Muslims. There is also a community of the weavers in Banaras. *This community is in many different ways different from other communities in the world*'[39] (italics mine).

III

I thought we would stay by our land, by out stock, by our Mussalman neighbours. No one can touch us, I thought. The riots will pass us by. But a man attacked our village—Oh, the screams of the women, I can hear them still. . . . I had a twenty-year-old brother, tall and strong as a mountain, a match for any five of them. This is what they did: they tied one of his legs to one jeep, the other to another jeep—and then they drove the jeeps apart. . . .

Mola Singh stands quite still. The men look away despite the dark. Their indignation flares into rage.

'God give our arms strength,' one of them shouts, and in a sudden movement, knives glimmer. Their cry, 'Bole so Nihal, Sat Siri Akal', swells into the ferocious chant: 'Vengeance! Vengeance! Vengeance!' The old Sikh sinks to his knees.

BAPSI SIDHWA, *The Pakistani Bride*

Interest in Partition has grown by leaps and bounds over the last few years: its legacy looms larger than ever before, the scars having proven to be deeper than the healing touch of freedom from colonial rule.[40] This revival of interest in India, according to the novelist Shama Futehally, began with the Babri Masjid dispute, which 'made it impossible, so to speak, to keep the lid on partition any more'.[41] Thereafter, social scientists began recognizing, after having neglected the subject for decades, that Partition is, indeed, the defining moment for understanding India's modern history and specially the current turmoil over religion.[42] Some even wonder 'why we didn't set up a museum to preserve the memory of partition', why 'we chose to live with communal hatred, rather than to objectify it'.[43]

The author Urvashi Butalia bemoaned a few years ago that 'the human history of Partition has a lesser status than the political history'.[44] This is no longer so. Her own book, based on oral narratives and testimonies, illuminates the 'underside' of Partition history.[45] In fact, the disconnection between the rarefied decisions leading to Partition, and the searing consequences in individual lives, remains one of the most powerful tropes that has been carried from Partition fiction into the work of historians and other social scientists.[46] So that, in part a response to the growing interest in 'history of beneath', the task of restoring a human dimension to the partition has received serious attention.[47] Alok Bhalla, editor of an anthology on Partition stories, painfully wonders why religious conflicts destroyed the subcontinent's communal life. The stories he puts together reveal how 'we fell out of a human world of languages, customs, rituals and prayers into a bestial world of hatred, rage, self-interest and frenzy'.[48]

My own writings recount the trauma of those caught up in the politics of hate and violence, the anguish of the silent majority which was invisible in national or provincial arenas of formal and institutional politics.[49] Moving further away from the meta-narratives of nationalism and communalism, I endeavoured to give a voice to the 'feelings and interests' of 'ordinary folks'. My aim was to emphasize the different meanings and perceptions of Partition, a theme that to the best of my knowledge had not been explored before, and to underline the pluralist view in which religious community is just one and not the sole source of identity. In particular, the two-volume anthology of short stories, poems, diaries, excerpts from autobiographical accounts, and interviews, serves as a reminder of how Partition cruelly displaced millions, divided India's past, wrecked its civilizational rhythm and unity, and left behind a fractured legacy.[50]

Elsewhere, my concern, which I share with my colleague M. Asaduddin, has been to examine how the stories invoke and construct images of Muslims, articulate many intimate yet historically unfamiliar points of reference, and represent the lived experiences of Muslim communities in different regions and socio-economic locations. It has been comforting to discover that, unlike so many historical accounts, the literary representations of Muslims and the nature of their life reveal a wide variety of forms, style, language and symbol adopted by different writers. Neither the forms nor the lives they portray derive from a supposedly homogeneous and unbroken tradition.[51] Sadly, this simple but important fact is lost sight of in constructing the Partition story.

Let me conclude this section with three axioms that have guided my research for nearly two decades. The first relates to the League's rhetoric, mouthed by the Jamaat-i Islami and a section of the Deobandi ulama, on Islam, the *Muslim* nation, and the birth of an *Islamic* society. Their battle-cry, though spurred by some leading Muslim intellectuals—notably Iqbal—and the resurgence of militant Hindu nationalism in certain spheres, had more to do with the political and economic anxieties of various social classes than with a profound urge to carve out an Islamic society and society.[52] This explains the conduct of, and the reasons why, Muslim landlords and professional groups in UP, Bihar and the princely state of Hyderabad, together with the small but upcoming trading and banking communities in western India, hitched their fortunes to the Pakistan demand. Muslim landlords of UP, having had no truck with the League until the 1930s and allied with their Hindu counterparts in their last-ditch battle against the Congress,[53] changed course once the Congress ministry, with its refurbished radical image, adopted the UP Tenancy Bill. Although they continued speaking in the name of Islam, their chief goal was to defend their landholdings, orchards, *havelis*, palaces, and the nawabi parapher-nalia built through the courtesy of their British benefactors. Their counterparts in Punjab, many of whom had been staunch supporters of Punjab's Unionist Party—a unique and successful experiment in class-based combination—also sensed the winds of change. They abandoned their erstwhile allies and adopted, by the end of 1945 and *not* before, the safe course of joining the League. Their strategy, one that suited the raj during and after World War II, was to project the Congress and the Unionists, their perceived rivals in the political world, as a *Hindu* party inimical to Islam. In a nutshell, the discordance between the League and the Congress politics in the final decade of the raj was caused by 'the sense of exclusion from the dominant sentiment of Indian nationalism, and not religious zeal, devoid of all temporal considerations'.[54] In the words of the historian Muhammad Mujeeb, whose family split in 1947, 'the needs which found political expression were not the needs of the community as a whole but those of a class, which consisted of big and small landlords, and the lawyers, doctors, government servants who belonged to the families of these landlords'.[55] Once the League bandwagon rolled on, other aggrieved groups, such as the *jotedars* in Bengal and peasant proprietors of the eastern and the ex-servicemen of its north-western districts in Punjab,[56] jumped into the fray as defenders of the faith. In neighbouring Sind, the influential pirs, having received assurances that their social and economic interests would be protected, flocked to the League: it was primarily their position as local leaders that drew them into party politics.[57]

My second axiom, though obvious enough, is scarcely recognized in nationalistic historiography. Pakistan was neither everybody's dream nor was Jinnah the Quaid of the socialists and Marxists,[58] the Khudai Khidmatgars, the ulama of Deoband, the Momins,[59] the Shias connected with the Shia Political Conference,[60] and scores of Muslim groups pushed to the periphery and surviving uneasily on the margins of mainstream national and provincial politics. Yet the standpoint of those, patronizingly referred to as 'Nationalist Muslims',[61] is wilfully ignored because of certain misplaced assumptions about Islam and nationalism and the insistence on projecting the so-called monolithic world view of the Muslim communities. Represented as weak and ineffective by religious and political orthodoxies, their voices, which were by no means inconsequential, have been stifled by 'imperial', 'secular' and 'communal' histories written before and after Independence. Thanks to active state patronage, we celebrate and valorize Muslim/Islam-baiters and rank Hindu communalists, but relegate secular and liberal-minded Muslims—from Badruddin Tyabji's generation to that of Rafi Ahmad Kidwai's—to a historian's footnote. I have been arguing for years that the historian of twentieth century Indian nationalism should foreground the so-called marginal voices among Muslims to rewrite the histories of nationalism, communalism, and Partition.[62]

There is, finally, the need to come to terms with the fact that most 'Hindus', 'Muslims' and 'Sikhs' had no feelings for national borders or the newly created geographical entities that were being laboriously created in 1947; the cartographic and political divisions constituted by Partition are 'the shadow lines' that the novelist Amitav Ghosh seeks to repudiate.[63] National borders, as argued elsewhere, were political constructs, and imagined projections of territorial power. Although they appeared in deceptively precise forms, they reflected, at least initially, merely the mental images of politicians, lawyers, and intellectuals.[64] Their practical consequences, which worked out so differently in various regions and for different classes, must be disaggregated from state-centred academic historiography.[65] Even though the trains had started carrying people to their death traps, large numbers of people, uprooted from their homes in search of a safe haven, were unclear whether Lahore would be part of India or Pakistan, or whether Delhi, the erstwhile imperial capital of the

Mughals and the British, would remain in Gandhi's India or Jinnah's 'moth-eaten' Pakistan. As the novelist Bapsi Sidhwa describes:

Hysteria mounted when the fertile, hot lands of the Punjab were suddenly ripped into two territories—Hindu and Muslim, India and Pakistan. Until the last moment no one was sure how the land would be divided. Lahore, which everyone expected to go to India because so many wealthy Hindus lived in it, went instead to Pakistan. Jullundur, a Sikh stronghold, was allocated to India. . . . [66]

Such descriptions point to an existentialist reality—the separation of people living on both sides who had a long history of cultural and social contact—and the paradoxical character of borders being a metaphor for the ambiguities of nation-building.[67] A lesser known but a highly gifted writer Fikr Taunsvi (1918-87) has poignantly captured this theme in one of his stories. It reads:

A few astrologers in 1947 made the heavenly bodies revolve in such a scientific manner that instead of having one border between them, India and Pakistan had two. Actually the word 'two' had befuddled their minds in such a way that now neither the stars moved in an orderly manner nor did their predictions come true. Exasperated by this very 'two' and swayed by their animosity to 'one' they became oblivious of the fact that the new unit they were trying to create was itself a derivative of one. . . .

The most interesting feature of the Wagah border was the shops set up for the organised sale of religion. A bearded Maulvi sat there with a huge pile of books, including the Vedas, Shastras, Granthas, Gitas and Upanishads . . . Sitting next to him was a Sardarji who sold copies of the Koran, *Fiqh* and *Hadith* and dozens of other writings in Arabic. All those books were a part of the loot that the two gentlemen had brought to sell. Otherwise, they would have been at each other's throats by now. But at Wagah they were selling their books peacefully. . . . If by selling religion one could have two square meals everyday, what could be better. . . .

I quietly took the army sentinel aside and asked: 'Well sir, a tree stood on the bank of the Wagah canal. Can you tell me whether it has been felled and thrown away or...?'

The sentry pointed his bayonet at me and staring at me said: 'Who are you to interfere in this business that concerns the two governments?'

And in the core of my heart I said: 'Listen good man, after all I am a branch of the same tree.'[68]

Saadat Hasan Manto's stories, on the other hand, question the intellectual underpinnings of state-centred national histories: most of his characters, especially Toba Tek Singh, are not reconciled to borders being drawn and people being uprooted from their social and cultural milieu. They remind us time and again that, regardless of religious passions being heightened by the politics of hate and separation and of the fragile nature of inter-community relations in the 1940s, most people had no clue whatsoever that their fate would be settled after Mountbatten's three days of 'diplomacy'; that a man called Cyril Radcliffe—whose credentials as an eminent British jurist is invoked to compensate for his lack of knowledge and experience of the subcontinent—would descend on Indian soil on a hot and sultry summer day and decide the frontiers in just seven weeks. Though diehard apologists of the raj—H.V. Hodson, the Reform Commissioner in 1941, Philip Ziegler, biographer of Mounbatten, & Co.— and their intellectual allies in the subcontinent have a different tale to tell, a creative writer, writing in the early 1980s, portrays the brutal consequences of a reckless though calculated imperial design:

Now that it was decided they would leave, the British were in a hurry to wind up. . . . Preoccupied with misgiving and the arrangements attendant on relocating themselves in their native land, by the agony of separation from regiments, Imperial trappings and servants, the rulers of the Empire were entirely too busy to bother overmuch with how India was divided. It was only one of the thousand and one chores they faced.

The earth is not easy to carve up. India required a deft and sensitive surgeon, but the British, steeped in domestic preoccupation, hastily and carelessly butchered it. They were not deliberately mischievous—only cruelly negligent! A million Indian died. The earth sealed its clumsy new boundaries in blood as town by town, farm by farm, the border was defined. Trains carrying refugees sped through the darkness of night—Hindus going one way and Muslims the other. They left at odd hours to try to dodge mobs bent on their destruction. Yet trains were ambushed and looted and their fleeing occupants slaughtered.[69]

Anguished by the communal riots, Nehru wrote in June 1947: 'It is curious that when tragedy affects an individual we feel the full force of it, but when that individual is multiplied a thousand-fold, our senses are dulled and we become insensitive.'[70] This was certainly not true of creative writers, many of whom reveal the other face of freedom, the 'freedom drenched in blood and gore'.[71] They bring to light, in a way that official chronicles do not, the plight of migrants, the woes of divided families and the trauma of raped and abducted women. Numerous texts, retrieve from the silence untold stories of women, stories that have died unspoken on the lips of their hapless protagonists.[72] Locating women at the centre (rather than the periphery) of discussions around Partition, argues Ritu Menon, casts a rather different light on the event and its consequences. In an engaging discussion of government policy on the recovery of abducted women by India and Pakistan, she explores the relationship of women to community identity and to the state and citizenship. Adult women, according to Menon, were forcibly 'recovered' purely on the basis of religious identity and in violation of all rights of citizens in a secular state.[73]

All said and done, literary narratives, whether in Hindi, Urdu, Bengali or Punjabi, are an eloquent witness to 'an unspeakable and inarticulatable history'.[74] Evoking the sufferings of the innocent, whose pain is more universal and ultimately a vehicle of more honest reconciliation than political discourse,[75] they provide a framework for developing an alternative discourse on inter-community relations. What lends greater credence to their creative imagination is their ability to unfold certain critically important dimensions without religion or community as the principal reference points. This is illustrated in Manto's literary vignettes, *Siyah Hashye* (Black Margins):

PRAISE BE TO THE LORD

The dancing session was over. The clients went away. That is when *Ustadji* said, having lost everything (during Partition) we came to this city. Praise is to Allah *Miyan* for having showered us with these riches in just a few days.

DOUBLE CROSS

Look buddy, you sold me petrol at black-market prices and not a single shop could be set on fire.

WHO ARE YOU?

The rioters wrestled hard with the landlord to drag him out of the house. He stood up, brushed his clothes and told them. 'Kill me for all I care. But I warn you not to touch my money—not a paisa.'

IV

Where do we go from here? asks the writer Bhisham Sahni.

Should people organize themselves on the basis of caste and community and fight collectively for their rightful demands? Or, should they ignore caste and community and fight on the basis of the deprived against the privileged, for there are both rich and poor among castes and communities? 'I believe the second course is still the right one, for it cuts across caste and community loyalties, and thereby weakens their stranglehold, and in consequence strengthens, in its own way, the pluralistic character of our polity. We certainly have a very long way to go.[76]

Today the historiography of Partition is hampered by mental laziness and pious rehashing even more than political ideology. Surely, it is time to strip it of the elementary significations it has bequeathed to its heirs, and to restore to it another *primum movens* of the historian, namely, intellectual curiosity and the free search for knowledge about the past.[77]

NOTES

1. It is common to connect the two-nation theory with the Aligarh reformer, Saiyid Ahmad Khan, and not his contemporary Dayanand Saraswati, the high priest of the Arya Samaj. The former appears to me to be far more tolerant, eclectic and broad-minded in his orientation and outlook than the latter. Beginning with the Arya Samaj movement and culminating in the writings of Veer Savarkar and Guru Golwalkar, the relentless search for a 'Hindu nation' and a 'Hindu identity' provided the underpinnings of the two-nation theory. Long before Jinnah appeared on the scene, Lala Har Dayal stated in 1925: 'I declare that the future of the Hindu race, of Hindustan and of the Punjab, rest on four pillars: (1) Hindu Sangathan, (2) Hindu raj, (3) *Shuddhi* of Moslems, and (4) Conquest and *Shuddhi* of Afghanistan and the frontiers. . . . The Hindu race has but one history and its institutions are homogeneous. But the Mussalmans and Christians are far removed from the confines of Hinduism, for their religions are alien and they love Persian, Arab and European institutions. Thus, just as one removes foreign matter from the eye, *Shuddhi* must be made of these two religions.' Quoted in Emily C. Brown, *Har Dayal: Hindu Revolutionary and Rationalist*, New Delhi, 1975, p. 233. This characterization of Christianity and Islam led Savarkar to write that, 'when the Muslims penetrated India, the conflict of life and death began'.

2. Adding a fresh dimension to the debate, Sumit Sarkar points out that constructions of Indian nationalism, Hindu unity and *Hindutva* were partly related, though in different ways, to efforts to respond to counter 'pressures from below' in the form of lower-caste aspirations. Sumit Sarkar, *Writing Social History*, Chap. 9.

3. Increasingly, this view is being challenged by regional and local studies. For example, Tazeen M. Murshid, *The Sacred and the Secular: Bengal Muslim Discourses, 1871-1977*, Calcutta, 1995, and the collection of essays in Mushirul Hasan (ed.), *Islam, Communities and the Nation*.

4. I have discussed this point at length in *Legacy of a Divided Nation*.

5. Larson, *India's Agony Over Religion*, pp. 183-4.

6. Akbar S. Ahmed, *Jinnah, Pakistan and Islamic Identity: The Search for Saladin*, Karachi, 1997, p. xviii. Notice, too, his comment: 'When a leader who commands respect in the Muslim community appears, and can focus on a cause, Muslims are capable of moving mountains', p. xxi.

7. I have borrowed this idea from Furet, *Interpreting the French Revolution*, p. 10.

8. Hasan (ed.), *India's Partition: Process, Strategy and Mobilization*.

9. Eric Hobsbawm, *Age of Extremes: The Short Twentieth Century 1914-1991*, London: 1994, pp. 219-20. Ian Talbot has examined the Punjabi Muslims support to the Muslims in the context of the War. *Punjab and the Raj, 1849-1947*, while Anita Inder Singh argues that the outbreak of War 'saved' the League and made it a representative Muslim body. Her contention is that the British deliberately built up Jinnah's prestige at the all India level for their war purposes, though at the provincial level they subordinated this objective to the prime necessity of operating the war machine with maximum efficiency. *The Origins of the Partition of India*, pp. 238, 241-2. The provincial scene is best surveyed in Jalal, *The Sole Spokesmen*.

10. Muhammad Amir Ahmad (brother of the raja of Mahmudabad) to Jinnah, 29 Nov. 1939, Shamsul Hasan Collection, Karachi.

11. Moon (ed.), *The Viceroy's Journal*, p. 267.

12. Quoted in Brown, *Gandhi: Prisoner of Hope*, p. 369.

13. 21 Sept. 1947, Alan Campbell-Johnson, *Mission with Mountbatten*, p. 201.

14. Bayly, *Rulers, Townsmen and Bazaars: North Indian Society in the Age of British Expansion*.

15. Sumit Sarkar, *A Critique of Colonial India*, Calcutta, 1985, p. 116.

16. Das, *Communal Riots in Bengal*, p. 207.

17. Sumit Sarkar, 'The Conditions and Nature of Subaltern Militancy: Bengal from Swadeshi to Non-Cooperation, c. 1905-22', in Ranajit Guha (ed.), *Subaltern Studies*, Vol. 3, New Delhi, 1984, p. 272. Rafiuddin Ahmed has shown how religious preachers prompted the masses to look beyond the borders of Bengal in quest of their supposed Bengali Islamic past and attach greater importance to their 'Muslim' as opposed to their local or regional identity. This new emphasis, according to him, proved crucial to the subsequent emergence of a measure of social cohesion in a diversified and even culturally polarised society. Ahmed, *The Bengal Muslims*, p. 184.

18. Robinson, *Separatism Among Indian Muslims*, Chap. 1.

19. The emergence of a corporate Sikh identity, according to Harjot Oberoi, was 'a sort of dialectical process', a response to what was happening to the Hindus and Muslims in terms of 'imagination, experience and cultural organization'. Historically, 'it is more precise to speak in terms of a simultaneity of religious identities rather than distinct, universal, religious collectivities'. *The Construction of Religious Boundaries: Culture, Identity and Diversity in the Sikh Tradition*, New Delhi, 1994, pp. 418, 424.

20. Nonica Datta's incisive study traces the emergence of Jat identity within the cultural context of rural southeast Punjab, arguing that identities are not just products of colonial institutions and economic changes but created by communities on the strength of inherited cultural resources as well as invented

traditions. So that the Jats were active participants in the construction of their own identity. *Forming an Identity: A Social History of the Jats*, New Delhi, 1999.

21. For Punjab, Gilmartin, *Empire and Islam*, p. 225.

22. Freitag, *Collective Action and Community*.

23. Ansari, *Sufi Saints and State Power: The Pirs of Sind, 1843-1947*, and Gilmartin, *Empire and Islam*, op. cit.

24. Datta, *Forming an Identity*, and her 'The "Subalternity" of Education: Gurukuls in Rural Southeast Punjab', in Hasan (ed.), *Knowledge, Power and Politics*; Kenneth W. Jones, *Socio-Religious Reform Movements in British India*, Delhi, 1994, and his *Arya Dharm: Hindu Consciousness in 19th century Punjab*, Berkeley, 1976.

25. See, for example, Christopher R. King, 'The Hindi movement in Banaras, 1868-1914', in Freitag (ed.), *Culture and Power in Banaras*.

26. Christophe Jaffrelot, *The Hindu Nationalist Movement and Indian Politics 1925 to the 1990s*, London, 1997, p. 6.

27. For Hinduism, Vasudha Dalmia, *The Nationalization of Hindu Traditions: Bharatendu Harischandrra and Nineteenth-century Banaras*, New Delhi, 1997, p. 1.

28. C.A. Bayly, 'The Pre-history of "Communalism"? Religious Conflict in India, 1700-1860', *MAS*, Vol. 19, 2, 1985, p. 202.

29. Bayly, *Saint, Goddesses and Kings*, and, Kate Brittlebank, *Tipu Sultan's Search for Legitimacy: Islam and Kingship in a Hindu Domain*, New Delhi, 1995.

30. For an incisive analysis of Gandhi's views, also in the context of the Partition, Bhiku Parekh, *Gandhi's Political Philosophy: A Critical Examination*, London, 1989.

31. Chakrabarty: 'Remembered Villages' in Low and Brasted (eds.), *Freedom, Trauma, Continuities*.

32. Anis Kidwai, 'In the Shadow of Freedom', in Hasan (ed.), *India Partitioned*, Vol. 2, p. 161.

33. For example, essays in T.N. Madan (ed.), *Muslim Communities of South Asia: Culture, Society, and Power*, New Delhi, rev. and enlarged edn., 2000, and his *Modern Myths, Locked Minds: Secularism and Fundamentalism in India*, New Delhi, 1997. Peter van der Veer, *Religious Nationalism: Hindus and Muslims in India*, Berkeley, 1994.

34. Introduction to Imtiaz Ahmad (ed.), *Ritual and Religion Among Muslims in India*, New Delhi, 1981, pp. 18-19; Barbara Daly Metcalf (ed.), *Moral Conduct and Authority: The Place of Adab in South Asian Islam*, Berkeley, 1984, p. 15.

35. *The Nawal El Saadwi Reader*, London, 1997, p. 127.

36. Quoted in Syeda Saiyidain Hameed (ed.), *India's Maulana: Abul Kalam Azad*, Vol. 2, New Delhi, 1990, and p. 161.

37. Hasan (ed.), *Islam, Communities and the Nation*.

38. Nita Kumar, *The Artisans of Banaras: Popular Culture and Identity, 1880-1986*, Princeton, N.J., 1988, p. 227.

39. Cited in Sudhir Kumar, 'Reconstructing the Nation: Image of the Nation in the Fiction of Muslim Writers', in *Studies in Humanities and Social Sciences* (Shimla), Vol. 1, Nov. 1994, p. 125.

40. Sugata Bose and Ayesha Jalal, *Modern South Asia: History, Culture, Political Economy*, New Delhi, 1998, p. 191.

41. *Indian Book Review* (New Delhi), Oct. 1993, p. 19.

42. Larson, *India's Agony Over Religion*, p. 183. Historians, in particular have taken the lead in challenging the old shibboleths dominating partition studies. As a result, we now have a better sense of, in the context of the transfer of power, the 'contradictions and structural peculiarities of Indian society and politics in late colonial India', 'the history that Partition creates' and the impact and representation of Partition violence. Some of the interesting works are by: Pandey, 'The Prose of Otherness', Arnold and Hardiman (eds.), *Subaltern Studies VII*; Shail Mayaram, 'Speech, Silence and the Making of Partition', in Shahid Amin and Dipesh Chakrabarty (eds.), *Subaltern Studies IX: Writings on South Asian History and Society*, New Delhi, 1996; Ranabir Samaddar (ed.), *Reflections on Partition in the East*, New Delhi, 1997.

43. Krishna Kumar, *Times of India* (Delhi), 10 Feb. 1999.

44. *Seminar* (Delhi), Aug. 1994.

45. Urvashi Butalia, *The Other Side of Silence: Voices from the Partition of India*, New Delhi, 1998, p. 10.

46. David Gilmartin, 'Partition, Pakistan and South Asian History: In Search of a Narrative', *The Journal of Asian Studies*, Vol. 57, No. 4, Nov. 1998, p. 1069.

47. See, for example, Ian Talbot, *Freedom's City: The Popular Dimension in the Pakistan Movement and Partition Experience in North-West India*, Karachi, 1996.

48. Alok Bhalla (ed.), *Stories About the Partition of India*, Vol. 1, New Delhi, 1994, pp. xxxii-xxxiii.

49. *Legacy of a Divided Nation*, Chap. 4.

50. Hasan (ed.), *India Partitioned*.

51. See Mushirul Hasan and M. Asaduddin (eds.), *Images and Representation: Stories of Muslim Lives in India*, New Delhi, 2000.

52. Brass, *Language, Religion and Politics in North India*, argued that Muslims of UP had a larger share of government jobs than their 14 per cent of the population warranted, and that Muslim politicians created the myth of 'Muslim backwardness' to protect their privileges and then selected divisive symbols to mobilise support for their own drive to power. Focussing on the landowning class, the economic mainstay of the Muslim elite, Lance Brennan demonstrated that, 'by mid-1939 the Muslim elite of UP had lost their illusion: the foundation they had fought so hard to build were shown to be straw. It was from this time that they began to embrace a new separatism. . . . Previously, they had aimed at striking a set of bargains with the Hindus in the province—now their objective was complete separation from the Hindus.' 'The Illusion of Security: The Background of Muslim Separatism in the United Provinces', Hasan (ed.), *India's Partition*, p. 360. Partha Chatterjee has, on

the other hand, argued that Muslim politics in Bengal in the period 1937-47 had a great deal to do with the structures and processes of the colonial state machinery. 'Bengal Politics and the Muslim Masses, 1920-47', in *India's Partition*, pp. 174-5.

53. Peter Reeves, 'Adjusting to Congress Dominance: The UP Landlords, 1937-1947', Sisson and Wolpert (eds.), Congress *and Indian Nationalism*, pp. 160-9.

54. Ayesha Jalal, 'Ideology and the Struggle for Democratic Institutions', Victoria Schofield (ed.), *Old Roads New Highways: Fifty Years of Pakistan*, Karachi, 1997, pp. 129-30.

55. M. Mujeeb, 'The Partition of India in Retrospect', in Philips and Wainwright (eds.), *The Partition of India*, p. 410.

56. Talbot, *Punjab and the raj*, p. 208.

57. Ansari, *Sufi Saints*, p. 122.

58. K.H. Ansari, *The Emergence of Socialist Thought Among North Indian Muslims 1917-1947*, Lahore, 1990.

59. Papiya Ghosh 'Partition's Biharis', in Hasan (ed.), *Islam, Communities and the Nation*, pp. 229-64.

60. Mushirul Hasan, 'Traditional Sites and Contested Meanings: Sectarian Strife in Colonial Lucknow', see above.

61. I have argued against the use of this expression in *A Nationalist Conscience*.

62. 'Those who got the worse of it, both in India and Pakistan', commented a well-known Urdu writer, 'were the honest, sincere Nationalist Muslims who, in the eyes of Hindus, were Muslims, and *vice versa*. Their sacrifices were reduced to ashes. Their personal integrity and loyalty were derided. Their morale was shattered like a disintegrating star; their lives lost meaning. Like the crumbling pillars of a mosque they could neither be saved nor used. India, for whose independence they had fought the British, refused to offer them refuge. So much so that they incurred the wrath of their own community. They were like that distant thunder which rises in the desert and then descends and disappears into the sand dumes.... For them the special day of independence was unusual, spent in the seclusion of the four walls of their homes. The League had made them untouchables to their fellow-Indians; they were reduced to the status of harijans in India.' Shorish Kashmiri, *Boo-i gul Naala-i dil Dood-i Chiragh-i Mehfil*, cited in Hasan (ed.), *India Partitioned*, Vol. 2, p. 145.

63. The reference to the novel *Shadow Lines* (Delhi, 1988) is drawn from Priya Kumar, 'Testimonies of Loss and Memory: Partition and the Haunting of a Nation', *Interventions*, 1999, p. 204.

64. Michiel Baud and Willem van Schendel, 'Towards a Comparative History of Borderlands', in *Journal of World History*, Vol. 8, 2, 1997, pp. 211-42.

65. See my 'Memories of a Fragmented Nation: Rewriting the Histories of Partition' above, and Ritu Menon, 'Cartographies of Nations and Identities: A Post-Partition Predicament', *Interventions*, London: Routledge, Vol. 1, 2, 1999.

66. Sidhwa, *The Pakistan Bride*, p. 4.

67. These lines are based on Baud and Schendel, 'Towards a Comparative History of Borderlands', pp. 211-42.

68. 'The Wagah Canal', in Hasan (ed.), *India Partitioned*, Vol. 1, pp. 250, 253, 255.

69. Sidhwa, *The Pakistan Bride*, pp. 17-18.

70. *SWJN*, Vol. 3, second series, p. 180.

71. Anis Kidwai, 'In the Shadow of Freedom', in Hasan (ed.), *India Partitioned*, Vol. 2, p. 161.

72. Deepika Bahri, 'Telling Tales: Women and the Trauma of Partition in Sidhwa's Cracking India', *Interventions*, 1999, p. 219.

73. Menon and Bhasin, *Borders & Boundaries*, and Veena Das, 'National Honour and Practical Kinship: Of Unwanted Women and Children', *Critical Events: An Anthropological Perspective on Contemporary India*, New Delhi, 1995, pp. 55-83.

74. Kumar, 'Testimonies', *Interventions*, 1999, p. 202.

75. Francisco, 'In the Heat of Fratricide', p. 250.

76. Bhisham Sahni, 'Images of Communities: Reflections of a Writer', *Studies in Humanities and Social Sciences*, Vol. 1, Nov. 1994, p. 5.

77. Francois Furet's plea to the historians of the French Revolution makes very good sense in the context of partition studies. See *Interpreting the French Revolution*, Cambridge, 1981, pp. 10-11.

PART IV

PART IV

14

Moradabad Riots, 1980:
Causes and Meanings

Between mid-August and early November 1980, Muslims in Moradabad experienced the most bloody orgy of violence.[1] Officially verified deaths, for which the government paid 'compensation' ran to about 400; a careful, responsible Muslim group estimated deaths at 2,500; other observers put the number between 1,500 and 2,000. This sustained, frenzied aggression was unmistakably engineered by the city policemen in uniform. The events were no less shattering for anyone who cares about the state of society in present and future India.

Various studies have revealed that these events were not so strange as to defy belief; previous riots from Ahmedabad to Pune and Sholapur presaged most of the themes.[2] Notable only are the intensity of the frenzy, the depth of official complicity, and the wholly unjustified confidence of the mass media—with but a few exceptions—in the official version of events. What happened in Moradabad has to be seen, however, in its historical setting, both in India as a whole and in the city of Moradabad. These pages seek to bring the events alive again, and reviewing the attitudes and actions in Moradabad might cause some of us to assess our own attitudes.

It is not, however, intended to provide an expose of events in Moradabad—although that is needed—but to illustrate several facets of contemporary Indian society. We wish to comment on the position of Muslims in north Indian society generally; we wish to advance a more candid examination of the tenor of Hindu-Muslim relationships in our past and our present; and finally, we wish to take notice of a chilling case of administrative regression, one that happens to illustrate more general tendencies around us too.

II

We begin with the general position of Muslims in north Indian society. There are enclaves of professional groups where one could almost forget whether one is a Muslim or a Hindu. We also know of areas like Chandni Chowk in Delhi where mutual understanding and exchange of services is widespread, if only because Muslim craftsmen have to rely heavily on the predominant Hindu trading community in the locality. To live apart—'within one's community', meaning kin or caste—is an old Indian pattern; but recent decades have seen a great deal of intermingling, especially in the new urban areas. Yet, one would not easily find many Muslims among the tenants or houseowners in the mixed, privately-owned urban localities. In part, as this reflects the Muslims' general economic position, obser-vations on this are not out of place.

The weakness of the Muslims' economic position, particularly in north India, is partly due to the fragmentation of the community in the wake of Partition, and the exodus of certain powerful professional groups, traders and bankers to the newly-born country. This is evident in their sparse representation in the upper echelons of commerce, industry, administra-tion, or the professions in India. Recent figures indicate that the percent-age of Muslims in the Indian Administrative Service is less than half their percentage in the total population; while barely 2 per cent of government officials at the highest levels and less than 0.5 per cent of government clerks and peons are Muslims (Table 14.1).

Table 14.1: Muslims in the combined gradation list of
IAS Officers 1948-74

Years	All	Muslims	Percentage
1948-52	149	1	0.67
1953-7	242	5	2.06
1958-62	361	5	1.38
1963-7	596	10	1.67
1968-72	500	9	1.80
1973-7	689	21	3.04
Total	2,537	51	2.01

Source: A.R. Shervani, 'Muslims in Indian Administrative Service, *Journal of Rabitat Al-Alam Al-Islami*, p. 33.

Precise figures are not available for the army, but they are usually said to be about the same as for the police. The figure commonly provided is that Muslims account for about 3 per cent of the total Indian police force. In the Provincial Armed Constabulory (PAC), notorious for its anti-Muslim venom, there are only 300 Muslims out of a force of 2 lakhs.

Politics is a rather special domain but if we ignore the decorative offices of president and vice-president, the 'Sarkari Muslims' who help the powers-that-be in sidestepping the major crises facing the country and concern ourselves with the substantative issues facing the Muslims, their weak base in politics would be plain. The same pattern is apparent in academia. Apart from institutions like Aligarh Muslim University,[3] and limited fields like Urdu and medieval Indian history, there is very little to cheer the Muslims. More distressing perhaps is the mushroom growth of *Dini Talim* schools—6,000 in UP with an enrolment of 6,00,000 students[4]—where the pupils are lulled into an illusion of education with Islamic texts.[5] The importance of such blockages goes far beyond statistics or particular persons' incomes. At stake are the informal access to certain kinds of information, the orientation to the wider social order commonly transmitted in the informal social relationships, and the sense of efficacy and competence that comes from knowing those who know and who can help put the 'official' seal of approval upon things happening the way you would like them to happen.

We realize, of course, the difficulty with categories like Hindu and Muslim in such matters: differentiation and inequalities within the categories may well be much greater than between the categories. If we choose, nevertheless, to employ these categories, this reflects our judgement that during the past three decades the Muslims in north India at different levels have had to cope with considerable hostile prejudices. Given the background to, and the fact of, Partition, the existence of some antagonism is not unexpected. What we need to recognize, however, is the co-existence of widespread public and private denial that any prejudice exists and the fact of its even more widespread, informal, active operation. To be sure, Muslims are not excluded from opportunity completely. It is merely that this happens often enough to make all the difference.

This difference is magnified by the rules by which we play the game. These rules are permissive enough for our competitive situations often permit assertive aggression without limits, with no holds barred. In such situations, a Muslim always has to reckon with the possibility that his religious identity might be thrown at him, publicly or privately, in a threatening manner. He would have grown up knowing the pain and the humiliation of being so insulted. More often than not, he chooses to withdraw, or at least not to press things to a point where the communal card would be played against him. The combination of active antagonism and this inclination to withdraw acts cumulatively to depress ambitions, especially in the generation which has been taught to take a constructive view of the prospects in the immediate milieu. As one Muslim observer pointed out: 'The demoralizing effect of such perceptions is that people give up the struggle to improve their competence. Consequently, whenever opportunity is available, they are left behind. Thus, the "self-fulfilling prophecy" comes true.'

The same point may be made from another angle. Economic weakness is by no means unique to the Muslims in north India. There are the scheduled castes and tribes, but the compensatory programmes have been useful at least in certain pockets within these categories; there are no counterparts to these for the Muslims, nor are any likely. Yet, other categories in the north Indian population—Kurmi, Yadav, Gujar—have been economically weak and have not had access to compensatory programmes; but they have in some measures sought to neutralize their weakness through mobilization in the political domain, using their numbers and voting strength to secure attention. To be sure, such mobilization, when it seeks politically allocated resources by way of job quotas, etc., has generated violent contentiousness in Bihar and elsewhere; but the magnitude of this contentiousness is small compared to the consequences that await Muslims when they seek to assert themselves, politically or otherwise. And this brings us to the general question of relations between Hindus and Muslims in these parts.

Concerning this relationship, various interpretations are abroad, often argued with intense passion. We have space here only to indicate our own understanding of the relationship in its historical context. We judge the relationship to have been highly ambivalent. The two traditions build upon widely divergent ideals concerning the nature of human beings and their relationship to the supernatural and to each other. In a milieu where the weight of religious orthodoxy has been variable, but always considerable, with religious precepts and observances influencing much in daily life, these divergent premises have inevitably led the two traditions to grate upon each other. Yet, most people have a large stake in the smooth flow of their daily life, and therefore, the appropriate accommodations, sometimes extending into syncretic sects, have generally been forthcoming.

It is nevertheless difficult to deny that considerable antagonism has resided in this relationship over the decades. To account for it, serious consideration should be given to Ratna Naidu's point that there is a history of mutual humiliation between those anchored in the two traditions in India. The urge to humiliate an adversary may be unusually strong and widespread in our society; whether this is so, and if so why, are questions worthy of enquiry. Insofar as this proclivity is expressed through attacks on religious symbols, one would imagine that the religious specialists of the affected side would interpret political attacks in religious terms and their interpretations would be handed down in myth and legend.

When myths and legends identify certain adversaries as posing grave threats to crucial social identities, the basis is laid for neurotic fears and anxieties such as would foist apocalyptic intentions upon the most ordinary of acts. It is necessary to posit some such mechanism in order to account for the heady rumours which invariably take wing during communal tension. Two examples will suffice. During the Ahmedabad riots in 1969, a widely circulated evening daily carried on its front-page lurid, though totally imaginary, details about the molestation of Hindu women in the Lal Mill area, and the All India Radio broadcast a false rumour about the poisoning of the city's milk supply in that communally charged atmosphere. In Moradabad in 1980, some activity on moving two *madaris* to more spacious grounds, and some talk of starting a third, led to the inference, published in a pamphlet, *Burning Moradabad*, that the Muslims were planning to turn the city into a fortress, in order to lay the basis for another Pakistan. Also, 'a college built with foreign money (reference to petro-dollars from Saudi Arabia and some Gulf States, in particular) will be (an) abode of foreign powers; one day this may even place our capital Delhi in jeopardy. . . . Though there is no objection to (the) spread of religious education . . . there is valid objection in setting up of religious forces convertible into armies.'[6]

Such fantasies are no monopoly of the Hindus: similar fears and anxieties lay behind the demand for a separate homeland in the 1940s, and, in more recent times, are served up by the Muslim communalist press, such as the *Dawat* daily and the *Radiance* weekly. We wish merely to stress that these anxieties and fantasies are often pathological. As with individuals so with societies, such complexes, to be resolved satisfactorily, need to be brought into our consciousness and tested against the probabilities in real life, not suppressed into the unconscious—as is often done by *both* communalists *and* secularists—for that merely makes their resolution that much more difficult.

To account for the particular course of events in Moradabad recounted below, one more element—the city administration—has to be kept in mind.

To expect to find a Solomon in every seat of local authority may be foolish. If communal fears are as deeply ingrained as the foregoing has suggested, one may take it for granted that these percolate in some measure into officialdom—which, as we have suggested, is invariably largely Hindu. We know that elsewhere the local officials and the guardians of law and order have often acted brutally towards the Muslims, for example in Aligarh. In Jamshedpur in April 1979, lapses on the part of the local officials, combined with the Bihar Military Force actively participating in the riot on the side of the Hindus, helped turn a minor fracas into the worst communal carnage since 1964 in that industrial metropolis (Singh 1979). Likewise Moradabad. The city's police, for long weeks, acted rather like a force organized to beat, loot, and kill the Muslims. The PAC, in particular, collaborated with communal elements and *goondas* in one community to bring about an open clash between Hindus and Muslims.[7] The PAC, reported a *Patriot* correspondent on 27 August 1980, 'has . . . earned for itself the rather dubious distinction of being the most hated organization in Moradabad'. This is not all. The various organs of administration including, alas, the judiciary appeared to act in a way supportive to the activities of the local police and the PAC.

We proceed now to consider the social setting in Moradabad and to recount the specific developments between August and November 1980.

III

The earliest known communal riot in Moradabad, once an administrative part of Rohilkhand division, occurred in 1848 on the occasion of the Muharram procession, followed by a more serious outburst in 1872. Similar riots in later years flowed from the structure of municipalities which were gradually being turned into arenas of intense communal battles. Tension arose in the 1980s over frequent reports of Muslims manipulating the electoral machinery to their advantage, leading the vice-chairman of the municipal board to complain that: 'Ever since the introduction of the principle of local self-government, the Hindus in Moradabad have had no share in Municipal administration, and are really worse off than they would have been if local self-government had never been granted to Moradabad.'

The result of such complaints, combined with the redrawing of ward boundaries that followed the 1900 Municipalities Act, destroyed the Muslim majority, a trend also noticeable in other Rohilkhand towns, such as Budaun and Chandpur. Such losses mattered a great deal, for the victorious community often used its dominance to assert its religious interests.

For instance, after the Hindus gained the upper hand in Moradabad, they compelled Muslim butchers to dry their hides outside the city; in Chandpur, they forbade cow-slaughter. Such pressure, often reinforced by the communal proclivities of national and provincial leaders, contributed to the growing communal animosity in Moradabad.[8]

In the late 1930s, the Muslim League gained a strong foothold in Moradabad; in 1946, it captured a majority of Muslim seats in the provincial elections. This astonishing success of an organization which had been so effectively displaced by the Congress in the 1937 elections reflected the widespread Muslim disillusionment with the Congress movement (Brennan 1977: 476). It also indicated the momentum gained by the League electoral machinery, which was geared up for the occasion by nawabzada Liaquat Ali Khan, and Khaliquzzaman, a 'deserter' from the Congress camp. In Moradabad, the initiative was wrested by Qazi Taslim Husain, a lawyer, who operated from the Muslim *Musafir Khana*—now frequented by the migrant Bihari workers and enthusiasts of the Tablighi Jamaat. Indeed, the *Musafir Khana*, located across the railway station in a predominantly Muslim area, was the focal point of Muslim 'separatist' politics in Moradabad.

Hindu communal groups, organized under the aegis of the RSS and the Arya Samaj, carried on their campaign against Muslims in general, and the Muslim League in particular. Raising the spectre of Muslim dominance, they organized *akharas* in the 1930s and revived the *shuddhi* and *sangathan* movements. Among those who joined such activities were traders, wealthy merchants, and some professional men who resented Muslim dominance in the law courts, in medicine, and in education. Following the Calcutta killing in 1946, such elements launched themselves with renewed vigour. After Partition, their growth was markedly enhanced and, in early January 1948, there occurred widespread riots.

During the August-November 1980 riots, the propaganda machinery made special reference to the 'Muslim atrocities' in the past in order to justify the killings in the present. Today, Moradabad is reached in a little over three hours by a fast train from Delhi; a fast bus takes an hour longer. Physically, the city offers a marked contrast between the Civil Lines, with its cluster of courts, administrative offices and neatly laid out residences, and the wealthy Punjabi exporters' new residences off Station Road and showrooms on Station Road (an area built after 1950) on the one hand, and the more crowded bulk of residential areas on the other. In many of these areas, little bits of industrial activity—a furnace here, a grinder there—are virtually part of family life; a cluster of lathes may be located in a separate room. It appears that in areas like Katgarh where the bulk of small-scale industrial work gets done—and where the population happens to be predominantly Muslim—civic neglect is the greatest; nearly every crossing has its mound of nightsoil and other rubbish, awaiting leisurely removal. In many of these areas, drainage was bad even during a dry January; during the monsoons we heard that some of these streets become open sewers, heavy with acid and other industrial waste from the workshops. Given these conditions, it is not surprising that some of the new wealth in Muslim hands, which we discuss later, should have sought to flow into new housing colonies, or that these colonies should have been given Muslim sounding names. The beginnings of a few such neighbourhoods set alarm bells ringing. Says the pamphlet *Burning Moradabad*: 'They have a dream of creating a Muslim State within UP, constituted of (the) western districts. . . . So they are creating the same conditions of panic and disorder for bending the knees of Hindus as they did in 1945, 1946 and 1947.'

Where does Moradabad's wealth come from? The city used to be a centre for making brass kitchenware in small scale units. After Partition, a number of Punjabi families, displaced from their ancestral homes in Pakistan, settled in Moradabad and, over the years, reoriented the industrial apparatus into producing decorative brassware—inlaid with other metals, wood, shell, and so forth—principally for export. The annual output, according to the *Patriot* (29 August 1980) is in the range of Rs. 100 crore, with about half exported. In recent years, the indigenous Muslims have been moving into this export business on a growing scale, attracting workers to the tune of 75,000 from different parts of UP and Bihar and providing employment to Muslims from the neighbouring towns of Sambhal, Chandausi and Budaun. But their offices tend to be located in their homes, usually alongside some production facility. The workshops are virtually all small-scale, each concentrating on one or another of the scores of manufacturing stages in the production of the intricate designs. At each stage the partly-finished goods move to a different locale.

The district population according to the 1971 Census was 24,28,971, while Moradabad city had a population of 2,72,355 in the same year. Moradabad has no elective municipal body.[9] Lying next to Rampur, a state formerly ruled by a Muslim prince, Moradabad district has long had a concentration of Muslims who, in pre-1947 days, congregated in towns as absentee landlords, officials, traders, artisans and weavers, and who played an important part in the life of most Rohilkhand towns. In the city, Muslims represented nearly 60 per cent of the population. In the district, they held

42 per cent of the land. Indeed, Muslims were more powerful in Moradabad than in any other district of UP. But this is no longer the case. Muslims have gradually lost out to the enterprising Punjabis, selling off their land and property. Many of the houses now lined up in Adarsh Nagar, Kothi Bal Nagar and the Civil Lines were purchased from depressed, absentee Muslim landlords who, under force of circumstances, have withdrawn into the countryside to guard their limited landholdings.

The Muslims of Moradabad have lagged behind in education. Except for a few families who insist on sending their children to the Aligarh Muslim University, the majority have stayed away from both government and privately-managed institutions, a fact noted by Mr Lawrence, vice-principal of Parker Intermediate College. Most of them flock to the five or six well known *madaris* which impart instruction in traditional Islamic learning. They are pathetically under represented in the degree colleges. Discrimination against Muslims in admission, combined with their own indifference to Western education, has caused much concern amongst the admittedly small Muslim intelligentsia. The answer, we were told, lay in imparting modern scientific-oriented education that would ensure Muslim representation in government service and the professions. Such words are expressed by, among others, the *Nazim* of Anjuman-i Madaris-i Arabia.[10]

The proportion of Muslims in the city appears to have been growing somewhat in recent years. The city's articulate Hindu opinion sees in this the Muslims' unrestrained fertility. How much of the growth is in fact due to immigration, to a preference for more children common to poor workers in the unorganized sector generally, and to a genuine fertility differential between Hindus and Muslims—this question we are unable to answer. Were elections to be held to municipal institutions, Muslims would probably be in a majority among those elected. The probability that in such a situation their political weight, however modest, might favour the Muslim exporters probably gives the Punjabi merchants an uneasy feeling. We shall discuss this matter later.

Since manufacturing in Moradabad is organized on a small-scale, and in subcontracting units, there are obvious difficulties in organizing the working class. We could not investigate the matter in depth, but we suspect that the exporters corner the lion's share of the surplus value, while the subcontracting workshop owner may often be a direct producer himself, sharing the worker's religious identity in a milieu seen to be hostile. When an active trade union organization has no clear focus, tensions of class conflict, may, therefore, often be felt as between Punjabi Hindu exporters and the local Muslim producers. There are Muslim exporters too; but these tensions, due to the reasons stated earlier, tend to be articulated through communal terms rather than class terms. In the elections to the state legislature in May 1980, for example, the principal contest was between a Congress(I) Muslim candidate and a RSS backed Punjabi candidate of the Bharatiya Janata Party, which drew political and financial sustenance from the rich brass merchants and grain traders of Moradabad, Sambhal and Chandausi.[11] The contest was turned by the Congress(I) organizations into one between the locals (of all religions) and the Punjabi outsiders, with somewhat menacing undertones of chasing the latter out of town. The Punjabis' connection with the RSS is said to be generally strong; they took the threat seriously.

These identities—Punjabi *versus* local, Hindu *versus* Muslim—are spacious enough to absorb varied other tensions too, e.g. those arising due to the substantial dent the Muslim traders are making by exporting to West Asia on their own account. In this 'free enterprise' economy, such ups and downs are routine—the Mahishyas in Howrah's small engineering sector outcompete the Brahmins and Kayasthas; Ramgarhia and other Sikhs in Punjab far outpace the Hindu Khatris in industry; Syrian Christians in Kerala buy up lands for plantations from the Nairs; aggressive Marwaris and Gujaratis often get the better of Parsis. But if the Muslims in Moradabad—or a handful among them—come into a measure of affluence, their rivals are quick to point to foreign money (a foreignness invisible in the Punjabi exporter's wealth), and to whip up communal frenzy resulting in large scale destruction of property and the migration of people from one area to another. A senior police official has rightly observed that 'adventurism can succeed best only in chaos and confusion, and the political and economic adventure knows that the best form of confusion, instability and panic can be generated only by a communal riot' (*Sunday* 17 May 1981).

If social consciousness in Moradabad is organized strongly along religious lines, this is not unconnected with the strong Islamic religious presence in town. There are two long established *madaris*, providing religious instruction for the future maulvis and other religious workers. Given the town's composition, there is a large number of mosques, and the calls to prayer go out on loudspeakers regularly. Our stay in Moradabad was too brief for us to judge the specifics of communal organization, Hindu or Muslim; but given the long history of communal conflict, with public force often poised against them in recent years, it would be surprising if the Muslims did not feel the need to secure for themselves a considerable measure of armed protection.

These engines of religious or communal consciousness are not much countered by secular institutions. We have noted the lack of elective municipal bodies and the weakness of trade union activity. There are a great many schools and a dozen colleges, these latter controlled largely by their Hindu patrons. We often heard of the damaging consequences of many kinds of commercialization for the content of education and for teachers' status. With a minor exception or two, these institutions are *not* neutral ground for discussing conflict or for mediating in disturbed situations. One meets articulate college teachers, but often hears only a communal view from them. We met only a handful of individuals able to view their social milieu critically, and to act upon it with disinterested passion.

IV

The bare bones of the events on Ramzan Id day, 13 August 1980, in Moradabad are fairly well known, but we recount them briefly to establish the context, relying largely upon the report in *Sunday* (24 August 1980) by the weekly's editor, M.J. Akbar, who reached the city on 15 August.

Some 80,000 Muslims had gathered at the Idgah, and the Id prayers were in progress. A pig wandered in, violating the Muslim sense of cleanliness appropriate to the sanctity of prayer. Some people asked the attending policemen why the pig had been let in, and were told that guarding pigs was not the job of the police. An altercation followed, and escalated so rapidly as to make any precise sequence difficult to establish.

Brickbatting from the crowd, firing by the police, an injured police officer, and scores of *namazis* shot dead, all these took place within about five minutes while the prayer drew to a close. 'The tragedy of Moradabad', declared an aggrieved Saiyid Shahabuddin in Parliament, 'is nothing but Jallianwala Bagh re-enacted. Both happened on a day of rejoicing. Both occurred in a closed place, and the firing in both instances took place, from the only exit and the point of entry that was there, against the people congregated there.'

A stampede followed the police firing, in which 50 more people lost their lives. The furious crowd surging out of the Idgah roughed up policemen in different localities. Later in the evening, a Muslim mob attacked the Gulshahid police *chowki*, killing two policemen, burning a portion of the *chowki*, and stealing two rifles. Nothing on that day can be construed as an attack by Muslims upon Hindus; it was rather the gross over-reaction of the police to the altercation at the Idgah, leading to Muslim fury, which in turn invited grotesquely brutal, escalatory reprisals by the police upon them, including in areas adjoining the police outpost of Gulshahid.

Before proceeding further, we may pause and wonder at the swift pace at which violence grew. Communal tension did not spring up overnight; the climate for its growth had been assiduously, if thoughtlessly, nurtured over the months with the knowledge and often silent consent of the district administration.[12] Our probes into such prior antagonisms between the Muslims and police brought mentions of various incidents a month or a year or two prior to this particular one on 13 August. Beyond that there is the petty tyranny of the neighbourhood policemen, which the ordinary Muslim is normally too weak to resist, but whose memory festers to prepare the ground for the ultimate explosion. Such an explosion is, in turn, immensely punitive and, after a while one returns to the workaday life. Normalcy appears to be restored at least on the surface.

To return to the aftermath of 13 August. The disturbances in the city were usually long drawn out, with fresh outbreaks beginning on 10 September and 20 October. The particular events touching these latter half are inconsequential. Important throughout is the immensely punitive stance taken by the city police and the PAC towards the Muslims. Hundreds of men were dragged out of their homes, beaten, and locked up.[13] Scores of men had their arms, knuckles, legs, and ankles broken by the police in cold blood. Except on the last occasion, curfew was enforced only against the Muslims; Hindus were free to roam at will.

M.J. Akbar's report and all other accounts agree that on 13 August and for several days after, there was no conflict between the Hindus—other than policemen—and the Muslims. The magnitude of police violence, however, had widespread repercussions in several towns in north India on 15 August; and the Moradabad police force appears to have been under pressure to divert attention from itself. It sought to do this by inciting Hindus to attack the Muslims, as in Barbaran *mohalla*, to simulate a communal riot. In this enterprise it may have received help from the group which had lost in the May 1980 elections; to have the socio-political boundaries reinforced in Hindu-Muslim terms would suit them too.

The police efforts succeeded. Several Hindus told us that policemen went around taunting Hindus to attack the Muslims, and, at least in one instance the PAC allowed students of K.G.K. College to launch an organized assault on the Muslims of Pul Paar Colony. Students of the same college are reported to have led a mob to Ram Talaiya, a village across the railway lines, and burnt alive 15 men, women and children (*Patriot* 29 August 1980).

To generate the requisite fire among the Hindus, diverse rumours were planted. The Hindu principal of a major college told us that he received a phone call, by someone who declined to identify himself, that the city's water supply had been poisoned; there were numerous such phone calls. A rumour announced that the Shiva temple next to the cremation ground had been demolished and its priest killed; in retaliation, Muslims living in the *line-paar* area lost their lives and a mosque in the neighbourhood was demolished.[14] In fact, neither the temple nor the priest had been touched.

The rumour on 14 August that a certain PAC platoon had been wiped out by the Muslims persuaded other PAC jawans to kill ten men who had been brought into the Kotwali by the police, by beating them to death with sticks. A leading advocate in the town told us that when on 16 August, in Patparsarai there was a rumour that Muslims were going to attack the area, Hindus assembled with whatever weapon they could lay their hands on. A police jeep came and shot a Hindu down. The advocate and some others who later asked the police the reason for their action were told that Muslims in police uniform, roaming around in a jeep, had done the killing! The victim's family was given Rs. 5,000 in compensation.

Another rumour was floated that a man, Sunil—no further detail—and a girl had been taken off a rickshaw; the listener could draw his own inferences. The (Muslim) MLA was rumoured to be distributing arms from a white Ambassador car. Muslims were credited with large arsenals, gathered in preparation for an uprising. Hindu *goondas* enjoyed immunity; they took Muslims off buses coming into the city bus-stand and killed them in broad daylight on Grand Trunk (GT) Road. The evidence of the frenzy among the Hindus being whipped up by the police is overwhelming. This is how communal frenzy is created.

During at least the first two bouts beginning 13 August and 10 September, curfew was enforced for Muslims alone. The police are reported to have made deals with Hindu *goondas* over sharing the spoils from the looting of Muslim shops. Some Hindu looters were arrested too, but charged with the light offence of merely breaking the curfew. The same advocate told us that a senior police official is reported to have said that some Hindus too had to be arrested in order to fill in the quota. Judicial action on the granting of bail and the like was generally such as to let the Hindus off lightly and to come down hard on the Muslims.

Clearly the Muslims were up against not only the police but also the judiciary. This applied to the news media too. Akbar's report in the *Sunday* (24 August 1980) is quite exceptional. Most reports were filed by newsmen who stayed away from Muslim areas, believing the administration's warning that their lives would not be safe there. These reports tended to reflect the police and the Hindu-communal view of what was happening in the city.

V

The events of Moradabad bear witness to the regression of a society and of its political, administrative, and judicial organs to a depth where one may no longer speak of the norms of a minimally civilized community. Within the city, to be sure, a few Hindus continued to help Muslims throughout the terror—among them Kishen Sharma, a trade unionist, and Umesh Caerey, a city journalist. They retained the Muslims' confidence throughout, and their good offices enabled us to reach a wide range of Muslims as well as Hindus during our brief visits. Such exceptions apart, what is striking about this bustling, 'prosperous' city is its woeful poverty in matters of head and heart, its lack of thought and effort over the manner in which life in the city might be organized, its lack of any feeling for a community of interests at any level.

How is it, one asks in despair, that the children of two great religious traditions, citizens of a country that lays claim to being a world leader, can be so inept and often so brutal in their mutual relations? Communal killings at Moradabad and elsewhere are discussed extensively, charges are traded, guilt proclaimed without any investigation, scapegoats sought, and appeals made for communal harmony. These shallow echoes of the poverty of thought, feeling, and effort noted earlier bespeak too profound a social crisis in Indian society, a crisis whose depths and dimensions we cannot consider here. It is evident, however, that even 'prosperous' urban centres like Moradabad lack the intellectual and moral resources needed to use what is available for creating a halfway civilized round of life for their inhabitants. We are persuaded that, if those of us who pride ourselves on our rational, secular world views are unable, or unwilling, to find ways to reach such centres, the malignancies being fostered there will, in quick time, come to engulf our metropolitan islands too.

NOTES

1. Since the publication of this article, the Moradabad riots have been extensively researched.
2. Some of the notable studies on communal riots are: Ratna Naidu, *Communal Edges to Plural Societies: India and Pakistan*, New Delhi, 1980; G.S. Bhargava, 'Structure of a Riot', *Seminar*, Jan. 1970.

3. Rasheeduddin Khan notes that the total number of Muslim students in the university is just about 5,000 out of a total enrolment of approximately 8,000. 'This should be indicative', he observes, 'of the fact that Aligarh is but an oasis in the vast desert-land of Muslim illiteracy. Its importance, in terms of the challenging task of spreading higher education for the Muslim masses is more symbolic than substantive.' 'Minority segments in Indian polity: Muslim situation and plight for Urdu', *EPW*, 2 Sept. 1978.

4. These figures are quoted in the articles by A.R. Sherwani in *Radiance* (Delhi) and *Mainstream* (Delhi). The articles provide interesting clues to the state of Muslim education in northern India.

5. For a survey of this literature see Satish Saberwal, 'Elements of Communalism', *Mainstream*, 28 Mar. 1981.

6. The pamphlet was reported to have been written by a group of Hindu lawyers.

7. This account was corroborated by our respondents.

8. Instances of communal squabbles in the municipalities of Rohilkhand can be found in Mushirul Hasan, *Nationalism and Communal Politics in India, 1916-1928*, New Delhi, 1977.

9. Uttar Pradesh is one of the several states where 'all civic bodies stand suspended, most of them for several years with no prospect of fresh elections being held' (*Indian Express*, 1981).

10. Interviews with Maulana Kalzum Ansari and S. Najmul Hasan, advocate. Most Muslims we interviewed were aware of the importance of *Angrezi talim* (Western education) and regretted that, in spite of the efforts of Sir Saiyid Ahmad Khan, the community was educationally backward.

11. We have not dealt with the role of the RSS because it was difficult to ascertain some of the facts pointing to its 'complicity' in the events leading to the communal outbreak in August. Some of the leading Congressmen were, however, closely associated with RSS activities. These included Vinod Gupta, a close associate of N.D. Tewari, Dinesh Rastogi, Mahesh Rastogi, a former MLA from Sambhal and Dayanand Gupta, president of the city congress committee. Professor B.S. Verma of K.G.K. College, Moradabad, told us that the RSS activitists published posters commending the role of the PAC and the CRP.

12. The background is provided in the *Sunday* (1981) and, more perceptively in the articles published in the *Patriot* (1980).

13. Such were the varied experiences of Babu Nabi Husain, Akhtar Jahan, Jamil Ahmad (his brother-in-law was murdered on 18 Oct. near the Katghar *thana*), Muhammad Hasan and Sadiq Hussain.

14. Interview with Fakir Chand, an activist of the Students' Federation of India.

15

Competing Symbols and Shared Codes:
Inter-Community Relations in Modern India

I'll tell you truth, oh Brahmin, if I may make so bold!
These idols in your temples—these idols have grown old;
To hate your fellow-mortals is all they teach you, while
Our God too sets his preachers to scold and to revile;
Sickened, from both your temple and our shrine I have run,
Alike our preachers' sermons and your fond myths I shun.
—In every graven image you fancied God: I see
In each speck of my country's poor dust, divinity.
Come, let us lift suspicion's thick curtains once again,
Unite once more the sundered, wipe clean division's stain.
Too long has lain deserted the heart's warm habitation—
Come, build here in our homeland an altar's new foundation,
And raise a spire more lofty than any of this globe,
With high pinnacles touching the hem of heaven's robe!
And there at every sunrise let our sweet chanting move
The hearts of all who worship, pouring them wine of love:
Firm strength, calm peace, shall blend in the hymns the votary sings—
For from love comes salvation to all earth's living things.[1]

MUHAMMAD IQBAL

The controversy over the Babri Masjid-Ramjanmabhumi issue did not just arouse deep religious passions but raised the fundamental issue of how best to allow competing religious symbols to co-exist in a society committed to the secular ideal. Admittedly, the pressing need is to resolve conflicting claims over the masjid at Ayodhya. But, in the long, run, all concerned citizens will need to marshal their intellectual resources so as to evolve a mechanism and, at the same time, define social codes for resolving controversies of this nature. Otherwise, the initiative, as always, will rest with those who manipulate both political institutions and processes to create and widen arenas of conflict.

It is not surprising that the flare-up, centred around the masjid in Ayodhya, caused such deep concern. After all, no other issue since India's Independence generated such violent passions, led to such widespread riots (Table 15.1),[2] gripped the people with panic, fear and anger, and threatened to destroy the democratic, secular consensus envisaged by the architects of the Indian Constitution. Sentiments were polarized to such an extent that two successive governments collapsed in the course of just a year, with the BJP succeeding in placing the mandir issue on the national agenda.[3] As the *Times of India* commented on 17 October 1989, 'Jettisoning once and for all its mumbo-jumbo about Gandhian values, the BJP, under Mr L.K. Advani's spirited leadership, has gone on the offensive with a strategy clearly designed to polarize life in the country along antagonistic religious lines.'

For the first time, religious zealots, bolstered by politically articulate groups, found both a cause and an opportunity to create a bonding among their divided and stratified constituency. In the *shilanyas* ceremonies, the Vishwa Hindu Parishad (VHP), backed by the BJP and the RSS, found a unifying symbol which had, for centuries, eluded Hindu reformers and

Table 15.1: Communal Riots from 1 September to 20 November 1990

State	No. of places	No. of deaths
Andhra Pradesh	4	27
Assam	1	7
Bihar	8	19
Delhi	–	8
Gujarat	26	99
Karnataka	22	88
Kerala	2	3
Madhya Pradesh	5	21
Maharashtra	3	4
Rajasthan	13	52
Tamil Nadu	1	6
Tripura	1	–
Uttar Pradesh	28	227
West Bengal	2	6
Total	116	567

preachers.[4] Through flamboyant demonstrations of religious worship and mindless retaliatory acts, these groups succeeded in stoking the fires of communal unrest.

On the other side of the spectrum, members of the Babri Masjid Action Committee (BMAC) acquired much political legitimacy and support. Some of its members, having tasted success over the Shah Bano case, reached out to the Muslim population, aired their long-standing grievances, and extracted concessions from political parties on the eve of the 1989 general elections. Given their capacity to mobilize Muslim opinion, especially in UP and Bihar, it was neither possible nor expedient to ignore the powerful imam of the Jama Masjid in Delhi or the renowned head of the prestigious Nadwat al-ulama. They represented a Muslim consensus which had been achieved only once in the history of Indian Islam, i.e. during the khilafat movement in the early 1920s.

Many contemporary aspects of the Babri Masjid-Ramjanmabhumi dispute remain shrouded in mystery. For example, why was a district judge in Ayodhya allowed to disturb the *status quo*? Was it to court the so-called Hindu constituency? Or, to mollify enraged feelings over the government's 'surrender' over the Shah Bano case? Even if these explanations are seemingly valid, it is still not clear why the VHP and their allies enjoyed the freedom to make political capital out of the judgement and launch a massive countrywide agitation which, in an extremely surcharged atmosphere, could only exacerbate tensions among the rival contestants? It would appear that the ruling party, already riven with dissension over the handling of the *shilanyas* ceremonies, lost the initiative to the VHP and failed to keep its leaders on a tight leash. Soon, the concern was not just confined to Rama's birthplace in Ayodhya. Amid the chanting of Vedic hymns and the ringing of temple bells, a general clamour was raised for 'recovering' other mosques, such as the ones in Varanasi and Mathura. Though such demands are being unabashedly voiced on public platforms and expressed in ominous terms,[5] they are also being contested with equal fervour by members of the BMAC and their vociferous supporters.

It is not uncommon to find scapegoats in history—to place the blame on the medieval sultans of Delhi who defiled and destroyed temples—and to attribute Muslim intransigence to the policies of the British government and its successor, the Congress party.[6] It is pointed out that the colonial rulers courted the Muslims by granting them privileges and special concessions in order to create their separate and distinct identity in Indian politics. It is also argued that the Congress succumbed to the League pressures in agreeing to the Partition of the country. After Independence, the Congress leadership continued to placate the Muslims and pandered to their sentiments for electoral reasons. In this way, secularism has merely served the interests of the minorities, especially the Muslims. The Hindus, on the other hand, have been at the receiving end. While their co-religionists in neighbouring Pakistan and Bangladesh have been relegated to the status of second-class citizens, Indian Muslims have been allowed to retain their personal law, conduct their proselytizing activities, and preach and practise their religion without inhibition.[7] This was the essence of the BJP's advertisements published in the national newspapers from 30 October to 1 November 1991.

Such generalized and simplistic formulations are backed by perspectives which dwell on the separateness and inherently contradictory nature of the Hindu and Muslim traditions and their estrangement, both in colonial and pre-colonial days. Thus the contest over the Babri Masjid-Ramjanmabhumi issue is seen as part of a recurring theme of conflict and tension in Indian history.

This is not the place to refute such ill-conceived theories. My main aim is to highlight certain broad aspects of Hindu-Muslim relations during the last decade of the nineteenth and the early decades of the twentieth centuries. In the final section, I focus on Faizabad/Ayodhya, a district with a long and chequered history, in order to outline the broad contours of local politics and to see if political linkages and socio-economic relations transcended religious cleavages or not.

II

Both as an ideology and as a movement, communalism derives ideological sustenance from the view, popularized by Henry Elliot and other colonial writers, that Islam and Hinduism, as indeed their followers, co-existed uneasily in India, and that religious conflicts rather than harmonious living was the hallmark of the medieval Indian ethos. In fact, the dominant images of the Muslim presence, nurtured by publicists and major literary writers, were concerned with the degradation of the Hindus through forcible conversions, imposition of the *jizya* (tax levied on non-Muslims to guarantee their safety and protection), strict application of the *Shariat*, and the desecration of Hindu temples.[8]

Admittedly, there existed a fragmented and differentiated form of religious consciousness which may have led the sultans and their ideologues to offend religious sensibilities. But religious solidarity was not the basis of collective socio-economic experiences. The ideology of the state, trimmed to suit the interests of the ruling elites, accommodated religious concerns. Yet, it did not rest on the notion of a unified 'community' with identifiable interests, which forms the main pillar of modern day 'communalism'. Moreover, while there were stray, localized and sporadic incidents of conflicts over religious symbols, integrative and syncretic forces were also at work amongst the elites as well as the common people. The dominant picture of the seventeenth and eighteenth centuries is not of the Hindus and the Muslims forming exclusive and antagonistic categories but of their cooperating in cultural life and social affairs.[9]

This scenario, however, gradually changed with the coming of the British. For the first time, signs of Hindu-Muslim friction surfaced in some areas and amongst certain groups. Now, the terms of dispute were articulated differently. The language and vocabulary of discourse changed. Muted expressions were replaced with angry exchanges. Mild protests took the form of violent outbursts. The reasons for this were quite numerous, ranging from the introduction of Western-style institutions to the emergence of religio-revivalist trends stimulated by powerful reform movements in Bengal, Punjab, and Maharashtra.

No summing up of late-nineteenth century trends can be complete without reference to the activities of the Arya Samaj, the spurt in cow-protection activity, and the vigorous campaign in support of the Nagri script and its use in government and law courts. These were not isolated assertions of militant, religio-revivalist tendencies, but manifestations of the new and burgeoning Hindu consciousness.[10]

Among the Muslims, the Graeco-Turkish war of 1897 stimulated pan-Islamic feelings. Islamization in Bengal and parts of northern India, inspired by Shah Waliullah and his successors and bolstered by the faraizis in Bengal, was an equally potent force. Insistence on a revitalized consciousness and identity, with its corresponding denigration of Islam's local roots, began to erode syncretistic traditions and undermine religious peace and understanding.[11] The massive communal rioting in 1893, preceded by sporadic but violent altercations, illustrated that the fabric of Hindu-Muslim unity was too fragile to withstand the onslaught of various revitalization movements. 'If the smouldering fire of religious enmity is not put out', warned an observer, 'it will before long be kindled into a mighty flame and destroy the noble edifice which the Congress has built with so much pains.'[12]

The prophecy did not come true. Though relations between certain sections of Hindus and Muslims were sometimes strained, their deterioration was neither deep nor irreversible. 'Nothing strikes the intelligent traveller in India more forcibly', observed a senior police official in 1894, 'than the friendly peaceable attitude of all castes and classes towards each other.'[13] He was right. Friction between religious groups was not ordinarily a major source of disturbance in the last quarter of the nineteenth-century.[14] During 1889-94, there was no violence in Bengal, except once in Calcutta and its suburbs.[15]

Such sporadic outbursts did not signify, as some writers are wont to suggest, the fragmentation of society along communal lines. Inter-community tensions and disputes were counterbalanced by the quiet, commonplace routines in which Hindus and Muslims intermingled with-out notice or incident and they could still be found involved in a range of 'religiously promiscuous' practices. In 1909, the *Imperial Gazetteer of India* stated that it was the regular practice of 'low-class Muhammadans' to join in the Durga Puja and other Hindu festivals; it mentioned Muslim consultation of Hindu almanacs, worship of Sithala and Manasa, use of vermilion and joint offerings to village deities before the sowing or trans-planting of rice seedlings.[16] Another inspiring legitimation of the more mundane expressions of peaceful co-existence came daily in the sounds of Muslim *shehnai* players joining in the *arti* at Hindu temples, including the *arti* of the Vishwanath temple in Banaras.[17] Sandria Freitag and Nita Kumar have shown how in this holy city of the Hindus, Muslim weavers actively participated in public ceremonials expressing a shared Banarasi culture, including 'the marriage of the Laut' (Bhairava), *Bharat Milap* and the day-today observances related to particular figures and shrines.[18]

Contemporary writings took note of the ongoing process of social and cultural fusion. The poet Iqbal shared the vision of a united India—one that was free of both alien domination and inner dissension. He called his land of birth a garden where the people inhabiting it were members of a *qaum* (nation), with the two circles of Islam and *watan* intersecting and at several places coalescing into a coherent whole. *Himala,* the first poem in *Baang-i Dara*, was inspired by the beauty of his land of birth. *Hindustani Bachhon ka Qaumi Geet* (National Anthem of Indian Children) and the *Tarana-i Hind* (The Song of India) were refined, and buoyant expressions of patriotic sentiments. In *Naya Shiwala* (New Temple), Iqbal chided both Hindus and Muslims for their narrow mentality and appealed to the keep-ers of the temple and the mosque to foster mutual goodwill and under-standing.[19]

Akbar Allahabadi, a merciless satirist equipped with an irrepressible sense of humour, had similar concerns. He subjected to ridicule, to scath-ing criticism or damning exposure the social and political strategy of imperialism and Saiyid Ahmad Khan's policy of loyal cooperation with the government. And, like Iqbal, he championed Hindu-Muslim unity. Both Hindus and Muslims, he wrote, have to bear the blows of those who wield the rod of worldly power, but they should respond by being like water on which the blows of a rod have only a momentary effect.[20]

Iqbal and Akbar stated the obvious. They recognized, as indeed did the others, that the direction in which patronage, economic welfare and authority flowed in everyday life indicated the continuing importance of cross-communal networks.[21] The Saiyid's Aligarh project was backed by the Hindus and Muslims alike. He encouraged, despite his misgivings over the Nagri resolution of 1900 (which sparked off a Hindu-Urdu controversy), a Hindu-Muslim *entente* in cultural and religious matters. His contemporary, Ajudhia Nath Kunzru, owed his fortunes as much to the wealthy Muslim landholders as to his extensive banking and commission agencies.[22] In east UP and Awadh generally, the dominant factor in the politics of the towns tended to be an Urdu-speaking élite connection based on landed interests. Communal considerations did not necessarily foul the path of politics.[23]

The competing units in early municipal politics were multi-factions, not antagonistic groups. In the composition of early municipal factions, caste and communal considerations played a secondary role to personal rivalries, family linkages, and economic ties. The lawyer, Maulvi Sirajul Islam, was elected from Chittagong to the Bengal legislative council largely on the strength of the 'Hindu vote'. Surendranath Banerjea, on the other hand, was backed by Muslims for a seat in the prestigious Calcutta corporation. Around the same time the Congress backed Hamid Ali Khan for a seat in the UP council.

Nor did communal divisions last long after they had been politicized. Soon after the violent eruptions in 1893, tempers began to cool everywhere and there was much display of 'mutual love and affection' in the riot-torn cities of UP.[24] Public statements and newspaper editorials on national unity and the commonality of Hindu-Muslim interests were matched by strenuous efforts of local reconciliation committees to resolve and defuse tensions.[25] When asked how the 'upper classes' of the two communities behaved when the riots occurred, the assistant magistrate of Gorakhpur replied: 'By taking leading Hindus and Muslims into confidence, matters are satisfactorily arranged. . . . In Aligarh, we left the whole matter to leading Hindus and Mussalmans and everything went off without hitch.'[26]

Such was the pattern everywhere. By the end of the nineteenth century, there was no sign of the Hindus and the Muslims going their separate ways. If anything, the lines of cleavage in north India were more sharply drawn between the Shias and the Sunnis rather than the Hindus and the Muslims.[27] Though expressed in exaggerated terms, there is merit in the observations of W.S. Blunt and Henry Cotton that the Hindu-Muslim animus was accentuated only after the government translated the principle of divide and rule into formal constitutional arrangements.[28]

With the onset of the twentieth-century, there was a tendency towards the use of religious solidarity as a basis of political action. It started with the Nagri resolution of April 1900 which created fissures among the professional classes in UP. The prospect of reforms and of a greater share in the expanding administrative and bureaucratic machinery triggered the Simla deputation and the establishment of the Muslim League in December 1906, while widespread religio-revivalist movements aided the growth of Defence Leagues, Anjumans, and Sabhas. The Turko-Italian war fanned pan-Islamic passions leading to intense religious activity.

Many of the controversies, both political and religious, subsided during the khilafat and non-cooperation movements when Gandhi cemented an extraordinary alliance between different segments of society.[29] But not long afterwards, the edifice of inter-communal unity, so passionately built by the Mahatma, began to crumble. The khilafat movement itself got bogged down in religious issues instead of concentrating on the consolidation and integration of anti-colonial forces. Consequently, a popular political movement, a gift of history, was a great opportunity absurdly wasted.

Still, it would be wrong to either conclude that the gulf separating the Hindus and Muslims was unbridgeable or that they were hopelessly polarized after Gandhi called off the non-cooperation campaign in February 1922. Most people, especially in the countryside, were unruffled by communal controversies and continued to live, as they had done in the past, in peace and harmony. This was so because of the bonds of socio-economic interests, centuries of common experiences, and shared memories. The governor of Bengal commented on the 'rank and file' of the two major communities in his province cooperating with each other in all 'daily business of life'; it was 'only at rare intervals, when religious feelings become inflamed, that they treat each other as enemies and clashes occur'. O.M. Martin, who served in the same province from 1915 to 1926, made similar observations. Hindu-Muslim unity, he added, was not a temporary occurrence but an old and cherished tradition.[30]

The pan-Islamic euphoria, which had caused so much excitement in the subcontinent, did not take much time to disappear as the Turkish nationalists began to rewrite their political agenda without a khalifa/

sultan. Faced with this reality, unpleasant though it was to committed pan-Islamists, there was an unmistakable reordering of priorities.[31] From then onwards, Islam was once more firmly rooted in the Indian subcontinent and the interests of its followers were much more closely linked with their country and their countrymen. That is why the ulama, based at Deoband and connected with the Jamiyat al-ulama, emerged as powerful advocates of composite nationalism and rejected the two-nation theory. Their arguments in defence of their position was backed by the theological weight of Islam.

It is assumed that the perspective of the Deobandi ulama, with its emphasis on composite nationhood, was rejected by the Muslim community and that the creation of Pakistan validated Jinnah's two-nation theory. These are questionable assumptions. The League's success neither vindicates nor legitimizes the ideological underpinnings of the two-nation theory, for the birth of Pakistan in that summer of discontent in August 1947 was neither imminent nor historically inevitable. It symbolized, more than anything else, Jinnah's personal triumph, his answer to the obdurate Gandhi-Nehru-Patel leadership which had persistently refused to treat him on equal terms or discuss with him the blueprint of a free and united India. Sadly, Indian nationalists of all shades, including the socialists and communists, failed to grasp this reality. As a result, they bowed to the mounting pressure of the League and acquiesced in India's partition, though for different reasons.

One final point. In the debates that preceded and followed the birth of Pakistan, communal rivalries alone were projected as *the* stark Indian reality. It is necessary to provide a corrective to this approach, for there still existed, despite the trauma and agony that accompanied the vivisection of the country, large areas of Hindu-Muslim cooperation and tangible expressions of cultural fusion and religious syncretism. Most people, Hindus and Muslims alike, clung to their inherited ideas, traditions and customs. This was so in the case of, for example, the Meos, the Malkana Rajputs, the Khojas, Bohras and Memons in western India and the Mappilas in Malabar.[32] Given their long, uninterrupted history of social mingling and cultural fusion, it is hard to conceive of a different scenario. Similar trends, syncretic and composite, were at work elsewhere.

True, the rise of communal and 'separatist' politics diminished the importance of certain religio-cultural symbols which had, in the past, transcended caste and community distinctions. Yet, one could still find Hindus observing Muharram—which marks the martyrdom of Prophet Muhammad's grandson and his seventy-two companions.[33] Thousands continued to gather around shrines of the Sufis and other venerated men and sought their intercession to avert calamities, cure diseases, procure children for the childless, or even improve the circumstances of the dead.[34] Frederick Graham Cracknell, magistrate and collector of Etawah and Kanpur, reported that the *mela* commemorating Shah Madaar, who settled at Makanpur in Bilaur *tahsil* in the fifteenth-century, was attended by 50,000 people, mostly Hindus. Unmoved by a Hindu-Muslim fracas in the area in 1931, Hindus and Muslims flocked to his shrine in equal numbers. The pattern was largely the same elsewhere.[35]

Faizabad district in UP, once the capital of the Awadh nawabs and an important Muslim centre, mirrored national and provincial trends in large measure. The Muslim population was relatively small—11.11 per cent in 1901. Most of them belonged to the weaving community, followed by the Sheikhs who held considerable land in Mangalsi, Haveli, Awadh and Khandansa, and the Saiyids whose vast estates lay in Pirpur, Samanpur, and Bhadarsa. In fact, Faizabad was among those districts of UP where a large proportion of land was held by Muslims. There were 2,051 separate estates at the beginning of 1905. Of these, 1,115 were owned by Rajputs, 366 by Brahmins, and 286 by Muslims.

In general, Faizabad and its adjoining areas, including Ayodhya, were no different from other places in UP: they were equally affected by religious and revivalist currents. The militancy of the cow-protection agitation, which led to widespread rioting in 1893 in Azamgarh and the neighbouring districts of Bihar, also caused much excitement in Faizabad. Yet, there was no outbreak of violence. When the 'cow-question' surfaced in 1906 it was amicably settled by local leaders. During 1910-12, however, the consensus broke down largely in reaction to extensive cow-riots in certain areas of eastern and western UP.[36] Although a 'snowball plan', based on the 'heavenly voice' heard at Hanumangarhi in Ayodhya, circulated in Faizabad district,[37] its impact was blunted by alert district officials. Backed by the UP government, local and provincial leaders, including the raja of Mahmudabad, were able to soothe frayed tempers. By September-October 1915, the provincial government, headed by James Meston, evolved a compromise formula acceptable to various contending groups.[38]

Hindu-Muslim relations in Faizabad were only marginally soured by the cow-protection movement and the great 'communal' debates that started with Saiyid Ahmad Khan's crusade against the Congress and culminated in the Lahore resolution of 1940. A major source of irritation was the mosque at Ayodhya which was allegedly built on the site of an ancient temple raised on the actual spot of Rama's birth. Evidence on the destruction of the temple is disputed.[39] Most historians at the Centre for Historical Studies, Jawaharlal Nehru University, point out that neither Abul Fazl, the sixteenth-century author of *Ain-i Akbari*, nor Tulsidas, a celebrated devotee of Rama, mention the demolition of a temple at the site of Rama's birthplace. They conclude, 'It is in the nineteenth century that the story circulates and enters official records. These records were then cited by others as valid historical evidence on the issue.'[40] H.R. Neville, who compiled the *District Gazetteer of Fyzabad*, recorded a view widely shared by British civil servants. He observed:

The materials of the old structure were largely employed, and many of the columns are in good preservation; they are of close-grained black stone, called . . . *basauti*, and carved with various devices. Their length is from seven to eight feet, and the shape square at the base, centre and capital, the rest being round or octagonal. The mosque has two inscriptions, one on the outside and the other on the pulpit; both are in Persian and bear the date 935 Hijri. Of the authenticity of the inscription there can be no doubt, but no record of (Babur's) visit to Ajodhya is to be found in the Musalman historians.[41]

What is perhaps not in dispute is that Ayodhya was, well before the sixteenth-century, a centre of pilgrimage for the Buddhists, the Jains, and the Hindus. It is known that Hindu worship remained possible in the compound of the Babri Masjid and the activities of the Brahmin *pandas* of Ayodhya are recorded by the first European visitor to the place, William Finch, between 1608 and 1611.[42] When Ayodhya first became an important pilgrimage centre in the eighteenth-century it was as much due to the activities of the Ramanandi sadhus as to the patronage of the nawabi court. The diwan of nawab Safdarjang, raja Naval Rai, built and repaired several temples in Ayodhya, while Safdarjang himself gave land for building a temple on what is known as the Hanuman's hill. Asaf ud-Daula's diwan, Tikayat Ray, supported the building of the important temple-fortress Hanumangarhi on this land. Peter van der Veer refers to documents indicating that Muslim officials of the nawabi court gave away gifts for rituals performed by the *pandas*,[43] i.e. Hindu priests on the site of pilgrimage centres.[44]

Peter van der Veer observes that, when the power of the nawabs gradually eroded due to the influence of the British in Awadh politics, the peaceful co-existence of Hindus and Muslims in Ayodhya came to be threatened.[45] Michael H. Fisher and J.R.I. Cole have shown how the changes in the configuration of forces under Wajid Ali Shah deepened religious conflicts and, in 1833 and 1855, nearly exploded into civil war.[46]

Though the last nawab of Awadh dealt with the recalcitrant forces, headed by Amir Ali, he did not emerge unscathed from the incident. His power and authority, already clipped by the British, waned as the firebrand agitators chose the reckless course of waging a holy war against each other. The British intervention in the mandir-masjid fracas was decisive. Hence, an ambivalent nawab was goaded into taking action. At the same time, it sealed his fate and gave the British an excuse to annex the kingdom of Awadh.

The confrontation in 1855 was serious, bitter and violent. But it did not take long for the wounds to be healed. Apart from litigation between 1883 and 1886,[47] the mandir-masjid dispute remained dormant until 1934 when a communal riot near Ayodhya, triggered by cow-slaughter, inflamed passions. Again, between 1950 and 1984 there was no movement to demand the occupation of Rama's birthplace, except for legal actions destined to remain endlessly unfruitful.

There can be no doubt that the Ayodhya mosque was a powerful symbol of communal mobilization in UP. Yet, it was not strong enough to polarize sentiments to a degree where Hindus and Muslims in the province or in the locality would be arrayed against each other. Even when religious sentiments ran amok in the towns of UP from 1 February 1986 onwards, Ayodhya remained unaffected by communal frenzy. 'It is remarkable', reported a newspaper correspondent, 'that while the controversy surrounding the Babri Masjid-Ramjanmabhumi has aroused religious passions elsewhere, Ayodhya and its surrounding areas have been able to maintain communal peace.'[48]

This was not an uncommon feature in Ayodhya. For nearly a century, most Hindus and Muslims in the area did not allow their daily lives to be influenced by the mandir-masjid controversy. They conducted their affairs and performed their usual chores without being swayed by religious passions. Their political life was not moulded by religious considerations alone. In the 1989 elections, for example, the majority of voters voted for the Communist Party of India (CPI) candidate who opposed the communalization of Faizabad polity and society by 'outside' forces. In this way communal groups and parties were humbled soon after the *shilanyas* ceremony. This was an extraordinary development, especially in the light of the fact that the then ruling party capitulated on that occasion and, in the process, legitimized the activities of the VHP, the RSS, and the Shiv Sena.

Generally speaking, political affairs in Faizabad were conducted on a supra-communal network. Before Independence, this process was aided by professional ties, cultural links and common landed interests that bound the Urdu-speaking élites and helped create a strong and powerful composite cultural tradition. More often, caste loyalties rather than religious affiliation moulded public life. This is illustrated by the strong links between the Kayasthas, who occupied one-quarter, and the Muslims, who held two-fifths, of the municipal board seats in the last quarter of the nineteenth-century.[49] Between 1905 and 1911, Muslims, in general, were attracted to Balak Ram and his Kayastha party whose *taluqdari* links gave it a class dimension, a more cosmopolitan, and a cross-communal image.[50] Until after the first general elections in 1952, municipal bodies in Faizabad-*cum*-Ayodhya remained in control of the Kayastha party and its Muslim allies.[51]

In the late 1930s and 1940s, however, there were visible strains in such cross-communal alliances. This was largely due to the failure of the Congress to thwart the communal forces. It allowed the Muslim League to wrest the initiative, as in the 1937 elections to the Faizabad-Sitapur-Bahraich urban constituency, when the Congress literally surrendered the seat to its adversary. What happened in the 1946 elections is a different story altogether. Like the rest of the country, Faizabad district was communally polarized. Here, as elsewhere, the success League's was a foregone conclusion.

Harold Gould has shown how, after Independence, the district became the focal point of a political showdown between Acharya Narendra Deva, the socialist leader, and his Congress rival Baba Raghava Das. In the course of the by-election campaign in 1948, Pandit Govind Ballabh Pant visited Ayodhya and declared that the Acharya did not believe in the divinity of Rama as proven by the fact that he did not wear the *choti* (topknot), displayed by all devout, genuine Hindus. Baba Raghava Das, for his part, moved among his followers distributing *tulsi* leaves to emphasize the spiritual difference between him and his socialist adversary. Ayodhya voted overwhelmingly for the Baba. This is how, concludes Gould, the 'Ayodhya strategy' had worked to perfection.[52]

It is easy to establish the connection between this election campaign and the event on the night of 22 and 23 December 1949 when an idol of Rama suddenly appeared in the Babri Masjid, which had been guarded by a posse of policemen. Baba Raghava Das and his Congress patrons in Lucknow not only revived but exploited the mandir-masjid issue which had remained dormant for decades. They pressed into service the Bairagis and the Mahants who, in subsequent years, headed a vigorous movement to 'liberate' the mosque at Ayodhya. In this way, the Congress introduced a discordant note in an otherwise harmonious society of Faizabad.

The 'Ayodhya strategy' was also used in a different context but with similar results. In May 1986, Rajiv Gandhi capitulated to the strident clamourings of some Muslim groups by introducing the retrograde Muslim Women (Protection of Rights on Divorce) Bill.[53] The motive was simple: the rising tide of anger over the Shah Bano verdict had to be stemmed to retain Muslim votes which, in the wake of the momentous Supreme Court judgement, had tipped the balance in favour of the opposition parties.[54] At the same time, the growing Hindu sentiment over the Ayodhya mosque, voiced by the VHP, the Bajrang Dal, the Shiv Sena and the RSS, had to be assuaged. Rajiv Gandhi's former associate and ministerial colleague, whose own conduct in the murky happenings on 1 February 1986 is not beyond reproach, is reported to have stated the following:

In early 1986 the Muslim Women's Bill was passed to play the Muslim card; and then came the decision on Ayodhya to play the Hindu card. It was supposed to be a package deal. I knew it was a dangerous thing to do and I did not agree. . . . When I asked Mr. Rajiv Gandhi who is showing the worship in the disputed shrine at Ayodhya on Doordarshan two days after it was unlocked, he did not reply; he merely smiled and observed it was tit for tat for the Muslim Women's Bill.[55]

The 'Ayodhya strategy' worked in 1948, but not in 1989. The Congress gained a prestigious seat in a constituency then but was thrown out of office in 1989. The goodwill of the Muslims, achieved in 1986 through cynical means, was frittered away by a reckless act. 'The alienation of the Muslims', commented a newspaper editorial, 'will undoubtedly rank as the most grievous lapse of the Rajiv Gandhi government.' The paper added:

In retrospect the laying of the foundation stone of the Rama temple in Ayodhya on November 9 can be seen to be a dangerous turning point in the history of independent India. The seeds for a disintegration of the secular vision of the country were sown on that day. History cannot easily pardon the Congress for its direct and indirect contribution to the spectacular growth of Hindu chauvinist forces today and for the tightening hold of the fundamentalists on the Muslim community.[56]

The use of the 'Hindu card' by a party that laid claims to the secular legacy of Gandhi and Nehru proved counterproductive. The BJP rather than the Congress benefitted from an ill-conceived and ill-advised electoral plan.[57] Communal mobilization not only divides people but often devours its own protagonists.

Competing symbols supposedly cause friction and create cleavages. Not so in Faizabad, where the people, with some exceptions, have withstood the communal onslaught for well over a century. There is much room for optimism that they will be able to weather the present storm. The people of Faizabad have done so in the not so distant past; there is no reason why they cannot do so now.

The real issue is not the future of the Babri Masjid or of Rama's birthplace; in fact, the seemingly endless debate among scholars over the existence of a temple on the present site of the mosque or the actual birthplace of Rama is not even of much academic interest. The main concern of the people of Faizabad and their brethren in other parts of the country must be to create an ethos and a social order in which competing symbols can be blended into a harmonious whole. Individuals and groups have quite successfully done so in the past, and there is no reason why it cannot be done in our times.

All said and done, India's hope lies in areas like Faizabad where shared memories and common historical experiences should slowly but steadily promote consensus and accommodation between different segments of society.[58] Even though strewn with obstacles and difficulties, it is worth fighting for the realization of such an ideal.

NOTES

1. Mujeeb, *Indian Muslims*, p. 485.
2. The official count of the deaths due to communal riots in 1990 put the number at 831. A report compiled by the Delhi unit of People's Unit for Democratic Rights (PUDR) lists 116 places where riots took place in the wake of the *rathyatra*. An agonized journalist commented, 'The 831 or 1,662 or more deaths due to the mandir-masjid row were not due to material causes, and the dead did not belong to an alien land. Think in the way poets think, and you are hit by the indicting realization that Indians as a nation are not growing, but diminishing. . . . The only way we can grow, individually and nationally, is by struggling to stop this *tandava nritya* (devil's dance) of communal violence.' Sudheendra Kulkarni, 'India Brutalised', *Sunday Observer*, New Delhi, 30 Dec. 1990. Also, see editorial comments, 'Bestiality in Bhagalpur', *Sunday Observer*, 5 Nov. 1989; 'Stop the Carnage'; *Times of India*, 17 Oct. 1989; 'Anguished India'; *Times of India*, 31 Oct. 1990.
3. Rajiv Gandhi conceded that '*shilanyas* played a crucial role in the (Congress) debacle', *Times of India*, 30 Nov. 1989 and 15 Dec. 1989 for analysis of the UP elections where seven of the nine Muslim candidates elected to the Lok Sabha belonged to the Janata Dal. Zafar Agha, 'UP Muslims Desert Congress-I', ibid., 26 Nov. 1989.
4. This view has found much support and is echoed in the writings of leading journalists like Chandan Mitra, then editor of the *Sunday Observer*, and

Swapan Dasgupta, then assistant editor of the *Times of India*. Dasgupta has argued that the fragmentation of India can only be arrested by creating alternative focal points of national consolidation. For this reason, he backs the 'movement in Ayodhya', pointing out that the defeat of the BJP on this issue 'will, in one important sense only aggravate the crisis of Indian nationalism'. 'Nationalist Disarray: Renewed Importance of Ayodhya', *Times of India*, 10 Sept. 1990. Also, 'Journey to Ayodhya: Hindu Nationalism Comes of Age', ibid., 23 Oct. 1989. However, the views of Swapan Dasgupta have been effectively challenged in the columns of the *Times of India* itself. For example, Arvind N. Das, 'Pathology of Uncivil Society: Ritualism United Mandal-Mandir Moves', 5 Oct. 1990; Praful Bidwai, 'BJP in a Clef Stick: Yatra's Success is a Liability', 12 Oct. 1990; Harish Khare, 'Sparring with Communalism: Why Sadhus are Setting National Agenda', 20 Oct. 1990; H.M. Seervai, 'NF-BJP Divorce: Hinduism Not Above the Constitution', 2 Nov. 1990.

5. The Jagatguru Shankaracharya of Dwarka Peeth announced that, 'as long as the three sacred places, which the Muslims had destroyed to build mosques, are not restored to the Hindus, no peace or communal harmony is possible'. *Times of India*, 9 Sept. 1990. L.K. Advani, president of the BJP, and his colleagues have also made similar statements. While announcing his plan of undertaking the *rath-yatra* from the Somnath temple to Ayodhya, the BJP president declared, 'So far as the question of the birthplace of Lord Rama in Ayodhya and Lord Krishna in Mathura and the Kashi Vishwanath temple is concerned, the Hindu community cannot compromise'. Ibid., 13 Sept. 1990.

6. See the collection of essays in, *Hindu Temples: What Happened to Them,* New Delhi, 1990.

7. Balraj Madhok, 'Persecuted or Pampered', *Illustrated Weekly of India*, 9 Jan. 1983. The thrust of this article is that Indian Muslims 'have no legal or moral claim or right on [*sic*] this country'.

8. Hasan, *Nationalism and Communal Politics*, Chap. 8.

9. Satish Chandra, *Parties and Politics at the Mughal Court 1707-1740*, New Delhi, 1972, pp. 261-6.

10. McLane, *Indian Nationalism and the Early Congress*, pp. 271-331 (for an insightful account of the cow-protection movement). Robinson, *Separatism Among Indian Muslims*, pp. 66-78, for a sensitive analysis of revivalist tendencies, including the development of the Hindi-Urdu conflict and the campaign for Hindi.

11. Roy, *The Islamic Syncretistic Tradition in Bengal*, p. 251; and Rafiuddin Ahmed, *Bengal Muslims*, 1981, p. 184.

12. *Al Waqt*, Gorakhpur, 21/26 February 1894, Selections from Native Newspapers, UP.

13. T.C. Arthur, *Reminiscences of an Indian Police Official*, London, 1894, p. 145. Both British and Indian witnesses before the Public Service Commission testified to the harmonious relations between the Hindus and Muslims

and took note of the cross-communal links. See *Public Service Commission*, NWP & O Sub-Commission, Calcutta, 1888, pp. 15, 23, 26.

14. McLane, *India Nationalism*, p. 318.

15. Rajat Kanta Ray, *Social Conflict and Political Unrest in Bengal 1875-1927*, New Delhi, 1984, p. 121. The commissioner of Dacca noted the 'extraordinary fact' that in five years 'not a single riot of any description should have occurred'.

16. *Imperial Gazetteer of India*, pp. 48-9.

17. Judy F. Pugh, 'Divination and Ideology in the Banaras Muslim Community', Ewing (ed.), *Shariat and Ambiquity in South Asian Islam*, p. 289.

18. Freitag (ed.), *Culture and Power in Banaras*, pp. 13-14, 168-9.

19. See the collection of essays in Hafeez Malik (ed.), *Iqbal: Poet-Philosopher of Pakistan*, New York, 1971.

20. Ralph Russell and Khurshidul Islam, 'The Satirical Verse of Akbar Allahabadi (1846-1921)', *MAS*, 1974, Vol. 8, 1, pp. 44-6.

21. Notice the comment on Banaras: 'It should be explained that in Benaras the Mahomedan population is nearly entirely dependent upon the Hindus. With the exception of a few members of the old Mahomedan aristocracy, who are now in straitened circumstances, the entire community lives a hand to mouth existence. . . . The weavers are without exception dependent on the goodwill of their Hindu employers. The two communities are therefore closely bound to each other by economic ties.' Quoted in Freitag, *Culture and Power in Banaras*, p. 13. Nita Kumar has argued that what seems more influential in promoting harmony is the fact that Hindus and Muslims of 'lower classes' share a similar lifestyle and ideology of work, leisure and public activity. 'Work and Leisure in the Formation of Identity: Muslim Weavers in a Hindu City', in Freitag, *Culture and Power*, p. 169.

22. Henry Sender, *The Kashmiri Pandits: A Study of Cultural Choice in North India*, New Delhi, 1988, p. 244.

23. Robinson, *Separatism Among Muslims*, p. 79.

24. Hasan, *Nationalism and Communal Politics*, p. 50.

25. Ibid., pp. 50-1.

26. *Public Service Commission*, NWP & O, Evidence, p. 158.

27. Mushirul Hasan, 'Sectarianism in Indian Islam: The Shia-Sunni Divide in the United Provinces', *The Indian Economic and Social History Review*, Vol. 27, No. 2, Apr.-June 1990.

28. Henry Cotton, *India and Home Memoirs*, London, 1911; Blunt, *India Under Ripon*, p. 94.

29. See the collection of essays in *Communal and Pan-Islamic Trends in Colonial India*, New Delhi, 1985.

30. Earl of Lytton, *Pundits and Elephants*, p. 172; 'Memoirs of O.M. Martin' (typescript), CSAS.

31. Hasan, *A Nationalist Conscience*, 1987, Chap. 6.

32. Mujeeb, *Indian Muslims*, pp. 10-20; and the collection of essays in Imtiaz Ahmad (ed.), *Caste and Social Stratification Among the Muslims*, New Delhi, 1984.

33. *Census of India*, 1931, United Provinces of Agra and Awadh, Vol. 1, Appendix E, p. 515.
34. See, for example, P.M. Currie, *The Shrine and Cult of Muin-al-din Chishti of Ajmer*, New Delhi, 1989.
35. Cracknell papers, CSAS.
36. Home (Political), B, File No. 109-14, April 1913, NAI.
37. Home (Political), A, File No. 1-4, Dec. 1913, NAI.
38. Home (Political), A, File No. 258-9, Oct. 1915, NAI.
39. R.S. Sharma, *Communal History and Rama's Ayodhya*, New Delhi, 1990. Asghar Ali Engineer (ed.), *Babri Masjid-Ramjanmabhoomi Controversy*, New Delhi, 1990.
40. The document was generally appreciated. 'All those', wrote a leading journalist, 'who have given up neither their belief in secularism nor the hope that Indians will one day stop killing one another should be grateful to Professors S. Gopal, Romila Thapar, Bipan Chandra and other historians of Jawaharlal Nehru University.' Praful Bidwai, 'Appeasing Hindu Bigotry', *Times of India*, 20 Nov. 1989. But there was adverse criticism as well, much of which, quite predictably, coming from the ideologues of the BJP and the RSS. The debate was conducted in the letters to the editor column of the *Times of India* (15, 21, 23 Dec. 1989), as well as in the *Indian Express*. Within the Centre for Historical Studies, Majid H. Siddiqi alone struck a discordant note with the view that 'it is not for historians to "prove" or "disprove" as right or wrong every instance of an assertion made by a political or cultural group as social winds blow this way or that'. Siddiqi, who did not sign the document, concluded with the exhortation: 'Historians must discard their personae as historians if they are to intervene in the dispute without at the same time endangering the very basis of their intellectual stand. They must exhibit intellectual self-confidence in their discipline and determine their own agenda in terms of their own questions and not allow the existence of communalism in this society . . . to force its agenda upon them.' 'Ramjanmabhoomi-Babri Masjid Dispute: The Question of History', *EPW*, 13 Jan. 1990.
41. *District Gazetteer of the United Provinces of Agra and Oudh, Fyzabad*, Vol. XLIII, Allahabad, 1905, pp. 173-4.
42. Peter van der Veer, 'God must be Liberated! A Hindu Liberation Movement in Ayodhya', *MAS*, Vol. 21, No. 2, 1987, p. 287.
43. For their importance in Ayodhya, see Peter van der Veer, 'The Concept of the Ideal Brahmin as an Ideological Construct', Günther-D. Sontheimer and Hermann Kulke (eds.), *Hinduism Reconsidered*, New Delhi, 1989, pp. 71-7.
44. Peter van der Veer, 'God must be Liberated', p. 288.
45. Ibid.
46. Fisher, *A Clash of Two Cultures*, pp. 228-36; Cole, *Roots of North Indian Shiism*, pp. 244-9.
47. S.K. Tripati, 'One Hundred Years of Litigation', in Engineer (ed.), op. cit., pp. 15-27.

48. Kuldip Kumar, 'Ayodhya Ready for Compromise', ibid., p. 106. Likewise, several neighbouring areas, such as Akbarpur in Sultanpur district, remained undisturbed. Suneet Chopra, 'Akbarpur: An Island of Communal Unity', *Times of India*, 3 Nov. 1989.

49. Robinson, *Separatism Among Muslims*, p. 64.

50. Harold A. Gould, *Politics and Caste*, Vol. 3, New Delhi, 1990, p. 49.

51. Ibid., pp. 48-9.

52. Ibid., pp. 76-7.

53. See Zoya Hasan, 'Minority Identity, Muslim Women Bill Campaign and the Political Process', *EPW*, 7 Jan. 1989.

54. Mushirul Hasan, 'Indian Muslims Since Independence: In Search of Integration and Identity', *Third World Quarterly*, London, Vol. 10, No. 2, Apr. 1988.

55. Arun Nehru quoted in A.G. Noorani, 'The Babri Masjid-Ramjanamabhoomi Question', in Engineer (ed.), op. cit., p. 57.

56. *Times of India*, 28 Nov. 1989.

57. Harish Khare, 'Rise of the BJP: Reemergence of the Right', *Times of India*, 6 Dec. 1989. Notice that in Maharashtra the BJP-Shiv Sena won fourteen seats and emerged as the only credible opposition to the Congress. *Sunday Observer*, 3 Dec. 1989.

58. 'Patient and sustained efforts of right thinking writers, researchers and educators can foil the communalist attempt to use the past as a wedge to divide the people into warring camps.' R.S. Sharma, 'Communal History and Rama's Ayodhya', op. cit., p. 32.

16

The Changing Position of the Muslims and the Political Future of Secularism in India, *c.* 1947-1986

> The scenes will return, like deranged ghosts, to haunt those of us who were at the graveside to witness the burial of a secular dream. The screams of exultation with each blow of a pickaxe, each thrust of a rod, each dome that came crashing down. If there were no implements, the frenzied hordes would have used their bare hands to the same effect, so powerful was the poison that coursed through their veins in those few hours of madness.
>
> AWASTHI, 1992: 15

> Something . . . basic took place at Ayodhya—a massive assault on the very foundations of Indian culture and civilization, its very identity, its *sanskriti*, the very tradition and inheritance that these *kar sevaks* and their political leaders thought they were upholding. . . . How India will survive this dual onslaught remains to be seen . . . I, for one, doubt if it can. Not the India we have known.
>
> KOTHARI, 1992: 26

> Hindutva, once an abstract article of faith of a handful of determined crusaders on the margins of political life, is on the verge of becoming the new *mantra* of civil society . . . [The] impossible has almost happened and that Hindutva has succeeded in linking the past, present and future, and the individual, family, community and nation into a powerful expression for change.
>
> DASGUPTA, 1993: 8

What lies behind the Ayodhya catastrophe? Does it mark the end of India's tryst with destiny; a snapping of ties with its secular past? Will the votaries of *Hindutva* rewrite the nation's agenda, foist a Hindu *rashtra*, and reduce religious minorities to the status of second-class citizens? If

so, what is in store for the secular and democratic forces which are already
in a state of disarray?

What accounts for the politics of *Hindutva* and its extraordinary appeal in the Hindi heartland? Explanations are sought in the weakening of
secular forces, and the Congress turning away from its own 'unique institutional and ideological enterprise'. Some writers question the wisdom of
the enterprise itself, palpably based on mistaken assumptions and on a
distorted Western-orientated version of secularism. There is, furthermore,
talk of a 'Hindu backlash' in reaction to 'Muslim appeasement', the political nurturing of the minority vote-bank, and the dogged refusal of Muslims to join the 'national mainstream'. Finally, the *Hindutva* movement,
spearheaded by the BJP, is seen as an expression of cultural nationalism
and Hindu awakening, hitherto stifled by 'pseudo-secularists' and by the
politics of minorityism. These formulations are no longer of academic
interest alone. They have acquired new meaning and relevance, especially
to those who have a stake in preserving India's democratic and secular
fabric.

The votaries of *Hindutva* are, moreover, haunted by the presence of a
ramshackle coalition of Muslim bodies acting as conscience-keepers and
guardians of the community, and by the fact that Muslims possess a strong
impulse to act as a separate, monolithic entity and advance their interests
through religious networks and their representatives in parliament and
state legislatures. I have tried to examine these propositions in relation to
the political trajectory plotted by influential Muslim groups in the first
decade after Independence, the nature of their interaction with the community and the nation, and their responses to the evolution of democracy
and secularism. This is followed by a discussion of how Nehru's endeavour to lend a secular thrust to government policies was thwarted
by his own party's ambivalence towards the very conception of civil
society based on secularism. It is necessary to understand the nature
of this ambivalence owing to its implication for the general communal
situation and for the Congress party's own long-standing commitment
to secularism.

The Future of Secularism

For well over a decade now, social scientists and political commentators
have introduced a discordant note in the discourse on secularism, equating
secularism with either Western liberalism or minority appeasement. It
is often argued that the Western concept of state and civil society is

intrinsically out of place in India where primordial loyalties, reinforced by the colonial experience of well over two centuries and the bitter legacy bequeathed by Partition in August 1947, exercise a pervasive influence in the public and private domain, and where religion is not just recognized as a mediating force in political and social affairs but legitimized through private and state intervention. That is why the secularizing forces, which conventional wisdom associates with literacy, urban growth, and industrial expansion, are said to have only touched the fringes of urban life.

Thus, Ashis Nandy (1990a: 69) challenges 'the hegemonic language of secularism popularized by the westernized intellectuals and middle classes exposed to the globally dominant language of the nation-state'. As an avowed 'anti-secularist', he believes that both the ideology and politics of secularism 'have more or less exhausted their possibilities and . . . we may now have to work a different conceptual frame which is already vaguely visible at the borders of Indian political culture' (Nandy 1990a: 73).

He has also written that 'modern India has a lot to answer for. So have the cosmopolitan intellectuals in this part of the world. They have failed to be respectful to the traditions of tolerance in Indian society. These traditions may have become creaky but so is, it is now pretty dear, the ideology of secularism itself' (Nandy 1990a: 85). In such writings, secularism tends to be dismissed as an import from the West grafted on a traditional society. It is written-off because of its limited appeal among the Western-educated élite. If one were to follow this intrinsically flawed logic, should India repudiate nationalism, parliamentary democracy, and free speech? The central issue is not the Western provenance of an idea but its place and relevance in a plural society.

The essence of the secular idea, flowing from the historical experiences of Western societies in the era following the French revolution, lies in drawing a sharp distinction between the symbols of a modern state and the Church, and of keeping the public domain free from religious interference. The inspiration behind this exercise, as also the impulse for creating a secular polity, rested on a refined conception of civil society, on restructuring community relations without reference to scriptures or religious texts, and on developing a scientific temper without being encumbered by the weight of scholasticism and religious traditionalism. In this schema, religious tolerance and religious neutrality undoubtedly occupied a central place, but many more inputs were required to lend meaning and weight to secularism.

It is possible to trace the roots of the 'secular' idea to the ancient Hindu and Buddhist texts, the Bhakti movement, and the religio-cultural syncretism evolved by Akbar, the sixteenth-century ruler, and Dara Shikoh, the Mughal prince. Still, it is perhaps inappropriate to equate those undifferentiated and undefined ideas and trends with the modern concept of secularism. *Sarva dharma sambhava* is a laudable notion, as it probably encapsulates the trajectory plotted by the state and society in pre-colonial India. At the same time, while *sarva dharma sambhava* forcefully conveys the spirit of religious tolerance, it does not imply a disjunction between the state and religion. Rooted in religion and spirituality and sustained by the ecumenical traditions of Hinduism, *sarva dharma sambhava* exuded the 'low-born', the *mlechhas* or those who were outside the *varna* system.

The chief ideologues of the nationalist movement generally refrained from adopting *sarva dharma sambhava* as their motto. Most of them, seeking refuge in the Western variant of secular nationalism, designed their mobilization campaigns accordingly. After Independence, too, India adopted, by and large, the Western model of secularism. It gave itself a secular constitution, one based on a broad national consensus.

The architects of the secular constitution were not always drawn from a particular intellectual ethos, designated as 'Western' in the recent trendy social science literature, but came from mixed and diverse traditions. Some were rooted in the soil, so to speak, and had powerful 'indigenous' cultural moorings. Aware of traversing the path of secularism, they believed it to be the only viable and acceptable course open to them. They knew full well, notwithstanding their ideological predilections, that a secular state was the surest way of preserving national unity and containing centrifugal tendencies that threatened to undermine, in the aftermath of a bloody Partition, an already fractured social structure.

No wonder secularism, along with democratic socialism, occupied a central place in their discourse. It also constituted, at least in public pronouncements and party manifestos, a key item on their agenda. Invoking secular symbols and slogans drew the political support of the trade union movement and the growing urban intelligentsia. To be non-secular, on the other hand, carried a stigma. To adopt 'non-secular' postures was considered an act of political blasphemy, an unforgivable sin. These trends conveyed the impression that the nation as a whole surged ahead, despite the grumblings of certain political leaders, in its quest for a secular state and society, and that the relevance and utility of the secular experience had gained wide acceptence. It is in this light that the resolution passed by the All India Congress Committee in May 1964 acquires significance. It reiterated that secularism was a priceless heritage and constituted the foundation on which a progressive modern state could be built for the welfare of all.

There is, however, little doubt that the secular ideology has been in a state of steady decline since the demise of Nehru, and that its appeal has diminished even among the 'Westernized intellectuals and middle classes' who are supposed to have popularized the 'hegemonic language of secularism' (Hasan 1991). The prospects for secularism appear to be fairly dim in the light of the events that have jolted Indian society since the demolition of the mosque at Ayodhya. There are other disturbing signs as well—the passive role of the Congress in allowing the anti-secular forces to run amok and seize the initiative in the public domain, the deconstruction of the secular paradigm by overtly communal parties, and the legitimacy accorded to *sadhus*, *mahants* and *mullahs* in the course of feeble efforts to resolve the deadlock aver the Babri Masjid issue. These are indeed ominous signs. Still, it is hard to agree with Nandy's denial of a place for secularism on the nation's political agenda.

The broad survey attempted in this chapter points to certain tangible gains and identifies certain bright spots in the slow progress made by India in its march towards the goal of a secular polity and society. One should, of course, not be wary of working out alternative frameworks preferably rooted in 'indigenous' traditions and tied to the legacy of the nationalist movement. But, in the end, Indian society, the liberal intelligentsia included, will have to restore the democratic, secular consensus of the 1950s and 1960s, and subscribe to the *ideal* of a composite and plural society with secularism as is masthead.

In this scheme of things, Nehru's secular manifesto, an outcome and prized legacy of the anti-colonial struggle, needs to be reiterated. The reason for this lies not in any intrinsic merit secularism may possess, but rather in its role in outlining the contours of India's historical development and providing a *rational ground* for a reconciliation of diverse and conflicting sectarian and communitarian perceptions and goals. The manifesto may bear the imprint of ambiguity; it may well be tailored and trimmed to suit the rapidly changing realities of political life. Yet, the ideological underpinnings of the democratic, secular consensus envisaged by the architects of India's Constitution and so assiduously forged by the country's first prime minister, are as relevant today as they were during the 1950s and 1960s. There may be differences of opinion about the nature of the secular consensus, and on the most effective way of rooting out communalism. One would, however, like to believe that there would be no divergence of views on the imperative of carrying out the secular and democratic provisions of the Constitution itself.

The mainstream of Indian nationalism has a decidedly secular orientation. That is why, when the newly created state of Pakistan was fostering its Islamic image in 1947-8, India was engaged in reconstructing a democratic and secular polity amidst the brutal and bloody violence that accompanied Independence and Partition. After more than four decades of Independence, this secular experiment needs to be reviewed for its implications both for other plural societies endeavouring to tackle their ethnic, regional, and religious problems in Asia and Africa, and for India's Muslims who form the largest minority in the country. My analysis will not lose sight of the obvious fact that the differentiating features that characterize Indian society as a whole are also to be found within the Muslim community. At the same time, my concern is to uncover certain broad trends amongst Muslims, excluding regional, local, and class nuances from the analysis.

During the 1940s, Jinnah led a powerful movement to advance the interests of Muslims after the withdrawal of the colonial power from the subcontinent. But the final outcome of his campaign proved catastrophic to the more than 35 million Muslims who remained in India after Partition. Leading industrial families, trading groups, and practitioners of various professions shifted base to Pakistan in order to improve their fortunes, and left behind a socially fragmented and economically depressed Muslim community. UP and Bihar were the areas most affected by the riots, the exodus to Pakistan, and a considerable 'skimming off' from the professional classes; a process that continued until the early 1960s. As a result, there were hardly any Muslims left in the defence services, in the police force, in universities, law courts and in the vast central secretariat in Delhi (Parthasarathi 1987). Likewise, the urban artisan and entrepreneurial class east and south of Delhi was reduced by riot and migration (Qureshi 1970). In Delhi itself, the *karkhandars*, petty traders, and shopkeepers suffered heavily at the hands of refugees dispossessed of their homeland in west Punjab.

The dissolution of the princely states impoverished a large percentage, if not the majority, of the upper and middle classes. With sources of patronage rapidly disappearing, prospects of securing employment in places such as Rampur, Bhopal, and Hyderabad deteriorated. The abolition of the *zamindari* system reduced the rural influence of the former Muslim landlords even more than that of their Hindu counterparts, because of the smaller number of Muslim peasants in the north and the greater number of urban *rentiers* among the Muslim landlords (Brass 1974; Husain 1965). The smaller landlords, as in the case of the Kidwais in Bara Banki district, lost much of their land to the tenants who acquired legal rights over the land they cultivated. The great *taluqdari* estates of Awadh declined due to families being divided, one branch migrating and the other electing to stay. Such was the fate of the Mahmudabad estate, the second largest *taluqdari* in Awadh after Balrampur. The raja hurried to Pakistan, leaving behind his wife, son, brother, and his vast estates in Bara Banki, Sitapur, and Bahraich districts.

Finally, politics for Muslims as Muslims had no *raison d'être*. With the Muslim League dissolved in the north and its leadership located in Pakistan, the political trajectory of the Muslims had to be defined within the broad democratic and secular framework; a framework that had evolved through a painful and tortuous process and depended on the consensual model that the Congress was attempting to create in the aftermath of Independence and Partition.

Rhetoric of Communal Solidarity:
The Politics of the Jamaat

In 1957, W.C. Smith commented on an Indian Muslim community, battered by inward circumstances and gripped inwardly by dismay (Smith 1957). A decade later, Percival Spear tried to assess its 'inner life or soul in the New India' (Spear 1967). In recent years, scholars have defined the distinct ethos of Islam and pointed out how the ideal of the Islamic community shapes their apprehension of what is legitimate, desirable and satisfactory political action (Robinson 1985: 373).

These formulations rest on questionable assumptions. There is, for example, no justification for perpetuating an exclusive political and religious category, created by the raj in its various constitutional arrangements, or to *create* an 'Islamic community' with a self-image and unified self-perception, supposedly its alone. One is even wary of using the expression 'Indian Muslim community', though one does so in this chapter with an implied recognition of socio-economic differentiations, multiple ideological strands, and diverse cross-currents both in the realm of thought and action.

Given their divisions and diversities, Indian Muslims, in general, could neither harness their inner resources to evolve a common vision nor work as a collective group in pursuit of shared goals. After Independence, in particular, the options of exercising 'free will', as it were, diminished. *The*

Destiny of Indian Muslims, the title of Abid Husain's work (1965), had to be defined within established parameters and in relation to newly-created democratic structures. This involved a redefinition of the Islamic community in the Indian environment, a task attempted by Maulana Azad and Rafi Ahmad Kidwai in the political domain, and by Zakir Husain, Mohammad Mujeeb, K.M. Ashraf, Humayun Kabir, K.G. Saiyidain, and Abid Husain in the realm of ideas.

The Congress Muslims of Azad's generation remained wedded to the concept of composite nationalism and pleaded for greater Muslim participation in nation-building (Hasan 1987; 1992). They envisaged a new role for themselves, not as leaders of Muslims but as members of a new political elite. With the disappearance of separate electorates and reserved seats, they were no longer required to woo the Muslim voter. Indeed, with their enlarged constituency, they began to enjoy the trappings of power, oblivious of their vulnerability in a system in which communal considerations continued to mould political life.

The co-option of Congress Muslims in governmental structures restricted their ability to keep up their links with large segments of the Muslim people. This need not have been so. With their vast and rich experience of public life, they were ideally placed to lead the Muslims in a critical phase of transition and prevent their alienation. But they did not take advantage of the opportunity presented to them after Independence. Instead, they settled for a soft option. Having been integrated into the vast Congress party machinery and assured of Nehru's backing, they developed a vested interest in defending the status quo. They eschewed involvement in all issues which were seen to be specifically Muslim and were likely to leave them vulnerable to charges of promoting sectarian causes. In particular, during the first three general elections 'the nomination and election processes work[ed] to put into the legislatures Muslims who [were] inclined to be docile and not raise embarrassing issues too persistently, lest they either not "[got] the ticket" next election or [were] shifted to less safe constituencies' (Wright 1966: 110). Even someone of Azad's stature, though deeply aggrieved by the communal posture of some of his own colleagues, avoided the more public forms of protest.

While the Congress Muslims nursed their political wounds after Independence/Partition, the political initiative was wrested from them by the Jamiyat-i-ulama-i Hind and the Jamaat-i Islami. Though competing for political supremacy, their members had the same high stakes in making the most of the newly created social and political structures. They recognized the need to mould their political strategy and to restore their hold over their followers, which was slackened by the fragmentation of leadership and by deep ideological schisms.

The Jamiyat, founded in 1919 amid the khilafat enthusiasm, plotted a nationalist, anti-colonial course in alliance with the Congress. In the 1940s, the Jamiyat, under Husain Ahmad Madani's leadership, opposed Partition wholeheartedly and identified itself with the forces of composite nationalism. After Independence, the Jamiyat met in April 1948 to 'chalk out the path to be traversed by the community for reconstruction [and to march] shoulder to shoulder with members of other communities inhabiting the country' (Qasimi n.d.: 1).

Its leaders acclaimed the democratic and secular principles of the Constitution, interpreting it as a *muhaadih* (social contract), comparable to the concordat between the Prophet of Islam and the Jewish people in Medina (Qasim n.d.: 2-3).[1] The emphasis, as in the past, was on promoting fraternal links between the two estranged communities, on political cooperation with the Congress under Nehru's secular leadership, and rejection of all previous demands. The latter included separate electorates and reservation of seats, and raised the spectre of 'Muslim separatism'. The Jamiyat expressed the view that Indian Muslims 'should [also] realize that in a country like India it is only this brand of secularism which can provide safeguards for their culture and religious freedom and can give strength to their status as a religious minority. It is, therefore, in their own interest to support the secular ideal envisaged in the Constitution with sincerity and ardour' (Faruqi 1966: 144).

The political manifesto of the Jamiyat was set out by Husain Ahmad Madani in September 1951. Writing to a correspondent who was troubled by the events in the aftermath of Partition, Madani made the following characteristically candid observation:

My respected friend (*mere muhtaram*)! You [certainly] entertain laudable religious sentiments. But why do you forget where you are and under what circumstances? Would the problems that we are facing today have arisen if the country had not been partitioned? The Muslims would then constitute 37 per cent of the population of the Republic of India. As an influential minority, they would number 100 million. But today they number only 40 million and constitute only 9 or 10 per cent. It is precisely because of such things that the Jam'iyya opposed partition, but our voice was not heard. Communalist (*firma parast*) Hindus wholeheartedly wish that not even one Muslim remain in India and that they may do whatever they please. . . . As you have brought about the partition of the country, what is the reason for your anger? It is an act of generosity on the part of the Hindus that they establish secularism in the country. Failing this, the decisions and actions of the League and of yourself call for a situation in which the Hindus do in their area of majority whatever they wish without your being able to utter a word. Likewise, in Pakistan you can do whatever you please and nobody can say a word. If you plan to hold a convention and wish the Muslims to leave India if their demands are not conceded—then this is precisely what the Hindus want! And again, are you saying that these 40 million Muslims will migrate from here? Even if you and I and several thousands of people like us will leave—will all follow us? And even if they did—which country will provide them with a permanent home?

What was the migration movement which took place during the khilafat (in comparison with the migration that took place after partition)? What calamity descended upon the Muslims who left the UP, Bihar, East Punjab and other places after the partition of the country and in what calamity do they remain! Not hundreds, not a thousand or two thousand, but hundreds of thousands of Muslims can find no home. . . . As for Afghanistan and the Arab countries—what can they do and what sympathy do they feel towards you or towards the Indian Muslims? Please, look at the situation thoughtfully.

Provincial bigotry (*subajati ta'assub*) of the worst kind is being practised in Sind, Punjab and Bengal against the Muslims of UP, Bihar and other provinces. . . .

This is not *der al-islam*. It was partitioned by our own hands. You and I did it Our forefathers chose to live here in cities, towns and villages before Mahmud of Ghazna [*sic*] and Muhammad b. al-Qasim. To what extent is the situation of that time different from the present one? Yet our forefathers did not make observations such as 'we are one thousand or two thousand, one hundred thousand or two hundred thousand and the country is full of infidels. They are extremely hostile to us. God knows what will happen and when.' But today—looking forward makes you so restless!

When the Muslims became stronger and their armies entered India, at that time they were also a negligible minority. Today you number 40 million. Were the vicissitudes of time (*irqilabat-i-zamana*), which may happen at any time, not taken into consideration by those early Muslims? But today the Muslims fear from such vicissitudes. Were the polytheists at that time their friends, did they not entertain polytheistic sentiments (*mushrikana jadhabat*) or were the vicissitudes of time absent? Granted that they have acquired power, but who could ensure that it would continue? Still, they remained here, propagated Islam and converted millions of people. Today you lose courage and are prepared to leave the country.

My respected friend! When Madina became *dar al-islam* and the [Koranic] verses relating to jihad were revealed and the battles of Badr and Uhud took place—the *sura* of Al' Imran was revealed. At the end of this *sura* there is the following verse: 'Assuredly you will be tried in your property and in your persons and will hear much wrong from those who were given the Scripture before you and from the idolators. But if you persevere and fear God, then that is of the steadfast heart of things.' If at that time the [divine] commandment was to endure, then what import does it have today? To act with fortitude and endurance, perseverance and high-mindedness, to be assiduously engaged in strengthening Islam is our and your duty. . . . (quoted in Friedmann 1971: 177-80)

In general, thus, the Jamiyat acted within a broadly secular framework. Its leaders were closely allied with the Congress which, in turn, helped them to secure seats in parliament and in state assemblies. Prominent amongst them were Maulanas Asaf Madani, Ishaq Sambhali, and Hifzur Rahman. Theodore Wright has indicated that 10 of the 21 traditionally trained men were among the 20 legislators who claimed adherence to the Jamiyat al-ulama in their Who's Who entries (Wright 1964: 259).

The Jamaat-i Islami, on the other hand, was an organization with a difference. It surfaced in 1941, nearly two decades after the birth of the Jamiyat al-ulama, and was founded not by a traditional *akim* but a scholar-journalist. Saiyid Abul Ala Maududi was tutored in the nationalist traditions of the Jamiyat al-ulama before he embarked on a mission to create a righteous group which, in turn, would effect a political and social transformation on an Islamic pattern. Though initially opposed to the aspirations of the Muslim League, Maududi and his spirited band of followers migrated to Pakistan where they mounted a campaign for creating a truly Islamic state. Their argument was that as Pakistan had been fought for and won in the name of the Muslims and their Islamic aspirations, was it not the duty of the leadership to create a state and a society based upon Islamic ideology, following Islamic policies, and actively striving towards an Islamic ideal (Adams 1966: 376).

The Jamaat was barely in its infancy when it was overwhelmed by the trauma of Independence and Partition. Its leadership in India was depleted, the command structures fractured, and the ideological equilibrium, which Maududi had so zealously maintained, was disturbed.[2] Above all, the Jamaat faced the daunting task of reconciling its ideology with the democratic and secular order in India. India was no *Dar al-Islam*, an ideal close to the heart of the undivided Jamaat leadership; but it was neither a *Dar al-harb*. The constitutional provisions, though warily implemented, guaranteed certain basic, fundamental rights to the minorities which were denied to their counterparts in Pakistan.

The Jamaat's early history after 1947 is shrouded in mystery, though there is fragmentary evidence of a debate over democracy, nationalism, and secularism. Maududi regarded nationalism as a Western phenomenon resting on the false philosophy of Western civilization. For this reason, he attacked the ulama of the Jamiyat al-ulama for a nationalism that ran counter to Islam and also, in tactical terms, risked the socio-cultural absorption of Muslims into Hindu society.[3] In May 1947, he published his political manifesto which, in large measure, served as a guide to his devoted band of followers in the subcontinent.

We are opposed to the 'secular, national, democratic' system. On whichever country or nation this curse falls we will warn all God's creatures living therein to beware of it and avoid it scrupulously. As against those three principles we put forward another three principles, and appeal to the conscience of all men to observe and test for themselves ... (a) as against secularism is the principle of submission and obedience to God; (b) as opposed to nationalism is humanism; and (c) as against democracy or sovereignty of the masses is the sovereignty of God and the vice-regency [khilafat] of the people. (Maududi, n.d.: 25)[4]

The Jamaat has remained, despite its protestations to the contrary, a retrograde and reactionary force, deriving ideological sustenance and financial support from conservative and semi-feudal regimes in West Asia. It is opposed to social reform, enforces strict adherence (taqlid) to the tenets of Islam through their vast network of madaris and makatib, and has stalled Muslim participation in the democratic processes.[5] Though continuing to equate secularism with irreligiousness, the Jamaat leaders have, at the same time, pinned their hopes on the survival of a democratic and secular society. 'In contrast to other totalitarian and fascist modes of government', declared an official Jamaat publication, 'the ... secular democratic mode of government in India should endure' (Wright 1979: 86).[6]

Muslim Participation in India's Secular Democratic
Political Process: 1947-1962

The rhetoric of communal solidarity often obscures the fragmented character of Muslim political formations. Divided on ideological grounds, the Jamiyat al-ulama and the Jamaat-i Islami pursue separate goals and follow independent political trajectories. Though seemingly united on some issues, they have yet to find a meeting ground for common action. This is equally true of the Ittehad al-Muslimeen and the Tamir-i Millat in Hyderabad, and the Shia Political Conference and the Muslim Majlis in Lucknow. The supposedly monolithic structure of the Muslim leadership and organization does not exist either at the national or the local level. This is not to deny the absence of community consciousness or of communal solidarity, but to emphasize that a separate communitarian consciousness was not always translated into any tangible political reality.

The All India Muslim Convention (AIMC), held at Aligarh in October 1953, was ineffective. Likewise, the initiative taken in 1964, leading to the formation of the Majlis-i Mushawarat, petered out after much fanfare. The Majlis, stigmatized as a sinister, incipient revival of the old Muslim League, legitimized Hindu communalism in UP and pushed more votes towards candidates who appealed to Hindu sentiments (Hasan 1988: 824-5).

The message was loud and clear. Political mobilization along communitarian lines carried serious risks, because it hardened communal attitudes among majority segments and deepened insecurity amongst the minorities. The alternative, then, was not to function as a separate political entity but to take advantage of the diverse political formations. In fact, the tendency to assume national party identifications and to lend electoral support to secular-orientated parties pointed to the effectiveness of the democratic forces among large segments of the Muslim population.

Rising Tide of Communalism in India: 1967-1980

Only 15 years after Independence, the communal forces, long kept under check by Nehru's leadership, surged forward, causing serious stress to India's secular fabric. The Jamaat-i Islami and the Ittehad al-Muslimeen gained legitimacy from the wave of communal violence sweeping through much of north India. Spearheaded by the cadre-based RSS and its political wing, the Jana Sangh, Hindu communalism, with its repudiation of secularism and the Congress 'appeasement' of Muslims under the camouflage of secularism, gained considerable support; a fact reflected in the electoral advances made by the Jana Sangh during the period 1952-67 (Baxter 1968).

In the 1962 general election, the party more than doubled its strength in parliament and in the state assemblies. In the general election, the Jana Sangh's share of the total vote was double that in 1952 for the Lok Sabha and nearly 150 per cent for the various state assemblies. In UP and Madhya Pradesh, the Jana Sangh became the second largest party—with 49 seats to the Congress party's 248 in the UP state legislative assembly; and 41 seats to the Congress party's 142 in the Madhya Pradesh state legislative assembly (Smith 1963: 474-5). This upward trend continued, especially in UP where the party polled 21.53 per cent of the total votes and gained 98 seats at the fourth general election (1967). The *Hindustan Times* (12 March 1962) regarded the extension of Jana Sangh's influence to the rural areas as 'the most significant development of this election in Uttar Pradesh'.

Another indication of the rising tide of communal forces was the steady rise in the incidence of Hindu-Muslim rioting. During the 1950s, the number of violent communal disorders fell steadily, reaching a low of 26 in 1960.

The number rose to 92 in 1961; the worst year was when the disappearance of a religious relic from the Hazratbal mosque in Srinagar on 26 December 1963 triggered off extensive riots. There were, moreover, the notorious January (1964) riots in Calcutta which spread to 215 villages around the metropolis, where, according to one estimate, 1,500 Muslims were killed. The worst rioting took place at TELCO—the locomotive and truck factory operated by Tatas in cooperation with Mercedes-Benz. In Rourkela, about 5,000 Muslims were killed (Zinkin 1971).

During the period 1965-7, 515 outbursts of violence were recorded (Brass 1974: 219) in which Muslims suffered at the hands of rampaging communal mobs, headed all too often by RSS volunteers. Nehru declared that, from his own inquiries, it appeared that local Congress leaders had made no attempt whatsoever to calm the communal frenzy which seized Jabalpur and other cities and towns of Madhya Pradesh during the riots of February 1961.[7] They simply sat in their houses like '*purdah* ladies' as the situation deteriorated (*Hindustan Times*, 24 April 1961). The pattern was no different in the communal catastrophe at Ahmedabad in September 1969. Over a thousand people, mostly Muslims, lost their lives.

The communal upsurge during the decade of the 1960s represented a sharpening of existing caste, class, and community cleavages, reflecting the limitations of the secularization process which had been boldly initiated through democratic processes, progressive social legislation, rapid industrialization, and a massive adult literacy campaign. These cleavages were kept under some control during the anti-colonial struggle, but not after Independence. The Congress was no longer at the head of a movement: it was turned overnight into a political party whose principal aim was to exercise control and dominance over the levers of power and authority. Devising electoral strategies became its prime concern, whilst populist slogans, radical rhetoric, and diffused socio-economic policies were its answers to growing caste/class tensions and increased communal animosities. 'The image of Indian unity', warned the *Economic and Political Weekly*, 'cannot be built merely of eye-catching laces and frills: it must also have the supporting "stays" of harder material.'

The Congress was singularly lacking in ideological coherence, as signified by the presence of communal and revivalist elements entrenched in the states and districts, and their uneasy relationship with Nehru who was committed to the destruction of communalism and the establishment of a secular state and society. It surged ahead without isolating such elements,[8] without developing any formal or informal structures to effect social transformation, and without evolving instruments to widen the social basis of secularism and thus assuage the fears of the minorities whilst satisfying the rising aspirations of various social groups. Nehru was no doubt aware of these limitations, but he also prevaricated on vital issues. He either took or failed to take certain steps which contradicted his promotion of secularism.

An easy solution to the communal impasse was to woo sectional and parochial interests and to make occasional friendly gestures towards the minorities, even if it meant heightening their community consciousness. In his keenness to win Muslim confidence, Nehru allowed Muslims a voice in the debate about the provision of equality before the law to all Indian women and the promulgation of a common civil code, thus damaging the prospects of progressive legislation in either of these spheres. He stated in 1954 that he thought a unified civil code was inevitable, but that the time was not ripe to push it through in India. Again, he failed to press his own initiative for the banning of communal parties. The banning of cow-slaughter was also a matter on which Nehru failed to act according to his convictions. Legislation imposing a total ban on cow-slaughter was enacted in UP, Bihar, Madhya Pradesh, and Rajasthan. All these states were ruled by the Congress.

In dealing with communalism, Nehru himself was not proud of his government's record. Rajendra Prasad, his lifelong political comrade and the Indian Republic's first president, was swayed by Hindu reactionary opinion. So were some of his own ministers and chief ministers. Yet, Nehru did little to curb or counteract their influence. He expressed pious sentiments, but his pronouncements were not backed by any administrative action or an ideological cleansing of the party he led with such authority. Many of his ideas and plans could not be translated into practice partly because of his preoccupation with other domestic and international affairs and partly because they were 'hacked into mincemeat' by the hatchet men in the Congress (Tyabji 1971).

In relation to Urdu, Nehru betrayed a marked tendency to compromise with his ideological adversaries. The cause of Urdu was no doubt dear to him and he was much distressed by the hostility of Hindu chauvinists towards a language which, in his view, symbolized the rich and composite traditions of the Indo-Gangetic belt. Yet, he hesitated when it came to implementing electoral promises and constitutional guarantees. It was during his first term as prime minister, when his detractors were few and his position unassailable, that Pant and Sampurnanand launched their assault on Urdu.

Urdu lost its place in UP in 1951, when Hindi was declared the sole official language of the state. Acharya Kripalani performed the final rites in 1961 with his anti-Urdu, anti-minorities, and anti-Muslim report. Nehru remained silent. Sensitive to the communally vitiated atmosphere, he was wary of pressing the case of Urdu and taking the lead in delinking the question of Urdu from communal controversies. He repeatedly said that Urdu was not the language of Muslims alone but was also spoken by Hindus and Sikhs. Yet, he did precious little to promote this idea among the rank and file of his own party (Parthasarathi 1987: 379).[9]

Consider the anti-Urdu campaigns spearheaded by the Hindi Sahitya Sammelan before and after Independence. Its leaders were instinctively hostile to any trace of Muslim/Islamic inheritance, and hence Hindustani, which they saw as a mask for Urdu, was anathema to them. They depicted Urdu as a Muslim language, which it was not, identified it with the Pakistan movement and claimed that its style was distinctly 'unnational', if not anti-national. The position of Hindi was assured after the Constituent Assembly declared it as the national language, Urdu was not its rival. Yet, active and aggressive campaigns were mounted to suppress the language of Mir and Ghalib, spoken by millions of people of all religious creeds and a vital and graceful aspect of a vibrant composite tradition in the Indo-Gangetic belt.

Not much has changed over the last five decades. The establishment-oriented Urdu speakers boast of numerous Urdu academies and translation bureaus, housed in elegant buildings with plenty of funds to dole out to friends and admirers. Some take pride in Urdu being the language of Bollywood; others draw satisfation from awards and scholarships given to literary figures in the glittering halls of the Raj Bhawans and the Rashtrapati Bhawan. Some derive comfort from the mere fact that *mushairas*, where sections of the audience pronounce Ghalib as Galib and applaud poor quality romantic 'poetry', attract larger audiences than the *kavi sammelans*.

In reality, Urdu has been marginalized in the country as a whole. Even the democratic and secular forces have not shown much inclination to defend a language that symbolizes our composite heritage. In UP, the then chief minister, V.P. Singh, after failing to act on repeated promises, finally issued an ordinance in 1982 granting Urdu the status of a 'second language' (not second official language). His government did not convert the ordinance into legislation. Five years later, when the Vidhan Sabha adopted the Official Language (Amendment) Bill in 1989 amid unruly scenes, the BJP MLAs stormed into the well and raised slogans like 'Urdu Bill Murdabad' (Death to the Urdu Bill) and '*Ek Rajya, ek Bhasha, nahi chahiye dusri Bhasha'* (One state, one language, a second language not required).

Urdu survives lazily in the alleys and by-lanes of Muslim localities. It has lost its position in Osmania University, Hyderabad, Delhi's Jamia Millia, and the Aligarh Muslim University. An Urdu university languishes in Aligarh; another one is in the making at Hyderabad. Except for some districts in UP and Bihar, Urdu has ceased to be the language of administration, the judiciary and the police. Even symbolic attempts to promote Urdu have led to a violent backlash. Thus, riots were triggered off when the UP government made Urdu the state's second official language in 1989. Ten-minute Urdu television news bulletin in Bangalore led to riots in October 1994, leaving 30 dead.

Urdu poetry? How can there be Urdu poetry when there is no Urdu language left? It is dead, finished. The defeat of the Mughals by the British threw a noose over its head, and the defeat of the British by the Hindi-wallahs tightened it. So now you see its corpse lying here, waiting to be buried. This is not just the anguish of a living Urdu poet in Anita Desai's novel, but a summation of the grievance of Urdu-speakers all over the country. The story of a weak, gasping poet in *In Custody* is, indeed, the story of Urdu language and poetry.

Nehru's ambivalence is further reflected in his handling of the Kashmir problem, which has been historically linked with the communal question because of the 'third party', namely Pakistan. His understanding, to say the least, was distorted by misleading reports from dubious quarters in the Kashmir valley. That is why he committed the colossal blunder of dismissing Sheikh Abdullah and putting him in jail. The Sheikh was no ordinary politician; it was not for nothing that his people idolized him as 'Sher-i Kashmir'. He was a political giant, his place in history assured by the dogged tenacity with which he led the struggle for the political and social emancipation of his people, Kashmiri Pandits and Muslims alike. Who could have known these facts better than Nehru? Yet, he chose to stifle the voice of the people. It is not important who were the guilty men—Patel, Rafi Ahmad Kidwai, Bakshi Ghulam Mohammad, or D.P. Dhar. The ultimate responsibility for this political blunder rests with Nehru.

Erosion of Secular Democracy and
The Economic Decline of Muslims[10]

The last phase of Indira Gandhi's government witnessed an unprecedented intensification of religious fervour, an exacerbation of sectarian feuds, and an increased polarization of Indian society not along class lines, as Nehru had envisaged, but on purely communal grounds. Approximately 4,000 persons were killed in communal riots during the 1980s. This is almost four times the figure for the 1970s, which had witnessed a relative lull after the bloody rioting in Ahmedabad in 1969.[11] The number of districts affected by communal rioting increased from 61 in 1961 to 250 in 1986-7 (out of a total of just over 350 districts). From February 1986 to June 1987, nearly 60 'major' and 'minor' riots broke out in UP alone. Over 200 people were killed and 1,000 injured. Damage to property was estimated in the region of Rs. 15,00,00,000.

Equally significant was the growth of communal organizations with militant overtones. They numbered less than a dozen in 1951; by 1987 there were over 500, with an active membership running into several million. The newly formed Hindu militias were the *trishuldharis* of the Akhil Bharatiya Shiv Shakti Dal (ABSSD) which boasted 3,000 followers and 60 branches between Delhi and Saharanpur; the Hindu Manch (HM), activated after the highly publicized conversions to Islam of a few hundred Harijans in the Tamil Nadu village of Meenakshipuram in 1981, with a following of 20,000 among the lower middle classes; and the Shiv Sena (SS) with strong supporters among the Hindu migrants from Punjab. All these bodies, combined with the VHP and the Virat Hindu Sammelan (VHS) which are at the apex of several right wing organizations, have been vying with each other to emerge as the greatest champion of Hindu communal causes, and are now in the forefront of an aggressive campaign to 'liberate', along with the Babri Masjid, 450 other mosques in north India alone.

Thus the secular consensus, an imprimatur of the Nehru era, was all but discarded by the dominant Congress leadership, eager to accommodate revivalist and obscurantist tendencies in order to isolate and deflect the emergence of alternative political forces surfacing in various parts of the country. This was most certainly the perception of politically sensitive Muslim groups. What angered them most was the systematic neglect of their material interests and the steady decline of economic opportunities. The view that the economic weakness of the Muslims must be seen in the context of the society as a whole, where development is slow, wages are low, and unemployment is on the rise, carries no conviction with most Muslim activist groups who argue that opportunities for economic advancement are specifically blocked for their community which has borne the consequences of official neglect and discrimination.

The causes of the economic decline of the Muslims are debatable. But there is no doubt that they have occupied the lowest rung of the ladder in terms of the basic categories of socio-economic indicators of development (Faridi 1965). In modern industry and trade, except for isolated instances, they have not owned large-scale industry or business. Until 1985, there was not a single Muslim house among 50 industrial groups, whilst at the lower end of the scale most Muslims are poor and backward (Khan 1978). The position remains unchanged at the time of writing.

No benefit has accrued to the Muslims from various government schemes aimed at improving the conditions of disadvantaged sections of society. Of the houses allotted by state governments to lower and middle income groups, until 1985 only 2.86 per cent went to Muslims. Of the licences issued for fair price shops, only 6.9 per cent were awarded to them. Finally, Muslims received just 0.25 per cent of the tangible benefits extended to artisans by the Khadi and Village Industries Commission (KVIC).[12]

The cooperative sectors fared no better. Of the loans advanced by financial institutions, only 3 per cent of those between Rs. 50,000 and 1,00,000 went to Muslims. Of those between Rs. 1,00,000 and 2,00,000, less than 2 per cent was received by Muslims. Of loans between Rs. 2,00,000 and 10,00,000 the figure was under 1 per cent.

In the sphere of employment, Muslims complain that they have been reduced to the position of 'the hewers of wood and the drawers of water'. Muslims settle for discrimination as a convenient explanation, though much of the problem in UP and Bihar has arisen out of the depletion of the Muslim middle classes in the aftermath of Partition and the abolition of Urdu as a language of administration and education, the latter adversely affecting the very section of the middle classes that sought employment at the clerical level, in lower government service, or in educational institutions. Widespread abandonment of Urdu has also made it difficult for a great many Muslim candidates whose mother tongue is Urdu to take competitive examinations for government posts. This accounts for the fact that very few Muslims take the examinations at all; another reason, of course, is a constant fear of discrimination if they do.

The plight of the Muslims is compounded by the occurrence of 'major' communal riots in towns where they have attained a measure of economic success through their traditional artisanal and entrepreneurial skills.[13] Ashutosh Varshney has recently shown that Hindu-Muslim violence has been primarily an urban phenomenon, as also highly locally concentrated. In fact, his study reveals (Table 16.1) that eight cities account for a disproportionate share of communal violence from 1950 to 1995; nearly 46 per cent of all deaths. This is the lesson of Aligarh where Muslims own

Table 16.1: Hindu-Muslim Riots in 28 Indian Cities (1950-95)[a]

Minimum of 15 deaths in 3 riots over 2 five-year periods[b]	Minimum of 20 Deaths in 4 riots over 3 five-year periods[c]	Minimum of 25 deaths in 5 riots over 4 five-year periods[d]	Minimum of 50 deaths in 10 riots over 5 five-year periods[e]	Total deaths 1950-95
Bombay	Bombay	Bombay	Bombay	1,137
Ahmedabad	Ahmedabad	Ahmedabad	Ahmedabad	1,119
Hyderabad	Hyderabad	Hyderabad	Hyderabad	312
Meerut	Meerut	Meerut	Meerut	265
Aligarh	Aligarh	Aligarh	Aligarh	160
Jamshedpur	Jamshedpur	Jamshedpur		198
Bhiwandi	Bhiwandi			194
Surat				194
Moradabad	Moradabad			149
Vadodara	Vadodara	Vadodara	Vadodara	109
Bhopal	Bhopal	Bhopal		108
Delhi	Delhi	Delhi	Delhi	93
Kanpur	Kanpur	Kanpur		81
Calcutta	Calcutta	Calcutta	Calcutta	63
Jabalpur				59
Bangalore	Bangalore	Bangalore		56
Jalgaon	Jalgaon	Jalgaon		49
Sitamarhi				47
Indore	Indore	Indore		45
Varanasi	Varanasi	Varanasi		42
Allahabad	Allahabad	Allahabad		37
Nagpur	Nagpur	Nagpur		37
Jaipur	Jaipur			32
Aurangabad	Aurangabad	Aurangabad		30
Srinagar	Srinagar	Srinagar		30
Ranchi				29
Malegaon	Malegaon			23
Godhra				18

Source: Ashutosh Varshney, 'Ethnic Conflict and Civil Society', World Politics, 53, April 2001, 3, 362-89.

Notes: [a] Total number of deaths from riots for all of India, 1950-95 = 7,173, of which 3.57 per cent of deaths took place in rural India.

[b] Total number of deaths from riots in these cities = 4,706. This is approximately 66 per cent of deaths from riots throughout India and 69 per cent of all deaths in urban riots during these periods.

[c] Total number of deaths from riots in these cities = 4,359. This is about 61 per cent of deaths from riots throughout India and 64 per cent of all deaths in urban riots during these periods.

[d] Total number of deaths from riots in these cities = 3,887. This is about 54 per cent of deaths from riots throughout India and 58 per cent of all deaths in urban riots during these periods.

[e] Total number of deaths from riots in these cities = 3,263. This is 45.5 per cent of deaths from riots throughout India and 49 per cent of all deaths in urban riots during these periods.

lock manufacturing industries and have recently moved into producing building materials; Varanasi, where Muslim weavers established their hold over the silk saree trade and tried to obtain ownership of the industry itself; Moradabad, where the industrial apparatus was reorientated into producing decorative brassware for export to rich Arab countries; Bhiwandi in Maharashtra, where Muslims gradually bought up small-scale textile units; Meerut in western Uttar Pradesh, where Muslim weavers became entrepreneurial and have done well in iron foundries, furniture manufacture, scissors-making, and lathe operations; and in the walled city of Delhi, where the traditional Hindu mercantile community resents Muslim intrusion into its commercial enclave. 'Hindus tend to raise their eyebrows at the assertion of an equal status by a community which they have been used to looking down upon as their inferiors in the post-Independence era', concludes a report on the Delhi riots of May 1987 (PUDR 1987: 2).

This 'economic resurgence' is often ascribed to Islamic fundamentalism and to a new sense of confidence among Muslims, now that their co-religionists in the Gulf have acquired wealth and considerable global influence. The connection is at best tenuous, though the Hindu petty bourgeoisie has not hesitated to use this argument to whip up communal sentiments. The motive is to displace the emerging Muslim entrepreneurial class in certain crucial areas of trade and business, and to reduce the possibility of keen competition. This was attempted in Moradabad and Meerut where Muslims witnessed the destruction of their hard-earned capital, invested in small factories.[14] A similar pattern can be seen in Ahmedabad and Bhiwandi (Engineer 1984), important centres of textile manufacturing. Yet, the more bizarre theories in circulation include the suggestion that riots at these centres were fuelled by petro-dollars funnelled through various Muslim organizations.

Communal riots, though by no means uncommon when Nehru was prime minister, were sporadic, localized, and easily controllable. Not so afterwards. Since the communal outburst in Ahmedabad (September 1969), riots have tended to be bloodier and more prolonged, with areas like Aligarh, Ahmedabad, Vadodara, Moradabad, and Meerut in a state of near perpetual tension.

The apathy, negligence, and complicity of local officials has also grown over the years; wherever public authority is compliant to anti-Muslim forces, the administration has offered weak or inadequate protection to the Muslims. This was a crucial variable in Ahmedabad, where the Congress administration delayed a crackdown on rioters for several days. It was the same a decade later in the steel township of Jamshedpur. In UP, on the other hand, the police and the PAC have often acted as if they were a force expressly organized to beat, loot, and kill Muslims (as for example, in Moradabad, and Malliana, a township dose to Meerut city). 'The massacre of Malliana [conducted by the PAC]', wrote an angry journalist, 'will go down in the history of this once-proud city as an unimaginable instance of sadism and brutality'. Amnesty International indicted the PAC for its brutalities in Malliana and in the Hashimpura area of Meerut.

Congress-Muslim Relations and Muslim Interests

The articulation of minority interests is often constrained, even in a democracy, as is illustrated by the case of India's Muslims whose identification with the Muslim League movement in the pre-Independence period has inhibited them from voicing their grievances in a sustained and organized manner. The formation of the All India Muslim Convention (AIMC) and the Majlis-i Mushawarat were bold initiatives, but the strategy of working through the electoral process backfired. The bitter controversy over Urdu, faced by the non-Congress governmental coalitions in Uttar Pradesh and Bihar after 1967, reinforced the proposition that parties identified with minority causes risked alienating their own constituents. Indira Gandhi was quick to learn this lesson when she spoke of a 'Hindu backlash' against any further 'pampering' of the minorities.

Though parliament and the state legislatures have remained important fora, the part played by Muslim legislators has not been seen in a favourable light by most Muslims. Muslim legislators, though often elected from Muslim-populated constituencies and sponsored as minority representatives, have eschewed the more public forms of protest and rebuffed petitions for help on minority causes. As a result, sponsored mobility has improved the political fortunes of a few chosen legislators without advancing the interests of their constituents. Hence, when scholars or publicists prepare impressive lists of the Muslim candidates elected over a number of years, they may contribute to group pride, but they signify not more than a pyrrhic victory (Schermerhorn 1978: 177-8).

Some formal and informal channels of articulation existed because of Nehru's close links with certain sections of the Muslim leadership, especially in the Jamiyat al-ulama, his long-standing association with Muslim nationalists, and his personal commitment to providing equal opportunities to the minorities and ending discrimination against them. Sensitive to the demands of the minorities, he pressed his colleagues to offer adequate representation to Muslims in the armed forces and civil services (*Statesman* 12 May 1958), instructed chief ministers, to submit quarterly reports of official recruitment (Gopal 1979: 206), advocated justice for the Urdu language, and warned that communalism, especially of the majority, was the greatest of all the dangers facing India. He was unsparing in criticizing senior party members who were unfriendly towards Muslims, pulled up Charan Singh for his reported remarks against Muslims, expressed unhappiness over the anti-Muslim bias of Pant, UP's chief minister (who subsequently became home minister of India), and was disappointed that Vallabhbhai Patel, India's first home minister, had lapsed into his old attitude of suspecting the loyalty of Muslims in India. 'All of us', he wrote sadly, 'seem to be getting infested with the refugee mentality or, worse still, the RSS mentality. That is a curious finale to our careers.'[15]

Though Nehru's exhortations went unheeded and the grievances of the minorities remained unredressed, Muslims continued to maintain confidence in his leadership and recognized the Congress as the principal vehicle of their aspirations. The AIMC, revived in June 1961 by Maulana Hifzur Rahman of the Jamiyat al-ulama, acted within the Congress framework and appealed to Muslims to 'stand shoulder to shoulder with their non-Muslim brethren inside secular political and social organizations'. Pro-Congress sentiment was also strong within the Majlis-i Mushawarat. Under the influence of Saiyid Mahmud, Nehru's contemporary at Cambridge, the Bihar unit of the Majlis did not go along with Faridi's anti-Congressism and supported as many as 50 Congress candidates for the 1962 assembly elections (Brass 1974: 251).

After Nehru's death, Congress-Muslim relations strained, and the links that India's first prime minister had established with the minorities were either weakened or altogether severed. Having supported Indira Gandhi in her early years of political dominance, Muslims slowly but steadily drifted away from her to swell the ranks of, for example, the National Conference (JKNC) in Kashmir, the Lok Dal (LD) in UP and Bihar, and the parties constituting the Left Front government in Bengal. The internal Emergency (1975-7) and its accompanying excesses were the last straw. 'The incongruous coalition of traditionalists, secularists, and repentant former Muslim League modernists', who had supported the Congress in previous elections, was broken up by forced sterilization, *jhuggi* clearance, slum removal, police firing on Muslims, and the suspension of civil liberties, which included the banning of the Jamaat-i Islami (Wright 1977).

Indira Gandhi's efforts to win over the Muslims during the 1980 elections were only partially rewarded. In the two crucial states of UP and Bihar, the LD rather than the Congress emerged as a powerful political force. The LD won 12 out of the 23 Muslim constituencies in UP and secured 33.3 per cent of the Muslim vote as against 34.4 per cent gained by the Congress party. Even in Bihar, where the Congress did exceptionally well in Muslim constituencies, the LD did better (23.4 per cent) in the Muslim constituencies than in the state as a whole (16.6 per cent).

Weiner (1984) contests the popular view that Muslims voted for the Congress(I) party. His conclusion is that a substantial number of Muslims who had voted for other parties in 1977 voted for the Congress(I) in 1980, but in no greater proportion than other communities (and except for Bihar and West Bengal, possibly even less).

The Rise of Communal Forces among Muslims?

The gradual weakening of the Congress base amongst Muslims made it possible for the religious-orientated Muslim groups to occupy the political vacuum, while frequent riots and unending discriminatory practices against Muslims legitimized their activities. This is a familiar pattern. During the 1940s, the Muslim League success was, in some measure, linked to Muslim estrangement from the Congress after the Quit India movement of 1942. Capitalizing on the 'wrongs' done by the Congress during the period 1937-9, when it held office in eight provinces, the League persuaded Muslim splinter groups to join it. Nearly three decades later, Muslim organizations of different shades of opinion extended their base of support by dwelling on the Congress failure to stem the communal tide and assuage the fears of the minorities. The rise of the Ittehad-ul Muslimeen in Hyderabad, the political intervention of the Jamaat-i Islami in Kashmir, and the increased support enjoyed by the Muslim League in Kerala must be seen against this background. They remain, as always, the principal force behind Muslim conservatism and political reaction.

It is hard to delineate the principal contours of Muslim conservatism, though its basic aim has remained unchanged since the advent of British rule in India: the preservation of cultural and religious identity within the defined Islamic framework. Its more tangible manifestation has been the resistance to modern education, opposition to the composite and syncretic trends in Indian Islam, and the tendency to thwart reformist initiatives. Thus, Muslim organizations and institutions have led successful mobilization campaigns centering on these issues, and insulated the community from the process of social change and modernization so as to resist the secularizing tendencies generated during and after colonial rule. This phenomenon was unique to Indian Islam, for reformist ideas and movements have not been inconsequential in Muslim countries like Egypt, Turkey, and Iran.

Conservative reaction after Independence has been most pronounced in opposing the demand for a uniform civil code—an issue which unites the three principal organizations in India which are otherwise opposed to each other on fundamental doctrinal matters. These are:

1. Tablighi Jamaat, established by Maulana Muhammad Ilyas to unite all sections of the community and 'make them realize their common bond of religion';
2. Jamaat-i Islami, founded in 1941 by Saiyid Abul Ala Maududi to create a state and a society based upon Islamic ideology, following Islamic policies, and actively striving towards an Islamic ideal; and
3. Jamiyat al-ulama, born in the throes of the massive khilafat upsurge and dominated by the ulama connected with the Dar al-ulum at Deoband.

Though radical in its political orientation, the Jamiyat has regarded 'modernism' as the most dangerous heresy of the day, and its leaders have challenged it vigorously.

The Jamaat-i Islami, which takes the most militant position on the issue of change in the personal law, argues that even a ban on polygamy cannot be accepted, because Muslims are sure it will be only 'the first step in the direction of erasing every symbol of a separate Muslim culture in India' (quoted in Brass 1974: 220). The Jamiyat al-ulama agrees, arguing that any attempt to alter the personal law would be an infringement of the 'covenant' of composite nationalism which binds Muslims to India and its Hindu countrymen. This was echoed at a convention organized in December 1974, and is repeated at every annual session of the Jamiyat (Qasimi, n.d.). Following this convention, an All India Muslim Personal Law Board was set up as a watchdog body to monitor and actively resist any changes in the *Shariat*. Just over a decade later, the AIMPLB spearheaded a campaign which signified a massive fundamentalist upsurge, unprecedented in post-Independence India.

The immediate provocation for this was provided by a Supreme Court judgement (on 23 April 1985) which criticized Islamic law and Koranic concepts in granting maintenance rights to Shah Bano, a 69 year old Muslim woman divorced by her husband after 43 years of marriage.

Several Muslims groups considered this judgement as an assault on the *Shariat* which, in their opinion, makes no such provision in the event of a divorce, and as 'the thin end of the wedge for securing the extinction of the Muslim personal law and its substitution by a common civil code'.[16] They took to the streets to register their protest and accused the Supreme Court of sacrilegious trespass.

The Rajiv Gandhi government capitulated to the strident clamourings of some Muslims by introducing the retrograde Muslim Women (Protection of Rights on Divorce) Bill in May 1986. This was done to stem the rising tide of anger over the Shah Bano verdict which was losing the Congress party its Muslim votes. The electoral defeats of the Congress after the momentous Supreme Court judgement were sharp reminders of this. Assam, Bijnor, and Kishanganj,[17] Bolpur, Kendrapara, and Vadodara were all areas where the Muslim vote tipped the balance in favour of the opposition parties. With Assam, West Bengal, UP, Bihar, Jammu & Kashmir, and Kerala having a substantial Muslim population, the stakes were obviously far too high.

The 'victory' tasted over the Shah Bano issue encouraged Muslim reaction in several different ways. In early January 1987, Saiyid Shahabuddin, editor of *Muslim India* and a member of parliament, called upon Muslims to stay away from the Republic Day celebrations on 26 January. This was followed by a call for an all-India strike (*bandh*) on 1 February 1987, the first anniversary of the day when, by an order of the district magistrate, the gates of the Babri Masjid in Ayodhya were thrown open for Hindus to offer worship in the mosque's inner sanctum.

The same forces which had exerted pressure on Rajiv Gandhi to undo the 'wrong' done by the Supreme Court judgement in the Shah Bano case incited communal frenzy amongst Muslims. As a result, violence spread to several towns of UP and Bihar, culminating in a massive congregation of over 3,00,000 Muslims in Delhi demanding justice and an end to discrimination against their community. The centre stage was once more occupied by, among others, Saiyid Abdullah Bukhari, the mercurial imam of Delhi's Jama Masjid and the 'messiah' of the Muslim backlash during the tumultuous general election of 1977. Organizer of a Muslim militia, Adam Sena, the imam was also the moving spirit behind the widely publicized incident on the night of 14 April 1987, when thousands of Muslims forced their way into several of the protected national monuments in the capital under the charge of the Archaeological Survey of India, to offer prayers on the occasion of Shab-i Baraat, a Muslim festival observed only in the subcontinent.

Such stirrings in the Muslim communities, which are only remotely related to fundamentalist movements in the Islamic world, symbolize their alienation from the wider democratic and secular processes in the country. The Indian people must wake up to the dangers of allowing their alienation to grow. It may be that Nehru's secular model, battered and bruised by India's troubled history after Independence, is still the answer to India's present communal impasse.

NOTES

1. Qasimi rejected the Jamaat-i Islami's slogan of *Hukumat-i Ilahiya* as 'a baseless optimism with which the sentimental sections of Muslims were fooled'.
2. The Jamaat claimed in 1959 to have 183 local units and a membership of 1,318 ('Introducing the Jamaat-e-Islami Hind', quoted in Brass 1974: 241). It owned two papers. *Dawat* (in Urdu) and *Radiance* (though not officially) in English.
3. Such views were echoed in *India after Independence* (Siddiqi 1952; Hasan 1988: 821).
4. This is an oft-quoted extract from Maududi's speech. Research on the Jamaat-i Islami is wanting in many respects, though one can still turn to the researches of Adams, Binder, and Kalim Bahadur for background information. Their writings, however, fail to make full use of the vast corpus of Jamaat literature and provide limited insight into the organizational structures.
5. While giving the Jamaat a clean chit, Wright ignored the fact that ideology and policy positions are as important as 'behaviour', the theme of his paper. In any case, a content analysis of *Dawat*, the Jamaat's organ, is hardly a satisfactory way of arriving at a meaningful conclusion (Wright 1979: 84-5).
6. The Jamaat had categorically stated on several occasions that, under the circumstances prevailing in India, it wanted a secular form of government to continue. Some writers have suggested that the Jamaat's aim of attaining *Hukumat-i Ilahiya* was dropped in 1962 in favour of the 'establishment of deen' (religion). It is not clear why this was done and which individuals or groups were responsible for this significant shift.
7. The Communist Party of India shared this view, especially in relation to the disturbances in western UP in 1961 (*Hindustan Times*, 10 Oct. 1961).
8. Acharya J.B. Kripalani, a senior Congress leader, warned that the Congress authorities will not tolerate the presence in the party's ranks of people who neither believed in socialism nor in secular democracy.
9. For Hindi-Urdu controversy, see Brass (1974: 119-276).
10. The empirical information contained in this section is drawn from national newspapers and periodicals, and not specifically attributed item by item.
11. In May 1979, the minister of state for Home Affairs reported in the Lok Sabha a threefold rise in deaths due to riots since 1977, with UP heading the

casualty list from 10 in 1977 to 65 in 1978 (*Times of India*, 4 May 1979).

12. Only four units were owned by Muslim industrialists, in a group of 2,832 industrial houses owned by large corporate units, each with a minimum annual turnover of Rs. 5,00,00,000.

13. Some would argue that riots tend to occur in medium-sized towns with a relatively large entrepreneurial class competing with and challenging the monopoly of the Hindu trading and business class. This has led them to conclude that communalism is essentially a by-product of competition between rival segments of the petite bourgeoisie in medium-sized towns (Engineer 1983; Alam 1983).

14. It is worth noting that since the riot, Mo radabad has experienced a slump in its traditional trade in brass. Exports dropped from Rs. 720 million in 1980 to Rs. 300 million in 1985 (Chowdhury 1986).

15. This quotation is taken from one of Nehru's letters to Mohanlal Saxena, dated 10 Sept. 1949.

16. Maulana Saiyid Asad Madani delivered the presidential address at the session convened by the Jamiyat al-ulama (Bombay: 14-16 Jan. 1983). See also Nadwi (1969) for a discussion of the Jamiyat's opposition to change and reform.

17. Saiyid Shahabuddin, fighting purely on the strength of his fundamentalist posture, won this constituency by an impressive margin of 73,000 votes.

REFERENCES

Adams, C.J., 1966: 'The Ideology of Maulana Maududi', in D.E. Smith (ed.), *South Asian Politics and Religion*, Princeton, N.J., pp. 371-97.

Alam, J., 1983: 'Dialectics of Capitalist Transformation and National Crystallisation: The Past and Present of National Question in India', *EPW*, 18 (29 Jan.): 5, pp. PE 29-46.

Awasthi, D., 1992: 'Ayodhya December 6, 1992: A Nation's Shame', *India Today* (Special Issue) (31 Dec.), pp. 15-27.

Baxter, C., 1968: *The Jana Sangh: A Biography of an Indian Political Party*, Philadelphia.

Blair, H.W., 1979: *Voting, Caste, Community, Society Explorations in Aggregate Data Analysis in India and Bangladesh*, Delhi.

Brass, P.R., 1974: *Language, Religion and Politics in North India*, Cambridge.

————, 1985: *Caste, Faction and Party in Indian Politics*, New Delhi.

Chowdhury, N., 1986: 'Growing Assertiveness', *Statesman* (19 Apr.).

Das, V. (ed.), 1990: *Mirrors of Violence: Communities, Riots and Survivors in South Asia*, New Delhi.

Das Gupta, S., 1993: 'Right Angles', *Sunday* (28 Feb.-8 Mar.): 8, p. 89.

Engineer, A.A., 1983: 'Socio-economic Basis of Communalism', *Mainstream* 21 (16 Jul.): 45, pp. 15-18.

————, (ed.), 1984: *Communal Riots in Post-independence India*, Hyderabad.

Faridi, S.N., 1965: *Economic Welfare of Indian Muslims*, Agra.

Faruqi, Z.H., 1966: 'Indian Muslims and the Ideology of the Secular State', in Smith (ed.), 1966, pp. 138-49.

Friedmann, Y., 1971: 'The Attitude of the Jamiyyat-i ulama-i Hind to the Indian National Movement and the Establishment of Pakistan', *Asian and African Studies* 7 (Jerusalem): I, pp. 157-80.

Gopal, S., 1975, 1979, 1984: *Jawaharlal Nehru: A Biography* (in 3 vols.), London.

———, 1989: *Jawaharlal Nehru: A Biography* (Abridged Edition), New Delhi.

Gould, H.A., 1966: 'Religion and Politics in a UP Constituency', in Smith (ed.), pp. 51-73.

———, 1990: *Politics and Caste, Volume 3: The Hindu Caste System*, New Delhi.

Hasan, M. (ed.), 1985: *Communal and Pan-Islamic Trends in Colonial India*, New Delhi.

———, 1987: *A Nationalist Conscience: M.A. Ansari, the Congress and the Raj*, New Delhi.

———, 1988: 'In Search of Identity and Integration: Indian Muslims since Independence', *Third World Quarterly*, 10 (Apr.): 2, pp. 818-42.

———, 1991: 'Changing Orientation of the State and the Emergence of Majoritarianism in the 1980s', in Panikkar (ed.), 1991, pp. 142-52.

———, (ed.), 1992: *Islam and Indian Nationalism: Reflections on Abul Kalam Azad*, New Delhi.

Husain, S.A., 1965: The *Destiny of Indian Muslims*, New Delhi.

Khan, R., 1978: 'Minority Segments in Indian Polity: Muslim Situation and Plight of Urdu', *EPW*, 13 (2 Sept.): 35, pp. 1509-15.

Kogekar, S.V. and R.L. Park (eds.), 1956: *Reports on the Indian General Elections 1951-1952*, Bombay.

Kothari, R., 1992: 'Pluralism and Secularism: Lessons of Ayodhya', *EPW*, 27 (19-26 Dec.): 51-2, pp. 2695-8.

Krishna, G., 1967: 'Electoral Participation and Political Integration', *EPW*, 2 (Feb.): 3-5, pp. 179-90.

Madan, T.N., 1987: 'Secularism in its Place', *Journal of Asian Studies* 46 (Nov.): 4, pp. 747-60.

———, 1990: 'Religion in India', *Daedalus* 118 (Fall): 4, pp. 115-46.

Mason, P. (ed.), 1967: *India and Ceylon: Unity and Diversity*, London.

Maududi, A.A. (n.d.): *The Political Theory of Islam*, Pathankot.

Nadwi, Maulana Abul Hasan Ali, 1969: *Western Civilisation: Islam and Muslims* (transl. from Urdu: M.A. Kidwai), Lucknow.

Nandy, A., 1990: 'The Political Culture of the Indian State', *Daedalus* 118 (Fall): 4, pp. 1-26.

———, 1990a: 'The Politics of Secularism and the Recovery of Religious Tolerance', in Das (ed.), 1990, pp. 69-93.

Panikkar, K.N. (ed.), 1991: *Communalism in India: History Politics and Culture*, New Delhi.

Parthasarathi, G. (ed.), 1987: *Jawaharlal Nehru: Letters to Chief Ministers: 1947-1964*, Vol. 3, New Delhi.

People's Union For Democratic Rights (PUDR), 1987: *Walled City Riots: A Report on the Police and Communal Violence in Delhi, 19-24 May 1987*, New Delhi.

Philips, C.H. and M.D. Wainwright (eds.), 1970: *The Partition of India Policies and Perspectives, 1935-1947*, London.

Qasimi, M.A.H. (n.d.): *The Community in Retrospect*, New Delhi.

Qureshi, I.H., 1970: 'A Case Study of the Social Relations Between the Muslims and the Hindus, 1935-1947', in Philips and Wainwright (eds.), 1970, pp. 360-8.

Robinson, F., 1985: 'Islam and Muslim Separatism', in Hasan (ed.), 1985, pp. 344-81.

Schermerhorn, R.A., 1978: *Ethnic Plurality in India*, Tucson.

Siddiqi, M.M., 1952: *After Secularism, What?*, Rampur, Maktaba-i Jamaat-i Islami Hind.

Smith, D.E., 1953: *India as a Secular State*, Princeton, N.J.

——, (ed.), 1966: *South Asian Politics and Religion*, Princeton, N.J.

Smith, W.C., 1957: *Islam in Modern History*, Princeton, N.J.

Spear, P., 1967: 'The Position of the Muslims, Before and After Partition', in Mason (ed.), pp. 30-50.

Tyabji, B., 1971: *The Self in Secularism*, New Delhi.

Weiner, M., 1984: *India at the Polls 1980: A Study of the Parliamentary Elections*, New Delhi.

Varshney, A., 2001: 'Ethnic Conflict and Civil Society: India and Beyond', *World Politics* 53 (Apr.): 3, pp. 362-89.

Wright (Jr.), T.P., 1964: 'Muslim Legislators in India: Profile of a Minority Elite', *Journal of Asian Studies*, 23 (Feb.): 2, pp. 253-67.

——, 1966: 'The Effectiveness of Muslim Representation in India', in Smith (ed.), 1966, pp. 102-37.

——, 1977: 'Muslims and the 1977 Indian Elections: A Watershed?', *Asian Survey*, 17 (Dec.): 12, pp. 1207-20.

——, 1979: 'Inadvertent Modernisation of Indian Muslims by Revivalists', *Journal of the Institute of Muslim Minority Affairs* (Jeddah) 1 (Summer): 1, pp. 80-92.

Zinkin, T., 1971: *Challenges in India*, New York.

PART V

PART V

17

India and Pakistan: Why the Difference?

The irony of history is that the last battle of our war of independence in
1947 was not fought against the foreign rulers . . . but between the two
major religious communities living in the subcontinent. . . . In the river of
blood which flowed during the twilight days of the British Empire in India,
not a drop of foreign masters' blood could be discerned [*sic*]; it was purely
South Asian. The Britishers left with all their prestige and goodwill and
their colonial legacy intact.

RAO RASHID, *Snobs and Spices: The True Face of*
Pakistani Politics 1990-1996

An elemental force had burst its confines (on the stroke of midnight on
August 14, 1947) and swept like a flood across the land. Would it also wash
away the cobwebs, the inertia and deadness of centuries? Would it create
overnight a brave new country in which everything would be perfect?
Anything seemed possible. Next morning, the sun rose in the eastern sky to
reveal the same squalor, the staggering poverty and hunger, the deep
inequalities as the day before. Myriad of flowers, yellow and orange marigolds
and pink rose petals, lay scattered on the ground, stale, scentless, trampled.
The municipal sweepers came and swept away the street, and the blossoms
mingled in the dust.

KUSUM NAIR, *Blossoms in the Dust*

Three years ago the Human Development Centre in Islamabad described
South Asia as the 'poorest, the most illiterate, the most malnourished, the
least gender-sensitive—indeed, the most deprived region in the world'.[1]
India and Pakistan account for the bulk of South Asia's population. Arguably, these two countries, in varying degrees, fit into the paradigm of
soft states proportionate to their respective level of institutional slump,
governance crises, and domestic conflicts. Generally speaking, nation

states in recent decades have been weaker than ever before. Indeed, the old concept of omnipotent sovereignty is dwindling, and indeed, the ecology of statehood itself has been shifting—sovereignty is no longer The Holy Grail, and state power is migrating to a variety of non-state institutions.[2]

Let me begin with the judgement that Pakistan—with years of half baked or controlled democracy, followed by full-fledged military dictatorships—is less than a nation state on account of its failure to resolve issues of integration and identity.[3] Is this the Pakistan envisaged by Muhammad Ali Jinnah or dreamt of by a people who proclaimed their faith in a partition of their patrimony, asks the columnist Mazhar Ali Khan. 'How can we return to the ideals that inspired the fight for freedom and revive the principles and purposes that the Quaid bequeathed to us?'[4] The task is an awesome one: 'too much time has been lost, and too many resources squandered in the attempt to fashion a nation-state from the social milieu that makes up the country'.[5]

Some had expected that General Zia-ul-Haq, 'one of the three Bonapartes who cast their malign shadows across the national horizon after 1947', to be the last dictator.[6] But General Parvez Musharraf has dashed this hope to the ground.[7] A democratically elected prime minister, whose descent from power proved to be as precipitous and quick as his ascent had been two years earlier, languished in jail, before being exiled to Saudi Arabia. The parliament, where he enjoyed a two-thirds majority, is closed; the Constitution put in cold storage. The fragile nature of democracy is evident from the opposition parties and their followers welcoming the coup in the first flush of excitement. This is how it has always been since October 1958, when Ayub Khan took over as martial law administrator.

Ayesha Jalal, having questioned some of the certitudes about post-Independence states and societies in South Asia, reminds us that Pakistanis have the 'state' if not quite the 'nation' of their collective imaginings. She draws attention to the hollowness of civil society, the weakness of the institutions of the state, and the ideological contradictions in the self-projections and self-perceptions of the Pakistani state. Created on the strength of Muslim solidarity, Pakistan almost immediately gave birth to its own minorities, the Bengalis in East Pakistan (now Bangladesh), the *muhajirs* in Sind, the Baluchis and Pathans in the North West Frontier Province. Each of these collectivities defines its linguistic regions as its homeland. Regional and linguistic diversities have provided through much of Pakistan's turbulent history, the highest common denominator of the multifaceted grievances of the people, denied as most of them have been of democratic rights and of basic rights of citizenship. Declaring the Ahmadiyyas as a 'minority' in the 1970s created a precedent for exclusion, exposing the state's claim of inclusionary nationalism.

Exclusive nationalism, argues Ayesha Jalal, is no substitute for nationalism based on equal citizenship rights, the nation state's main claim to legitimacy. Pointing to the inherited colonial structures that were not realigned with the dominant conceptions that had fired the Muslim struggle for equality, solidarity and freedom, she underlines how, for example, Muhammad Iqbal's lofty equation of Islam and civil society has been lost sight of in the litany of confusion surrounding conceptions of national identity and state sovereignty. Incidentally, in the 1960s, the scholar Fazlur Rahman expressed the view that Iqbal's philosophical legacy had not been followed, partly because of what he had said but largely because he was both misunderstood and misused by his politics-mongering followers.[8]

What has contributed to Pakistan's woes is the absence of a social coalition of the three main segments—the underprivileged, the middle class and the élite. For this, the power élites—professional groups, merchant capitalists and the big landowners drawn mostly from Punjab and Sind—must share the blame. Though repeating *ad nauseam* the rhetoric of Muslim nationalism, they abandoned the Pakistani ship adrift in turbulent waters. They squandered the opportunity to reshape the country, to break the stranglehold of the civil-military oligarchy, and to create a multi-party system that would aggregate and synthesize the interests of many disparate groups. Zulfiqar Ali Bhutto, riding on the crest of an unprecedented popular wave, promised much in his 1970 election manifesto but delivered little. 'The Himalayas will weep, if I am harmed', a beleaguered Bhutto told his prosecutor in jail. But the mountains did not cry when Zia-ul-Haq, who ruled from 1977 to 1988, signed his death warrant.

Benazir Bhutto's legacy was a country torn apart by intense regional rivalries, sectarian animus, and ethnic strife in Karachi. Her successor, Nawaz Sharif, won a landslide victory in February 1997 and declared his intention to keep faith with the people.[9] But he turned out to be a reckless country politician with no sensitivity to the elementary principles of governance. Instead of breaking loose from the military-bureaucracy nexus, the chief cause of the previous crises, he subverted established political institutions. As was the case during the dark days of the Emergency in India (1975-7), the Big Brother arrived with his rabble-rousers, judges and executioners, ready to strike down any one who deviated from the legislated code of conduct. Instead of concentrating on economic discontent and a recession unprecedented in Pakistan's history, he chose to go nuclear. Washington responded angrily; Nawaz Sharif lost face with his people. Instead of diffusing widespread social unrest, he used the rhetoric of Islamization to buy peace. If he had read his country's history, he would have discovered the merit in what Iskander Mirza had said, 'We can't run wild on Islam; it is Pakistan first and last.'[10] He should have sensed, moreover, that Islam offers 'agency' to its adherents in the sense that the sociologist Anthony Giddens uses the terms—an individual's or groups capability to intervene, or to refrain from intervening, in a series of events so as to influence their course. But religio-political fundamentalism is different: so often in Pakistan, as indeed in the annals of public life elsewhere, it has devoured its own protagonists.

There are numerous prescriptions, starting with the long forgotten recommendations of the Munir commission (1953) to the bold journalistic and scholarly assertions in recent years.[11] Some scholars call for sustained debates on citizenship rights towards forging a collective ethos as a nation state, and a national dialogue to create the necessary consensus to begin rebuilding anew. Who is to initiate this dialogue is by no means clear. Besides, with the General having ruled out an early return to democracy (a referendum is being held at the time of finalizing this draft for publication) and the former prime minister in exile, it may not be easy to achieve such goals. The writer Feroz Ahmad pleads for rejecting 'legalistic shibboleths' and 'unsubstantiated hypotheses' in order to 'get down to the nitty gritty of how to materially transform this country into a voluntary association of equal, prosperous and happy peoples'.[12] While this concern is widely felt, the main issue is whether or not the current wave of ethnic and religious movements will be partially outgrown, partially domesticated, and partially mediated by the political process in the near future. 'Much may be lost,' comments a concerned Pakistani citizen, 'but the situation is not irretrievable.'[13]

Some of these concerns, if not all, are relevant to India as well. The rise of Hindu nationalism poses a major threat to pluralism and multiculturalism. Violence against religious minorities,[14] intolerance towards dissenters,[15] saffronization of education, exemplified in rewriting of history textbooks[16] and the appointment of the BJP-RSS ideologues to prestigious centres of learning,[17] and the review of the Constitution constitute a frightening trend. Reviewing certain aspects of the Constitution may not, after all, be such a bad thing, yet attempts to tinker with state structures, according to the noted columnist Harish Khare,

... would be tantamount to an assault from above on the legitimacy of the Indian state. Simply put, the Vajpayee regime does not have the credentials to review the Constitution because it lacks the legitimacy that accrues to a leadership either on account of participation in a nationalist struggle, or from an overwhelming popular acceptance, or from demonstrated outstanding performance and competence. After all, the efficacious exercise of any constitutional authority is to be negotiated through the democratic idiom. Only through a vigorous democratic engagement can we temper our constitutional arrangement against political expediencies. The clamour for a Constitution review is a subterfuge from non-democratic temptations; but this authoritarian project will also fail because it is intended to bypass the egalitarian assertiveness from below.[18]

Already, the new RSS chief K.S. Sudarshan has launched a diatribe against conversions and the 'Anglicization' of Indian society.[19] He favours a new code of conduct (*dharma*) based on Hindu philosophy and a 'Hindu way of development'. In an interview to the RSS mouthpiece *Organiser*, he described Bharat as a *Hindu rashtra*, based on *dharma*. Its identity, according to him, lies in one motherland, one *sanskriti* (culture), common ancestry and heritage. 'It is these three that constitute the national culture.' Pointing to 1989 as a milestone, he said that the situation had undergone a 'total metamorphosis'. While the Berlin wall was being dismantled brick by brick, Bharat was witnessing the *shilanyas* at Ramjanmabhumi, 'which in a sense was a symbol of the nation as an edifice'. The incident, stated Sudarshan, instilled a new-found self-confidence in Hindus, though some anti-*Hindutva* elements had ganged up in total disregard of 'this sublimation of society'. But, prophesied the RSS chief, 'it is going to be the last gasp of those haunted by the spectre of defeat. . . . There is yet another epic war between Hindus and anti-Hindus, a veritable *Mahabharat* in which sometimes Abhimanyu will fall, sometimes Ghatotkacha or it may be Jayadratha's turn yet another day.'[20]

II

Churchill [Winston] said that India wasn't a nation, just an 'abstraction'. John Kenneth Galbraith, more affectionately and more memorably, described it as 'functioning anarchy'. Both of them, in my view, underestimated the strength of the India-idea. It may be the most innovative national philosophy to have emerged in the postcolonial period. It deserves to be celebrated—because it is an idea that has enemies, within India as well as outside her frontiers, and to celebrate it is also to defend it against its foes.

SALMAN RUSHDIE, *Time*, 11 August 1997

Watching the Republic Day parade in 1955, India's first prime minister had a sense of fulfilment 'in the air and of confidence in our future destiny'. Two years later, Nehru told the chief ministers: 'If we look about to various countries which have recently attained freedom . . . India compares favourably with them, both in regard to our stability and the progress we have made in these last 10 years. The record is a creditable one, and this is increasingly recognized by other countries of the world.' Recent commentators echo the same optimism. According to an editorial comment,

At fifty, the crisis of the sovereign Republic of India cannot be purely biological. No mid-life crisis this, for fifty years in the life of a nation is an occasion to worry about the cellular stability of nationhood. And India this morning shows no signs of 'the state withering away'. Rather, the Republic is seemingly confident, not irredeemably subordinated to tradition, and it is not looking back with nostalgia. The popular will still continues to drive national destiny. No singular man's paranoia or fantasy has succeeded in repudiating that will. Democracy, with all its chaos and anarchy, has not only survived. It has thrived beyond the limits of an average Indian's expectation.[21]

Likewise, *The Hindustan Times* observed on Republic Day:

The first Republic Day of the Year 2000 sees India emerging in a far more confident frame of mind than in the recent past. Once again the country has recovered the mood of marching ahead with great elan as it did in the period immediately after Independence. The difference is that, this time, it is based less on hope and surmise than on a realistic assessment of what is possible. . . . India is poised to take a great leap forward as its economy is unshackled and the burden of a false ideology is abandoned. In the process, the country is also bound to emerge as a centre of stability—and modernity—in an area where military, communist, one-party and medieval fundamentalist regimes thrive, fostering indiscriminate terror, and vicious civil wars that drag on indefinitely. In contrast to its neighbours, India's normality stands out like a beacon.

If this were the whole story it would be hard to explain the mounting unrest in Kashmir and the north-east, the growing socio-economic inequities, the escalation of social tensions, and the violence against Dalits, minorities and women. More than 50 years after Independence, more than 40 per cent of the rural households are either landless or own less than 0.2 hectare of land. Less than 1 (0.8) per cent of the households own 14 per cent of the land.[22] There has been an increase in the number of people below the poverty line—from 305.87 million in 1987-8 to 314.66 million in 1993-4—an increase by an average of 1.76 million a year.[23] Poverty alleviation programmes are underfunded and insufficiently implemented; thus public food distribution has poor rural coverage. Funding for primary education, an aspect Amartya Sen has ever so often repeated,[24] declined from 56 per cent of all education expenditures in the First Five Year Plan (1951-6) to 29 per cent in the Seventh Five Year Plan (1985-90).[25] In short, traditional faultlines of social deprivation—based on class, caste and gender—continue to characterize patterns of social deprivation. A Constitution may indicate the direction in which we are to move, but the social structure will decide how far we are able to move and at what pace.[26]

No wonder, on the eve of the Golden Jubilee of the Republic, president K.R. Narayanan called for an 'honest self-analysis and self-questioning about where we, as a people and a society, are headed?' Drawing attention to the sullen resentment among the masses against their condition, often erupting in violence, he cautioned that these voices of resentment should not go unheard.

Violence in society has bared a hundred fangs as advertisement-driven consumerism is unleashing frustrations and tensions in our society. The unabashed, vulgar indulgence in conspicuous consumption by the nouveau riche has left the underclass seething in frustration. One half of our society guzzles aerated beverages while the other half has to make do with palmfuls of muddied water. Our three-way fast lane of liberalization, privatization and globalization must provide safe pedestrian crossings for the unempowered India also.

The president talked of the raw deal given to women—'our greatest national shame'—and the indifference towards Dalits. There were signs, he added, that the privileged classes were getting tired of the affirmative action provided by the Constitution.[27] On the eve of Independence Day on 14 August 2000, the president spoke yet again of the 'dark clouds of prejudice and callous unconcern' over the problem of rape and atrocities against women and suggested rewriting of laws to deter such crimes.

Few will deny the enormous gains of the last 50 years,[28] a point underscored by the president. Political power has moved downward. A democratic empowerment of the lower castes, the chief catalyst for what has been described as the second democratic upsurge, has made India's democracy more inclusive and participatory. Writing a decade ago, Paul Brass concluded that, despite the evident decay over time, the performance of India's political institutions compares favourably in many respects with those of its neighbours or with most other post-colonial societies. Indeed, the Indian political regime is one of the most democratic in the world by most conventional measures of political participation, electoral and party competition, and persistence of parliamentary institutions.[29]

These developments need to be located in the context of, though not always as a sequel to, the larger political processes at work. After all, scholars and generalists alike have commented on the decline of the Congress[30] and its decimation in UP, the most populous state,[31] the crisis of governability,[32] the unreconstructed bureaucracy,[33] the political decay,[34] and the many institutions associated with liberal democracy looking messy, worn out and frayed at the edges.[35] The failure to assure substantive democracy and equitable development for significant segments of civil society has resulted in the discrediting and delegitimization of state-sponsored nationalism.[36] Analysts have pointed out the changes taking place in the familiar world of modern politics after Nehru's death and the passing away of the leadership of the national movement.[37] Sometimes they bemoan the absence of strong political and social actors; on other occasions, they invoke the names of Gandhi, Jawaharlal Nehru, Vallabhbhai Patel, B.R. Ambedkar, Jinnah and Sheikh Mujibur Rahman to contrast their spirited role with the decline in public standards and the poor quality of leadership. 'Where are the heirs to the great political tradition bequeathed by them' (Jinnah, Maulana Azad, Abdul Ghaffar Khan and Mian Iftikhar-ud-Din), asks a leading Pakistani columnist. Lamenting that 'the mantle of leadership lies neglected, tattered and torn, frequently defiled by unworthy hands', he asks, 'who will pick up the banner, cleanse it to its pristine purity, and then raise it aloft so that the people can recognise it as the symbol of their redemption and follow it to bring the country to its salvation?'[38]

Analysts question the efficacy and the appropriateness of focusing on high politics, and yet they cannot deny that the electorate in South Asia continues to repose confidence in its leaders, many of whom have inherited the political and intellectual legacy of the anti-colonial struggles.[39] True, leaders have mostly failed to deliver; yet their followers pin their hopes on their ability to deliver.[40] This is not surprising. Compared to the Pakistani élite, the Indian élite, largely connected with the Congress movement, represented a much wider range of interests, and its social composition and political aims were far more heterogeneous than what the British or some historians dominated by the official mind have argued.[41] Undeniably, members of this élite jockeyed for positions in the colonial structures, captured important positions in the post-colonial state, jealously safeguarded their political interests, and made the most of the economic opportunities that came their way. At the same time, they developed over a period of time an agenda setting out national goals and aspirations and guided some of the more important social and political movements. Thus, the limited repertoire of the early Congress was enlarged in the aftermath of the Swadeshi agitation. With the Mahatma energizing the rural poor in places like Champaran and Kheda, the party gradually developed an organizational structure starting with village and taluqa units at the bottom and then, in ascending order, district, provincial and all-India committees, each elected by the lower units. The Rowlatt satyagraha (1919) and the khilafat and non-cooperation movements (1919-22) deepened Congress' support in urban and rural areas, and led to a partial radicalization of its politics. It was at Nagpur (December 1920), wrote the kisan leader Swami Sahajanand, 'that the Congress forsook the time-honoured procedure of begging for something . . . and instead took to the path of self-respect'.[42] Starting with its feeble demand for dominion status, the party began to clamour, as in 1921 and 1929, for complete independence (*purna swaraj*). 'When the resolution on full and complete Independence was passed,' noted Sahajanand, 'it seemed as though a new world had come into being.'[43] 'No one can describe the great enthusiasm which pervaded the Congress,' Sahajanand was to write, 'wave after wave of enthusiasm was visible.' As he listened to the Mahatma with rapt attention, he noticed that 'every word that came out of his mouth was like a thunderbolt against the government. It seemed that Shiva, the God of Destruction, was raging and that soon the great deluge would follow.'[44] 'Quit India', Gandhi's final cry in August 1942, laid to rest the lingering doubts over the timing of the British withdrawal from Delhi's viceregal lodge.

The estrangement of many Muslims and the disillusionment of the underclasses marred the ascendancy of the Congress. But the energy generated by some of its leaders had its glorious moments as well. In 1920, for instance, when Gandhi's personal charisma, rhetoric and mobilization strategies heightened countrywide excitement. Again, when the same frail man, aged 60 years, accompanied by his 78 followers, walked 241 miles from his Sabarmati Ashram to the shores of Dandi. This was nationalism, pure and simple, on the move. Rabindranath Tagore commented that the influence emanating from Gandhi's personality was ineffable, like music, like beauty. Its claim upon others was great because of its revelations of a spontaneous self-giving. Not only did the Mahatma awaken the villages to a sense of their power, but also his novel conception of motion, exemplified in the Dandi March, shot across the changeless horizon.[45] One of his British followers remarked that this march was 'the beginning of a revolution'.[46] It was not. Yet, the Dandi March set Indian nationalism on a new course. Nehru noticed the extraordinary enthusiasm of the people during a frenetic 130 days tour in 1937. As he moved about, 'often in remote parts of the country, addressing enormous audiences every-where . . . and probably covered over fifty thousand miles by railway train, motor car and aeroplane', he found himself addressing as many as a dozen meetings and upwards of 1,00,000 people a day, and at the end reckoned he had addressed something like 10 million people all told.[47] No wonder, the Congress won overall majorities in the provincial elections in 5 of the 11 provinces of India (Madras, Bihar, Orissa, CP, and UP): it had after all, claimed the general secretary, Acharya Kripalani, the biggest individual membership that any organization had, the world over.[48] An elated Nehru told Strafford Cripps:

As a whole India is wide awake and expectant. . . . My extensive touring has been a revelation to me of the suppressed energy of the people and of their passionate desire to be rid of their burdens. The Congress is supreme today so far as the masses and the lower middle classes are concerned. . . . It has hardly ever been in such a strong position.[49]

From 1937 to 1939 their supporters and detractors subjected the Con-gress ministries to critical scrutiny. They were justified in doing so; in fact, satyagraha campaigns were mounted in some districts of Bihar against the ministry, resulting in the arrest of a number of kisan sabha volunteers. Yet, it is undeniable that the ministries, having performed poorly in some areas, brought about some major shifts in the political, social and economic spheres. Doubtless, they diluted or tailored policies and programmes, as in the case of the 1939 UP Tenancy Act, to meet political exigencies.[50] But this was not unexpected in the case of a party that had no pretension of heralding a socialistic era. The critical issue is that the leadership, though riven with dissension and lacking in internal cohesion on policy matters, endeavoured to build a consensual base for itself, a fact that has been crucial for its own survival. Social engineering was a daunting prospect, but at least some political actors, both at the national, regional and local levels, willy-nilly brought together a cross-section of intellectuals and activists, all of whom contributed in varying degrees to the formulation of its agenda. Men like Baba Ramchandra and Swami Sahajanand had worked, however uneasily, with the Congress before the parting of ways took place. Walter Hauser's thesis hints—in his discussion of the charisma of the Swami—at the ideological link between nationalist leaders and peas-ants.[51] The young socialists, fiery and idealistic, drafted the Fundamental Rights Resolution as well as the Congress party's 1936 agrarian programme. They, too, drifted apart in due course. The efforts of the Communist Party resulted, at least in some periods, in the wider participation of the trade unions, peasant and other organizations. This arrangement was also short-lived.

Navigating between the demands of political incumbency and the dictates of economic development, the post-colonial Congress governments tried implementing, though not without considerable conflicts of principle and tussle of interests, the unfinished agenda of the ministries. The Constituent Assembly, with an abundant faith in the common man and the ultimate success of democratic rule, sought to breakdown the provincialism of local loyalties through the provision for direct election by adult suffrage.[52] To many, these urges and the initial moves towards their fulfilment captured the spirit and essence of nationalism.[53] Arguing for the moral value and legitimacy of nationalism in a form compatible with liberal democratic principles and institutions, Nehru underlined in 1951 that India had infinite variety and there was absolutely no reason why anybody should regiment it after a single pattern. In this context, a written constitution turned out to be

the first-ever attempt in the last 2,000 years of our collective civilizational existence to put in place a quintessentially egalitarian polity and a pluralistic social order. It is this promise of egalitarianism that garnered for the Indian state a modicum of democratic legitimacy and popular acceptance, despite all the aberrations and anti-poor biases in the ruling and governing classes.[54]

True, the notion that loyalty to the people came before loyalty to the party or government—in the nineteenth century European sense where nationalism was associated with the idea of popular sovereignty—did not find favour in India. Yet, the urge to clear the debris of the raj and to fashion a dynamic nation state was central to the post-colonial project. Democracy bestowed an aura of legitimacy on modern political life: laws, rules and policies appeared justified when they were democratic. Leaders differed in intellectual outlook and leadership style; yet, they shared a single vision of the system of rule that was to guide the new nation. It was a parliamentary system, and its leaders answerable to the people through elections.[55] That is why, in what can be called a gentle rap on the knuckles for the ruling BJP-led government which has been clamouring for reviewing the Constitution, president Narayanan saluted the 'far-sighted vision and arduous labours' of the Constitution's founding fathers. Reminding the nation that 'Republic' meant 'supreme power is exercised not by some remote monarch, but by the people', Narayanan wanted the nation to use the occasion of the Golden Jubilee to hail that proclamation and commitment. He subtly rebuffed all those who wanted to free the 'Executive' from the rigours of accountability.

A qualitative agrarian transformation took place during the Nehruvian era. Morris-Jones commented, in the early 1970s, on the vast social and economic changes being accomplished and being accommodated and digested by and within a political structure which was successfully flexible, and 'politically multi-lingual'.[56] Though ravaged by the effects of Partition, Punjab made rapid strides in the consolidation of landholdings. This contributed to the progress in agricultural productivity.[57] In 1948, the government of Madras moved to under-cut communist support among the Andhra peasants by passing the Madras Estate Abolition and Conversion into Ryotwari Act. The legislation abolished all *zamindari* and *inamdari* estates and gave the *ryot* the *pattas* of their lands over 30 per cent of the areas in the Andhra district.[58] The communist government in Kerala adopted the Agrarian Relations Bill on 10 June 1959, only a few days before the Centre imposed presidential rule.[59] Nehru was able to push through legislation abolishing *zamindari* in UP and Bihar, though the Zamindari Abolition Act did little to alleviate the suffering of the former tenants; equally, the goals set in the First Five Year Plan for pursuing land reforms were not accomplished.[60] In Punjab, legislation was enacted but too late to prevent landlords from taking the necessary precautionary measures.[61] In Bihar, a land of villages with nearly 85 per cent of its population living in about 67,000 villages, the feudal classes jettisoned land reforms.

On balance, the economic and political power of the *zamindars* was curtailed in some states where the very structure of power in the countryside was redesigned by reforms of land tenure and credit.[62] Besides, the state took up on itself the responsibility for transforming the economy,[63] and sought to deliver new services, education, public health, sophisticated agricultural technology and cooperative marketing to half a million villages. The initiatives, though sometimes ill conceived and poorly coordinated, produced results in some areas, but not everywhere. Despite two Five Year Plans, the economy of UP, with its 74 million people in 1961, was characterized by agricultural stagnation and industrial decline.[64] According to the Planning Commission estimates for 1960-1—after the first decade of planning—50 to 60 per cent of the rural population, or approximately 211 million people, could not afford minimum levels of consumption, calculated primarily in terms of calorie intake necessary to avoid the onset of malnutrition.[65] Here and elsewhere, the basic malaise was that the colonial apparatus of governmental administration was not even tinkered with. Likewise, the basic structure of civil and criminal law remained largely unchanged.[66] Clearly, there were many contested visions of nationhood and alternative frameworks for its realization. This meant two things: the absence of structural transformation and the lack of a composite long-term vision. Yet, the overarching authority of the state and the goods and services it was able to provide consolidated unity and the democratic tradition. A weaker or a more disengaged state may not have been able to motivate the people to have faith in the country or to participate in its political dynamic.[67] This requires elaboration.

Unlike Pakistan, the Indian national movement bequeathed a leadership that was somewhat better equipped to cope with the changes ushered in by the upheaval caused by Partition. In this respect, Nehru's leadership made a significant difference. Like Lord Krishna who lured the *gopis* (milkmaids) with his flute, the charismatic Nehru lured India's masses with the magic of his name.[68] Despite his failures and weaknesses, he managed to lead a truncated nation through an extremely difficult phase of nation-building. He failed to put into practice many of his own ideas and proved weak and indecisive in dealing with his ideological adversaries, but he set modern goals for his otherwise ideologically divided party and government. Though all that glittered in the refurbished parliament was not gold, Nehru did not allow regional, linguistic and religious/communal cleavages to get out of hand. While Pakistan moved dangerously close to becoming an Islamic theocracy, Nehru relentlessly pursued, despite the opposition of some comrades, the secular projects. 'For all of us in India', he told the chief ministers in May 1950, 'the issue of communal unity and a secular state must be made perfectly clear. We have played about with this idea sufficiently long and moved away from it far enough. We must go back and go back not secretly or apologetically, but openly and rather aggressively.'

Similarly, while Pakistan's political leadership in the early years searched for secular and unifying symbols, Nehru painstakingly referred to the Mahatma's message of inter-community peace and his courage in extinguishing the flames of religious hatred. In so doing, he tried to settle the issue whether the government and the party were going to adhere to old Congress principles in regard to communalism or whether the country as a whole was going to drift away from them. He did not waver in his belief that religious and caste strife must be fought tooth and nail no matter what the cost or how daunting the opposition; in fact so frequently did he inveigh against communalism, linguism, casteism and the like that the composers of newspaper headlines were hard-pressed to make the theme arresting.[69] In the words of Sarvepalli Gopal: 'To a whole generation of Indians he was not so much a leader as a companion who expressed and made clearer a particular view of the present and vision of the future. The combination of intellectual and moral authority was unique in his time.'[70] The historian Walter Hauser 'followed him more than once in 1957 as he swept out of Anand Bhawan (in Allahabad) in his black, convertible Buick, moving swiftly to one of the neighbouring villages to engage the peasants about the meanings of the new India. It was always a magnetic moment to be sure, and that Nehru did it on some regular basis in the eight or nine months I was in Allahabad was in itself impressive, but the encounter always had for the peasants certainly, something of a *darshan* quality. *Which in itself told us much about the nature of the relationship, and about the quality of the freedom movement itself at this level of engagement*'[71] (italics mine).

Some fumed and fretted against Nehru's exertion to change the fabric of Hindu society, his lenient policy towards Pakistan, and his undue tenderness for the Muslims, but most recognized that the country's first prime minister enjoyed countrywide support and legitimacy. This was especially true after Vallabhbhai Patel's death in 1950. To Patel goes the remarkable feat of integrating the princely states into the Union. It is to Nehru's credit that the language issue was amicably resolved, whereas it led to riots in East Pakistan in protest against the central government's attempts to impose Urdu as the only official language.[72] The reorganization of states in 1956 along linguistic lines was a masterstroke: if the first prime minister had been a linguistic naivete rather than a linguistic sophisticate like Nehru, then we would have had today not a unified India with a strong government at the Centre but an India weakly divided along linguistic and cultural lines into two or three semi-autonomous regions. The unity of India would be as a faded dream. In creating linguistic states, Nehru provided a vernacular political milieu that was conducive to the flowering of many linguistically rooted cultures and thereby evolved a system, which greatly enriched the cultural life of the nation as a whole.[73]

III

We are only a four-month-old child. You know somebody would like to overthrow us. I know you would say we have not done such and such thing, but we are only four-month-old.

JINNAH on 14 December 1947

In so many different ways, the first decade of Nehru's government stands in contrast to developments in neighbouring Pakistan. In 1947 India went on to consolidate itself as a democracy; the enthusiastic members of the Constituent Assembly burnt the midnight oil over a period of two years and adopted a constitution on 26 November 1949, which came into force on 26 January 1950. On the other hand, Pakistan's Constituent Assembly took nine years to agree to a constitution. No national elections were held under the 1956 Constitution, however. Two years later, Pakistan fell prey to military rule. The *coup d'etat* was followed by the dissolution of the National Assembly. Parliamentary elections, scheduled for early 1959, were cancelled.[74]

Jinnah died on 11 September 1948. The Muslim League, having led the demand for and achieved a Muslim homeland, declined thereafter. The ideological cement that held it together dissolved once Pakistan was achieved. If the League had institutionalized itself or provided the leadership essential for underwriting stability or democracy, it could well have devised a programme or a mechanism to adjust the conflict of interests that existed between different social and economic classes.[75] But that was not to be. In 1954, the party was routed in provincial elections in East Pakistan. This is where 54 per cent of Pakistan's population lived. The Muslim League was likened to

a virtuous lady who has fallen into bad times and is forced by circumstances to become a courtesan. As such, she is now ever ready to serve as a concubine of any adventurer who is in a position to pay her the right price. . . . After the death of Quaid one adventurer followed another to claim her hand. Muslim League lost her innocence and became a handmaiden of every charlatan who came to seize the reins of power in Pakistan.[76]

A Hindu fanatic assassinated the Mahatma on 30 January 1948. But the Congress survived not only as a powerful organization but also its pragmatic leadership created a democratic and secular polity, and accommodated, through a policy of conciliation and compromise, diverse social and political forces in its own ranks.[77] The Congress in Bihar, for example, enjoyed a virtual monopoly over two important 'vote banks', that of the scheduled castes and the Muslims. Moreover, the party coopted aspiring politicians from the Yadav and Kurmi caste groups and prevailed upon the leaders of the Bhumihars and the Rajputs to subordinate personal ambitions to party unity.[78] In the south, a relatively peaceful lower caste revolution, pioneered by the Daravida Munnetra Kazhagam (DMK), was well underway.[79]

Elected governments in Pakistan, by contrast, held power at the discretion of what Hamza Alavi has described as the all-powerful military-bureaucratic oligarchy.[80] The problem was further compounded: in an area where religious passions had been heightened to create a Muslim nation, Jinnah's belated plea for a secular society did not strike a favourable chord. Whereas the Hindu Mahasabha and the RSS were discredited and isolated, more so after Gandhi's assassination, the Jamaat-i Islami, a party wedded to Islamic theocracy, was out in the open ready to seize power in order to enforce the *Shariat*. Its leader maulana Abul Ala Maududi began flexing his muscles and made his intentions known during the anti-Ahmaddiya riots that the Jamaat-i Islami instigated. It was the first major blow to the Quaid's dream of a united Pakistan. Meanwhile, in India, the first Backward Classes Commission was appointed on 29 January 1953 under the chairmanship of a former disciple of Gandhi, Kaka Kalelkar. Although Nehru's government rejected its recommendations, the issue of backward caste empowerment soon became the nation's preoccupation.[81]

Why have the experiences of India and Pakistan been so different since their Independence? Various explanations already exist. Ayesha Jalal's emphasis on the structural and ideational features of colonialism in the post-colonial era is valid. But her attempt to obfuscate the dichotomy between democracy in India and military governments in Pakistan and Bangladesh does not carry conviction. Similarly, her attempt to discover the common strand of authoritarianism in the political experiences of India and Pakistan reveals her insensitivity to the important achievements of Indian democracy.[82]

The subaltern historians argue that Indian democracy was not the outcome of a national-popular revolution but a passive one carried out by the Gandhian-led Congress that enabled the bourgeoisie to institute its hegemony over the subaltern groups, but without a formal confrontation with them. Most other writers ascribe Indian democracy to a developed political culture, viable institutions, dedicated élites, unique organizational skills on the part of the Indians, a tradition of compromise and accommodation, the success of the Congress in having institutionalized itself in state and society, and the British role in bequeathing tutelary democracy to India. Conversely, the breakdown of democracy in Pakistan is attributed to a backward political culture, unseasoned or corrupt leaders, ethnic and group frictions, weak institutions debilitated further by stresses arising from the exigencies of nation building in a new state, the incompatibility of Islam and democracy,[83] and the contradictions between the Islamic notions of community and the recently instituted idea of electoral politics.[84]

What these theories fail to sufficiently underline are the differences in the social bases, ideological orientations, and the contrasting styles of leadership in India and Pakistan. Although the structures and social composition of formal political parties mattered substantially, more so in post-colonial societies, the striking contrast between India and Pakistan, as also between military rulers in West Pakistan and the Awami League leaders in East Pakistan (later Bangladesh), was not just the charisma, popular appeal and moral authority of some Congress leaders, notably Nehru and Patel, but their legitimacy across regions, castes and classes. Indeed, they inscribed their preferences in the routinized practices of quotidian politics. That is why, even in so divided and fragmented a society, people sought a resolution of their dilemmas and predicaments in their leader's policies and pronouncements. Unlike Pakistan, where regional parties were weak, the Lucknow, Calcutta or Patna-based actors kept intact their caste, class and community linkages and patronage networks. This gave them considerable leverage in local, regional and, in some cases, national politics. Consequently, Sri Krishna Sinha, who first served as chief minister between 1937 and 1939, ruled as chief minister of Bihar from the formation of the Congress ministry in 1946 until his death in 1961. Such leaders also enjoyed greater latitude in choosing from a menu of institutional options. After Nehru's death in 1964, the influence of the chief ministers increased, though the pattern was already well established during the Nehru era. Some of it was exercised through the National Development Council (formed in 1956), under which all the chief ministers met members of the Planning Commission several times a year to discuss development problems for the country as a whole.[85]

The person who probably made the greatest difference of all was Mohandas Karamchand Gandhi, who, in the words of Nehru, 'was like a powerful current of fresh air that made us stretch ourselves and take deep breaths, like a beam of light that pierced the darkness and removed the scales from our eyes'. To people like Nehru, he did not descend from the top but seemed to emerge from the millions of India. Although assassinated just when the country had tasted the fruits of freedom, his legacy lived on in the hearts and the minds of the people (if not the government), whom he had served with such singular devotion. Many aspects of the Constitution itself bore the imprint of his personality.

There is no denying that Gandhi possessed a sharp and intuitive mind and had the ability to marshal his resources towards ends clearly discerned and goals clearly defined. He was an innovator and synthesizer of diverse political and philosophical traditions. He was therefore able to develop a political theory grounded in the unique experiences and articulated in terms of the indigenous philosophical vocabulary. Sustaining collective action in interaction with powerful opponents marks his movements off from the earliest forms of protest or contention in the late nineteenth and early twentieth centuries. On balance, his engagements developed out of his concern to articulate the interests of different castes, communities and regions. He was a devout Hindu but not a *Hindu* leader, a distinction not recognized by the estranged Muslim leadership in the 1940s. He turned to popular religious traditions, including some Hinduized symbols, to unite and not to divide the fairly broad-based constituency that he had created during the khilafat movement. No wonder, the pan-Islamic leader Mohamed Ali stated in the early 1920s: 'It is Gandhi, Gandhi, Gandhi that has got to be dinned into the peoples ears, because he means Hindu-Muslim unity, non-cooperation, *dharma* and *Swaraj*.' Mohamed Ali became Gandhi's most relentless critic in the late 1920s, but the Mahatma maintained, 'I have nothing but kindly feelings about him.' He continued: 'and I feel that time will remove misunderstandings. Having no feeling either against Islam or Mussulmans, I feel absolutely at ease.'[86]

Jinnah's role should not be interpreted from the lofty heights of majoritarianism. Nor should he be vilified for rejecting the Congress creed or held solely responsible for the vivisection of India. The nationalist rhetoric can no longer obscure the part played by some key Congress and Hindu Mahasabha players in signing united India's death warrant. What is undeniable, however, is Jinnah's self-imposed isolation from the Gandhian-led movements, and his distaste for the socialist programme of the Congress. He did not approve of the *purna swaraj* resolution, adopted by the Lahore Congress in 1929, and blamed Gandhi 'for this sudden outburst of political hysteria'.[87] The civil disobedience movement, according to him, 'has struck the imagination mostly of the inexperienced youth, the ignorant and the illiterate. All this means complete disorganization and chaos.'[88] By the time Gandhi launched the Quit India movement, Jinnah, having descended from the heights of Malabar Hills, was soldiering on to accomplish his mission of creating a Muslim homeland.

Jinnah relished debating, in the traditions of British parliamentary democracy, finer points of law and legal processes and performed with his characteristic élan in Home Rule Leagues and the cozy chambers of the Central Legislative Assembly. He stayed clear of the dusty roads, the villages inhabited by millions of hungry, oppressed and physically emaciated peasants, and the British prison where so many of his countrymen were incarcerated for defying the colonial government. Like Mohamed Ali, he enjoyed the trappings of power. But, unlike the volatile khilafat agitator, he was ill equipped to lead the masses from the front. While Gandhi walked barefoot to break the Salt Law and to galvanize the masses by culturally resonant and action-oriented symbols, a pensive and restless Jinnah waited in London to occupy the commanding heights of political leadership in Delhi. While Gandhi treaded the path fouled by Hindu and Muslim zealots in the riot-stricken areas of Bihar and Bengal, Jinnah was being crowned as the governor-general of Pakistan. For the Mahatma, it was a moment of deep anguish and agony; for the Quaid the fulfilment of his dream.

For much of his public life Jinnah had operated, entirely out of choice, on the periphery of national politics. He made no enemies but cultivated no friends either. But, having finally returned to India in October 1935, he expected a miracle to occur in the 1937 elections. This did not happen. He was dismayed to discover that Gandhi's Congress and not the Muslim League was the people's party. Yet, he was not one to lick his wounds: he launched the League version of the Muslim mass contact campaign, upbraided the Congress ministries for their anti-Muslim bias, and chided Gandhi and Nehru for their intransigence. As a dogged lawyer who had built up a fine reputation in the British-Indian courts, he bounced back, with active British support, to extract major political concessions from a beleaguered wartime government. That was the time when Gandhi, his chief *bete noire*, languished in British jails. His own personal and professional skills were many, but he used them to humble rather than win over his adversaries or potential rivals. He enticed the provincial Muslim bosses in Punjab, Sind and Bengal before destroying their own power base.[89] That is because he liked being on the winning side, even if it meant sacrificing his own cherished principles. Whenever he negotiated with the Congress, he did so not to arrive at a modus vivendi but to vindicate his own stand.[90] With Nehru it was a clash of personalities; with the Mahatma it was a titanic clash of ideologies. 'The two mountains have met,' the viceroy Wavell referred to the Gandhi-Jinnah talks in September 1944, 'and not even a ridiculous mouse has emerged.'[91] Earlier, Jinnah's call to observe 'Deliverance Day' in 1939, or his later appeal for 'Direct Action Day', conformed to Tej Bahadur Sapru's description of him as a 'spoilt child'.[92] In the end, the fruits of freedom were split between the two nations, born in the throes of ugly violence and bloodshed.

Gandhi and Jinnah, brought up in Gujarat and nurtured in British legal schools, should have been able to make sense of each other. In reality, their life-story ran a parallel course. They were distanced from each other long before their acerbic exchanges in the late 1930s. True, the anglicized Jinnah, whose English speech as governor-general of Pakistan to a *Jirgah* of the Pakhtuns in the frontier was translated into Pushtu by the British governor, George Cunningham, was not a devout Muslim or an Islamist.[93]

Somebody accustomed to living in Hampstead and moving in the company of British lawyers and judges could not have felt comfortable before the rustic maulvis or the erudite Muslim theologians, who began to throng the Muslim League sessions after 1940. Yet, he, rather than the ulama of Deoband or Nadwat al-ulama, expounded the idea of a civilizational unity among Muslims and counterpoised it against the heterodox religious and cultural traditions. Having advocated multiculturalism until the mid-1930s for which he earned the title 'Ambassador of Hindu-Muslim unity' from Sarojini Naidu, he authored the two-nation theory in complete disregard of his early conviction.

Grounded in the historical experiences of two mutually incompatible entities engaged in creating their separate destinies, Jinnah questioned, something he had not done before, the very *idea* of unitary nationalism being foisted on different nationalities. For him, the idea of Pakistan, though vaguely defined and interpreted in the early stages, was the only way out of the Muslim predicament. And for the colonial rulers, who had precipitated the Hindu-Muslim divide and had no qualms in seeing the fragmentation of a nation, Jinnah was a trump card to be used against the Congress during the War. He had been ignored and rebuffed on previous occasions, but his newly acquired status in the mid-1940s as the 'sole spokesman' suited imperial designs. While paying lip service to India's unity and bemoaning its imminent division, British policies ensured, particularly in the aftermath of the War, the creation of not one but two nations in 1947.

It was easy to split people and divide territory, but the more challenging task was to *create* a nation out of highly disparate and unevenly developed communities in Pakistan: 'The final truth for man', wrote W.C. Smith in his incisive chapter on Islam, 'lies not in some remote and untarnished utopia, but in the tension and struggle of applying its ideals to the recalcitrant and obstructive stuff of worldly sorrow.'[94] It was easy to project Islam as the cementing bond, a politically motivated exercise that did not find favour with the leading ulama of the period, especially those connected with Deoband and the Jamiyat al-ulama. Realistically speaking, the real task was to initiate new rounds of state building under conditions of intense conflict that divided the élite and militated against compromise, to lay down ground rules for building a state system divorced from the rhetoric of the mullahs, and to accommodate divergent interests in the unreformed bureaucratic and institutional structures. Creating such a system and its long-term effectiveness depended on the capacity of the élites to distance themselves from the theologians, devise an economic strategy to curb the power of the landowning class, and evolve mechanisms to defuse mounting linguistic, sectarian and ethnic tensions.

In other words, instead of attempting to homogenize Pakistan society on the basis of Muslim nationalism, the compelling need was to lay bare the outlines of a pluralist society. That was one way of meeting the various demands of the Bengalis in East Pakistan, the Baluchs and Pathans in the North-West Frontier Province, the Sindhis in Sind, and the *muhajirs* in Karachi, capital of the same province. Mere references to Islamic solidarity, as Jinnah's successor Liaquat Ali Khan discovered the hard way, were no substitute for the hard imperatives of building a new central government machinery for Pakistan's western and eastern wings.[95] As a result, tensions between the dominant and subordinate regions, rather than the purported unities of a common religion, characterized Pakistan's polity for well over two decades.[96] The ruling élites, vying with each other for the pickings, had no intellectual resources to draw upon, and no cadres to translate their nebulous plans into action. The commitment and enthusiasm generated by the Pakistan movement left little of any substantial political value behind on which the post-Jinnah political leadership could rely for support.[97]

The ailing and beleaguered founder of Pakistan had neither the time nor the intellectual reserves to define his long-term agenda. Although he led, organized and conducted powerful mobilization campaigns under the aegis of the Muslim League, he made no attempt to discuss and devise an economic programme. In fact, Nehru noted in 1938 that Jinnah did not show much interest in the economic demands of the masses and the all-important question of poverty and unemployment. During his lifetime, he thwarted even feeble attempts to propose democratic reforms and economic policies. New ideas breaking out among fiery young idealists were nipped in the bud.[98] Those who asked fundamental questions about Pakistan's future trajectory were either told that the time was not appropriate or that they had raised them to pursue partisan interests.[99]

IV

Have you not heard what happened to Mansur?
Here, if you speak, they crucify you.

MIR TAQI MIR

Given the historical role of the Congress and Muslim League activists and their contrasting legacies, Pakistan would have probably plotted a predictable course with or without Jinnah. Its fate or destiny was not, however, predetermined. Nor was its survival as a national entity at stake. For Pakistan's ruling classes, the more pressing issue was to negotiate the terms of a post-1947 social contract with the migrants who had moved from their birthplace in search of better opportunities. Given Pakistan's *raison d'être*, this arrangement would have been workable. But the dynamics of power politics, combined with the leadership crisis and the fundamental tension between an autocratic centre and regional interests,[100] belied the expectations raised by Muslim nationalism. The country was unable to work out the four institutionalized arrangements that define the developmental capacity of the state: state-society relations, the nature of the bureaucracy, state fiscal practices, and patterns of state economic intervention.[101] Powerful landlords in Sind and Punjab, having helped Jinnah realize his goal, showed no inclination to share power or agree to land redistribution. There was no Nehru or his socialist comrades to push through land reforms. In 1970, Bhutto's Pakistan People's Party promised to destroy the power of the feudal landowners; but in 1977 the PPP sought to preserve the *status quo*. The Noons and Tiwanas of Sargodha, the Maliks of Mianwali, the Qureshis of Multan, the Hayats of Rawalpindi and Campbellpur, the Legharis and Mazaris of Dera Ghazi Khan were back in the political arena as its candidates.[102]

Similarly, the nascent bourgeoisie, drawn mainly from the migrant entrepreneurs belonging to the ethnic minorities, notably the Memons, Khojas and Bohras, had no stake in democracy. Rather, it relied on the authoritarian state structures to expand and consolidate its position. Finally, the leadership could not rein in the ulama, who demanded a theocratic state. No wonder the ideal of an Islamic state and society, though vaguely defined in the Objectives Resolution in 1952, was ultimately consummated years later during the inglorious regime of Zia-ul-Haq. The contestation between the modernist and traditionalist world views imposed severe strains on a nation that was still trying to find its feet after the untimely death of its founder.[103]

Jinnah, in a broadcast in February 1948, stated: 'Islam and its idealism have taught us democracy. It has taught equality of man, justice and fairplay to everybody. . . . In any case Pakistan is not going to be a theocratic state—to be ruled by priests with a divine mission.' Equally, some leaders and intellectuals talked of 'the nightmare of Pakistan's going back to a rigid, backward, narrow country'. 'For us, the intellectuals, the problem is that Pakistan shall not go back. That it should not become simply an extension of Afghanistan. It is a nightmare for us. The danger of the mullahs coming to power is serious; it would be calamitous. This is the terror.' Yet, the secular project remained dormant, exposing the liberal and secular voices to the fundamentalist fury of the Jamaat-i Islami. The ulama desired the state to be declared Islamic, which the first Constitution, adopted in 1956, declared it to be. Later, they attacked the progressive Muslim Family Laws Ordinance, promulgated by Ayub Khan on 2 March 1961. In the First Amendment Act of 1964, the name of the country was again changed from the Republic of Pakistan to the Islamic Republic of Pakistan.

The PPP fared no better. When Bhutto was caught up in his own quagmire, he resorted to repression. As a practitioner of realpolitik and moving according to the conception of what was most advantageous in the gaining and maintaining of power, he cultivated conservative and religious elements. In 1974, he declared the Ahmadiyas, or Qadianis, a non-Muslim sect, banned alcohol, gambling and night-clubs, and replaced Sunday with Friday as the weekly holiday. Zia-ul-Haq's Islamization programme covered judicial reforms, the introduction of an Islamic penal code, the creation of a federal *Shariat* court, and an educational policy incorporating Islamic tenets. But his main project was the Federal Court, the product of twelve Presidential Ordinances promulgated between 1980 and 1985 and grafted onto the 1973 Constitution.[104] These measures legitimized the power of the ulama, institutionalized theocracy against the wishes of most people, and, in the process, increased the divisions, ruptures and bitterness within an already insecure nation.

The Pakistan scholar Fazlur Rahman, who was exiled from his own country, had pointed out that the slogan, 'in Islam religion and politics are inseparable, is employed to dupe the common man into accepting that, instead of politics or the state serving the long-term objectives of Islam, Islam should come to serve the immediate and myopic objectives of party politics'. Since then, the failure of successive leaderships has led to a deep and justified scepticism on the part of much of Pakistan civil society regarding their leaders, and the political rhetoric behind which they camouflage their failings.

Military dictatorships, even without divine missions, are bad enough. When imbued with the spirit of religious fundamentalism, they suffocate the creative impulses of a society.[105] Though committed to the Islamization Bill after assuming office in February 1997, Nawaz Sharif had no immediate political compulsions, regardless of America's cruise missile attack on Afghanistan, to introduce the Fifteenth Amendment Bill in the Assembly on 28 August 1999. He should have learnt his lesson from his country's bitter experiences in the past. He should have known that the essence of

Table 17.1: Indicators of Development for India and Pakistan

	Year	India	Pakistan	South Asia	All developing countries
Human Development Index (value)	1997	0.545	0.508	0.544	0.637
HDI Rank	1999	132	138	–	–
Real GDP per capita (PPP$)	1997	1670	1560	1803	3240
Female real GDP per capita (PPP$)	1997	902	701	950	2088
Male real GDP per capita (PPP$)	1997	2389	2363	2606	4374
Life Expectancy (value)	1997	0.63	0.65	0.63	0.66
Life Expectancy of Birth (Years)	1997	62.6	64.0	62.7	64.4
Female Life Expectancy at Birth (Years)	1997	62.9	65.1	63.1	66.1
Male Life Expectancy at Birth (Years)	1997	62.3	62.9	62.3	63.0
Education Index (value)	1997	0.54	0.41	0.52	0.67
Adult Literacy Rate (%)	1997	53.5	40.9	52.2	71.4
Female adult literacy rate (%)	1997	39.4	25.4	38.6	62.9
Male adult literacy rate (%)	1997	66.7	55.2	65	80
Female gross enrolement ration (combined) [%]	1997	47	28	44	55
Male gross enrolment ration (combined) [%]	1997	62	56	60	64

Gender-related Development Index (value)	1997	0.525	0.472	0.630
GDI Rank	1997	112	116	–
Gender empowerment measure (value)	1997	0.240	0.176	–
GEM Rank	1997	95	101	–
Seats in Parliament held by women (% of total)	1997	8.3	2.0	10.0
Human Poverty Index (value) [%]	1997	35.9	42.1	27.7
HPI Rank	1997	59	71	–
Population without safe water	1990-7	19	21	28
Population without health services	1981-92	25	15	NA
Population without sanitation	1990-7	71	44	NA
Real GDP per capita of poorest 20% (PPP$)	1980-4	527	907	57
Real GDP per capita of richest 20% (PPP$)	1980-4	2641	4288	–
Richest 20% to poorest 20%	1980-4	5.0	4.7	–

Source: UNDP, 1999, *Human Development Report 1999*, New York.

a democratic order lies in letting people follow their moral and religious codes, and that state authority should not be used to prescribe, in the light of a religious text, what is right and to forbid what is wrong.

Today, Pakistan can ill-afford to either nurture or acquire the role of a vanguard for a fundamentalist vision of Islam. It may succeed in becoming an Islamic state. Or it may transfer its loyalty to some new ideal. Or it may fail. Each of the alternatives is momentous; and the choice between the people is searching and inexorable.[106] Yet, history is no longer a very effective guide for defining Pakistan's *raison d'être*; too much has happened since 1947. The country is half its original size; culturally, socially, and economically, it is now less a part of South Asia than before. It is in these very changed circumstances that the people of Pakistan will need to find a direction for themselves and for their country,[107] and think in terms of a comprehensive social action—aggregating people with different demands and identities and in different locations in concerted campaigns of collective action. This solution involves, first, mounting collective challenges; second, drawing on social networks, common purposes, and cultural frameworks; and, third, building solidarity through connective structures and collective identities to sustain collective action. These, according to Sidney Tarrow, are the main processes of social movements.[108]

Out of various contradictory tendencies the Pakistanis must find the capacity to create a secularized state and confront the powerful trends towards authoritarianism. If the past is any indication, they have an uphill struggle ahead of them. Yet their 'case, with all its specificities, will be relevant to other countries trying to cope with daunting external circumstances and beset with internal problems.

NOTES

1. Quoted in *The Economist* (US), 22 May 1999.
2. M. Rashiduzzaman, 'Is Bangladesh Soft State?', *Daily Star*, 2 Feb. 2000.
3. Norman D. Palmer, 'Pakistan: The Long Search for Foreign Policy', in Lawrence Ziring et al. (eds.), *Pakistan: The Long View*, Durham, N.C., 1977, p. 413.
4. 17 Aug. 1989, *Pakistan the Barren Years: The Viewpoint Editorials and Columns of Mazhar Ali Khan, 1775-1992*, Karachi, 1998, p. 63. See also Ghulam Kibria, *A Shattered Dream: Understanding Pakistan's Underdevelopment*, Karachi, 1999.
5. Lawrence Ziring, *Pakistan in the Twentieth Century: A Political History*, London, 1997, p. 614.

pointed out candidly, 'after all, there is a Congress Ministry in the Province (Bombay) with the greatest proportion of Muslims, and 1 million votes were cast *against the Muslim League at the recent election as compared with about 6 million for the League*'[35] (italics mine). Jinnah was on an equally weak turf in demanding the exclusion of the Congress Muslims from the interim government. They may not have been, in Nehru's description, the 'soul of the Congress', but they had occupied an important enough position in the country's liberation struggle. They may not have always played a pivotal role, but they remained a priceless asset to the Congress movement. Their presence vindicated the Congress stand of representing the Indian nation rather than a segment of it. How could the Congress, then, forsake its close allies for the illusory prospect of an accord with the League? How could Gandhi and Nehru, in particular, sacrifice personal friends and political expediency? 'It has now become clear', wrote the viceroy on 1 October 1946, 'that Congress are unwilling to give way on the Nationalist Muslim issue.'[36] The problem, he told Pethick-Lawrence, 'is an extraordinary intractable one'.[37] This was so because of Jinnah's obstinacy, and his refusal to give way.

Sensing the mood in the Congress circles, Cripps and Wavell urged Jinnah to give way on the question, and, in exchange, secure his other points.[38] Wavell went to the extent of explaining that the Congress would not, in fact, appoint a 'Nationalist' Muslim in the end, if Jinnah conceded their right to do so. The Congress had not given any such assurance.[39]

Azad and his Muslim comrades may have been comforted by the Congress stand, but not by the vicious communal atmosphere that gripped the country. The League campaign gathered momentum day after day, and the country was, consequently, caught up in a bitter and violent confrontation. With their limited constituency, which had steadily shrunk over the years, Azad and his followers could do little to influence the course of events. The inexorable march towards the vivisection of the Indian nation could neither be halted by an individual or a group. Nor could the communal tide be stemmed by the Mahatma or the Maulana. Besides, once the Congress agreed to the Partition Plan, the tide turned against the Congress Muslims. Ghaffar Khan protested loudly and passionately; others did so quietly. Azad maintained his studious silence and aristocratic poise at the Congress Working Committee meeting on 2 June 1947, when the Mountbatten plan for the Partition was ratified. He could do little at the time to prevent this 'abject surrender', particularly after Gandhi and Nehru dithered in the face of the communal onslaught.[40] Dispirited, defeated and detached from the humdrum of political happenings, Campbell-Johnson recorded the details of a meeting on 16 September 1947. 'Throughout this long meeting, Maulana Azad, the Moslem elder statesman in the Congress, sat silent and impassive, as he always does, looking, with his pointed beard, just like Cardinal Richelieu.'[41]

The dawn of freedom had arrived. But 'the sad face of Maulana Azad, to whom the occasion was something of a tragedy, sticking out from the sea of happy faces like a gaunt and ravaged rock'.[42] Azad could well have recalled his own passage from *Ghubar-i Khatir* which summed up the story of his life.

In religion, in literature, in politics, in everyday thought, wherever I have to go, I have to go alone. On no path can I go with the caravans of the day.... Whichever way I walk, I get so far ahead of the (caravan) that when I turn to look back, I see nothing, but the dust of the way, and even that is the dust raised by the speed of my own passage.

NOTES

1. Kenneth Cragg, *Counsels in Contemporary Islam*, Edinburgh, 1965, pp. 132-3, and Ian Henderson Douglas, *Abul Kalam Azad: An Intellectual and Religious Biography*, eds. Gail Minault and Christian W. Troll, New Delhi, 1998, p. 29; Abdur Razzaq Malihabadi, *Zikr-i Azad*, Calcutta, 1965, pp. 132-3. See the collection of articles in Rasheedyddin Khan (ed.), *Abul Kalam Azad: Ek Hamageer Shaksiat*, New Delhi, 1989.

2. Cragg, *Counsels*, p. 134.

3. Mujeeb, *The Indian Muslims*, p. 302.

4. For example, the *fatwa* on the boycott of government-aided educational institutions. *Khilafat*, 1 Nov. 1920.

5. Douglas, *Abul Kalam Azad*, p. 180.

6. Ibid.

7. For Azad's early political life, Rajat K. Ray, 'Revolutionaries, Pan-Islamists and Bolsheviks: Maulana Abul Kalam Azad and Political Underworld in Calcutta, 1905-1925', Hasan (ed.), *Communal and Pan-Islamic Trends in Colonial India*, pp. 101-24.

8. *Al-Hilal*, 23 Oct. 1912.

9. Mohamed Ali, *My Life*, pp. 163-4.

10. Douglas, *Abul Kalam Azad*, p. 76.

11. *Comrade* (Calcutta), 14 Jan. 1911.

12. Mohamed Ali, *My Life*, p. 46.

13. To Tilak, 12 Nov. 1916, *Mohamed Ali in Indian Politics*, Vol.1, p. 292.

14. Hasan, *Mohamed Ali: Ideology and Politics*, pp. 28-9.

nationalism ever made from a Congress platform—reaffirmed his secular vision and rebutted the two-nation theory. It could well have served as a political manifesto for those Congress Muslims who were, after Ansari's death in May 1936, in search of a leader and a programme to steer their ship through the rough currents of communalism.

In April 1940, Azad placed proposals for overcoming the constitutional deadlock and, at the same time, challenged the League's claim to be the sole representative of the Muslims. The conference resolution included a declaration beginning: 'India, with its geographical and political boundaries, is an indivisible whole and as uch it is the common homeland of all citizens, irrespective of race or religion, who are joint owners of its resources'.[24]

As the Congress president, a position he had already occupied in 1923, Azad sought to narrow down the ever-increasing gulf separating the Congress and the League. He also conducted negotiations with Stafford Cripps and the viceroy, Wavell, and again, after the War, with the cabinet mission. It was a role he enjoyed most. Cripps and Wavell thought well of him and counted on his support for their plans and proposals. The former thanked Azad for his help and friendship and the 'really marvellous way in which you stuck to your guns'. He was 'absolutely convinced' that, but for the Maulana, 'no arrangement would have been come to'.[25] Wavell found Azad 'very moderate and friendly'. He added: 'I have a great respect for him, and if all these politicians were of the same quality matters would be comparatively easy'.[26] Azad reciprocated these sentiments. Complimenting Cripps for his 'courtesy, tact and resourcefulness', he referred to his own part in the negotiations. 'I may tell you', he wrote on 22 July 1946:

that my attitude was throughout governed by two considerations. I regard the advent of the Labour Party to power an event of historic importance. For the first time in history, there is the prospect of a peaceful transition to a Socialist order. I also feel that the Labour Government have on the whole been following a policy of democracy and freedom, and working for peace and stability in the modern world. I therefore felt it my duty to do everything possible to help it towards a peaceful settlement of the Indian problem.[27]

On the other hand, sections of the Congress leadership doubted Azad's negotiating skills; in fact, Nehru's election as Congress president in 1946 is said to have been an expression of lack of confidence in Azad's ability to follow the dictates of the Congress Working Committee.[28] The judgement is unfair. Azad was, as Alan Campbell-Johnson recorded on

21 December 1947, just a 'titular head of the movement during the vital negotiations with both the Cripps and the Cabinet Missions'.[29] Others like Gandhi and Nehru, backed by Patel, Rajagopalachari and Rajendra Prasad, called the shots, though Azad could bring round the AICC and the CWC to his point of view on a few issues, including the formation of a coalition government composed of both Congress and the League.[30] But, in general, Azad was expected to perform a subservient role. His own initiatives were not welcomed. On occasions, they were thwarted.[31]

In a sense, Azad's position was similar to that of his Congress Muslim comrades who held positions of authority but were rarely allowed to influence major policy decisions. This was so in 1930 when Gandhi ignored the wishes of Ansari and his Nationalist Muslim Party in launching the civil disobedience movement. Again, the Congress in general, and Nehru in particular, ignored the views of Azad on the formation of a Congress-League coalition ministry in UP. On reflection, Azad concluded that 'if the League's offer of co-operation had been accepted the Muslim League party would for all practical purposes merge with the Congress, Jawaharlal's action gave the League in UP a new lease of life'.[32] Azad may not have been right in his assessment, but he, at least implicity, gave vent to the feeling that the upper echelon of the Congress leadership paid no heed to the 'Nationalist Muslim' perspective.

Dealing with the Muslim League posed an added problem: the stout refusal of its diehards to recognize the position and status of the Congress Muslims. The Aligarh students and teachers, who had once idolized the Maulana when their pan-Islamic passions were heightened, turned against Azad. The Barelwi ulama, averse to the Jamiyat al-ulama-Congress alliance, were his sworn critics. And Jinnah, of course, refused to meet him and showed no sympathy for his viewpoint. 'Cannot you realize', he told Azad in July 1940, 'you are making a Muslim show-boy Congress president to give it colour that is national.'[33] In this way, recorded Campbell-Johnson:

Maulana Azad, a great scholar and a man of retiring disposition, has during the past ten years been a central figure of controversy. He embodied in his position and person perhaps the most important symbol of the Congress aspiration to be a nationalist as against a communal party. His status was thus the focal point of Gandhi's clash with Jinnah, who always maintained that politically no one but a member of the Muslim League could represent Muslim interests.[34]

Jinnah displayed lack of realism in insisting that the League solely represented the Muslim community. How could it be in the light of the poor performance of his party in the 1937 elections? Besides, as Wavell

8

'Congress Muslims' and Indian Nationalism, Dilemma and Decline
c. 1928-1934

In the aftermath of the Nehru report controversy, the Congress had to reckon with Jinnah's 'Fourteen Points'. Gandhi tried to soothe suspicions with the assurance that swaraj did not mean Hindu raj, and engaged with him in February and August 1929 to explore possible avenues to peace. But Lajpat Rai, Malaviya, Jayakar, B.S. Moonje, working president of the Hindu Mahasabha (1927-35), and N.C. Kelkar, urged him not to reach a solution outside the terms of the Nehru report.[1] Lajpat Rai refused to accept any modification,[2] while Jayakar pressured Gandhi not to yield on the ground that the government, as in 1919, would deliberately make any concessions part of a constitution.[3] Gandhi wrote to Motilal Nehru in anguish: 'How that can be done [resolving the communal deadlock] or whether it should be done, you know best. My mind is in a whirl in this matter. The atmosphere is too foggy for me to see clearly.'[4]

With the failure of the Gandhi-Jinnah talks and the crusade against the Nehru report gathering momentum, the Lahore Congress let the report lapse, and decided not to accept any solution of the communal problem without the concurrence of the minorities.[5] Gandhi hoped the declaration of complete independence and the launching of civil disobedience would enable leaders of various shades of opinion to draw their followers into the anti-colonial struggle. He wrote in *Navajivan*: 'If we have true freedom we will shed communal fear. Hindus and Muslims will cease to fear one another.'[6]

But soothing Muslim feelings was not enough. The issue at stake was to arrest their growing alienation from the Congress. The process, having begun soon after the khilafat movement came to a halt, was attributed to a

wide range of factors, including the failure of the Congress to curb assertive and militant expressions of Hindu nationalism. Such had been the
burden of Abdur Rahim's speech at the 1925 Muslim League session. He
argued that the Congress would jettison Muslim interests in any future
scheme of swaraj, and that their 'salvation' lay in either forging an alliance
with the government or in pursuing independent political action.[7] Such
views, echoed both in Bengal and Punjab, struck a favourable chord in
certain Muslim circles and led to, here and in other provinces of British
India, a steady decline in Muslim participation at annual Congress sessions and in national, provincial, and district committees.

Table 8.1 indicates the attendance of Muslim delegates at Congress
sessions from 1918 to 1923. Clearly, the number of Muslims gradually
dwindled from a few hundred to less than a score. Muslim representation
in the AICC was impressive, showing an increase from 11.1 per cent in
1919 to 24.5 per cent in 1923 (Table 8.2). In 1922-3, 84 of the 338 AICC
members were Muslims. By 1928, however, their number was reduced to 54
out of 332.[8] Provincial and district committees also had very few Muslim
members. In UP, only 7 Muslims served on various district committees:
1 each in Gonda, Allahabad, Jhansi, Moradabad, Faizabad, Azamgarh, and
2 in Bara Banki.[9]

In 1922-3, Motilal Nehru built his support among an influential group of
Lucknow and Allahabad based professional men: T.A.K. Sherwani, Rafi
Ahmed Kidwai, Khaliquzzaman and M.H. Kidwai.[10] In Bengal, C.R. Das
lured the khilafatists into supporting the Swaraj party by offering a set of
extravagant concessions. In consequence, his party swept the November
1923 polls, capturing an overall majority of seats, including half the
Muslim seats. Muslim backing was strongest in the eastern division
of Chittagong and the northern division of Rajshahi, the storm centres of
the khilafat movement in Bengal. Likewise, the swarajists won 10 of the

Table 8.1: Attendance of Muslim delegates at the Congress sessions, 1918-23

Year	Total no. of delegates	No. of Muslim delegates
1918	3,975	205
1919	6,717	314
1920	13,532	1,050
1921	4,201	521
1922	NA	NA
1923	1,550	111

15. Iqbal, *Life and Times of Mohamed Ali*, p. 308.
16. 'India's Message to France', Iqbal (ed.), *Writings and Speeches*, p. 158; *Comrade*, 13 May 1913.
17. 'A People's Right to Live', ibid., p. 171.
18. Mohamed Ali to Chelmsford, 24 Apr. 1919, MAP.
19. Mohamed Ali observed: 'Islam united Muslims by offering a set of common ideals and offered the only rational basis for unity and co-operation among its followers. The sympathies of a Muslim are co-extensive with his religion because they have been bred into him by the inspiring spirit of his creed.' *Comrade*, 12 Apr. 1913.
20. Nehru, *An Autobiography*, p. 117.
21. *Comrade*, 16 Oct. 1925; Afzal Iqbal (ed.), *Select Speeches*, pp. 331-2, 337.
22. Douglas, *Abul Kalam Azad*, p. 223.
23. Abul Kalam Azad, *India Wins Freedom: the complete version*, New Delhi, 1988, p. 248.
24. Nicholas Mansergh (ed.), *The Transfer of Power* (hereafter *TP*), 1942-7 (London: His Majesty's Stationery Office), Vol. 1, p. 293. For an account of the Conference, Humayun Kabir, *Muslim Politics, 1906-42*, Calcutta, 1944.
25. *TP*, Vol. 8, p. 103.
26. Wavell to J. Colville, 8/9 July 1946, and Note by Wavell, 19 Aug. 1946, ibid., p. 23; Datta, *Maulana Azad*, p. 171.
27. To S. Cripps, 22 July 1946, ibid., Vol. 8, pp. 102-3.
28. Sarvepalli Gopal, *Jawaharlal Nehru: A Biography 1889-1947*, Vol. 1, New Delhi, 1975, p. 326.
29. Alan Campbell-Johnson, *Mission with Mountbatten*, London, 1951, p. 254.
30. To Wavell, 9 July 1946, *TP*, Vol. 8, p. 24.
31. On differences between the Mahatma and the Maulana, first over the Quit India movement, and later over the conduct of the negotiations with the cabinet missions, see Datta, *Maulana Azad*, pp. 168, 174, 175, 176. For Gandhi's unfavourable response to Azad's proposal for alleviating Muslim fears, see Jenkins to Abell, 28 Aug. 1945, reporting on an intercepted letter from Gandhi to Azad, *TP*, Vol. 6, p. 76. Azad's own version of his differences with Nehru is quite revealing. For a refutation of the Maulana's thesis, see Gopal, *Jawaharlal Nehru*, Vol. 1, pp. 227-9, and S.R. Mehrotra, 'Nehru and the Partition of India, 1935-47', in Philips and Wainwright (eds.), *The Partition of India*, pp. 178-9.
32. *India Wins Freedom*, p. 170.
33. Datta, *Maulana Azad*, pp. 164,171; Douglas, *Abul Kalam Azad*, p. 295.
34. Campbell Johnson, *Mission with Mountbatten*, p. 254.
35. Wavell to A. Clow (Bombay), 7 Oct. 1946, TP, Vol. 8, p. 675.
36. To Pethick-Lawrence, 1 Oct. 1946, ibid., p. 634.
37. To Pethick-Lawrence, 1 Oct. 1946, ibid., p. 636.

38. Wavell to Abell, 1 Oct. 1946, ibid., p. 631.
39. Wavell to Pethick-Lawrence, 29 Sept. 1946, ibid., p. 625.
40. Pethick-Lawrence to Cripps, 30 Sept. 1939, ibid., p. 629.
41. Campbell-Johnson, *Mission with Mountbatten*, p. 194.
42. Douglas, *Abul Kalam Azad*, pp. 232-3 and 238.

spheres. And, yet, it indicates the overall thrust of their political concerns in relation to the community, the region and the nation at large. Some like Azad and Husain Ahmad Madani, head of the Dar al-ulum at Deoband, interpreted Islam as a religion of freedom and equality, of justice, and of cooperation with and respect for all mankind.[23] Thus Madani defended full and individual Muslim participation in a struggle for India's freedom by advancing a theory of territorial nationhood for India rather than by appealing to concepts of safeguards and community confederation. He expressed his ideas in a public controversy with Iqbal shortly before the latter's death in 1938.[24]

For those trained and tutored at the Aligarh College or the institutions in Allahabad, Patna and Calcutta, the Congress expressed the popular yearning for political freedom and independence. 'If I were asked why I have such an abiding faith in Indian nationalism,' stated the Bihar lawyer-politician Ali Imam, 'my answer is that without that India's freedom is an impossibility.'[25] Such men accepted the Congress as a viable vehicle for social change rather than the communal organizations. By joining it in large numbers, observed Maulvi Mujibur Rahman at the Bakarganj District Muslim Conference in May 1931, the Bengali Muslims would take a greater part in the freedom struggle.[26] Khan Abdul Ghaffar Khan announced at a public meeting in December 1931 that the Congress party alone would free the country, feed the hungry, and clothe the naked.[27] The *Jirgah* of India, he reaffirmed, was called Congress—a common *Jirgah* of all the communities of India. Justifying his alliance with Congress he said: 'In order to save himself from the enemies did not the Holy Prophet make alliance with the Jews and the Politheists [*sic*]?'[28] His audience beamed approvingly.

Such individuals and groups spanned several provinces of British India. The Khudai Khidmatgars headed a nationalist and socially progressive movement in the frontier province. Within two years of its creation they were 2,00,000 strong.[29] Quotations from the Koran against slavery served as rallying points for nationalist enthusiasm, and the struggle to liberate the country from foreign rule became the rallying cry. 'No section of India', observed W.C. Smith, the historian of Indian Islam, 'has been more thoroughly nationalist.'[30] During civil disobedience in 1930-1 Khudai Khidmatgar activism was linked with the Congress—the connection was strengthened in August 1931 when the Afghan *Jirgah* merged with the provincial Congress committee. The local *Jirgahs* became the local Congress committees, while 'Red Shirt' volunteers merged with the Congress bodies at various levels. The whole movement was conducted in accordance with the Congress constitution, and the flag used was the Congress flag. The 'Frontier Gandhi' explained:

People complain against me for having joined the Congress by selling my nation. The Congress is a national and not a Hindu body. It is a jirga composed of Hindus, Jews, Sikhs, Parsis, and Muslims. The Congress as a body is working against the British. The British nation is the enemy of the Congress and of the Pathans. I have therefore joined it and made common cause with the Congress to get rid of the British.[31]

The intensity of civil disobedience was reflected in the number of prosecutions and convictions. Until September 1932, the figure was 5,557 in a total population of 25 lakhs. In neighbouring Punjab, the number was 1,620, though the population was more than eight times that of the N.W.F.P.[32] Convictions were also higher than the Bombay presidency (see Table 8.3). Ghaffar Khan's motto: 'We are Pakhtuns but until we attain freedom we do not deserve to be called Pakhtuns'[33] remained the rallying slogan of his followers.

The Majlis-i Ahrar-i Islam, organized in 1929 by a group of Muslims in Punjab, had its base amongst the well-to-do peasantry and the lower-middle classes. The Ahrars combined economic grievances and religious passions to formulate their militant policies,[34] thus expressing something of the old khilafat movement tradition: an ardent and explicit enthusiasm for freedom. And like the Khudai Khidmatgars, the Ahraris steadily and fervently went to jail in large numbers.[35] In Delhi, they combined with the Jamiyat al-ulama activists to organize processions, public meetings, and picket liquor shops. Clashes with the police on 11-13 March 1932 led to the arrest of Azad and Maulvi Kifayatullah and twenty-five other Muslims. Reminiscent of scenes during the Rowlatt satyagraha was a mammoth meeting at the Fatehpuri Masjid, where 4,500-5,000 Muslims endorsed Gandhi's civil disobedience movement.[36]

Table 8.3: Convictions in Bombay and the N.W.F.P.

	Conviction in January-February 1932	Convictions in March-September 1932	Total
Bombay	5,165	6,311	11,476
N.W.F.P.	4,318	1,239	5,557

Source: Home Poll. File No. 5/72, 1932, NAI.

Table 8.2: Composition of AICC, 1919-23

Religion	1919 (161 Members)	1920 (163 Members)	1921	1922 (338 Members)	1923
Hindus	139	133	124	242	248
Muslims	18	21	33	84	83
Sikhs	-	2	2	9	8
Parsees	3	4	2	-	-
Christians	1	2	2	3	3

Source: Gopal Krishna, 'The Indian National Congress, 1918-1923', D. Phil. thesis, Oxford, 1960, p. 747.

15 Muslim seats in the Calcutta Corporation elections. The Muslim vote was strongest in the city's central mercantile wards with its up-country Urdu-speaking merchants, property owners and artisans who had formed the backbone of the khilafat movement.[11]

This support was eroded once the Bengal Congress repudiated the Das pact. There were 15 Muslim swarajists in 1923; there were none in 1926. The *Mussalman* rejected the Swaraj party 'as the party which turned out to be inimically disposed towards the Mussalmans,'[12] while Husayn Suhrawardy and Abdul Karim, leading negotiators of the Das pact, led their followers in Calcutta deeper into the labyrinth of distinctly communal politics.[13] The picture was not very different in UP.[14] As against 11 Muslims nominated and 4 elected in 1923, 6 were renominated in 1926 and only 1 returned. Of the 8 swarajist Muslims returned in 1923 to the Central Assembly, only 3 were elected in 1926. Irked by Motilal Nehru's attitude towards reforms in the N.W.F.P., Saiyid Murtaza, a swarajist from Madras, accused him of sacrificing the Frontier Muslims in order to woo Lajpat Rai on the eve of the 1926 elections.[16] Muhammad Shafee Daoodi's indictment was equally harsh: 'Temporary success in your political endeavours has got greater value for you than the more enduring rapprochement of the two great communities of India.' He charged that the Congress, having gradually drifted towards the Mahasabha since 1923, had reduced itself to being its tool.[17] Both Murtaza and Daoodi quit the Swaraj party in 1926. The feeling of insecurity was so widespread that some Muslims, who had in the recent past contributed to Congress's popularity, were now arrayed among its enemies.[18]

Yet, political activity among Muslims was sporadic and fragmented. Conflicting regional, local and class interests—a consequence of the uneven development of the Muslim communities—deepened conflicts and divisions only to expose the hollowness of the leader's claim to represent all Muslims. This was reflected in the formal split between the Jinnah and the Shafi factions in the Muslim League. Any new party, whether cobbled together by the khilafatists or the Leaguers, promised to be a rickety, splintered structure that could collapse at any moment. Such was the fate of the All-Parties Muslim Conference after 1932. The organizers, like the Dutch army, were all generals but no soldiers. Members of the land-owning class, none of them was prepared to spreadhead the movement or to follow the other.[18]

Similarly, Jinnah's brave attempts to infuse some life into the Muslim League were poorly rewarded; its total membership rose from a mere 1,093 in 1922 to 1,330 in 1927.[19] 'We are disgusted', wrote the *Mussalman*, 'with the Muslim League on account of its culpable inactivity. . . . The provincial Leagues have imbibed the inactivity and the character of the parent body.'[20]

Within the Congress ranks were, however, a number of groups, who were described as 'Nationalist Muslims'. Most had been associated with the party from the days of the Rowlatt satyagraha, though the distinction between them and their detractors—the Ali brothers, Muhammad Shafi and the other organizers of the All-Parties Muslim Conference—gained currency in the mid-1920s. 'They are men', said Ansari, the principal spokesman of the Congress Muslim, 'to whom the freedom of the country from alien rule comes merely as a bad second to communal privileges.'[21]

Though the label 'Nationalist Muslim' communicates the ideology and politics of those wedded to Indian nationalist aspirations, its exclusive application to Muslims, as discussed in the introduction to this book, conjures up the false image of a community largely communally-oriented with only a handful integrated with the dominant nationalist trend. Such a label also does not account for the subtle but extremely important differences between a professed nationalist and a so-called communalist. It is thus not easy to place Mohamed Ali in this supposed dichotomous framework. Though a critic of the Congress and the Nehru report, he remained committed to swaraj. Ansari conceded that, in spite of being led into the 'camp of national reaction', the Ali brothers had not 'surrendered their loyalty to the fundamental principle of Indian politics, freedom from foreign domination'.[22]

How, then, does one describe the many Muslim groups connected with the Congress movement at various levels? It is convenient, for descriptive purposes, to identify them as Congress Muslims, though the term does not quite embrace the range of their activities in the social and education

Mujibur Rahman, Akram Khan, K. Nooruddin and Abdur Razzack (the latter two were Calcutta Corporation Councillors) the Calcutta branch. Local branches in Bogra and Faridpur were controlled by a scattering of others who had been active in the khilafat and non-cooperation movements.[53]

On the strength of this network, the NMP claimed to represent the 'entire Muslim intelligentsia'.[54] Ansari scoffed at the League, pointing out that it had long ceased to be a reality, while the khilafat committee, once so powerful, 'was now but a shadow of its former self'. He concluded his party as the 'real representative group of the Musalmans of India today'.[55]

Such claims were exaggerated, and yet the NMP had the potential of emerging as a powerful force.[56] Hence, Ansari and his comrades staked their claim to represent the Muslims at the Round Table Conference in London. Gandhi insisted on demonstrating Congress's representative position,[57] and told the viceroy that without Ansari he would be 'perfectly helpless' in conducting Hindu-Muslim negotiations.[58] But the viceroy did not acquiesce. The Mahatma said in London that, whoever prevented Ansari from being selected as a delegate, committed a 'fatal blunder'.[59]

Actually, it was Fazl-i Husain, member of the viceroy's council, who vetoed Ansari's participation. Backed by the Muslim Conference and a section of the Urdu press, the Punjabi leader questioned the NMP's claim to represent the Muslims. 'The Muslim press has already stated', he wrote in July 1931, 'that Ali Imam and Ansari should not go as representatives of Muslims. This is the right line to take, and if it is right, there is no reason why it should not succeed.' He admired Ansari, adding, however, how 'during the last few weeks he [Ansari] seems to have done his best to convince all his friends and admirers that [his] partisanship of the Congress has deprived him of any sense of fair-play and propriety'.[60] Fazl-i Husain reserved his harsh comments for Gandhi. 'To confuse the issues, to indulge in irrelevance and to begin to talk of Muslim demands, and then talk of Congress Muslims of Dr. Ansari and so on', he wrote to friends in October 1931,

all are devices with which Hindus as well as Muslims are quite familiar . . . Gandhi's insistence upon Dr. Ansari's inclusion and his parading readiness for complete surrender in case complete unity is forthcoming have nothing new about them. They are the very old devices which the Congress, Gandhi and the Indian Hindus have been condemning in the British Government and the British statesmen. They are doing now exactly what they alleged Lord Birkenhead was doing—asking for complete unanimity and resorting to the well known principle of Divide and Rule; but Gandhi should know that the people are not so unsophisticated today as they used to be and that the game he is now indulging in is one which has been played out for some time.[61]

Ansari hated being drawn into the controversy. Gandhi, he wrote on 28 September, 'is harking back on me and wanting me even at this eleventh hour to be invited. . . . It is like a baby crying for his wetnurse'. Convinced that the government would keep the NMP unrepresented,[62] he stated:

I am positive that the government has deliberately left the Nationalist Muslim Party unrepresented . . . because they do not want the Hindu-Muslim question to be settled without their intervention. And they know that if there is any party in India which can bring about Hindu-Muslim unity it is the Nationalist Muslim Party. It is, therefore, against their interest to have the representatives of that party at the Round Table Conference, for they would be able to cement the unity of the various parties in India and thus deprive the government from playing their trump card against the representatives of India who are pressing hard for complete freedom from the British tutelage.[63]

He felt that Gandhi should not insist on his inclusion, but Jawaharlal Nehru dissuaded him not to be 'so rash as to cable him to do what he chooses'.[64] In early October, Gandhi changed gear, arguing that Ansari will be of no use unless the Muslim delegation endorsed his selection as a delegate.[65]

Meanwhile, the NMP secured the adherence of influential Muslims who had built their reputation through years of selfless political work. Its meetings at Lucknow (18-19 April 1931), Faridpur (27-8 June 1931) and Lahore (24 October 1931) were well-attended, and its policies conveyed some sense in the N.W.F.P., Punjab, UP and Bombay.[66] 'One of the most gratifying signs of the times', commented the *Leader*, 'is the rapid growth of nationalism among Indian Muslims. . . . The impressive gathering of the nationalist Muslims at Lucknow from all parts of the country tells its own tale.'[67] The editor of the *Indian Annual Register* expressed similar views.[68]

Ansari worked feverishly to weld together the various Muslim factions and persuade them to accept the NMP's proposals. They were mainly two: joint electorates and adult suffrage;[69] on other issues there was no fundamental difference between Jinnah's 'Fourteen Points' and the NMP resolution adopted in Lucknow on 18-19 April 1931.[70] Political problems, argued the Bihar lawyer Ali Imam, were a reflex of social forces. 'If you erect an iron wall between community and community in their politics, you destroy the social fabric. . . . Nationalism can never evolve from division and dissension.'[71] Ansari, too, refused to countenance separate electorates. He wanted the measure and method of representation in

The Ahrar party, also active in Kashmir, agitated against the Dogra ruler, maharaja Hari Singh, seeking redressal of the grievances of the Muslim subjects.[37] These were set out in the memorial submitted to the maharaja on 19 October 1931,[38] and taken note of by B.J. Glancy, chairman of a commission to enquire into the demands of the memorialists.[39] Led by Mazhar Ali, Habibur Rahman of Ludhiana, Abdur Rahman Ghazi, and Ataullah Shah Bukhari, the Ahrars sent *jathas* of red-uniformed *razakaars* (volunteers) from parts of Punjab, especially Sialkot, to Kashmir to bear pressure on the maharaja to meet their demands.[40] Large-scale rioting in Jammu on 2 November 1931, and violent clashes at Mirpur between the *jathas* and state forces, followed. British troops were deployed to quell the disturbances.

The spurt in political activity profoundly influenced Kashmir's future history. With the Ahrar agitation petering out, the Jammu and Kashmir Muslim Conference, founded in 1932, wrested the political initiative. The conference, stated its founder Shaikh Muhammad Abdullah, though Muslim in name, was 'in spirit national and concerned with the welfare of all communities.'[41] He declared in 1931 and, again, in 1935, that the country's progress depended on harmonious communal relations,[42] and that he fought for the country's emancipation. 'Let us all rise above petty communal bickerings and work jointly for the welfare of the masses,' he said.[43] In the years to come, the Muslim Conference formulated a radical 'New Kashmir' plan, and spurned the rising tide of Muslim nationalism.

In Bombay, Saiyid Abdullah Brelvi, editor of the *Bombay Chronicle*, launched the Congress Muslim Party on 8 July 1929 to induce Muslims to join the Congress.[44] His chief support lay among the urban-based politicians, such as Yusuf Meharally, editor of the English weekly *Vanguard*, Abbas Tyabji, a lawyer with a long-standing association with the Congress movement, and M.C. Chagla, also a lawyer who came to the forefront as a vociferous champion of the Nehru report. Gandhi blessed the party with the message: 'If it is fully supported and does not go to sleep, it may prove a tower of strength to the Congress and an instrument of real service to India generally and to Mussalmans in particular.'[45]

The Congress Muslim Party, though assailed by Shaukat Ali and his followers among the Urdu-speaking Muslims, garnered a fair measure of support for civil disobedience: thus, Brelvi, backed by several Muslim mercantile associations, led a mile-long procession on 2 June 1930 and chaired a meeting of about 10,000, including Hindus.[46] 'Conspicuous amongst organizers of procession and speakers at meeting', noted a government report, 'were certain Maulanas and Muslim propagandists from other provinces. To this extent, [the] procession must be regarded as success of Congress propaganda and it must be admitted that during the last *fortnight many Muhammadans have been gathered into the Congress fold*'[47] (italics mine). This is not to deny that, compared to 1920-1, Muslim enthusiasm in Bombay and elsewhere was much less. But, then, the religious passion stirred by the khilafat question was out of the extraordinary: no such issue in the early 1930s evinced the same degree of fervour.

II

The All-India Nationalist Muslim Party was formed on 27-8 July 1929. This was a sequel to the AICC meeting at Allahabad where delegates, reflecting on the political struggle being weakened by inter-communal conflicts and the attempts being made in to wean Muslims away from political activities, resolved to form themselves into a group.[48] They attributed the 'disruption' among politically-minded Muslims and their consequent apathy to a 'confused appreciation of the political obligations implicit in the fact of the community being a part of the Indian nation. Muslim political activity is now confined under the auspices of the existing Muslim institutions, to winning political responsibility as the main objective, and with freedom for the country as merely incidental thereto. Hence the need for the new party.' The NMP set out to develop a mentality above communalism, inspire into the Muslim communities greater confidence in nationalistic ideas, and create harmonious Hindu-Muslim relations.[49]

Khaliquzzaman claimed to be the founder of the NMP,[50] though existing historical evidence points to Ansari as its architect. Others closely associated with him were Rafi Ahmed Kidwai, Sherwani, Azad, Ghaffar Khan, Brelvi, Abdul Majid Khwaja, Mujibur Rahman, Saifuddin Kitchlew, and Abdul Bari of Bihar. Maulvis Kifayatullah, Muhammad Sajjad and Ahmad Said represented the Jamiyat al-ulama, while Maulana Qutubddin Wali belonged to Firangi Mahal.[51]

At its first meeting held at Sherwani's home in Allahabad on 27 July 1929, a central body was constituted: 28 members were elected from Bengal, 27 from Punjab, 3 from the N.W.F.P., 24 from UP. Committees were set up in Lucknow, Rae Bareli, Allahabad, Banaras, Faizabad, Hardoi, Bijnor, Saharanpur, Bareilly, Mahoba, Meerut, Aligarh, and Shahajahanpur.[52] In Punjab, NMP committees functioned in eight districts. There were ten in Bihar, and at least four in Bengal—Calcutta, Dacca, Bogra and Faridpur. Shamsul Huda and Ghulam Qadri headed the Dacca committee;

there is still some ground for fear that is a matter for safeguards, not of opposing a just demand.

We are therefore of opinion that even communal grounds justify the separation of Sind. If the Hindus stand to lose thereby and the Muslims stand to gain, of which we see no chance, such risk of loss by the one and the chance of gain by the other community will not, we hope and trust, be allowed by either to endanger the larger cause. We shall deal with the general aspect of the question later. We would note here that our colleague Mr. Aney does not agree with all the above views but agrees with our conclusion.

CHAPTER III

RESERVATION OF SEATS

ALTERNATIVE PROPOSALS

Coming now to the question of reservation of seats, it was found that each party held strongly to its own opinion and was not prepared to give in. Muslims were insistent on the reservation of seats for the Muslim majorities in the Punjab and Bengal, and the Hindu Maha Sabha and the Sikh League were equally strongly opposed to this. The Committee considered various proposals, among them being:

1. Reservation of seats on population basis for majorities as well as minorities.
2. Part reservation for majorities with freedom to contest other seats.
3. Proportional Representation.
4. Amalgamation of the Punjab and N.W.F. Province, with no reservation of seats.
5. No reservation, but special safeguards in the constitution for educational and economic advance of backward communities.

Before considering these proposals, some of which were new, the Committee was of opinion that representatives of the principal organizations concerned might be consulted. An invitation was therefore sent on June 11th to the Hindu Maha Sabha, the All India Muslim League and the Sikh League to send one or two representatives to meet the Committee on June 21st. The response to these invitations was not very encouraging. The secretary of the Hindu Maha Sabha wrote to express his inability to send any representative on that date, and the secretary of the Muslim League did not send any answer at all. The Sikh League were prepared to send representatives but as the Maha Sabha and Muslim League were not sending any one, our colleague Sardar Mangal Singh did not think it necessary to trouble the Sikh representative to come. Some others who had been personally invited could not come. We had the privilege however of conferring with Dr. M.A. Ansari, who took the trouble to come and assist us with his advice.

The proposals set out above were discussed at two consecutive sittings at which Dr. Ansari was also present. No agreement could be reached on the first proposal, but decisions were taken on the remaining four. It will be convenient to deal with these latter before taking up the main proposal.

PART RESERVATION

The suggestion was to have part reservation of the majority community in the Punjab and in Bengal with freedom to contest the other seats. This part reservation was granted to the non-Brahmans in the south and is still continuing. But even in the case of the non-Brahmans it has been found to be wholly unnecessary as they have always, so far as we are aware, captured a far larger number of seats on the strength of their votes and have had no need to invoke the aid of the reservation clause. It is not the case of any one in the Punjab or Bengal that the Muslim majority will not succeed in capturing a large number of seats. What is feared by the Muslims, unreasonably most of us think, is that they may not capture the majority of seats. In any event they will capture enough seats to make them if not a clear majority at least a strong minority just short of a majority. If they are sure of capturing, let us say, 45 per cent of seats the need for part reservation disappears. We are not opposed to part reservation for majorities or minorities, with freedom to contest the remaining seats, but we feel that in the case of Bengal and the Punjab it is unnecessary and does not materially affect the situation either way.

PROPORTIONAL REPRESENTATION

The next proposal is that of Proportional Representation. The sub-committee appointed by the All Parties Conference to consider this method of election and representation has presented no report but some individual members have sent their separate notes. Sardar Mangal Singh has supported the proposal, but the others, while favouring the system, are of opinion that under present circumstances in India it will not work. We feel strongly attracted to this method and are of opinion that it offers the only rational and just way of meeting the fears and claims of various communities. There is a place in it for every minority and an automatic adjustment takes place of rival interests. We have no doubt that proportional representation will in future be the solution of our problem.

How far is it immediately practicable? Great stress is laid on its intricacy and of the general illiteracy of the electorate in India. We are told that it is impossible to work this system, desirable as it may be, so long as the electorate is not educated up to understanding its significance. We recognize this difficulty. It is considerable. And yet we feel that it is a little exaggerated. Proportional Representation requires not so much a high standard of intelligence in the voters, as expert knowledge in the returning officers and the people who count and transfer votes from one head to another. There can be no doubt that there is a sufficiency of Indians who are competent enough to do this work of counting of votes satisfactorily. As for the general electorate it is very true that a standard of intelligence is necessary for a proper choice to be made in order of merit. But a certain standard is also necessary to exercise the right of vote even in a single member constituency. It is notorious that even in highly democratic England that standard is lacking and votes are given not for high matters of policy or considerations that are really important, but for trivial matters or even sometimes most objectionable considerations which the exigencies of election times force to the front. A general election has turned in the past on the cry of hanging the ex-Kaiser or on a forged letter, and the men, who were to govern an empire and influence largely world events, have been elected for reasons which make every intelligent person despair of democracy. In India the standard of intelligence of the vote will, to begin with at least, be lower than that of the English voter. But these are reasons against democracy, not so much against Proportional Representation.

We are told that another strong argument against Proportional Representation is that for the illiterate voter it would do away with the secrecy of the ballot. We think that the device of three boxes of the same colour for each candidate with different symbols painted on each box to indicate the first, second and third choice, would remove this objection. But it applies in equal measure to the illiterate voter at most of the ordinary elections today. In Malta, where there is a large majority of illiterate voters, Proportional Representation has been tried with success, but of course we cannot compare the little island of Malta to our enormous country with its millions.

Most of us feel that there are no insuperable difficulties in the way of giving a trial to Proportional Representation in India. There are drawbacks and risks, but no proposal which we have considered is free from objection, and some of these involve a departure from principle which may bring greater difficulties in its train. Some of our colleagues however are not satisfied that Proportional Representation can be introduced at this stage in India. We therefore refrain from recommending it.

AMALGAMATION OF PUNJAB AND N.W.F. PROVINCES

It was suggested that the N.W.F. province be amalgamated with the Punjab and that there should then be no reservation of seats in this province. We have no objection to this proposal but we do not know how far this will meet the different view points of the parties concerned. If it does meet with their approval, we would gladly recommend it. There is no special principle involved in it. Its acceptance or otherwise depends entirely on whether it is approved or not. Our colleague Sardar Mangal Singh does not approve of the proposal and we understand that some other people also are of his opinion. We therefore make no recommendation in regard to it.

AMALGAMATION OF PUNJAB N.W.F.P.,
SIND AND BALUCHISTAN

A similar but more far reaching proposal was made to us, namely, that the Punjab, the N.W.F. Province, Baluchistan and Sind should all be amalgamated together and that there should be no reservation of seats, unless the minority desires it, in this area. We were unable to entertain this proposal. It would mean the creation of an unwieldy province sprawling all over the north and north-west.

NO RESERVATION IN THE PUNJAB

Another proposal in regard to the Punjab was that there should be no reservation whatever but that special safeguards in the constitution for educational and economic advance of backward communities may be provided. We would cordially welcome such a solution if it was agreed to. But we have to recognize that a unanimous acceptance of this proposal is at present unlikely, otherwise there would have been no communal friction. In our draft constitution we have included many safeguards for minorities and provisions for the educational and economic advance of backward communities. We would gladly add to these safeguards and provisions if thereby we could remove feelings of insecurity in any community and do away with reservation of seats and other communal expedients. It seems unnecessary to pursue the subject any further in the present atmosphere.

RESERVATION OF SEATS ON POPULATION BASIS

We now come to the main question, the reservation of seats on the basis of population, both for majorities and minorities.

GENERAL

It was never seriously denied that reservation of seats for communities was as bad in principle as communal electorates, but, for various reasons of expediency, such reservation was recommended for a time to serve as a transitional stage between communal electorates and general mixed electorates without any restrictions. The idea was that during the interval the distrust of one community of the other would be very much lessened if not altogether removed. Similar arguments were used when the Lucknow pact was arranged, but the actual experience of the last 12 years has belied the expectations then formed. Communal electorates might or might not be responsible for the increasing communal tension of recent years but they have certainly failed to pave the way to a better understanding between the communities as was hoped. General reservation of seats for any community whether found in a minority or a majority is a full recognition of communalism and differs little from communal electorates.

RESERVATION FOR MAJORITIES

Reservation of seats for majorities has been fiercely opposed—both on grounds of theory and fact. The question arises only in the provinces of the Punjab and Bengal where the Muslims are in a slight majority over all others. It has not been claimed for any other majority in any other province. We have therefore to consider the Punjab and Bengal only in this connection.

We should have thought that of all the provinces of India the Punjab and Bengal were the most fortunate in that the distribution of population was such that there was little chance of one community or group dominating over another or harassing it and preventing its growth in any way. Although one community is in an absolute majority in both of these provinces the others are strong enough to protect their own interests and prevent any oppression.

Reservation for a majority is indefensible in theory. It is in artificial restriction on the growth both of the majority and the minority and must necessarily retard national progress. It is, we feel, specially injurious to the majority itself for it makes it rely on legislative provision to keep up its position and not on its own inherent strength. After a period of reservation such a community is bound to lose in self-reliance and all the qualities that contribute towards building up a people and adding to their creative energy. Ordinarily a majority captures seats in excess of its population strength unless the method of election is by Proportional Representation. This is evident as the majority may be so spread out as to be in a commanding position in each or at any rate most of the constituencies. It is this danger of the majority capturing far more seats than its population strength entitles it to, and thereby encroaching on the limited preserves of the minority, that leads to the protection of minority interests.

A majority reservation or other fixation of seats is incompatible with real representative and responsible government. It obviously interferes with the right of the electors to choose whom they like. Further, it is bound to come in the way of other and more natural groupings in and outside the legislature and it will give a longer lease of life to communalism. Everybody regrets the communal spirit and desires to exorcise it from the body politic. But it is clear that it cannot go merely by talking about unity and indulging in pious platitudes which take us nowhere. Communalism can only go when the attention of the people is directed in other channels, when they begin to take interest in questions which really affect their daily lives rather than in fancied fears based on an artificial division of society. We must therefore try to create this new interest in the people and we must put no barriers in the way of the development of this interest. There can be no doubt that a majority reservation and fixation of seats is such a barrier.

METHODS OF RESERVATION

An examination of the methods by which reservation for a majority can be secured will show that it is not only a negation of representative government but is in direct conflict with the principle on which responsible government rests.

THE MONTAGU-CHELMSFORD METHOD

One of these methods has been applied in the Madras and parts of the Bombay presidency to secure a partial reservation for the overwhelming majorities of non-Brahmans in those presidencies. This large community which forms over 96 per cent of the population of the Madras presidency succeeded in inducing the government, on the recommendation of the Southborough Committee, to reserve for them 28 seats out of a total of 98 to protect them from the small minority of Brahmans who did not exceed 2½ per cent of the whole population. The manner in which this reservation was secured was that two purely non-Brahman constituencies, each returning a single member, were created and, of the remaining constituencies, 25 were made plural, each returning three or more members, two of whom must be non-Brahmans in Madras City, and one must be a non-Brahman in each of the remaining 24. The rule on the subject is thus stated:

When the counting of the votes has been completed the Returning Officer shall forthwith declare the candidate or candidates as the case may be, to whom the largest number of votes has been given, to be elected: provided that if one or more seats are reserved the Returning Officer shall first declare to be elected the non-Brahman candidate or candidates, as the case may be, to whom the largest number of votes has been given.

To illustrate this rule take the case of Madras City where out of six seats in a mixed electorate two are reserved for non-Brahmans. Assume that no non-Brahman candidate has secured enough votes to be placed among the first six who have polled the largest number of votes and that the only non-Brahman candidates who have secured any votes are to be found somewhere near the bottom of the list. Under the rule just quote two of these non-Brahmans would be at once declared to be duly elected and the 5th and 6th candidates on the list who are not non-Brahmans would have to give place to them. Thus in the case of non-Brahmans the choice of the electorate is wholly set aside even though a majority of their own community voted against them. The question is whom would these two non-Brahmans represent. It is clear that they do not represent the majority of the electorate nor possibly even a majority of non-Brahmans. They have come in by an artificial rule based on no principle whatever. Happily the fears of the non-Brahmans in Madras turned out to be unfounded and we are informed that there never was a single occasion to put the rule into practice.

It is bad enough to have 28 members of this kind in a representative house of 98 members, but when the majority of members are elected in this manner and the ministry is formed from out of them, representative government becomes a farce.

'SIND PACT' METHOD

Another method of reservation of seats both for the majority and the minority has been suggested by the promoters of what is called the 'Sind Pact'. This method is thus described in clause 5 of the 'Pact':

In order to make the system of joint electorates truly effective, there shall be one common electoral roll for each constituency and the election of Muslim and non-Muslim representatives should be held separately but on the same day, so that the whole electorate, Muslim and non-Muslim, shall have the right and opportunity to vote at both these elections separately, whereby the members so elected shall have been returned by the entire constituency and not only by the voters of their own communities.

The only merit claimed for this method is that the 'members so elected shall have been returned by the entire constituency and not only by the voters of their own communities'. For this purpose it would not be necessary to hold the elections separately as in a single election also the whole electorate—Muslim and non-Muslim—would have the right and opportunity to vote. The real object of the clause seems to be to avoid competition between the Hindu and Muslim candidates and thus secure to them reservation of seats according to their numbers. Apart from the fact that such competition is essential for the exercise by the elector of his free choice, the method proposed entirely shuts out all opportunity for a Hindu elector to vote for a Muslim candidate in preference to a candidate of his own community and *vice versa*.

It is obvious that the result of two separate ballots for each group of candidates can never be the same as that of a single ballot for both and that there will always be much greater chance at separate elections for the majority community to secure the return of their mandatories from among the minority community by concentrating their votes on them.

BOTH METHODS UNSATISFACTORY

It will thus be seen that neither of the two methods discussed above is likely to give satisfactory results. The third and the only remaining method of which we are aware is that of separate communal electorates which we have already discussed. The doing away of communal electorates is intended to promote communal unity by making each community more or less dependent on the other at the time of the elections. But reservation for a majority community in a mixed electorate will take away much of the incentive for communal unity, as the majority community as a whole would under all circumstances be assured of its full quota without the help of the other communities. There is no doubt some advantage to be gained by individual candidates of either community having to canvass the other community as against their rivals of the same community but this small advantage will probably not be availed of in times of acute communal tension.

It is absurd to insist on reservation of seats for the majority and claim full responsible government at the same time. Responsible government is understood to mean a government in which the executive is responsible to the legislature and the legislature to the electorate. If the members of the executive with the majority behind them have all got in by reservation and not by the free choice of the electorate there is neither representation of the electorate nor any foundation for responsible government. Reservation of seats for a majority community gives to that community the statutory right to govern the country independently of the wishes of the electorate and is foreign to all conceptions of popular government. It will confine minorities within a ring-fence and leave them no scope for expansion.

Defects of Elections

We have based the foregoing observations on the principles generally applied to representative government. We are aware that those principles have in practice been found far from perfect and that serious objections have been raised in certain quarters against democratic government itself. We can hardly enter into these considerations in this Committee and must at this stage of our evolution accept the principles governing elections in most of the advanced countries of the world. We are also aware that the system of election we have recommended has sometimes failed to establish the rule of the majority, as in the case of the last British elections, which resulted in the return of an overwhelming majority of members who had only the support of a minority of electors. This we believe was mainly due to inequalities in voting strength and the wastage of votes on candidates who did not need them. The only remedy is proportional representation which for the reasons already mentioned we have refrained from recommending at present.

Facts and Figures

We have so far considered the question of reservation for majorities on principle but the strongest argument against such reservation is furnished by the facts as they are. We are indebted to Pandit Jawaharlal Nehru for the figures given in Appendices A and B which he has compiled with great industry from the reports of the last census relating to Bengal and the Punjab—the only two provinces in which the Muslims are in a majority. These figures conclusively show that there is no foundation in fact for the fears entertained by the Muslims in these two provinces, and indeed no occasion for any adventitious aid to secure to them the full benefit of their natural majority. The argument is that Mussalmans will not obtain adequate representation and the slight majority they have will be more than counter-balanced by their educational and economic backwardness in these provinces. The whole force of this argument, which is based on the total population of the two provinces, disappears when we examine in detail the figures relating to the administrative divisions and the districts composing them.

It appears from an analysis of the population figures of the Punjab and Bengal that Muslims can certainly have nothing to fear from a free electorate, without any reservation of seats, in these two provinces. It will be clear from the figures given in the appendices that in both the Punjab and Bengal the distribution of population is such that the Muslim majority in most of the geographical and administrative areas comprising these provinces is much greater than it appears when the whole province is taken as a unit. We find that there are natural areas of reservation for the different communities which ensure the representation of each community far more effectively than any artificial reservation can do.

THE PUNJAB

Thus in the Punjab, we have a Muslim zone in the north and north-west of the province, where the Muslims are overwhelmingly strong and where no other community can encroach on their preserve. We find also a smaller area in the south, the Hindu zone, where the Hindus and Sikhs are equally strong. Between the two there is a third area where the Muslims are predominant, but not overwhelmingly so. This analysis leads us to the conclusion that Muslims are bound to capture over 47 per cent of the total seats in the Punjab from their special zone alone, whilst the Hindus and Sikhs will jointly capture nearly 30 per cent. The remaining 23 per cent of seats will lie in either a predominantly Muslim area or in districts where the Muslims are the strongest single community. Allowing for every contingency we cannot conceive of Muslims not capturing enough seats in this area to give them a clear majority in the provincial legislature.

We have discussed these population figures for each Punjab district in detail in our note attached (Appendix A). We may here however refer to some of these figures.

The population of the Punjab (British territory) at the last 1921 census was as follows:

Muslims	11,444,321	55.3%
Hindus	6,579,260	31.8%
Sikhs	2,294,207	11.1%
Others (mainly Christians)	367,236	1.8%
Total Punjab population	20,685,024	100.0%

There are 29 districts in all. We have divided these into four zones:

I. Fifteen districts in the overwhelmingly Muslim zone. The percentage of Muslims in one district is nearly 91; in nine districts it is between 80 and 90; in two districts it is 71 or over; and in three it is 63.3, 61.9 and 60.7. We have included the last three districts in this zone as, although the Muslim percentage is not so high as in the adjoining districts, it is very high compared to the Hindus and Sikhs combined. Thus in one (Sheikhupura) Muslims are 63.3%, Hindus 16.0% Sikhs are 15.9%; in Sialkot, Muslims are 61.9%, Hindus are 19.5% and Sikhs are 8.0%; in Lyallpur Muslims are 60.7%, Hindus are 18.1% and Sikhs are 16.4%.
It should be remembered that the non-Muslim minority in all these districts consists not of one group but of several communities Hindus, Sikhs, Christians and others.
If we give one member of the legislatures to every 1,00,000 popu-lation as we have suggested elsewhere, we find that 98 members will be returned from this Muslim zone alone. This amounts to 47.3 per cent of the total membership of the legislature.

II. There are two districts (Lahore and Gurdaspur) which might be called the predominantly Muslim zone. Here the Muslims are greater than Hindus and Sikhs combined—in Lahore they are 57.3% of the total—but they are not so many as in zone I. The number of members of the legislature for these two districts are 19½ or 9.4 per cent of the total membership.

III. There are three districts where no community is predominant but even here the Muslims are the strongest single community. The number of members of the legislature for these districts is 27½ that is, 13.3 per cent of the total.

IV. There are nine districts which might be called the overwhelmingly

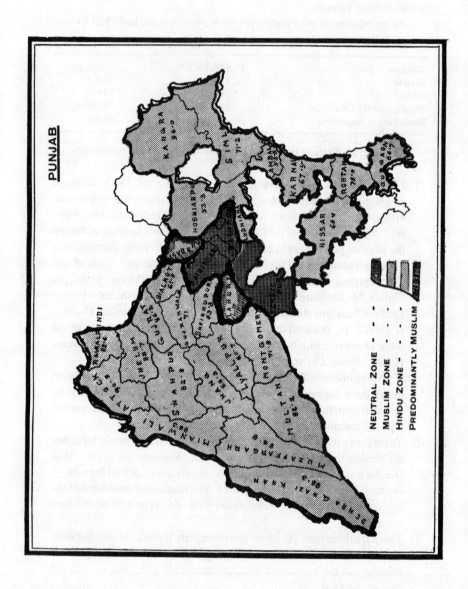

PUNJAB

NEUTRAL ZONE - - - - -
MUSLIM ZONE
HINDU ZONE
PREDOMINANTLY MUSLIM

Hindu-Sikh zone. The number of members for this zone is 61½ or 29.7 per cent of the total.

We thus see that Muslims are certain of 47.3 per cent seats; have a good chance of capturing the majority of at least 9.4 seats; and a fair chance of some seats out of the 13.3 per cent of group III. They are thus, humanly speaking, assured of a clear majority in the legislature.

BENGAL

In Bengal the figures are even more illuminating. These are discussed in full detail in the separate note attached (see Appendix B). We give here only a brief summary. The population figures are:

Muslims	25,210,802	54.0%
Hindus	20,203,527	43.3%
Others (chiefly tribal religions and Christians)	1,281,207	2.7%
Total Bengal population (British territory)	46,695,536	100.0%

Here also we find definite zones as in the Punjab.

I. Overwhelmingly Muslim zone. There are 13 districts with 282 members of the legislature or over 60 per cent of the total.
II. Predominantly Muslim zone—two districts with 23 members or 5 per cent of the total.
III. Neutral or predominantly Hindu zone. Four districts with 42 members or 9 per cent of the total.
IV. Overwhelmingly Hindu zone. Nine districts with 118 members or 25 per cent of the total.

Thus in Bengal from the overwhelmingly Muslim zone alone, not taking into consideration the predominantly Muslim zone, Muslims are assured of over 60% seats in the legislature. The Hindu minority, although it is a very big minority, is highly likely to suffer in numbers in an open general election without reservation.

BENGAL DISTRICT BOARD ELECTIONS

This has recently been demonstrated in a remarkable manner by the figures of the last District Board elections in Bengal, printed in Appendix C.

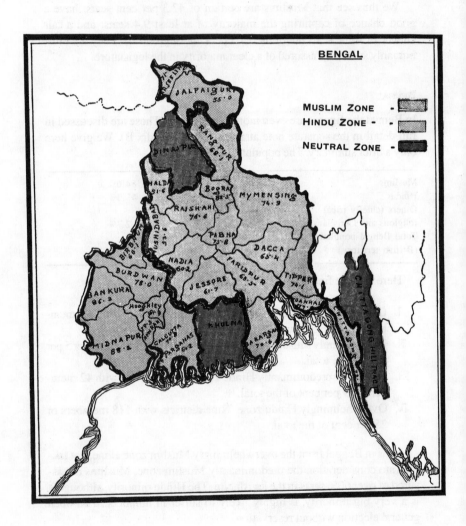

BENGAL

MUSLIM ZONE -
HINDU ZONE -
NEUTRAL ZONE -

JALPAIGURI 55·0

RANGPUR 66·1

DINAJPUR

MALDA 51·6

BOGRA 88·2

MYMENSING 74·9

RAJSHAHI 74·6

MURSHIDABAD 55·5

PABNA 75·8

DACCA 65·4

BIRBHUM

NADIA 60·2

FARIDPUR 65·5

TIPPERA 74·1

BURDWAN 66·0

JESSORE 61·7

NOAKHALI 77·7

BANKURA 96·2

HOOGHLEY

CALCUTTA 74·9

KHULNA

24 PARGANAS 78·6

CHITTAGONG HILL TRACTS

CHITTAGONG 76·5

MIDNAPUR 88·2

PARGANAS 64·2

The electorates for these boards are mixed Hindu and Muslim, but the electoral roll being based on a property or tax paying franchise does not maintain the population proportions of the two communities. We expect that the voting strength of the Muslims, who are economically weaker than Hindus, is much less than it would be with adult suffrage and yet we find that they made a clean sweep of the Hindu minority in three districts—Mymensingh, Chittagong and Jessore. In the first two of these not a single Hindu was elected though the Hindus are about 24 per cent of the population, and in the third only one Hindu managed to get in though the community forms 38.2 per cent of the population. As against this we find that Muslims, where they are in insignificant minorities of 3 and 4 per cent, have managed to send one to three representatives to the District Board. We have also very interesting examples of what happens when the two communities are found in about equal strength. The cases of Khulna and Dinajpur are in point. In the former the non-Muslims being 50 per cent of the population carried 11 seats as against 5 taken by Muslims who were 49.8 per cent. In the latter the Muslims being 49 per cent of the population carried 14 seats as against 4 of the Hindus who were over 44 per cent. Actual population is not a safe guide in the absence of exact figures showing the voting strength of the two communities, but we think it can safely be inferred that the Muslims in Bengal need no protection from all the non-Muslims put together. The case of Jessore is particularly interesting. As long as the Muslim majority did not take much interest in the local affairs of the district the Hindu minority had it all its own way. Once roused to action the Muslims not only swept the polls but for the first time in the history of their District Board gave it a Muslim chairman and a Muslim vice chairman, both members of the Bengal Council. We are informed that the last elections for the District Boards in Bengal have opened the eyes of both communities and that Muslim opinion is now veering round to mixed electorates. It is one of the tragedies of communal hostility that men shut their eyes to facts and fight against their own best interests. We commend a careful study of the figures we have given in Appendices A, B and C to those who are flooding the country with elaborate manifestos and memoranda in support of communal electorates for the Punjab and Bengal.

ECONOMIC AND EDUCATIONAL STANDARDS

We find therefore from an analysis of the actual figures that Muslim fears in the Punjab and Bengal are largely imaginary. These fears are based on the superior economic and educational standards of the Hindus and Sikhs.

We have seen that this superiority has not helped the Hindus of Bengal at the District Board elections and we are sure that the result of council elections will be even more strikingly in favour of Muslims. But there is no doubt that Muslims are backward both in education and in wealth, specially in Bengal, as compared to the other communities. There is also no doubt that the power of wealth is great in the modern State. It is so great indeed that it seldom troubles to contest seats in the legislature as it can pull the strings from behind the scenes. Reservation of seats or separate electorates, or any other device of this kind, cannot materially reduce this power. So long as people think and act in terms of communalism, so long will they not face the real problem. And if they will not face it, they will not solve it.

We are not here called upon to advise on a new structure of society where the economic power is not concentrated in the hands of a few. We take it that the communal organizations which aggressively demand special rights and privileges for their respective communities are not desirous of attacking the basis of the existing structure. If this is admitted then all we can do is to provide safeguards and guarantees for education and economic advancement, specially for all backward groups and communities.

Parties in Free India

We are certain that as soon as India is free and can face her problems unhampered by alien authority and intervention, the minds of her people will turn to the vital problems of the day. How many questions that are likely to be considered by our future legislatures can be of a communal nature? There may possibly be a few now and then, but there can be no doubt that the vast majority of the questions before us will not be communal in the narrow sense. The result will be that parties will be formed in the country and in the legislature on entirely other grounds, chiefly economic we presume. We shall then find Hindus and Muslims and Sikhs in one party acting together and opposing another party which also consists of Hindus and Muslims and Sikhs. This is bound to happen if we once get going.

Hindu and Sikh Minorities

Looking at it purely from the Hindu point of view however, we can well imagine that a reservation of seats for the Muslim majorities in the Punjab and Bengal, may actually benefit the Hindus, and it may be Sikhs also,

more than no reservation. The facts and figures we have stated demonstrate that the Muslim position in the Punjab and Bengal is so strong that
in all likelihood they will gain in a joint electorate with no reservation more
seats than their population warrants. Thus the Hindu and Sikh minorities
may find their representation even reduced below their population ratio.
This is a possible and indeed a likely contingency. But it is impossible to
provide for such contingencies. The safest and most obvious course is to
have an open election with such safeguards as we can devise.

INFORMAL CONFERENCE

The considerations set out above were fully discussed at the informal
conference to which reference has already been made and the following
resolution was unanimously adopted, subject to a note by our colleague
Sardar Mangal Singh on the second part of the resolution:[1]

We are unanimously opposed to the reservation of seats in the legislatures either
for majorities or minorities and we recommend that no such reservation should be
provided for in the constitution. But if this recommendation is not accepted and an
agreement can be arrived at only on a reservation of seats on the population basis
we recommend that such reservation be made for majorities or minorities without
any weightage and with a clear provision that it shall automatically cease at the
expiry of ten years or earlier by the consent of the parties concerned.

The note of Sardar Mangal Singh runs as follows:

I agree with the first part of the above proposition, namely that there shall be no
reservation of seats either for majorities or minorities in the legislatures of the
country. But I am very strongly opposed to the creation of statutory communal
majorities by reservation of seats for majorities on population basis under all
circumstances and for any time howsoever short it may be. If the agreement can
only be reached by reservation of seats I will recommend that the case of the Sikhs
be considered as that of an important minority and adequate and effective representation, far in excess of their numerical strength, be given to them in the Punjab
on the basis adopted for Muslim minorities under the Lucknow Pact in Behar and
other provinces. And I further suggest that special weightage be given to Sikhs for
representation in the central legislature.

It will be seen that the first part of the resolution contains the actual
recommendation of the informal conference and the second part deals
with a contingency which can happen, if at all, only when that recommendation is rejected in favour of an agreement by all the parties concerned on reservation of seats on the population basis. There has not

only been no such agreement among the members of this Committee but they have definitely expressed themselves in the first part of the resolution to be unanimously opposed to reservation. It is highly unlikely that the agreement referred to in the second part of the resolution will be reached in the All Parties Conference. But if by any chance such an agreement is arrived at, it would be binding on all those who join it and in that case all that the second part provides is that it should not be given effect to for more than ten years. We cannot be taken to have recommended what we have expressly opposed. But we recognize the value of a compromise between parties and communities however wrong it may be in principle, and if such a compromise is arrived at in spite of ourselves, we can do no more than try to limit its operation. This is exactly what we have done. As regards the special claim of the Muslims and Sikhs for greater representation than their population would justify, it is enough to say that in the view we have expressed above, no such claim is admissible on the part of any community however important it may consider itself to be.

We shall have to revert to the resolution of the informal conference in considering the question of reservation for minorities to which we now address ourselves.

RESERVATION FOR MINORITIES

Muslims in provinces other than the Punjab and Bengal are in small minorities and in some parts of India almost negligible, though in the total population of India the proportion is over 24 per cent.

RESERVATION FOR MUSLIM MINORITIES IN PROPORTION TO POPULATION

After the resolution of the informal conference referred to above was passed it was pointed out to us that it would work great hardship on the Muslim minority which would in all probability be able to elect no more than 30 or 40 Muslims from the Punjab and Bengal, and perhaps one or two from the U.P. and Behar, to the central legislature of 500 members, and that there was little chance of any of the other provinces with less than 7 per cent of the population returning a single Muslim. The result, it was argued, would be that Muslims, who form nearly one fourth of the total population of British India, would have no more than one tenth of representation in the central legislature. The same reasoning, it was urged, applied to the legislatures of provinces where the Muslims are in small minorities. We recognize the force of this argument and it is here that we feel compelled by force of circumstances to introduce a temporary element of communalism in the electoral system of the country. We are therefore unable to adopt the resolution of the informal conference of the 7th July in its entirely as our recommendation. In provinces other than the Punjab and Bengal we must make an exception in favour of Muslim minorities by permitting reservation of seats, if so desired by them, in proportion to their population both in the central and the provincial legislatures. The retention of communal representation to this extent for some time to come is in our opinion a necessary evil. It will be seen that by making this concession in favour of Muslim minorities we are not introducing the anomalies arising out of reservation for majorities. A minority must remain a minority whether any seats are reserved for it or not and cannot dominate the majority.

WEIGHTAGE NOT PERMISSIBLE

Representation in excess of their proportion in the population fixed for Muslims in a number of provinces under the Lucknow pact, as well as the Montagu-Chelmsford reforms, will disappear under our scheme. Such representation is only possible in separate electorates and has no place in joint or mixed electorates. It is of course not physically impossible to reserve a larger proportion of seats for Muslim minorities than their population would justify but, apart from the obvious injustice of such a course not only to the majorities but to the other minorities as well, it will in our opinion be harmful to the development of Muslims themselves on national lines. We have allowed them their full share on the population basis by reservation and anything over and above that share they must win by their own effort. We do not propose to impose any restrictions on their right to contest a larger number of seats than those reserved for them. The main consideration which has guided us in accepting reservation for their minority is that we are not thereby putting it in a ring-fence beyond which it cannot advance however competent it may be to do so. It is in our opinion more important to secure a free and open field for the expansion of the political activities of all communities large or small than to reserve a maximum number of seats for them even in excess of their numbers. Such reservation will never bring them in open competition with any community other than their own and the inevitable result will be stagnation. It is true that a Muslim candidate will have to canvass non-Muslim votes to defeat his Muslim rival but this is not calculated to advance the Muslim on national lines. It will always be a question of whether Muslim A is better than Muslim B without regard to the fact that non-Muslim C is better or worse than both.

Muslims cannot reasonably claim reservation of seats beyond their strict proportion to population along with the right to contest additional seats, and the question for them to consider is which of the two is likely to be of greater advantage to them. We have no doubt that when they carefully weigh the pros and cons of the reservation of a larger number of seats than they are entitled to on the population basis *without* the right to exceed that number, against the pros and cons of reservation in proportion to their population *with* the right to contest as many more seats as they like, they will find that the latter is by far the better choice. As we have already pointed out, reservation to the fullest extent deprives mixed electorates in a considerable measure of their utility in promoting national unity. Whatever inducement a Muslim candidate may have to approach the non-Muslim voter to defeat his Muslim rival, so far as his community as a whole is concerned, it will have its full quota assured to it with or without the help of the non-Muslim voters, and at times of extreme communal tension it will be easy both for Muslims and non-Muslims to run their elections quite independently of each other without either losing a single seat. It is only by maintaining the interdependence of the two communities that we can hope to minimize their differences.

MUSLIMS IN U.P.

Having regard to the actual conditions prevailing in the U.P., where the Muslim minority is the largest, we are convinced that the Muslims stand to gain more seats under our scheme than the number fixed for them under the present system. In several urban areas in the U.P. they are in majorities and in others they have strong and influential minorities. They may perhaps lose a few seats in some other provinces but the net result of a general election in the country as a whole is likely to be fairly satisfactory to all.

RESERVATION FOR MUSLIMS IN
THE CENTRAL LEGISLATURE

So far as the Muslim demand is concerned it only remains for us to deal with that part of it which relates to reservation of one third of the total number of seats in the central legislature for Muslims. This point was not directly raised or discussed at the informal conference, but we think that it is concluded by the general recommendations we have made in regard to reservation of seats. The principle we have adopted is that wherever such reservation has to be made for the Muslim minority it must be in strict proportion to its population. The Muslims are a little less than one fourth of the total population of British India and they cannot be allowed reservation over and above that proportion in the central legislature. It must be remembered that they have the right to contest additional seats both for the central and provincial legislatures in provinces other than the Punjab and Bengal, and that in the two last mentioned provinces their right is unfettered to contest any number of seats they like for both legislatures. In the case of provincial legislatures we have substituted this right for the present weightage they enjoy. In the central legislature the Muslims do not at present enjoy any definite weightage and their numbers to be returned by the provinces are fixed on a more or less arbitrary basis. The actual number of the Muslim members falls short of one third of the total strength of the Assembly. There is thus no foundation for the demand even in existing conditions. A little reflection will show that it is far better to have a free hand than to be tied down to the difference between $\frac{1}{3}$ and $\frac{1}{4}$. But as we have already observed we cannot depart from the principle we have accepted for the Muslim minorities in the provincial legislature. Besides the question of principle there are practical difficulties in the way. How are we to secure this one third reservation in the central legislature without restricting the Punjab and Bengal majorities to definite numbers of members and allowing weightage in the other provinces all round? And on what principle is the excess in the number of members in the provinces to be allotted to each province? We have given our best consideration to the matter but we regret we are unable to recommend reservation of one third of the total number of seats for Muslims in the central legislature.

RECOMMENDATION

For these reasons we recommend reservation of seats, when demanded, for Muslim minorities both in the central and provincial legislatures in strict proportion to their population, with the right to contest additional seats for a fixed period of ten years. We would add, however, that our colleague Mr. Shuaib Qureshi does not agree with some of the arguments and conclusions given above. He is of opinion that the resolution of the informal conference, referred to above, should be adopted in its entirety.

He further desires that one third of the seats in the central legislature
should be reserved for Muslims.

NON-MUSLIM MINORITIES IN N.W.F. AND BALUCHISTAN

As regards non-Muslim minorities the only provinces which deserve consideration are the N.W.F. and Baluchistan where they are in much the same
position as the Muslim minorities in Madras and the C.P. We recommend
that the same concession be made to them as to the Muslims in provinces
other than the Punjab and Bengal.

OTHER NON-MUSLIM MINORITIES

Turning to the other non-Muslim minorities we find that there is no such
sharp cleavage between them and the majorities among whom they live as
there unfortunately is between Hindus and Muslims. We do not think that
any protection by way of reservation is either necessary or desirable in
their case. They will realize that we are recommending such protection to
Muslim minorities under very special circumstances and for a limited
period only. The latter have sooner or later to stand on their own legs. We
shall indeed be glad if they will make up their minds to do without reservation from the beginning.

There is no analogy between the Muslim and non-Muslim minorities
in India. The latter are nowhere when the total population of India is considered. Leaving out the case of Buddhists, who are to be found chiefly in
Burma and are in a majority there, the percentage of the population of
other non-Muslim minorities to the total population of India is as follows:

Christians	1.2%
Sikhs	1.0%
Jains	.2%
Others (besides tribal religions in hill tracts)	.2%

It will thus appear that so far as the central legislature is concerned the
reservation of seats for non-Muslim minorities on a population basis will
hardly help them to any appreciable extent and that there is no occasion to
reserve seats for minorities, other than those in the N.W.F. Province and
Baluchistan, even in the provincial legislature. Any attempt to do so will
only cause confusion and will in our opinion be a very doubtful advantage to the communities concerned.

We have not mentioned the Hindu minorities in the Punjab and Bengal as by no stretch of the imagination 32 and 45 per cent of the population can be regarded as small minorities.

SIKHS

Among the non-Muslim minorities the Sikhs deserve special consideration. They are concentrated in the Punjab and the position they occupy in that province is very similar to that of the Muslims in the U.P. The latter being about 15% of the population are in fact more numerous in the U.P. than the Sikhs in the Punjab where they are only 11%. Under the existing system they have their separate electorate and are given considerable weightage. We recognize that Sikhs are a distinct and important minority which cannot be ignored and we have, all along, been giving our best consideration to the point of view of the Sikhs as expressed by our colleague Sardar Mangal Singh. It must be said to their credit that they have shown an admirable spirit of self-sacrifice by their decision to give up these communal advantages in the general interest of the country. Throughout the communal controversies that have raged round the question of representation in the legislature during recent years they have taken their stand on joint electorates with no reservation for any community. Our colleague Sardar Mangal Singh has drawn attention to the fact that the Sikhs do not form the majority of the total population of any district in the Punjab, and that the strongest position they occupy is in Ludhiana district where they are the strongest single community. Even in this district they are only 41.5% and are not in a majority. In every other district they are outnumbered either by Muslims or Hindus, and usually by both. It is obvious that situated as the Sikhs are in the Punjab . . . subject to all the disadvantages of a minority in a joint mixed electorate based on the wide adult suffrage we have recommended. In these circumstances they have in the Punjab at least as strong a case for reservation both in the provincial and central legislatures as the Muslims have in the U.P. There is however a third and a very potent factor to be taken into account and that is the presence of the strong Hindu minority side by side with the Muslim majority and the Sikh minority. It is this circumstance in the Punjab which, apart from general considerations has so far defied all attempts at a satisfactory adjustment on the basis of reservation for any community. The Punjab problem has assumed an all India importance and we cannot look at it as an isolated case arising in a single province. The only effective way of avoiding complications and giving full play to the forces of nationalism is to eradicate the virus of communalism from the body politic of the Punjab. Our colleague, Sardar Mangal Singh, who has discussed the matter very fully and frankly with us shares our difficulty. We believe that nothing is farther from the wishes of the Sikh League than to introduce any complications directly or indirectly in the solution of the communal problem. They could, if they had insisted on any special advantage, have caused endless difficulties in the adoption of a uniform rule of representation. They fully realized this and voluntarily gave up all their claims with the sole object, we are assured, of preventing an impasse. We appreciate this spirit and congratulate them on their patriotic resolve.

The Only Alternative

The only alternative to the proposal we have made is to adopt the recommendation of the informal conference and have no reservation for any minorities, including Muslims, in any legislature. But this will cause considerable dissatisfaction to Muslims without conferring any special benefit on non-Muslims. It must be remembered that besides reservation by means of communal electorates the Muslims at present enjoy considerable weightage in every province. We are offering them the right to contest additional seats in lieu of this weightage and we cannot very well do away with reservation in their case. We see no hardship in this to non-Muslim majorities or minorities. Endless complications will arise if we recommend reservation for all minorities. Besides the existing well defined minorities such as Christians, Parsis, Jews, fresh groups from among the Hindu castes and sub-castes will claim the right and it will be a perpetual source of trouble.

The communal question is essentially a Hindu-Muslim question and must be settled on that basis. We shall indeed be doing poor service if in our attempt to settle it we let communalism loose on the country to swallow up communities and sub-communities most of whom have not even dreamt of it.

Non-Brahmans

There remain two important communities included in the Hindu majority— the non-Brahmans and the depressed classes. The sharp division between Brahman and non-Brahman is to be met with only in the south and is unknown in other parts of India. Where the non-Brahmans as such are found, they are either an overwhelming majority as in Madras or a very strong minority as in parts of Bombay. They need no protection in the matter of representation in the legislatures as has been established by the elections held in recent times. Their grievances against Brahmans are all traceable to the ascendency gained by the latter in the political and social life of the country. This is the natural result of their intellectual ascendency which is now seriously threatened by the rapid advance of non-Brahmans.

'DEPRESSED' CLASSES

The problem of the 'depressed' or 'suppressed' classes has come to the front in recent years and their present condition is put forward as an argument against the political advancement of India. We are certainly of opinion that the Hindus are chiefly responsible for this suppression of a large class, but we are equally clear that the solicitude for this class which the British government has endeavoured to show has its basis on reasons other than humanity or love for this class. This solicitude is of very recent growth. As the national movement has grown in the country, so has the political value of the 'depressed' classes grown in the eyes of the government. It is only since 1917 that their numbers have been separately given in the official reports on education and reference has been made to the educational facilities offered to them. The solicitude of government has so far brought little relief to these classes. It has resulted in giving them some nominated seats in the legislatures and some minor contributions for special schools.

Far more serious and effective attempts have been made by non-official Indian agencies to raise these classes. The Christian missions have also helped in this task. The Congress made the abolition of untouchability one of its principal planks in 1920 and, as is well known, Mahatma Gandhi has thrown himself with all his great powers and energy into the movement. Other political organizations, and we are glad to find even communal organizations, have with equal emphasis declared against untouchability. The practical work done and the considerable results achieved already make it quite clear that these declarations were not mere pious wishes. We realize that there are still conservative elements in the country which are strong enough to put obstacles in the way and retard the progress of the movement. But we are convinced that untouchability is doomed.

In our suggestions for the constitution we have not made any special provision for the representation of the 'depressed' classes in the legis-

latures. This could only be done by way of special electorates or by nomination. We have dealt fully in another place with the question of special
electorates and reservation of seats. We are not prepared to extend this
unsound and harmful principle if we can help it, nor do we think that we
will do any good to these classes by ensuring some seats for them in this
way. We are still more opposed to nomination. This can only result, as it
has resulted, in the government of the day nominating some one who will
support it through thick and thin, and will not represent anybody.

We feel strongly however that the 'depressed' classes must be abolished or rather that they should be raised socially and economically so
that they may take their proper place in the community. The only effective
way to do this is to give them educational and other facilities for this
advance and to remove all obstacles in the way of this advance. Some of
the articles in the Declaration of Rights, which we have recommended, will
go a long way to remove the disabilities from which these classes suffer
and will give them an opportunity to go ahead. The proposal that we
should have adult suffrage will also automatically raise their level and
increase their political power. Finally, we have strongly recommended that
the education of all backward classes should be a special concern of the
state. If all these recommendations are acted upon we are convinced that
the 'depressed' classes will rapidly disappear and will be replaced by a
self-reliant and progressive group, co-operating with other groups in the
welfare of the entire community.

APPENDIX A

AN ANALYSIS OF THE POPULATION FIGURES OF
THE PUNJAB ACCORDING TO RELIGION

*Being a note on the population figures of the Punjab with special
reference to the probable extent of the representation of various religious groups in the legislature*

This note is based on the following assumptions:

1. That there is ordinary territorial representation with what are called
    joint or mixed electorates and without any reservation of seats.
2. That there is adult franchise, or at any rate some franchise which
    ensures that the numbers of electors of the various communities
    bear the same ratio to each other as the population figures of those
    communities.

The figures and calculations in these notes are based entirely on the 1921 census. It may be mentioned however that the ratio of increase of Muslims in the Punjab is slightly greater than that of Hindus. This according to the census report is not due now to conversions but to certain social causes—widow remarriage and a higher marriage age amongst the Muslims. Infantile mortality is greater amongst the Hindus owing to early marriages. Hence it is probable that the Muslim population in the Punjab today is slightly greater proportionately than is evidenced by the 1921 census figures. The next census may show this increase. This means that the calculations in these notes are conservative figures so far as the Muslims are concerned, and the actuality is more favourable to them.

It is not possible to arrive at any accurate conclusion regarding representation in legislatures on population figures from a census report. A great deal must depend on the grouping of constituencies. It is also by no means certain, and it certainly is most undesirable, that in a joint electorate a Hindu should always vote for a Hindu, and a Muslim for a Muslim. But it is not possible to make allowances for this in these calculations. As the question is being considered in its communal aspect we must presume that as a general rule votes will be cast on communal lines. The constituencies not having been formed the only alternative is to examine the figures for the individual districts. It is likely that either a whole district or a part of it will form a single constituency.

The population of the Punjab (excluding Indian States) in 1921 was 2,06,85,024. This was made up as follows:

Muslims	1,14,44,321	55.3%
Hindus	65,79,260	31.8%
Sikhs	22,94,207	11.1%
Others (mainly Christians)	3,67,236	1.8%
	2,06,85,024	100.0%

Thus the Muslims are in a clear but not a great majority over all others combined. If the distribution of population is more closely examined it will be seen that the Muslims are in an even stronger position than the all Punjab figures might indicate. This is due to the fact that the Hindus and Sikhs are present in large numbers in the southern part of the province—Ambala and Jullundur divisions. Muslims are in a minority in these two divisions but they make up for it by increasing their majorities elsewhere.

The Punjab can be divided roughly into three natural belts or areas (1) the predominantly Muslim area (2) the neutral area but with Muslim majority and (3) the Hindu-Sikh area. If we take the existing divisions as corresponding approximately to these areas we have the following three belts:

I.   Rawalpindi and Multan divisions forming the Muslim zone with Muslims in very great majorities (86.9% and 76.9% respectively).

II.   Lahore division forming the neutral zone, but Muslims in a majority (57.0%) over all others combined.

III. Ambala and Jullundur divisions forming the Hindu-Sikh zone. Muslims are in a minority (26.3% and 32.8%) respectively.

We can form some rough idea of the representation in the legislature on the basis of these communal zones. Allowing one member for every hundred thousand of population we have:

		Population in thousands	Members of legislatures	
Punjab. . . .		20,685	207	
I.	Rawalpindi division	3,461	35	⎰ 77
	Multan division	4,218	42	⎱
II.	Lahore division	4,997	50	50
III.	Ambala division	3,827	38	⎰ 80
	Jullundur division	4,182	42	⎱
			207	

We may presume that the Muslims will capture all the seats in the Muslim zone and Hindu-Sikhs all the seats in the Hindu-Sikh zone. In the Lahore division there may be a division of the spoils. This of course cannot and should not happen in its entirety. It is not desirable that each division should be represented by one community only. But in making a rough calculation one may presume this much—the seats gained by the Muslims in the Hindu-Sikh area will probably be counter-balanced by the seats gained by the Hindu-Sikhs in the Muslim area. As a matter of fact there is more chance of the Muslims gaining a seat in the Hindu-Sikh area than the reverse, as the Muslim majorities in Rawalpindi and Multan divisions are tremendous (86.0% and 76.9%).

Thus we arrive at the conclusion that the Muslims are bound to get 77 seats in their zone, and the Hindu-Sikhs combined 80 seats in their zone. The third zone—Lahore division—will probably be divided between the two, but the division is likely to be very much in favour of the Muslims. They are 57.0% of the population, the Hindus being 20.7% and the Sikhs 16.2%. Christians, etc., amount to 6.1% but they may be left out of consideration here as presumably they have no special affiliations to the major communities and can certainly not be considered as being anti-Muslim or as belonging to the Hindu-Sikh *bloc*. Hindus and Sikhs together amount to 36.9% as against the 57.0% of the Muslims. The Muslims are thus more than one and a half times stronger than the Hindu-Sikh group. The difference is considerable and the Muslim strength must make itself felt in an election. The Muslim majority in this division should ordinarily gain more seats than it is entitled to on basis of population. But even if it got seats exactly in proportion to its population in the division, it would have 29 seats. This added to the 77 seats in the Muslim belt gives the figure 106 which gives a small but clear majority in the legislature of 207, over all other communities and groups combined. The majority will really be much greater over the Hindu-Sikh *bloc* as the 'others' may also be in the minority.

All this proceeds on the basis that Hindu and Sikh interests are identical and the two groups hang together on all occasions. This of course is not a justifiable presumption and it is more than likely that they may not always act together. In such a contingency each community's hopeless minority in the face of the solid Muslim majority will become even more obvious.

As the Lahore division is likely to be the critical one, it may be examined in greater detail. Out of the 6 districts in this division three districts—Sialkot, Gujranwala and Sheikhupura—have very substantial Muslim majorities. And as 'others' (Christians, etc.) are present in appreciable numbers in these districts the Muslim majorities *vis-a-vis* the Hindu-Sikh *bloc* become even greater and are really overwhelming.

The figures are:

Sialkot district		
Muslims	61.9%	
Hindus	19.5%	
Sikhs	8.0%	9½ seats
Others	10.5%	

The Hindu-Sikh *bloc* totals 27.5% as against the 61.9% of the Muslims. The latter thus are considerably more than double the number of the Hindus and Sikhs combined.

Gujranwala district		
Muslims	71.0%	
Hindus	15.8%	
Sikhs	8.2%	6¼ seats
Others	5.1%	

The Hindu-Sikh *bloc* totals 24.0% as against the 71.0% of the Muslims. The latter are thus nearly three times the number of Hindus and Sikhs combined.

Sheikhupura district		
Muslims	63.3%	
Hindus	16.0%	5¼ seats
Sikhs	15.9%	
Others	4.8%	

The Hindu-Sikh *bloc* totals 31.9% as against the 63.3% of the Muslims. The latter are thus just double the number of the Hindus and Sikhs combined.

In these three districts the Muslims are in an impregnable position. Indeed they really form part of the Muslim zone and should be considered along with it. These districts will be entitled to send 21 members to the legislature. These can be added to 77 members from the Muslim zone giving the total 98.

In the other districts of Lahore division the position is as follows:

Lahore district		
Muslims	57.3%	
Hindus	21.5%	11 seats
Sikhs	15.9%	
Others	5.3%	

Here the Hindu-Sikh *bloc* totals 37.4% as against the 57.3% of the Muslims. The Muslim majority is not so great as in the northern districts but it is substantial. The Muslims greatly outnumber the Hindus and Sikhs, being over one and a half times their number.

Amritsar district		
Muslims	45.6%	
Hindus	21.6%	9 seats
Sikhs	30.9%	
Others	1.8%	

In this district the Hindus and Sikhs combined amount to 52.5% and are in a fair majority over the 45.6% Muslims.

Gurdaspur district		
Muslims	49.6%	
Hindus	26.0%	8½ seats
Sikhs	16.2%	
Others	8.2%	

Here the Muslims outnumber the Hindus and Sikhs combined—49.6% against 42.2—but the majority is not great. The position in Amritsar district is reversed. There are a fair number of 'others' here.

Thus in these three districts, the Muslim position is strong in Lahore, fair in Gurdaspur and weak in Amritsar. But even in the last mentioned place the Muslims are by far the strongest single community.

It is highly likely that Muslims will capture some seats in these districts, specially in Lahore.

The Lahore division will thus be largely represented by Muslims and this representation added to that from the Muslim zone in the north and west ought to give them a clear majority.

This question can be considered from another point of view. Instead of looking at the divisions as a whole the individual districts may be taken. This will probably give a more accurate idea of the result.

There are 29 districts in the Punjab. These may be divided into four groups (1) overwhelmingly Muslim districts where the Muslim position is impregnable: (2) predominantly Muslim districts, where there is a Muslim majority but not so great as in (1); (3) districts where there is no special predominance of any community; and (4) overwhelmingly or predominantly Hindu-Sikh districts.

I. *Overwhelmingly Muslim districts*

		Percentage of Muslims given after districts	No. of members in legislatures
1.	Gujrat	86.2	8
2.	Shahpur	82.8	7
3.	Jhelum	88.7	5
4.	Rawalpindi	82.6	6
5.	Attock	90.9	5
6.	Mianwali	86.3	4
7.	Montgomery	71.8	7
8.	Lyallpur	60.7	10
9.	Jhang	83.3	6
10.	Multan	82.2	9
11.	Muzaffargarh	86.8	5½

12.	Dera Ghazi Khan	88.3		5
13.	Sialkot	61.9		9½
14.	Gujranwala	71.0		6
15.	Sheikhupura	63.3		5
				98

II. *Predominantly Muslim districts*

1.	Lahore	H.	21.5	
		M.	57.3	11
		S.	15.9	
		O.	5.3	
2.	Gurdaspur	H.	26.0	
		M.	49.6	8½
		S.	16.2	
		O.	8.2	
				19½

III. *Districts with no special predominance of any community*

1.	Jullundur	H.	29.4	
		S.	25.1	8
		M.	44.5	
		O.	1.0	
2.	Ferozepur	H.	27.6	
		S.	27.6	11
		M.	43.9	
		O.	.9	
3.	Amritsar	H.	21.6	
		S.	30.9	
		M.	45.6	9
		O.	1.8	
				28

Even in these three districts the strongest single community is the Muslim.

IV. *Overwhelmingly or predominantly Hindu-Sikh districts*

1.	Hissar	H.	66.1	8
2.	Rohtak	H.	78.0	8
3.	Gurgaon	H.	66.7	7
4.	Karnal	H.	67.5	8
5.	Ambala	H.	53.8	7
6.	Simla	H.	71.2	½
7.	Kangra	H.	94.0	8

8.	Hoshiarpur	H.	53.3	9
9.	Ludhiana	H.	23.6	
		S.	41.5	
		M.	34.0	6
		O.	00.9	
			61½	

According to this the Muslims get from their special zone of 15 districts where they are impregnable   98

The Hindus similarly get from their zone   61½

Two districts predominantly Muslim return   19½

Three districts more or less neutral,
but Muslims strongest single community in each   28
                                                                                    207

104 seats give an absolute majority in the legislature.

The result of the analysis of the figures for the districts leads us to the following conclusions:

1.   From the Muslim zone alone, where the
     Muslim position is unassailable, the Muslims get
     98 seats or   47.3 of the
                                                                                      total
                                                                                      seats

2.   From the Hindu Sikh belt where the Hindu-
     Sikh position is very strong the Hindus and
     Sikhs get 61½ seats or   29.8   -do-

3.   In two districts where Muslims are pre-
     dominant there are 19½ seats or   9.4   -do-

4.   In 3 districts the strength of the various com-
     munities is more or less evenly balanced but
     Muslims are the strongest single community in each,
     total 28 seats or   13.5 of the
                                                                                      total
                                                                                      seats
                                                                           100.0

It is exceedingly likely that from group II above, which is predominantly Muslim, the Muslims will get at least 10 out of the 19½ seats. This added to their seats from their particular zone gives them 108 seats which is a clear majority in the legislature. In group III above the Muslims should also get some seats as they are the strongest single community. They might safely count on 12 out of the 28. This raises the Muslim number in the legislature to 120 out of 207 or 58% if the total. Thus on a conservative estimate Muslims are highly likely to have 58% of the seats in the legislature.

PUNJAB (BRITISH TERRITORY)

Detailed population figures

Punjab

Total population	2,06,85,024	100.0	per cent
Muslims	1,14,44,321	55.3	"
Hindus	65,79,260	31.8	"
Sikhs	22,94,207	11.1	"
Others (mainly Christians)	3,67,236	1.8	"

PUNJAB DIVISIONS

(Population figures in thousands)

Ambala Division

	Populations	Percentage	No. of members in legislatures 1 for 100,000
Total	3,827	100	
H.	2,556	66.6	
M.	1,006	26.3	38
S.	158	4.2	
O.	106	2.8	

Jullundur Division

Total	4128	100	
H.	1893	45.0	
M.	1370	32.8	42
S.	880	21.0	
O.	40	00.9	

Lahore Division

Total	4997	100	
H.	1033	20.7	
M.	2849	57.0	50
S.	813	16.2	
O.	303	6.1	

Rawalpindi Division

Total	3461	100	
H.	296	8.5	
M.	2973	86.0	35
S.	153	4.4	
O.	38	1.1	

Multan Division

Total	4218	100	
H.	602	14.3	
M.	3246	76.9	42
S.	290	6.9	
O.	80	1.9	

Note: H = Hindu   M = Muslim   S = Sikh   O = Others

PUNJAB DISTRICTS

I. *Overwhelmingly Muslim Districts*

District	Population in Thousands	Percentage	No. of members in legislature
1. Gujrat	T.	824	100	
	H.	59	7.2	
	M.	710	86.2	8.2
	S.	49	6.0	
	O.	6	.7	
2. Shahpur	T.	720	100	
	H.	79	11	
	M.	596	82.8	7.2
	S.	30	4.2	
	O.	15	2.1	
3. Jhelum	T.	477	100	
	H.	33	6.9	
	M.	423	88.7	4.8
	S.	19	4.0	
	O.	2	.4	
4. Rawalpindi	T.	569	100	
	H.	55	9.7	
	M.	470	82.6	5.7
	S.	32	5.6	
	O.	12	2.1	
5. Attock	T.	512	100	
	H.	25.5	5.0	
	M.	465.5	90.9	5.1
	S.	20	3.9	
	O.	1	.2	

6. Mianwali	T.	358	100	
	H.	45	12.6	
	M.	309	86.3	3.6
	S.	3	.8	
	O.	1	.3	
7. Montgomery	T.	714	100	
	H.	92	12.9	
	M.	513	71.8	7.1
	S.	96	13.4	
	O.	13	1.8	
8. Lyallpur	T.	980	100	
	H.	177	18.1	
	M.	595	60.7	9.8
	S.	161	16.4	
	O.	47	4.8	
9. Jhang	T.	570	100	
	H.	84	14.7	
	M.	475	83.3	5.7
	S.	9	1.6	
	O.	2	.4	
10. Multan	T.	890	100	
	H.	129	14.5	
	M.	732	82.2	8.9
	S.	18	2.0	
	O.	11	1.2	
11. Muzaffargarh	T.	568	100	
	H.	66	1.6	
	M.	493	86.8	5.7
	S.	5	.9	
	O.	4	.7	
12. Dera Ghazi Khan (including Biloch tract)	T.	496	100	
	H.	54	10.9	
	M.	438	88.3	5.0
	S.	1	00.2	
	O.	3	00.6	
13. Sialkot	T.	938	100	
	H.	183	19.5	
	M.	581	61.9	9.4
	S.	75	8.0	
	O.	99	10.5	
14. Gujranwala	T.	623	100	
	H.	98	15.8	
	M.	443	71	6.2
	S.	51	8.2	
	O.	31	5.1	

15.	Sheikhupura	T.	523	100	
		H.	84	16.0	
		M.	331	63.3	⎱ 5.2
		S.	83	15.9	
		O.	25	4.8	
15	Districts				97.6

II. *Predominantly Muslims Districts*

(Where Muslims are greater than Hindus and Sikhs combined but
are not so many as in I above.)

1.	Lahore	T.	1,131	100	
		H.	243	21.5	
		M.	648	57.3	⎱ 11.3
		S.	180	15.9	
		O.	60	5.3	
2.	Gurdaspur	T.	852	100	
		H.	222	26.0	
		M.	423	49.6	⎱ 8.5
		S.	137.5	16.2	
		O.	69.5	8.2	
2	Districts				19.8

III. *Districts in which there is no special predominance of any community but Muslim community strongest single group*

1.	Jullundur	T.	822.5	100	
		H.	242	29.4	
		M.	366.5	44.5	⎱ 8.2
		S.	206	25.1	
		O.	8	1.0	
2.	Ferozepur	T.	1098	100	
		H.	303	27.6	
		M.	482	43.9	⎱ 11
		S.	303	27.6	
		O.	10		.9
3.	Amritsar	T.	929	100	
		H.	201	21.6	
		M.	424	45.6	⎱ 9.3
		S.	287	30.9	
		O.	17	1.8	
3	Districts				28.5

IV. *Overwhelmingly or predominantly Hindu-Sikh Districts*

1.	Hissar	T.	817	100	
		H.	540	66.1	
		M.	216	26.4	⎱ 8.2
		S.	46	5.6	
		O.	15	1.8	

2.	Rohtak	T.	772	100	
		H.	602	78.0	
		M.	125	16.2	7.7
		S.	1	.1	
		O.	44	5.7	
3.	Gurgaon	T.	682	100	
		H.	455	66.7	
		M.	217	31.8	6.8
		S.	1	.1	
		O.	9	1.3	
4.	Karnal	T.	829	100	
		H.	560	67.5	
		M.	236	28.5	8.3
		S.	12	1.4	
		O.	21	2.6	
5.	Ambala	T.	682	100	
		H.	367	53.8	
		M.	206	30.2	6.8
		S.	98	14.4	
		O.	11	1.6	
6.	Simla	T.	45	100	
		H.	32	71.2	
		M.	7	15.5	0.4
		S.	1	2.2	
		O.	5	11.1	
7.	Kangra	T.	766	100	
		H.	722.3	94.0	
		M.	38.3	5.0	7.7
		S.	2	.3	
		O.	3.4	.7	
8.	Hoshiarpur	T.	927	100	
		H.	494	53.3	
		M.	289	31.2	9.3
		S.	133	14.3	
		O.	11	1.2	
9.	Ludhiana	T.	568	100	
		H.	134	23.6	
		M.	193	34.0	5.7
		S.	236	41.5	
		O.	5	.9	
9	Districts				60.9

These figures demonstrate that quite apart from any artificial reservation of seats there is a natural reservation in more than three-fourths of the Punjab. In less than one-fourth there is some chance of free play. The distribution of population favours the majority community, Muslims, considerably.

Appendix II

❖◆❖

Report of the Working Group on 'Empowering the Minorities' constituted by the Planning Commission in the context of formulation of the Tenth Five Year Plan (2002-2007) 10 May 2001

CHAPTER I

BACKGROUND

The Central Government notified Muslims, Christians, Sikhs, Buddhists and Parsis as religious minorities for the purpose of the National Commission for Minorities Act, 1992. These communities constitute about 17% of the country's total population numbering about 14.5 crore as per the 1991 census. Community-wise population is estimated as Muslims—12%, Christians—2.3%, Sikhs—2%, Buddhists—0.77% of the population of country while the Parsis are about 1.0 lakh in number. 41 Minority Concentration Districts (MCDs) spanning 11 States have been identified based on significant minority population.

    1.2 India has the third largest Muslim population next only to Indonesia and Pakistan. Muslims constitute a majority in the Union Territory of

*In December 2000, the Planning Commission constituted a Working Group on 'Empowering the Minorities' under the Chairmanship of Prof. Mushirul Hasan. The Working Group in its first meeting held on 30 January 2001 decided to constitute Sub-Groups in order to examine the issues in detail and provide necessary inputs for the report of the Working Group. This edited version is based on their findings and recommendations.

Lakshadweep (94.31%) and in Jammu & Kashmir (64%). In three other States their population is much above the national level average, viz., Assam (28.43%), West Bengal (23.61%) and Kerala (23.32%). The States having the sizeable Muslim population are Uttar Pradesh (2.50 crore), West Bengal (1.80 crore) and Bihar (1.30 crore). The total Muslim population of the country is approximately 11 crore. . . .

ECONOMIC STATUS

1.8   An analysis has been carried out by Prof. Abusaleh Shariff, Principal Economist, National Council of Applied Economic Research (NCAER), on the relative position in economic, educational and health areas according to poverty line classification between the majority community, the SCs, STs and the Muslims. The study has been carried out on the basis of the survey of 33,000 nationally representative rural sample on household income and a range of human development parameters (comparative data is given in Table II.1). The study reveals that:

(i)   SC/ST (including Buddhists in the context of the minorities) are the most poverty-stricken group and the Muslims are next only to them compared with all India average.

Table II.1: Comparison of various Parameters among Different Groups

	STs	SCs	Hindus	Muslims	All
Household Income (Rs.)	19,556.0	17,465.0	25,713.0	22,807.0	25,653.0
Per Capita Income (Rs.)	3,504.0	3,237.0	4,514.0	3,678.0	4,485.0
Work Male	51.6.0	52.8	52.3	48.0	51.9
Participation Ratio Female	27.7	23.0	19.3	9.6	18.4
Source of Agriculture	55.6	37.7	56.1	44.1	55.0
Income Artisanship	2.7	5.7	4.3	8.3	4.5
Salaried	14.8	15.2	16.4	14.7	16.5
Land Holding Reporting	4.3	2.8	4.6	3.6	4.5
Household (Acres)					
% of Kutcha House	74.0	66.6	55.2	65.9	55.4
% of Electric Connection	29.7	30.7	43.2	30.0	42.9
% Protected Water	61.6	72.8	71.1	78.1	72.0
% Piped Water	17.2	22.6	25.3	19.4	24.8
% Having Toilet	12.2	8.3	13.2	26.7	15.3
% Using PDS	37.5	32.1	34.1	21.8	33.2
Poverty Head Count	51.0	50.0	39.0	43.0	39.0
Capacity Poverty %	68.0	60.0	–	56.0	52.0

Source: India Human Development Report of the 1990s.

(ii) SC/STs (including Buddhists in the context of the minorities) and the Muslims can be considered as the economically deprived population groups. However, there is wide gap in the per capita income amongst *the Muslims* because of their larger family size as compared to the other groups.

(iii) The Muslims are largely engaged as artisans and as workers in the industrial sectors. Their involvement in agriculture and allied activities is much lower.

(iv) The Work Participation Rate (WPR) amongst the Muslims is the least, both for male and females, suggesting a relatively higher unemployment rate. WPR amongst the Muslim women is as low as 10% compared with the all-India average of 18%.

EDUCATIONAL STATUS

1.9 In its report submitted in 1983, a panel, appointed by the Ministry of Home Affairs in 1980 and headed by Dr. Gopal Singh, identified Muslims and Neo-Buddhists as educationally backward at the national level.

1.10 As per the National Family Health Survey (1998-9), incidence of illiteracy, female illiteracy among Muslims continues to be significantly high (Table II.2).

Table II.2: Educational Status of Women (15-49 years)

Religious community	Educational Level	
	Illiteracy (%age)	Higher Secondary & above (%age)
Hindus	59.3	6.8
Muslims	60.5	3.5
Christians	32.9	16.7
Sikhs	38.9	13.8
Jains	6.8	30.4
Buddhists/Neo-Buddhists	44.7	7.9
Others	70.3	2.1
No religion	51.2	8.0
Overall	58.2	6.8

Source: National Family Health Survey 1998-9 (89, 199 women respondents).

Table II.3: Fertility Rate, Infant Mortality Rate and Current use of Family Planning Methods

Religious community	Total fertility rate	infant morality rate	Using FP methods
Hindus	2.78	77.1	49.20
Muslims	3.59	58.8	37.00
Christians	2.44	49.2	52.40
Sikhs	2.26	53.3	65.20
Jains	1.90	(46.7)	65.10
Buddhists/Neo-Buddhist	2.13	53.6	64.70
Others	2.33	80.3	48.60
No Religion	3.91	(77.6)	30.10
Overall	2.85	73.0	48.20

Source: National Family Health Survey 1998-9 (89, 199 women respondents).

HEALTH AND SOCIAL STATUS

1.11 The effects of low literacy level are also reflected in terms of poor health, large families, high fertility rates leading to socio-economic backwardness as evident from the National Family Health Survey (1998-9) (important health indicators for various communities are given in Table II.3).

1.12 A document entitled 'Status of Muslim Women in India' brought out by the National Commission for Women stated that, 'Muslim women are the weakest link in the generally disempowered chain of Indian womanhood.'

EMPLOYMENT

1.13 It appears that the Muslims, in particular, have not been able to take advantage of the Government schemes on account of their educational backwardness. In a sample of 73 Public Sector Undertakings, only 1.2% of the Directors were Muslims. The proportion of Muslim Directors in private corporate sector appears to be even lower. Likewise, the percentage of Muslims employed in the executive, supervisory or worker cadres is extremely low. In addition to the low representation of Muslims in employment, particularly at the decision making or decision influencing levels, Muslims as a community lag behind others in self-employed categories of activity (*Source: Study on Muslim Potential In India* by Sh. K.M. Arif, President United Economic Forum, Mumbai).

PERCEPTION OF ISOLATION AND INSECURITY

1.14 Despite the constitutional safeguards, the minorities feel insecure and suffer from a sense of isolation and deprivation. With this background, the Minorities Commission was set up in 1978. In May 1992, the National Commission for Minorities Act, 1992, was enacted giving statutory status to the erstwhile Minorities Commission. . . .

1.16 Realizing the need for instilling security and for ensuring the rapid socio-economic development of the minorities, a special 15-point programme was proclaimed by the then Prime Minister in May 1983. The 15-point programme was based on a 3-pronged approach, viz. (i) to tackle the situation arising out of communal riots and prevent communal riots, (ii) ensuring adequate representation of the minority communities in employment under Central and State Governments as well as Public Sector Undertakings and (iii) introducing other measures, such as under various development programmes, maintenance and development of religious places, Wakf properties, and redressal of minority grievances.

CHAPTER II

REVIEW OF ACTION TAKEN IN THE PREVIOUS PLANS,
SUCCESS, LIMITATIONS AND THE PRESENT SCENARIO

The Ninth Plan was committed to empowering the minorities as the agents of socio-economic change and development. It suggested a fresh approach envisaging efforts to create an enabling environment that would be conducive for their welfare, progress and prosperity.

EDUCATION SECTOR

2.2 Education, being the most effective instrument of empowerment, received serious attention. It was envisaged that all-out efforts be initiated to improve the educational status of these groups, especially women and the girl child, through the universalization of primary education by the year 2005. In brief, the Planning Commission suggested the following strategies for removing educational backwardness among the minorities:

    (i) Universalization of primary education by 2005;
    (ii) Strengthening of the Maulana Azad Educational Foundation;
    (iii) Provision of additional facilities to minority schools, colleges and hostels;

   (iv) Remedial coaching for under-achieving students;

   (v) Upgrading the existing institutions and networking with vocational and technical education;

   (vi) Provisions for *scholarships/fellowships*;

   (vii) Provision of educational facilities with appropriate infrastructural support in those areas where educationally backward Muslims, particularly women, are concentrated;

   (viii) Modernization of existing traditional institutions, such as the Madarsas;

   (ix) Expansion of pre-examination coaching centres in minority concentrated districts;

   (x) Promotion of the minority languages and protection of their cultural identity. Also, safeguarding and promoting the linguistic and cultural identity of the Muslims.

2.3   The following interventions already existed at the commencement of the Ninth Plan:

   (i) The Maulana Azad Education Foundation was set up in 1989, under the aegis of the Ministry of Welfare, to promote education amongst the educationally backward minorities, especially Muslims;

   (ii) An Area intensive scheme was under implementation at the block level in all the 41 Minorities Concentration Districts to provide basic education and related infrastructural facilities under the Department of Education;

   (iii) Community Polytechnics were set up in 41 Minorities Concentration Districts to impart technical skills to eligible persons belonging to Minority communities under the Department of Education.

   (iv) The Ministry of Labour set up Industrial Training Institutes in 19 out of the 41 districts and introduced trades relevant for the minority artisans and workers;

   (v) Pre-examination Coaching Centres in 21 Universities and 32 Colleges by the University Grants Commission;

   (vi) A special scheme of pre-examination coaching was launched by the Ministry of Welfare in 1992-3. Under this scheme, 1,888 institutions provided coaching to 9,480 candidates for competitive examinations. . . .

2.5   The major programmes for the educational upliftment of the minorities are reviewed in the following paragraphs.

AREA INTENSIVE PROGRAMME FOR
EDUCATIONALLY BACKWARD MINORITIES

2.6   This Central scheme was the direct outcome of the action points contained in the Programme of Action as part of the revisions in the strategies for implementation. It was launched in May 1993, to provide basic infrastructure and facilities in areas where educationally backward minorities were concentrated, which do not have provision for elementary and secondary education. Under the scheme, 100 per cent financial assistance is provided to State Governments and the voluntary organization for the following programmes:

(i)   Establishment of new primary/upper primary schools, non-formal education centres where such a need is felt and viability established on the basis of a school mapping exercise.

(ii)   Strengthening of educational infrastructure and physical facilities in the primary/upper primary schools.

(iii) Opening of multi-stream residential Higher Secondary Schools for girls to impart studies in Sciences, Commerce, humanities and vocational courses.

2.7   Since the inception of the scheme, i.e. from 1993-4, financial assistance of Rs. 6068.80 lakh has been released. The scheme has so far been implemented in 12 States, though the number of blocks covered in each district varies. The State-wise break-up of the grant released so far under the scheme is given in Table II.4.

2.8   On analysis of various aspects of implementation of the scheme, the Working Group observed the following:

(i)   School Mapping exercise was not carried out to determine the needs for schools, though this was an underlying condition for the opening of new schools.

(ii)   Substantial amount of financial assistance with the State Governments has not been utilized.

(iii) No time schedule has been fixed by the State Governments to complete the projects.

(iv)   Often, sanctions for grant-in-aid were given almost at the close of the financial year, and the State Governments were expected to seek permission to carry over the grants to the next financial year.

Table II.4: Scheme of Area Intensive Programme for Educationally Backward Minorities–Grant released during the period 1993-4 to 2000-1 State-wise

(in Rs. lakh as on 31.12.2000)

Name of State/Trust	1993-4	1994-5	1995-6	1996-7	1997-8	1998-9	1999-2000	2000-1
Andhra Pradesh	–	–	–	–	42.91	–	42.9062	–
Assam	–	–	–	–	37.50	21.00	29.35	–
Bihar	–	–	–	–	–	–	439.64	–
Gujarat	–	4.30	–	–	–	–	–	–
Haryana	2.08	–	–	–	15.015	22.275	2.08	45.90
Karnataka	68.42	9.00	–	69.03	76.765	9.265	58.50	38.32
Kerala	–	105.48	–	–	17.98	–	–	–
Madhya Pradesh	20.88	15.30	–	–	9.30	17.32	6.00	20.36
Rajasthan	65.62	12.71	27.64	112.305	55.60	–	–	–
Tamilnadu	–	–	–	–	–	72.81	–	–
Uttar Pradesh	45.00	83.71	173.06	38.665	597.87	855.74	551.43	1371.85
West Bengal	13.00	6.70	19.30	–	146.00	354.51	12.00	194.25
R.A. Kidwai Trust	–	5.00	–	–	–	–	–	–
Total	215.00	242.00	220.00	220.00	1099.00	1352.00	1142.90	1670.00

(v) The schools have not been recognized by the State Governments. This has given rise to a number of problems such as:

(a) Merit scholarships and special scholarships given to girl students are also denied to them.

(b) Transfer Certificates issued by the schools are not considered valid.

(c) Teachers of these schools are not included in the DPEP programmes.

(d) Students of these schools are also not included in the common programmes of the departments, such as the Youth Festival, sports and games, science festival, etc.

(e) These schools have been instructed by the State Governments not to collect any fees.

(f) The teaching and non-teaching staff of these schools are qualified but are unpaid. Their services are not counted because the schools are not recognized.

(g) The mid-day meal is also denied.

(h) There has been little effort on the part of the State Governments to monitor the scheme at the gross-root level.

(i) Some States have poorly responded to the scheme.

SCHEME FOR THE MODERNIZATION OF MADRASAS

2.9 The other major scheme of the Department of Education is Modernization of Madrasas, initiated in 1993-4 to introduce Science, Mathematics, Social Studies, Hindi and English. The basic objective was to improve the standard of Madrasa education at par with the general education so that Muslim children studying in Madrasas may obtain education that will equip them to compete in every walk of life. Under the scheme, 100 per cent financial assistance is provided to State Governments/Union Territories and voluntary organization for the following programmes:

(i) Financial assistance to the extent of 100% for appointing qualified teachers for the teaching of Sciences, Mathematics, Social Studies, and Languages.

(ii) Assistance for establishment of Book Banks and strengthening of libraries in the Madrasas for these subjects.

(iii) Provision of Science kits, mathematics kits, essential equipment, etc.

Table II.5: Details of year-wise Outlay and Expenditure under Scheme of
Modernization of Madrasas during the Ninth Five Year Plan

(in Rs. crore)

1997-8		1998-9		1999-2000		2000-1		2001-2	
Out-lay	Actual Exp.	Out-lay	Actual Exp.	Out-lay	Actual Exp.	Out-lay	Actual Exp.	Out-lay	Actual Exp.
7.00	1.73	7.00	6.74	10.00	4.61	12.00	6.61	12.00	–

2.10 During the Ninth Five Year Plan, Rs. 48 crore was earmarked out of which only Rs. 19.69 crore has been released in the first four years. The Year-wise breakup of the outlay and actual expenditure during the Ninth Five Year Plan is given in Table II.5.

2.11 The Working Group on Minorities for the Ninth Five Year Plan had recommended Rs. 91.65 crore in the Ninth Five Year Plan for Madrasa Modernization Scheme. However, only Rs. 48 crore was earmarked in the Ninth Five Year Plan. The scheme has been expanded recently. Its main features are:

(i) Salary to two teachers instead of one Grant of assistance to State Madrasa Education Boards to prepare text books and to organize teachers training programme.

(ii) Increase on time Grant for purchase of Science/Maths kits from Rs. 4,000 to Rs. 7,000.

(iii) One time grant of Rs. 7,000 for books and the strengthening of libraries.

2.12 Analysis of the implementation of the scheme of Modernization of Madarsas indicates the following:

(i) Against Rs. 91.65 crore recommended and Rs. 48 crore provided in the 9th plan, only Rs. 19.69 crore was released in the four years.

(ii) The Madarsas, which have been assisted under the scheme, fall in three categories:

(a) Madarsas affiliated and assisted by Arabic Persian Examination Board in UP/or with other respective Madarsas Education Board by their State Govts.

(b) Madarsas affiliated to the Board but not assisted by it.

(c) Madarsas not affiliated to the Board.

(iii) In Uttar Pradesh, Science and Mathematics kits were issued only in 31 out of 699 Madarsas covered by the scheme, while books and furniture were issued to 109 Madarsas. No effort has been made to train teachers in the utilization of these kits.

(iv) In many cases, the buildings housing the Madarsas are in a dilapidated condition.

(v) Adequate ground work needs to be done to ensure success of the scheme. Detailed guidelines are needed about the modern subjects to be taught and the time to be assigned to each of them in the Timetable. This would avoid wide discrepancies between the different Madarsas and ensure some measure of uniformity of standards.

MAULANA AZAD EDUCATION FOUNDATION

2.13 The Maulana Azad Education Foundation was strengthened during the Ninth Plan by augmenting its Corpus Fund from Rs. 30.01 crore to Rs. 70.01 crore. The interest earned on the corpus is utilized for promoting

Table II.6: Grant-in-aid Sanctioned by MAEF (up to 31.3.2001)

S. No.	State/UTs	Amount sanctioned (Rs.)	No. of NGOs
1.	Andaman	10,00,000	01
2.	Andhra Pradesh	03,37,75,000	23
3.	Assam	01,00,00,000	06
4.	Bihar	04,01,51,800	25
5.	Delhi	1,07,15,500	07
6.	Goa	25,00,000	01
7.	Gujarat	03,22,11,800	17
8.	Haryana	85,00,000	04
9.	Jammu & Kashmir	91,42,000	06
10.	Karnataka	05,10,66,800	32
11.	Kerala	03,38,80,000	17
12.	Madhya Pradesh	61,90,000	06
13.	Maharashtra	02,79,41,800	21
14.	Manipur	19,00,000	01
15.	Orissa	10,32,000	04
16.	Punjab	61,67,000	06
17.	Rajasthan	65,00,000	04
18.	Tamil Nadu	01,06,00,000	05
19.	Uttar Pradesh	17,51,73,740	149
20.	West Bengal	03,00,40,000	20
	Total	49,84,87,440	355

education among the educationally backward minorities by providing grant-in-aid for the establishment/expansion of School/Colleges, Girls Hostel, Residential Schools, opening remedial coaching, upgrading the existing professional and technical institutions.

2.14 Since its inception, the Foundation has sanctioned grant-in-aid amounting to Rs. 49.85 crore to 355 NGOs spread in 20 States/Union Territories. The State-wise breakup of the grant sanctioned and released so far under the scheme is given in Table II.6.

2.15 It is observed that the assistance released to States like West Bengal, Bihar is much less than the proportion of minority population. The Working Group felt that there is a need to popularize the scheme in all States and also to cover all the minority communities under the scheme.

EDUCATIONAL DEVELOPMENT SCHEMES OF
THE CENTRAL WAKF COUNCIL

2.16 The Central Wakf Council (CWC) is a statutory body established by the Central Government under sub-section (1) of Section 9 of the Wakf Act, 1995. It advises the Government on matters relating to the working of the Wakf Boards and the proper administration of wakfs.

2.17 The Central Wakf Council collects 6% as donation on loan advanced by it to Wakf Institutions under the scheme for the Development of Urban Wakf Properties. The amount thus received is deposited in the 'Education Fund'. The interest earned on the bank deposits, as well as interest accrued from the Revolving Fund, is credited to the Education Fund. This Education Fund is utilized in financing:

(i) Scholarship to students undergoing technical/professional degree course (B. Tech., MBBS, BUMS, B. Pharma, MCA. etc.) @ Rs. 6,000 per annum.

(ii) Ad-hoc grant to the poor and needy students of general degree courses Rs. 3,000.

(iii) Matching grant to State Wakf Boards for scholarships to students of diploma courses in technical education, higher secondary and Madarsa education.

(iv) 50% matching grant to the technical institutes for starting fresh courses or strengthening the existing trade courses.

(v) Financial assistance for vocational training courses.

(vi) Financial assistance to book banks in school libraries and reading rooms.

2.18   For the year 2000-1, budgetary provision of Rs. 210 lakh was earmarked for the educational programmes of the Council out of which Rs. 105.87 lakh had been sanctioned (by December 2000) in respect of programmes like scholarship to students in respect of professional/technical degree courses, ad/hoc grant to students of general degree course, matching grant to State Wakf Boards for educational programmes, 50 per cent matching grant to technical institutes and financial assistance to Library and Vocational Training Centres.

ECONOMIC SECTOR

2.19   The mid-term appraisal of the Ninth Five Year Plan has recognized that the Indian economy has reached a stage where there would be greater demand for skilled manpower rather than for clerical positions in white collar professions. The expansion in government jobs will be limited, as compared to its growth during the last 40 years. More jobs will be created in factories, small business and crafts where minorities and OBCs have an edge over other communities. Therefore, they would do well by taking advantage of the new opportunities that might come their way.

CREDIT AVAILABILITY

2.20   Evaluation studies on the credit flow by the banking sector/financial institutions to minority communities in the minority concentration districts, conducted by the Ministry of Social Justice and Empowerment, reveal the following:

(i)   The share of institutional credit has increased considerably in the rural as well as in the urban areas.

(ii) Maximum credit was availed under the general credit scheme of the banks, followed by IRDP, Crop loan scheme, PMRY, Differential rate of Interest scheme, DWACRA, special schemes of the State Govt./ Central Govt. Co-operative banks, Co-operative societies, etc. There is no target fixed for the poor amongst the minority community and the credit available to them is along with other weaker sections under the priority sector lending.

(iii) Persons facing difficulties in accessing loans on account of complicated procedures is much more in the case of commercial banks, regional and rural banks as compared to the co-operative banks and co-operative societies.

(iv) Generally, no rural/urban bias has been observed in extending credit, though some complaints have been reported.

(v) High incidence of poverty, unemployment, big family size, more expenditure, indebtedness were the major factors that compelled the poor, including the members of the minority community, to take institutional or non-institutional credit for generating extra income.

(vi) Major share of the institutional credit has been cornered by the upper strata in rural areas. The poorer section resort to taking credit from non-institutional sources, even though the rate of interest they have to pay is very high.

(vii) Literate beneficiaries have utilized the fund in a better manner than the illiterate beneficiaries.

(viii) Illiterate and low income people engaged in marginal occupations, such as livestock and agricultural labour, have proven to be most vulnerable. Credit utilisation and repayment have been low in the case of such groups.

(ix) Apprehension amongst the poor of losing land and other assets if given as *collateral or mortgaged* against the requirement of bank for security against loan. This restricts the poor from availing bank credit. Source study conducted on credit facilities to minorities in minority concentration district of Rampur (U.P.), Mumbai and Aurangabad (Maharashtra) and Kutch (Gujarat).

CREDIT FROM PUBLIC SECTOR BANKS

2.21   The priority sector lending schemes of different Ministries/Departments are being implemented through the scheduled banks. These constitute a major portion of credit flowing to the poorer sections of the different communities. The priority sector schemes being implemented through the banks include the PMRY, IRDP, JRY, Swarna Jayanti Gram Swarojgar Yojana. Besides, the banks also provide credit under their normal business. The poorer section of the minority community are also benefited from the credit being extended by the scheduled banks. Compilation of data on the number of persons covered under the bank credit has been started by the Reserve Bank of India at the behest of the National Commission for Minorities, though the banks still do not ask for the religious demonication of the applicant/loanee. The data on the bank credit flow to the minorities is being reported in the half-yearly progress reports by the RBI to National Commission for Minorities. The data pertains to the overall flow of credit to the minorities and does not segregate between the credit extended under priority sector lending or loans given under normal course by the banks. Analysis of data on flow of credit to the minorities, made available by the RBI to the NCM, has been analysed in four separate tables.

2.22   The performance of Nationalized Banks in providing credit to Minorities has been found to vary (Table II.7). The State Bank of India, followed by the Canara Bank and the Punjab National Bank, lead in advancing credit to Minorities. At present, the Nationalized Banks provide credit to the tune of Rs. 11,789 crore through about 64 lakh accounts.

Table II.7: Credit to Minorities by Nationalized Banks in the Country

(in Rs. crore)

S. No.	Name of the Bank	Credit extended during March '99	Credit extended during Sept. '99
1.	State Bank of India	3,014.17	3,134.90
2.	State Bank of Hyderabad	141.11	164.42
3.	State Bank of Bikaner and Jaipur	82.13	93.11
4.	State Bank of Mysore	50.92	50.93
5.	State Bank of Patiala	496.24	411.37
6.	State Bank of Saurashtra	43.44	49.06
7.	State Bank of Travancore	540.62	590.46
8.	State Bank of Indore	30.46	35.72
9.	Andhra Bank	45.59	43.86
10.	Allahabad Bank	169.68	177.75
11.	Bank of India	588.61	604.92
12.	Bank of Baroda	535.63	535.97
13.	Bank of Maharashtra	82.05	87.36
14.	Canara Bank	859.19	923.99
15.	Central Bank of India	351.96	338.93
16.	Corporation Bank	104.99	121.80
17.	Oriental Bank of Commerce	419.05	447.07
18.	Punjab and Sindh Bank	682.24	704.40
19.	Dena Bank	116.23	111.01
20.	Indian Bank	156.37	142.68
21.	Indian Overseas Bank	413.54	402.66
22.	Punjab National Bank	1,161.55	1,160.86
23.	Syndicate Bank	331.57	339.57
24.	Union Bank of India	406.03	474.21
25.	United Bank of India	177.71	178.20
26.	Uco Bank	244.84	244.70
27.	Vijay Bank	195.98	200.14
	Total	11,445.01	11,789.07
	Number of Accounts	6,130,279	6,407,346.00
	Average Credit per Account	18,600	18,400.00

2.23　Table II.8 gives the State-wise position of credit given to minorities compared with percentage of the minority population. In Orissa (5.15%), Arunachal Pradesh (29.82%), Tamil Nadu (11%), Pondicherry (21.57%) and UT of Chandigarh 25.62%), the share of credit flow to the minorities

Table II.8: State-wise Position of % Credit and average amount per Account Extended to Minorities Compared to % of Minority Population

S. No.	Name of State/UT	% of Population	March '99		September '99	
			% of Credit	Avg. amt. per Actt.	% of Credit	Avg. amt. per Actt.
1.	Andhra Pradesh	10.8	6.62	9,000	7.6	9,300
2.	Arunachal Pradesh	24.7	16.78	13,000	29.82	13,000
3.	Assam	32.11	11.14	11,000	10.8	11,000
4.	Bihar	15.88	9.19	6,700	8.55	6,300
5.	Delhi	15.31	7.9	1,40,000	6.08	1,29,000
6.	Goa	35.22	25.4	49,000	25.63	48,000
7.	Gujarat	9.31	2.99	21,400	3.48	22,000
8.	Haryana	10.56	8.5	29,000.	8.76	30,000
9.	Himachal Pradesh	4.06	3.64	29,000	3.94	31,000
10.	Jammu & Kashmir	–	29.35	14,000	51.54	36,000
11.	Karnataka	13.73	9.94	21,000	9.04	25,000
12.	Kerala	42.66	37.96	11,000	39.71	11,000
13.	Madhya Pradesh	6.18	5	17,000	4.71	10,000
14.	Maharashtra	17.45	5.33	29,000	5.28	26,000
15.	Manipur	41.49	28.97	20,000	28.59	20,300
16.	Meghalaya	68.35	49	31,700	58.54	29,000
17.	Mizoram	94.27	77.74	98,500	87	85,000
18.	Nagaland	89.28	48.76	30,000	54.35	25,000
19.	Orissa	4.01	4.9	11,000	5.15	13,400
20.	Pondicherry	13.78	20	50,000	21.57	48,000
21.	Punjab	65.36	45.59	39,000	43.33	36,500
22.	Rajasthan	9.61	5.26	20,000	5.23	20,400
23.	Sikkim	31.49	19.05	7,000	23.09	9,300
24.	Tamil Nadu	11.17	10.47	17,500	11	17,000
25.	Tripura	13.49	8.75	7,500	9.09	7,600
26.	Uttar Pradesh	18.12	14.32	18,000	13.53	19,000
27.	West Bengal	25.56	13.34	10,500	12.41	10,500
28.	A. & N. Islands	32.16	5.7	22,000	9.41	26,400
29.	Chandigarh	23.91	12.19	79,000	25.62	72,000
30.	Daman & Diu	–	6.12	36,000	7.22	38,000
31.	Lakshadweep	95.47	41.2	14,000	36.73	12,000
32.	Dadra & Nagar Haveli	–	17.61	5,41,000	11.19	3,46,000
	All India	17.17	12.46	18,600	12.25	18,300

Source: National Commission for Minorities.

is comparable to their percentage population. Whereas in the rest of the States/UTs, the percentage of credit flow to the minorities is less than their percentage of population. At the all India level also the flow of credit to the minorities is 12% of the total credit. Their population percentage, on the other hand, is 17%.

2.24   Table II.9 gives the region-wise position of credit facilities. It is observed that the average amount of credit per account is highest in the

Table II.9: Region-wise Flow of Credit to Minorities in the Country

Region	State/UTs Region	March '99		September '99	
		Amt. in crore	Credit per Actt.	Amt. in crore	Credit per Actt.
North East	Assam, Mizoram Arunachal Pradesh Nagaland, Manipur Sikkim, Tripura	183.18	14,000	182.51	14,000
Eastern	Bihar, West Bengal Orissa and A. & N.	1,088.68	9,000	1,088.09	9,000
Western	Gujarat, Maharashtra, Daman & Diu, Goa, D. & N. Haveli	982.04	28,000	979.64	27,000
Central	UP & MP	1,421.72	18,000	1,505.32	16,200
Southern	Andhra Pradesh Karnataka, Lakshadweep, Tamil Nadu Kerala, Pondicherry	3,576.76	14,000	3,816.03	14,000
Northern	Delhi, Punjab Haryana, Chandigarh J&K, HP, Rajasthan	4,192.62	38,000	4,217.47	38,000
		11,445.00		11,789.06	

Source: National Commission for Minorities.

Northern region at Rs. 38,000 followed by Rs. 27,000 in the case of the western region. Though reasonable also in the north east, central & southern regions, it is quite low in the eastern region at Rs. 9,000.

2.25   Table II.10 gives information on credit offered to minority groups in the 41 Minority Concentration Districts. Percentage of credit to minorities under lending programmes of the scheduled banks is limited to *around 13-14%* of the total credit flow in the minority concentration districts whereas the percentage of minority population in these areas ranges *from 25 to 50%*. Also, in the Minority Concentration Districts the share of

Table II.10: Credit Flow in Minority Concentration Districts

Communities	March '99		September '99	
	Amt. in crore	% to Total	Amt. in crore	% to Total
Muslims	1,392.71	71.69	1,388.18	72.87
Christians	277.03	14.26	274.32	14.40
Sikhs	172.58	8.88	173.58	9.12
Buddhists	62.74	3.23	52.05	2.73
Parsis	37.65	1.94	16.79	0.88
Total	1,942.71	100.00	1,904.92	100.00
All Communities	14,131.86	13,469.49		
% of Minorities to Total Credit flow	13.75	14.14		

Source: National Commission for Minorities.

credit to each minority community as in Sept. 1999, is Muslims (72.87%), Christians (14.40%), Sikhs (9.12%), Buddhists (2.73%) and Parsis (0.88%).

2.26   The above information indicates that the percentage of minority accounts may not be in proportion to their percentage of population. This necessitates capacity building so that more and more persons of the minority community can access bank credit. Per account loaning is also less, as minority groups do not own big business/industries and the quantum of loaning is small.

2.27   Some reference of credit flow to minorities has also come under the financing schemes of Prime Minister Rojgar Yojana (PMRY) under the Ministry of Small Scale Industries. Though no specific targets are fixed, separate data is available about the credit flow to the minorities. This scheme is being implemented in collaboration with the banks. The banks provide 95% of the project cost as loan; the balance of 5% is brought by the beneficiary in his business. The government provides 15% of the funds (subject to a maximum of Rs. 7,500) as subsidy. This is adjusted by the banks against the repayments made by the loanee.

PRIME MINISTER'S ROZGAR YOJANA (PMRY)

2.28   Though in a span of 7 years, the total credit flow under PMRY scheme has been nearly Rs. 9,500 crore, no separate earmarking has been made by either the Govt. or the Banks for capacity-building of the loanees. This adversely affects the loan absorption capacity of the loanees and, with poor recoveries, burdens the banks with non-performing assets. This is reflected in terms of diminishing number of suitable applicants for loans.

2.29   The details of the assistance provided to the minorities under PMRY is given in the following Table II.11.

Table II.11: Assistance to Minorities under PMRY

S. No.	Year	Total	Minori- ties	% (Col 4/3)	Total	Minori- ties	% (Col 7/6)
1	2	3	4	5	6	7	8
1.	1993-4	18,673	1,318	7.06	14,001	950	6.79
2.	1994-5	114,846	9,457	8.23	84,565	6,715	7.94
3.	1995-6	281,968	22,334	7.92	201,144	15,419	7.67
4.	1996-7	270,811	22,201	8.20	181,646	14,950	8.23
5.	1997-8	288,316	25,957	9.00	182,472	16,383	8.98
6.	1998-9	299,061	29,140	9.74	178,083	17,581	9.87
7.	1999-2000	255,222	24,692	9.67	152,188	14,435	9.48
Total		1,528,897	135,099	8.84	994,099	86,433	8.69

(a)   Sanction and disbursement to the minorities is hovering around 9% of the total credit provided during the period.

(b)   Share of credit to the minorities has been found to be *quite low* in Andhra Pradesh, Uttar Pradesh and Kerala. These states have a sizeable minority proportion.

(c)   Achievement is satisfactory in those states where the religious minorities have a major share of population, such as Punjab, Jammu & Kashmir, Mizoram, etc.

(d)   Special steps need to be initiated to increase the share of the minorities.

(e)   Separate data about credit flow to minority groups under other schemes of priority sector lending is not maintained.

NATIONAL MINORITIES DEVELOPMENT & FINANCE CORPORATION (NMDFC)

2.30   Besides the general credit mechanism of the banking sector and the Government, the National Minorities Development & Finance Corporation (NMDFC) extends credit for self-employment to the minorities. NMDFC was set up in 1994 under the Ministry of Social Justice & Empowerment to promote welfare and economic development of the poorer sections amongst them. The paid up share capital of NMDFC so far is Rs. 238 crore, of which the Union Government has contributed Rs. 202 crore and the States/UTs have provided Rs. 36 crore.

2.31   The main focus of NMDFC has been to provide loans for self-employment at concessional rates of interest. These are lower than the bank rates, though other promotional programmes, such as vocational training, skill upgradation and marketing support, are also provided.

2.32   NMDFC operates through a networking with the State Govt. bodies called the State Channelising Agencies (SCAs). These SCAs are the main links in the implementation mechanism of NMDFC, as they identify the applicants and disburse the loans. They are also responsible for the utilization of loans and repayment of funds to NMDFC. Presently, there are 32 SCAs (among them 28 being operational in 21 States and 2 UTs). These include 9 State Minorities Finance Corporations or Backward Classes Financial Corporations or some other Corporations. The maximum amount of loan given by NMDFC is upto Rs. 5 lakh. As most of the borrowers are from the poorer sections, quite often the loans are very small (depending upon the need of the borrowers). NMDFC has been able to disburse loans worth Rs. 296.79 crore to over 86,874 beneficiaries. At the same time, inadequate infrastructure of the SCAs—both administrative and financial—has constrained the implementation of NMDFC's programmes.

2.33   The existing system has not been able to cover the poorest of the poor whose credit needs were small but recurring in nature. These were the poorest men and women in our villages and towns who were mostly illiterate and could not hope to avail of loans from the banks or even the SCAs because of the procedures involved. Their need was an informal and flexible credit delivery mechanism at their doorstep. Also to make credit really a means of empowerment, a more active intervention in their lives was felt necessary. The *micro-financing* scheme itself has been modelled on the credit system of Bangladesh Gramin Bank and the Rashtriya Mahila Kosh, which are the pioneers in this field. This scheme is being implemented as a parallel strategy of NMDFC and is taken up directly through the NGOs, which have proven record in this field. As of now, NMDFC has evolved linkages with 84 NGOs in different parts of the country and has brought nearly 20,000 beneficiaries under its purview. Apart from giving small loans for income generation, support is also given for the promotion and sabilization of SHGs. The concept of Self Help Groups among the minorities is a relatively novel concept.

CREDIT THROUGH COMMUNITY BASED ORGANIZATIONS

2.34   Religious organizations also extend credit to members of the minority community. There are about 200 Islamic credit institutions in India operating (as per the tenets of Koran). They do not charge interest on the loan extended by them. As they do not conform to the rules of conventional banking, they function as societies, trusts, etc. However, they have wide acceptability amongst the minorities and, with a degree of restructuring and development of administrative/infrastructural base, they can play an important role in channelizing funds to the targeted minority groups.

EFFICACY OF EXISTING DELIVERY MECHANISM

2.35 The 15-point programme for the minorities emphasizes that care be taken to see that in various development programmes, including the 20-point programme, minorities secure a fair and adequate share of benefits. This has sought to be achieved through the NMDFC. But, on a wider plane, minorities form only a part of the overall target group of the socio-economic developmental schemes being taken up by the government and the banking sector. Unlike the SCs/STs, no specific targets are fixed for the minorities, which consequently results in diluting the focus in ensuring that the benefits reach these segments of society. Even the specific flow of information about the quantum of benefits that have reached the minorities is not always available.

2.36 Credit to the minorities is reaching predominantly through the general banking structure. It also includes the efforts being complemented by specialized agencies such as SIDBI, NABARD, etc. There has not been any evidence of any bias observed in the flow of credit to the minorities. The comparatively lower percentage of credit flowing to the minorities as compared to their population percentage has been mainly on account of illiteracy and lack of capacity to avail loan. Thus capacity building should be made part of the loaning programme targeting the poorer sections including the minorities. A training module should be developed for skill development focussed to the needs of the cluster area/target group with inbuilt flexibilities and involvement of the local community.

2.37 The weaker sections need comparatively smaller loans whereas the conventional systems and attitudes followed by the banks and other financial institutions are more or less the same as for larger quantum of loans. As these systems and procedures are not attuned to the credit needs of the poor small loanees, the same are responsible for adversely affecting the credit flow to them. This also applies to the minorities. Thus what is required is that the system of financing for schemes targeting the vulnerable sections of the society should be made simple and easy to execute, less cumbersome and time consuming, guarantee norms should be made more flexible and compliable.

TRADITIONAL OCCUPATIONS OF MINORITIES
AND RELATED ISSUES

2.38   A sizeable section of the Muslim population, which comprises the predominant group amongst the minorities are good artisans and are involved in handloom and handicraft activities, such as the brass work in Moradabad, glasswork in Firozabad, leather industry in Agra and Kanpur, carpet and banarasi sarees industry in Mau/Varanasi/Bhadohi/Mirzapur, Chikan work in Lucknow, and so on. About 38% of the weavers in the country are Muslims. Buddhists are also engaged in the traditional handicraft and handloom activities. It is a well known fact that the poor artisans are fleeced by middlemen and do not get remunerative prices for their work. In addition, these handloom and handicraft items are being edged out on account of higher prices in areas where they have to compete with articles made by machine and powerlooms. Also due to *poor profit margins*, the working capital has been depleted. As a result, the artisans do not have the wherewithal to carry on further and are gradually moving away from their traditional activities and are looking up for other avenues for their livelihood. Further, the problem of the children engaged in these activities also requires specific attention for ensuring that they are not deprived of education and protection.

2.39   It is felt, that in order to support such artisans, they may be provided with necessary inputs, such as the design developments to match with the current market requirements, introduction of new techniques, infusion of fresh credit in the sector and market tie-up. Socio-economic development of the artisans is given priority on the agenda of a number of financial institutions and Govt. Departments. However, due to lack of co-ordination among these Departments the reach and effectiveness of their programmes is limited. Better co-ordination is required between agencies such as the offices of Development Commissioner Handicraft and Handlooms with the various financial institutions. The services of the good Primary and Apex Handloom Weavers Co-operative Societies and the National Award Winning Master Craftsmen can also be utilized.

MANAGEMENT OF WAKFS

2.40   The Institution of Wakf is a striking feature of Islamic jurisprudence. The word 'Wakf' applies to any property movable or immovable, dedicated for purposes recognized by the Muslim Law as religious, pious or charitable. Apart from their religious aspect, the Wakfs are also instruments of socio-economic upliftment. The benefit from the Wakfs flow to the needy persons for their socio-economic, cultural and educational development. Income from Wakfs also plays an important role in providing community services. There are about 3 lakh Wakfs in the country. Improvement in management of Wakfs is crucial not only for the preservation of religious and charitable institutions but also for educational and economic development of the Muslim community. Wakfs constitute a national asset as a very large number of them support schools, colleges, technical institutions, libraries, reading rooms, charitable dispensaries, musafir-khanas, etc., which benefit the general public irrespective of their caste or creed.

2.41 To improve the financial position of the Wakfs and Wakf Boards and to enable them to enlarge the area of their welfare activities, the Central Government has been giving, from 1974-5, annual grants-in-aid under a Non-Plan scheme to the Central Wakf Council. The projects involve construction or reconstruction of commercially viable buildings on Urban Wakf Lands. The budget provision and utilization under the scheme during the Ninth Five Year Plan period (Table II.12) indicate that the utilization of funds under this scheme has been satisfactory.

Table II.12: Development of Urban Wakf Properties

(in Rs. crore)

	1997-8	1998-9	1999-2000	2000-1
Budget estimate	1.40	1.49	1.70	2.00
Revised estimate	1.40	1.49	1.70	1.80
Actual expdr.	1.08	1.49	1.70	1.80

CHAPTER III

RECOMMENDATIONS

STRATEGIC IMPERATIVES

During the Tenth Five Year Plan the strategy for empowering the minorities has to be moulded against the backdrop of the emerging social and economic scenario in the country. The 1990s saw a shift from the socialistic pattern of economic development to a policy based on globalization, liberalization, and privatization. The private sector is being consciously promoted to take up the production and commercial activities, while the role of the government and the government-aided sector is getting restricted to core activities. Thus, employment opportunities are likely to come up mainly in the private sector in the coming years.

3.2 Coupled with the changes above, the sectoral composition has also undergone a fundamental change over the years. Agriculture, which used to contribute 55.4% of the national income in 1950-1, accounted for only 25.5% in 1999-2000. On the other hand, the share of the services sector has increased from 31.8% in 1950-1 to 52.4% in 1999-2000. The expansion of the service sector has, thus, created new employment opportunities.

3.3 Following the 73rd and 74th amendments to the Constitution, Panchayati Raj bodies and local bodies have also started playing a major role. Further, various non-government bodies have come up as alternative modes of delivery of services. These institutions are required to be strengthened and actively associated in the implementation of the Plan. Importance of involving the community in the initiatives for their welfare needs to be recognized.

Data on development of the minorities, particularly those belonging to the economically weaker sections, indicates that among the minority communities, those who have taken advantage of the modern education. system have been able to achieve greater success in terms of exploiting the employment opportunities both in the government and private sectors. As such, adoption of regular educational curriculum and formal recognition from State Board of Education has to be taken as a major strategy for the upliftment of the educationally backward minorities during the Tenth Five Year Plan. In this context, while the curriculum followed in the religious institutions, such as Madarsas, will continue to be of significant, efforts should be made to also introduce courses that would enable the students to compete for employment in government and the professions. For this reason, the existing programme for modernizing the Madarsa education should be suitably re-oriented.

3.5 Analysis of the general trend of development indicates that States like Kerala which have better human development index in terms of a better literacy rate, better health and nutrition, and higher status of women, etc., have been able to tackle the population growth. In Uttar Pradesh, Bihar and Rajasthan, on the other hand, this is not so owing to the low human development indices. With a view to deal with unemployment and poverty effectively on one hand, and to develop the human resources which is the most important resource in India, making provision of social infrastructure such as education, primary health, sanitation, hygiene, etc., has to be given importance during the Tenth Plan.

3.6 This will be of special significance for the minority communities, whose rate of growth of population impinges adversely on their socio-economic well-being. While the concerned Departments (Ministry of Human Resource Development, Ministry of Health and Family Welfare, and Ministry of Urban Development) would be requested to gear up their activities, these programmes should be suitably supplemented by the Ministry of Social Justice and Empowerment. The Civil society at large, particularly, those of religious background should be actively associated in making various programmes acceptable to the community and ensuring their active participation.

3.7 On account of poor socio-economic condition, at times, children who represent future of the country, are subject to a lot of hardship and are forced to take up manual work. As a result, they are not only deprived of their childhood days but also the benefit of education. Specific efforts have to be made for ensuring that child labour in all forms is prohibited and the children are given full benefit of education along with nutrition and other support.

3.8 Sizeable population of the minority communities is engaged in traditional arts and crafts like handloom, handicraft, leather work, glass work, etc. With globalization, the new opportunities at the national and international level are likely to open up which can be exploited for their economic empowerment. Introduction of appropriate technology, development of entrepreneurship, and formation of self help groups hold the key for enabling the community to produce goods as per the market demand and exploit the market. Tenth Plan should emphasize this strategy for economic empowerment of the artisans belonging to minority community.

3.9 The working group recommends that in the above background, the Tenth Plan will have to envisage implementation of schemes and programmes for welfare of minorities for integrating them with the national mainstream—economically, socially and psychologically. The factors such as the content of the programmes, the quantum of resources allocated to the sector, and their delivery mechanisms are critical to their effective implementation. Based upon the review in the previous Chapters and in the context of the strategic imperatives outlined above, the recommendations of the Group are given below. The presentation has been made sector-wise for the sake of convenience. However there is some overlap between the sectors, which has arisen as no sector can be viewed in isolation.

RECOMMENDATIONS

EDUCATIONAL SECTOR

3.10   Among all the interventions deemed necessary for empowerment of minorities, the educational sector is the most important one and is required to be given specific attention during the Tenth Plan. Various plan and programmes for provision of education, including those minorities, are implemented by the Ministry of Human Resource Development, which is primarily responsible in this regard. Action taken by the Ministry of Social Justice & Empowerment are supplemental in nature for meeting the specific needs of the educationally backward minorities. In this regard civil society based institutions like the Maulana Azad Education Foundation and the Central Wakf Council assume special significance in view of their acceptance among the minorities.

SCHEMES IMPLEMENTED BY MINISTRY OF HUMAN RESOURCE DEVELOPMENT

AREA INTENSIVE PROGRAMME FOR
EDUCATIONALLY BACKWARD MINORITIES

3.11   The Group recommends the continuation of the Area Intensive Programme of the Department of Secondary & Higher Education during the Tenth plan. The Programme as currently being implemented covers only those educationally backward Blocks, where the minorities population is more than 20%. The Working Group recommends that in view of the educational backwardness prevailing among the minorities and its adverse impact on the employability, the basis for identification of blocks should be relaxed to cover all blocks having more than 12.5% of minority population.

3.12   While the precise number such blocks would have to be identified by a fresh District-wise survey in minority concentration areas, the Group has assumed that there are 600 such educationally backward Blocks in the country.

3.13   In addition to the number of the blocks to be covered, certain aspects of the ongoing scheme as indicated below also need revision for making it effective and purposeful. The standard of education also needs to be improved with focus on the quality of education, effective administration and periodic inspections.

(i) The whole purpose of a well intended scheme is lost if recognition is not granted to these schools.

(ii) School mapping exercises are required to be carried out immediately prior to opening of new schools.

(iii) State Governments should give wide publicity to the programme as well as the benefits that the targeted communities are getting from the programme.

(iv) Implementation of proposals under the scheme of Area Intensive Programme in a time bound manner.

(v) State-level Committees should exclusively monitor the implementation of the Area Intensive Programme. This is essential to ensure that the target group is benefited as per the objectives of the Scheme.

(vi) All States need to evolve a system by which to initiate the action as per the provisions of the National Education Policy and maintain an effective monitoring system.

(vii) Only those *NGOs* which have capacity to bear the cost of the expenses will be considered under the scheme. For the rest the assistance will be made available only when the State Govt. agrees to bear the cost of the recurring expenditure.

(viii) State Governments must pursue the implementation of the Scheme more vigorously.

3.14 Taking into account importance of education in empowerment of minorities and the prevailing scenario, the financial requirement for the Area Intensive Programme during the Tenth Plan will be as under:

(i) Construction of Primary and upper Primary Schools: 2,500 nos. at a cost of Rs. 5 lakh each

Total cost: Rs. 12,500 lakh

(ii) Construction of Secondary School buildings: 1,000 nos. at a cost of Rs. 7 lakh each

Total cost: Rs. 7,000 lakh

(iii) Construction of Multi-stream Residential Schools (10+2 level) for girls (boarding facility for atleast 200 girls): 150 nos. at a cost of Rs. 150 lakh each

Total cost: Rs. 22,500 lakh

(iv) Construction of additional classrooms/toilets, etc., for Primary/Upper Primary School: 5,000 nos. at a cost of Rs. 75,000 each

Total cost: Rs. 3,750 lakh

(v) Construction of additional classrooms/toilets for secondary school: 1,000 nos. at a cost of Rs. 1 lakh each

Total cost: Rs. 1,000 lakh

(vi) Upgradation of Primary Schools to Junior High Schools: 2,000 nos. at a cost of Rs. 3.50 lakh each

Total cost: Rs. 7,000 lakh

(vii) Supply of teaching/learning material to primary schools not covered by Operation Black Board : 10,000 nos. at a cost of Rs. 10,000 each

Total cost: Rs. 1,000 lakh

3.15 The total requirement of the Area Intensive Programme for Tenth Plan will be about Rs. 54,750 lakh.

SCHEME FOR THE MODERNIZATION OF MADRASAS

3.16 The Working Group feels that the ongoing scheme of Modernization of Madrasas implemented by the Department of Secondary and Higher Education has served a purpose in educational empowerment of the minorities. However it is required to be revised incorporating the following points for making it more effective:

(i) Considering the varying standards of Science, Humanities and English education in Madrasas, it is necessary that the syllabi followed by the State level recognized boards should be adopted. A Central Madarsa Board may be set up to coordinate with the States and to ensure quality of education in all relevant subjects.

(ii) The task of modernization of Madrasas involves the modernizing teaching methodology and broaden mental horizon of the teachers and managements of these institutions through exposing them to the new trends in the field of education, pedagogy, technology, psychology and educational management which may be relevant to them, and motivating them to make use of this knowledge in the teaching of their own traditional subjects so as to improve the quality of learning of these subjects. The in-service training of madarsa teachers in a modern University setting may be used for the modernization scheme. Such a project should expose madarsa teachers to new developments that have taken place both in the universe of knowledge as well as Indian society. The exposure programme may be *operationalized* either through a programme culminating in a degree like Bachelor in Education (B. Ed.) or basic education diploma, or else it may be a non-formal exposure programme for a lesser duration.

(iii) The teaching of modern subjects appears to be restricted to Class III to Class VIII. It should be extended to the school certificate (10+2) level covering all higher classes.

(iv) Provision of assistance for reconditioning and repair of these buildings are essential and should be provided in Tenth Plan.

(v) The funds under the scheme for modernization of madarsas have not been utilized fully for various reasons. These include lack of dissemination of information, particularly about the usefulness of such modernization, to the community and community leaders, lack of coordination between the Union and State Government agencies, absence of interaction with community leaders, delayed release of funds resulting in non-payment of salaries to teachers and consequent abandonment of the scheme, procedural hindrances like registration and recognition of institutions, non-availability of teachers, etc. Appropriate remedial measures may be taken for overcoming these constraints.

3.17   With a view to achieve the above stated objectives, the Group recommends the following provisions under the Scheme of Modernization of Madrasa Education during the Tenth Plan:

(i) Assistance to 2,500 Madrasas, i.e. @ 500 Madrasas every year for the plan period. The assistance should be based on the provision of an *average three teachers* per Madrasa @ Rs. 48,000 per annum per teacher (i.e. one teacher each for Sciences and Maths, English & Humanities, and Computer education).

Total cost: Rs. 3,600 lakh

(ii) Provision for assistance to State Madrasa Education Board/State Govt. to prepare *text books* during the Tenth Plan.

Total cost: Rs. 500 lakh

(iii) Provision for assistance to State Madrasa Education Board/State Govt. for organization of *teacher training Programme* for 2,000 Madrasa teachers every year @ Rs. 300 lakh per year.

Total cost: Rs. 1,500 lakh

(iv) *Provision of Computers* and accessories on a one time basis to 1,000 Madrasas at cost of Rs. 1.00 lakh per Madrasa covering 200 Madrasas each year.

Total cost: Rs. 1,000 lakh

(v) Provision of *laboratory equipment* at the rate of Rs. 25,000 to each of 500 High School level Madrasas, i.e. 100 Madrasas per year.

Total cost: Rs. 125 lakh

(vi) Supply of *teaching aids/learning material* on an one time basis to 2,500 Madrasas at cost of Rs. 10,000 for the plan period.

Total cost: Rs. 250 lakh

(vii) Priority for assistance to 2,500 Madrasas for reconditioning and repair of building and expansion of existing infrastructure at the rate of Rs. 5 lakh per Madrasa (one-time grant).

Total cost: Rs. 12,500 lakh

3.18   The total cost of the above proposals under the Scheme of Modernization of Madrasa Education during the Tenth Plan works out to Rs. 19,475 lakh.

Scheme of Community Polytechnics

3.19   The scheme of community polytechnics was started in 1978-9 as a Central Sector scheme. Community polytechnic is a wing of an existing polytechnic mandated to undertake rural/community development activities through manpower development, transfer of technology, provision of technical support/services and dissemination of information. Among men, training courses on house wiring, motor winding, repair of electronic consumer durables, repair of agricultural machinery, welding and fabrication, civil construction, vehicle repairing, etc., are popular. Among women, garment making, textile printing, screen printing, embroidery, food processing and secretarial work are popular. More than 500 community polytechnics have been established so far covering most of the 41 identified Minority Concentration Districts.

3.20   The Group recommends that coverage under this Scheme should be extended during the Tenth Plan for covering the remaining 100 other Districts having significant minority population with at least one such community Polytechnic per District and to include new and innovative trades as per the emerging market demand.

3.21   About Rs. 51.25 lakh will be required per polytechnic at the rate of Rs. 10 lakh for purchase of equipment and Rs. 5 lakh for creating infrastructure as one time grant basis and @ Rs. 7.25 lakh per annum for recurring expenditure. The total financial implication on this during the Tenth Plan will be Rs. 5,125 lakh.

SCHEME FOR PROVIDING ONE YEAR DIPLOMA
COMPUTER APPLICATIONS AND MULTILINGUAL DTP

3.22   The National Council for Promotion of Urdu Language, Ministry of Human Resource Development, Government of India has been conducting a two year course, namely, 'Calligraphy, Introduction to Computer and Desk Top Publishing', using Urdu. First year of the course deals with Urdu Calligraphy and fundamentals of computer and in the second year advance course on computer application and Desk Top Publishing is conducted. During the Ninth Plan Rs. 5.47 crore has been sanctioned for setting up of 160 computer centres and 10,002 students have been covered.

3.23   Keeping in view the emerging potential in the Information Technology sector, the Group feels that this scheme is very promising and has great potential for self-employment. Continuation of the scheme during the Tenth Plan is recommended for establishing 30 computer institutes every year. This will require a provision of Rs. 25 crore during the Tenth Plan.

SCHEME OF PROVISION OF URDU TEACHERS

3.24   Taking note of the fact that the Constitution of India seeks to safeguard the right of minorities for conservation of their language and culture, the Group recommends that in the Tenth Plan at least 5,000 schools must be assisted to have Urdu teachers, based on accepted parameters of the number of students wishing to learn the language. This scheme should apply equally to minority and non-minority (including government) educational institutions. The average number of Urdu teachers to be deployed may be 1.5 per school. For covering 5,000 schools during the Tenth Plan under this scheme at a cost of Rs. 26,400 per annum per teacher, the total expenditure for the Tenth Plan comes to Rs. 19.80 crore.

COMMUNITY COLLEGES

3.25   The Working Group further recommends that, with a view to enable the minorities to exploit the emerging job opportunities particularly in the services sector, vocationalization of education should be given emphasis by establishment of community colleges in Minorities Concentration Areas as has been envisaged in the Programme of Action of National Policy on Education.

Minority Educational Institutions

3.26   Minority Educational Institutions can play a more positive role in promotion of education among the educationally backward sections among minorities provided their growth is facilitated. The Rules guiding recognition of minority educational institutions for starting professional and technical courses should be simplified by the All India Council of Technical Education. Further, the Central and State Governments should grant permission to minorities for opening professional institutions such as Medical Colleges, vocational training institutions and teacher training institutions.

3.27   The State Governments should simplify the procedures *for issuance of recognition* of minority educational institutions. Complaints about delay in, or refusal to, issue Minority Status Certificates have come to notice in some States. Issue of certificate by the State Governments should be expedited. This would be in accordance with the Programme of Action (1992) and enable the enable minority educational institutions to exercise their legitimate rights which have been recognized in the National Policy on Education (1986).

3.28   Special efforts need to be made for the professional development of Managers, Principals and teachers of minority educational institutions including both initial training like B.Ed. and subsequent on the job orientation at regular intervals. Assistance of institutions such as the All India Association for Christian Higher Education, Aligarh Muslim University, Jamia Millia Islamia may be availed for the purpose.

Linguistic Minorities

3.29   In order to eliminate frustration and build a sense of confidence among minorities, it is essential that the State also plays a positive role to maintain cultural pluralism. Towards this purpose the facilities for teaching of minority language and protection of their cultural traditions should be made available outside the areas of their concentration. For example, Sikhs and Punjabis living outside Punjab, particularly in States of Delhi, U.P., Maharashtra, Bihar, Rajasthan, etc., where they are in substantial numbers, need to be provided facilities for Punjabi teaching in Schools. For this purpose schools, may be provided assistance for appointing teachers under the plan scheme. Also, creation and strengthening of cultural academies, like Urdu, Punjabi and Sindhi academies in Delhi may be considered in various States in due course.

3.30   Recommendations by various committees for instructions up to class V in mother tongue should be implemented for effective fulfillment of the constitutional right conferred upon the linguistic minorities under Article 350(A). For this, the greatest challenge is to develop curriculum and material in minority languages particularly in States other than minority concentration population.

3.31 Necessary arrangements for teaching of minority languages are also lacking. For example, it was brought to the notice the Group that in Leh district of Ladakh, Bhoti language has been introduced from 1971 in 272 Government Schools but only 37 Bhoti teachers posts have been created so far. Such glaring contradictions need to be attended urgently.

SCHEME OF REMEDIAL COACHING

3.32 The Remedial Coaching scheme has been under operation for enabling the minorities student to overcome their difficulties in specific subjects. This scheme is operated through UGC. The Group recommends that it should be continued in the Tenth Plan. The UGC scheme assists students at higher secondary level and above. At least 1,60,000 students may be assisted under the scheme during the Tenth Plan through 500 Institutes (@ 320 candidates per institute) at the rate of 100 Institutes per year. The cost of assisting 500 Institutes (at a rate of Rs. 7,65,200 per institute) will come to Rs. 3,826 lakh.

SCHEMES IMPLEMENTED BY MINISTRY OF SOCIAL JUSTICE & EMPOWERMENT

MAULANA AZAD EDUCATION FOUNDATION

3.33 According to the National Policy on Education 1986 (modified in 1992) the minority groups which are educationally deprived or backward need special interventions. For accelerated growth, intensive investment is required in the field of education, vocational training and upgradation of skills. There is an urgent need of additional focus in girl child and women empowerment.

3.34 The Maulana Azad Education Foundation has made considerable contribution towards this cause during the Ninth Plan so far, by sanctioning over Rs. 41 crore to 287 NGOs as grant-in-aid for establishment/expansion of schools/colleges, girls' hostels, residential schools, remedial coaching (for students at secondary level) and upgradation of the existing professional and technical institutions. The scheme has been received well as is evident from the large number of proposals (worth

Rs. 195 crore) pending with the Foundation for consideration.

3.35   As the impact of the scheme is substantial, the *Corpus Fund* of the Foundation may be *raised* from Rs. 70 crore to Rs. 200 crore. Thus the provision for this purpose required during the Tenth Plan would be Rs. 130 crore.

MERIT LINKED SCHOLARSHIP

3.36   With a view to ensure that the meritorious students among the minorities are able to pursue education at higher level at par with others, the Group feels it is necessary to introduce a *merit linked scholarship* scheme for students belonging to minorities at the earliest, as envisaged by the Ministry of Social Justice & Empowerment to formulate. The scholarship is conceived as a special intervention to improve the educational standards of educationally backward minorities to bring them at par with the rest of the community as they are not able to avail of the opportunities for higher and technical education. 10,000 scholarships are proposed to be given annually at a cost of Rs. 17 crore. The Tenth Five Year Plan outlay works out to Rs. 85 crore.

SCHEME OF HOSTELS FOR MINORITIES STUDENTS

3.37   The Working Group felt the need for having adequate hostel facility for enabling the minority students to pursue education at matric and post matric level in general and for the girl students, in particular. Ministry of Social Justice & Empowerment has been implementing schemes for construction of hostels for SC and OBC students. However there is no scheme for construction of hostel for the minorities. It was learnt that a proposal for merger of the two ongoing schemes for hostel for SC and OBC students and also the inclusion of minorities is under consideration. The proposed 'Centrally Sponsored Scheme of Sangati Hostels for students (Boys and Girls) belonging to Scheduled Castes, Minorities and Other Backward Classes' aims at integrating the weaker sections with the mainstream. The Group endorsed the proposal.

3.38   The Group recommends that, in the Tenth Plan period, a conscious effort be made to have *one hostel each for minorities boys and girls (capacity of 50 students each)* in the sub-divisional headquarters of all the 41 Minority Concentration Districts. At an estimated cost of Rs. 30 lakh per hostel (5 sub-divisions per district), the total cost works out to

Rs. 41 x 5 x 2 x 30 lakh or Rs. 12,300 lakh. Under this Centrally assisted scheme, State Governments/UT Administration as well as the Voluntary Organizations may be assisted for setting up hostels. Operation and maintenance cost should, however, be borne by the agency concerned. It may be stated that, as far as possible, the hostels should not be exclusive— that is—they should cater to all sections of the society; the minorities can be allotted a certain proportion of the seats available as envisaged under the proposed scheme of 'Sangati hostels'.

SCHEME FOR COACHING

3.39   The Group considered the progress, problems and potential of the scheme of Coaching Classes for competitive examinations operated by the University Grants Commission through selected Universities/Colleges and came to the conclusion that the scheme *should be continued in the Tenth Plan and specific efforts should be made for increasing the success rate* so as to ensure that the minority communities are adequately represented in the government services.

3.40   The *Ministry of Social Justice & Empowerment* also operates a pre-examination coaching scheme for weaker sections including minorities under which assistance is given to national and State-level NGOs of repute. During the Ninth Five Year Plan the Rs. 9.50 crore has been sanctioned to 222 institutions covering 17,750 beneficiaries under this scheme. It was learnt that the Ministry of Social Justice & Empowerment is contemplating to formulate a common coaching scheme for students belonging to Scheduled Castes, Other Backward Classes and Weaker Sections including Minorities and for widening the scope of the scheme for meeting the requirement of government as well as private sectors. The Group supports this initiative in view of the need for supporting students appearing for Professional courses. A provision of Rs. 50 crore, i.e. Rs. 10 crore per year may be made for the Tenth Plan.

EDUCATIONAL DEVELOPMENT SCHEMES
OF THE CENTRAL WAKF COUNCIL

3.41   The Central Wakf Council is at present implementing a scheme through the network of wakf institutions, for helping the minority students for pursuing education. The working group feels that the wakf organization has enormous potential in empowering the minority community educationally and recommends that the efforts of the Central

Wakf Council should be supplemented by the government during the tenth plan. The Council should be assisted for focusing on the elementary education, particularly on the girls education for achieving total literacy during the Tenth Plan with particular stress on common health and hygiene, sanitation, mother and child health, etc. A provision of Rs. 25 crore during the Tenth Plan @ Rs. 5 crore per annum is recommended for this new scheme.

VOCATIONAL TRAINING SECTOR

3.42   The Ministry of Labour (Directorate General of Employment Training) have been operating a scheme for upgrading Industrial Training Institutes (*ITIs*) in minority concentration areas under which 41 Minorities Concentration Districts have been covered so far. In view of the peculiar nature of problems faced by the minorities, the Working Group recommends the expansion of this scheme to 100 more Districts, having significant minority population, during the Tenth Plan. This would require a provision Rs. 1,000 lakh during the Tenth Plan assuming at the rate of Rs. 10 lakh per ITI.

ECONOMIC SECTOR

EMPOWERMENT OF WOMEN

3.43   Women are the weakest link amongst the minorities. With one of the lowest literacy and enrolment rates, burden of bearing large number of children leading to poor health and lowest Work Participation Rate (WPR), they need maximum focus. The most effective strategy to reach women and empower them economically should be through (i) organizing them to form Self Help Groups (SHGs) support; (ii) capacity building through increased income generation skills and, (iii) provide them micro-financing/ term loan for running micro enterprises/setting up production based activities suitable to women.

3.44   Considering inherent constraints of the conventional banking system in reaching the poor women, the financing institutions need to place a special thrust on micro-financing scheme. Besides allowing small loans for income generation, active support for promotion and stabilization of SHGs would be needed. To ensure grassroot level reach a networking of Governmental agencies and programmes with accredited organizations in the voluntary sector seems imperative. While involvement of Government agencies such as DRDA in DWACRA schemes has shown that if such agencies are decentralized and have flexible procedures they can play an important role, the main agents for micro-financing would have to be non-Governmental organizations. Such organizations can be encouraged by providing financial support by way of revolving funds or some specific project based activities. Considering the low level of skills and entrepreneurship qualities available among the women, it would also help them to encourage more and more production based activities by various NGOs/ Governmental organizations, which would ensure assured wage employment to them. While provisions for revolving funds can be a part of the normal credit operations by various organizations, special support can be provided by the Government to encourage training activities among the minority women.

3.45 The Working Group recommends a provision of Rs. 1,000 lakh for the Tenth Five Year Plan for making a breakthrough in this by assisting at least 100 NGOs of repute for organizing self-help groups, orientation and training.

3.46 For the enhancement of income generation skills of women, the ITIs and community polytechnics can play an important role. However, it has been observed that participation of women of minority communities in the polytechnics and the ITIs is negligible. The main reason is their inherent hesitation to study in co-educational institutions. Keeping in view this practical problem, the group recommends holding of separate vocational training course exclusively for women in the existing ITIs and community polytechnics in trades suited to them, to be started in the 41 minority concentration districts in the first phase during the Tenth Plan. For this purpose an amount of Rs. 205 lakh is envisaged at the rate of Rs. 5 lakh for district.

EMPOWERMENT OF ARTISANS

3.47 The Handloom and Handicraft sector is the biggest sector after agriculture in terms of employment. Sizeable population of the minorities are engaged in these activities for earning their livelihood. Thus this is the second most important area of focus for empowerment of the minorities.

3.48 As the needs of craft-persons are multifaceted, such as relating to design development, marketing, working capital, etc., promotional schemes should be integrated in nature with an in built element of flexibility. This would mean a change from the existing system in which several schemes are implemented by promotional agencies in a parallel manner with little coordination between different schemes of the same agency, not to speak of different ones. Steps in this direction have already been initiated by recent introduction of 'Deen Dayal Hatkargha Protsahan Yojana' and Baba Saheb Ambedkar Hastshilp Vikas Yojana respectively by the Development Commissioner (Handlooms) and Development Commissioner (Handicrafts).

3.49 A cluster based integrated project dovetailed with the promotional schemes and credit programmes of financial institutions would be more suitable to need of the artisans.

3.50 Due to its uniqueness the handlooms sector should be encouraged to concentrate in such project range and markets, which are not covered, by the powerloom and the mill sector. The elite section of the society and the export market should be targeted for higher returns. To tap this market fresh designs and adequate marketing facilities will be needed.

3.51 Growth centres with required forward and backward linkages for ensuring design development, bulk processing, quality control and export based production may be set up which will facilitate design development for marketable designs, processing, finishing, and quality control for meeting the requirement of domestic market as well as exports. Training on product diversification will also be imparted there. The Group recommends an outlay of Rs. 30 crore for setting up 200 such Growth Centres in the first phase the rate of Rs. 15 lakh per centre. This may be dovetailed with the programmes of the NMDFC and other financing institutions.

3.52 To meet the working capital needs of the artisans, *credit cards* on the lines of the cards for the farmers need to be started.

3.53 It is extremely important to provide permanent marketing outlays to the craft-persons, specially targeting the higher income group customers both domestic and foreign tourists. It is recommended to open Minority Craft Bazaars at selected places, similar to 'Dilli Haat'. To begin with in the Tenth Five Year Plan, three such craft bazaars are recommended to be opened at three centres on the 'Golden Tourist Cresent' on the roads leading from Delhi to Agra, Agra to Jaipur, and Jaipur to Delhi. The scheme could be implemented by the Ministry of Social Justice & Empowerment through the National Minorities Development & Finance Corporation with tie-up with the Development Commissioner (Handicrafts) and the Ministry of Tourism. The outlays for each craft bazaar are given below:

Cost of land	Rs. 1.00 crore
Cost of building	Rs. 2.00 crore
Common facilities	Rs. 1.00 crore
Total	Rs. 4.00 crore

Thus for three outlets an outlay of Rs. 12.00 crore would be required.

CAPACITY BUILDING THROUGH SKILL DEVELOPMENT TRAINING PROGRAMMES

3.54   It has been observed that the ventures of the beneficiaries often fail on account of lack of proper training required for the trade or their skills have become outdated and do not match with the current market needs. The current financing schemes of most of the financing institutions/banks, departmental schemes either do not have provision for capacity building or lack adequate allocation. It has also been observed that it is difficult for the financing institutions to find good training institutes where quality training could be imparted to those who can be considered for financing. On the other hand, there are Government Departments/Institutions which have been created to provide training and whose infrastructure is not utilized fully as sufficient avenues are not available for fruitful absorption of the trainees. Thus, there is need for better co-ordination between the financial institutions desirous of capacity building of their prospective beneficiaries and the training institutes. Also the infrastructure of the training institutes such as the ITIs needs to be upgraded, especially in the minority concentration districts. The norms of general vocational trades may be revised by DGET and those trades that are more popular with the minorities should be included in the course curriculum of these ITIs. Capacity building should be made part of the loaning programme targeting the poorer sections including the minorities. A training module should be developed for skill development focussed on the needs of the cluster area/target group with inbuilt flexibilities and involvement of the local community.

NETWORKING WITH NGOS

3.55   Lack of awareness and information have been found to be the major handicaps in the empowerment of the minorities, particularly the poorer sections of the community. Civil society, including the religious/charitable institutions, can play a vital role in disseminating information and educating the community about various welfare schemes of the Government. Assistance of such institutions should be availed fully in identification of beneficiaries, monitoring and recovery of dues, etc.

3.56   Women, especially belonging to the minority community, are particularly vulnerable and are often subject to immense hardship. Civil society can play an active role in organizing these women into Self-Help Groups (SHGs) and providing them required skill, entrepreneurial ability, credit, etc. Success achieved by the SEWA, Ahmedabad, the SEWA,

Bhopal Development Credit Bank, and the Annapurna Mahila Mandal indicates that the involvement of *Community Based Organisations* (CBOs) in developmental programmes has led to an effective implementation of self-employment schemes. The Working Group recommends that formation of SHGs with help of the civil society should be taken as a major plank of the strategy for empowerment of women belonging to the minorities during the Tenth Plan.

NATIONAL MINORITIES DEVELOPMENT & FINANCE CORPORATION (NMDFC)

3.57 The group recommends that National Minorities Development & Finance Corporation (NMDFC) should be adequately strengthened during the Tenth Plan. For the purpose, the authorised share capital of the corporation should be increased from Rs. 500 crore to Rs. 1,000 crore. The Central Government is expected to contribute almost its entire earmarked share of Rs. 300 crore by the end of Ninth Five Year Plan. The capital structure of NMDFC is such that it requires the contribution of the State Govt. and the interested groups in the equity of NMDFC. NMDFC has been trying to obtain contribution from the groups/individuals/institutions. However, no success has been achieved so far. As the contribution from this group is not likely to increase substantially, the group recommends that the capital structure of NMDFC should be revised with the share of Central Govt. being 75% and that of the State Govt./UT administration being 25% in the equity of NMDFC.

3.58 By the end of the Ninth Plan period, NMDFC would have extended loans of nearly Rs. 300 crore to about 1.30 lakh families. This is a small proportion of the approximately 1.20 crore minority families targeted to be assisted. Thus there is every need to increase the quantum as well as the pace of financing. It is proposed to double the level of financing during the 10th Five Year Plan period to Rs. 600 crore to cover 2.50 lakh families under the SCA programme. The achievements under the NGO programme have been very modest during the 9th Plan period as it has taken some time to gain sufficient expertise and stabilize. However, during the 10th Five Year Plan the Corporation can be expected to provide microcredit of about Rs. 100 crore to over 2 lakh families. Thus the financing programme of NMDFC is expected to be of the order of Rs. 600 crore under the SCA programme and another Rs. 100 crore under the NGO programme. The total financing programme is expected to be of Rs. 700 crore. During the 9th Five Year Plan period, an amount of nearly Rs. 300 crore is expected to be disbursed by NMDFC against the paid-up capital of Rs. 235.44 crore. Funds are disbursed by NMDFC for a maximum period of 5 years. It is expected that the disbursement of Rs. 300 crore made during 9th Plan will be recovered during the 10th Five Year Plan period. This NMDFC shall have Rs. 300 crore available with it for ploughing it back for further financing as per the projections of 10th Five Year Plan period. It may however, be seen that there will be a shortfall of Rs. 400 crore which shall have to be met primarily through contribution by the Central Govt. Thus the outlay for contribution towards the equity of NMDFC during the Tenth Five Year Plan is proposed at Rs. 300 crore (Rs. 60 crore per year) and the balance Rs. 100 crore will be contributed by the State Governments.

THRUST AREAS IN CREDIT DELIVERY MECHANISM

3.59 In various credit programmes of the banks as well as Government specific targets for the minorities should be fixed and monitored at various levels. This would help to ensure that necessary benefits reach the minorities as part of the general programmes.

   3.60   To have a wider reach and acceptability among the minorities, it is recommended that the financing institutions are encouraged to network with the financial institutions of the minorities. This would include the institutions which have been registered as Trusts or Societies and are taking up grass root activities among the beneficiaries specially those relating to income generation and credit, as well as traditional financial institutions like cooperative banks and cooperative societies of the minorities.

   3.61   Poor people need a personalized approach. Owing to their illiteracy or low literacy, there is a special need to making the channels of communication effective and transparent. The need for proper motivation and mobilization is foremost. Financial institutions would do well to opt for cluster based personalized approach to ensure that selected beneficiaries are not discouraged by cumbersome procedures and running around various Government offices/Banks for different purposes. The approach would also include the post disbursement follow up including timely recoveries. Involving local persons in various kinds of enquiry and scrutiny can prove to be extremely effective.

   3.62   Closer coordination between the promotional organizations like the Development Commissioner (Handlooms), Development Commissioner (Handicrafts) and financing institutions is required.

SOCIAL SECTOR

3.63   In the social sector the importance of religious and social institutions such as Churches, Mosques, Gurudwaras, Wakfs has to be recognized and their cooperation elicited for reaching out to the target groups in a more effective manner.

DELIVERY OF HEALTH SERVICES

3.64   It has to be ensured that health services including family welfare schemes provided by the Government reach out effectively to the minorities, especially the poor in both quality service and timely delivery. To achieve this objective, community involvement appears to be of critical importance in the strategy for delivery of health services to minorities as it will not only smoothens reach but also facilitate acceptance. Cooperation of religious and other social institutions among the minorities may be elicited for the effective implementation of the Information, Education and Communication (IEC) component in the health sector. The cooperation of institutions like the Central Wakf Council and the State Wakf Boards can also be obtained. It is felt that representation of the target communities among the implementing staff would improve delivery of services.

3.65   The Working Group appreciates the importance of the Indian Systems of Medicine and Homeopathy and recommends that the benefits of Ayurveda, Unani, Homeopathy, etc., systems may be availed of along with the greater involvement of the community for helping the minorities more effectively.

3.66   . . . The Working Group recommends that the NGOs should be encouraged to spread their activities in the areas/villages inhabited by educationally and economically backward minority communities for improving the delivery of health services as well as promotion of the small family norms.

MANAGEMENT OF WAKFS

3.67   As noted in Chapter-II, improvement in management of Wakfs is crucial not only for the preservation of religious and charitable institutions but also for the educational and economic development of the minority community. Since 1974-5 the Central Government has been giving grant-in-aid to the Central Wakf Council for the development of Urban Wakf Properties. The Council extends loan to Wakf institutions and charges 6% donation on the outstanding amount of loan repayable which is used to fund its programmes for educational development. The amount received as repayment of loan forms a revolving fund, which is used to fund minor development projects up to Rs. 20 lakh. Sizeable number of proposals are pending from State Wakf Boards and individual Wakf management for development of respective Wakf properties, which could not be processed due to inadequate fund. There is enormous potential for commercial development of wakf properties. The increased income can be utilized for the purposes of taking measures to protect the Wakf land/properties and construction of boundary walls around graveyards, Idgah (Prayer grounds), etc., instead of looking for government assistance.

3.68   In view of the procedure followed for availing bank loan and the legal aspects of management of wakf properties, the group recommends that the Non-Plan scheme of grant to the Central Wakf Council for *Development of Urban Wakf Properties* may be brought under the Plan and Rs. 25 crore may be provided during the Plan period.

3.69   The National Foundation for Communal Harmony (NFCH) was set up in 1992 under the aegis of Ministry of Home Affairs to undertake programmes for assisting children of families affected by communal violence, particularly for their physical and psychological rehabilitation including their education/vocational training, and for their assimilation into the mainstream. This scheme needs to be given wide publicity and the provision enhanced suitably. A corpus also needs to be established with all the State Governments and particularly the major riot-prone States, so as to enable them to make payment to the families of the victims as compensation for the loss of life and property.

BUILDING UP OF DATA BASE ON MINORITIES

3.70   It is observed that the data relating to demographic and socio-economic characteristics of the minorities is collected during the censuses but it is not collated. This has resulted in a significant information gap limiting the effectiveness of Government interventions. It is felt, for example, that State-wise and district-wise literacy figures for men and women among the minorities can be a useful pointer for prioritizing flow of assistance within these areas. The Registrar General & Census Commissioner of India may be requested to collate and publish the data on the basis of religion. In case it is not possible to do so for the entire country, the same needs to be done at least for the identified Minority Concentration Districts in the country.

ABSTRACT OF FINANCIAL OUTLAYS PROPOSED

3.72 . . . The abstract of outlays proposed under various schemes during the Tenth Plan for empowering the minorities is given in the following Table:

Abstract of Outlays proposed in Tenth Five Year Plan

S. No.	Details of the Scheme	Page No.	Para No.	Ministry/ Deptt.	Outlay (Rs. Lakh)
1.	Area Intensive Programme	39	3.15	HRD	54,750
2	Modernization of Madrasa Education	41	3.18	HRD	19,475
3.	Community Polytechnics	42	3.21	HRD	5,125
4.	Diploma Computer Applications and Multilingual DTP	42-3	3.23	HRD	2,500
5.	Provision of Urdu Teachers	43	3.24	HRD	1,980
6.	Remedial Coaching	45	3.32	HRD	3,826
7.	Maulana Azad Education Foundation	46	3.35	SJ & E	13,000
8.	Merit linked scholarship	46	3.36	SJ & E	8,500
9.	Scheme for Hostels	47	3.38	SJ & E	12,300
10.	Scheme for coaching	47-8	3.40	SJ & E	5,000
11.	Educational Schemes of the Central Wakf Council	48	3.41	SJ & E	2,500
12.	Vocational Training for Women	48	3.42	Lab./HRD	1,000
13.	Training for capacity building	50	3.45	SJ & E	1,000
14.	Vocational Training for Women	50	3.46	Lab./HRD	205
15.	Growth Centres for support to Craft-persons	51	3.51	SJ & E	3,000
16.	Craft Bazaars	51-2	3.53	SJ & E	1,200
17.	Equity support to NMDFC	54	3.58	SJ & E	30,000
18.	Development of Urban Wakf Properties	57	3.68	SJ & E	2,500

Total Rs. 1,67,861 lakh
or (say) Rs. 1,679 crore

CONCLUSION

The strategy for the empowerment of the minorities during the Tenth Five Year will be multi-faceted in nature and would involve effective interventions by the Central Government, State Governments, Panchayati Raj institutions, local bodies, and also the various minority institutions and religious bodies. Involvement of the civil society at large including NGOs, in particular, would play an important role in this strategy. It is through the wider interaction between the government, the institutions, and the community, and their combined efforts, that the goal of empowering the minorities and their mainstreaming can be achieved.

Index

Note: Some full names (with titles) which were difficult to insert into the text in the proof stage have been included in the index.